Western Philosophy

Western Philosophy
From Antiquity to the Middle Ages

James N. Jordan

Queens College
The City University of New York

Macmillan Publishing Company
New York

Macmillan Publishing Company
866 Third Avenue, New York, New York 10022

Collier Macmillan Canada, Inc.

Library of Congress Cataloging-in-Publication Data

Jordan, James N. (Nicholas).
  Western philosophy.

  Bibliography: p.
  Includes Index.
  1. Philosophy, Ancient. 2. Philosophy, Medieval.
I. Title.
B171.J65 1987   180   86-11711
ISBN 0-02-361450-1

Printing: 1 2 3 4 5 6 7   Year: 7 8 9 0 1 2 3

Credits Grateful acknowledgment is hereby made for permission to reprint in this
volume passages from:
Allan, D. J. *The Philosophy of Aristotle*. Rev. ed. London: Oxford University Press,
  1963. Reprinted by permission of Oxford University Press.
Anselm, Saint. Reprinted from *St. Anselm: Basic Writings*, translated by S. N. Deane,
  2nd ed., by permission of The Open Court Publishing Company, LaSalle, Illinois.
  Second edition copyright © by The Open Court Publishing Co., 1962.
Aristotle. *Nichomachean Ethics*. Reprinted by permission of the publishers and The
  Loeb Classical Library from *Nichomachean Ethics,* Aristotle, translated by H. Rack-
  ham, Cambridge, Mass.: Harvard University Press, 1934.
Aristotle. *The Works of Aristotle Translated into English*. Edited by J. A. Smith and
(continued on p. v)

ISBN 0-02-361450-1

W. D. Ross, 12 vols. Oxford: Clarendon Press, 1908–1952. Reprinted by permission of Oxford University Press.

Augustine, Saint. *The City of God.* Translated by Gerald G. Walsh, Demetrius B. Zema, Grace Monahan, and Daniel J. Honan. Abridged version edited by Vernon J. Bourke. Copyright © 1950, 1952, 1954, 1958 by Fathers of the Church, Inc. Reprinted by permission of The Catholic University of America Press, Washington, D.C.

Augustine, Saint. *Confessions.* Translated by R. S. Pine-Coffin. Harmondsworth: Penguin Classics, 1961. Copyright © 1961 by R. S. Pine-Coffin. Reproduced by permission of Penguin Books, Ltd.

Cicero. *The Nature of the Gods.* Translated by Horace C. P. McGregor. Harmondsworth: Penguin Classics, 1972. Copyright © 1972 by Horace C. P. McGregor. Reproduced by permission of Penguin Books, Ltd.

Cicero. *Selected Works.* Translated by Michael Grant. Rev. ed. Harmondsworth: Penguin Classics, 1971. Copyright © 1960, 1965, 1971 by Michael Grant. Reproduced by permission of Penguin Books, Ltd.

Cleanthes. "Hymn to Zeus." Translated by James Adam. In Whitney J. Oates, ed., *The Stoic and Epicurean Philosophers.* Copyright © 1940 by Random House, Inc. Reprinted by permission of Random House, Inc., New York.

De la Mare, Walter. *Complete Poems.* New York: Knopf, 1970. Reprinted by permission of The Literary Trustees of Walter de la Mare and The Society of Authors (London) as their representative.

Diogenes Laertius. Reprinted by permission of the publishers and The Loeb Classical Library from *Lives and Opinions of Eminent Philosophers,* by Diogenes Laertius, translated by R. H. Hicks, Cambridge, Mass.: Harvard University Press, 1925.

Epictetus. *The Discourses and Manual.* Translated by P. E. Matheson. Oxford: Clarendon Press, 1917. Reprinted by permission of Oxford University Press.

Epicurus. *Epicurus: The Extant Remains.* Translated by Cyril Bailey. Oxford: Clarendon Press, 1926. Reprinted by permission of Oxford University Press.

Hesiod. *Theogony, Works and Days.* Translated by Dorothea Wender. In *Hesiod and Theognis;* Harmondsworth: Penguin Classics, 1973. Copyright © 1973 by Dorothea Wender. Reproduced by permission of Penguin Books, Ltd.

Homer. Excerpt from Homer, *The Iliad,* translated by Robert Fitzgerald. Copyright © 1974 by Robert Fitzgerald. Reprinted by permission of Doubleday & Company, Inc., New York.

Hopkins, Gerard Manley. *Poems.* 3rd ed. Oxford: Oxford University Press, 1948. Reprinted by permission of Oxford University Press.

Kirk, G. S., and J. E. Raven. *The Presocratic Philosophers.* Corrected ed. Copyright © 1957 by Cambridge University Press. Reprinted by permission of Cambridge University Press.

Lucretius. *The Nature of the Universe.* Translated by R. E. Latham. Harmondsworth: Penguin Classics, 1951. Copyright © 1951 by R. E. Latham. Reproduced by permission of Penguin Books, Ltd.

Maimonides, Moses. *The Guide for the Perplexed.* Translated and with an introduction by M. Friedländer. New York: Dover, 1956. Reprinted by permission of Dover Publications, Inc.

Marcus Aurelius. *Meditations.* Translated by George Long. In Whitney J. Oates, ed., *The Stoic and Epicurean Philosophers.* Copyright © 1940 by Random House, Inc. Reprinted by permission of Random House, Inc., New York.

Philo. Reprinted by permission of the publishers and The Loeb Classical Library from *Philo,* translated by F. H. Colson and G. H. Whitaker, Cambridge, Mass.: Harvard University Press, 1929 (for Vols. 1 and 2), 1932 (for Vol. 4), 1935 (for Vol. 6).

Plotinus. Reprinted by permission of Faber and Faber, Ltd., London, from *Plotinus:*

To
Cathleen

Introductory Note

Twenty-six hundred years ago, among the Ionian Greeks, there arose the kind of reasoned inquiry after truth that characterizes philosophy in Western civilization. A path with many twists and turns (and desolate stretches as well) is traceable from this ancient beginning to the types of philosophy pursued in the West today. The aim of the present volume is to acquaint the reader with landmarks along this path as far as the end of the Middle Ages, until about 1350, when the Renaissance began its work of shaping the modern era. Western philosophers of the Ancient and Medieval periods have had great influence not only upon later philosophers but also upon the general culture of the West. Politics, religion, the arts, the sciences, the very notions that pass for common sense—all have been complexly affected, directly and indirectly, by the philosophical methods and findings of Pythagoras, Socrates, Plato, Aristotle, Cicero, Plotinus, St. Augustine, St. Thomas Aquinas, Ockham, and others to be examined herein. Some knowledge of these thinkers is essential to any real understanding of the whys and wherefores of Western cultural history. Moreover, because most of the philosophical issues investigated in modern times first came up in Ancient or Medieval discussions, a grasp of the latter is necessary to a just estimate of more recent discussions and to an avoidance of blind alleys and delayed insights in one's own philosophical reflections. It is also true that the ideas and intellectual careers of Ancient and Medieval philosophers are matters of absorbing interest on their own account. Simply as personalities these thinkers are extraordinary, and their respective contributions toward overcoming the "reign of chaos and old night" are among the noblest of human achievements.

Acknowledgments

To his colleagues at Queens College, Harvey Burstein, Keith Eubank, Hilail Gildin, Norman Goldman, Jason Jacobowitz, George Krzywicki-Herburt, Salvatore Miceli, and Frederick Purnell, Jr., and to the publisher's reviewers and editors, heartfelt thanks from the author for many valuable suggestions.

J.N.J.

Contents

The Pre-Socratic Philosophers

Ancient Western philosophy before Socrates (470–399 B.C.) was chiefly occupied with speculation about the world's origin and basic composition—matters which today are partly the concern of cosmology and metaphysics in philosophy, and partly the concern of natural sciences such as astronomy and physics. After Socrates, and owing largely to his influence, much more attention was given to problems of ethics and politics, and to issues regarding the nature and scope of human knowledge. In order to mark this change and his pivotal role in its occurrence, the philosophers before Socrates are customarily called "the Pre-Socratics." But this is not meant to suggest that Socrates' predecessors are of interest only as his predecessors. They are well worth examining in their own right, for among them—in less than two centuries—they developed ideas that have not been outdone in variety, richness, or stimulating power.

No complete work by a Pre-Socratic philosopher is known to have survived. For information about all of these early figures we have to rely upon the sketchy reports of later writers and upon the passages—mostly short fragments—that they quoted. It is not easy to reconstruct the original Pre-Socratic positions from these meager sources. The experts in the field often disagree. In what follows we shall keep to interpretations that are generally accepted, but the reader should bear in mind that there is controversy on many points.[1]

---

[1]The chief controversies are interestingly explained in the book by G. S. Kirk and J. E. Raven listed in the bibliography at the end of this volume. Following the bibliography, by the way, are notes to sources quoted in the text and to major works of reference.

CHAPTER 1

The Ionians

About 1000 B.C., people from the mainland of Greece, possibly in escape from invaders, crossed the Aegean Sea to the western shore of what today is Turkey. They settled upon some islands and a strip of coastline that together came to be called Ionia. Important trade routes passed through this region, and in time a dozen cities were built as centers of commerce. The greatest of these cities was the seaport of Miletus, which was sufficiently prosperous and cosmopolitan to provide for some persons the leisure and the incitement to engage in intellectual pursuits. The beginning of philosophy in Western civilization can be traced to three such persons, Thales, Anaximander, and Anaximenes, who all lived in Miletus between 600 and 500 B.C. and who are known collectively as "the Milesians."

The Milesians are mainly remarkable for their *cosmology,* that is, for their attempts to explain how the universe came to be what it is. Their guiding idea was that originally the universe was one substance. From this substance, as from a common ancestor, the universe and everything in it emerged and grew. The multitude of apparently unrelated things we see around us, from sticks and stones to the farthest star, the Milesians said, are but surface manifestations of this single permanent underlying stuff. All that arises and changes and perishes, all the restless flux of visible nature, has a common genealogy, a single source, indeed the same basic composition.

In some respects the idea that the universe arose from a single substance was very much older than the Milesians. As they may have known, the Egyptians and the Mesopotamians had long before formulated *theogonies* in which they traced the genealogies of their gods and goddesses, and in which the universe was described as having come out of a primordial stuff. In the Old Kingdom of Egypt (2850–2000 B.C.), there was a traditional belief that the universe emerged from a boundless watery abyss called Nūn. Above the waters, so the tales went, there appeared a hillock of mud; and upon this hillock, by his own power of self-creation, the god Rē-Atum came into being. From within himself Rē-Atum produced the god of air and the goddess of moisture, who in turn were the parents of earth and sky. In Mesopotamia, sometime around 1500 B.C., the Babylonian epic of creation, *Enuma Elish,* was composed. It describes the original state of the universe as a watery chaos in which three elements were in turbulent mixture: Apsu (fresh waters), Tiamat (salt waters), and Mummu

3

(clouds and mist). From the marriage of Apsu and Tiamat came the gods and goddesses of sky and earth, sun and wind. The Greek *Theogony* of Hesiod (composed around 700 B.C.), with which the Milesians were almost certainly familiar, follows the same general pattern and tells how, from the yawning void of Chaos, "the gods and earth arose at first, and rivers and the boundless swollen sea"—a tale of hair-raising savagery which features the castration of Ouranos (Heaven) by his son Kronos (a Titan) with the assistance of Gaia (Earth), who was mother of them both.

In Ionia itself, about 750 B.C., Homer is believed to have lived and fashioned his epic poem about the Trojan War, the *Iliad,* from traditional stories some of which may have been nearly as old as the events (occurring about 1200 B.C.) they described. From scattered passages in the *Iliad* it is possible to piece together what no doubt was a popular Greek view of the world. The sky is a great metallic bowl, filled with shining aether above and mist below, covering a flat, round earth. Earth, rooted in Tartarus, reaches as far down as the sky reaches above, and around its circular surface flows the mighty river Okeanos, the source of all waters. In one unusual passage whose interpretation is difficult, Homer appears to say that Okeanos is the source, the "begetter" or "forebear," not just of all waters but of everything that exists, the gods included.

From the absence of anything in the original Greek territories to suggest an earth-encircling river, some scholars have conjectured that the idea came to the Greeks from Egypt or Mesopotamia. The reference in Homer to Okeanos as the source of all things would seem to strengthen the supposition. In Egypt the land did indeed emerge from the waters, once a year, as the floods of the Nile receded. In Mesopotamia the land was actually formed from the marshes between the rivers Tigris and Euphrates and from the silt deposited at their confluence in the Persian Gulf. Having emerged from water, the land could still be imagined as surrounded by it, and this conception may have been assimilated by the Greeks, who modified it by having the earth rooted, not floating, and by making the encircling waters a vast river, not a limitless sea.

However that may be, it is at first a disappointment to learn that Thales of Miletus, first among the Seven Sages of Greece and Father of Western Philosophy, is most celebrated for his declaration that the source and substance of the visible universe is—water. What was novel in this? What more precisely did he say?

The Milesians

Thales

Hardly anything is known for certain about Thales. The only date that may safely be associated with him is 585 B.C. In this year, according to the Greek historian Herodotus, Thales predicted an eclipse of the sun which put a stop to a battle and so ended a war between the Lydians and the Medes. Modern astronomers have determined that an eclipse, visible in Asia Minor, did occur in 585 B.C.—on May 28, to be exact. Whether or not Thales actually predicted it, the story gives at least some indication of the period in which he was active and noticed. Through the haze of dubious anecdotes that tradition recorded of him, one can discern the shape of a plausible personality: well-connected parents; probable visits to Mesopotamia and Egypt; a wide acquaintance with Near Eastern lore in astronomy, geometry, and meteorology; a great reputation as a sage to be consulted on matters political, technical, and military; a man of long life and modest means who liked to say that he could have been rich if he had so desired (there is a story that he once cornered the market in olive oil to prove the point). According to one famous anecdote, which is not easily squared with his reputation for practical wisdom, he fell into a well while gazing at the stars. Another anecdote, which has a ring of greater authenticity, suggests how a Greek sage handled a delicate situation. Thales' mother is said to have urged him to consider marriage. He replied that the right time had not yet arrived. When later on she took the matter up with him again, he said that the right time had passed. There is, however, a story that Thales did finally marry and either had or adopted a son.

Thales is not known to have written anything. Our earliest information about his views comes from Aristotle, who was born some two hundred years after the eclipse that Thales is supposed to have predicted. The *most* there is evidence for saying is that Thales believed water to be what everything came from and continues to be composed of, that he believed motion and change in general to be attributable to a kind of life or soul inherent in water, and that he believed the earth (solidified water, presumably, like ice) to float upon water. His reasons for saying that everything is made of water were probably, according to Aristotle, physiological in character: the moistness of semen and nutriment, the damp warmth of living bodies. Aristotle mentions as doubtful the possibility that Thales drew upon ancient myths, and he does not even mention what one might have supposed to be a prime reason for considering water the basis of all things: its obvious capacity to assume the three states of liquid, solid, and vapor.

In spite of Aristotle's doubts, it is likely that old myths had some influence upon Thales. The importance of water in theogonies which Thales may be supposed to have known and compared (all the more if he went to Mesopotamia and Egypt) suggests that it was by abstracting this common feature from them that he first got the idea of water as the *original source* of everything. His belief that water is also what everything is *composed of*, that it is the permanent underlying stuff of which everything is made, could well have been generalized from observations of the sort Aristotle indicates. But an element of myth probably came in here as well.

The essential role of moisture in the life of organisms would invite the conclusion that water is basic to all things only if all things are imagined to be alive. This Thales appears to have believed. He is said to have thought that magnetic stones, in particular, possess souls, because they can move iron. Very old is the idea that souls or spirits are what account for any power of movement or growth that things appear to have—rivers, trees, winds, oceans, storms, and so forth. This ancient *animism,* prevalent in Greek mythology, seems to have been extended by Thales to things that look far less alive than rivers and trees. He may have reasoned that if something as apparently dead as a stone is alive after a fashion, then so is everything else. "All things," he is reported to have said, "are full of gods." There is, in other words, a great life-principle built into the universe as a whole, and since where there is life there is water, water is what everything is. And the reason why the universe we know arose in the first place, instead of remaining a motionless ocean, is that water is animated, a living being that spontaneously changes.

This interpretation of Thales is necessarily conjectural. The point to stress is the novelty of his central idea: notwithstanding many appearances to the contrary, the universe possesses (in living water) an underlying order. The seemingly different objects and processes of nature have something fundamentally in common. The world's multiplicity is the function of a basic unity, not apparent to the senses but discoverable nevertheless. The "many," as the Greeks liked to say, are essentially related to a "one" and can be explained in terms of it. In this way the confusing flux of events has under the surface an intelligible structure.

No idea has been of greater importance than this one in the development of both science and philosophy. Ridiculous as it might now seem that anyone could have taken water as the basis for explaining everything, Thales is to be congratulated for thinking that things may be explained by departing to any extent from traditional myths. The animistic side to his position, from what we can tell, had none of the usual features of myths—no gods and goddesses quarreling among themselves and unpredictable in their dealings with mortals, reflecting a sense that the world is largely in disorder. In attributing movement and change to a life-principle ("gods") inherent in the universe, Thales implicitly denied the relevance (if not also the existence) of supernatural agencies. Events in nature could be accounted for without attributing them to powers from outside. Instead of describing the parentage and exploits of a water-god, or fitting gods into a family tree that grew out of water, Thales adopted a perspective on nature that seems almost modern by comparison. Naive as his view was, it had the great merit of being open to tests of logic and evidence—tests whose laborious development was stimulated by the critical discussion his view invited.

A qualification should be made of our statement that the gods and goddesses of ancient mythology were depicted as being disorderly in their ways. This was not always true, and it is possible that Thales' views owed something to the exceptions. Let us see briefly how this may have been so. In Homer's *Iliad*—a work of the highest standing with the Greeks— the whole complicated story of warfare and horror is organized around the theme, announced in the opening verses, that the events it describes were "in fulfillment of the will of Zeus" and so part of a universal plan. The intelligibility of this plan, or at least the scope of its influence, is cast into doubt by frequent intrusions in the *Iliad* of a mysterious "fate"— a blind force governing events and on occasion apparently independent even of the gods. Indeed, it was by the "decree of fate," we are told, that Zeus himself was allotted, as his particular domain, "the broad sky and a home among the clouds," while his brothers, Poseidon and Hades, were allotted the sea and the underworld respectively. Nevertheless, in at least one passage Homer seems to have had in mind, as far as human affairs are concerned, a divinely established moral law:

> As under a great storm black earth is drenched
> on an autumn day, when Zeus pours down the rain
> in scudding gusts to punish men, annoyed
> because they will enforce their crooked judgments
> and banish justice from the market place,
> thoughtless of the gods' vengeance; . . .

And we find the same conception, expressed in remarkably similar words, in Hesiod's *Works and Days:*

> The deathless gods are never far away;
> They mark the crooked judges who grind down
> Their fellow-men and do not fear the gods.
> Three times ten thousand watchers-over-men,
> Immortal, roam the fertile earth for Zeus.

The notion of an inescapable rule of justice, administered by Zeus even-handedly and in keeping with a cosmic plan, could easily suggest regularity and order throughout the whole of nature. Possibly Thales was encouraged by this suggestion in his search for an underlying unity in the world. Perhaps even "fate" came into the picture, interpreted by Thales as an impersonal order of nature, but as similar to a rule of justice in being at least intelligible. We have no way of knowing about any of this. It is just worth noticing how these ideas in Homer and Hesiod might have figured in Thales' speculations.

Whatever precisely influenced him, Thales probably pored over a number of existing materials, took from them such ideas as seemed to him valuable in accounting for the world's origin and composition, developed these ideas in connection with observations and reflections of his own, and produced a result that, crude as it now looks, made him a pioneer. His conception of the world as fundamentally *one* begins a long tradition in philosophy of *monism* (one-basic-thing-ism, from the Greek *monas,* a "unit," a "one"). His belief that this one is a *material stuff* begins a protracted search, in philosophy as well as in science, for an *ultimate thing* (or species of things, in another type of monism), with all of the difficulties we will see this to involve. And with Thales the notion that the world is *orderly,* that it is, as the Greeks said, a "cosmos," begins to take on the shape in which we now know it.

All of these ideas will be challenged; about each of them there is much to examine. Thales' own immediate successors took issue with the role he assigned to water, as now we shall see.

Anaximander

From the scanty information that has come down to us from Aristotle and later sources, it appears that Anaximander was a younger associate of Thales'. His birth has been put at about 610 and his death at about 546 B.C. Like Thales, he was noted for a wide range of activities. He is said to have been in charge of an expedition that set up one of Miletus' trading posts on the Black Sea (*Pontos Euxeinos,* "hospitable sea," the Greeks called it). There is evidence that he took an interest in astronomical apparatus, in map making, in the prediction of earthquakes (common then as now in his region), in meteorological phenomena, and in zoological observations. He wrote at least one book, the first in prose, which according to tradition was entitled *On Nature.* This was lost at an early date; all that remains of it are a few words and part of a sentence.

Anaximander, like Thales, looked for a basic stuff from which the world we know derives. Water, however, seemed to him a poor choice. He questioned how water could yield so unwatery a thing as fire, for example, which is certainly an important feature of our world—only consider the sun. Water and fire are actually "opposites"—water extinguishing fire, fire evaporating water—just as fire (hot) is opposed to air (cold) and as air (light) is opposed to earth (heavy). If water were the source and substance of everything, fire could never have existed. Since fire obviously does exist, Thales' view implies a false consequence and so must itself be false.

In general, Anaximander reasoned, the stuff that is the origin of all things—of earth, air, fire, and water—cannot very well possess the specific nature of any of them. These opposites of which the world is composed must originate from something quite indefinite in itself, something that lacks any characteristics of its own—not cold or hot, moist or dry, heavy or light. And so Anaximander called the source of all things simply "the Indefinite" (in Greek, *to apeiron,* occasionally translated also as "the Boundless," "the Infinite," "the Indeterminate"), meaning by this something both inexhaustible in quantity and wholly devoid of specific qualities, an unlimited mass of characterless stuff having unlimited potential for assuming different specific forms.

From Aristotle's testimony, it appears that Anaximander viewed the Indefinite as "steering" all things and as "divine." It is divine because, like the gods in Homer, it is "immortal and indestructible." But unlike the gods, the Indefinite has always existed and was never born of some parent god or material. It is the permanent source and repository of all the perishable things of nature. The Indefinite "steers" the world by issuing things in such a way that they exhibit a great cosmic law. Specifically, this law operates in coordinating the opposites as they emerge from the Indefinite. The surviving sentence-fragment of Anaximander's book indicates how he conceived of this: the opposites arise from the Indefinite and return to it, he said, "according to necessity; for they pay penalty and retribution to each other for their injustice according to the assessment of Time."

By these figurative terms, Anaximander seems to have meant that order in the world consists of a cyclical process of compensation or adjustment by which the opposites are kept within bounds. The change of seasons may have been one of the things he had in mind. The cold wetness of winter seems in a kind of feud with the hot dryness of summer: each tries to monopolize the environment, never minding about the "rights" of the other. But just as everything is about to be swamped in water or burned to a crisp, the guilty party is brought to justice, and the injured party is given restitution—emerging from the Indefinite to carry on, no better than its former oppressor, as if the world belonged to it only. Were it not that each side is given, "according to the assessment of Time," a fixed span in which to run riot, affairs would deteriorate completely. Anaximander may have believed that a similar cyclical process is at work in long-term changes of sea level and climate. Cycles of seasons and climates may have been the pattern on which he interpreted the detailed changes in nature—the kindling and dying of fires, the formation and dissipation of clouds, and so on.

However he may have worked this out, the order in nature appears to have struck him as uneasy. "Injustice" elicits "injustice." It is only because of the way in which opposites are played off against one another, in accordance with a scheme of time, that a rough stability is preserved. Homer and Hesiod, we saw, spoke of an order of justice maintained by Zeus over human affairs. Anaximander seems to say that the Indefinite attempts something similar for nature as a whole, but the feuding opposites are incurably recalcitrant. One opposite or another is always being hauled into court for its criminal behavior. Heraclitus, a little later on, seems to have been criticizing Anaximander when he said that strife among opposites *is* justice—a view which Anaximander would probably have considered a rather lofty and cynical paradox.

The divinity that Anaximander attributed to the Indefinite, like the soul Thales attributed to water, involved the power of spontaneous life and movement. Owing to this, something was isolated in the Indefinite, or "separated off" from it, which produced the opposites that make up our world. At first there was a colossal ball of flame. This enclosed, "like bark around a tree," a mass of misty air, and from the air the earth was formed at the center of the ball. Then the ball of flame exploded, perhaps because of mounting pressure from the air it heated, and the flame broke up into circles that were engulfed by the mist or steam. The sun, the moon, the planets, and the stars are apertures in the mist through which the fiery circles are visible as they wheel around the earth. Eclipses and lunar phases occur because of blockages, total or partial, of these apertures. The earth is a short cylinder like a drum, supported by nothing, in motionless equilibrium with the heavenly bodies. Living creatures, which inhabit the "top" of this cylinder, arose from ocean mud as it was warmed by the sun. The first animals had spiny coverings like those of sea urchins, which they shed when they moved onto dry land. Humans were originally generated inside fish, where they remained and were nurtured, like the young of sharks, until they could fend for themselves.

Anaximander also worked out explanations of meteorological phenomena—thunderstorms, whirlwinds, typhoons—as well as estimates of the distances from earth and the relative sizes of the heavenly bodies. He may have held the view that our world is just one of an innumerable series of worlds, so that someday our world will be destroyed into the Indefinite and succeeded by a new one, which in turn will be destroyed, and so on forever. There is dispute about whether Anaximander really believed this, but at any rate it is the kind of remarkable conjecture of which he seems to have had an inexhaustible supply. For scope and depth of ideas, he has had few rivals. "Anaximander," G. S. Kirk says, "is the first of whom we have any concrete evidence that he made a comprehensive and detailed attempt to explain all aspects of the world of man's experience."

An especially noteworthy feature of Anaximander's attempt is his assigning ultimate reality not to any of the objects apprehended by the senses but to something that may be discovered only by a process of reasoning. Unlike a specific substance such as water, the Indefinite cannot be seen or touched or otherwise perceived. It has no observable qualities. Anaximander argued that it could not be the *source* of all observable qualities—of the "opposites" that make up the world of our sense-experience—if it had any such qualities itself. The underlying substance of all definite things must itself be quite indefinite. To argue in this way is to appeal to abstract reasoning in support of a conclusion as to what is ultimately real, and no one before Anaximander is known to have done this.

Anaximenes

Even less is known about Anaximenes than about his predecessors. He is said to have been a pupil of Anaximander's and in his prime around 546 B.C., which is approximately the year in which Anaximander died.

Like his teacher, he wrote at least one book of which nothing remains except a sentence and a couple of words. His style of writing was noted for its simplicity, in contrast to the style of Anaximander, which was thought—by the person who preserved the words we quoted—to be "rather poetical." From the testimony about Anaximenes' positions, one gets the impression that he had nearly the same breadth of preoccupations as Anaximander; neither earthquakes nor stars, nor much in between, escaped his curious attention. The difference in writing styles, however, reflects an important difference in perspectives. Anaximander pictured the cosmos as the scene of a perpetual drama in which "opposites" do violence to one another and are punished accordingly. Anaximenes, as far as we can tell, conceived of the cosmos in light of a mechanical process that has nothing to do with justice or injustice and that does not occur in order to fulfill any purpose of "penalty" or "retribution."

Anaximenes had his own theory about the originative stuff of the world. He said that it was *air*. Of course, air was one of Anaximander's "opposites," and at first it may seem that Anaximenes, heedless of his teacher's arguments, was taking a step backwards. Had not Anaximander demolished water as a candidate for this stuff of the world with arguments equally destructive to air? Did he not demonstrate once and for all that no substance with definite qualities could be the source of all things? Anaximenes thought not. He believed that he had discovered a way in which one "opposite," without losing its own nature, could produce all of the others; and his search for this was possibly prompted by a sense that "the Indefinite" was a confused idea.

Consider how indefinite "the Indefinite" is. If it really has no particular characteristics, there is no describing what it is or does. To describe what something is and what role it plays in relation to other things necessarily involves describing its characteristics. To be a *thing* at all is to have characteristics that make it something in particular and different in certain respects from other things. A "thing without characteristics" is a contradiction in terms. The force of this point is clear from Anaximander's own failure, hard as he may have tried, to be strictly indefinite about the Indefinite. In fact he attributed to it, directly or by implication, a number of characteristics: imperishability, gigantic size, powers of life and movement, disapproval of injustice, and so on.

The problem that the concept of the Indefinite was meant to solve is serious enough. How can an underlying stuff of which everything is supposed to be made possess any determinate nature of its own? How could *one* qualitatively definite material such as water become *many* qualitatively different materials such as earth, air, and fire? This is a version of the famous "problem of the one and the many" which comes up again and again in Greek philosophy. Anaximander could see no way out except by supposing that the "one" has no qualities whatever and is thus on a wholly different level from the "many."

Anaximenes, however, saw another possibility. Why could not differences in *kind* (hot-cold, wet-dry, and so on) be owing to differences in the *amount* of a single definite stuff? There would then appear to be many "opposite" sorts of things, but this would be just an appearance; in reality there would be only one sort of thing, varying in density from one locality to another. Changes of *quality* would be attributable to changes of *quantity* on the part of this one basic material.

Air, Anaximenes thought, is precisely the right thing. He imagined that when air is *condensed,* or reduced in volume by pressure, it assumes an increasingly more solid appearance, first as wind, then as clouds, water, earth, and stones. He understood the formation of clouds on the analogy of fel•ing—that is, the process by which loose fibers are interlocked by moisture and pressure so as to become felt—and so he evidently viewed streams of wind as fibrous. When the feltlike clouds are further compacted, the result is water in the form of rain. On the other hand, when air is *rarefied*—Anaximenes seems to have said "relaxed"—it takes on the appearance of fire. Temperature varies inversely with compression: the more compressed the colder, the less compressed the hotter. In support of this, Anaximenes is said to have observed that when one's breath is exhaled through puckered lips it is cool, and when exhaled with the mouth open it is warm.

It is condensation and rarefaction, then, by which the one becomes (apparently) the many. Why did Anaximenes select air? Why did he not return to Thales, equipped now with condensation and rarefaction, and view air as a "relaxed" appearance of water? Our only real clue comes from the sentence we have from his book: "As our soul being air holds us together and controls us, so does wind and air enclose the whole world." ("Does," not "do," because wind and air are the same.)

Air, like water, was in ancient times identified with life. The soul which animates the human body was associated all over the world with breath. Since any irregular expulsion of breath might jeopardize one's life, there were many curious practices designed to neutralize sneezes and yawns. "An offshoot of this idea," says Theodor Gaster, "was the custom of kissing the mouth of the dying in order to receive his soul." And Gaster cites as an example this passage from the Old Testament Book of Genesis: "And when Jacob had made an end of commanding his sons, he gathered up his feet into the bed, and yielded up the ghost, and was gathered unto his people. And Joseph fell upon his father's face, and wept upon him, and kissed him."

As air is the source of life and movement in us, so it is for Anaximenes in the cosmos as a whole. And since by condensation and rarefaction air can become fire, earth, and water, it is not simply what enlivens things and controls them; it is the substance of which everything is made—an animated stuff that transforms itself into different local appearances and thus gives rise to the objects and events of our experience. As the deathless and immeasurable source of the world, air had for Anaximenes aspects of divinity, but again he did not ascribe purposes to air in the way in which Anaximander ascribed a concern for justice to the Indefinite. The processes of the world do not happen for any reason; they just happen, in a mechanical way that we can discover. Nevertheless, Anaximenes did not deny that there are gods in the traditional sense. He held that they arise in some fashion from air, though it is not clear how he thought they do so or what place he thought they have in the overall scheme of things.

Much clearer are his accounts of the earth (condensed from air via water, it is flat and floats in air like a leaf), of the stars (rarefied from moist vapors arising from the earth, they are leaves of fire), of earthquakes (caused by mountains tumbling down when the earth dries and cracks, or gets wet and crumbles), and so forth. Conjectures like these, and the similar ones offered by Thales and Anaximander, rough and incautious as they are, show an attitude toward natural phenomena that seems positively scientific in comparison with the superstition and idolatry that elsewhere so largely prevailed. With the Milesians we feel that we have already come a great distance from the kind of ignorant fear of nature that consorts with magic, divination, and blood sacrifice. Their attempts to account for natural phenomena in natural terms, their belief that the world has an objective order which is discoverable by rational methods (especially as Anaximenes conceived it, whereby changes of quality are explicable on the basis of changes of quantity), together with their dawning sense of how beliefs about nature are to be measured against standards of logic and evidence—these are remarkable anticipations of modern natural science and required no little courage of spirit.

Of course, it is anachronistic to speak of "natural science," with however many qualifications, in connection with the sixth century B.C. The expression did not even exist until 1840, according to the *Oxford English Dictionary,* and the names for the particular sciences (physics, astronomy, and so on), in their current meanings, all came into use only after the sixteenth century. The old name for a scientist, which in our language dates from the period of Middle English (about 1150 to 1450), was "natural philosopher." So philosophy was distinguished from the sciences, and the sciences were distinguished from one another, only gradually and during fairly recent times. But more important than matters of nomenclature and specialization was the absence from Milesian thinking of certain essential ingredients of modern science: the use of controlled experiments, the formulation of hypotheses in exact mathematical terms, and the explicit recognition of the significance of what are called "negative instances," that is, cases in which the phenomenon in question does *not* occur, contrary to one's hypothesis. On this latter point, consider again Anaximenes' belief that temperature varies inversely with compression, so that as compression increases, temperature decreases, and vice versa. In support of this he cited his observation about breath. So far well and good, but what about phenomena that seem to point in the other direction—warm stones, for example? How is the belief about compression and temperature to be squared with them? If Anaximenes had adopted his belief tentatively, as an *hypothesis* likely to need modifying or replacing in light of a wider variety of relevant data, he would have come much closer to the method of science. And he would probably have come to see that the actual relation between compression and temperature, as far as gases are concerned, is roughly the opposite of what at first he had thought, so that in fact he had been misled by the observation concerning breath.

Anaximenes' followers, had there been any, could well have won through to a more circumspect method of inquiry. A kind of scientific school might have grown up in Miletus, pressing forward with the work that Anaximenes and his predecessors had so nobly begun, and after a few generations . . . But Miletus was sacked by the Persians in 494 B.C. The men were massacred; the women and children were made slaves. Although the city was later rebuilt on new ground and carried on as a seaport until early Christian times when the harbor silted up, she produced no more philosophers.[1] The rubble of the old city may be seen today on a bluff near the Maeander River, called Büyük Menderes by the Turks.

Xenophanes

In the Ionian city of Colophon, some forty miles north of Miletus, the poet Xenophanes was born in about 570 B.C. From the surviving fragments of his poems, it appears that he was aware of the philosophers of Miletus and was moved at least partly by consideration of them to dissociate himself, in a spirit of caustic iconoclasm, from the religious beliefs of his time. When the Persians moved to capture Colophon in 546 B.C., Xenophanes slipped away to the Greek colonies in Sicily, which for the rest of his life were the base from which he traveled around reciting his poems. He seems to have been one of those persons, quite uncomplicated in their own eyes, who have on the one hand an ironic contempt for popular opinions and on the other hand a puzzled sense of being insufficiently appreciated. Any athlete who happens to win a contest, he said, is provided with dinners and entertainments, with a good seat in the assembly, and with "some gift of lasting value." "Yet he would not deserve them as much as I deserve them; for surely a man's wisdom is superior to strength and speed." No doubt; and Xenophanes does after all seem to have won considerable favor among people in educated circles. One even begins to sympathize a little with his patrons and hosts when one sees how he must have taxed their resources. In a lengthy passage in which he delivered himself of rules pertaining to parties, he said that there is nothing wrong with drinking as much as you can hold, so long as you can still get home on your own. With all that, he lived well into his nineties, dying sometime around 475 B.C.

---

[1] With the possible exception of Leucippus. See p. 41.

Like the Milesians, and probably following their example, Xenophanes speculated about the nature of things, both in general and in detail. He had his ideas about the sun and the moon, the rainbow and the clouds. He was the first, as far as we know, to call attention to the geological significance of fossil shells, plants, and fishes. From examining them he arrived at Thales' probable view that dry land was once ocean and at Anaximander's view that life started from mud. He believed that the world goes through cycles of comparative wetness and dryness and that in his day a muddy period was setting in. Humankind would be destroyed, to arise again when the waters receded. Like Thales and Anaximenes, and unlike Anaximander, he seems to have believed that the underlying oneness of the world is of a definite material complexion, and like all the Milesians he ascribed to the "one," as the source of life and movement, some elements of divinity.

What material Xenophanes chose for the "one," whether water or something else, is unknown. He seems to have believed that the universe as a whole has the shape of an immense globe and has always existed as such, whereas the heavenly bodies, for example, are accounted for in Anaximenes' fashion as rarefied water vapor. When it came to the religious aspects of the matter, Xenophanes was very definite about what the "one" was not. With remorseless satire, he criticized the prevailing conceptions of deity, as drawn from Homer and Hesiod, for their *anthropomorphism,* that is, for their assigning to the gods a number of traits and features that are human, only too human. The gods were depicted as shameless thieves, adulterers, and liars. They were imagined as having been born, as having bodies like ours, as moving about and speaking as we do, and as wearing clothes. With solemn conviction the Greeks believed all this, never stopping to think how much it was simply a projection of themselves, just as the Ethiopians viewed their gods as snub-nosed and black and as the Thracians viewed theirs as having blue eyes and red hair. Indeed, Xenophanes said, if horses and cattle could draw pictures, then no doubt they would represent their gods as looking like horses and cattle.

In fact, according to Xenophanes, there is only one god, the globular cosmos as a whole—ungenerated, unmoving, everlasting, possessed of consciousness throughout, morally good, the cause by its mere thought of all that happens within it: "One god, greatest among gods and men, in no way similar to mortals either in body or in thought." This was an unusually refined conception of deity for its time and place, but there are two things especially to notice about it. First, Xenophanes did not distinguish, any more than the Milesians did, between the divine being and the world it animates and governs. The deity was not viewed as a spiritual entity separate and apart from the natural order, nor was it viewed as the creator of the natural order. God and nature were identical, and so Xenophanes was a monist, not a monotheist like his contemporary, the Second Isaiah in the Old Testament, who wrote: "Thus saith the Lord that created the heavens; God himself that formed the earth and made it; he hath established it, he created it not in vain, he formed it to be inhabited: I am the Lord; and there is none else."

Second, there is little or no indication in fragments or testimony that Xenophanes had an attitude of piety toward the god-cosmos. His language is not devotional either in tone or in substance; it is dry and matter of fact. Unlike *pantheists,* who typically identify God and the natural world in a spirit of awe and reverence, Xenophanes seems to have been mainly interested in promulgating a correct theory. Worship apparently did not strike him as appropriate. His monism, like that of his three predecessors, is a species of what is called *hylozoism* (from the Greek words for "matter" and "life," *hyle* and *zoe*), which is the generic name for theories according to which all matter is animated. For Xenophanes, as for Thales, Anaximander, and Anaximenes, the universe is at bottom a single living material thing (though for Anaximander the material was indefinite).

Despite the air of conviction with which Xenophanes expressed himself, he made a point of the limitations of human knowledge. We cannot be certain, he said, about the truth of anything, though with care we can arrive at *opinions* that more closely resemble the truth. People's beliefs and experiences differ too widely for us to be thoroughly confident of our own. God alone can be sure that he *knows.*

How did Xenophanes think that we can tell whether one opinion is closer to the truth than another? And if we cannot be certain of anything, how can we be certain that we cannot be certain? He does not seem to have considered these questions, but his distinction between knowledge and opinion set the stage for later philosophers to do so, and thus began the study in philosophy of *epistemology* (theory of knowledge).

Heraclitus _____

If Xenophanes had little patience with the opinions of others, his contemporary and near neighbor, Heraclitus of Ephesus, had even less. In fact, Heraclitus considered Xenophanes a mere dilettante. He thought that most persons were no better than asses and cattle. Later generations returned the compliment by fastening upon Heraclitus a number of unlikely and unflattering stories—for instance, that his contempt for society caused him to retire into the mountains and to feed upon grasses and plants, a diet that eventually killed him. But aside from the information that he came from an aristocratic family and was in his middle years around 500 B.C., we have no reliable details about his life. There is dispute about whether the sayings of his that we possess were parts of a book, and there is dispute about what some of his sayings mean. Apparently Heraclitus felt it was beneath him to use language that everyone could understand. As a result his utterances were often exceedingly cryptic, and in antiquity he was known as "the Riddler" and "the Dark."

Heraclitus believed that he alone had found the ultimate truth about things; while everyone else was "asleep," he was "awake." And the truth is that all the apparently unrelated happenings in the world are ordered in keeping with a comprehensive plan that he called "the Logos,"[2] which he personified as a deity, and which he identified with fire. If only we could rise above the limitations of our individual perspectives and see our experience for what it is, we would come, he was sure, to agree with him. Extremes of various sorts are essentially related to one another; day and night, winter and summer, death and life, war and peace, hunger and satiety are all simply different points up and down the same continuous road, not sharply separate or capable of existing alone. One extreme follows another within an overall arrangement of balance and proportion. As a single fire emits different fragrances when different kinds of incense are thrown into it, so the Logos is the abiding medium of the changing opposites of our experience. Or, to shift the metaphor, as there is an exact balance of opposing tensions in a well-adjusted bow or lyre, so the Logos adjusts the extremes in nature into a stable cosmic whole.

Radical change from one extreme to another is the way of the world. Heraclitus likened this to warfare, and contrary to Anaximander, he found nothing "unjust" in it. From the point of view of the Logos, he said, "all things are beautiful and good and just." "War is the father of all and king of all. . . . Right is strife and . . . all things happen by strife and necessity." Strife among opposites, controlled by the Logos, is what constitutes the order of the cosmos; being necessary to the existence of any world at all, it cannot wisely be condemned as wrong. Wisdom consists in accepting it as unavoidable anywhere, in human life as well as in the physical processes of nature, and in adjusting one's sense of values accordingly. To wish for an end to war is to wish for an end to everything.

Few philosophers have expressed as forcibly as Heraclitus the sense that everything is transitory—everything except the scheme of the Logos according to which transitions occur. He likened the universe as a whole to a great river whose waters are ever rushing on. The form and course of the river, fixed by the Logos, do not change; but its contents are in unceasing flux, so that in a sense you cannot step into the same river twice. However permanent a thing may seem, it is changing and will be swept away.

Nevertheless, what is lost in one place is made up for in another. The universe is in this way a self-restorative system, and fire, the embodiment of the divine Logos, is the agent that preserves the balance. The world is "an everliving fire, kindling in measures and going out in measures." "All things are an equal exchange for fire and fire for all things, as goods are for gold and gold for goods." As is clear from the second of

---

[2]The Greek word *logos*, for which there is no exact English equivalent, has a number of related meanings: anything said or written, a story or narrative, an account or explanation of something, a cause or reason, an argument, a general principle or rule, a ratio or proportion, and so on. It also means the power of reasoning. For Heraclitus it signified both human thought and the law which actively orders the universe.

these fragments, Heraclitus did not view fire in the way in which Thales viewed water or Anaximenes viewed air, as the source from which the world arose and the substance which continues to underlie it. Instead he imagined fire to be a kind of medium of exchange between equally eternal constituents of the world—sea and earth particularly. By "fire" he probably meant the fiery "aether" that, as in the case of Homer, Greeks commonly supposed to fill the upper sky. Ordinary fires would be mundane forms of this, and as there is measure and regularity in the process by which an ordinary fire consumes fuel and emits smoke and heat, so also the cosmic fire consumes vapor from the sea and sends back clouds and rain in exchange—all in accordance with a built-in scheme of fixed proportions. In one place sea turns into earth, in another earth turns into sea, but thanks to the measured way in which fire stabilizes the whole process, the total amounts of sea and earth and fire itself always remain the same.

Heraclitus believed, then, that the "many" are "one," not in the sense of deriving from a common material ancestor, as the Milesians had supposed, but in the sense of conforming to a single great principle of eternal flux and movement. He thought that our universe "always was and is and shall be," and so he abandoned the genealogical approach to cosmology, asking not what parent stuff the world came from but what common structure or pattern everything in the world eternally exhibits. In attributing the maintenance of this structure to a physical thing like fire, Heraclitus did in part follow the Milesians. At this early stage of philosophy, when no one seems to have recognized that a pattern may be distinguished from what fits or maintains it, Heraclitus naturally pictured the Logos in concrete material form. A fire, always changing and yet also the same, was a striking image for him to select; it vividly expressed his sense that there is an order in the ceaseless flow of events. When the notion of this order is abstracted from the things ordered, as later thinkers were to do, the idea of *natural law* begins to acquire its modern appearance. It is remarkable that Heraclitus anticipated this development as much as he did.

His own interests, however, were not mainly scientific. Unlike the Milesians, and more than Xenophanes, Heraclitus was concerned with the bearing of cosmology upon politics and upon personal issues of ethics and religion. To live as one ought requires wisdom, and wisdom consists in seeing "how all things are steered through all" by the Logos, which alone is perfectly wise. The soul which animates the human body and provides intelligence is itself a portion of the cosmic fire, taken in by breathing and by the organs of perception, and increased when wisdom has given one a clearer sight of the Logos. If the soul is to perform effectively, it must of course be kept in a dry condition: "For souls it is death to become water." Since drunkenness, for example, makes the soul moist, Heraclitus did not share Xenophanes' cheerful view of it. "A dry soul is wisest and best." Souls that are virtuously dry will survive bodily death and join the cosmic fire. Souls that have become too moist convert at death directly into water. But because the cosmic fire is constantly being exchanged in measures for sea and earth, probably Heraclitus did not think that even the driest souls would survive forever.

Like Xenophanes, Heraclitus ridiculed popular religious ideas and practices for being foolishly idolatrous, but he did concede that occasionally they contained elements of truth. For instance, there were certain rites in which Hades and Dionysus, the gods of death and of life respectively, were worshipped together. Heraclitus found this not wholly despicable, since it conformed with his own identification of opposites, as when in one of his darker utterances he said: "Immortal mortals, mortal immortals, living their death and dying their life." Sayings of this type were, to his way of thinking, exactly what the subject matter called for— veiled hints to the wise, not explicit statements that the unwise would only misunderstand. Accordingly he praised the famous oracle of Apollo at Delphi, who "neither speaks nor conceals, but gives a sign."

In his political remarks, Heraclitus expressed views that were conservative and aristocratic. The multitude, he said, are insolent, politically irresponsible, and resentful of genuine ability. They drive the best people away from the city, even though a single really capable person is worth ten thousand of the ordinary sort. Laws are to be defended no less vigorously than a city's walls, "for all the laws of men are nourished by one law, the divine law." We might have supposed that Heraclitus would have spoken with particular favor of laws of aristocratic governments, not with equal favor of all laws, on the grounds that only laws of aristocratic governments are adequate expressions among humankind of the Logos. Possibly, however, he believed that all laws reflect the Logos to some extent and that people are better off living by poor ones than in making a mess of things by trying, with their customary incompetence, to acquire better. Or possibly his opinion of laws in general, unlike his opinion of the intelligence of his fellows, was moderated by his belief that everything is "beautiful and good and just." It is difficult to say.

There is a story that Heraclitus resigned in favor of his brother from a post in Ephesus that was hereditary in his family—a ceremonial "kingship" which carried such privileges as a front seat at the games. Xenophanes, of course, desired things like that, as a matter of simple justice to poets, but Heraclitus would have none of them. Withdrawing from society, whether into the mountains or not, he became (one imagines) a lonely figure, a prophet who felt that he preached in vain. "I searched out myself," he said, and in doing so he found that the soul within him was continuous with the divine. As we shall see, the outcome of his search had upon later generations immeasurably more impact than it had upon his own.

CHAPTER 2

The Italians

In the Greek colonies of Italy a kind of philosophy flourished that had a vastly different orientation from that of the Milesians or Xenophanes or Heraclitus. It was not motivated simply by curiosity as to the nature of things; it was by no means hostile to traditional religious beliefs; it was not exasperated with human folly or disengaged from politics. On the contrary, it aimed with missionary zeal to reform government, to purify morals, and—above all—to save souls. Heraclitus, of course, had his words for the wise on matters of ethics and religion. The philosophy we have now to examine, however, was definitely not to his liking. He dismissed it in no uncertain terms as a case of philosophical malpractice.

Pythagoras

The founder of Italian philosophy was the famous Pythagoras, who was born around 570 B.C. on the island of Samos, just off the Ionian coast. His father Mnesarchus is said to have been an engraver of precious stones, and Pythagoras may have been trained in the same profession. Soon, however, he must have sensed that he had another and higher calling. As one whom his disciples subsequently deemed an incarnation of the god Apollo, he was not long content, one suspects, with a career in the family business. Precisely what role he played in the life of Samos is unknown, but whatever it was it put him at odds with the tyrant Polycrates, who took control of the island around 538 B.C., and Pythagoras found it advisable to emigrate. He went to Croton, a seaport in southernmost Italy, where he set up a school and became active in politics. For many years he and his band of followers were an increasing political force, securing important posts and pressing for reforms in keeping with their moral ideas. But finally, around 497 B.C., their opponents—both aristocrats and democrats, it seems—rose up to suppress them. In the ensuing turmoil Pythagoras, by then in his seventies, made his way to Metapontum, and there he is said to have died. His followers regrouped and carried on with his mission until the middle of the fifth century B.C., when a more wholesale persecution caused most of them to emigrate to the mainland of Greece.

The strange character of Pythagoras' school no doubt contributed to the trouble. It must have excited innumerable suspicions in the minds of the ordinary citizens of Croton. It was like a religious order, open to both women and men. It required a pledge of secrecy about its doctrines as a condition of membership. Members held all possessions in common, followed a strict daily routine, wore white robes, and observed a number of prohibitions that smacked of primitive magic and taboo. They could not stir a fire with a knife or wear a ring or eat beans; they had to spit on their nail-parings, to put on their right shoes before their left, to touch earth when they heard thunder, and so on. The rule against eating beans arose from their belief that beans are, among vegetables, an especial embodiment of the same universal life-spirit that is present in humans. Eating beans was for them a form of cannibalism.

In fact Pythagoras and his disciples believed that all life is akin—so much so that at death our souls can inhabit new bodies, animal as well as human. Naturally, then, they abstained from meat as well as from beans. This doctrine of *reincarnation* (also known as *transmigration* or *metempsychosis*) was central to the whole Pythagorean outlook. Their overriding concern was to live in such a way that their souls would be purified of all influences from the body, escape from the cycle of rebirth, and join once more the divine spirit from which they originally fell away. Philosophy for them was a way of life, a method of living so as to secure the best life here and hereafter. Pythagoras is said to have been the first to use the word *philosophy* in this sense.

He was hardly innovative, however, in preaching a way of salvation. In much of the Greek world during the seventh and sixth centuries B.C. there occurred a kind of religious revival. Alongside the traditional Homeric religion, according to which the human soul survives death only as a feeble shadow and the gods alone are truly immortal, there was a resurgence of old cults that were associated with deities of agriculture and in which human immortality was secured by secret rites. In the Eleusinian Mysteries, celebrated at Eleusis on the coast north of Athens, the procedure centered around a reenactment of the story of Persephone—goddess of barley and wheat—whose descent into Hades and glorious return gave assurance that her worshippers, like the crops, would also rise again. Candidates for initiation were led through an elaborate ritual, including a torchlight procession, an all-night vigil, and "a solemn communion with the divinity by participation in a draught of barley-water from a holy chalice" (Frazer). The rites culminated in a darkened room where a sacred stalk of grain was suddenly displayed in a blaze of light.

In the Orphic Mysteries, so called because the legendary poet Orpheus was supposed to have founded them, the rites were based upon a complicated myth concerning Dionysus Zagreus, the son of Zeus and Persephone, god of trees and grapevines. Initiation entailed partaking of the body and blood of the god, represented by a sacrificed bull or goat, in the course of a dramatization of his sufferings, death, and resurrection. This, however, was just the beginning. Immortality required not only a regular repetition of the rites but also a changed way of living. The earthly element in one's soul had to be refined out by observing a strict code of dress and behavior; otherwise one would be perpetually caught in the wheel of rebirth and never reach the Isles of the Blest. One had to wear a white garment, abstain from sexual intercourse, eat no meat (except for the flesh of the god), and comport oneself generally in an ascetic fashion.

The religious side of Pythagoreanism was therefore in particularly close affinity with the Orphic cult, which was practiced in southern Italy, among other places. The differences between them, however, are philosophically more important than their similarities. Pythagoras (like his critic Heraclitus) said that to purify (Heraclitus would have said "to dry") the soul it is necessary to contemplate the orderliness of the cosmos,[1] especially as this orderliness is shown in the motion of the stars. The cosmos, in its everlasting structural perfection, is divine. On the principle that we become like what we know, contemplation of the cosmos will reproduce this godly order in our souls, making them microcosms after the pattern of the perfect macrocosm and cleansing them of mortal dross. In his Parable of the Three Lives, Pythagoras compared the life of contemplation to attending games as a spectator—not as a contestant anxious for fame or as a concessionaire bent on making money. Fame and money are slavish aims; contemplation alone frees the soul and fits it for worthwhile action.

In line with this, Pythagoras sought widely to uncover the orderliness in things upon which contemplation should be fixed. Unlike Heraclitus, he was enormously impressed by the extent to which this orderliness could be formulated in mathematical terms. Although he was probably indebted to earlier Greeks and to the Mesopotamians and Egyptians for a good deal of what he knew,[2] Pythagoras was responsible for substantial advances in mathematics. He and his school did much to systematize arithmetic and geometry. One thing in particular seems to have fascinated him: the way in which musical harmony has a mathematical basis. He learned or discovered that, with a simple one-stringed musical instrument, the chief intervals of the Greek scale—the octave, fifth, and fourth— could be produced by stopping the string at half, at two thirds, and at three fourths of its length. The proportions in question (2:1, 3:2, and 4:3) caused him to attach a sacred significance to the number 10 (since it equals $1 + 2 + 3 + 4$) and to require his followers to swear their most binding oaths by it—or rather by the triangle of dots, called the Tetractys of the Decad, by which 10 was represented:

[1] "Cosmos" is a term that Pythagoras is said to have coined.
[2] For example, the so-called Pythagorean Theorem (that the square of the hypotenuse of a right-angled triangle is equal to the sum of the squares of the other two sides) has been found in cuneiform on a tablet from the time of the Mesopotamian king Hammurabi, about 1700 B.C., or roughly 1,130 years before Pythagoras was born.

From the facts of musical harmony, Pythagoras appears to have leapt to the generalization that the entire universe is composed of numerical proportions. How thoroughly he himself worked this out we are unable to tell, but his followers at any rate did so in considerable detail. According to Aristotle, "they supposed the elements of numbers to be the elements of things, and the whole heaven to be a musical scale and a number." They reasoned that, as harmony in music derives from imposing numerical limits upon an unlimited range of sound, so order and structure in the world at large depend upon Limit in general being introduced into the Unlimited in general. Limit shows up in various departments of nature as numerical oddness, the Unlimited as numerical evenness. Why Limit was identified with Odd and Unlimited with Even is shown by the patterns of dots (or the arrangements of pebbles) that the Pythagoreans used to represent the series of odd and even numbers:

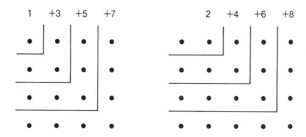

As dots are added to form the series of odd numbers, the pattern remains always a square, with length and height keeping the same ratio to one another (namely, 1:1). In the case of the even numbers, however, the ratio constantly changes (2:1, 3:2, 4:3, 5:4, and so on). Geometrically speaking, then, odd numbers are "limited," even numbers "unlimited." And we see why the Pythagoreans also called odd numbers "square" and even numbers "oblong."

Now, if you conceive of numbers as made up of units, and if you visualize units as dots having a small magnitude (not as dimensionless points), and if you suppose that "the elements of numbers are the elements of things," then you will take numerical dot-units to be the atoms of which the world is composed. Such apparently was the Pythagoreans' line of thinking. "Things are numbers," that is, things consist of the tiny material particles which are the units of numbers. Two of these make a line;

three make a surface (the triangle); four make a solid (called a tetrahedron); and solids make up the physical objects of our experience.

At the beginning of the world, the principle of Limit, which the Pythagoreans thought of as male, deposited the first unit into the Unlimited, which they thought of as female and as consisting of air. The details here are obscure, but apparently this unit grew by "inhaling" the Unlimited until it divided into two. These two then grew and divided, and so it went—numbers arising from units and the cosmos arising from numbers. The finished universe is a gigantic divine organism, living and breathing, and the souls that enliven creatures on earth are portions of the celestial breath.

Although the identification of the Unlimited with air makes one think of Anaximenes, the Pythagoreans' system was very different from his. They believed that *two* distinct principles are ultimate and underived, Limit and the Unlimited, whereas Anaximenes believed that air alone is the originative stuff of the world. In having dual ultimate principles, the Pythagoreans were *dualists* in their theory of reality, that is, in their metaphysics. Anaximenes, of course, was a monist. Like the Ionians in general, however, the Pythagoreans seem not to have considered the possibility that something could exist without being extended in space, that is, without being material. As Heraclitus identified the Logos with fire, so the Pythagoreans identified soul—whether cosmic or human—with air, into which Limit has brought numerical proportion. And while there is a point in saying that the Pythagoreans focused more upon the *structure* of the universe than upon its *matter*, it must be remembered that for them the one could not be abstracted from the other, and that in fact they recognized no such distinction. The structure was numerical, but numbers, to their way of thinking, were sets of concrete material entities. Units were bits of physical stuff distributed in air to form objects.

According to one Pythagorean tradition, the original unit remains at the center of the universe as a fire of great brilliance—the "Guard-House of Zeus," as it was called. Around this our entire solar system, including the earth, revolves. The earth was thus regarded, for the first time in history, not as the center of things but as a planet like any other. We cannot see the fiery original unit because our side of the earth is perpetually turned away from it, but it is reflected by the sun and the moon. The heavenly bodies, as they wheel in their orbits, produce a musical sound. We cannot hear this Harmony of the Spheres because, having had it in our ears from birth as a constant and unvarying "background" sound, we take it as silence.

Harmony occurs wherever the contrary principles of Limit and the Unlimited are present in the right proportions. The many pairs of "opposites" in nature, as species of Limit and the Unlimited, are brought into unity by blending and mixture in accordance with precise numerical ratios. Everything depends upon keeping a middle course between too much and too little. Thus health in the human body requires a proper mingling of the hot and the cold, the wet and the dry; and on this basis, the Pythagoreans developed notions of medicine that dominated medical theory and practice for many centuries. Beauty in art, virtue in ethics, justice in politics—all consist in observing rules of due proportion; and the Pythagoreans were quick to supply numbers even for general concepts such as these. Justice, for example, was said to be a property of the number 4. Goodness in general was identified with Limit, badness with the Unlimited. Because, as we have seen, femaleness was also considered Unlimited, it is a matter for wonder that women were neither excluded from nor unwilling to join Pythagoras' school. Possibly the Pythagoreans held that, since all concrete individuals are constituted alike by factors of Limit and the Unlimited, actual women are not as such any more "bad" than actual men; but one would give a great deal to know what Pythagorean women had to say about the Unlimited. The name of one of these women, Theano, has come down to us. She is said to have been one of the local Crotonians who first joined the school and to have become a celebrated figure. Unfortunately, history is silent about her views.

Both the particular doctrines of Pythagoreanism and its "mathematical metaphysics" in general were to have remarkably far-reaching effects upon philosophy and the sciences. Thus as late as the sixteenth century of our era, we find Nicolaus Copernicus saying that it was by reading reports of Pythagorean astronomy that he was encouraged to see whether he could improve upon existing theories of the motion of the heavenly bodies by supposing that the earth is itself in motion. And Johannes Kepler, a little later, was so taken with the Pythagorean idea of the Harmony of the Spheres that he went to great lengths trying to express the mathematical relations among planetary orbits in terms of musical notation.

It happened, however, that the next major Greek philosopher in Italy, although he may have adhered for a time to Pythagoreanism, came up with a position that was as far removed from Pythagorean dualism as it is possible for a position to be. He was Parmenides, the most thoroughgoing monist to date.

Parmenides

In the dialogue of Plato that bears his name, Parmenides is said to have visited Athens and to have conversed with the young Socrates. From what Plato tells about their relative ages, and from what is known about Socrates' dates, it seems likely that Parmenides was born sometime between 515 and 510 B.C. In his youth he appears to have associated with a Pythagorean named Ameinias, and there is a story that when Ameinias died Parmenides built a shrine in his memory. At what point he broke with Pythagoreanism is uncertain. There may or may not be something to the hypothesis that he was prompted to do so by an acquaintance with Xenophanes. In any case he moved from the vicinity of Croton (presumably) to the Greek colony of Elea, which had been founded on the west coast of Italy in 540 B.C., and there he gained a reputation as a legislator, attracted followers (of whom more presently), and thus founded the "Eleatic school" of philosophy. Plato described him in his middle sixties as "quite gray-headed and of distinguished appearance." Other sources say that he was of noble birth and independent means and that the laws he gave to Elea were so admirable that the citizens annually swore to uphold them.

Parmenides put his philosophy into the form of a poem, 154 lines of which have survived. The poem begins with a prologue in which Parmenides describes himself as ascending in a chariot from darkness into light, where he is greeted by a goddess who takes his hand and states that she is going to disclose to him "the unshaken heart of well-rounded truth." There are, she says, only two possible ways to proceed when truth is your goal. Either you suppose that whatever you can think of exists, or else you believe that you can think of what does not exist. But the second alternative is out of the question. What does not exist is a mere nothing, the goddess points out, and a mere nothing cannot be an object of thought. To think of literally nothing is the same as not thinking at all. Whatever you can think of must exist, just as whatever exists you can think of. This is the Way of Truth.

To interrupt the goddess for a moment, it does of course seem perfectly possible to think of what does not exist—trees on the moon, for example. Why does she so firmly deny this? The answer may lie in the meaning commonly borne at the time by the Greek verb translated as "think of" (*noein*). To "think of" something primarily meant to apprehend or recognize something directly, as by seeing or by a mental process like seeing. As seeing requires something to be seen, so thinking requires something to be thought—something which exists, not blank nothing. To think of what does not exist may therefore have been, in the goddess's vocabulary, a simple contradiction in terms.

At all events, she has established to her satisfaction that "it is the same thing that can be thought and can be," and she proceeds to caution Parmenides against a confusion which is both dangerous and common. Most mortals, devoid of judgment as they are, think that existence and nonexistence are the same—that is, they believe that a thing which exists at one time may not exist at others and that a thing may change and become different from what it was before. Thus clouds seem capable of forming where none existed previously, and of changing and finally vanishing. People constantly believe in this way that "things that are not are." It all comes from trusting one's senses, whereas reason alone is reliable.

When reason is consulted, the goddess says, we find that nothing comes into being or passes away, that nothing moves or changes, and that no more than one thing can possibly exist. The Way of Truth, remember, is that what exists, and only what exists, can be thought of. If anything came into being or passed away, it would not exist before it came into being or after it passed away. We would thus have to think of a time before which, and of a time after which, it was "nothing." Similarly, if anything changed its qualities or its location, it would acquire new qualities or new relations to other things which were "nothing" in its case before, and the old qualities or relations which these replaced would vanish into "nothing." And if more than one thing existed, there would have to be some empty space between however many things there were in order for them to be distinguishable from one another. But empty space would be space in which there was "nothing." In each case, therefore, we would need to think of "nothing," and this we cannot possibly do. To think at all is to think of what exists.

We are driven to the conclusion that only One Thing can possibly exist and that this One Thing is uncreated, unchangeable, indestructible, and immovable. Plurality, creation, change, destruction, and motion are mere appearances. In reality there is only the One (as we may call it for short), and about it there are two further points to notice. First, it is perfectly uniform in composition, the same throughout. We cannot think that there is more of it in one place than in another, for this would involve our thinking that the additional amount of it in the one place was nonexistent (or "nothing") in the other. And we cannot think that in one place it has some quality (say, a shade of color) which is nonexistent (or "nothing") in another place. Second, past and future have no meaning for the One; to say even that "it always was and will be" is a mistake, for this implies that it lasts forever while the years come and go. But if nothing changes, nothing comes and goes—time itself is unreal—and the only correct statement to be made about the One is simply that "it is." In short, it is not "everlasting" (as if it existed through all time); it is *eternal* (not in time).

The Milesians, Xenophanes, Heraclitus, and Pythagoras were therefore guilty of a common mistake: they trusted their senses and believed in the reality of change and of things that change—air that condenses and rarefies, cycles of wetness and dryness, exchanges of fire for earth and water, inhalings of the Unlimited by Limit, and so on and so forth. The Milesians and Xenophanes, as monists, were right as far as they went, but they were wrong in stopping short of treating plurality and change as simply unreal. They tried to explain the (apparently) many things of the world as modifications of a single underlying stuff. What they should have seen is that there is nothing to explain.[3] Only the One exists; the rest is sheer illusion. There can be no question of the One's being "condensed" or "rarefied," or of anything's "separating off" from it. Its unity is changeless. Only this more wholesale type of monism can satisfy the demands of reason.

Xenophanes perhaps came closest to this, in conceiving the universe at large as a single motionless eternal being, and he may have prompted Parmenides toward the extreme conclusion that motion and plurality do not exist. At any rate Parmenides seems to have agreed with Xenophanes in picturing the One as having the shape of a colossal ball. His argument for this may show also some traces of his former Pythagorean beliefs. "It is not lawful," he (or the goddess) says, "that what is should be unlimited. . . . It is bounded on every side like the bulk of a well-rounded sphere, from the center equally balanced in every direction; for it needs must not be somewhat more here or somewhat less there." The One is full and complete, and since whatever is Unlimited is incomplete, the One must exhibit the principle of Limit. Since, moreover, the One is equally full and complete in every direction, which is what a sphere is, the One must be spherical.

This extraordinary position developed itself in Parmenides' mind as a thing inspired by divine assistance. It was not as a mere literary device that he put his arguments into the mouth of a goddess: he evidently felt, as the poets of his time often felt, that his words came to him in a kind of mystical trance. As far as philosophy is concerned, however, what is special about his poem is the careful way in which his arguments were developed step by step. Having laid down his main starting point or premise ("that which can be spoken and thought of needs must be"), and having disposed of alternatives, he proceeded to deduce in orderly sequence his conclusions about the One. This example of *deductive reasoning,* so novel in its explicit formulation, was to have a powerful effect upon subsequent philosophers. Of equal impact, upon Plato in particular, were Parmenides' specific positions: his sharp distinction between reason and the senses, and his insistence that the former gives truth and the latter gives error; his belief that only what is changeless is real and knowable; his contrast between what is eternal in the sense of being timeless and what is everlasting in the sense of enduring for all time.

However careful his reasoning, Parmenides arrived at a conclusion that seems outrageous. The entire world of common experience—of chairs and

---

[3] Parmenides' goddess does, however, supplement her account of the Way of Truth with an account of a Way of Seeming, which she represents as the least implausible, though still wholly erroneous, theory taking plurality and change as realities. Not much survives of this part of the poem. Apparently the Way of Seeming was a cosmology in which two "opposites," Fire and Night, figure as the originating elements of heavenly bodies, of the earth, and of all things on the earth. The goddess tells Parmenides that she wants him to understand how plurality and change, on the (false) assumption that they are real, could best be accounted for, so that he would not be at a loss when arguing with opponents on their own terms.

tables, suns and moons, days and nights—is to be dismissed as a complete mistake. Not a scrap of it really exists. If this is where the Way of Truth leads us, we may well wonder how it differs from the slope of madness. But Parmenides had a follower who aimed to show that what passes for sanity and common sense is actually a heap of absurdities.

Zeno

When Parmenides spoke with Socrates in Athens, he was accompanied by his friend and follower Zeno—then "nearly forty," Plato says, and "tall and fair to look upon." Like Parmenides, Zeno was a citizen of Elea, originally a Pythagorean, and active in politics. The simple life of Elea is said to have been more to his liking than the "arrogance" of Athens, which he seems to have made a point of visiting as infrequently as possible. On one occasion, however, affairs in Elea were not so simple. Although the details differ from one account to another, it appears that Zeno's involvement in politics included his taking part in a plot to overthrow a tyrant. He was arrested and interrogated under torture as to who his accomplices were. Showing a courage for which he became famous, but with what success we do not know, he named the tyrant's own friends. Of Zeno's dates, we know only that he was born about 490 B.C.

Zeno wrote a book in defense of Parmenides that contained dozens of ingenious arguments. In general his strategy was to maintain that, however absurd Parmenides' conclusions may seem, it is really the beliefs of his opponents that are ridiculous. Zeno would assume for the sake of argument that some statement at odds with Parmenides was true; then he would show that this statement leads of necessity to one or more other statements that opponents of Parmenides must admit to be false. The opponents' position would thus be undermined by a "reduction to absurdity" (*reductio ad absurdum*). This method of argument, which Aristotle later called "dialectic" and of which Zeno was a pioneer, can be used with stunning effect. Beliefs that seem perfectly straightforward, even indispensable, are shown to be riddled with paradox.

A good deal of laughter must have greeted Parmenides' announcement that plurality and motion are mere illusions. What could be more obvious than that many things exist and that some of them move from one place to another? Enter Zeno with his paradoxes, one battery of them directed against plurality and another directed against motion. We will describe a representative example of each.

First, let it be assumed, contrary to Parmenides, that many things exist. Suppose, for example, that among other things a medium-size wooden table exists. Now the table could, if we wanted, be sawed into chunks, and each chunk could be sawed into sticks, and each stick could be reduced to splinters. Could the process of cutting go on forever, resulting in smaller and smaller pieces? In theory it would seem to be possible, for every piece would have some size, however tiny, and whatever has any size at all is divisible in principle (even though we may lack sufficiently fine tools to divide it). But if the process could go on forever, this means that the table has infinitely many parts of some size; and since whatever is composed of infinitely many parts of some size must be infinitely large, the table must be infinitely large. Of course it is not. We must have been wrong in saying that the process of cutting it up could go on forever. At some point, we will now say, we would arrive at pieces that would be indivisible in principle. But they could not be indivisible in principle unless they had no size, and since to have no size is to be nothing, they must be nothing. The table, then, in being composed of little pieces of nothing, is itself nothing. So if the table is not infinitely large, it does not exist.

A similar argument can be developed for any object that we care to take. If it has no size, it is nothing. If it has any size it is divisible, at least in principle, and then we are led to the conclusion that it is either infinitely large or nonexistent. Since this is where the belief in plurality leads us in the case of any particular object, the belief in plurality must be wrong. Parmenides must have been right when he said that only the One exists.

Second, and again contrary to Parmenides, let it be supposed that motion occurs. To take a specific case, imagine that Achilles is in a race against a tortoise. As the chivalrous competitor that he is, Achilles gives the tortoise a head start of 100 feet. He knows and we know that he will still have no difficulty in overtaking and passing the tortoise within a very short time. Suppose that Achilles can run a 4-minute mile (or 15 miles per hour). It will take him only 4.5 seconds to cover the 100 feet to where the tortoise starts. Now, in these 4.5 seconds the tortoise can make a little distance. If she crawls, say, an inch per second (or .057 mile per hour), she will move 4.5 inches. Achilles, running steadily at top speed, will cover these 4.5 inches in no more than .017 second. During this .017 second, however, the tortoise will move .017 inch—not much, but she will still be ahead of Achilles. Without breaking stride, Achilles will cover the .017 inch in .000064 second flat. But during the .000064 second, the tortoise will move .000064 inch. Achilles will cover the .000064 inch in .00000024 second. But during the .00000024 second, the tortoise will move .00000024 inch.

It looks like Achilles is in trouble. Although his speed is over 263 times that of the tortoise, she will always maintain a slight lead. Her lead will become smaller and smaller, but it will never vanish completely. No matter how fast Achilles runs, he cannot cover any distance without taking at least some time, and in this time the tortoise can always move a little and stay ahead. So Achilles cannot overtake and pass the tortoise after all. And since on the assumption that motion exists we are led to this obviously absurd conclusion, our assumption must be false. The appearance of things moving is to be discounted as an illusion. Motion, like plurality, does not exist. Parmenides is vindicated.

These famous paradoxes have intrigued philosophers for centuries. One may be sure that there is something terribly wrong with each of them; the problem is to determine precisely what is wrong, and about this there has been wide disagreement. Modern attempts to "resolve" the paradoxes have drawn upon the revolutionary work concerning infinite classes or sets done by mathematicians toward the end of the nineteenth century, particularly by Georg Cantor (1845–1918). Many would now say that the argument concerning plurality is mistaken, for one thing, in assuming that whatever contains infinitely many parts of some size must be infinitely large. In the case of Achilles and the tortoise, however, there is much less agreement, and the full solution is still hotly disputed.[4]

Melissus

Pericles (about 495–429 B.C.), the great political and military leader of Athens, had a mistress by the name of Aspasia whom he dearly loved. "The story goes," Plutarch said, "that every day, when he went out to the market-place, and returned, he greeted her with a kiss." Now Aspasia was a native of Miletus, and Miletus and Samos went to war over the possession of the city of Priene, which lay near to them both. When it became apparent that the Samians were going to win, it was Aspasia (so at least it was commonly supposed) who prevailed upon Pericles to intervene on behalf of Miletus. He got the Athenians to decree that the combatants should cease hostilities and submit their differences to arbitration in Athens. When the Samians refused, Pericles (in 440 B.C.) mounted a naval expedition to reduce them to submission. Ultimately he was successful, but not before losing two sea battles to "Melissus, the son of Ithagenes, a philosopher who was then in command of the Samian forces."

Melissus had written a book in which, with some important exceptions, he had followed Parmenides closely. It is not known whether he actually studied with Parmenides or whether he simply came by a copy of Parmenides' poem. Indeed, all we know about the life of Melissus is what has just been said. But ten fragments of his book, including two lengthy ones, have survived.

The reader may have noticed that Zeno's argument against plurality is hazardous to the user. Much as it was intended to silence those who ridiculed Parmenides, it backfires against the One at the same time that it demolishes tables and chairs. Parmenides said that reality, the One, is spatially extended and has a definite shape. It is an immense globe, with a center and a circumference. But in that case it is as divisible, at least

---

[4] Those who are curious about modern work on Zeno's paradoxes will find an authoritative treatment, not unduly technical, in the article "Zeno of Elea" by Gregory Vlastos in *The Encyclopedia of Philosophy*, ed. Paul Edwards (New York: Macmillan, 1967).

in principle, as an orange or a billiard ball. Melissus evidently saw this and tried to adapt Parmenides' theory accordingly. He said that the One has no "body" and no "thickness" or "bulk." In denying these qualities of it, he seems to have been feeling his way toward a conception of the One as incorporeal, that is, as having no qualities related to space or as being nonspatial—a strictly spiritual being, like God on standard monotheistic doctrine. And if he had arrived at this conception or had kept to it, then certainly the problem raised by Zeno's arguments would have been avoided. If something is nonspatial, there can be no question of dividing it up into parts, endlessly or otherwise.

Melissus does appear to have been unwavering in his insistence that the One is intangible, invisible, and without boundaries in space. But in the course of reflecting upon another problem for Parmenides, he nevertheless fell back into (or never quite succeeded in freeing himself from) conceiving it as extended in space. He said that it is *infinite* in spatial extent. He arrived at this by noticing that if the One has the definite boundaries of a sphere (or, for that matter, any other definite boundaries), the question arises as to what it borders on. Empty space? No, because Parmenides has shown that empty space does not exist. Then does it border on some other reality besides the One? No, because Parmenides has proved that the One is all there is. So it "borders on nothing." This, however, is just another way of saying that the One has no borders whatever, no spatial configuration, and must accordingly be infinite in extent. Parmenides was wrong in giving it a shape. In every direction it goes on forever.

Yet if the One is spatially extended at all, even infinitely, it must have some kind of body and bulk. Otherwise there would be nothing to it; it would be no different from empty space, which has been shown to be nonexistent. And if it has some kind of body and bulk, then you can take any particular region of it and apply Zeno's argument. Even with Melissus' adaptations, Parmenides' position remains vulnerable to those who would turn Zeno's argument against it. The One is infinitely extended? Very well, let us take at random a cubic foot of it. Is this infinitely divisible or not? If you say yes, the cubic foot is infinitely large. If you say no, it is nothing.

As far as we know, the Eleatics never got beyond this unsatisfactory state of affairs. Contemporary with Melissus there were philosophers who, without fully meeting the Eleatics' objections, developed pluralistic theories in which motion and change were not dismissed as mere illusions. These philosophers agreed with Parmenides to the extent of saying that whatever exists has always existed and will never pass away. But they held that the world is composed of a number of ultimate physical elements and that it is these that are everlasting. The movement and change that we perceive around us are accounted for in terms of combinations of these elements. Melissus himself insisted that, even if one abandons Parmenides' monism and believes instead in a plurality of things, each of them "would have to be of the same kind as I say that the One is"— namely, uncreated, unchangeable, and indestructible. Of course, Melissus did not think that there was any good reason to believe in a plurality of things, and the failure of those who did believe this to refute Parmenides' main arguments would not have escaped him.

CHAPTER 3

The Pluralists

Empedocles

First among the proponents of pluralism was Empedocles, who was born around 492 B.C. in Acragas (now Agrigento) on the southern coast of Sicily. Tradition has it that he went to Elea, where he and Zeno were fellow students of Parmenides', and that after a time he took up with the Pythagoreans. It is said that, having divulged some of the Pythagoreans' secret doctrines, he was forbidden to attend any more of their meetings. Back home in Acragas, he went into politics and—in spite of his own aristocratic upbringing—led a democratic movement that overthrew a tyrant and kept down an oligarchy. Like Pythagoras, he appears to have had a charismatic personality in which modesty was not a conspicuous trait. "Hail, friends!" he said in one of his poems. "I come among you no longer as a mortal but as an immortal god, rightly honored by all, and crowned with fillets and floral garlands. When I enter a flourishing town, with my attendant youths and maidens, I am received with reverence; great throngs of people press upon me, seeking benefits." Prophecies, medicinal remedies, raisings of the dead, and changes of weather were among the benefits sought and—so we are told—provided by Empedocles. One might suppose that, with all this to his credit, Empedocles would have won the universal esteem of his fellow Acragantines. Such, however, was not the case. He had political enemies who, during a trip he took abroad, managed to secure a vote prohibiting his return. He died in exile around 432 B.C. The impression he made upon the popular mind may be gauged from the other stories, less probable but more sensational, that were told about his death. According to one, he threw himself into the crater of Mount Etna; according to another, he vanished in a blaze of light when a great voice called his name.

This remarkable figure composed two lengthy poems of which a number of fragments have survived. One of these poems, *On Nature,* reflects his interests as philosopher-scientist. The other, *Purifications,* gives us the religious prophet and mystic. But these two sides of Empedocles were so closely fused that scholars have difficulty in determining whether some fragments belong to the one poem or to the other.

On Nature stresses the limitations of human knowledge in general. Reason, despite Parmenides' high opinion of it, is as feeble an instrument as the senses. Both, however, can apprehend some things clearly. We can see, for example, Empedocles says, that Parmenides was right in denying that empty space can exist and in denying that anything can literally be created from, or destroyed into, "nothing." But it was equally clear to Empedocles that Parmenides was wrong in so distrusting his senses as to conclude that reality is a motionless One. Without, as far as we know, giving explicit criticisms of Parmenides' and Zeno's arguments to the contrary, he declared that motion and plurality exist—although ordinary experience of them does not reveal their true nature. Close investigation shows that at bottom the world is made up of four elements or "roots" (*archai*)—earth, air, fire, and water. These are uncreated, indestructible, unchangeable in quality, and alive; as such they may be associated with the deities Aidoneus, Hera, Zeus, and Nestis respectively. Invisible particles of these divine elements compose the objects we perceive, and changes in their mixture account for the changes of color, texture, shape, temperature, and so on in the objects we perceive. Visible motion occurs when one cluster of these particles changes places with another. Since there is no empty space, such changes of place involve a circular movement, whereby the last in a series of things takes the place of the first.

Empedocles likened the composition of the world to the painting of a picture. As a painter can portray any number of plants and animals by mixing a few basic colors (Greek painters in fact worked with four: red, yellow, black, and white), so the things we perceive are different mixtures of the four basic elements. The mixing and remixing of the elements is attributed to two imperishable powers—a power of attraction called Love (or Aphrodite) and a power of repulsion called Strife. Empedocles viewed these powers as both physical and psychological. They spread through space, inducing among the divine elements exactly the same feelings of affection and enmity that they do among people. There is some evidence that Empedocles, following the example of Pythagoras' principles of Limit and the Unlimited, saw Love as the cause of good in general and Strife as the cause of evil.

The continual struggle between Love and Strife makes for a continual shifting of the particles of earth, air, fire, and water. In a never-ending cosmic cycle, the two powers alternately achieve dominance—Love blending all the particles together into one undifferentiated spherical mass, Strife segregating them into four separate masses. "A double tale will I tell: at one time it [the universe] grew to be one from many, at another it divided again to be many from one. There is a double coming into being of mortal things and a double passing away." Our world has arisen during a period when Strife is overcoming Love. Empedocles describes how the earth and the heavenly bodies were formed as Strife separated the elements from the original mixture. He goes on to tell how human beings evolved from certain primitive "whole-natured forms" composed of earth mixed with water and fire and in which there was no distinction of sex. (It is in the reverse cosmic phase, when Love overcomes Strife, that there occur such deformities as his famous "man-faced oxen." It is also in his description of that phase that he describes biological evolution as a matter of the survival of creatures that happen to be fitted to cope with their surroundings.) He offers a number of conjectures as to the growth of plants, the process of human reproduction, and the factors at work in nutrition and respiration—all in keeping with his theory of the four basic elements.

Consciousness, in Empedocles' view, is shared by everything. The four divine elements experience desire and aversion. Love and Strife are conscious powers. Human thought, however, is particularly associated with blood in the vicinity of the heart. Empedocles came to this conclusion by way of the principle that like is known by like. In order for us to apprehend anything in thought, our thought must be like the thing we apprehend. Now everything is composed of earth, air, fire, or water, or of some combination thereof. Accordingly, that in us which apprehends everything must contain all of these elements, and Empedocles thought that our blood contains them in nearly equal proportions. The things around us, "from the continual motion of a ceaseless flux," are always giving off some of their constituent particles in the form of filmy replicas of themselves—"effluences," as Empedocles called them. When these pass through the pores of our bodies, they are registered, so to speak, by corresponding particles in our blood, and when the blood reaches the heart, thoughts occur.

A similar process accounts for sense-perception. Effluences from things outside us meet with like particles in our eyes, ears, noses, and so forth. "For with earth do we see earth, with water water, with air bright air, with fire consuming fire; with Love do we see Love, Strife with dread Strife."

In his *Purifications,* Empedocles tells how each human soul goes through a cycle parallel to the cosmic cycle of Love and Strife. There is first a state of innocence, corresponding to the rule of Love, in which one's body has not yet developed a head or limbs; "rather is he only a holy, unspeakable mind, darting with swift thoughts over the whole world." This blessed condition is lost, however, when the sin of bloodshed is committed. The soul is banished (remember Pythagoras) to a series of incarnations lasting 30,000 seasons, in which its bodily forms are in succession airy, watery, earthy, and fiery. One thus becomes "a fugitive from the gods and a wanderer." Empedocles says of his own case that "already have I once been a boy and a girl, a bush and a bird and a dumb sea fish." Having now ascended the scale of incarnations to the point where he is among "prophets, bards, doctors, and princes," he expects soon to be free at last from the cycle of rebirth and to become a god, "sharing with the other immortals their hearth and their table, without part in human sorrows or weariness." We should all, Empedocles says, live with this goal before us.

On the face of it, the soul's immortality is incompatible with Empedocles' view that human consciousness is a function of the blood. How could the soul survive the death of the body? Scholars have always felt that there is a great problem here. Perhaps, however, the solution is that Empedocles actually identified the soul with that portion of Love which unites the elements in one's blood. One's body dies when Love's unifying force is overcome by Strife, but one's portion of Love—one's soul—is imperishable.

Anaxagoras

The second pluralist, Anaxagoras, was actually eight or ten years older than Empedocles and would on this basis be entitled to first consideration. There is evidence, however, that Empedocles' views were in circulation first, for Anaxagoras pretty clearly takes issue with one of them in the only book we know him to have written—a short volume of which about a thousand words have survived. Born around 500 B.C. in the Ionian city of Clazomenae (near the present Turkish city of Izmir), Anaxagoras was the opposite of Empedocles in temperament. Like the Milesians, his chief motive in philosophizing seems to have been simple curiosity. There was nothing in him of the prophet, the mystic, or the wonder-worker. His attitude was strictly scientific. And although he came from a wealthy family and could have had a career in politics, he gave away his inheritance and went off to Athens (when he was about twenty) to pursue his researches. He remained in Athens for thirty years, the first philosopher to reside there, making his living as a teacher. Among his students was Pericles, whose dignity of spirit, nobility of speech, and freedom from superstition are said to have been owing to Anaxagoras' influence. Teacher and student came to be close friends, with the result that Anaxagoras was subjected to slanderous allegations from political opponents who wanted to embarrass Pericles. As it happened, both Anaxagoras and Aspasia (Pericles' mistress) were charged at about the same time with the same offense—"impiety." The specific charge against Anaxagoras was that he openly denied the traditional belief in the divinity of heavenly bodies ("he called the sun a fiery stone"). Aspasia was charged not only with impiety but also with operating, for Pericles' especial benefit, a house of ill-repute. Pericles managed to win an acquittal for Aspasia, but Anaxagoras was convicted, fined, and forced into exile. He went to Lampsacus, on the Hellespont, where he lived for some years in great honor and died about 428 B.C. The anniversary of his death was long observed as a holiday in Lampsacus for school children.

Like Empedocles, Anaxagoras accepted without reservation the Parmenidean principles that empty space is impossible and that nothing can literally be created or destroyed. And also like Empedocles, Anaxagoras could by no means accept Parmenides' conclusion that reality is a motionless One. Plurality and motion exist, and they need to be accounted for. But Anaxagoras evidently believed that Empedocles' theory of the four elements could not satisfactorily account for them. The trouble was that, in spite of Empedocles' good intentions, he unwittingly violated the principle that nothing can literally be created or destroyed.

It is easy to see what Anaxagoras probably had in mind. Everything, according to Empedocles, is composed of particles of no more than four elements. The human body, for example, is supposed to be analyzable in terms of three of the four elements, namely, earth, fire, and water, so that a piece of flesh could in theory be separated into tiny fragments of these, with nothing left over. But think what this means. These fragments would not be bits of flesh; they would be separate bits of earth, fire, and water, with nothing fleshy about them. Where fleshiness existed before, we would have earthiness, fieriness, and wetness instead. Fleshiness would have disappeared. It would have vanished into "nothing," and this is flatly at odds with Parmenides' principle. It is impossible for anything to be literally destroyed.

Or consider the process of nutrition, which seems to have especially aroused Anaxagoras' curiosity. In the words of Walter de la Mare:

> It's a very odd thing—
> As odd as can be—
> That whatever Miss T. eats
> Turns into Miss T.

"How," Anaxagoras asked, "could hair come from what is not hair or flesh from what is not flesh?" Bread, for example, is a nourishing substance, but how could bread "turn into" hair? On the basis of Empedocles' theory, bread is composed of some of the same elements as hair, and in the process of digestion Love and Strife interact in such a way as to separate the elements in bread and to join the appropriate ones to the like elements in hair. This, however, involves two impossibilities: the "destruction" of bread by its separation into elements of which none is bready (but, we will suppose, earthy, airy, and wet instead), and the "creation" of hair by the conjunction of elements of which none is hairy (but, let us say, earthy and airy instead). In the one case breadiness goes clean out of existence; in the other case hairiness just suddenly pops in. Neither of these can possibly be what happens.

No, when bread, as we loosely say, "turns into" hair, an entirely different process must be at work. Nothing comes from nothing, and if hair comes from bread, that is because bread contains hair in the first place—an amount too small to be seen, of course, but there nevertheless. The same goes for flesh and bones; if they are nourished by bread, then bread also contains little pieces of them.

The lesson here applies to our thinking about nature generally. It is a mistake to single out certain forms of matter as the "elements" of everything. There are infinitely many different substances in the world, and no one of them can be derived from any combination of the others. The characteristics of hair, flesh, bone, wood, gold, marble, wheat, turnips, grapes, and so on, cannot be accounted for in terms of some mixture of *other* things such as earth, air, fire, and water. Every distinguishable type of stuff must always have existed.

The world is a scene of perpetual transformation. Things are always, as we say, "changing into" other things. It stands to reason, then, that "all things have a portion of everything." If bread "turns into" hair, it must contain a portion of hair to start with; likewise if wood becomes ashes, if grapes become wine, if wine becomes vinegar, if vinegar becomes vapor, and so on. Any given thing, Anaxagoras thought, will sooner or later "turn into" every other kind of thing; thus any given thing must contain portions of all the infinitely many substances that exist. A turnip, for example, contains portions of flesh, gold, and wheat, to name but a few, in addition to its distinctively turnipy components. The reason why we call it a turnip instead of wheat is that its turnipy components outnumber the wheaty ones.

So in order to account for change without violating the principle that nothing can literally be created or destroyed, we must take it that in everything there is a share of everything else—of each of the infinitely many things that exist. This will be true of every part of a thing, however small, not just of a thing as a whole, because parts can change, too. If you dice a turnip, each piece will contain the same proportions of flesh, gold, and wheat—in addition to the dominant turnipy factor—as the turnip as a whole.

Zeno's argument against plurality comes up at this point. How far, in theory, can you go in cutting up a turnip? Is it infinitely divisible, or would you eventually arrive at bits that are indivisible? Anaxagoras opted for the first alternative. "Of the small," he said, "there is no smallest, but always a smaller. . . ." And he acutely observed that, if this is so, the number of pieces in a little thing (however little) is the same as the number of pieces in a big thing (however big). If everything is infinitely divisible, no matter what size it is, then everything has an infinite number of parts, just as the number of points in an inch is as infinite as the number of points in a mile, since between any two points there is always another. Thus he said that "each thing, in relation to itself, [is] both large and small"—"large" in that it has infinitely many parts, "small" in that for every part there is one smaller. Whether Zeno would, or should, have been content with this as an answer to his argument is for the reader to consider.

At any rate, Anaxagoras held that the world was not always the way it is now. There was once a time when everything was so mixed together that nothing could be distinguished. "There was not even any color plain, for the mixture of all things prevented it." Pieces of hair, flesh, bones, wheat, turnips, gold, wood, and infinitely many other things, each too small to be seen, were jumbled up in a kind of cosmic stew. These bits of stuff, which Anaxagoras called "seeds," would always have remained in this mixed condition had not a certain force caused them to start "separating off." And here we come to the point for which Anaxagoras is most famous: he called this force "Mind" (*Nous*, in Greek).

Mind, he said, "is the finest of all things and the purest, it has all knowledge about everything and the greatest power. . . ." With this Anaxagoras came close to the notion of an incorporeal being, of an intelligence without body or parts, but he did not go all the way. Mind, for him, still has extension in space and can be spoken about in quantitative terms, as when he says that it is "all alike, both the greater and the smaller quantities of it." (It is "all alike" in having nothing mixed with it, so that its activity is unhindered.) And although Mind "knows" and "arranges" everything, it does not act with any purpose in view. It is not as if Mind wishes to arrange everything "for the best," say, nor did Anaxagoras refer to it as caring about values or as having holy attributes. In some way which the surviving fragments do not explain, Mind imparted a rotary movement to a small area of the primordial mixture. Once started, the movement widened under its own steam so as to encompass more and more of the mixture, and in the process our world was formed by things' being "separated off." What was at first the work of Mind became purely mechanical. The centrifugal force of the rotation, which increased to a terrific velocity, caused similar "seeds" to come together. "The dense and the moist and the cold and the dark came together here, where the earth now is, while the rare and the hot and the dry went outwards to the farther part of the aether." "The sun, the moon, and all the stars are red-hot stones which the rotation of the aether carries round with it."

Plants come from "seeds" in the air which rain carries down to earth. Animals first arose in "the moist." In the beginning Mind was dispersed evenly throughout the primordial mixture of "seeds," but as soon as plants and animals began to exist, it became associated just with them. Thus Mind presently controls all things, both the greater and the smaller, that have life. And here we have an exception to the rule that everything contains a portion of everything. More accurately, "In everything there is a portion of everything *except Mind;* and there are *some* things [namely, living things] in which there is Mind as well."

Anaxagoras was praised in antiquity for seeing that motion requires a cause separate from the things that move and for saying that this cause is Mind. To Aristotle, "he seemed like a sober man in contrast with the random talk of his predecessors." The purposeful order and arrangement of things bespeak an intelligence that controls them. But the limited role that Mind plays in Anaxagoras' theory, as merely what initiates motion and enlivens plants and animals, was too limited for both Aristotle and Socrates. In a famous passage in Plato's *Phaedo,* Socrates describes the delight with which he learned that Anaxagoras had said that "Mind was the disposer and cause of all." He supposed that Anaxagoras had explained how everything is disposed "for the best" and how the best for human life is determined accordingly. "What expectations I had formed," he said, "and how grievously was I disappointed! As I proceeded, I found my philosopher altogether forsaking Mind or any other principle of order, but having recourse to air, and aether, and water, and other eccentricities." Or, as Aristotle put it: "Anaxagoras uses reason [that is, Mind] as a *deux ex machina* for the making of the world, and when he is at a loss to tell from what cause something necessarily is, then he drags reason in, but in all other cases ascribes events to anything rather than to reason." There is no denying, however, the ingenuity of Anaxagoras' theory of matter or the influence of his conception of Mind upon subsequent philosophers—Plato and Aristotle included.

Leucippus and Democritus

Of Leucippus, the founder of Greek atomism, exceedingly little is known. His dates and his birthplace (variously given as Miletus, Elea, and Abdera) are wrapped in obscurity. Possibly he did, and possibly he did not, "associate with Parmenides" or "study under Zeno," as some sources relate. What is fairly certain is that he ended up with a school at Abdera in Thrace (now Avdira in northeastern Greece). Abdera was founded in about 650 B.C. by colonists from Clazomenae. Its inhabitants acquired a reputation for being so deplorably stupid that "Abderite" became a term of ridicule among the Greeks. Perhaps Leucippus felt that the town was ripe for his services. In any case, a native Abderite called Democritus became one of his students, and it is Democritus about whom we know more. He was born around 460 B.C. and lived to an advanced old age— over a hundred, according to one source. In a career devoted to elaborating his teacher's principles, Democritus produced no fewer than fifty-two separate works in a variety of fields ranging from physics to music (which in those days included language and literature, as well as "music" in our sense). His investigations entailed a good deal of foreign travel, upon which he prided himself. "I am the most widely traveled man of all my contemporaries," he said, "and have pursued inquiries in the most distant places; I have visited more countries and climes than anyone else, and have listened to the teachings of more learned men." One anecdote has it that he traveled as far as India, where he associated with certain "naked philosophers." If he spent so much time in distant places, it is not surprising that when he went to Athens he found that "no one knew me." Apparently he was famous for uncanny powers of observation. In one story he paid a visit to Hippocrates, the great physician, "and there was a young maidservant of Hippocrates, whom Democritus on first arrival greeted with 'Good morning, Maiden!' but on the next day with 'Good morning, Madame!' As a matter of fact it turned out that the girl had been seduced during the night." Of course, this story permits of more than one interpretation.

Leucippus wrote two works—one called *The Great World-System* and the other *On Mind*—of which only one sentence (from the latter) survives: "Nothing occurs at random, but everything for a reason and by necessity." Fortunately a number of fragments have survived from Democritus' writings—which included, incidentally, one called *The Little World-System*—and because Democritus seems to have elaborated Leucippus' views with only a few minor refinements of his own, we can take Democritus as generally speaking for them both. Like Empedocles and like Anaxagoras (whom Democritus may have known), they accepted Parmenides' denial of literal creation and destruction while rejecting Parmenides' conclusion that reality is a motionless One. Motion and plurality exist; the problem is how to account for them. But here they took issue with both Empedocles and Anaxagoras in two important respects: they asserted the existence of empty space or "void" as essential to motion and plurality, and they maintained that both the "elements" of Empedocles and the "seeds" of Anaxagoras were to be rejected in favor of "atoms."

Parmenides held that if empty space does not exist, there can be no movement and no separation or distinction between one thing and another. And he argued that because empty space would be space in which nothing exists, and because "nothing" is strictly unthinkable, there can be no empty space. Leucippus and Democritus, however, seem to have argued that because movement and separation obviously do exist, the empty space which is indispensable to them must also exist—in spite of the fact that empty space is "nothing." "Nothing" or "not-being" must in some sense exist and be thinkable. "Since the void exists no less than body, it follows that not-being exists no less than being."

This void or empty space is of infinite extent, and scattered throughout it are infinitely many particles of matter or "body," which have "being." These particles are indivisible, either because they are "too small" to be divided (as Leucippus may have said) or else because, having no empty space in them, they are "too compact" (as Democritus may have said).[1] Now the Greek word for "indivisible" is *atomos* (*a-*, "not"; *tomos,* from *tomnein,* "to cut"), and so it is that this position is called *atomism* and is summed up in the saying that what exists are "atoms and the void."

The atoms are uncreated, unalterable, and indestructible. They are too small to be seen. They differ from one another only in shape, size, and position. Empedocles' "elements" and Anaxagoras' "seeds" differed in all sorts of additional respects: fire is hot and dry, water is cold and wet; bits of turnip are white, bits of gold are yellow. But Leucippus and Democritus followed Parmenides more closely in denying that such differences of quality can really exist. Given that there is a plurality of things, they must all be (as Melissus had insisted) like the One of Parmenides in hav-

---

[1] In either case, however, the atoms would still have some size and would therefore have parts that could be distinguished at least in thought, so that Zeno would insist that his argument against plurality has not been met.

ing a uniform composition. Hotness, dryness, coldness, wetness, whiteness, yellowness, and so on, are mere subjective appearances to us of different complexes of atoms, which in themselves have none of these characteristics. All the objects of our everyday experience are atom-conglomerates. Differences in the shapes, sizes, amounts, and arrangements of the atoms in these conglomerates account for our perception of differences of other kinds. In short, apparent differences of quality arise from real differences that are only quantitative.

How does it happen that the infinitely many atoms in the infinite void cluster together so as to form what appear to be animals, vegetables, and minerals? Why is not each atom an infinite distance from every other, as in an infinite void each atom could be? The answer is that the atoms are constantly moving in various directions, so that in the course of time they collide. Occasionally it chances that a vast number of collisions will occur in the same general vicinity, and a great cloud of atoms will be formed. If the atoms have the right shapes and velocities, their impacts will result in a vortex or rotary movement within the cloud that has the effect of sorting the bigger atoms from the smaller ones.[2] "Those that are fine go out towards the surrounding void as if sifted, while the rest 'abide together' and, becoming entangled, unite their motions and make a first spherical structure."[3] Such a structure represents the beginning of a world, and in the case of our world the upshot was the earth (which is flat) and its encircling heavenly bodies. But other worlds beyond number are formed in the infinite void—some like ours with suns and moons and moisture and living creatures, others dark and barren—and the worlds destroy one another in stupendous collisions.

So everything comes about thanks to the collision of atoms. The process is strictly mechanical. It is not initiated or guided by any intelligent power, and it has no meaning or purpose. It happens "by necessity," as Leucippus said, and in saying also that "nothing occurs at random, but everything for a reason," he meant a mechanical "reason"—not a purpose, but a cause—a cause having to do with the shape, size, and velocity of atoms.

Visible objects are formed when atoms are so shaped as to stick together when they collide. As Aristotle explained the theory, "Some of [the atoms] are angular, some hooked, some concave, some convex, and indeed with countless other differences; so . . . they cling to each other and stay together until such time as some stronger necessity comes from the surrounding and shakes them apart." The changes that we perceive in things

---

[2] It would appear that Leucippus and Democritus are considerably indebted to Anaxagoras at this point. The atoms have always been in motion and do not require a Mind or anything else to start them moving, but the sorting action of rotary movement is in keeping with Anaxagoras' theory.

[3] Weight, it seems, is the tendency of larger atoms to move to the center of a vortex— the larger the atom the stronger the tendency and the greater its weight. Atoms not caught in a vortex have no weight. Two ordinary objects of the same size will differ in weight when they have different amounts of void mixed in with their constituent atoms.

are owing to losses or gains in their constituent atoms, such losses or gains being caused by impacts with other atoms in the neighborhood. No matter how stuck together two atoms may be, they always retain their separate identities and never merge into one. If this were not true, there would be literal creation and destruction as one atom came to exist where two existed before. Similarly, one atom can never become two. "The many does not come from the one nor one from many," as Aristotle put it, "but rather all things are generated by the intertwining and scattering around of these primary magnitudes."

If nothing exists apart from atoms and the void, then the soul which might be supposed to animate a living body can at most be a temporary complex of certain atoms. Such is what Leucippus and Democritus said. A soul consists of especially small atoms that are spherical in shape—the better to move with ease among the atoms composing the body. A human mind, which is the thinking portion of a human soul, is an accumulation of spherical atoms in the head. At death the soul-atoms are scattered, and consciousness is lost. The same sort of atoms are associated with fire, and in fact one keeps one's soul-atoms in stock by inhaling fire-atoms from the atmosphere (remember Heraclitus). Human sensation and thought are both simply impacts and movements of atoms. Vision, for example, is attributed to "certain images, of the same shape as the object, which [are] continually streaming off from the objects of sight and impinging on the eye" (remember Empedocles). The images seen, like the eyes that see them, are complexes of atoms which in reality possess only shape, size, and position. There are no colors, nor are there any sounds, smells, tastes, or temperatures. All such sensory qualities are mere appearances that we mistakenly assign to things in keeping with general custom. "By convention are sweet and bitter, hot and cold, by convention is color; in truth are atoms and the void." Sensory awareness is therefore called, by a considerable understatement, "obscure." Fortunately we have another, and a "genuine," means of knowing: by an intellectual process, involving action directly upon mind-atoms by images that are too tiny for the senses to pick up, we can go beyond sensory "convention" and grasp things as they are. Once aware of the true composition of objects, we can interpret our sensory awareness of changing colors, sounds, and so forth, as representing changes at the atomic level.

Little beyond this has survived as to Leucippus' and Democritus' theory of knowledge. Our ancient sources were much more interested in Democritus' contributions to ethics—a field in which Leucippus, as far as we know, was silent. Nearly three hundred fragments from Democritus' ethical writings were preserved. Now ethics, in its search for general principles by which we ought to live, presumes that how we live is something for which we can be responsible. And such responsibility would seem to require, at a minimum, that we possess a capacity for purposeful actions that are not literally identical with purposeless collisions among atoms. Democritus, however, appears not to have seen any problem here. He simply proceeded to state the goal that he believed we should all aim at in our lives and to describe the means by which he thought we could attain it. This goal, he said, is cheerfulness or contentment (*euthymia,* in Greek), by which he meant a state of soul that is serene, imperturbable, and unagitated by emotion. Such a soul is virtuous, and it achieves this condition by restraining bodily appetites, by focusing on what is attainable, by cultivating refined pleasures, and by eradicating even the wish to do wrong. Although Democritus' ethical remarks contain a good many commonplaces on the order of "Constant delay means work undone," there are others more original and arresting. "Good and true are the same for all men, but pleasant differs from one man to the next"—which makes it plain that Democritus, unlike the Epicureans who were later to borrow much of his philosophy, was not a hedonist. "Magnanimity consists in enduring tactlessness with composure"—as urbane a maxim as one is likely to find. To live badly is "not to live badly, but to spend a long time dying." In politics Democritus was a thoroughgoing democrat: "Poverty under democracy is as much to be preferred to so-called prosperity under an autocracy as freedom to slavery."

Some of Democritus' ethical remarks express positions for which Socrates and Plato were famous: "The wrongdoer is more unfortunate than the man wronged"; "The cause of error is ignorance of the better." Because Democritus and Socrates were contemporaries, either of them could have influenced the other, but we have no means of telling what actually happened. In other respects, as we shall see, the two men had very little in common.

The atomism of Leucippus and Democritus had a long life. As modified by Epicurus within a generation or two of Democritus' death, and as elaborated by Lucretius in the first century B.C., atomism survived to play an important part in the development of modern science. The great physicist and chemist Robert Boyle (1627–1691) is an outstanding example. He found the old atomism presented in the writings of the English philosopher Francis Bacon (1561–1626) and the French philosopher Pierre Gassendi (1592–1655), and he proceeded enthusiastically to employ it in formulating his revolutionary theory of chemical elements. Subsequent developments in physics and chemistry have of course radically changed the manner in which atoms are conceived. No longer are they taken to be ultimate, indivisible units of matter. Beginning with the discovery of electrons at the end of the nineteenth century, atoms have been found to consist of more and more subatomic particles, and now over 150 different ones are known. The distant influence of Leucippus and Democritus might be said to be at work, however, in the current debate as to whether the known subatomic particles are all simply combinations of a single, more elementary kind of particle called "quarks." As for the divisibility of atoms, that was displayed with terrible clarity at Hiroshima on August 6, 1945, and at Nagasaki three days later.

PART II

The Great Days of Athens

Thus saith the Lord, thy redeemer,
and he that formed thee from the womb,
"I am the Lord that maketh all things; . . .
That saith of Cyrus, 'He is my shepherd,
and shall perform all my pleasure':
even saying to Jerusalem, 'Thou shalt be built';
and to the temple, 'Thy foundation shall be laid.' "

In these words Second Isaiah refers to Cyrus the Great, king of the Persians, who conquered Babylon (538 B.C.) as the prophet foretold and freed the Jews from their Babylonian Exile. Cyrus and his successors, Cambyses and Darius, went on to amass the largest empire the world had ever seen. It stretched from Ionia in the west to India in the east, and from Thrace in the north to Egypt in the south. In due course Darius made preparations for the conquest of mainland Greece, whereupon the Athenians went to the aid of a revolt in Ionia and burned down Sardis (499 B.C.), the Persians' regional headquarters. When Darius heard the news, he first asked "who the Athenians were," and then, according to Herodotus, "on being told, gave orders that his bow should be handed to him. He took the bow, set an arrow on the string, shot it up into the air and cried: 'Grant, O God, that I may punish the Athenians.' Then he commanded one of his servants to repeat to him the words, 'Master, remember the Athenians,' three times, whenever he sat down to dinner."

Remember them he did. By 493 B.C. Darius had reduced Ionia and destroyed Miletus in the process. In September of 490 B.C., the Persian general Datis landed with an immense force on the Greek coast at Marathon, about twenty-five miles north of Athens. Here, in an afternoon, the battle was fought that first checked the Persian tide. The Greeks under Miltiades lost 192 men; the Persians lost 6,400. "Had Persia beaten Athens at Marathon," Sir Edward Creasy said, "she could have found no obstacle to prevent Darius . . . from advancing his sway over all the known Western races of mankind."

Ten years later, under Darius' successor Xerxes, the Persians tried again and were defeated again—at Salamis, Plataea, and Mycale. Athens emerged in 478 B.C. as the leader of a military alliance called the Delian League (from the island of Delos, where its treasury was kept). From funds contributed by the various cities composing the League, Athens maintained a powerful navy, supposedly for the common defense against Persia, but which she lost little time in using to advance her own commercial and colonial interests. For the next forty-seven years, until her imperial ambitions resulted in the ruinous Peloponnesian War with Sparta (431–404 B.C.), Athens was the scene of an unparalleled flowering of culture. During this period there lived the playwrights Aeschylus, Euripides, Sophocles, and Aristophanes; the historians Herodotus, Thucydides, and Xenophon; the architects Ictinus and Callicrates (designers of the Parthenon); the sculptor Phidias (supervisor of the Parthenon's frieze); the philosophers Anaxagoras, Socrates, and others soon to be mentioned.

Pericles, the leading statesman in Athens for much of this period (from about 457 to 429 B.C.), delivered an oration at the funeral of those who were killed in the first year of the Peloponnesian War. In this oration, as reported by Thucydides, he described the principles of action by which Athens rose to power, "and under what institutions and through what manner of life our empire became great." Athens in her heyday is brought to life in words of noble simplicity:

> Our form of government [Pericles said] does not enter into rivalry with the institutions of others. We do not copy our neighbors, but are an example to them. It is true that we are called a democracy, for the administration is in the hands of the many and not of the few. But while the law secures equal justice to all alike in their private disputes, the claim of excellence is also recognized; and when a citizen is in any way distinguished, he is preferred to the public service, not as a matter of privilege, but as the reward of merit. Neither is poverty a bar, but a man may benefit his country whatever be the obscurity of his condition. There is no exclusiveness in our public life, and in our private intercourse we are not suspicious of one another nor angry with our neighbor if he does what he likes; we do not put on sour looks at him, which, though harmless, are not pleasant. While we are thus unconstrained in our private intercourse, a spirit of reverence pervades our public acts; we are prevented from doing wrong by respect for authority and for the laws, having an especial regard for those which are ordained for the protection of the injured, as well as for those unwritten laws which bring upon the transgressor of them the reprobation of the general sentiment.
>
> And we have not forgotten to provide for our weary spirits many re-

laxations from toil; we have regular games and sacrifices throughout the year; at home the style of our life is refined; and the delight which we daily feel in all these things helps to banish melancholy. Because of the greatness of our city the fruits of the whole earth flow in upon us, so that we enjoy the goods of other countries as freely as of our own.

Then, again, our military training is in many respects superior to that of our adversaries. Our city is thrown open to the world, and we never expel a foreigner or prevent him from seeing or learning anything of which the secret if revealed to an enemy might profit him. We rely not upon management and trickery, but upon our own hearts and hands. And in the matter of education, whereas they from early youth are always undergoing laborious exercises which are to make them brave, we live at ease, and yet are equally ready to face the perils which they face. . . .

If, then, we prefer to meet danger with a light heart but without laborious training, and with a courage which is gained by habit and not enforced by law, are we not greatly the gainers? Since we do not anticipate the pain, although when the hour comes, we can be as brave as those who never allow themselves to rest; and thus too our city is equally admirable in peace and in war. For we are lovers of the beautiful, yet simple in our tastes, and we cultivate the mind without loss of manliness. Wealth we employ, not for talk and ostentation, but when there is a real use for it. To avow poverty with us is no disgrace; the true disgrace is in doing nothing to avoid it. An Athenian citizen does not neglect the state because he takes care of his own household; and even those of us who are engaged in business have a very fair idea of politics. We alone regard a man who takes no interest in public affairs, not as a harmless, but as a useless character; and if few of us are originators, we are all sound judges of a policy. The great impediment to action is, in our opinion, not discussion but the want of that knowledge which is gained by discussion preparatory to action. For we have a peculiar power of thinking before we act, and of acting too, whereas other men are courageous from ignorance but hesitate upon reflection. And they are surely to be esteemed the bravest spirits who have the clearest sense of the pains and pleasures of life, but do not on that account shrink from danger. . . .

To sum up, I say that Athens is the school of Hellas, and that the individual Athenian in his own person seems to have the power of adapting himself to the most varied forms of action with the utmost versatility and grace. This is no passing and idle word, but truth and fact; and the assertion is verified by the position to which these qualities have raised the state. For in the hour of trial Athens alone among her contemporaries is superior to the report of her. No enemy who comes against her is indignant at the reverses which he sustains at the hands of such a city; no subject complains that his masters are unworthy of him. And we shall assuredly not be without witnesses; there are mighty monuments of our power which will make us the wonder of this and of succeeding ages: we shall not need the praises of Homer or of any other panegyrist, whose poetry may please for the moment, although his representation of the facts will not bear the light of day. For we have compelled every land, every sea, to open a path for our valor, and have everywhere planted eternal memorials of our friendship and of our enmity.

CHAPTER 4

The Sophists

If Athens was, as Pericles said, the "school of Hellas," the most notable educators of Athens itself were certain foreigners known professionally as "Sophists"—a name that may be translated as "Wisdom Experts." These were men of cosmopolitan background and miscellaneous knowledge who traveled from city to city lecturing for a fee on various subjects of popular interest and giving courses of instruction for the young. Hitherto the education of children had consisted simply of the rudiments of reading, writing, and arithmetic, together with gymnastics and some music and poetry. Such meager attainments became more and more inadequate as the complexities of Greek life increased. The growth of democracy in the various independent city-states, and above all at Athens, called for a more thorough training in one field especially—public speaking. This training the Sophists aimed particularly to furnish.

In Athens, after the reforms of Cleisthenes (508 B.C.) and his grandson Pericles (462 B.C.), ultimate political authority was vested in the Assembly, which comprised all the adult male citizens—about 30,000—and which met monthly to transact legislation. Only those who possessed the oratorical skill to sway this multitude could rise to positions of power. Moreover, judicial functions at Athens were performed by juries (which were judges and juries at once), varying in size from 101 to 1,001, chosen from the Assembly by lot. Plaintiffs and defendants had to plead their own cases in court; there were no professional attorneys. Since lawsuits were a routine method of getting money, the need for persuasive public speaking, on the part of those who wanted to retain wealth no less than on the part of those who wanted to acquire it, was all the greater.

This need the Sophists professed to meet, at least for those who could afford their services. The young sons of well-to-do families were sent to them in order that they might learn the poise and polish, the all-round impressiveness of bearing and utterance, to shine in debate and to excel in politics. A brief look at three considerable figures will give an idea of what the Sophists offered.

Protagoras

First among the Sophists, both in date and in reputation, was Protagoras. He lived from about 490 to 420 B.C., and like Democritus, he was a native of Abdera. For forty years he practiced his profession, accumulating a fortune in fees and tuition. In Athens, where he often appeared in his travels, he was considered the foremost speaker of his time. Pericles was so impressed with Protagoras' political sagacity that he commissioned him to draft a legal code for one of Athens' colonies. In the dialogue of Plato that bears his name, Protagoras is depicted in his later years as a man who has quite overcome a certain stigma attached by Athenian society to "foreigners" who come to town and hire themselves out as teachers. Thoroughly confident of his powers and his position, he makes no bones about what he can provide his pupils, namely, "political virtue."[1] A young man who comes to him, he says, "will learn that which he comes to learn. And this is prudence in affairs private as well as public; he will learn to order his own house in the best manner, and he will be able to speak and act for the best in the affairs of the State. . . . And I give my pupils their money's worth, and even more, as they themselves confess."

As part of his curriculum in "political virtue," Protagoras naturally included under "speaking for the best" a substantial amount of attention to techniques of debate. And it is no surprise to find him reported as having said that there are two sides to every issue and as having composed a volume of pro-and-con arguments, called *Antilogiae,* to illustrate the point. What is remarkable are the notions of truth and reality in light of which he viewed the differing beliefs on any issue. Like Parmenides, and possibly under Parmenides' influence, he held that it is impossible to think of what does not exist, of what is literally "nothing," since "thinking of nothing" is the same as not thinking at all. Whereas Parmenides used this to argue that change and plurality are illusions and that popular opinions to the contrary are false, Protagoras used it to argue for the diametrically opposite conclusion that *whatever anyone believes is true*—true, that is, for the person who believes it. If to think at all is necessarily to think of what exists or is real, then none of your thoughts or beliefs can for you be false. If something appears true to you, then for you it is really true. Another person may, of course, believe differently, in which case that person's belief is true, too—true for that person. Neither of you is wrong, for neither of you can be believing what is unreal and false. And this means that there is no objective truth independent of what people believe, no reality distinguishable from how things

---

[1] "Virtue" is the usual English translation of the Greek word *arete,* whose primary meaning was "practical efficiency or skill." An implement or tool could have *arete,* in the sense of being well adapted to perform its function. An artisan or craftsman could have *arete,* in the sense of being skilled at his trade. When used generally of a man or a woman, without reference to a particular skill or task, *arete* designated an all-round excellence in one's civic and domestic roles, in both public and private life, including moral goodness or "virtue." The "political virtue" of which Protagoras goes on to speak has this wider meaning; he teaches not only skill in politics as such, but also a general excellence in managing one's affairs, in keeping with customary moral ideas.

appear. If the wind, for example, feels warm to you and cold to me, then it *is* warm (for you) and cold (for me). There are two sides to every issue, at least two, and both of them are right—for those who take them.

In short, reality and truth are relative to individual persons, to particular thinking subjects. This position, which is called *relativism* (or *individualistic relativism,* to be more precise) with respect to metaphysics and epistemology, is summed up in a famous sentence which stands at the beginning of Protagoras' book *On Truth:* "Man is the measure of all things, of the existence of things that are, and of the nonexistence of things that are not." That is to say, "Things are to you such as they appear to you, and to me such as they appear to me."

Protagoras did not hesitate to apply this maxim to ethics and to politics. Of moral rightness and political justice each man is also the "measure." On the level of the state as a whole, "whatever appears to a state to be just and fair, so long as it is regarded as such, is just and fair to it." It follows that if a majority are of one opinion and a minority of another, as regards right and justice, both are correct; and the majority are correct if they think that the minority ought to conform to their opinion, while the minority are correct if they think that they ought not to conform.

Two questions immediately come up. If one person's opinion is as true as another's, how can anyone justifiably claim, as indeed Protagoras claimed, to be wiser than others and to deserve handsome fees as a teacher? And if each person is the measure of what is right and just, does not this mean that "anything goes" in morality and politics—even the most complete ruthlessness, for those who are so minded? Protagoras seems to have answered the first question by saying that although all opinions are equally true, some are "better" or "sounder" or "more expedient" than others, and it is these which a Sophist offers. Using words as a physician uses medicines, a Sophist persuades people to adopt new opinions which they themselves will feel are better—"better" as judged by themselves on the basis of whatever standards they happen to accept. The Sophist is adept at convincing them in this way to accept as "stronger" arguments that at first appear to them "weaker." And as regards the second question, Protagoras seems to have believed that people will normally find it better— "only better, and not truer"—to live by the traditional values of their communities and by "the laws which were the invention of good lawgivers living in the olden time." These values and laws generally express, in ways suitable to particular local circumstances, certain natural human tendencies toward friendly and harmonious social relations, which it is in the common interest to maintain. Justice, honesty, piety, and self-control, as defined by the established morality and instilled by the customary educational methods, are elements of the "virtue" that the ordinary citizen will find it "best" to have. The Sophist, however, may see that the prevailing code can be amended in respects which he can persuade the majority to consider as "better," and in any case he is professionally qualified to articulate this code in ways that will most effectively supplement the traditional education. "A teacher of this sort I believe myself to be," Protagoras says in Plato's dialogue.

So it was that a theory of knowledge which in other hands could be used to sanction anarchy was brought by Protagoras into line with an essentially conservative position. As we shall see in a moment, however, other hands were ready.

On the score of religion, Protagoras confessed to being a skeptic. Life is too short, he said, and the subject is too obscure, for him to know whether the gods exist and, if they do, what they are like. Although, in keeping with his general conservatism, he seems to have spoken up for the traditional religion as a civilizing force, his doubts about its literal truth may finally have gotten him into trouble. There is a story, which is possibly true, that he was prosecuted in Athens for impiety and that he drowned in a shipwreck on his voyage away from the city.

Gorgias

Gorgias of Leontini, in Sicily, was only a few years younger than Protagoras and not much behind Protagoras in fame. He is said by all authorities to have lived for over a hundred years, which would put his death sometime after 380 B.C. Like Protagoras, he was a free-lance teacher who practiced in various cities, but he was late in coming to Athens. His first appearance there, in 427 B.C. when he was already about sixty, was occasioned by an attack upon Leontini by Syracuse. Gorgias was sent as head of an official mission to persuade Athens to come to the rescue. The mission was a success, and Gorgias managed also to pick up a little something on the side. "By general consent," Plato reported, "he spoke most eloquently before the Assembly, and in his private capacity, by giving demonstrations to the young and associating with them, he earned and took away with him a large sum of Athenian money." It was a special feature of Gorgias' appearances that he would challenge his audiences by stating that he was prepared to give convincing answers to any questions they wanted to ask. "I may add," he says in Plato's *Gorgias,* "that many years have elapsed since anyone has asked me a new one."

Unlike Protagoras, Gorgias did not promise to teach "virtue." In fact he seems to have been amused by the idea that anyone would promise this. He denied that there is some one human quality of which "virtue" is the name, so that actually there is nothing specific under this name to be taught. Instead there are many different "virtues" appropriate to the various situations and callings in life—obedience for the young, courage for soldiers, leadership for statesmen, and so forth. As a Sophist, Gorgias promised only to teach the art of rhetoric or oratory—the ability "to speak and to persuade the multitude"—on any subject at hand and for whatever purposes one may wish. He made much of the power this can give; and while recognizing that it can be put to improper uses, he denied that he was blameworthy if his students did so. This, he said, would be like blaming a boxing trainer if one of the trainer's protégés should punch his mother in the nose. The Sophist meant his instruction to be employed for good ends, and he assumed that his students knew the difference between right and wrong. (The Gorgias in Plato's dialogue is forced into a corner by Socrates and made to say that, after all, he will teach a student the difference if the student does not already know; but it is doubtful that the real Gorgias ever said this.)

Like Protagoras, Gorgias interpreted the role of oratory in light of relativistic views of truth and reality. There are no objective truths valid for everyone, only various opinions that are true for those who are persuaded of them. (The master persuader, of course, was the Sophist.) That truth is relative seems to have occurred to Gorgias in part because of the radical disagreements he found among philosophers. From Thales to Democritus, philosophers claimed one after another to have discovered the underlying structure of the universe, but they were hardly unanimous about what it is. Some said this and some said that. A natural explanation for their disagreements is that there is no reality with a structure to be discovered, no definite nature of things to be known, and that what philosophers proclaim as the truth is simply what strikes them personally as convincing. There is nothing objective to which human beliefs must conform if they are to be true. Truth and reality are relative to the beliefs of each person.

With the aim of making this position all the more persuasive, Gorgias concocted an intricate parody of the arguments by which Parmenides and Zeno tried to prove the opposite. Whereas the Eleatics had argued that only the One exists and that popular opinions based on appearances to the contrary are false, Gorgias used the same sort of arguments to prove that *nothing* exists, that even if anything *did* exist no one could comprehend it, and that even if anyone *could* comprehend it this comprehension could not be communicated. "In contending with adversaries," Gorgias said, "destroy their seriousness with laughter." The joke began with the title he gave to his parody, *On the Non-Existent: On Nature,* which is the reverse of the title of Parmenides' poem, *On Nature: That Which Is.* But the joke had a serious moral: if Parmenides' and Zeno's methods of argument can prove things so much at odds with their distinctions between appearance and reality, opinion and knowledge, then no such distinctions can be made. Reality for each of us just *is* what appears to us, and "knowledge" is merely another name for opinion. (This presumes that the Eleatic arguments are as good as any available on the subject, so that if they fail others will fare no better.)

In arguing that nothing exists, Gorgias displayed a kind of mastery of his opponent's position and deftness at turning it inside out that must have dazzled his audiences. A concise abridgment will show how he proceeded: If anything exists, he said, it must be either the existent or the nonexistent. The latter alternative is out of the question; the nonexistent does not exist, so what exists must be the existent. Now the existent must be either many or one. It cannot be one, because (as Zeno said) whatever exists has size, whatever has size is divisible, and whatever is divisible is not one. But it cannot be many, because whatever is many consists of an addition of ones, and we have just seen that nothing which exists can be one. Because, then, the existent can be neither many nor one, the existent cannot exist. In other words, nothing exists.

Thunderous applause, we are told, greeted Gorgias' rhetorical performances. "When persuasion joins with speech," he said, "it can affect the soul in any way it wishes." As evidence of this he cited philosophical debates, "in which mental agility is what determines the acceptance of opinions." And in keeping with his own particular profession, he cited the way in which an advocate in court can sway the jury, "not because of the truth of what he says but by the sheer power of speech and its skillful composition."

Upright as Gorgias himself may very well have been, the art of rhetoric as he taught it was open to unscrupulous uses that his relativism would have done nothing to discourage. If persuasive opinions are to count as the truth, then whatever you take to be right is right for you, and whatever you can persuade others to take as right is right for them. The dangerous possibilities are clear. Dissatisfaction with this side of Sophism on the part of certain influential Athenians was responsible for the derogatory associations that still cling to the word *sophistry* today. Thus Aristophanes, in his comedy *The Clouds* (first performed in 423 B.C.), attacked the Sophists' system of education with satire as damaging as it was (and is) funny. Strepsiades is being sued by his creditors for immense debts that his son Pheidippides has run up. A solution occurs to him in the nick of time: he will take himself to the "Thinking-Shop" (the *Phrontisterion*) of the Sophists, where he will learn "to conquer in speaking, right or wrong, . . ." and thereby

> escape clean from my debts, and appear to men to be bold, glib of tongue, audacious, impudent, shameless, a fabricator of falsehoods, inventive of words, a practised knave in lawsuits, . . . a thorough rattle, a fox, a sharper, . . . a dissembler, a slippery fellow, an imposter, a gallows-bird, a blackguard, a twister, a troublesome fellow, a licker-up of hashes. . . .

When Strepsiades proves to be a poor student, he sends Pheidippides to the Thinking-Shop instead, and Pheidippides has no trouble learning his lessons. With delight he exclaims: "How pleasant it is to be acquainted with new and clever things, and to be able to despise the established laws!"

Callicles

Gorgias is said to have maintained that rhetoric is superior to the other arts because it dominates in every field, not by violence but by bringing people into willing submission. Be that as it may, violence is hardly inconsistent with the relativism upon which both Gorgias and Protagoras based their practice of rhetoric. If truth is a matter of personal opinion, some persons are of the opinion that "might makes right"; and according to relativism, their opinion is not incorrect—not for them.

Among those who held this opinion was a certain man named Callicles. It was in Callicles' house that Gorgias stayed on the occasion described in Plato's *Gorgias,* and in fact all of our information about Callicles comes from this dialogue. He was at the time (about 405 B.C.) a wealthy young Athenian gentleman looking forward to a political career. Like Pheidippides, he was not going to let "established laws" get in his way. Pericles, in his Funeral Oration, spoke with pride of the "spirit of reverence" which pervaded the public life of Athens and of the "respect for authority and for the laws" which especially protected the injured. Protagoras held that such reverence and respect are produced by cultivating certain human tendencies that are natural. Callicles, however, frankly declared that he found all this a matter of mere "convention" (*nomos,* in Greek), certainly not anything sanctioned by "nature" (*physis*). For example, "convention" has it that all men are to be treated as equals, that doing wrong is worse than suffering it, and that moderation is a very great virtue. According to "nature," precisely the opposite is true in each instance. Most men are weak—weak in intelligence, in spirit, in courage, and in impressiveness of character—and the customary laws and moral rules are meant simply to protect them from exploitation by those who, in these respects, are strong. Society's norms are so many charms and spells for taming and enslaving the noble spirits (whom Callicles likens to "lions") that occasionally appear. As is plain, however, from both the behavior of animals and the broad course of human history, the Law of Nature is that "justice consists of the superior ruling over and having more than the inferior." A man with sufficient natural strength will break out of the cage that society puts around him: "He would trample underfoot all our formulas and spells and charms, and all our laws which are against nature: the slave would rise in rebellion and be lord over us, and the light of natural justice would shine forth." He will have the command of politics and the absence of scruple to do what he likes; he will live on a grand scale, helping his friends and harming his enemies, giving free play to his appetites, stopping at nothing that would give him satisfaction. Everyone would prefer to live like this, if only everyone knew how; but such is the weakness of most people that out of resentment, as a matter of sour grapes, they praise moderation and self-control. In fact, "luxury and intemperance and licence, if they are provided with means, are virtue and happiness—all the rest is a mere bauble, agreements contrary to nature, foolish talk of men, nothing worth."

In the sixteenth year of the Peloponnesian War (or about ten years before the probable date of the discussion in Plato's *Gorgias*), Athens sent a military expedition against the Spartan colony on the island of Melos. When the troops had landed, representatives were first sent to negotiate with the Melians. Thucydides recorded the substance of what was said. Would the Melians forsake their alliance with Sparta and join the Athenian confederacy on a tribute-paying basis? The Athenians said that they were not going to mince words. The Melians knew as well as they did that in such situations the strong do what they have the power to do and the weak accept what they must. It is a general and necessary law of nature, they said, a law fixed for all eternity and followed even by the gods, that he should rule who can. The Melian troops were badly outnumbered. "Think it over," the Athenians said, "and let this be a point that constantly recurs to your minds—that you are discussing the fate of your country, that you have only one country, and that its future for good or ill depends on this single decision which you are going to make."

The Melians decided to fight for their liberty, trusting that the gods would come to their assistance because the right was on their side. In the end, the Athenians put to death all the men of military age and sold the women and children as slaves.

Many examples of Callicles' view in action could be cited from the history of later centuries, including the present one.

CHAPTER 5

Socrates

Socrates' Life and Character _____

In a sentence that has often been quoted, Cicero said that it was Socrates who "first called philosophy down from the sky, set it in cities and even introduced it into homes, and compelled it to consider life and morals, good and evil." Now it is only fair to acknowledge that Protagoras and Gorgias, who were Socrates' seniors by about twenty years, had already broken with the tradition of Thales. Instead of speculating about the heavens and the cosmos at large, they focused upon matters pertaining to the individual and society; and much general controversy was excited by the issues they raised—whether virtue can be taught, whether morality and law are mere conventions, whether reality and truth are relative to opinion, whether persuasive rhetoric is a legitimate instrument of politics. Nevertheless, Cicero had a point if by "philosophy" he meant, as no doubt he did, a methodical search for *knowledge* on the issues in question. It was Socrates' position that opinion is one thing, knowledge another; and he believed that he had arrived at a method by which knowledge in ethics and politics could be obtained, or at least approximated. His opposition to the Sophists was in this respect complete, and his method, as developed by Plato and Aristotle, had an impact upon Western philosophy—and thence upon Western culture—which is beyond calculation.

He was born in Athens in 470 or 469 B.C., the son of Sophroniscus, a sculptor, and Phaenarete, a midwife. After receiving the usual education, Socrates pursued an interest in natural science by joining the school of Archelaus, who was the successor in Athens to Anaxagoras. Like Gorgias, however, he came to distrust the scientific theories of his day because of their many disagreements with one another, and he felt besides that no one except Anaxagoras understood that what above all needs explaining is *why*—for what purpose—things in nature happen as they do. Ultimately, as we saw, he was dissatisfied with Anaxagoras too for his failure to employ his conception of *Nous* or Mind to show how the world is intelligently ordered for the best and how the best for human life fits in with this. A growing conviction that cosmological speculation is irrelevant to human problems culminated, probably sometime in his thirties, in a crisis from which Socrates emerged with the sense of having a new mission. One event in particular appears to have figured in this. An impetuous admirer of Socrates' named Chaerephon went to the shrine of Apollo at Delphi and put a question to the priestess there who transmitted oracles from the god. "Is anyone," he asked, "wiser than Socrates?" When Chaerephon told Socrates that the god (via the priestess) had said "No," Socrates, who knew that he was not wise, could only suppose that the god was, as usual, speaking in riddles.

With an eye to confirming this, he proceeded to interview those whose reputations for wisdom were such as to make him think that they were certainly wiser than he. But all of them turned out to be disappointing, because on the important subjects in which they fancied themselves wise they were in fact very ignorant. The god, he concluded, could only have meant that human wisdom is in general a poor affair and that he, Socrates, had an edge over others only in knowing this. His vocation for the future, he further concluded, must be to serve the god by going to his fellow Athenians—"individually, like a father or an elder brother"—exhorting them all to care less for "money and honor and reputation" and to care more for "wisdom and truth and the greatest improvement of the soul." "And," Socrates said in Plato's *Apology,* "if the person with whom I am arguing says: Yes, but I do care; then I do not leave him or let him go at once; but I proceed to interrogate and examine and cross-examine him, and if I think that he has no virtue in him, but only says that he has, I reproach him with undervaluing the greater and overvaluing the less."

His pursuit of this mission occupied the remaining thirty-odd years of his life. During the first decade of the Peloponnesian War he saw considerable army service and got married to a woman named Xanthippe, but neither experience seems to have much interrupted him. Because he was a *hoplite* (a heavily armed infantryman) in the army, and because at Athens only those who were in a financial position to buy their own weapons were liable to this service, Socrates must for a time have been fairly prosperous. Plutarch reports a story that he owned a house and had an income from money that he had invested. If so, he must have gotten these things by inheritance, for according to our best evidence he never had a craft or profession. He made a point of not accepting money as a philosopher, in part because he did not want to deprive himself of his freedom to converse with anyone he chose. The Sophists, in demanding fees, were obliged to converse only with those who could pay, and Socrates considered this the intellectual equivalent, as he said, of "slavery." Owing probably to the general financial crisis brought on by the war, together with his absorption in his mission, Socrates was reduced to extreme poverty in his old age.

In the turbulent politics of Athens at the end of the Peloponnesian War, several men who had associated with Socrates in their youth played key roles in an antidemocratic revolution (the oligarchy of the Thirty Tyrants in 404–403 B.C.) that was short-lived but bloody. Socrates risked his life in withstanding their attempts to implicate him in their crimes, but when democratic government was restored he was nevertheless viewed with great distrust. He was already notorious for embarrassing the leaders of earlier days with his incessant interrogations. Now he was seen by respectable citizens as a teacher of traitors and a menace to society. Since a general amnesty had been declared by the new government, he could not be charged on political grounds. Thus charges were trumped up to the effect that he had committed crimes against the state religion and had corrupted the youth. The penalty of death was demanded in hopes of forcing him into exile. There was no real desire that he be executed.

He was determined, however, to stand his ground. Conscious only of having benefited his city in line with the god's command, and convinced that no real harm can happen to a good man either in life or after death, he remained in Athens and allowed his case to come to trial. In court, according to Plato's *Apology,* he refused on principle to make the kind of tearful appeals that might have won him an acquittal. The jury of 501 found him guilty by a margin of 60 votes. Afterward, in prison, according to Plato's *Crito,*[1] he turned down an offer by a wealthy friend to arrange for his escape into Thessaly. He pointed out, among other things, that his long residence in Athens amounted to a solemn promise to abide by her laws and by the judgments of her courts, and that escaping would be inconsistent with his duty of gratitude to Athens for all the benefits she had given him. And so in 399 B.C., one evening at sunset, Socrates drank the hemlock.

He left no record of his own as to his thought or activity. The only thing we have about him that was written before he died is *The Clouds* of Aristophanes, which was first performed when Socrates was forty-six or forty-seven. Aristophanes poked fun at Socrates (they appear to have been old friends) by putting into the play a character with his name and general appearance as the head, no less, of the Thinking-Shop. This burlesque of Socrates as a Sophist, harmless as it may have seemed at the time, came back to haunt him later on. At his trial he attributed much of the animosity against him to the misleading impression that the comedy had created years before in the minds of the general public. Partly to clear his reputation and partly to preserve his memory, several of Socrates' young friends composed dialogues after his death in which his character and conversation were depicted. Of these only the dialogues of Plato and Xenophon have survived intact (both first met Socrates when he was in his late fifties and they were in their teens).

These dialogues portray an eccentric man of ill-favored appearance but of hypnotic vitality and force. He had protruding eyes, a flat nose, a potbelly, and a strutting walk. He wore the same garment year round and always went barefoot. From childhood he had strange experiences in which

---

[1] The titles of most of Plato's dialogues, as in this case, are taken from the names of persons in them with whom Socrates converses.

he believed that a "divine voice" spoke to him, warning him not to do something he had planned to do. On more than one occasion he was seen to fall into a sort of trance, sometimes for hours, in which he appeared to be absorbed in thought. He rarely drank, but when he did, he would consume prodigious quantities of wine without getting drunk. During his military service he was notably cool and courageous: Alcibiades, in Plato's *Symposium* describes him during the Athenians' headlong retreat at Delium as "stalking like a pelican, and rolling his eyes, calmly contemplating enemies as well as friends, and making very intelligible to anybody, even from a distance, that whoever attacked him would be likely to meet with a stout resistance." His physical robustness was such that when he died, at seventy or seventy-one, the youngest of his three children was only a baby.

By all accounts the effect of Socrates upon others was at first exceedingly uncomfortable. His questioning tended to reduce everyone to a state of numb helplessness. Many were so irritated at having their ignorance shown up that they were ready, he said, to "bite him." More than a few of these simply made a point of avoiding him in the future. Others, however, recovered from the shock to find themselves with an anxious desire for knowledge and with a strong conviction that the only way to acquire it was by spending as much time as possible with Socrates. For his part, Socrates always insisted that because he was far from wise himself he could not help these people by teaching them anything (another reason why he did not charge for his services). The only possible role for him, he said, was to follow the example of his mother and serve as a kind of midwife—assisting others to bring forth their own thoughts and to examine whether they were true or false. "Dire are the pangs," he said, "which my art is able to arouse and to allay in those who consort with me, just like the pangs of women in childbirth; night and day they are full of perplexity and travail which is even worse than that of the women."

Socrates' Method

Socrates' art of midwifery (*maieutics,* in Greek) consisted of adroit questioning (*elenchus*) with a view to discovering precisely what, if anything, someone had in mind in using certain general ethical terms. A good illustration is given in Plato's *Meno.* Socrates and the young Meno fall into conversation, and Meno raises a question which—thanks to the Sophists—is being much discussed: how is virtue acquired—by instruction, by practice, by nature, or what? In the sly or "ironic" fashion for which he was famous, Socrates replies that he is hardly in a position to say, because he does not even know what virtue[2] is and has not met

---

[2] See the note about "virtue" on p. 52.

anyone else who does either. Perhaps Meno will be kind enough to inform him? No problem, says Meno, for Gorgias has already told us: "Every age, every condition of life, young or old, male or female, bond or free, has a different virtue: there are virtues numberless, and no lack of definitions of them; for virtue is relative to the actions and ages of each of us in all that we do." But, Socrates asks, do all of these virtues have nothing in common? Health and strength may vary in degree, but in kind they are the same for everyone; why should virtue be different? Surely the same specific virtues, such as temperance and justice, are expected of all virtuous persons, irrespective of their ages, sexes, and occupations, and this suggests that virtue in general is of the same identical pattern or form (*eidos*) in everyone who possesses it. What is this pattern?

Meno says that if Socrates insists upon having a single definition, he supposes that virtue is the power of governing mankind. This response, however, is obviously worthless on two counts, as Socrates proceeds to explain. In the first place it is too narrow as a definition because it leaves out, for example, children. In the second place it is too broad as a definition because it includes, for example, tyrants; and Meno will have to amend it at least to the extent of saying that virtue is the power of governing mankind *with justice*. Yet because Meno admits that justice is one particular virtue among others, this is no nearer to telling us what virtue is in general, and besides it is circular to state that virtue consists in doing something in keeping with a virtue. In fact, Meno has confused a whole (virtue) with one of its parts (justice), as if he had said that figures are circles or that color is whiteness.

Meno tries again. Virtue, he now proposes, is the desire of good things and the ability to procure them. Socrates, however, hardly finds this an improvement. It implies that someone might *not* desire good things, that someone might actually desire what he or she knew to be *evil*, and this is out of the question. After all, to desire something is to want to possess it; and to know that something is evil is to know that it is harmful; and to know that something is harmful is to know that, in proportion to its harmfulness, it will make one miserable. Knowingly to desire something evil would thus entail wanting to be miserable. But, as Meno agrees, no one wants to be miserable. Insofar as anyone desires what is evil, he or she must be unaware of the fact that it is evil. Everyone desires what is good, understanding that what is good is personally beneficial, and so the desire of good things cannot be a feature that distinguishes virtuous persons from others.

Accordingly, the first part of Meno's definition is useless and should be discarded, leaving us with "virtue" defined simply as the *ability to procure* good things. It comes out that by "good things" Meno has in mind such things as wealth, status, and honor. Now all of these can be acquired by dishonest means. Is it Meno's position, then, that robbers and frauds are virtuous? No, of course not, Meno says. Naturally he means that virtue is the ability to procure good things *honestly*. Very well, Socrates says, but is not honesty, like justice, a *part* of virtue? Has not Meno once again equated a whole with one of its parts? And, anyway, how does Meno expect us to know parts of virtue until we know virtue itself? "Did I not ask you," Socrates says, "to tell me the nature of virtue as a whole? And you are very far from telling me this, but declare every action to be virtue when it is done with a part of virtue, as though you had told me and I must already know the whole of virtue, and this, too, when frittered away into little pieces. And, therefore, my dear Meno, I fear that I must begin again and repeat the same question: What is virtue?"

The dialogue continues, but this is enough to illustrate the main points of Socrates' method. As Aristotle said, Socrates was always "busying himself about ethical matters . . . seeking the universal. . . ." In the *Meno* he was after the distinctive qualities, the common pattern or form, exhibited universally in each and every case of virtue. Other general ethical terms come in for the same type of investigation in other dialogues of Plato's: temperance in the *Charmides,* courage in the *Laches,* friendship in the *Lysis,* piety in the *Euthyphro,* love in the *Symposium,* justice in the *Republic,* and so on. Socrates believed that a general term should be used in reference to a multiplicity of specific things only when those things have distinctive qualities in common; otherwise nothing but confusion results—potentially very serious confusion in discussions of ethical and political issues. And he believed that unless we know these common qualities and can give a reasoned account of them, we are in no position to make trustworthy judgments of value or to withstand the persuasion and propaganda of those who would like to exploit us. Knowing what qualities, what pattern or form, must be present if any action is to be morally right or virtuous, we are in firm possession of a universal principle that will serve us reliably as a criterion or standard of judgment.

What we must do, then, is to compare particular instances of virtue, for example, and see what qualities are common and peculiar to them. This procedure, which Aristotle called "induction" and credited Socrates with first using systematically, will enable us to formulate a universal definition of "virtue" that will hold for all times, places, and persons. There will be nothing subjective or relative about it. In his dialectic of question and answer, Socrates would commonly appeal to analogies in order to bring his interlocutors to see that universal definitions of ethical terms are possible. (Virtue varies according to age, sex, and occupation? But health and strength do not vary, not in kind, and why may not virtue be like them?) And when Socrates' midwifely methods finally delivered someone of an attempt at a universal definition, this would be subjected to several tests. Is it too narrow? Too broad? Can we, in other words, think of counterexamples—of things the definition erroneously excludes (say, children) or includes (tyrants)? Is the definition circular? (Virtue consists in doing something virtuously?) Does it equate a genus (like virtue) with a species (like justice or honesty)? Does it in any other way imply something we know to be false? (Virtue consists in desiring good things? Then is it possible to desire evil things?)

As the dialogue proceeded, Socrates' partners in discussion would increasingly, if reluctantly, have the sense that ethical concepts and principles are not, as the Sophists had said, relative matters. Less and less would all opinions look equally respectable. One felt that one was being drawn by Socrates' questions ever closer to an objective "form" of (say) virtue, to an essential nature of moral goodness which is what it is independently of varying attitudes and circumstances, and to which one personally had to measure up. One's intensifying awareness of *not* measuring up could be most unsettling, as witness the testimony of Alcibiades. Socrates, he said,

> has often brought me to such a pass that I have felt that I could hardly endure the life which I am leading . . . and I am conscious that if I did not shut my ears against him, and fly as from the voice of the siren, my fate would be like that of others—he would transfix me, and I should grow old sitting at his feet. For he makes me confess that I ought not to live as I do, neglecting the wants of my own soul, and busying myself with the concerns of the Athenians; therefore I hold my ears and tear myself away from him. . . . For I know that I cannot answer him or say that I ought not to do as he bids. . . . Many a time have I wished that he were dead, and yet I know that I should be much more sorry than glad if he were to die: so that I am at my wit's end.

In the dialogues of Plato that appear to represent Socrates most faithfully, no fully satisfactory conclusions are ever reached. He is shown convincing his interlocutors of their ignorance by criticizing and rejecting one after another the definitions he encourages them to produce. The conversation is never tidily wrapped up by Socrates' saying flatly what he thinks is true. This can be explained partly by a genuine belief on his part that he lacked the necessary knowledge and that his own strength lay in examining the views of others. Also, however, he evidently believed that the best way to foster enlightenment in others is not by a direct attempt to instruct them but by demolishing their self-complacency, by whetting their curiosity, and by showing them from the example of his conversation that, and how, progress toward knowledge is possible.

Socrates' Views

Despite the inconclusiveness of Socrates' recorded conversations, it is possible to gather from them an idea of where he stood on several matters relating to ethics. Again and again he came back to one point in particular: everyone, without exception, means to get what is *good,* to fare *well* and to attain *happiness* (*eudaimonia*). In the case of anything else, someone could conceivably be satisfied with a substitute. The outward show of, say, power or wealth might do as well as the genuine article. When it comes to happiness, however, to authentic personal well-being, *no one* prefers a mere appearance; everyone wants the real thing. Of course, people often choose what in fact is bad for them, but this is always a result of ignorance or miscalculation of what is good for them. Given sufficient wisdom about their best interests, they would always act as they really desire and fare as well as they possibly could. They would get full benefit of their opportunities and abilities, and realize the best that is in them. Lives of true excellence, of "virtue" in the richest sense of the word, would be the inevitable result, for what is truly best for any individual is the best in itself and absolutely. The essential thing is to understand how this is so.

Virtue is knowledge. To know the good is to do it. Wrongdoing is involuntary, a matter of ignorance. These statements are known as the "Socratic paradoxes" because they seem very much at odds with common opinion on the subject. It is commonly said that one can believe a thing to be beneficial and reject it, and that one can believe a thing to be harmful and pursue it. In this way human nature is said to be *sinful,* and in a Psalm of the Bible we find the lament, "I know my transgressions, and my sin is ever before me." But sin, as an ingrained tendency to transgress limits that are *recognized* to be right and advantageous, is psychologically impossible in Socrates' view. There can be no conflict, indeed there can be no real distinction, between what one *apprehends as beneficial* and what one *wills to do,* since the second (as Socrates believes) is always constituted by the first. What above all is needed is the *wisdom* to apprehend what really is beneficial.

Socrates' reasons for attributing crucial importance to wisdom are given in the following excerpt from Plato's *Euthydemus.* Socrates is telling of a conversation he has had with a Sophist by the name of Cleinias.

> Do not all men [Socrates asks] desire happiness? And yet perhaps this is one of those ridiculous questions which I am afraid to ask, and which ought not to be asked by a sensible man, for what human being is there who does not desire happiness?
>
> There is no one, said Cleinias, who does not.
>
> Well, then, I said, since we all of us desire happiness, how can we be happy? That is the next question. Shall we not be happy if we have many good things? And this, perhaps, is even a more simple question than the first, for there can be no doubt of the answer.
>
> He assented.
>
> And what things do we esteem good? No solemn sage is required to tell us this, which may be easily answered: for everyone will say that wealth is a good.
>
> Certainly, he said.
>
> And are not health and beauty goods, and other personal gifts? . . . Can there be any doubt that good birth, and power, and honors in one's own land, are goods? . . . And . . . what do you say of temperance,

justice, courage: do you not verily and indeed think, Cleinias, that we shall be more right in ranking them as goods than in not ranking them as goods? . . .

They are goods, said Cleinias.

And should we be happy by reason of the presence of good things if they profited us not, or if they profited us?

If they profited us, he said.

And would they profit us if we only had them and did not use them? For example, . . . would an artisan who had all the implements necessary for his work, and did not use them, be any better for the possession of them? . . . Would a carpenter be any the better for having all his tools and plenty of wood, if he never worked?

Certainly not, he said.

And if a person had wealth and all the goods of which we were just now speaking, and did not use them, would he be happy because he possessed them?

No indeed, Socrates.

Then, I said, a man who would be happy must not only have the good things, but he must also use them; there is no advantage in merely having them?

True.

Well, Cleinias, but if you have the use as well as the possession of good things, is that sufficient to confer happiness?

Yes, in my opinion.

And may a person use them either rightly or wrongly?

He must use them rightly. . . .

Now in the working and use of wood, is not that which gives the right use simply the knowledge of the carpenter? . . . And in the use of the goods of which we spoke at first—wealth and health and beauty—is not knowledge that which directs us to the right use of them, and regulates our practice about them?

He assented.

And tell me, I said, . . . what do possessions profit a man, if he have neither good sense nor wisdom? Would a man be better off, having and doing many things without wisdom, or a few things with wisdom? . . . If he did fewer things would he not make fewer mistakes? if he made fewer mistakes would he not have fewer misfortunes? and if he had fewer misfortunes would he not be less miserable?

Certainly, he said. . . .

Then, I said, Cleinias, the sum of the matter appears to be that the goods of which we spoke before are not to be regarded as goods in themselves, but the degree of good and evil in them depends on whether they are or are not under the guidance of knowledge; under the guidance of ignorance they are greater evils than their opposites . . . and when under the guidance of wisdom and prudence, they are greater goods, but in themselves they are nothing?

That, he replied, is obvious.

What then is the result of what has been said? Is not this the result—

that other things are indifferent, and that wisdom is the only good, and ignorance the only evil? . . . [And] seeing that all men desire happiness, and happiness, as has been shown, is gained by a use, and the right use, of the things of life, and the right use of them . . . is given by knowledge—the inference is that everybody ought by all means to try and make himself as wise as he can?

Yes, he said.

Our happiness or well-being depends upon our making the right use of our gifts and attainments, and this is a matter of wisdom. Wisdom alone guarantees that we actually get benefit from whatever is potentially beneficial. It alone is incapable of harmful misuse, since it consists in knowing what benefits us, and we always pursue what benefits us insofar as we know what it is. For these reasons Socrates concluded that "wisdom is the only good, and ignorance the only evil," by which he probably meant that wisdom is the only thing beneficial, and ignorance the only thing harmful, *without condition*. Wealth, health, beauty, power, and so forth, are beneficial or harmful *on condition* that they are used rightly (wisely) or wrongly (ignorantly); intrinsically, they are "indifferent." But where does this leave happiness or well-being? If wisdom is "the only good," is happiness or well-being "indifferent," or even bad? This cannot be what Socrates had in mind. He surely believed that happiness or well-being is good in itself, or else he would not have set such store by wisdom as the only reliable guide to attaining it. His position would best be stated in terms of a threefold distinction among types of good things: (1) things beneficial *under certain conditions* (wealth, for example); (2) things beneficial under *any* conditions (wisdom is the sole instance of this type); and (3) things with which our benefit is to be *identified* (happiness or well-being is everything here).

Notice that, in listing "good things" of the first type, Socrates included temperance, justice, and courage along with such equivocal possessions as power and money. He was referring to popular notions of these virtues, according to which they have little to do with wisdom, have no necessary relation to one another, and often do more harm than good. Courage, for example, tends to be identified with simple obstinacy or daring or boldness; it can be fanatically intemperate and thoroughly unjust. But as Socrates argues in Plato's *Protagoras* (after the Sophist says that "many a man is brave and not just"), this sort of "courage," often being the opposite of beneficial for all concerned, cannot be what anyone could really admire as an excellence or virtue of human character. We all desire what we think is beneficial. It is certainly beneficial for anyone to have the power to face up to opposition and peril when enduring them is correctly seen as necessary to achieve a great good or to avoid a great evil. This, when we come to think of it, is what we really mean by "courage" and esteem as a virtue. Now since this calls for sound judgment about comparative goods and evils, for a sure sense of when backing down in a tight situation would be the truly dangerous thing, courage is inseparable from wisdom. A close examination of justice and temperance will lead to the same conclusion: they, too, involve an accurate understanding of moral values and reliable judgment about what is at stake in particular circumstances. In fact, "courage," "justice," and "temperance" are three different names for precisely the same thing—wisdom.[3] As Xenophon says in his *Memorabilia,* "Socrates made no distinction between wisdom and temperance. . . . He also said that justice, as well as every other kind of virtue, was wisdom."

This *unity of virtue* was one of Socrates' most characteristic positions. It means that to speak of one virtue apart from the others is wholly artificial. Either you have all of them together or you have none. Courage involves self-possession ("temperance") in rough waters; temperance involves poise and staying power ("courage") in withstanding temptations; justice involves steadfast restraint of one's desires ("courageous temperance") out of respect for the rights of others. All of these are just so many manifestations of wisdom in the varied situations of life—of wisdom and the pursuit of genuine well-being that wisdom unfailingly produces.

Wisdom, then, is the identical pattern or form (*eidos*) discoverable in all cases of virtue and only in them. This is the definition of "virtue" for which Socrates was searching with Meno. When Meno said that virtue is the ability to procure good things, he was proceeding in the right direction, for virtue consists of wisdom in all of our procuring and using. Where Meno went wrong was in thinking that money and status are good things (at least if they are honestly gotten), whereas these are just potentially good (and much more than honest getting is necessary if they are to be beneficial).

In examining with Cleinias the case for wisdom, Socrates brought in the analogy of a carpenter. As the carpenter's knowledge is essential for the right use of his tools and lumber, so wisdom is essential for the right use of anyone's gifts and possessions. Analogies from various arts and crafts were a favorite device of Socrates',[4] and they make clearer what he meant by "wisdom"—not just theoretical knowledge of moral principles but an expertise at applying them which is a matter of considerable practice.

In Plato's *Gorgias,* after Callicles has extolled the life of "luxury, intemperance, and licence" as the happiest life imaginable, Socrates man-

---

[3] Wisdom, justice, courage, and temperance were the four "cardinal virtues" traditionally recognized by the Greeks. In Christian times, the three "theological virtues" of faith, hope, and charity (or love) were added to the list. See St. Paul's First Epistle to the Corinthians, 13:13.

[4] Xenophon says that during the antidemocratic revolution of "the Thirty," an attempt was made to hush up Socrates by enacting a law against "teaching the art of argument." When Socrates innocently inquired whether it was *unsound* reasoning that the law forbade—in which case "obviously one must try to reason soundly"—an official angrily warned him especially to "avoid asking about cobblers, builders, and metalworkers, for I think that they have already been worn out and exhausted by you."

ages to extract from him an admission that some pleasures are harmful and some pains are beneficial, so that happiness can hardly be just a matter of amassing pleasures and avoiding pains. We should choose the beneficial pleasures and pains and avoid the harmful ones, but the right selection demands "art or knowledge of them in detail"—an art comparable to medicine in knowing the conditions of genuine well-being, not one like pastry cooking that aims only at momentary gratification. Of course, the techniques of medicine, and even of carpentry, can be put to harmful uses. Only wisdom, the craft of well-being, is incapable of being misused.

Socrates did not claim to possess this wisdom, only a method by which it could be approximated—the dialectic method of question and answer which one can carry on with oneself as well as with others in discussion. In seeking by this method to define the essential nature or "form" of any kind of thing, we must consider, he thought, the *function* or *purpose* of that kind of thing. Discovering what something *is* amounts to discovering what it is *for*. To understand what hammers and saws are, you must understand their function as tools of carpentry and how by having "virtue" as adapted to perform this function they are what they are. To understand what a carpenter is, you must understand his craft and how by having "virtue" as skilled therein he is what he is. Now to understand what *you* are as a *human being*, you must understand what you are "for" and by what skill or excellence or virtue you may achieve this purpose. "The unexamined life is not worth living," Socrates said, because your well-being is not a thing which you can begin to take care of as long as you are ignorant of your nature—your function or purpose.

Developing further the analogy of arts and crafts, Socrates argued that the idea of "taking care" of yourself, when closely inspected, unfolds into the idea that the *you* whose well-being is at stake is your *soul* (*psyche*). This is best conveyed in the dialogue called *Alcibiades I*, attributed by ancient sources to Plato but by some modern scholars to some other (unknown) associate of Socrates, or to an (unknown) follower of Plato's. In any case, as all agree, it is an able exposition of Socrates' views. As we join them, we hear Socrates asking Alcibiades:

What is the meaning of a man taking care of himself? and when does he take care? Does he not take care of himself when he takes care of what belongs to him?

I should think so [Alcibiades says].

Does a man take care of his feet when he takes care of what belongs to them—his shoes? And is it by shoemaking, then, that he takes care of his feet, or is it by some other art?

By some other.

And the same art improves the feet which improves the rest of the body, namely, gymnastic?

Certainly.

Then by gymnastic we take care of our feet, and by shoemaking of that which belongs to our feet?

Very true.

Then in taking care of what belongs to you, you do not take care of yourself. And now let me ask you what is the art with which we take care of ourselves?

I cannot say.

Should we ever have known what art makes a shoe better if we did not know a shoe?

Impossible.

And can we ever know what art makes a man better if we do not know what we are ourselves?

Impossible.

And is self-knowledge such an easy thing, and was he to be lightly esteemed who inscribed the text ["Know Thyself"] on the Temple at Delphi? Or is self-knowledge a difficult thing, which few are able to attain?

At times I fancy, Socrates, that anybody can know himself; at other times the task appears to be very difficult.

But whether easy or difficult, Alcibiades, still there is no other way; knowing what we are, we shall know how to take care of ourselves, and if we are ignorant we shall not know.

That is true.

Come now, I beseech you, tell me with whom you are conversing?— with whom but with me? That is to say, I, Socrates, am talking? And I in talking use words?

Certainly.

And the user is not the same as the thing which he uses? The shoemaker, for example, uses a square tool, and a circular tool, and other tools for cutting; but the tool is not the same as the cutter and user of the tool?

Of course not.

Does the shoemaker cut with his tools only or with his hands? And does he use his eyes?

He does.

Then the shoemaker is to be distinguished from the hands and eyes which he uses?

Clearly.

And does not a man use the whole body?

Certainly.

And that which uses is different from that which is used?

True.

Then a man is not the same as his own body?

That is the inference.

What is he, then?

I cannot say.

Nay, you can say that he is the user of the body. And the user of the body is the soul?

Yes, the soul.

And the soul rules?

Yes.

Then he who bids a man know himself would have him know his soul?

That appears to be true.

He whose knowledge only extends to the body knows the things of a man and not the man himself? And he who cherishes his body cherishes not himself but what belongs to him?

That is true.

But he who cherishes his money cherishes neither himself nor his belongings, but is a stage yet further removed from himself?

I agree.

And if the soul, my dear Alcibiades, is ever to know herself, must she not look at the soul and especially at that part in which her virtue resides, and to any other which is like this?

I agree, Socrates.

And do we know of any part of our souls more divine than that which has to do with wisdom and knowledge?

There is none.

Then this is that part of the soul which resembles the divine; and he who looks at this and at the whole class of things divine, will be most likely to know himself?

Clearly.

In that mirror you will see and know yourself and your own good, and so you will act rightly and well?

Yes.

But if you act unrighteously, your eye will turn to the dark and godless, and being in darkness and ignorance of yourself, you will probably do deeds of darkness?

Very possibly.

If you as a soul are to be distinguished from your body and its appurtenances, then your happiness or well-being as a soul cannot be identified with catering to bodily interests. Thus, in Plato's *Gorgias,* Socrates goes so far as to say that suffering even the worst injustice is always preferable to *doing* injustice, because in doing injustice the soul becomes corrupted and diseased, which makes it "far more miserable a companion" than an injured body. For the same reason, being cured of injustice through suitable corrective punishment is always preferable to getting away with injustice. A life of "luxury, intemperance, and licence," devoted to the maximum satisfaction of bodily appetites, heedless of justice and concerned only with not getting caught, is a life of complete disorder—ruled by random cravings that can never be satisfied. Anyone who, like Callicles, thinks this the ideal is totally in the dark about what makes any sort of thing worth having. For anything to be good of its kind—a painting, a house, a ship—various elements must be arranged into a consistent and organized whole, in keeping with the specific nature and function of that kind of thing. It is no different with the soul, for its function is to rule the body and the body's vagrant impulses, and its characteristic excellence is an internal order fashioned by wisdom and expressed as justice, temperance, and courage. So it was that, as Socrates said at his trial, "I do nothing but go about persuading you all, old and young alike, not to take thought for your persons or your possessions, but first and chiefly to care about the greatest improvement of the soul."

The true self is the soul. This is one's reason or intelligence viewed as a thing unto itself, different in kind from the body, employing the body as a craftsman employs his tools. In its capacity for wisdom, the soul resembles "the divine" and can best know itself as mirrored therein. Here we have an indication of Socrates' religious views, which are given more fully in Xenophon's *Memorabilia* and in Plato's *Apology*. Although he often referred in the traditional Greek way to "the gods" in the plural, Socrates also spoke of one supreme Divine Intelligence "who controls and orders the whole universe" and who "sees and hears everything at once, is present everywhere, and is concerned with everything." As the human soul controls the body, so "universal thought disposes of everything as it wishes." This Divine Being, who is invisible like the human soul, created and loves and assists mankind, and sees to it that no evil happens to those who are virtuous—no evil "either in life or after death." These views appear to represent an effort to advance beyond the popular polytheism of the day and a determination to hold out for the conception of Mind—as ordering everything intelligently and for the best—that Socrates had hoped to find elaborated in Anaxagoras. When Socrates gave up cosmological speculation, he evidently retained his belief in a supreme Mind as a matter of simple faith and probably viewed "the gods" as just so many different manifestations of this.

If the human soul is distinguishable from the body, if the soul's well-being is consistent with the body's suffering the worst injustices, if the soul has a divine counterpart that watches over it both in life and after death, then it would certainly look as if the soul must survive the death of the body. In Plato's *Phaedo,* Socrates is depicted as having no doubts about the matter and as giving several arguments in proof of it. These arguments appear to be Plato's own, however, for in the *Apology* Socrates says only that he believes immortality is possible, not a proven fact, and the *Apology* is generally considered the more faithful representation of his actual views. What he says there is that death is one of two things, neither of which is to be feared: either unconsciousness like a dreamless sleep or else "a change and migration of the soul from this world to another." Now some have understood Socrates to be saying that he inclines toward neither alternative and simply suspends judgment, because indeed he disclaims any real knowledge of which is true and says that he is wiser than others about "the world below" only in knowing that he knows nothing on the subject. But to others, including the present writer, it seems clear that Socrates' sympathies are with the hope of immortality, however little proof he had for it. Plato would not have been likely to put his own arguments for immortality into Socrates' mouth if Socrates had not himself expressed confidence in it. And the tone of what Socrates says in the *Apology* about the soul's possible career is hopeful:

> If death is the journey to another place, and there, as men say, all the dead abide, what good, O my friends and judges, can be greater than this? If indeed when the pilgrim arrives in the world below, he is delivered from the professors of justice in this world, and finds the true judges who are said to give judgment there, Minos and Rhadamanthus and Aeacus and Triptolemus, and other sons of God who were righteous in their own life, that pilgrimage will be worth making. What would not a man give if he might converse with Orpheus and Museaus and Hesiod and Homer? . . . Above all, I shall then be able to continue my search into true and false knowledge; as in this world, so also in the next; and I shall find out who is wise, and who pretends to be wise and is not. . . . In another world they do not put a man to death for asking questions—assuredly not. For besides being happier than we are, they will be immortal if what is said is true.
>
> Wherefore, O judges, be of good cheer about death, and know of a certainty that no evil can happen to a good man, either in life or after death. He and his are not neglected by the gods, nor has my own approaching end happened by mere chance. But I see clearly that the time had arrived when it was better for me to die and be released from trouble, wherefore the oracle gave me no sign. . . .
>
> The hour of departure has arrived, and we go our ways—I to die, and you to live. Which is better God only knows.

God only *knows;* but Socrates believes that death is better, "wherefore the oracle gave me no sign"—that is, the "divine voice" which has reliably guided him so far issued no warning as he made his way to court.

In sentencing Socrates to death for "corrupting the youth," that is, for inciting young men to become antidemocratic revolutionaries, the court was right on one point. Socrates had no very high opinion of democratic government as practiced at Athens. The choosing of judges and administrators by lot, the control of the legislative Assembly by clever speakers, made little sense to him. No one, he pointed out, would dream of selecting an architect or a sea captain by lot or by consulting the ignorant multitude, and yet mistakes in architecture and navigation are not nearly as disastrous as mistakes in ruling a state. Ruling is a high art. It calls for considerable knowledge of law, finance, agriculture, and so on. It demands wisdom about what is truly beneficial for the state as a whole. Most persons have neither the ability nor the opportunity to acquire this knowledge and wisdom. They should recognize that the few who do are the only ones to whom governmental office should be entrusted. Kings and rulers, Socrates said, "are not those elected by the electorate or chosen by lot, nor those who gain power by force or treachery; rather, they are those who know how to rule." Thus Socrates was disposed to favor monarchy or aristocracy, maintained not by force but by common consent, and based not upon birth or wealth but upon competence.

He was far from advocating violent revolutionary methods. He maintained that only two choices are open to someone who is dissatisfied with the existing form of government: either get the laws changed by peaceful persuasion, or emigrate to another country. Violence and lawbreaking produce only more of themselves. In Plato's *Crito,* when Socrates is considering the offer of escape from prison, he imagines "the laws and the government" speaking to him: " 'Tell us, Socrates,' they say, 'what are you about? Are you not going by an act of yours to overturn us, the laws and the whole state, as far as in you lies? Do you imagine that a state can subsist and not be overthrown in which the decisions of law have no power, but are set aside and trampled upon by individuals?' " That he has been unjustly condemned is immaterial. His escape would encourage disrespect for law in general. No state can exist in which each citizen takes it upon himself to decide which laws and legal decisions he will honor. Beyond this, as we saw earlier, Socrates believed that it is always wrong to return injustice for injustice, no matter what the provocation. It corrupts and maims the soul. Thus in the *Crito* he says: "We ought not to retaliate or render evil for evil to anyone, whatever evil we may have suffered from him. . . . Neither injury nor retaliation nor warding off evil by evil is ever right." And what if this is to invite death? "The difficulty, my friends, is not to avoid death, but to avoid unrighteousness, for that runs faster than death."

The Minor Socratics _____

Socrates encouraged his associates to think for themselves. His associates, however, were not unnaturally spellbound by him—by his personality, above all, and by what they could gather of his views. The different positions at which they arrived were reflections of the different aspects of Socrates that fascinated them. Only Plato had the philosophical gifts to grasp Socrates' concerns as a whole and to develop a balanced position of his own that did justice to them. The others, who are aptly called "the Minor Socratics," were men of limited perception and creativity, and the views that Socrates inspired in them were exceedingly one-sided. Thus Antisthenes (about 455–360 B.C.), who started as a pupil of Gorgias' but became a fanatical admirer of Socrates, was so taken with Socrates' abstemious habits and meager possessions that he identified virtue with self-denial and happiness with independence from all worldly goods and pleasures. Diogenes of Sinope (about 412–323 B.C.), who thought that Antisthenes did not sufficiently practice what he preached, carried this independence so far as to live in a tub and to imitate only too closely the behavior of a dog. "The Dog," in fact, was what he called himself; and from *kynikos,* the Greek for "doglike," came the name of "Cynics" which was given to his disciples.[5]

By contrast, Aristippus (about 435–360 B.C.) was evidently impressed by Socrates' ability to enjoy himself, as in his occasional drinking, without being overcome by pleasures. He therefore identified happiness with bodily gratification and virtue with the self-control to avoid being mastered by it. If you have the proper attitude toward pleasure, he said, you can plunge into it safely, just as you could safely jump into a volcano if your body were fireproof. When he was reproached for his relations with a famous courtesan named Lais, he is said to have replied: "I possess Lais; she does not possess me." Aristippus was a native of the Greek colony of Cyrene in North Africa, and so it was that his followers were called "Cyrenaics."

Euclides (about 450–375 B.C.) seems to have been gripped less by the personality of Socrates than by certain conclusions to which so many of Socrates' discussions plainly tended—the unity of virtue as wisdom and the unique value of wisdom as the only thing always beneficial. These conclusions Euclides summed up in the statement that "the good is one." Now Socrates had declared his faith in a supreme Divine Intelligence of which wise human souls are imperfect likenesses. If the good is one, what is perfectly good is one Supreme Being. This appears to have suggested to Euclides that Socrates' ethics and religion could be combined with the metaphysics of Parmenides, with benefit all around. Parmenides proved that One Being exists. Euclides interpreted the "one" in "the good is one" to be the One Being of Parmenides, which in turn he took to be the Divine Intelligence of which Socrates spoke. If the good is one, the One is the good. In this way, he seems to have thought, Socrates' views can be set upon the firm basis of Parmenides' metaphysics, while Parmenides' One is enriched by the ethical and religious insights of Socrates. Since Parmenides also proved that *only* One Being exists, Euclides concluded that "things opposed to the good"—evil things—simply do not exist. Such was the extreme position at which he arrived. His followers, called "the Megarians" after his birthplace of Megara, developed a number of arguments reminiscent of Zeno's in support of Parmenides, and they contributed to the study of logic by inventing some paradoxes that still trouble logicians today—for example, the paradox of Eubulides about whether a man who says "I am lying" is saying something true or false.

---

[5]The current usage of "cynic," to mean a person disposed to deny and sneer at the sincerity or goodness of human motives and actions, dates only from the late sixteenth century A.D.

CHAPTER 6

Plato

Plato was born in 427 B.C., two years after the death of Pericles, four years after the beginning of the Peloponnesian War. He was the youngest son of Ariston and Perictione, both of whose families had long been prominent in the politics of Athens. Ariston died while Plato was still a child, and Perictione remarried her uncle Pyrilampes, who had been a friend and supporter of Pericles. Growing up in such a political household, Plato expected as a matter of course that he too would have a career in public life. His association with Socrates, which is likely to have begun in his late adolescence, did not by itself prompt him to become a philosopher. After probable military service during the last five years of the Peloponnesian War—from his eighteenth to his twenty-third year—he was invited to join the government of the revolution of 404–403 B.C., in which his uncle Charmides and his cousin Critias were leaders. The deterioration of Athenian politics had reached a point where control by autocratic reformers seemed to many the only possible solution. Plato, however, waited to see what their policies would be, and before long he was disgusted by their lawless violence and by their attempt to intimidate Socrates into complicity with them. The restored democracy, whose comparatively moderate treatment of the revolutionaries made it look promising to Plato at first, turned out to be even worse, for it put Socrates to death.

Having seen what a man who would be honorable can expect from democrats and antidemocrats alike, and badly shaken by the execution of Socrates, Plato—then twenty-eight—forsook politics and left Athens. How long he stayed away, where he went, and what he did are matters on which there is little solid evidence. The tradition that he traveled widely around the Mediterranean is likely enough, although the stories that were handed down about this are probably inaccurate in many of their details. During this period he must have accumulated a wide knowledge of the governments of the day while composing his early dialogues of Socrates; and in the process he must have concluded that his own mission was to carry on with Socrates' work, but in a way that would be expressly calculated to raise the level of Greek politics. Thus, sometime around his fortieth year (387 B.C.) he was back in Athens setting up a school about a mile from the city. From a nearby grove sacred to the hero Academus, the school was called "the Academy," and its purpose was to offer a philosophical education to potential statesmen. It was Plato's view that wise

77

statesmanship calls for persons whose minds have first been developed by the disinterested pursuit of knowledge for its own sake. To this end the Academy's curriculum included mathematics and astronomy—fields in which great developments were made by the specialists Plato recruited for his faculty—as well as philosophy proper.

The Academy's success was considerable: students came from all over Greece and the Greek colonies, and many of them returned to their home cities to play important roles as legislators and political reformers. Twice Plato was persuaded against his better judgment to visit Syracuse in Sicily, with a view to converting the tyrant there to sounder principles of government, and with no more success than Plato expected; but otherwise he spent the last forty years of his life presiding over the Academy. He died in 347 B.C. at the age of eighty. As far as we know, he never married. His Academy continued to exist for over 900 years, until the Roman Emperor Justinian, who felt himself divinely appointed to protect the Christian religion, had it closed in 529 A.D. as a "pagan" institution. No other school has existed for so long.

Some thirty-six dialogues have been attributed to Plato at one time or another. Nine of these are now generally considered to be spurious. The twenty-seven remaining,[1] all of which have come down to us complete, add up to the finest body of work that any philosopher is known to have produced. For depth and scope of thought, expressed with consummate literary art, these dialogues are matchless. Yet Plato did not himself ascribe the greatest significance to them. He viewed them, at least for the most part, as popular reading, and he reserved his most important views for delivery in lectures and discussions at the Academy. Of these "unwritten doctrines" of Plato we have only a few obscure hints in Aristotle and what we can guess by reading between the lines of the dialogues. And in the dialogues themselves, where Plato never appears by name and the chief role is usually given to Socrates, the problem is to determine when Socrates is functioning simply as a spokesman for views that were actually original with Plato—popularly put or not.

Knowledge and Its Objects

Aristotle, who was a member of the Academy for twenty years, is our best source on the relation of Plato to Socrates. In his *Metaphysics* he says that Plato studied in his youth with a philosopher of extreme Heraclitean persuasion named Cratylus, who taught him that the whole of existence is in such radical flux that everything escapes our attempts to comprehend it. Nothing remains the same or stands still long enough for us to say anything even approximately accurate about it.[2] Heraclitus had

---

[1] Counting Plato's letters as one unit.
[2] It would seem that Cratylus rejected Heraclitus' notion of the Logos as a principle by which the flux is ordered and made intelligible.

declared that you cannot step into the same river twice. Cratylus insisted that you cannot step into it even once, so incessantly is everything changing in every respect. Socrates, for his part, did not concern himself with this sort of issue; he was occupied exclusively with ethical matters, particularly with finding general definitions of ethical terms. Now Plato, Aristotle says, fully agreed with the importance of this, but he saw that Socrates' procedure was incompatible with the teachings of Cratylus. Socrates' definitions were supposed to express the distinctive patterns or forms exhibited in all instances of goodness and virtue. But if the world were as Cratylus said, with nothing the same from one moment to the next, distinctive patterns or forms would simply not exist—neither in human life nor anywhere else. There would be no persons or things with definite characteristics in which they could resemble one another. General definitions as to what all virtuous persons and good things have in common would be out of the question. The world would be a meaningless chaos. Socrates' whole enterprise would be bankrupt.

This conflict between the lessons of Socrates and of Cratylus appears to have been what moved Plato to work out his own views of knowledge and reality. The ethical knowledge for which Socrates inquired had to be shown to be possible; and this led Plato to investigate the nature of knowledge in general because the problem raised by Cratylus was general.

The *Theaetetus* is the dialogue in which Plato, going beyond Socrates but still using Socrates as his spokesman, takes up the nature of knowledge directly.[3] He begins by considering the idea that knowledge consists merely of perception by the senses—sight, hearing, touch, and so on. He shows how Protagoras' relativism about knowledge may in part have been based upon some such view, with perception understood as Cratylus understood it. Protagoras had said that each man is his own "measure" of what exists and that whatever seems true for any given person *is* true for that person. There is no objective truth over and above the varying opinions of people. This position would be a natural consequence of taking knowledge to be perception and of taking perception to be the very subjective affair it must needs be if Cratylus were right. Perception arises from a relation between an organ of perception and an object—between an eye, say, and an apple. But if eyes and apples are constantly changing, no two persons will see quite the same thing at any instant. There will be as many different perceptions as there are people, and none of these

---

[3]Scholars have placed the *Theaetetus* in the second or third of three chronological groups (early, middle, and late) into which Plato's dialogues may be sorted on the basis (largely) of differences in language and style. The early group includes such dialogues as the *Euthyphro, Apology,* and *Crito,* in which the words given to "Socrates" seem to represent more or less faithfully the mind of the actual Socrates. The middle group (including the *Phaedo* and *Republic*) and the late group (including the *Timaeus* and *Laws*) have "Socrates" or another character functioning mainly as a spokesman for Plato. For an excellent introduction to the problems involved in establishing the chronology of the dialogues, see G. C. Field's *Plato and His Contemporaries,* 3rd ed. (London: Methuen, 1967), ch. 5.

perceptions will be any truer than the others. In this way, each man will be his own measure of what exists, on the supposition that knowledge of what exists is a matter of perception.

That there is something very mistaken in all this seemed clear to Plato. In general, he thought, it can hardly be true that one person's opinion is as good as another's, because this type of relativism actually refutes itself. Most of humankind believe that some persons are decidedly wiser than others. In a storm at sea, for example, a ship's passengers look up to the captain as if he were a kind of god. They certainly suppose him to be wiser than themselves about keeping ships afloat, and by "wiser" they mean that he has true thoughts on the subject, whereas such thoughts as they may have are probably false. Protagoras, of course, spoke as if he intended to deny the rightness of this way of looking at the matter. All opinions, he said, are equally true. Let us suppose that he meant what he said, bizarre as it is. He cannot consistently deny that those who disagree with him are correct; their opinion is that some opinions are just false, and this opinion of theirs must be true if all opinions are true. Putting it differently: the truth of all opinions implies the truth of the opinion that *not* all opinions are true. In short, Protagoras' relativism implies its own falsity.[4]

Accordingly, there must be some error in the views which lead to this relativism. Either knowledge is not just a matter of perception by the senses or Cratylus was wrong in holding that everything is literally always changing. Plato, in fact, argues for both. If everything were always rushing to become something else, our very perceptions themselves would be swept away in the universal flux. Seeing and hearing, as perceptual processes, would be obliterated. There would be nothing the same for any length of time that the words "seeing" and "hearing" could name, just as there would be nothing for seeing to see or for hearing to hear. In that case, Plato says, "we must not speak of seeing any more than of not-seeing, or of any other perception more than of any not-perception"; and if this is what we have produced when asked to define knowledge, "we [have] no more answered what is knowledge than what is not knowledge." Of course, the world of our sense-experience is a scene of change, of motion and alteration, but it cannot be totally devoid of stability in the way that Cratylus supposed. The perception of change in things does

---

[4] Protagoras could reply that what he meant and said was that all opinions are true *for those who hold them,* which implies only that his position is false for those who believe it is, not that it is false absolutely. Plato, in turn, could observe that this only brings up another difficulty. If Protagoras' position is supposed to be true for those who believe it and false for those who do not, then *believing it* must exclude *not believing it*; and the truth of *this* at least must be independent of its being believed. One's believing could not constitute the truth of "believing excludes not believing," since the truth of "believing excludes not believing" would be presupposed in taking "I believe that believing excludes not believing" to exclude "I do not believe that believing excludes not believing."

not indeed amount to knowledge. Such perception does, however, occur, and the fact of its occurrence refutes the extreme position of Cratylus.

If by "perception" we mean the bare awareness of sensory qualities such as colors and sounds, and if by "knowledge" we mean judgments about these qualities that are as accurate as possible, we can easily see that perception does not amount to knowledge. The judgments which make up "knowledge" in this sense always involve general concepts that cannot be provided by perception.[5] Socrates, speaking for Plato, develops this in conversation with Theaetetus:

> Then, now, Theaetetus, take another view of the subject: you answered that knowledge is perception?
>
> I did.
>
> And if anyone were to ask you: With what does a man see black and white colors, and with what does he hear high and low sounds?—you would say, if I am not mistaken, "with the eyes and with the ears."
>
> I should.
>
> The free use of words and phrases, rather than minute precision, is generally characteristic of a liberal education, and the opposite is pedantic; but sometimes precision is necessary, and I believe that the answer which you have just given is open to the charge of incorrectness; for which is more correct—to say that we see or hear with the eyes and the ears, or through the eyes and through the ears?
>
> I should say "through," Socrates, rather than "with."
>
> Yes, my boy, for no one can suppose that in each of us, as in a sort of Trojan horse, there are perched a number of unconnected senses which do not all meet in some one nature, the mind, or whatever we please to call it, of which they are the instruments, and with which through them we perceive objects of sense.
>
> I agree with you in that opinion.
>
> The reason why I am thus precise is because I want to know whether, when we perceive black and white through the eyes, and again, other qualities through other organs, we do not perceive them with one and the same part of ourselves, and, if you were asked, you might refer all such perceptions to the body. Perhaps, however, I had better allow you to answer for yourself and not interfere. Tell me, then, are not the organs through which you perceive warm and hard and light and sweet, organs of the body?
>
> Of the body, certainly.
>
> And you would admit that what you perceive through one faculty you cannot perceive through another; the objects of hearing, for example, cannot be perceived through sight, or the objects of sight through hearing?
>
> Of course not.
>
> If you have any thought about both of them, this common perception cannot come to you either through the one or through the other?

[5] *A priori* concepts, as much later these general concepts will be called.

It cannot.

How about sounds and colors: in the first place, you would admit that they both *exist?*

Yes.

And that either of them is *different* from the other and the *same* with itself?

Certainly.

And that both are *two* and each of them *one?*

Yes.

You can further observe whether they are *like* or *unlike* one another?

I dare say.

But through what do you perceive all this about them? For neither through hearing nor yet through seeing can you apprehend that which they have in common. Let me give you an illustration of the point at issue: If there were any meaning in asking whether sounds and colors are salty or not, you would be able to tell me what faculty would consider the question. It would not be sight or hearing, but some other.

Certainly; the faculty of taste.

Very good; and now tell me what is the power which discerns, not only in sensible objects but in all things, *universal notions* such as those which are called being and not-being and those others about which we were just asking—what organs will you assign for the perception of these notions? . . .

Indeed, Socrates, I cannot answer; my only notion is that these, unlike objects of sense, have no separate organ, but that the mind, by a power of her own, contemplates the universals in all things. . . .

You have done me a kindness in releasing me from a very long discussion if you are clear that the soul views some things by herself and others through the bodily organs. For that was my own opinion, and I wanted you to agree with me.

I am quite clear.

The common thoughts we have about the objects of different senses—that they exist, are two, are different, and so on—represent an activity of judgment on the part of our minds, not simply a passive awareness of these objects by means of our senses. And these common thoughts or "universal notions"—being and not being, sameness and difference, and the rest—are not such as any of our senses can supply. They are grasped by the mind through its own resources, without any special bodily organ. Any judgment we make about what we perceive will contain one of these universal notions. "This color exists" contains the notion of "existence" or "being." "This color is different from that one" contains the notion of "difference" and implies that of "twoness." As far as our sense-experience is concerned, what is commonly called "knowledge" consists of judgments like these. Therefore, such "knowledge" cannot just be equated with perception.

Is it correct, however, to view judgments about what we perceive as constituting genuine knowledge? Granted that most persons think so, are they right? Plato thought not, and his reasons begin to emerge as the discussion between Socrates and Theaetetus continues:

And to which class would you refer being or essence? For this, of all our notions, is the most universal.

I should say to that class which the soul aspires to know of herself.

And would you say this also of like and unlike, same and other?

Yes.

And would you say the same of the noble and base and of good and evil?

These I conceive to be notions which are essentially relative, and which the soul also perceives by comparing in herself things past and present with the future.

And does she not perceive the hardness of that which is hard by the touch, and the softness of that which is soft equally by the touch?

Yes.

But their essence and what they are, and their opposition to one another, and the essential nature of this opposition, the soul herself endeavors to decide for us by the review and comparison of them?

Certainly.

The simple sensations which reach the soul through the body are given at birth to men and animals by nature, but their reflections on the being and use of them are slowly and hardly gained, if they are ever gained, by education and long experience.

Assuredly.

And can a man attain truth who fails of attaining being?

Impossible.

And can he who misses the truth of anything have a knowledge of that thing?

He cannot.

Then knowledge does not consist in impressions of sense, but in reasoning about them; in that only, and not in the mere impression, truth and being can be attained.

Clearly.

And would you call the two processes by the same name when there is so great a difference between them?

That would certainly not be right.

And what name would you give to seeing, hearing, smelling, being cold, and being hot?

I should call all of them perceiving—what other name could be given to them?

Perception would be the collective name of them?

Certainly.

Which, as we say, has no part in the attainment of truth any more than of being?

Certainly not. . . .

Then perception, Theaetetus, can never be the same as knowledge? . . .

Clearly not, Socrates; and knowledge has now been most distinctly proved to be different from perception.

But the original aim of our discussion was to find out rather what knowledge is than what it is not; at the same time we have made some progress, for we no longer seek for knowledge in perception at all, but in that other process, however called, in which the mind is alone and engaged with being.

Knowledge is to be found not in judgments about our perceptions but solely in reflections upon the universal notions that come into these judgments. This is because knowledge concerns truth, because truth concerns what things really are, and because what things really are—their "being" or "essential nature"—is understandable only by universal notions. For example, what hardness and softness really are, what in themselves their "being" and "opposition" amount to, cannot be learned from particular sensations of touch. "Being" is a universal notion, the most universal of all, and "difference" (or "opposition") is another. If these notions are not gotten by perception, as earlier we saw they cannot be, then the "being" and "difference" of hardness and softness cannot be matters of perception either. The mind may be stimulated by sensations of touch to "review and compare" their similarities and differences in respect of hardness and softness, but the true natures of hardness and softness are decided by a process of thinking "in which the mind is alone and engaged with being." Strictly speaking, perception "has no part in the attainment of truth," and thus no judgment about perception actually amounts to knowledge, in spite of what people commonly suppose.

The "universal notions" mentioned in the *Theaetetus* are what Plato elsewhere calls "forms" (*eide,* the plural of the Greek *eidos*) or "ideas" (*ideai,* the plural of the Greek *idea*).[6] Socrates had inquired after forms in the field of values, without investigating their precise nature or their importance to knowledge in general. For him they were the distinctive common patterns exhibited more or less faithfully in particular instances of justice, temperance, and so on. His assumption of their existence must have seemed to him justified by the success of his dialectical method in identifying them, at least approximately. Plato, however, had to come to terms with Cratylus' extreme theory of flux, according to which common patterns are completely absent from the world. In the *Theaetetus* he argues that even the simplest judgments of perception involve a reference to forms and that genuine knowledge concerns forms alone. This, if correct, shows that there can be no general objection to the possibility of forms of values, say, in ethics and politics. But it also shows that any such forms, if we are genuinely to know them, must be viewed separately

---

[6] As is now customary, we shall use "forms" instead of "ideas" in discussing Plato's theory. The English "idea" is misleading because it suggests that the things in question exist only "in the mind," which for Plato is definitely the *wrong* "idea."

from the actions of particular persons and the governments of particular communities. Forms of values in ethics and politics would no more be knowable from observing particular persons and communities than the forms of being and not-being or sameness and difference are knowable from perceptions of sight or touch. Both kinds of forms exist over and above the particular things we perceive with our senses.

Plato explains this more fully in his *Republic*. In a manner that shows the influence upon him of Parmenides, he lays it down that what we know when we know anything must be something real, "something that is." Of blank nothing, "that which is not," there can be only blank ignorance. Now for anything to be real and fully to exist, and thereby to be truly knowable, it must have constancy and permanence as well as a fixed and definite character. Thus in our ordinary experience we take a thing's shadow to be less real than the thing itself, because by comparison the shadow is shifting and indefinite and lacks any stable configuration. You can assign no particular shape or size to a shadow; both qualities are radically variable and depend on how the object casting the shadow is positioned relative to the source of light. Because it cannot be said that a shadow has one shape or size any more than an indefinite number of others, there is nothing specific to know about a shadow in and of itself; and where there is nothing specific to know, nothing fully exists. In general, the more variable and relative we find anything, the less real and knowable we consider it to be.

What Plato points out is that the objects we perceive through our senses, however real we may think them, are nearly as variable and relative as their shadows. There is no use in asking whether any given sensible object is definitely heavy or light, big or little, hard or soft, a unity or a multiplicity, concave or convex, straight or crooked, or one color or another. Everything depends upon one's point of view, one's standards of comparison, and the particular circumstances of the moment. Thus a certain chair seems big and heavy in comparison with a footstool but small and light in comparison with a table; it is a unity as one chair among others, but a multiplicity as composed of many parts; it is one color when viewed in daylight but another color when viewed in candlelight. One cannot say that the chair absolutely *is* any one of these things as opposed to the other. It has an equally good claim to both of each pair of opposite designations, and so it is with any sensible object you care to consider: every one of them has the same ambiguous character.

We arrive at a similar result when we examine things from the standpoint of our estimates of their value. Aesthetic appraisals of beauty may be taken as an example. Even a cooking pot, when "smooth and round and properly fired," could be said to have a certain beauty; but if we view it alongside a beautiful human figure, its beauty seems quickly to fade. In fact, it may look quite ugly by comparison. The most beautiful of human figures, however, might well appear ill-favored if a god or goddess were suddenly to materialize in the vicinity. Physical beauty is a comparative matter. Regardless of what it is, "the beautiful will in some point of view be found ugly." Or consider a judgment in morality or politics about the rightness of some action or the justice of some law. Here, too, everything depends on the circumstances. Other things being equal, it is right, for example, to return what we have borrowed; but other things are not equal if what we have borrowed is a knife and if the person from whom we borrowed it has in the meantime taken leave of his senses. Returning what we have borrowed is thus sometimes right and sometimes wrong. The same kind of relativity infects laws, so that a law that is warranted in one set of circumstances (say, a law about rationing foodstuffs in wartime) would be wholly unwarranted in another. Of all the many actions and laws that we deem right and just, there is none that, under changed conditions, will not appear wrong or unjust.

So with matters of value it is as with matters of fact: the things of our experience suffer from an inherent ambiguity. Every question about them has a "yes and no" answer, because in and of themselves they are no more one thing than something else—no more unities than multiplicities, big than little, beautiful than ugly, right than wrong. And we see on reflection that we cannot affirm completely the reality of what has this kind of equivocal status, nor can we claim genuinely to know it. Knowledge must be of "something that is," and none of the things of our experience really *is* or has *being* as one thing rather than another. Of course, tables and chairs, pots and human figures, actions and laws are not *nothing*. We are aware of them after a fashion, and we cannot be aware of what is literally nonexistent. Here Plato definitely parts company with Parmenides, for whom a thing either absolutely *is* or absolutely is *not*. There is, Plato says, a third alternative—a sort of twilight region, neither perfectly real nor utterly unreal, in which objects of sensation are found "tossing about." And as a name for the kind of awareness we have of these objects, "belief" is suitable as indicating something "darker than knowledge, but lighter than ignorance."

Accordingly, our judgments about what we perceive through our senses never amount to more than beliefs. The forms or universal notions that figure in these judgments are never exhibited unambiguously or for long in the objects we perceive. The most we can hope for in making these judgments is to catch things on the wing with judgments that will for a while and from one point of view be approximately correct. If Cratylus were right, of course, we could not hope even for this: the instability of things would be too great for our judgments to catch them at all. As it is, however, the objects and actions and communities of our experience do in a transitory and equivocal way partake of the forms of fact and of value— of being and not-being, sameness and difference, unity and multiplicity, hardness and softness, bigness and littleness, beauty and ugliness, rightness and wrongness, justice and injustice. Nothing we perceive ever *is* any of these things permanently or uniquely, and to that extent Cratylus was right. What looks beautiful at one time or from one point of view will look ugly at another time or from another point of view. For genuine knowledge we have to look elsewhere—to the forms themselves, as we saw before—but if beliefs are not as luminous as knowledge, they are also not as dark as ignorance; and as we shall see in a moment, they can be distinguished as better and worse.

It is not just that the things we perceive are inconstant in the forms they have. More importantly, perhaps, they never have any of them completely. Plato illustrates this point in the *Phaedo,* where he considers the example of equality. Two sticks or stones, however equal they may at first seem in size or in weight, will be found to fall short of perfect equality. Perfect equality, like perfect straightness or squareness or circularity, never shows up in our experience. The best we can expect is an approximation that is tolerably close. We always allow for a certain "margin of error," and exactly the same thing is true when it comes to matters of value. Perfectly just laws and perfectly virtuous dispositions are as elusive in our experience as perfectly circular circles.

We can, however, *think* of the perfect forms of all of these things. If we could not, we would be unable to estimate the comparative imperfection of the things we see and touch. Our ability to rank various diagrams on the basis of the different degrees to which they share in perfect circularity, for instance, shows that we have an awareness of perfect circularity and that we employ it as a standard.

Circularity itself, the perfect form, has a completely definite and objective nature, in no way relative to time, circumstance, or point of view. A perfect circle is a two-dimensional figure all the points of whose circumference are the same distance from its center. In thinking of this form, we are not thinking of a "mere abstraction" or of anything imaginary or simply "in the mind." Plato, following Parmenides, holds that whatever we can know must be "something that *is,*" and as we can certainly know circularity itself (its definition was given two sentences ago), it follows that circularity itself really exists. It is the particular figures we see through our eyes that are not fully real, since they have no fixed and abiding character. The figures drawn above, for one thing, will vanish when this page is destroyed, but circularity itself is not the kind of thing that can be destroyed, or created either. It is what it is eternally, whether any mind exists to know it or not. Circularity itself, like the One of Parmenides, is not a member of the changing world of space and time. What comes into being and passes away is not "something that *is*," not something that exists without qualification and is eternally the same, such as circularity itself.

All of the forms possess full reality. As eternally unchanging, they exist independently of the things we perceive through our senses. Sensible things are real insofar as they measure up to, or resemble, or participate in, the forms, and they are unreal insofar as they do not. Because judgments about sensible things always involve a reference to one or more forms, these judgments are possible only because sensible things do to some extent measure up; but because they never fully measure up, these judgments always fall short of knowledge and constitute only beliefs.

It is by virtue of their all resembling or participating in the same form to varying degrees that a number of different sensible things can appear to be more or less alike. Different diagrams will look more or less circular when they all participate more or less in circularity itself. Different actions or laws will seem more or less right or just when they all participate more or less in rightness or justice itself. Different faces and figures will seem more or less beautiful when they all participate more or less in beauty itself.

The moral as regards our getting knowledge is plain. One who loves knowledge, that is, a philosopher, will seek to penetrate the approximations of experience and to lay hold of the realities beyond. Socrates, in the *Republic,* reports his conversation with Glaucon as follows:

> Who then [Glaucon asked] are the true philosophers?
>
> Those, I [Socrates] said, who are lovers of the vision of truth. . . .
>
> I should like to know what you mean [Glaucon said].
>
> To another, I replied, I might have a difficulty in explaining; but I am sure that you will admit a proposition which I am about to make.
>
> What is the proposition?
>
> That since beauty is the opposite of ugliness, they are two?
>
> Certainly.
>
> And inasmuch as they are two, each of them is one?
>
> True again.
>
> And of just and unjust, good and evil, and of every other class, the same remark holds: taken singly, each of them is one; but from the various combinations of them with actions and things and with one another, they are seen in all sorts of lights and appear many?
>
> Very true.
>
> And this is the distinction which I draw between the sight-loving, art-loving, practical class and those of whom I am speaking, and who are alone worthy of the name of philosophers.
>
> How do you distinguish them? he said.
>
> The lovers of sights and sounds, I replied, are, as I conceive, fond of fine tones and colors and shapes and all the artificial products that are made out of them, but their mind is incapable of seeing or loving absolute beauty.

True, he replied.

Few are they who are able to attain to the sight of this.

Very true.

And he who, having a sense of beautiful things has no sense of absolute beauty, or who, if another lead him to a knowledge of that beauty is unable to follow—of such an one I ask, Is he awake or in a dream only? Reflect: is not the dreamer, sleeping or waking, one who likens dissimilar things, who puts the copy in the place of the real object?

I should certainly say that such an one was dreaming.

But take the case of the other, who recognizes the existence of absolute beauty and is able to distinguish the form from the objects which participate in the form, neither putting the objects in the place of the form nor the form in the place of the objects—is he a dreamer, or is he awake?

He is wide awake.

The process of awakening to the reality of the forms is described in keeping with a fourfold classification of levels of awareness. (I) Lowest of all is the state of mind that Plato calls "illusion" (*eikasia*), an inferior type of believing (*doxa*) in which one takes as real the mere "images" of sensible things. These include shadows and reflections as well as secondhand opinions, which are shadows and reflections in words. Suppose one were content to gather one's ideas about justice from some misleading description of actual laws. One would be at three removes from the truth because one would have (1) an inaccurate impression of (2) the laws in question, and one would wrongly suppose that those laws were (3) justice itself. This would be like taking the shadow of a cart wheel as a basis for knowledge of circularity itself. "We are all in a state of *eikasia* about many things," R. L. Nettleship says, "and to get a general idea of the sort of views that Plato had in mind when he spoke of shadows and reflections, we must think how many views there are which circulate in society and form a large part of what we call our knowledge, but which when we examine them are seen to be distorted, imperfect representations of fact, coming to us often through the media of several other men's minds, and the media of our own fancies and prejudices."

(II) When one realizes that images are images, one rises to the level of "belief" proper (*pistis*) and supposes that truth is to be found in direct personal experience of objects and actions and institutions, of "the animals which we see and everything that grows or is made." A wheelwright, for example, may believe that his long experience in making cart wheels has acquainted him with all there is to know about circularity; or a legislator may believe that his experience of lawmaking has fully informed him as to the nature of justice. Both may be tolerably close to the truth on certain points. The wheelwright may have found that the circumference of a cart wheel is a little over three times its diameter (precisely how much has not so far concerned him). The legislator may have found, as Pericles did, that justice requires extending to all citizens equal protection under the laws (although he may not yet have been prompted to examine very closely what "equal" calls for in this connection). Neither man has knowledge, however, but only belief, as long as he is content with less than a precise and reasoned understanding of the relevant forms. Either may run into practical difficulties that will stimulate his curiosity and cause him to wonder exactly what the story is as regards circularity or equal justice.

(III) The pursuit of knowledge (*episteme*) commences with what Plato calls "thinking" (*dianoia*). Here one begins to discern the nonsensible (or "intelligible") forms that are imperfectly exhibited in sensible objects, although to some extent one still finds it necessary to look to sensible objects for purposes of illustration. Plato cites geometry as an example. With one foot in the sensible world, geometry is full of diagrams of circles, triangles, and squares; but with its other foot in the intelligible world, geometry employs these diagrams only to set us *thinking* about the perfect forms of circularity, triangularity, and squareness, "which can only be seen with the eye of the mind." The method of geometry is hypothetical, and in this also it is typical of the present stage of knowledge as a whole. One starts in geometry from certain unquestioned assumptions or hypotheses—from definitions and postulates, and from axioms such as "things which are equal to the same thing are equal to one another." On the basis of these one reasons deductively to prove conclusions (theorems) about the geometrical forms represented roughly by diagrams. The assumptions or hypotheses, however, are not themselves proved within geometry. In this sense the whole procedure is hypothetical. Something similar takes place in thinking about forms of value. From certain assumptions about the form of human virtue in general one might work to conclusions about the form of justice, and all along one might have one's eye on a specific political constitution as a sort of imperfect "diagram."

(IV) When one seeks proof for the assumptions or hypotheses of thinking and no longer needs help from visual illustrations, one is on the road to what Plato calls "intelligence" *(noesis)*, or "knowledge" in the strict sense *(episteme)*. This knowledge "reason herself attains by the power of dialectic, using the hypotheses not as first principles, but only as hypotheses—that is to say, as steps and points of departure into a world which is above hypotheses, in order that she may soar beyond them to the first principle of the whole; and clinging to this and then to that which depends on this, by successive steps she descends again without the aid of any sensible object, from forms, through forms, and in forms she ends." Employing Socrates' dialectical method of philosophical discussion, one searches for ever higher and wider principles by which the assumptions made in the different spheres of thinking can be proved. The ultimate goal, whose achievement is described as "a task which is really tremendous," is to discover "the first principle of the whole"—one supreme form to which all the more special forms governing particular branches of knowledge owe their existence. By reference to this all of our assumptions, from geometry to ethics, are coordinated and justified. As the source of all being and truth, this supreme form does not itself either allow of or require explanation. It is the ultimate principle of all explanations, and in and of itself it is perfectly certain and intelligible.

Plato calls this supreme form "the form of the good," or "the good" for short. He is unable to describe this, he says, except in terms of an analogy. The good is related to the intelligible world of forms and to our knowing as the sun is related to the visible world of living things and to our seeing. The sun makes possible both seeing and the living things that are seen. The good makes possible both knowing and the forms (the truths) that are known. The sun, as the cause of light and of living things, is not itself light or life. The good, as the cause of knowing and of truths, is not itself knowledge or truth. The objects of knowledge derive from the good "not only their power of being known, but their very being and reality"; and yet the good "is not the same thing as being, but even beyond being, surpassing it in dignity and power."

From Plato's brief and figurative references to the form of the good, it is difficult to see exactly how he understood it. The goodness shared by moral qualities—by the forms of justice, temperance, courage, and so on— would in Plato's view naturally be explained by their common relation to the form of the good. But it is not clear how he could view the forms in other branches of knowledge—in geometry, for instance—as related to the good. Are the axioms of geometry what they are because they are good in the same sense in which justice is good? The attempts of scholars to determine what Plato meant have given rise to an enormous body of literature. He himself says that an understanding of the good comes only with long philosophical training and as a kind of revelation, when the "eye of the soul" is lifted up "to gaze on that which sheds light on all things." What the soul sees Plato will not try to say, for as with all the "most important points" there is "no way of putting it in words." Acquaintance with such a thing, he says, "must come rather after a long period of attendance on instruction in the subject itself and of close companionship, when, suddenly, like a blaze kindled by a leaping spark, it is generated in the soul and at once becomes self-sustaining."

A hint as to his view, however, is perhaps given in his *Phaedo,* where he describes sensible objects as "striving to be like" the forms and as "doing their best to resemble" them. These expressions suggest that every sensible object, no matter how lifeless, is to be accounted for teleologically—by reference to a purpose (*telos*)—and that the purpose of any kind of thing is to be as perfect an instance of that kind of thing as it possibly can be. For anything to be as perfect as possible of its kind is for it to come as close as possible to the forms that constitute perfection for that kind of thing—hardness and roundness in the case of a pebble, let us say. Now, because anything that is as perfect as possible of its kind is *good* of its kind, the forms in question (hardness and roundness, for instance) could be said to constitute *the good for that kind of thing.* All of the forms together could be said to constitute the good for *every* kind of thing—a fact that Plato would express by saying that all of the forms share in the higher form of goodness-of-a-kind in general, that is, in the form of the good in general. This would be as true of the forms of geometry (the good for sensible shapes) as of the forms of human virtue (the good for the souls of humankind). If, then, we could comprehend the form of the good, we would understand why all the other forms are as they are, just as we understand why sensible things are as they are, insofar as they *are* at all, by looking to the forms they "strive" to resemble. (Plato did not think that sticks and stones are literally "striving" for perfection, as from a sort of unconscious desire to be good. As we shall see when we come to his cosmology, he attributed purposiveness in the world to a divine architect, who takes the good as his model.)

Close companionship with a Socratic teacher is said to be necessary if one is to attain real knowledge of "the most important points." Failing this, however, something can still be done to indicate what the experience of progressive enlightenment is *like*. Thus Plato composed myths, in order to suggest figuratively what words cannot express literally. His superb poetic gifts are shown in the great Myth of the Cave, which is an allegory upon the four levels of awareness that have just been described. Socrates is still reporting, in the *Republic,* his conversation with Glaucon:

> And now, I said, let me show in a figure how far our nature is enlightened or unenlightened: Behold! human beings living in an underground den, which has a mouth open towards the light and reaching all along the den; here they have been from their childhood, and have their legs and necks chained so that they cannot move, and can only see before them, being prevented by the chains from turning round their heads. Above and behind them a fire is blazing at a distance, and between the fire and the prisoners there is a raised way; and you will see, if you look, a low wall built along the way, like the screen which marionette players have in front of them, over which they show the puppets.
>
> I see.
>
> And do you see, I said, men passing along the wall carrying all sorts of vessels, and statues and figures of animals made of wood and stone and various materials, which appear over the wall? Some of them are talking, others silent.
>
> You have shown me a strange image, and they are strange prisoners.
>
> Like ourselves, I replied; and they see only their own shadows, or the shadows of one another, which the fire throws on the opposite wall of the cave. . . . And of the objects which are being carried, in like manner they would only see the shadows. . . . And if they were able to converse with one another, would they not suppose that they were naming what was actually before them?
>
> Very true.
>
> And suppose further that the prison had an echo which came from

the other side, would they not be sure to fancy when one of the passers-by spoke that the voice which they heard came from the passing shadow? . . . To them . . . the truth would be literally nothing but the shadows of the images. . . . And now look again, and see what will naturally follow if the prisoners are released and disabused of their error. At first, when any one of them is liberated and compelled suddenly to stand up and turn his neck round and walk and look towards the light, he will suffer sharp pains; the glare will distress him, and he will be unable to see the realities of which in his former state he had seen the shadows; and then conceive someone saying to him that what he saw before was an illusion, but that now, when he is approaching nearer to being and his eye is turned towards more real existence, he has a clearer vision— what will be his reply? And you may further imagine that his instructor is pointing to the objects as they pass and requiring him to name them—will he not be perplexed? Will he not fancy that the shadows which he formerly saw are truer than the objects which are now shown to him?

Far truer.

And if he is compelled to look straight at the light, will he not have a pain in his eyes which will make him turn away to take refuge in the objects of vision which he can see, and which he will conceive to be in reality clearer than the things which are now being shown to him? . . . And suppose once more that he is reluctantly dragged up a steep and rugged ascent and held fast until he is forced into the presence of the sun himself, is he not likely to be pained and irritated? When he approaches the light his eyes will be dazzled, and he will not be able to see anything at all of what are now called realities. . . . He will require to grow accustomed to the sight of the upper world. And first he will see the shadows best, next the reflections of men and other objects in the water, and then the objects themselves; then he will gaze upon the light of the moon and the stars and spangled heaven; and he will see the sky and the stars by night better than the sun or the light of the sun by day. . . . Last of all he will be able to see the sun, and not mere reflections of him in the water, but he will see him in his own proper place and not in another; and he will contemplate him as he is. . . . He will then proceed to argue that this is he who gives the seasons and the years, and is the guardian of all that is in the visible world, and in a certain way the cause of all things which he and his fellows here have been accustomed to behold?

Clearly, he said, he would first see the sun and then reason about him.

And if they were in the habit of conferring honors among themselves on those who were quickest to observe the passing shadows and to remark which of them went before, and which followed after, and which were together; and who were therefore best able to draw conclusions as to the future, do you think that he would care for such honors and glories or envy the possessions of them? Would he not say with Homer, "Better to be the poor servant of a poor master," and to endure anything rather than think as they do and live after their manner? . . . Imagine once more . . . such an one coming suddenly out of the sun to be replaced in his old situation; would he not be certain to have his eyes full of darkness?

To be sure, he said.

And if there were a contest, and he had to compete in measuring the shadows with the prisoners who had never moved out of the den, while his sight was still weak and before his eyes had become steady (and the time which would be needed to acquire this new habit of sight might be very considerable), would he not be ridiculous? Men would say of him that up he went and down he came without his eyes; and that it was better not even to think of ascending; and if anyone tried to loose another and lead him up to the light, let them only catch the offender, and they would put him to death.

No question, he said.

This entire allegory, I said, you may now append, dear Glaucon, to the previous argument; the prison-house is the world of sight, the light of the fire is the sun, and you will not misapprehend me if you interpret the journey upwards to be the ascent of the soul into the intelligible world according to my poor belief, which, at your desire, I have expressed—whether rightly or wrongly God knows. But, whether true or false, my opinion is that in the world of knowledge the form of the good appears last of all and is seen only with an effort; and when seen is also inferred to be the universal author of all things beautiful and right, parent of light and of the lord of light in the visible world, and the immediate source of reason and truth in the intelligible; and that this is the power upon which he who would act rationally either in public or private life must have his eye fixed.

I agree, he said, as far as I am able to understand you. . . .

But then, if I am right, certain professors of education must be wrong when they say that they can put a knowledge into the soul which was not there before, like sight into blind eyes. . . . Our argument shows that the power and capacity of learning exists in the soul already; and that just as the eye was unable to turn from darkness to light without the whole body, so too the instrument of knowledge can only by the movement of the whole soul be turned from the world of becoming into that of being, and learn by degrees to endure the sight of being, and of the brightest and best of being, or in other words, of the good.

In saying that it is a mistake to suppose that knowledge can be put into a soul that was not in it before, Plato seems to be alluding to a notion of his that is not stated explicitly in the *Republic*. It is rather in his *Meno, Phaedo,* and *Phaedrus* that we find the remarkable view that learning is a matter of *recollecting* an acquaintance we made with the forms in a previous state of existence. When at birth our souls entered our present bodies, we forgot this acquaintance, but the stimulus of sense-experience and of dialectical questioning will call it into consciousness again. In the *Meno* this is offered in explanation of the feat of an unschooled slave boy, who comes up with the solution to a geometrical

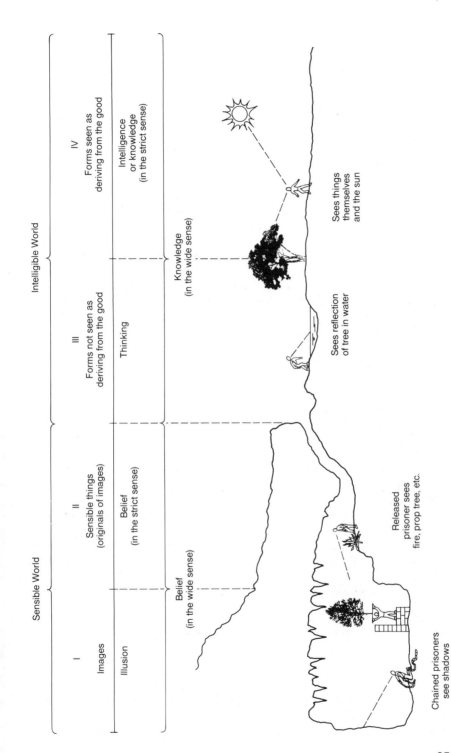

Sensible World

Intelligible World

I	II	III	IV
Images	Sensible things (originals of images)	Forms not seen as deriving from the good	Forms seen as deriving from the good
Illusion	Belief (in the strict sense)	Thinking	Intelligence or knowledge (in the strict sense)

Belief (in the wide sense)

Knowledge (in the wide sense)

Chained prisoners see shadows

Released prisoner sees fire, prop tree, etc.

Sees reflection of tree in water

Sees things themselves and the sun

95

problem when Socrates merely asks him some questions about a diagram. And in the *Phaedo* this is said to explain how it is that we may compare sticks and stones with reference to a standard of perfect equality which no sense-experience can provide, because none fully bears it out. Sense-experience and Socratic questioning serve only to *remind* us of what subconsciously we already know but temporarily have forgotten. In the Myth of the Cave the process of reminding is expressed in the simile of turning the soul away from the sensible world of becoming and toward the intelligible world of being.

Whether Plato meant "recollection" (*anamnesis*) literally is a disputed question. Some believe that this so-called "doctrine" of his was a deliberately figurative presentation, in terms of Orphic and Pythagorean ideas, of a much less colorful thesis, namely, that we must possess substantial nonbodily souls in order to apprehend, as in *this* life we do, nonsensible forms. Others, however, see no reason to doubt that Plato meant "recollection" literally, at least at the time he composed the dialogues in question. Perhaps the best comment on the matter is the one given by Socrates in the *Meno:* "I shouldn't like to take my oath on the whole story, but one thing I am ready to fight for as long as I can, in word and act: that is, that we shall be better, braver, and more active men if we believe it right to look for what we don't know than if we believe there is no point in looking because what we don't know we can never discover." In other words, the main thing is to recognize that knowledge of the forms is possible. Recollection, as an account of this possibility, is less certain and less important.

Note the accompanying diagram of the parallels between the four levels of awareness and the stages of the prisoner's progress in the Myth of the Cave.

The line here that is divided into four segments is used by Plato himself in describing the four levels of awareness, and he attaches some significance to the way in which the segments are marked off. The segment representing the sensible world (I + II) is shorter than that representing the intelligible world (III + IV) in order to indicate the inferior reality and truth of the sensible world. Each of these two main segments is subdivided in the same proportion as the whole line, so that the proportion of I to II and of III to IV is the same as the proportion of I + II to III + IV. This indicates the inferiority of I to II and of III to IV.

Ethics

Plato's theory of forms, in showing how knowledge in general is possible, was in particular a vindication of Socrates' search for objective truths in ethics. The practical effect of knowing these truths seemed to Plato exactly what it did to Socrates: to know them is to strive to follow them, once it is understood that following them is personally beneficial. But how many people are really capable of knowing them? Granted that no one deliberately courts self-harm, is everyone able to see for himself or herself what is truly beneficial and right?

Socrates was hopeful. As we saw, he thought that he had been divinely commissioned to serve as a gadfly to Athens by reproaching all and sundry, young and old alike, for caring too much about "money and honor and reputation" and too little about "wisdom and truth and the greatest improvement of the soul." He believed that if he confronted people one by one, he could bring them to see how their ignorance thwarted their well-being, how "money and honor and reputation" are dangerous possessions unless the soul which uses them is informed about its own best interests. This realization, he thought, would excite in anyone a strong desire for self-knowledge—a desire that could always be satisfied, given only normal intelligence and the opportunity for philosophical discussion. Once self-knowledge was attained, people would govern themselves by personal insight into the conditions of genuine happiness, by that wisdom which is also courage and temperance and justice. "So . . . I tried to persuade each of you not to think more of practical advantages than of his mental and moral well-being, or in general to think more of advantage than of well-being in the case of the state or of anything else."

To Plato it did not seem this simple. From his own experience of men and affairs, and in particular from the fate of Socrates himself, he concluded that most persons have little capacity for moral wisdom—or indeed for genuine knowledge of any kind. They pass their lives entirely in the Cave, kept there by insurmountable limitations of character and intelligence that mainly they inherit from their parents. To "inborn disposition" Plato attributed the strength of one's desire for truth itself, as well as certain traits essential to getting at the truth—good memory, for one thing, and a propensity to view things in accurate perspective that comes from an inward "measure and grace." Most persons suffer from a congenital inability to see things clearly and to keep things straight; irrelevant wishes and fears are always clouding their minds, and by nature they are preoccupied with "those pleasures of which the body is the instrument" and of which money is the provider. They are "lost in the mazes of multiplicity and change," content with mere beliefs (with *eikasia* and *pistis*) of varying degrees of everyday adequacy, and deaf to the news that wisdom and truth pertain to an unchanging order of eternal principles that "men have not heard, nor perceived by the ear, neither hath the eye seen." These views, which are given in Plato's *Republic,* are presented again and more explicitly in his *Laws,* where his conviction of the importance of heredity shows up in his counsel to the potential father: "During the whole year and all his life long, and especially when he is begetting children, he ought to take care and not intentionally do what is injurious to health, or what involves insolence and wrong; for he cannot help leaving the impression of himself on the souls and bodies of his offspring, and he begets children in every way inferior."

A few children have the good fortune to be born with the wherewithal to attain wisdom. Most of these, however, are corrupted by irresistible pressures to conform to the false values of the society around them. "The multitude can never be philosophical . . . it is bound to disapprove of all who pursue wisdom," and most children are infected early and permanently with the likes and dislikes of the multitude. "The remnant who are worthy to consort with philosophy will be small. . . ." "You may be sure that, in the present state of society, any character that escapes and comes to good can only have been saved by some miraculous interposition."

From Plato's point of view, then, it is inaccurate to say that wrongdoing is always a function of ignorance, if by "ignorance" is meant something that education could remedy. The preponderance of wrongdoing is to be attributed instead to simple vice or wickedness. This indeed is no less involuntary than the wrongdoing that comes of "ignorance" in the sense just specified. None would be wicked who knew the personal cost and the intrinsic evil of wickedness, but the earmark of the wicked is precisely their incapacity for such knowledge. All they can appreciate is coercion of one sort or another—"chastisement," Plato calls it in the *Sophist*. His spokesman in this dialogue, who is identified only as a "Stranger from Elea," converses with Theaetetus as follows:

In the soul [the Stranger declares] there are two kinds of evil.

What are they? [Theaetetus asks].

The one may be compared to disease in the body, the other to deformity.

I do not understand.

Perhaps you have never reflected that disease and discord are the same.

To this, again, I do not know what I should reply.

Do you not conceive discord to be a dissolution of kindred elements, originating in some disagreement?

Just that.

And is deformity anything but the want of measure, which is always unsightly?

Exactly.

And do we not see that opinion is opposed to desire, pleasure to anger, reason to pain, and that all these elements are opposed to one another in the souls of bad men?

Certainly.

And yet [as elements of the soul] they must all be akin?

Of course.

Then we shall be right in calling vice [or wickedness] a discord and disease of the soul?

Most true.

And when things having motion, and aiming at an appointed mark, continually miss their aim and glance aside, shall we say that this is the effect of symmetry among them, or of the want of symmetry?

Clearly of the want of symmetry.

But surely we know that no soul is voluntarily ignorant of anything. . . . And what is ignorance but the aberration of a mind which is bent on truth, and in which the process of understanding is perverted?

True.

Then we are to regard an unintelligent soul as deformed and devoid of symmetry?

Very true.

Then there are these two kinds of evil in the soul—the one which is generally called vice, and is obviously a disease of the soul. . . . And there is the other . . . ignorance. . . .

I certainly admit what I at first disputed—that we ought to consider cowardice, intemperance, and injustice to be all alike forms of disease in the soul, and ignorance . . . to be deformity. . . .

And in the case of the body are there not two arts which have to do with the two bodily states?

What are they?

There is gymnastic, which has to do with deformity, and medicine, which has to do with disease.

True.

And where there is insolence and injustice and cowardice, is not chastisement the art which is most required? . . . Again, of the various kinds of ignorance, may not instruction be rightly said to be the remedy?

True.

Ignorance is cured by instruction in the way in which bodily deformity, that is, a poor physique, is remedied by physical training. Vice or wickedness, on the other hand, is like a disease (either congenital or contracted in childhood); and the only cure for it, insofar as it is curable, is the medicine of punishments and threats. In many cases, no doubt, this treatment will be effective against only the symptoms of the disease, by way of discouraging overt wrongful actions, and the soul behind the actions will be little the wiser about happiness and virtue. Unfortunately, there is nothing else to be done.

As disease is really a sort of civil war among "kindred elements" in the body, so vice or wickedness is a matter of discord among elements in the soul. "Opinion is opposed to desire, pleasure to anger, reason to pain." Such an account of the vices of "cowardice, intemperance, and injustice" was impossible on Socrates' view of the soul, for he identified the soul simply with one's reason or intelligence, and in this he saw no complexity of elements that could be at odds with one another. Socrates believed that when the soul perceives that something is beneficial and right, it could not encounter within itself any obstacle to acting accordingly.

To an extent Plato agreed with Socrates that the soul lacks inner complexity. Considered apart from the body that it enlivens, the soul, Plato thought, is a unitary stock of psychological energy, a single undifferentiated force. He conceived of this more precisely as a quantity of desire (*eros*), capable of being directed toward many specific goals and of moving the body in pursuance thereof. A human body cannot move itself: like any other physical object, it moves only when something else starts it moving. A chief feature of the soul, however, and one that distinguishes it from everything physical, is its power of moving itself and the body without being caused to move by anything else. ("Self-initiating motion" is Plato's definition of "soul" in the *Laws*.) But in spite of its unity when considered by itself, the soul exhibits complexity in its association with the body. This single stock of energy is directed like a stream into three separate channels, each of which constitutes an element of the soul.

In the *Republic* Plato identifies these three elements by analyzing the experience of conflicting desires. He takes the example of a man who feels very thirsty but who is unwilling to drink because he understands that drinking would be bad for him. There must be two different factors at work in the man's soul—one urging him to drink without heeding the consequences, the other holding him back out of prudent reflection. Such an experience of conflict cannot be explained on the supposition that the soul is unitary, for the same thing cannot act in opposite ways at the same time; nor can it be explained if the soul is purely reason or intelligence, since the urging to drink is irrational. The conflict is between reason and appetite, between a rational element in the soul and an appetitive element, between a desire to act with wisdom and forethought on the basis of accurate knowledge and a desire merely to satisfy a bodily craving. This example is typical of situations with which everyone is familiar. The bodily appetites—for drink, food, sex, and money as a means of obtaining them—are a "many-headed beast," always trying to run out of control and not infrequently succeeding.

Fortunately, there is a third factor in the soul that is a natural ally of reason in its struggle to keep the appetites within bounds. This is what Plato calls the "spirited" element, or "spirit," and it is characterized by the desires for honor and reputation, for self-esteem and respect from others, and for cutting a fine figure in life generally. We feel that whatever is inconsistent with these desires is unworthy of us, beneath us, a threat to our integrity, just not the kind of thing with which we should be associated. Thus we are annoyed with ourselves if we contemplate succumbing to some base appetite, and disgusted with ourselves if we actually succumb. Thus also we are angry and indignant with others if we believe they have violated our rights or ignored our prerogatives. Spirit takes the side of reason inasmuch as it never champions a bodily appetite if reason decides against it, nor does it ever make us angry with ourselves for doing what reason perceives to be right. Spirit can, however, get out of hand: we can get unreasonably angry with ourselves and others, we can be too jealous of our prerogatives, too anxious about our reputation, too ambitious and self-assertive. The difference between spirit and reason is shown by cases like these and also by observing that children and even animals, while short on reason, are full of spirit.

The human soul is therefore composed of three elements—reason, spirit, and appetite—each of which has its own characteristic desires. The conflict among them makes up the drama of our inner lives. In the *Phaedrus* Plato employs mythical imagery of great force to illustrate a trial of strength between sexual lust on the one hand and spirit in alliance with reason on the other.

Of the nature of the soul [Socrates says], though her true form be ever a theme of large and more than mortal discourse, let me speak briefly and in a figure. And let the figure be composite—a pair of winged horses and a charioteer. Now . . . one of [the horses] is noble and of noble breed, and the other is ignoble and of ignoble breed. . . . The right-hand horse [corresponding to the spirited element of the soul] is upright and cleanly made; he has a lofty neck and an aquiline nose; his color is white and his eyes dark; he is a lover of honor and modesty and temperance and the follower of true glory; he needs no touch of the whip but is guided by word and admonition only. The other [corresponding to the appetitive element] is a crooked lumbering animal put together anyhow; he has a short thick neck; he is flat-faced and of a dark color, with grey eyes and blood-red complexion; the mate of insolence and pride, shag-eared and deaf, hardly yielding to whip and spur.

Now when the charioteer [corresponding to the rational element] beholds the vision of love, and has his whole soul warmed through sense, and is full of the prickings and ticklings of desire, the obedient steed, then as always under the government of shame, refrains from leaping on the beloved; but the other, heedless of the blows of the whip, plunges and runs away, giving all manner of trouble to his companion and the charioteer, whom he forces to approach the beloved and to remember the joys of love. They at first indignantly oppose him and will not be urged on to do terrible and unlawful deeds; but at last, when he persists in plaguing them, they yield and agree to do as he bids them. And now they are at the spot and behold the flashing beauty of the beloved, which when the charioteer sees, his memory is carried to the true beauty, whom he beholds in company with Modesty like an image placed upon a holy pedestal. He sees her, but he is afraid and falls backwards in adoration, and by his fall is compelled to pull back the reins with such violence as to bring both the steeds on their haunches, the one willing and unresisting, the unruly one very unwilling; and when they have gone back a little, the one is overcome with shame and wonder, and his whole soul is bathed in perspiration; the other, when the pain is over which the bridle and the fall had given him, having with difficulty taken breath, is full of wrath and reproaches which he heaps upon the charioteer and his fellow steed for want of courage and manhood, declaring that they have been false to their agreement and guilty of desertion.

Again they refuse and again he urges them on and will scarce yield to their prayer that he would wait until another time. When the appointed hour comes they make as if they had forgotten, and he reminds them, fighting and neighing and dragging them on, until at length he, on the same thoughts intent, forces them to draw near again. And when they are near he stoops his head and puts up his tail, and takes the bit in his teeth and pulls shamelessly. Then the charioteer is worse off than ever; he falls back like a racer at the barrier, and with a still more violent wrench drags the bit out of the teeth of the wild steed and covers his abusive tongue and jaws with blood, and forces his legs and haunches to the ground and punishes him sorely.

And when this has happened several times and the villain has ceased from his wanton way, he is tamed and humbled and follows the will of the charioteer, and when he sees the beautiful one he is ready to die of fear. And from that time forward the soul of the lover follows the beloved in modesty and holy fear.

It is in light of his three-element (or "tripartite") analysis of the soul that Plato, in the *Republic,* identifies the forms of the chief moral virtues. One has *wisdom* when the rational element governs the entire soul from knowledge of what is best for each of the three elements and for all of them together. (So the charioteer, knowing that true beauty is the friend of modesty only, reins in his horses—one willingly, the other not so willingly.) One has *courage* when the spirited element fears only what reason determines to be really fearful—not disappointed appetites but the loss of the soul's integrity. (So the right-hand horse, "under the government of shame," remains true to his allegiance with the charioteer.) One has *temperance* when conflict among the three elements has given way to harmony and solidarity, to their unanimous consent that reason shall govern. (So the left-hand horse finally agrees with his companion and with the charioteer to walk for the future "in modesty and holy fear.") One has *justice* when not only has conflict been overcome but each element fulfills its own proper function with maximum effectiveness and with due respect for the functions of the others—with the result that the soul as a whole achieves excellence. (So at last the chariot is rightly driven, with charioteer and horses working expertly together.) "The just man," Plato says, "does not permit the several elements within him to interfere with one another, or any of them to do the work of the others. He sets in order his own inner life, and is his own master, and his own law, and at peace with himself; and when he has bound together the three principles within him . . . [he] is no longer many, but has become one entirely temperate and perfectly adjusted nature. . . ." Just and honorable conduct in any sphere of activity, private or public, is behavior that "preserves and cooperates with this harmonious condition."

Justice and the other virtues constitute the soul's health, whereas injustice and the other vices are its diseases. To ask why one should be virtuous is therefore to ask why one should be healthy instead of diseased, and Plato considers this a ridiculous question. The inward harmony of virtue is desirable in and of itself. The inward disharmony of vice is undesirable in and of itself. That is all that needs to be said. Still, it can be shown, Plato believes, that a virtuous life will for anyone also be pleasanter than a life of vice. Distinctive pleasures accompany the activities of each of the three elements in the soul. Only if the elements work together in temperance and justice can pleasures of the highest quality be gotten for each element in the maximum attainable quantity. Should appetite, for example, seize control of reason and spirit, so that one's whole object in life becomes the gratification of its cravings, the inevitable outcome will be more pain and less pleasure than one would otherwise have experienced. The expectation in such cases is always that bodily pleasures will give satisfaction that is lasting and cumulative, but what one actually gets is transitory and adds up to little. Thankless as they are, the appetites reward one's devotion only by multiplying their number and raising their demands, until finally one is a slave to their insatiable greed. The pleasures of the rational element, on the other hand, really do get us somewhere, for knowledge and wisdom are progressive, are not gone as soon as they are arrived, and afford durable satisfaction of the finest type. But the moral is not that we should forgo the pleasures of appetite; it is that "all the desires both of the gain-loving [appetitive] and of the ambitious [spirited] part of our nature will win the truest pleasures of which they are capable, if they accept the guidance of knowledge and wisdom and pursue only those pleasures of which wisdom approves."

These views in the *Republic* were supplemented by a more detailed account in the *Philebus* of the role of reason in relation to appetite. There Plato proposes that the good for human life may be identified as something perfect or complete and therefore wholly sufficient and supremely desirable for all who can apprehend it. Judged by this criterion, neither pleasure alone nor wisdom alone can be the good. This may be seen by considering each of them by itself. Take pleasure first:

> Would you choose [Socrates asks] to live all your life long in the enjoyment of the greatest pleasures?
>
> Certainly I should [Protarchus replies].
>
> Would you consider that there was still anything wanting to you if you had perfect pleasure?
>
> Certainly not.
>
> Reflect; would you not want wisdom and intelligence and forethought, and similar qualities? . . .
>
> Why should I? Having pleasure I should have all things.
>
> Living thus, you would always throughout your life enjoy the greatest pleasures?
>
> I should.
>
> But if you had neither mind, nor memory, nor knowledge, nor true

opinion, you would in the first place be utterly ignorant of whether you were pleased or not, because you would be entirely devoid of intelligence. . . . And similarly, if you had no memory you would not recollect that you had ever been pleased, nor would the slightest recollection of the pleasure which you feel at the moment remain with you; and if you had no true opinion you would not think that you were pleased when you were; and if you had no power of calculation you would not be able to calculate on future pleasure, and your life would be the life, not of a man, but of an oyster. . . . Could this be otherwise?

No.

But is such a life desirable?

I cannot answer you, Socrates; the argument has taken away from me the power of speech.

We must keep up our spirits. Let us now take the life of mind and examine it in turn.

And what is the life of mind?

I want to know whether any one of us would consent to live, having wisdom and mind and knowledge and memory of all things, but having no sense of pleasure or pain, and wholly unaffected by these and the like feelings?

Neither life, Socrates, appears desirable to me, or is likely, as I should imagine, to be chosen by anyone else.

What would you say, Protarchus, to both of these in one, or to one that was made out of the union of the two?

Out of the union, that is, of pleasure with mind and wisdom?

Yes, that is the life which I mean.

There can be no difference of opinion; not some but all would surely choose this third rather than either of the other two. . . .

But do you see the consequence?

To be sure I do. The consequence is that two out of the three lives which have been proposed are neither sufficient nor desirable for man or for animal.

Then now there can be no doubt that neither of them has the good, for the one which had would certainly have been sufficient and desirable for every living creature or thing that was able to live such a life; and if any of us had chosen any other, he would have chosen contrary to the nature of the truly desirable, and not of his own free will, but either through ignorance or from some unhappy necessity.

Certainly that seems to be true.

So the good for human beings, and indeed for any creatures who have the capacity for it, is a life in which there is a blend of "pleasure with mind and wisdom." Now there are roughly two kinds of pleasure and two kinds of knowledge, and the question is whether to put all four of these possible ingredients into the blend, and if so, how much of each. First let us see what they are. Pleasures are either mixed or unmixed. *Mixed* pleasures are those which are experienced in contrast with more or less painful sensations and emotions—the pleasure of drinking, for example, which depends upon a painful (or at least an uncomfortable) feeling of thirst; or the pleasure of expressing our anger at someone who has displeased us. *Unmixed* pleasures are those that do not depend upon any preceding or accompanying pain (discomfort, unpleasantness), as when we take delight in certain patterns, colors, tones, and fragrances, or when we simply enjoy finding out about something. Mixed pleasures differ from unmixed ones in three noteworthy respects: in themselves they have nothing that limits the degree of intensity to which they can be pushed (thus the temptation to run after "more" of them); their pleasantness can be offset more than one supposes by the pains that precede or accompany them (and the greater the pleasure the greater the pain necessary for contrast); and they are less genuine or true to type as pleasures because of the pains with which they are mixed up—just as a muddy patch of white is less genuinely white than a clear one. (So much by way of an impression of Plato's examination of pleasure, which is remarkably subtle and detailed.)

As for the two kinds of knowledge, one is technical and the other is cultural. *Technical* knowledge is concerned with producing and making, and it is found in arts and crafts—in carpentry, music, agriculture, medicine, military tactics, and so forth. Chiefly because measurement is not equally feasible in all of them, these arts and crafts differ considerably in the exactness of their methods and in the assurance they can give of definite results. Carpentry is thus in a better position than medicine (in which much depends upon guesswork and luck), and it more deserves the title of "knowledge." Strictly speaking, of course, all the arts and crafts involve only what Plato calls "belief"; he here calls them kinds of "knowledge" in a loose sense and out of courtesy. But *cultural* knowledge, that is, knowledge which has to do with the *cultivation* of the soul, is "knowledge" properly so called. This is philosophical dialectic, "the knowledge which has to do with being and reality, and sameness and unchangeableness, [and] is by far the truest of all."

Such are the possible ingredients of the best life. Now it can be seen without further ado that dialectic is certainly needed, for without that we should lack the wisdom to get the benefit of anything else. If we do not know the forms of excellence (the virtues) that constitute our well-being or happiness, we shall hardly know how arts and crafts are to be employed instead of misemployed—and all of them have potential for evil as well as for good. Given wisdom, however, technical "knowledge" is also plainly essential to a life that human beings can find complete and sufficient, and all of it may safely be introduced into the blend. This takes care of the "sober water" of knowledge; now for the "honey" of pleasure. What of that should go in? The unmixed pleasures, which are the truest, present no problem. Having scant tendency to monopolize the soul, they are "good and innocent." But the mixed pleasures are a horse of a different color: they are a species of what Pythagoras called "the Unlimited," with powerful imperialist designs upon the entire soul. Once they get loose (like, in fact, the dark horse in the myth), they stop at nothing and never are satisfied. For a life that we can feel is complete and sufficient, a principle of intelligent Limit, of definite "measure and proportion," needs to be introduced into the Unlimited; so that only those mixed pleasures are indulged which "consort with health and temperance, and . . . attend upon virtue in general, following her everywhere as their divinity."

A life thus composed will exhibit measure and proportion throughout; the blend of ingredients will be a true blend, Plato says, instead of a "mess." Measure and proportion, as Pythagoras suggested, are what confer goodness upon any complex of elements, whether in music where goodness is harmony, or in the body where goodness is health, or in the soul where goodness is happiness. And because any complex having measure and proportion will have beauty as well as goodness, we see how much is owing to reason as the controlling element that institutes and maintains measure and proportion. And what is true in human life is true in the universe at large, where the order, beauty, and regular motion of the heavenly bodies are such that we can account for them only by supposing a "presiding cause of no mean power, which orders and arranges years and seasons and months, and may justly be called wisdom and mind . . . the king of heaven and earth." Our souls, as Pythagoras said, are really fragments of this divinity and as such have a commission to promote in our sphere the same kind of beauty and goodness that he promotes in his. "Then, Protarchus, you will proclaim everywhere, by word of mouth to this company, and by messengers bearing the tidings far and wide, that pleasure is not the first of possessions, nor yet the second, but that in measure, and the mean, and the suitable, and the like, the eternal nature has been found."

We saw that Plato understood the human soul to be a single stock of psychological energy in the form of desire (*eros*), which in its association with the body appears as appetite, spirit, and reason. And we have seen how Plato identified human well-being as a coordination of these elements in keeping with justice and temperance, which are instances of that "measure and proportion" upon which goodness and beauty everywhere depend. In his *Symposium,* however, Plato views all this from a different angle. There he explains how those with philosophical gifts can so redirect and concentrate their energies, by refining their appetitive and spirited desires, as to fulfill in the highest degree their rational desire for wisdom. This is not so much a coordination of the elements as a sublimation of two of them in the interests of facilitating the third. The pinnacle of knowledge is insight into the form of the good. Earlier the process of achieving this insight was said to be one of intellectual cultivation through philosophical dialectic. In the *Symposium* we have the other side of the matter: training of desire is necessary as well—or rather is an essential part of the same process. Here the form of the good is represented under its aspect as *beauty:* the form of the good is also the form of the beautiful; and it is as beauty, we are told, that the good is desired. Everyone desires not only to possess what is good, as Socrates had said, but to possess it perpetually and to fare well always—truly always, by being immortal. This is what everyone seeks, what everyone *loves* in the sense of longing for it. Such love expresses itself in a host of particular ways—in desires of appetite and of spirit and of reason—but in each case the good that is loved is apprehended as some type of beauty, however imperfect its likeness to the form of beauty itself. And the encounter with beauty by any element of the soul excites in us an activity whose aim is *procreation* in one fashion or another, for thus do we show our longing for immortality.

The appetitive desire to be forever on intimate terms with physical beauty (which is *eros* in a narrow sense) expresses itself as the longing for offspring and in concern for their well-being. "There is something divine about the whole matter; in procreation and bringing to birth the mortal creature is endowed with a touch of immortality." The spirited desire for a glorious (or "beautiful") reputation expresses itself in ambitious striving for accomplishments that will ever be honored by posterity. The rational desire for noble (or "beautiful") works of knowledge, whether "technical" or "cultural," expresses itself in the activities of craftsmen and artists, statesmen and educators. So it is that "spiritual children," in the form of pottery and verse, laws and ideas, are the fruit of *eros* no less than sons and daughters.

The foregoing are love's "lesser mysteries" which, in the *Symposium,* are disclosed to Socrates by a certain Diotima of Mantinea, "a woman wise in this and in many other kinds of knowledge, who in the days of old, when the Athenians offered sacrifice before the coming of the plague, delayed the disease ten years." As for the "greater mysteries" that crown these lesser ones, Diotima is not sure that Socrates is able to enter into them.

> But [she says] I will do my utmost to inform you, and do you follow if you can. For he who would proceed aright in this matter should begin in youth to visit beautiful forms; and first, if he be guided by his instructor aright, to love one such form only—out of that he should create fair thoughts; and soon he will of himself perceive that the beauty of one form is akin to the beauty of another; and then if beauty of form in general is his pursuit, how foolish would he be not to recognize that the beauty in every form is one and the same! And when he perceives this he will abate his violent love of the one, which he will despise and deem a small thing, and will become a lover of all beautiful forms; in the next stage he will consider that the beauty of the mind is more honorable than the beauty of the outward form. So that if a virtuous soul have but a little comeliness, he will be content to love and tend him, and will search out and bring to the birth thoughts which may improve the young, until he is compelled to contemplate and see the beauty of institutions and laws, and to understand that the beauty of them all is

of one family, and that personal beauty is a trifle; and after laws and institutions he will go on to the sciences, that he may see their beauty, being not like a servant in love with the beauty of one youth or man or institution, himself a slave mean and narrow-minded, but drawing towards and contemplating the vast sea of beauty, he will create many fair and noble thoughts and notions in boundless love of wisdom; until on that shore he grows and waxes strong, and at last the vision is revealed to him of a single science, which is the science of beauty everywhere. To this I will proceed; please to give me your very best attention:

He who has been instructed thus far in the things of love, and who has learned to see the beautiful in due order and succession, when he comes toward the end will suddenly perceive a nature of wondrous beauty (and this, Socrates, is the final goal of all our former toils)—a nature which in the first place is everlasting, not growing and decaying, or waxing and waning; secondly, not fair in one point of view and foul in another, or at one time or in one relation or at one place fair, at another time or in another relation or at another place foul, as if fair to some and foul to others, or in the likeness of a face or hands or any other part of the bodily frame, or in any form of speech or knowledge, or existing in any other being, as, for example, in an animal, or in heaven, or in earth, or in any other place but beauty absolute, separate, simple, and everlasting, which without diminution and without increase, or any change, is imparted to the ever-growing and perishing beauties of all other things. He who from these ascending under the influence of true love, begins to perceive that beauty, is not far from the end. And the true order of going, or being led by another, to the things of love, is to begin from the beauties of earth and mount upwards for the sake of that other beauty, using these as steps only, and from one going on to two, and from two to all fair forms, and from fair forms to fair practices, and from fair practices to fair notions, until from fair notions he arrives at the notion of absolute beauty, and at last knows what the essence of beauty is.

This, my dear Socrates, . . . is that life above all others which man should live, in the contemplation of beauty absolute; a beauty which if you once beheld, you would see not to be after the measure of gold, and garments, and fair boys and youths, whose presence now entrances you; and you and many an one would be content to live seeing them only and conversing with them without meat or drink, if that were possible—you only want to look at them and to be with them. But what if man had eyes to see the true beauty—the divine beauty, I mean, pure and clear and unalloyed, not clogged with the pollutions of mortality and all the colors and vanities of human life—thither looking, and holding converse with true beauty simple and divine? Remember how in that communion only, beholding beauty with the eye of the mind, he will be enabled to bring forth, not images of beauty, but realities (for he has hold not of an image but of a reality), and bringing forth and nourishing true virtue to become the friend of God and be immortal, if mortal man may. Would that be an ignoble life?

Such is the culminating vision of philosophy, wherein the good, which was formerly likened to the sun, is beheld as beauty, which is likened to a "vast sea." One thinks of how much sun and sea dominate the environment of Greece and of the particular importance to Greek life of the sea. Xenophon tells in his *Anabasis* of the heroic Retreat of the Ten Thousand through the mountains of Armenia in search of a route home. "Always cold and sometimes freezing, always hungry and sometimes starving, and always, always fighting, they held their own. No one by now had any clear idea where they were. One day, Xenophon, riding in the rear, putting his horse up a steep hill, heard a great noise in front. A tumult was carried back to him by the wind, loud cries and shouting. An ambush, he thought, and calling the others to follow at full speed, he drove his horse forward. No enemy was on the hilltop; only the Greeks. They were standing, all faced the same way, with tears running down their faces, their arms stretched out to what they saw before them. The shouting swelled into a great roar, 'The sea! The sea!' They were home at last. The sea was home to a Greek."

Politics _____

Certain "institutions and laws" and "fair practices" are said to provide steps upon which the philosopher can mount up to the final vision. Among these Plato would certainly have included a principle that plays a key role in his *Republic* and that he believed to have great relevance to politics. This has been called the "principle of reciprocity" by R. L. Nettleship, and it goes something like this: since we are none of us self-sufficient but must depend upon others to supplement our limitations, we should all *reciprocate* by doing our best to supplement the limitations of others. And "doing our best" particularly entails our getting as proficient as we can in some one line of work for which we are fitted by talent and temperament, and by which others will be benefited. Only in this way can the well-being of all be effectively promoted. At the economic level this principle calls for division of labor according to natural aptitudes, so that the basic material needs of everyone for food, clothing, and shelter may be duly satisfied. A farmer, for example, who had to make his own clothes and implements from scratch would have too little time for his crops, even supposing (what is highly unlikely) that he were adept at spinning, weaving, sewing, tanning, shoemaking, iron-mining, smelting, blacksmithing, and so forth. And because human needs are not merely material, the same principle calls at a higher level of culture for specialization as regards the graces of life—art, poetry, music, and so on, as well as "all sorts of household gear, including everything for women's adornment." On the score of military defense, the principle calls for professional "guardians," not a citizen militia, since "in no form of work is efficiency so important as in war; and fighting is not so easy a business that a man can follow another trade, such as farming or shoemaking, and also be an efficient soldier."

These defenders should be spirited and strong, formidable against an enemy but gentle and well disposed to one another and to the civilian population. Personalities having the requisite combination of attributes can be discovered and nurtured only by means of a system of education specially designed for the purpose. Plato goes into this at great length, explaining how until about their eighteenth year children should be educated in literature, music, and elementary mathematics, in accordance with a curriculum designed to bring out such grace, harmony, and rhythm ("measure and proportion") as may be latent in their souls. He believes that children learn chiefly by imitation and learn best when their lessons take the form of play, which "will also help you to see what they are naturally fitted for." He further believes, much ahead of his time, that ability alone, not sex, should determine who receives how much education and goes into what kind of work. It is irrelevant whether someone is male or female, even when it comes to soldiering. At eighteen or so, all are to undergo two or three years of physical training in order that the spirited element in their souls may be developed to the point, and only to the point, where it will complement the development that reason has received from literature, music, and elementary mathematics. Various tests and trials will then be administered to find out which young men and women are really dedicated to protecting and promoting the interests of the commonwealth, in spite of all temptations to misuse for their own selfish purposes the authority with which they may be entrusted.

At this point in the *Republic,* Plato moves from the specific issue of military defense to wider considerations of political leadership. He remarks that those who excel at their studies and who pass every test with distinction will have the makings of more than good soldiers. With further training, they should be exactly the right persons to serve as rulers, performing the legislative and deliberative functions in the state. They will be the real Guardians, looking out for the well-being of the state as a whole. Others, a step lower in ability, should be Auxiliaries of the Guardians—their agents for military defense and also for government administration. Plato is still applying the principle of reciprocity: limitations are to be supplemented by strengths. Only a few persons are born with a sufficient element of reason (which Plato likens to gold) in their souls to become wise and incorruptible rulers. Somewhat more, but still a minority, are gifted with enough spirit (silver) to become courageous and loyal soldiers and government administrators. A large majority will always come into the world with appetite (iron) as the dominant element in their souls; and they will make their best contributions, and be happiest, in occupational fields where it is permissible (as in government and the military it decidedly is not) for material gain to be a prime consideration—manufacturing, commerce, various arts, and agriculture. These three classes of persons, identifiable by their respective temperaments, are permanent and salient features of the human landscape. In the best of societies the persons of each class would be occupied in doing what they do best, with full respect for the occupations of the others. And when it comes to virtues or excellences of character, a state is only an individual "writ large." As the moral virtues of an individual soul consist in the right relations among its three elements, so the political virtues of a state consist in the right relations among its three classes of citizens. A state will be *wise* when it is ruled by Guardians in accordance with laws and policies that are framed for the common good, *courageous* when the common good is defended and the laws are administered by ever-loyal Auxiliaries, *temperate* when all hands are in harmonious agreement about who should rule and who should obey, and *just* when every citizen performs some beneficial function for which he or she is by nature well suited.

A wise Guardian is a philosopher invested with supreme political authority—a "philosopher-king." Likely candidates for this position should at twenty begin a ten-year course of study in the mathematical sciences. This is designed to turn them away from the sensible world of belief and toward the intelligible world of knowledge, acquainting them with mathematical forms as preparation for philosophical dialectic. Those who score high in this will devote five years to dialectic, and then, at thirty-five, they will be sent out for fifteen years of practical experience as public servants in subordinate positions. Finally, at fifty, "those who still survive and have distinguished themselves in every action of their lives and in every branch of knowledge [will] come at last to their consummation; the time has now arrived at which they must raise the eye of the soul to behold the universal light which lightens all things, and behold the absolute good; for that is the pattern according to which they are to order the state and the lives of individuals, and the remainder of their own lives also; making philosophy their chief pursuit, but, when their turn comes, toiling also at politics and ruling for the public good, not as though they were performing some heroic action, but simply as a matter of duty; and when they have brought up in each generation others like themselves and left them in their place to be governors of the state, then they will depart to the Islands of the Blest and dwell there. . . ."

Political power tends to corrupt anyone. It especially tends to corrupt those who want it. Philosopher-kings would have the advantage of *not* wanting it, since anyone who has beheld the form of the good would far rather remain on the heights, contemplating all time and existence, than return to the Cave and look after the prisoners. But however little they like kingship as compared with philosophy, it is still advisable to require of them a special manner of living in which they will experience the fewest possible temptations to abuse their power. Plato stipulates that they should possess nothing whatever beyond a few "necessaries" of a personal nature, that they should never be allowed even to touch silver or gold, that they should dine on simple fare at a common table, and that they should live in a barrackslike dwelling as one family. They are to have no "private property" in women or children, and sexual intercourse is to be strictly controlled for eugenic purposes. To the objection that these people will not be particularly happy living like this, Plato replies that the chief thing is not to make any one segment of the community specially happy but to secure the greatest possible happiness for the community as a whole. If philosophers cannot be persuaded to meet their responsibilities, then they must be forced to do so. The stakes are tremendous: "Until philosophers are kings, or the kings and princes of this world have the spirit and power of philosophy, and political greatness and wisdom meet in one, and those commoner natures who pursue either to the exclusion of the other are compelled to stand aside, cities will never have rest from their evils—no, nor the human race, as I believe."

Is it likely that any philosopher will ever be made king, or that any king will ever become a philosopher? Neither, Plato admits, is at all likely, but both are *possible*. Somewhere and sometime a community might be persuaded to insist upon having a philosophical ruler, or a royal family might produce an heir to the throne who has philosophical abilities that somehow or other develop properly. In any case, the pattern of a perfectly just, wise, courageous, and temperate society is the ideal by which political action should be guided, and it is the standard by which existing governments are to be ranked as better and worse. Reforms are certainly feasible that would bring existing governments *closer* to the ideal, but of course only if reformers know what the ideal is—otherwise, unless they are lucky, they will just make things worse.

The closer a society is to the ideal, the sounder will be its basic constitution, and the fewer will be its laws and regulations. In the *Republic* Plato observes with much amusement how in unhealthy societies you find the legislators passing more and more laws in the vain hope of effecting a cure, "always fancying that by legislation they will make an end of frauds in contracts and . . . other rascalities . . . not knowing that they are in reality cutting off the heads of a hydra." A true legislator would not trouble himself with the drafting of a mass of detailed regulations, since he would know that they are useless if the society is sick and unnecessary if it is healthy. Instead he would set about producing a wholesale reformation of the society's fundamental institutions, especially its practices of child rearing and its system of education. Once a good start has been made in these respects, there can be assurance of steady improvement throughout the body politic. "If a sound system of nurture and education is maintained, it produces men of good disposition; and these in their turn, taking advantage of such education, develop into better men than their forebears, and their breeding qualities improve among the rest, as may be seen in animals." With intelligence and good sense increasing in the general population, more and more things previously hedged about with laws and regulations could be left to take care of themselves.

Ideally, laws and regulations would vanish completely, and philosopher-kings would "legislate" as necessary by rendering specific judgments to meet specific cases. The trouble with the law as an instrument for the public good is that it is exceedingly blunt: it necessarily addresses people in general and cannot take account of the innumerable variations of individual character and circumstance. Plato explains this in the *Statesman* (or the *Politicus,* as it is sometimes called). His spokesman here is once again the "Stranger from Elea," who is conversing with a young friend of Socrates' who happens to be named "Socrates" also.

> There can be no doubt [the Stranger says] that legislation is in a manner the business of a king, and yet the best thing of all is not that the law should rule, but that a man should rule, supposing him to have wisdom and royal power. Do you see why this is?
>
> Why? [asks young Socrates].
>
> Because the law does not perfectly comprehend what is noblest and most just for all and therefore cannot enforce what is best. The differences of men and actions, and the endless irregular movements of human things, do not admit of any universal and simple rule. And no art whatsoever can lay down a rule which will last for all time.
>
> Of course not.
>
> But the law is always striving to make one—like an obstinant and ignorant tyrant, who will not allow anything to be done contrary to his appointment, or any question to be asked—not even in sudden changes of circumstances, when something happens to be better than what he commanded for someone.
>
> Certainly, the law treats us all precisely in the manner which you describe.
>
> A perfectly simple principle can never be applied to a state of things which is the reverse of simple.
>
> True.

Government by philosopher-kings would mean a great reduction in the number of laws, but unfortunately not even they could eliminate laws entirely. Being mortals, not gods, they could not be everywhere at once so as to give personal attention to every problem that came up. Some laws they would have to lay down—for their Auxiliaries to administer and enforce. They would not, however, have an "obstinant and ignorant" attachment to these laws. If a law became outdated, they would abolish it. If exceptions to a law were in order, they would authorize them.

> Let us put to ourselves [continues the Stranger] the case of a physician, or trainer, who is about to go into a far country, and is expecting to be a long time away from his patients—thinking that his instructions will not be remembered unless they are written down, he will leave notes of them for the use of his pupils or patients.
>
> True.

But what would you say if he came back sooner than he had intended, and owing to an unexpected change of the winds or other celestial influences, something else happened to be better for them—would he not venture to suggest this new remedy, although not contemplated in his former prescription? Would he persist in observing the original law, neither himself giving any new commandments, nor the patient daring to do otherwise than was prescribed, under the idea that this course only was healthy and medicinal, all others noxious and heterodox? Viewed in the light of science and true art, would not all such enactments be utterly ridiculous?

Utterly.

And if he who gave laws, written or unwritten, determining what was good or bad, honorable or dishonorable, just or unjust, to the tribes of men who flock together in their several cities, and are governed in accordance with them; if, I say, the wise legislator were suddenly to come again, or another like to him, is he to be prohibited from changing them? Would not this prohibition be in reality quite as ridiculous as the other?

Certainly.

So although philosopher-kings could not avoid the necessity of making laws, they would themselves be "above" all laws. Their wisdom would confer upon them the right—in fact the obligation—to nullify, amend, or permit exceptions to any law whatsoever, given sufficiently different or special circumstances. No political constitution should be seen as limiting their power to bind and loose, for their wisdom is the only true constitution. "Nor can wise rulers ever err while they, observing the one great rule of distributing justice to the citizens with intelligence and skill, are able to preserve them, and as far as may be, to make them better from being worse."

Now rulers of this caliber are few and far between. "Kings do not arise in cities in the natural course of things in the way in which a royal bee is born in a beehive." In the absence of a philosopher-king—in other words, for all practical purposes—we must be content with what is second best: a government of *laws* that "imitate" as closely as possible the laws that a philosopher-king, if we had one, *would* lay down.

> The idea which has to be grasped by us is not easy or familiar, but we may attempt to express it thus. Supposing the government of which I have been speaking [that is, the government of philosopher-kings] to be the only true model, then the others must use the written laws of this. In no other way can they be saved; they will have to do what is now generally approved, although not the best thing in the world.
>
> What is this?
>
> No citizen should do anything contrary to the laws, and any infringement of them should be punished with death and the most extreme penalties; and this is very right and good when regarded as the second-best thing. . . . To go against the laws, which are based upon long

experience and the wisdom of counsellors who have graciously recommended them and persuaded the multitude to pass them, would be a far greater and more ruinous error than any adherence to written law.

Certainly.

Therefore, as there is a danger of this, the next best thing in legislating is not to allow either the individual or the multitude to break the law in any respect whatever. . . . The nearest approach which these lower forms of government can ever make to the true government of the philosophical ruler is to do nothing contrary to their own written laws and national customs.

Second-best government (or, as Plato calls it, "untrue" government) may be government by one (monarchy), by a few (aristocracy), or by many (democracy). When a monarch takes the law into his own hands, however, monarchy becomes tyranny and the monarch a tyrant. Similarly, aristocracy can become oligarchy and the aristocrats oligarchs. There is no special name, Plato says, for a democracy that becomes lawless, but altogether there are six broad types of second-best or untrue government—three law-abiding, three not.

Then the question arises: which of these untrue forms of government is the least oppressive to their subjects, though they are all oppressive; and which is the worst of them? . . . Monarchy, when bound by good prescriptions or laws, is the best of all the six, and when lawless is the most bitter and oppressive. . . .

True.

The government of the few, which is intermediate between the one and the many, is also intermediate in good and evil; but the government of the many is in every respect weak and unable to do either any great good or any great evil, when compared with the others, because the offices are too minutely subdivided and too many hold them. And this therefore is the worst of all lawful governments, and the best of all lawless ones. If they are all without the restraints of law, democracy is the form in which to live is best; if they are well-ordered, then this is the last which you should choose. . . .

A few years before he died, Plato presented in his *Laws* a detailed scheme for what he then considered the outstanding second-best form of government. This is not constitutional monarchy, as the *Statesman* would lead one to expect, but a mixture of what he says are elements of monarchy and democracy. "If you are to have liberty and the combination of friendship with wisdom, you must have both these forms of government in a measure." His actual scheme, however, is more a mixture of *aristocracy* and democracy: a balance of power is struck between "the few" who are comparatively wise and "the many" who are not, the goal being to insure that all citizens remain subjects of the law. "For that state in which the law is subject and has no authority I perceive to be on the highway to ruin; but I see that the state in which the law is above the rulers, and the rulers are the inferiors of the law, has salvation, and every blessing which the gods can confer." What Plato has in mind may be illustrated by some of his provisions for the administration of justice. All citizens should take part in this, he says, since "he who has no share in the administration of justice is apt to imagine that he has no share in the state at all." He therefore stipulates that there shall be large popular courts selected by lot. In Athens, as we saw, this was the procedure actually followed; but Plato insists upon two highly significant innovations: the popular courts are not to have jurisdiction in capital cases, and they are not to have final authority. He sets up a small Supreme Court to which cases heard in the popular courts may be appealed. This is to be elected annually by the various boards of public officials from their own number. Capital cases are to be tried by a special court consisting of the Supreme Court and thirty-seven Guardians of the Law (elected by military veterans from nominees who are subject to approval by the citizens at large). As a check upon arbitrary and illegal action by public officials, Plato creates a board of Examiners, empowered to issue indictments, who will keep them under continual observation and issue periodic reports on their conduct. Those officials who feel that the Examiners have wrongly indicted them may appeal to the Supreme Court. Anyone who feels wronged by any official, *or by any judge,* may sue for damages. As G. L. Morrow says, "One can hardly imagine a more dramatic remedy against judicial injustice than a suit for damages against the judge; and there is, so far as we know, no historical counterpart in the procedure of any Greek state. . . ."

In his final work on politics, then, Plato believes that in practice the best government is one in which judicial power is so divided that every group of officeholders is legally answerable to another and independent body. It is a "mixed" government of "checks and balances" in which sovereignty is accorded to the laws alone, not to any person or persons. "If a man were born so divinely gifted that he could naturally apprehend the truth, he would have no need of laws to rule over him; for there is no law or order which is above knowledge, nor can mind, without impiety, be deemed the subject or slave of any man, but rather the lord of all. I speak of mind, true and free, and in harmony with nature. But then there is no such mind anywhere, or at least not much; and therefore we must choose law and order, which are second best."

Soul and Cosmos

Human Immortality

Whether the human soul survives the death of the body is, Plato says, an issue of the greatest difficulty. Instead of plunging into the fog of controversy surrounding it, one might well prefer to take no position one way or the other, or to wait perhaps for some divine illumination that would clear the matter up once and for all. Yet there would be something weak-spirited about so passive an attitude toward so important a question. Life is a dangerous voyage for which we should equip ourselves as well as we can; and if there are reasons for believing that it leads to a safe harbor at the end, we should obviously try to discover these reasons. "In fact we ought to achieve one of two things: either to find for ourselves, or learn from some other, the truth about these matters: or else, if that is impossible, to seize upon the best and most irrefutable doctrine that mankind can offer. . . ."

We can best sample Plato's arguments on the subject by seeing how he addressed a particular type of objection to immortality. In his day there were people who believed, as in our day there are still people who believe, that the mental events—the thoughts, desires, and feelings—attributed to the mind or soul are entirely the outcome of certain *bodily* factors. Recent versions of the theory maintain that the factors in question are to be found in the brain or central nervous system. An ancient version held that they are to be found in certain mixtures of bodily elements—"the hot" and "the cold" (fire and earth), "the moist" and "the dry" (water and air). Mental events occur when and only when these pairs of "opposites" are properly balanced in the body, just as harmonious sound comes from a lyre when and only when its strings are properly tuned.[7] As harmonious sound is terminated when a lyre is put out of tune or broken, so mental events are terminated when a body's elements are unbalanced (as in some diseases) or dissociated (in death). There is no "soul" aside from the "harmony" of these bodily "strings"; the "soul" is merely a by-product or derivative phenomenon (*epiphenomenon*) of physiological states. Accordingly, there can be no question of its continuing to exist after the body has died, and of course the same conclusion follows from modern versions of epiphenomenalism (as the theory is called), which say that the "strings" involved are chemical processes in the brain and nervous system.

This theory is put forward in Plato's *Phaedo* by a certain Simmias of Thebes. Plato, through Socrates, responds to it by focusing closely upon its use of the idea of harmony:

> Do you imagine [Socrates asks] that a harmony or any other composition can be in a state other than that of the elements out of which it is compounded?
> Certainly not [Simmias replies].
> Or do or suffer anything other than they do or suffer?
> [No.]

---

[7] The origins of this view are obscure. It may in part have been derived from Empedocles' theory of the four elements and from Pythagoras' notion of harmony; but in its denial of immortality, it was at odds with both Empedocles and Pythagoras.

Then a harmony does not, properly speaking, lead the parts or elements which make up the harmony, but only follows them. . . . For harmony cannot possibly have any motion, or sound, or other quality which is opposed to its parts.

That would be impossible. . . .

[Now] is one soul in the very least degree more or less, or more or less completely, a soul than another?

Not in the least.

[And that is] equivalent to admitting that harmony is not more or less harmony, or more or less completely a harmony?

Quite true.

And that which is not more or less a harmony is not more or less harmonized?

True.

And that which is not more or less harmonized cannot have more or less of harmony, but only an equal harmony?

Yes, an equal harmony.

Then one soul, not being more or less absolutely a soul than another, is not more or less harmonized?

Exactly.

And therefore has neither more or less of discord, nor yet of harmony?

She has not.

And having neither more nor less of harmony or of discord, one soul has no more vice or virtue than another, if vice be discord and virtue harmony?

Not at all more.

Or speaking more correctly, Simmias, the soul, if she is a harmony, will never have any vice; because a harmony, being absolutely a harmony, has no part in the inharmonical.

No.

And therefore a soul which is absolutely a soul has no vice?

How can she have, if the previous argument holds?

Then if all souls are equally by their nature souls, all souls of all living creatures will be equally good?

I agree with you. . . .

And can all this be true, think you? . . . For these are the consequences which seem to follow from the assumption that the soul is a harmony?

It cannot be true.

In other words, the theory that the soul is a harmony of bodily elements leads to the conclusion that no two persons can differ in respect of moral virtue; and since we are far surer that this is false than that the theory is true, we should reject the theory. If the soul were a harmony of bodily elements, then moral attributes could only be aspects of this harmony. But one harmony cannot be more of a harmony than another (either strings are in tune or they are not), and therefore one soul could not possess any moral attribute that was not equally possessed by every other soul. All persons would be fully virtuous—not vicious, because vice is a matter of disharmony; and on the theory before us, where there is disharmony there is no soul at all.

So the mental events attributed to the soul cannot be understood to depend upon some "harmony" of bodily elements; and for all we can tell, these events may continue to occur after the bodily elements have been dispersed by death. Is it correct, however, to attribute these events to a soul or mind—to a substantial *thing,* different in kind from the body, which thinks thoughts and experiences desires, which initiates action and moves the body, and which in short is one's *self*—the seat of one's personality? Plato thought so, and we saw in his *Theaetetus* part of his case for this. There he argued that judgments about what we perceive through our senses must be the work of a unitary mind or soul that coordinates and compares this information in light of universal notions or forms. In order to understand how we can make these judgments, we have to view *ourselves* as different from our bodily senses and as employing our senses as *instruments* of our awareness. This recalls the way in which Socrates argued, in conversation with Alcibiades, that one's self is to be distinguished from the body which one *uses,* that the soul is the *user* of the body as a craftsman is the user of his tools, and that the soul is really "the man himself." Judgment involves *activity* on our part, not simply a passive awareness of sensory data; and such activity requires a mind or soul which *acts.*

The same conclusion, Plato thought, may be reached by an analysis of our experience of moral conflict. He explains this in his further remarks in the *Phaedo* about the "harmony" theory of the soul:

What ruler is there of the elements of human nature other than the soul, and especially the wise soul? Do you know of any?

Indeed, I do not.

And is the soul in agreement with the affections of the body? or is she at variance with them? For example, when the body is hot and thirsty, does not the soul incline us against drinking? and when the body is hungry, against eating? And this is only one instance out of ten thousand of the opposition of the soul to the things of the body.

Very true.

But we have already acknowledged that the soul, being a harmony, can never utter a note at variance with the tensions and relaxations and vibrations and other affections of the strings out of which she is composed. She can only follow, she cannot lead them?

It must be so. . . .

And yet do we not now discover the soul to be doing the exact opposite—leading the elements of which she is believed to be composed; almost always opposing and coercing them in all sorts of ways throughout life, sometimes more violently with the pains of medicine and gymnas-

tic; then again more gently; now threatening, now admonishing the desires, passions, fears, as if talking to a thing which is not herself, as Homer in the *Odyssey* represents Odysseus doing in the words—
"He beat his breast, and thus reproached his heart:
Endure, my heart; far worse hast thou endured!"
Do you think that Homer wrote this under the idea that the soul is a harmony capable of being led by the affections of the body, and not rather of a nature which should lead and master them—herself a far diviner thing than any harmony?

Yes, Socrates, I quite think so.

Then, my friend, we can never be right in saying that the soul is a harmony, for we should contradict the divine Homer, and contradict ourselves.

True. . . .

The most striking feature of our moral experience is the conflict between rational judgment and irrational appetite. This conflict could scarcely occur if rational judgment were simply the effect of bodily causes in the way in which appetite may be conceded to be. If rational judgment were a "harmony" of bodily "strings," how could it utter so much as a single note that was at variance with their "tensions and relaxations and vibrations?" As it is, of course, we are regularly in the position of having to repress or threaten, refine or admonish, our desires and passions and fears. Our understanding in such situations is that reason can and should be the leader of the body's "affections." We identify ourselves with this leadership (with the charioteer of the myth in the *Phaedrus*), and we view the body with its troublesome demands *not* as ourselves but as something with which we have to contend. Consistently with this, we can only maintain that the true self is the soul—a nonphysical (or immaterial, or incorporeal) *agent* capable of more or less enlightened directive activity. Any other view—the "harmony" view in particular—would not be "in harmony" with the facts of our experience. (Never one to let his opportunities slip, Socrates observes that "there surely ought to be harmony in a discourse of which harmony is the theme.")

Suppose we grant, then, that the true self is the soul, that the soul is distinguishable from the body, that what is distinguishable from the body may not die with the body, and that the true self may therefore survive death. But what reason is there to suppose that the soul, the true self, *will* survive—and survive forever? Perhaps, sooner or later, it would wear itself out; so that even if it outlasted the body, it would not be literally immortal but would finally dwindle away? In the *Phaedo*, Plato answers this by producing a complicated argument based upon his theory of forms. Briefly put, the argument is that a soul is what it is by virtue of its participating in the form of life; and since the form of life is the contrary of the form of death, the former will always exclude the latter in the case of a soul.

Another argument to the same general effect, but more interesting and influential, is given briefly in the *Phaedrus* and more elaborately in the *Laws*. We saw that Plato believed it to be a distinctive feature of the soul that it can initiate motion without being caused to do so by anything else. It is a distinctive feature of physical objects, on the other hand, that they cannot do this; one of them can move another only if it has itself first been caused to move by something else. Thus there are two kinds of motion—the kind that is generated *spontaneously* by souls and the kind that is *communicated* by objects whose own motions have been externally caused. Imagine two billiard balls. One moves forward and hits the other, causing it to move also. This is an example of *communicated* motion. The first ball, needless to say, did not start moving by itself. Billiard balls are lifeless, and nothing lifeless—that is, nothing that lacks a soul—can move by itself. The first ball started moving because you (let us say) struck it with a cue, intending to make that particular shot. Here we have *spontaneous* motion, initiated by intelligent design; and if something of the kind had not entered the scene, the two billiard balls would have been motionless forever. Now what is true of this particular situation is true of the cosmos as a whole. *Communicated motion is always the product of spontaneous motion,* of the activity of soul, human or divine. If it were true of any given soul that sooner or later it would exhaust its energy and fade away, then there would come a time when all souls will have died and all movement in the cosmos will cease. "The whole universe, the whole of that which comes to be, would collapse into immobility, and never find another source of motion to bring it back into being." But Plato believes that this state of affairs is impossible. Motion is so essential a feature of any universe we can conceive that we must count its absence as entailing the annihilation of everything; and the annihilation of everything—that is, the existence of nothing at all—is strictly unthinkable. Consequently, we cannot suppose that any given soul, human or divine, will ever perish. Eternal life for souls is assured.

When the soul is freed from the body, the energy devoted to that (appetitive) element of itself which was invested in the business of the body will revert to the working capital of reason. The energy devoted to spirit, which was reason's ally in managing the affairs of appetite but which tended also to be ambitious of worldly success, will likewise be restored to the firm's chief operation—now its only operation—the pursuit of wisdom and of converse with the divine. Justice and the other virtues will no longer be a matter of coordinating distinguishable elements of the soul, for such elements will no longer be distinguishable. What precisely the soul and its excellence will be like it is difficult to tell. All we can say is that "when she has regained the pure condition which the eye of reason can discern, you will then find her to be a far lovelier thing and will distinguish more clearly justice and injustice and all the qualities we have discussed."

Souls that have not in this life striven after goodness and virtue cannot, however, be expected to enjoy the fullest blessings in the next life, at least not immediately. Plato's dialogues feature several accounts in mythical terms of a day of reckoning for the souls of the departed. Toward the end of the *Gorgias,* for example, we are told of three divine judges, Minos, Rhadamanthus, and Aecus, who give judgment "in the meadow at the parting of the ways, whence the two roads lead, one to the Islands of the Blessed and the other to Tartarus." Each soul appears before these judges in all its nakedness, stripped of any fine appearance of body or raiment, so that the judges may unerringly see what were its natural gifts and what it has done with them. A soul that has abused its gifts and become disfigured with wickedness is pronounced to be either curable or incurable, and it is sent to Tartarus to be punished accordingly. Now punishment may rightly serve either of two different purposes. For those whose wickedness is curable, punishment is an essential instrument of *reform.* In the case of those whose wickedness is incurable, punishment is necessary in order to *deter* others from following in their footsteps. Most of the incurables, Plato says, are found to have been "tyrants and kings and potentates and public men, for they are the authors of the greatest and most impious crimes, because they have the power." These are to be punished eternally as "a spectacle and a warning to all unrighteous men." Not many politicians, as it happens, are allowed by the judges to proceed to the Islands, "for where there is great power to do wrong, to live and die justly is a hard thing, and greatly to be praised, and few there are who attain to this." On the other hand, the judges look "with admiration on the soul of some just one who has lived in holiness and truth; he may have been a private man or not; and I should say . . . that he is most likely to have been a philosopher who has done his own work, and not troubled himself with the doings of other men in his lifetime."

The Divine Craftsman

"The heavens declare the glory of God, and the firmament showeth his handiwork," says the Nineteenth Psalm; and Plato, in his *Philebus,* expresses a similar view. It cannot be supposed, he says, that the universe is the product of "unreason and chance medley," in the way that Democritus believed everything arose from random collisions of atoms in the infinite void. The beauty and regular motion of the heavenly bodies, the orderly cycle of years and seasons and months, are powerful evidence of a "marvelous intelligence and wisdom" in the shaping of cosmic events. In his *Timaeus,* Plato endeavors to outline a religious cosmology in keeping with this basic conviction, but also in keeping with his recognition that the best we can expect in this field is a theory that will be probable, not certain. Human intelligence is too limited; and the subject itself, which concerns the sensible world of becoming and change, precludes genuine knowledge even in principle. Knowledge can be had only of intelligible forms. So it is that "the father and maker of all this universe is past finding out"—for sure, that is—and we must be content with the most likely story we can discover.

The events we perceive through our senses—the movements and alterations, the comings and goings—all have causes. "Everything that becomes or is created must of necessity be created by some cause." And what is true of every particular event can be no less true of the entire world of events: the whole cosmos of planets, moons, and stars must have been produced by some cause—a cause having the immense power and intelligence to bring about so vastly complex and well ordered and beautiful an arrangement as (on the whole) we find in the universe. Plato calls this cause God, and also the Divine Craftsman or Artificer (the Greek word for which is *demiourgos,* and "Demiurge" is an English version of this which is often employed). Unlike the God of the Judeo-Christian tradition, the Craftsman of the *Timaeus* is not described as being omnipotent or all-powerful in the sense of creating the cosmos out of nothing,[8] nor is he described as creating it according to a plan of his own devising. Like a human craftsman, the Divine Craftsman worked with a preexisting raw material, and he followed a plan that was already laid down. The raw material consisted of a completely formless, chaotic, and indefinite "matrix" of stuff in space having the potential of assuming a multitude of specific characters—in particular the characters of earth, air, fire, and water. The plan consisted of the eternal forms, or at any rate of those among them that are related to the form of animal life, for the cosmos that the Craftsman fashioned is pictured by Plato as an organic entity, a living creature of stupendous size and (remember Xenophanes and Parmenides) spherical shape. The Craftsman, seeing the utter disorder of the matrix, desired that it should become as perfect in every respect as possible, and in doing so should become as much like himself as possible.

He was good, and the good can never have any jealousy of anything. And being free from jealousy, he desired that all things should be as like himself as they could be. This is in the truest sense the origin of creation and of the world, as we shall do well in believing on the testimony of wise men: God desired that all things should be good and nothing bad, so far as this was attainable. Wherefore also finding the whole visible sphere not at rest but moving in an irregular and disorderly fashion, out of disorder he brought order, considering that this was in every way better than the other. Now the deeds of the best could never be or have been other than the fairest; and the creator, reflecting on the things which are by nature visible, found that no unintelligent creature taken as a whole was fairer than the intelligent taken as a whole; and that intelligence could not be present in anything which was devoid of soul. For which reason, when he was framing the universe, he put intelligence in soul, and soul in body, that he might be the creator

---

[8] That anything could come from nothing seemed to all the ancient Greek philosophers an absolute impossibility.

of a work which was by nature fairest and best. Wherefore, using the language of probability, we may say that the world became a living creature truly endowed with soul and intelligence by the providence of God.

The Craftsman, then, proceeded to fashion in the matrix an intelligent living creature (our cosmos) that would resemble as closely as possible the perfect form of creaturely existence (the form of "living being" or "animal"). As receptive of this formative activity, the matrix is called "the Receptacle," and within the Receptacle the Craftsman formed the visible body and the invisible soul of the cosmos. Under inspiration from both Pythagoras and Empedocles, Plato says that the body of the cosmos was formed when the Craftsman introduced into the Receptacle such tiny geometrical structures (composed of copies of triangle-forms) as would give rise to the visible properties of earth, air, fire, and water, which he then combined in accordance with strict mathematical proportions so as to produce an harmonious spherical whole. In language that is exceedingly obscure and variously interpreted, Plato seems to say that the soul of the cosmos was made by a mathematically precise blending of three ingredients: intermediate Sameness ("intermediate," that is, between the intelligible form of Sameness and its sensible appearances), intermediate Difference, and intermediate Being. The main point is that "measure and proportion," which everywhere constitute goodness for Plato, are markedly shown in the composition of the cosmic soul as an everlasting creative agency intermediate between the eternal realm of the forms and Craftsman, and the sensible realm of becoming and perishing. Once produced, the cosmic soul was divided by the Craftsman into parts that would be individually responsible for causing and maintaining the different revolutions of the stars and planets. The immortal part of human souls (their rational element) is made of the same ingredients as the cosmic soul, but "diluted to the second and third degree." The mortal parts of human souls (their spirited and appetitive elements), as well as human bodies, are made by the intelligent souls that the Craftsman has given to the heavenly bodies, which are celestial gods, and whom the Craftsman addresses in these remarkable words:

> Gods, children of gods, who are my works, and of whom I am the artificer and father, my creations are indissoluble, if I so will. All that is bound may be undone, but only an evil being would wish to undo that which is harmonious and happy. Wherefore, since ye are but creatures, ye are not altogether immortal and indissoluble, but ye shall certainly not be dissolved, nor be liable to the fate of death, having in my will a greater and mightier bond than those with which ye were bound at the time of your birth. And now listen to my instructions:—Three tribes of mortal beings remain to be created [birds, sea and land animals, including humans]—without them the universe would be incomplete, for it will not contain every kind of animal which it ought to

contain if it is to be perfect. On the other hand, if they were created by me and received life at my hands, they would be on an equality with the gods. In order then that they may be mortal, and that this universe may be truly universal, do ye, according to your natures, betake yourselves to the formation of animals, imitating the power which was shown by me in creating you. The part of them worthy of the name immortal, which is called divine and is the guiding principle of those who are willing to follow justice and you—of that divine part I will myself sow the seed, and having made a beginning, I will hand the work over to you. And do ye then interweave the mortal with the immortal, and make and beget living creatures, and give them food, and make them to grow, and receive them again in death.

The dominant theme of the *Timaeus* is that the cosmos, in general and in detail, is for the most part providentially ordered and is to be explained *teleologically,* by reference to the beneficial purposes which things are wisely calculated to serve. One might think, Plato says, that the processes associated with human vision, for example, are to be explained simply in terms of the bodily factors involved, which factors are ultimately reducible to earth, air, fire, and water. This, however, is a mistake. Bodily elements are just "secondary and cooperative causes"; completely unintelligent, they produce by themselves only "chance effects without order or design," and must be combined with intelligence—the "prime cause"—if anything like a human eye is to be made from them. It is the *purposes* for which we were given eyes that finally explain their existence and operations; and "God invented and gave us sight to the end that we might behold the courses of intelligence in the heaven [the celestial deities], and apply them to the courses of our own intelligence which are akin to them, the unperturbed to the perturbed; and that we, learning them and partaking of the natural truth of reason, might imitate the absolutely unerring courses of God and regulate our own vagaries."

To a large extent the Craftsman succeeded in his efforts to bring order out of chaos, to introduce into the Receptacle a perfection that would do justice to the eternal form of creaturely existence. But as Plato indicates by saying that the Craftsman desired that all things should be good "so far as this was attainable," complete perfection in the cosmos is *not* attainable. This is because the Receptacle, the matrix of raw material with which the Craftsman has to work, has built into it an irrational factor that resists complete determination by "measure and proportion." Plato calls this factor "necessity" or the "errant (or variable) cause." It is owing to this that the physical elements of earth, air, fire, and water produce "chance effects without order or design" apart from the control of intelligence, and far too often even in spite of this control. "Necessity" means for Plato "what lacks purpose"; and to his way of thinking, to say that something lacks purpose is to say that it "just happens," randomly or by chance, in an "errant" or "variable" fashion. "The creation is mixed," Plato says, "being made up of necessity and mind." The Craftsman, representing mind, has "persuaded necessity to bring the greater part of created things to perfection," fashioning them "by form and number" so as to make them "as far as possible the fairest and best, out of things which were not fair and good." But the inherent intractability of the matrix frustrates the intentions of the Craftsman, and "in a manner contrary to nature" there occur all manner of evils in the lives of animals and humans, and "few are the goods of human life, and many are the evils, and the good is to be attributed to God alone—of the evils the causes are to be sought elsewhere, and not in him."

Beginning with Plato's immediate followers and continuing down to the present day, there has been much dispute as to how literally he intended his "likely story" to be taken. A major issue is whether he really wished to be understood as maintaining that the cosmos was created, that there actually was a time before which it did not exist, and that it was formed by stages beginning at some point in the distant past. Many commentators have argued that Plato cannot have meant this. They hold that the creation story was simply his allegorical way of saying that the cosmos, which has always existed, depends for its goodness and order upon divine wisdom and power. The point then is that the Craftsman *sustains,* by a continuous process of creation, a cosmos that exists throughout all time; he did not begin his creative activity at some particular time. This interpretation has often been said to be necessary because of what Plato himself says about time:

> When the father and creator saw the creature [the cosmic whole] which he made moving and living, the created image of the eternal gods, he rejoiced, and in his joy determined to make the copy still more like the original [the ideal form of creaturely existence]; and as this was eternal, he sought to make the universe eternal, so far as might be. Now the nature of the ideal being was everlasting, but to bestow this attribute in its fullness upon a creature was impossible. Wherefore he resolved to have a moving image of eternity, and when he set in order the heaven, he made this image eternal but moving according to number, while eternity itself rests in unity; and this image we call time. For there were no days and nights and months and years before the heaven was created, but when he constructed the heaven he created them also. They are all parts of time, and the past and future are created species of time. . . . Time, then, and the heaven came into being at the same instant. . . .

Now if "time . . . and the heaven came into being at the same instant," how could there have been a time *before* the Craftsman created the heaven? That, it seems, would be contradictory; and many commentators have therefore concluded that Plato did not in fact mean for us to take literally the many expressions in the *Timaeus* stating that there *was* such a time. Instead, they say, we must understand Plato's remarks about creation as intentionally metaphorical. There never was a time before the cosmos existed, but the cosmos depends upon the Craftsman for its "measure and proportion" at every time. That must be what Plato intended to convey. Other commentators, however, have argued that this interpretation is in error and that the "contradiction" in question vanishes when more careful account is taken of what Plato meant by "time" (*chronos,* in Greek). As is clearly shown in the passage above, Plato identified *chronos* with the movement "according to number" of the heavenly bodies, particularly with the periodic revolutions of the sun and the moon, which produce the recurrence of days and nights, months and years—the "parts," he says, of which *chronos* is made up. So without the heavenly bodies in their orbits, there cannot be *chronos;* but it does not follow that there cannot be "time" in another sense—a sense of which Plato undoubtedly had a conception, even though he did not call it *chronos.* This is "time" in the sense of succession or duration, simple beforeness and afterness, which is what *we* commonly say is *measured* by celestial motions and by man-made clocks. Beforeness and afterness as measured by celestial motions is what Plato calls *chronos.* When he spoke of the Craftsman, the forms, and the matrix as having "existed . . . before the heaven," he was surely thinking of beforeness and afterness as *not* measured by celestial motions. In this way Plato can be shown to have been consistent with himself in maintaining, as the most likely story, that the cosmos has not always existed but was literally created.

Controversy on the point is likely to continue. The intrinsic interest and the historical importance of the *Timaeus,* together with its relevance to a number of issues of perennial concern such as this one, make it among the most studied of Plato's dialogues. A Latin translation of about half of it, which was made by a certain Chalcidius in the early fifth century A.D., survived into the Dark and Middle Ages and inspired a great deal of work in cosmology, including attempts to square Plato's account of creation with the one in Genesis. Yet the glorification in the *Timaeus* of the rational beauty of the cosmos was fundamentally at odds with prevalent Church doctrines in the spirit of I John 2:15: "Love not the world, neither the things that are in the world. If any man love the world, the love of the Father is not in him." And it is a distinctive feature of the Renaissance that Plato's attitude was then revived, and philosophers expressed with reawakened feeling the reverence toward the world of Plato's conclusion to the *Timaeus:* "Here at last let us say that our discourse concerning the universe has come to its end. For having received in full its complement of living creatures, mortal and immortal, this world has thus become a visible living creature embracing all that are visible and an image of the intelligible, a perceptible god, supreme in goodness and excellence, in beauty and perfection, this Heaven single in its kind and one."

CHAPTER 7

Aristotle

Aristotle was born in 384 B.C. in Stagira, now called Stavrós, in north-eastern Greece. His father, Nichomachus, was physician to Amyntus II, King of Macedon. Both his father and his mother, Phaestis, died when he was a child, and he was brought up in the household of a relative named Proxenus. At seventeen he was sent to Plato's Academy in Athens, where he stayed for twenty years, having so distinguished himself as a student that he was made a member of the faculty. Plato is said to have considered him "the mind of the school." Upon Plato's death in 347 B.C., Aristotle went to Assos in order to join some followers of Plato's who had gathered around the ruler Hermias—himself an alumnus of the Academy and a classmate of Aristotle's. After Aristotle had been some three years in Assos, Hermias was murdered by Persian forces against whom he was planning an assault with Macedon. Aristotle and his colleagues fled from the city, taking with them Hermias' niece and adopted daughter Pythias, who soon became Aristotle's wife (and who bore him a daughter whom they named Pythias). The couple settled in Mitylene on the island of Lesbos, where another graduate of the Academy, Theophrastus, was living.[1] Their residence in Mitylene was not a long one, however, for in 343 B.C. Aristotle was summoned by Philip, successor to Amyntus II as King of Macedon, to educate his thirteen-year-old son Alexander. This is the same Alexander, subsequently known as "the Great," who united Greece against the Persian Empire and subjugated Egypt and much of the Near East before his death at thirty-three. When Alexander ascended the Macedonian throne in 336 B.C., Aristotle made his way to Athens and set up a school in the Lyceum, a gymnasium attached to the temple of Apollo Lyceus. (Since much of the instruction was given under the gymnasium's covered portico—*peripatos*, in Greek—the school became known as the Peripatos and its members as Peripatetics.) In adjacent buildings Aristotle assembled a notable library and a museum of natural history, the latter with the help of a grant of money from Alexander and of specimens that Alexander ordered to be sent in from around his empire. For twelve or thirteen years Aristotle directed the activities of the school, encouraging research in a wide variety of fields, while giving the lectures for which his surviving works are evidently the notes. When Alexander died in 323

---

[1] Theophrastus was later to become Aristotle's most famous follower.

B.C., there was a reaction in Athens against Macedonian influence, and Aristotle, as the emperor's teacher, came under attack. The capital charge of "impiety" or "crimes against the state religion" was leveled against him on the ridiculous grounds that some verses he had written on the occasion of Hermias' death made his friend out to be a deity. Unlike Socrates, he did not stay in Athens for his trial. Not wishing to let the Athenians, as he said, "sin twice against philosophy," he turned his school over to Theophrastus and withdrew to Chalcis, a town under Macedonian control. There he was soon overtaken by an illness of long standing, and he died at the age of sixty-three.

Pythias having died some years before, Aristotle was living with Herpyllis, a lady from Stagira by whom he had a son named Nichomachus. As is clear from Aristotle's will, which was preserved by an ancient biographer, he was a man of deep affection, devoted to Herpyllis and to his children but still close in his thoughts to Pythias—beside whom he directed that he should be buried. In appearance Aristotle is said to have been bald and thin-legged, with small eyes and a lisp, but with a remarkably stylish wardrobe. We are also told that he was a man of considerable wit and had a mocking disposition that showed in his expression.

Plato's views were the starting point from which Aristotle gradually developed positions of his own—sometimes diverging from Plato, sometimes refining or elaborating upon Plato, and sometimes investigating matters to which Plato had given little attention. Only a few fragments remain of the graceful dialogues that Aristotle wrote during his years at the Academy, when he still adhered closely to Plato. What survived approximately intact are compilations of his lecture notes—twelve volumes in the standard English edition—which show him working out his own ideas in terse and unadorned language that has nevertheless, as Schopenhauer said, a certain "brilliant dryness." The scope of these writings is tremendous. Included are works on logic, metaphysics, natural science, psychology, ethics, politics, and aesthetics. Especially striking is the enthusiasm shown in them for observations of fact and for scientific classification as regards the animal kingdom. "Every realm of nature is marvelous," Aristotle said, and even "the humbler animals," when closely inspected, "will reveal to us something natural and something beautiful." In spirit Aristotle remained faithful to Plato's *Timaeus,* stressing the extent to which "absence of haphazard and conduciveness of everything to an end are to be found in Nature's works," but he went far beyond Plato in investigating from this point of view the actual phenomena of nature.

Logic and Method

Aristotle, like Plato, was intent upon the discovery of knowledge—both theoretical knowledge of what actually exists, which he says is worth having for its own sake, and practical knowledge of what is to be done, individually and collectively, in order to achieve the best lives of which we are capable. Metaphysics, physics, and mathematics, according to Aristotle's classification, are the sciences in which theoretical knowledge is the goal; and their distinctive principles are found in the realities which they investigate, not in the persons who do the investigating. In ethics and politics, however, where the aim is practical knowledge for the sake of action, the starting point and "first principle" is to be found not in external reality but "in the doer"—that is, in the persons themselves who act.

Success in obtaining theoretical knowledge, Aristotle insists, requires first of all an understanding of the principles of logic that serve as instruments in getting it.[2] He remarks with a certain asperity that "the attempts of some of those who discuss the terms on which truth should be accepted are due to a want of training in logic; for they should know these things already when they come to a special study, and not be inquiring into them while they are listening to lectures on it." Logic is "the science which inquires into demonstration and science"—the systematic investigation of the standards of reasoning and evidence that pertain to theoretical knowledge in general. Inasmuch as Aristotle himself first developed the subject and showed great creative genius in doing so, it is startling and amusing to find him referring to logic as though it were a long-established field in which one might naturally be expected to have done some work.

Reasoning on any topic, Aristotle maintains, is built up from simple true-or-false statements in which something is spoken about—the *subject* in question—and something is said about the subject, or "predicated" of it, which is therefore called the *predicate.* Such statements are called *propositions,* and a standard example is "Socrates is mortal," where "Socrates" indicates the subject, "mortal" indicates the predicate, and "is" (which later logicians called the *copula*) indicates the connection that is asserted to hold between them. Aristotle believes that, no matter how complex a pattern of reasoning may be, it can be broken up into propositions having this simple subject-predicate form. An *affirmative* proposition like "Socrates is mortal" is true when and only when the subject spoken about does indeed have the predicate that is affirmed of it. A *negative* proposition like "Socrates is not mortal" is true when and only when the subject spoken about does indeed not have the predicate that is denied of it.

In his theory of *categories,* given in a treatise of that name, Aristotle sets forth what he takes to be the basic types of predicates that can be affirmed or denied of subjects. His fullest list comprises the ten categories of *substance, quantity, quality, relation, place, time, position, state, action,*

---

[2]*Organon,* the Greek word for "instrument," has since the sixth century A.D. been used as a general title for Aristotle's six logical treatises.

and *affection*. "To sketch my meaning roughly," he says, "examples of *substance* are 'man' or 'the horse,' of *quantity*, such terms as 'two cubits long' or 'three cubits long,' of *quality*, such attributes as 'white,' 'grammatical.' 'Double,' 'half,' 'greater,' fall under the category of *relation;* 'in the market place,' 'in the Lyceum,' under that of *place;* 'yesterday,' 'last year,' under that of *time*. 'Lying,' 'sitting,' are terms indicating *position*, 'shod,' 'armed,' *state;* 'to lance,' 'to cauterize,' *action*, 'to be lanced,' 'to be cauterized,' *affection*." Each and every proposition, then, affirms or denies of some subject either a predicate concerning what the subject is (a predicate under the category of substance like "man"), or its quantity, or its quality, or its relation to something else, and so on.

In his theory of *predicables*, given in the *Topics*, Aristotle classifies propositions according to the types of relations between subject and predicate which they affirm or deny. Consider, by way of illustration, the collective term *men* as a subject. In the proposition "All men are animals," the predicate "animals" denotes a wider group—that is, a genus—in which men are included along with many other species of creatures. On the other hand, in "All men are capable of discourse," the predicate "capable of discourse" is an essential *difference* that sets men apart from all other animals. And when genus and difference are explicitly mentioned together, as in "All men are animals capable of discourse," the predicate is a *definition* of the subject, denoting that species of the genus which contains all and only men, and giving the really essential distinctive feature—the essence, in short—of men. But every species of things will be found to have distinctive or peculiar features that are not really essential to it—*properties*, Aristotle calls them. For example, the capacity for learning the multiplication table may be peculiar to men, but it is not an essential aspect of their nature, not a difference that constitutes part of their essence; it is only one of their properties. Finally, there are predicates that are not at all distinctive of a species, because even though it may have them, it need not, and other species may have them as well. These Aristotle called *accidents*, and as examples in the case of men he cites the predicates "sitting," "two-footed," and "asleep."

So there are five "predicables," that is, five types of relation that a predicate may bear to a subject—the relations of being a *genus* ("All men are animals"), a *difference* ("All men are capable of discourse"), a *definition* ("All men are animals capable of discourse"), a *property* ("All men are capable of learning the multiplication table"), or ·an *accident* ("All men are two-footed").

Aristotle did not view his categories and predicables merely as ways in which we happen to think or speak about things but, rather, as ways in which things actually exist. The categories of substance and quality, for example, or the predicables of definition and accident, characterize the basic structure of reality as well as the propositions which figure in our reasoning—they have metaphysical as well as logical significance. What actually exist are particular substances having qualities, and certain qualities (expressed in definitions by genus and difference) are actually essential to any species of substances, whereas others (accidents) are not. The whole of nature is organized along the lines of the categories and predicables; and all of our reasoning concerns propositions that contain predicates from one or another of the ten categories and related to subjects in accordance with one or another of the five predicables.

Now reasoning, to put it very generally, consists of "argument in which, certain things being laid down, something other than these necessarily comes about through them." Thus if it be "laid down" (or *premised*) that all animals are mortal and that all men are animals, there "necessarily comes about" the *conclusion* that all men are mortal. Much in reasoning obviously depends upon what exactly is "laid down." If the premises of an argument are at all doubtful, the conclusion that follows from them cannot be less doubtful insofar as the premises constitute our evidence for the conclusion. When the premises are *known* to be true, we have an argument of the kind that Aristotle calls a *demonstration,* because it will conclusively demonstrate or prove the truth of the conclusion. If, however, the premises are not known to be true, but are just commonly *believed* to be true, the argument is *dialectical;* and if the premises are not even commonly believed to be true but just *seem* to be commonly believed, or are *said* to be commonly believed, the argument is *contentious.*

The simplest type of argument, and the type of which Aristotle believes all more complex arguments are composed, is what he calls the *syllogism.* A syllogism is an argument having just two propositions as its premises and one as its conclusion, for example:

> All animals are mortal.
> <u>All men are animals.</u>
> Therefore, all men are mortal.

Notice that this syllogism has a pattern or form which can be duplicated by any number of other syllogisms, as by this one:

> All marsupials are vertebrates.
> <u>All opossums are marsupials.</u>
> Therefore, all opossums are vertebrates.

The form that these two syllogisms have in common may be represented as follows:

> All B's are C's.
> <u>All A's are B's.</u>
> Therefore, all A's are C's.

The symbols A, B, and C stand for the innumerably many different *terms* that can be put into this form of syllogism. Aristotle calls B the *middle term* because it "comes in the middle" and is "contained in another and contains another in itself"; that is, B comes between A and C (called the *minor* and *major* terms respectively) in that the B's are said to be included among the C's and to include the A's, like this:

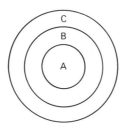

As the diagram makes all the plainer, the terms in this form of syllogism are so related that, whatever they may be, the conclusion ("All A's are C's") will certainly be true if the premises are true—a fact which later logicians expressed by saying that any syllogism having this form will be *valid*. The several different forms that make for valid syllogisms and the principles upon which these depend are examined in Aristotle's *Prior Analytics*. Few books have been as influential as this one. Only in the last hundred years or so has it come to be generally recognized that Aristotle's account of syllogisms does not exhaust the possible types of *deductive* argument—argument, that is, in which the conclusions cannot possibly be false if the premises are true.

A demonstration, for Aristotle, consists of a valid syllogism whose premises are known to be true, and such a syllogism gives what he means by theoretical or scientific knowledge. The connection between the two terms in the conclusion is established and explained by means of the middle term in the premises. All A's are shown to be C's inasmuch as one premise affirms that the A's are B's, while the other premise affirms that the B's are C's. In this way the premises identify the *reason* or *cause* of the fact stated in the conclusion. All men are mortal because all men are animals and all animals are mortal—their essential animality is the reason or cause of men's mortality. Broadly speaking, the aim of all the sciences is to discover middle terms that will explain why given subjects (say, "men") have certain predicates (say, "mortality") and not others. "In all our inquiries," Aristotle says, "we are asking either whether there is a 'middle' or what the 'middle' is: for the 'middle' here is precisely the cause, and it is the cause that we seek in all our inquiries." Middle terms of the required type express some element of the essential nature (the definition) of the subject in a syllogism's conclusion, owing to which the subject *necessarily* possesses the predicate (as one of its properties). Considerable scientific imagination is needed for the discovery of these middle terms. "Quick wit," Aristotle says, "is a faculty of hitting upon the middle term instantaneously. It would be exemplified by a man who saw that the moon has her bright side always turned toward the sun, and quickly grasped the cause of this, namely that she borrows her light from him; or observed somebody in conversation with a man of wealth and divined that he was borrowing money, or that the friendship of these people sprang from a common enmity. In all these instances he has seen the major and minor terms and then grasped the causes, the middle terms."

The premises of a demonstrative syllogism, in giving the essential nature of the subject in the conclusion, will be *necessarily* true; for to state the essential nature of any kind of thing is to state what necessarily belongs to it. Only propositions that are seen to be necessarily true are really *known,* according to Aristotle; and when we see that a proposition, though true, could possibly have been false, we have only *opinion.* We know only what we understand could not possibly have been otherwise than it is. The accidents of a thing, in not belonging to it necessarily, cannot therefore be known to belong to it, only believed to do so. Height and weight, for example, are accidents of men; they could have been other than they are for any person at any time, and they vary for any person with the passage of time. There is an instability about the accidents of things, whereas their essential natures remain ever the same; and Aristotle, like Plato, insists that knowledge requires absolute stability in its objects. "Opinion," he says, "is unstable, and so is the kind of being that we have described as its object," but scientific knowledge "proceeds by necessary connections, and that which is necessary cannot be otherwise."

The necessary connections in question are given in propositions that are *universal,* such as "All men are animals," not in propositions that are *particular,* such as "Some men are animals," or *singular,* such as "Socrates is an animal." A connection between being a man and being an animal could not be necessary if some men were animals and some were not. To know that the connection is necessary is to know that it holds in all cases, and the way to express this knowledge is to assert an affirmative universal proposition. Nor could "Some men are animals" (or "Socrates is an animal") serve as a premise in a syllogism intended to explain, for example, why all men are mortal. "All men are mortal because all animals are mortal and some men are animals" is not a valid syllogism and does not contribute to the growth of scientific knowledge.[3] The goal of scientific knowledge is to account for things by showing that propositions about them follow with logical necessity from necessarily true premises about all things of the kind.

How can we be sure that a universal proposition of the form "All A's are B's" is necessarily true? One way is to demonstrate it by showing that it follows from premises of whose necessary truth we are sure. Thus "All men are animals" might be demonstrated from the premises "All

---

[3] The syllogism commits the fallacy known as Illicit Process of the Minor Term, drawing a conclusion about all men from a premise giving information about only some.

mammals are animals" and "All men are mammals." But these premises are also universal, and now the question is how we are sure of them. "All men are mammals" might be demonstrated from the premises "All viviparous creatures are mammals" and "All men are viviparous creatures." (A viviparous creature is one that brings forth its young alive, instead of laying eggs.) There must, however, be a way in which we can be sure of some universal propositions without having to demonstrate them by syllogisms. We cannot go on forever constructing syllogisms to prove the premises of other syllogisms. We must be able to find some "first principles" or "primary premises," as Aristotle calls them, to which chains of syllogisms may be fastened.

These are found, Aristotle says, by *induction*. This is a matter of directly apprehending ("intuiting") universal truths as exemplified in the particular data of our sense-experience. Having perceived that particular A's are B's, we are able in certain cases to determine, without any process of reasoning, that "All A's are B's" is necessarily true, that whatever has the characteristic of being an A will necessarily also have the characteristic of being a B.[4] The characteristic of being an A or a B (a viviparous creature, say, or a mammal), which can be embodied in an indefinite number of particular things, is what Aristotle calls a *universal*. What happens in induction is that a necessary connection between two universals is detected immediately in reflection upon concrete instances, and we just see that in no instance could one of the two possibly occur apart from the other. Intuitions of this kind occur to us thanks to our capacity for discriminating and remembering the recurrent characteristics of things—the universals that are stabilizing unities amid the otherwise chaotic multiplicity of our perceptions. Aristotle describes induction in a famous passage:

> All animals . . . possess a congenital discriminative capacity which is called sense-perception. But though sense-perception is innate in all animals, in some (those having the power of memory) the sense-impression comes to persist, in others it does not. So animals in which this persistence does not come to be have either no knowledge at all outside the act of perceiving, or no knowledge of objects of which no impression persists; animals in which it does come into being have perception and can continue to retain the sense-impression in the soul; and when such persistence is frequently repeated a further distinction at once arises between those which out of the persistence of such sense-impressions

---

[4] Aristotle does not mean by "induction" what is commonly meant by it today, namely, a kind of argument in which a universal proposition is supposedly shown to be probable relative to particular data. Aristotle's "induction," in the sense in question here, is not a kind of *argument* at all; and it supposedly gives certainty, not just probability. (In another context Aristotle uses "induction" in another sense for a kind of argument that gives certainty. This is the procedure of concluding that all A's are B's after examining *all* the A's—"perfect induction," so called, the scientific importance of which is usually slight even when it is feasible.

develop a power of systematizing them and those which do not. So out of sense-perception comes to be what we call memory, and out of frequently repeated memories of the same thing develops experience; for a number of memories constitute a single experience. From experience again—i.e., from the universal now stabilized in its entirety within the soul, the one beside the many which is a single identity within them all—originate the skill of the craftsman and the knowledge of the man of science, skill in the sphere of coming to be and science in the sphere of being.

We conclude that these states of knowledge are neither innate in a determinate form, nor developed from other higher states of knowledge, but from sense-perception. It is like a rout in a battle stopped by first one man making a stand and then another, until the original formation has been restored. The soul is so constituted as to be capable of this process.

Let us now restate the account given already, though with insufficient clearness. When one of a number of logically indiscriminable particulars has made a stand, the earliest universal is present in the soul: for though the act of sense-perception is of the particular, its content is universal—is man, for example, not the man Callias. A fresh stand is made among these rudimentary universals, and the process does not cease until the indivisible concepts, the true universals, are established: e.g., such and such a species of animal is a step towards the genus animal, which by the same process is a step towards a further generalization.

Thus it is clear that we must get to know the primary premisses by induction; for the method by which even sense-perception implants the universal is inductive.

By induction, then, we directly grasp the necessary universal truths that are the starting points of theoretical knowledge. Being of a high degree of generality and abstractness, these are less familiar to us than "objects nearer to sense"; but once we have become aware of them, we find that their truth is the clearest of all. These "first principles" are of two kinds—*axioms* common to all or several sciences, and *theses* peculiar to each science. An axiom common to all sciences is a proposition we must know if we are to know anything; for example, the proposition "A cannot be both B and not B," which is true whatever A is, and which is not so much a premise *from* which we reason as a principle *in accordance with* which we reason.[5] An example of an axiom common to several sciences, but not to all, is "Take equals from equals and equals remain," which holds for such mathematical sciences as arithmetic and geometry.

---

[5] "A cannot be both B and not B" came to be called the Principle of Contradiction. Another of Aristotle's axioms is "A must either be B or not be B," later known as the Law of Excluded Middle. These two, together with the Law of Identity, "A is A," have traditionally been called the Three Laws of Thought; but Aristotle believes that the reason why they are to be observed in our *thinking* is that they are necessary truths about all *things,* including those of which we might think.

Theses peculiar to each science include basic *hypotheses,* which assert the existence of the kind or genus of things the science investigates, and basic *definitions,* which set forth the essential characteristics of that kind or genus of things. From these starting points, known intuitively by induction, a scientist proceeds by means of syllogisms to deduce necessary conclusions as to the properties of the things in question, thereby establishing that, and explaining why, those things must have those (and just those) properties—why the interior angles of triangles add up to two right angles, why viviparous creatures are mammals, why the moon has her bright side always turned toward the sun, and so forth and so on.

Such in outline is Aristotle's understanding of the instruments of theoretical knowledge. The science that in his own day used these instruments with greatest success was geometry, of which the classical exposition was given about twenty years after Aristotle's death in the *Elements* of Euclid. How far these instruments are adequate outside mathematics, and indeed how far they are adequate even within mathematics, were to become topics of extensive controversy. Nevertheless, there is little dispute that Aristotle's logical treatises are the source from which the main stream of logic has flowed ever since, so that the richer symbolic logic of today only "carries forward to a high level of generality the same undertaking which Aristotle's *Organon* accomplished on a much more limited scale" (Eaton).

Metaphysics _____

That branch of theoretical knowledge which has to do with first principles common to all special sciences is called "First Philosophy" by Aristotle. The fourteen "books" (sets of lecture notes) in which Aristotle is mainly concerned with First Philosophy came to be known as his *Metaphysics* simply because an early editor, in a collection of Aristotle's writings which he made, placed them after (*meta,* in Greek) Aristotle's writings on physics. Knowledge of first principles deserves more than anything else to be called "wisdom," Aristotle says, because this knowledge alone has the characteristics that are generally considered to be wisdom's earmarks, in particular comprehensiveness, authoritativeness, and desirability on its own account. It is comprehensive ("the wise man knows all things, as far as possible") in that it enlightens us about the ultimate "whys" or causes of all classes of things. It is authoritative in that it determines the ends or purposes for which every class of things exists—"the good in each class and in general the supreme good in the whole of nature." It is desirable on its own account in that it satisfies our native curiosity about "the greater matters" and thereby is worth having irrespective of any question of its practical advantages.

For it is owing to their wonder that men both now begin and at first began to philosophize; they wondered originally at the obvious difficulties, then advanced little by little and stated difficulties about the greater matters, e.g., about the phenomena of the moon and those of the sun and of the stars, and about the genesis of the universe. And a man who is puzzled and wonders thinks himself ignorant (whence even the lover of myth is in a sense a lover of wisdom, for the myth is composed of wonders); therefore since they philosophized in order to escape from ignorance, evidently they were pursuing science in order to know, not for any utilitarian end. And this is confirmed by the facts; for it was when almost all the necessities of life and the things that make for comfort and recreation had been secured, that such knowledge began to be sought. Evidently then we do not seek it for the sake of any other advantage; but as the man is free, we say, who exists for his own sake and not for another's, so we pursue this as the only free science, for it alone exists for its own sake.

Hence also the possession of it might be justly regarded as beyond human power; for in many ways human nature is in bondage, so that according to Simonides "God alone can have this privilege," and it is unfitting that man should not be content to seek the knowledge that is suited to him. If, then, there is something in what the poets say, and jealousy is natural to the divine power, it would probably occur in this case above all, and all who excelled in this knowledge would be unfortunate. But the divine power cannot be jealous. . . .

The first principles that are wisdom's subject matter are universal propositions as to the most basic characteristics that anything must have if it is to *exist* at all, if it is to be *real* or to have *being*. Aristotle expresses this by saying that First Philosophy is the "science which investigates being as being and the attributes which belong to this in virtue of its own nature." Special sciences such as physics and mathematics investigate the necessary attributes of limited aspects of reality. Metaphysics, however, takes the whole of reality, "being as being," as its field of inquiry. It aims to articulate the fundamental structure of reality in general—of reality "as such."

There are many different senses, Aristotle says, in which things can be said to exist—as many, in fact, as there are categories of predicates that can be affirmed of subjects. The different categories of predicates are just so many different ways in which things can have being. Within these, however, two major ways are to be distinguished. Things have being as substances when, like men and horses, sticks and stones, they are *concrete and specific individuals*. Things have being as quantities, qualities, relations, places, times, positions, states, actions, and affections when they are *characteristics* of concrete and specific individuals. Whatever has being does so in one or the other of these two basic ways—as an individual substance or as a characteristic of an individual substance. The being of individual substances is therefore that "which is primary and on which the others depend." Things that are *not* individual substances exist *only* as "affections of substance, [or] processes towards substance, or destructions or privations or qualities of substance, or productive or generative of substance, or-. . . . relative to substance, or negations of some of these things or of substance itself." Since individuals, or substances, are the fundamental constituents of reality, "it will be of substances that the philosopher must grasp the principles and the causes"—substances in general, that is, not any special kind such as men or horses, sticks or stones.

Although Aristotle includes substance among his categories of predicates, he does not mean to suggest that an individual such as Socrates can be "predicated" of some other individual taken as a subject. "A is Socrates," where A is the name of some *other* specific individual (William Howard Taft, say) would obviously be nonsense. It is not as though Socrates were a sort of characteristic which some other individual could possess, like a shade of color. It is of the nature of a substance, in the primary sense of a specific individual, never to be a predicate but always to be only a subject *of which* predicates are affirmed or denied. We can, however, speak of "substances" in a secondary sense when it comes to real *species* of concrete individuals such as men or horses; and these *can* be predicates, as in "Trigger is a horse," where the idea is to affirm that Trigger is a member of the species of horses ("a class with a certain qualification"). It is only predicates of this sort, referring to species of individuals, that Aristotle means to include under his category of substance.

What is especially distinctive of individual substances, Aristotle says, is that they remain one and the same throughout changes in many of their characteristics (in their "accidents," to be precise). A particular horse galloping is the same horse that a moment ago was standing still. Galloping and standing still are *contraries* in the sense that nothing can do both at the same time, but of course it is perfectly possible for the same horse to do both at different times. This capacity for possessing contrary characteristics at different times is the outstanding peculiarity of substances. "From among things other than substance, we should find ourselves unable to bring forward any which possessed this mark. Thus, one and the same color cannot be white and black. Nor can the same one action be good and bad: this law holds good with everything that is not substance. But one and the selfsame substance, while retaining its identity, is yet capable of admitting contrary qualities. The same individual person is at one time white, at another black, at one time warm, at another cold, at one time good, at another bad." Now to be capable of admitting contrary qualities or characteristics is to be capable of *change,* and it is in terms of the loss or gain of characteristics by substances that change is to be understood. Characteristics of quantity, quality, relation, place, and so forth, do not change in and of themselves; it is *substances* that change, by losing and acquiring characteristics, while remaining numerically the same substances. Alterations and processes and movements of whatever kind take place in and among individual substances, which are the fundamental realities in the universe.

There is a limit, however, to the amount of change that any individual substance can undergo and still retain its identity. It cannot remain the same if it loses the characteristics that constitute its essence or definition, for these are precisely what distinguish it fundamentally from things of other species. If a human being, for example, is essentially an animal capable of discourse, then loss of the capacity for discourse would entail loss of humanity. For every species of substances there is a fixed set of characteristics that constitute the nature of those substances, and Aristotle calls this their *form*. It is because of their different essential *forms* that substances of different species *are* different, for Aristotle believes that all of them are at bottom made of the same elements of *matter*—namely, earth, air, fire, and water. The form of an individual substance is the principle (or "formula") by which these elements are so combined as to produce that specific kind of thing. Earth, air, fire, and water are themselves four different forms of an "ultimate substratum" of matter[6] that is the same for them all—the underlying "what," in itself quite characterless, that has the forms of earth, air, fire, and water embodied in it.

An individual substance, then, is a "compound of form and matter" in which the aspect of form is what makes all the difference. The form is also the object of scientific knowledge, for it consists of characteristics or universals—"being an A," "being a B"—between which we can, in induction, detect necessary connections expressible in propositions of the form "All A's are B's." The form that makes one individual what it is can be duplicated in any number of other individuals, which thus will constitute a species, and it is with species that scientific knowledge is concerned.

Aristotle is at pains to make it clear that he does not agree with Plato's particular theory of forms. Plato, he says, mistakenly conceived of forms as though they were things separate and apart from concrete individuals, as though the forms of circularity and animality, for example, were existences on their own account to which particular circles and animals were related in an external fashion. The precise nature of this relation Plato never indicated at all clearly; he spoke of particular circles and animals as "imitating" or "copying" or "trying to be like" the forms of circularity and animality, as "participating in" the forms or "resembling" or "partaking of" them. But all of these expressions, in Aristotle's opinion, are just "empty words and poetical metaphors" employed in an attempt to characterize a relation that does not and could not exist. Forms such as circularity and humanity exist only as *characteristics* of particular concrete individuals, not as some abstract type of thing over and above them. Plato really pictured forms as being a special kind of substances, existing in some supersensible realm of their own, far removed from the everyday world of changing and imperfect sensible things. In fact, however, forms exist only as aspects of concrete individuals—the most important aspects, to be sure, for it is the form embodied in a substance that

---

[6] Also called the "primary substratum," whence the expression "prime matter" in later discussions of Aristotle.

gives a specific character to its matter, but forms exist only as *embodied*. Plato certainly believed that it is by virtue of their relations to forms that particular things possess such comparative stability and determinateness as they do; but what he should have recognized is that such comparative stability and determinateness are unintelligible unless forms are viewed as principles of organization *within* particular things. It is impossible that what constitutes the very nature and inmost essence of a particular thing should exist apart from it.

The error of viewing forms as separate from particular things is shown, Aristotle maintains, by several very awkward consequences that follow from doing so. Now Plato himself was not unaware that some such consequences at least seem to follow from his theory. He points them out in his *Parmenides*. One of the arguments that Plato states there concerns the difficulty of understanding how *many* particular things can "partake of" *one and the same* form. Particular beautiful things, for example, are alike in being beautiful because (so says Plato's theory) they all "partake of" one and the same form of beauty. But what does this mean? Does it mean that each particular beautiful thing has, so to speak, its own individual *share* of the one form of beauty? This cannot be right, for if the form is single it cannot provide "shares" of itself. Perhaps, then, particular beautiful things "partake of" the one form of beauty in the sense that the *whole* of it exists in each of them? But this cannot be right either, for one and the same thing—the single form of beauty—cannot belong wholly to each of a number of different things at the same time. The conclusion would seem to be that particular beautiful things cannot "partake of" the form of beauty at all, since none of them can have either a share of it or all of it and obviously there is no third alternative. The same sort of argument can be given for any form one cares to consider. In general the theory of forms appears to leave unsolved the old problem of "the one and the many."

Plato did not explain what he made of this argument that he himself presented. Probably he did not believe that it was unanswerable, but whether he tried to answer it and, if so, how, have long been matters of debate. Aristotle, for his part, saw the argument and others like it as clear indications that Plato's theory of forms was misguided. The only possible solution to the "one-many" problem lies in conceiving of forms simply as *characteristics* of particular substances, not as existences on their own account to which particular substances are somehow related. Particular substances are members of the same species when they have essential characteristics in common, but their having these in common cannot be accounted for by saying that they all "partake of" or "resemble" things over and above themselves. Why A's have in common the characteristic of being B's can perhaps be explained by showing that "All A's are B's" follows by syllogisms from certain axioms and theses. Why there are any substances *at all* with common characteristics cannot, however, be explained; that is just an ultimate fact of reality, a first principle of "being as being," and should simply be accepted as such. On this understanding of the matter, the one-many problem does not even come up; for there is no "one" apart from the "many" as to whose relations with the "many" there could be any problem. Only the "many" exist, with characteristics in common. By induction we are able to arrive at abstract concepts of these common characteristics and to apprehend necessary relations among them. Each of these *concepts* is "one" (one *concept*) and "separate" (in our *minds*) from the "many," but Aristotle is not suggesting that the "many" derive their common characteristics by "partaking of" our concepts. It is the other way around: our concepts derive by inductive abstraction from the common characteristics of the "many," which alone objectively exist—forms embodied in matter.

Aristotle's use of the distinction between form and matter is ingenious. He counts as matter whatever is incompletely developed from the point of view of some finished condition of form suitable to it. What in this way is identified as matter, however, may itself be viewed as finished in form relative to its own constituents, so that what is matter from one point of view is form from another. For example, a crucible of molten bronze is matter in relation to the finished form of the statue that is about to be cast from it, whereas the bronze is finished in form relative to the matter of the copper and tin of which it is an alloy. The tissues and bones of a foal are matter in relation to the finished form of a fully developed horse, whereas the foal's tissues and bones are finished in form relative to the matter (as Aristotle believes) of its mother's blood. What is matter relative to a particular form is called the *proximate matter* of that form. Processes of manufacture and of natural growth consist of distinguishable stages at each of which a fresh form is imposed upon, or develops within, a proximate matter which itself is a compound of a more elementary form and a more elementary matter.

Parmenides, as we know, took the position that changes of any kind, including those associated with processes of growth and manufacture, are wholly illusory. To suppose that some quantity of matter could change in the sense of acquiring a new form is, to his way of thinking, simply preposterous. A new form would be one that, as far as the matter in question is concerned, did not exist and was "nothing" before. It is impossible, however, to think of what once was "nothing," for to "think of 'nothing' " is precisely the same as not to think at all; and that of which it is impossible to think can hardly be thought to come into existence.

Aristotle provides what in effect is a reply to this. It is a mistake, he maintains, to think that when a quantity of matter comes to have a new form, something comes into existence where there was "nothing" before. Something *does* exist before, namely, a *potential* in the matter for acquiring the new form, and a potential is not a mere "nothing." The *potential* in A for becoming *actually* a B consists not of the mere absence in A of the characteristics of B but of specific conditions in A for developing these characteristics. This distinction between the potential and the actual, or between potentiality and actuality, can be grasped by considering illustrations.

> We say [Aristotle observes] that potentially, for instance, a statue of Hermes is in the block of wood and the half-line is in the whole, because it might be separated out, and we call even the man who is not studying a man of science, if he is capable of studying; the thing that stands in contrast to each of these exists actually. Our meaning can be seen in the particular cases by induction, and we must not seek a definition of everything but be content to grasp the analogy, that it is as that which is building is to that which is capable of building, and the waking to the sleeping, and that which is seen to that which has its eyes shut but has sight, and that which has been shaped out of the matter to the matter, and that which has been wrought up to the unwrought. Let actuality be defined by one member of this antithesis, and the potential by the other.

So obvious and elementary may this distinction seem that it might be difficult to believe that an Aristotle was needed to make it explicit and to call attention to its philosophical significance. Such was the case, however, and it seems obvious now chiefly because of the influence of Aristotle's writings upon Western ways of thinking. As he employed the distinction, potentiality is associated with undeveloped capacities in the matter of a substance, actuality with a finished condition of form in which these capacities are fully developed. Thus a mature oak is the actuality, the finished form, of which the undeveloped matter of the acorn was the potentiality. A house is the actuality of which the matter of bricks and mortar were the potentiality. All processes of natural growth and of human production are understood by Aristotle along these lines—as the progressive actualization of form in matter having the potential for development in specific directions. The existence in any given matter of definite conditions of development is particularly clear from the fact that although some new aspects of form are possible for it, others are not. An acorn can grow into an oak but only into an oak. Bricks and mortar can be worked up into a house but not into swords or shoes. And it is only because any given matter has specific latent capacities that it makes sense to speak of it as being "deprived" of some aspect of form that it has not got. There is a deprivation (or "privation," as Aristotle says) of treeness in an acorn only because it has the wherewithal and the natural tendency (which circumstances may nevertheless thwart) to develop into a tree. It cannot aptly be said to be "deprived" (in the same sense) of chickenhood, for an acorn has neither the wherewithal nor the tendency to hatch into a chicken. It simply lacks the potential.

Entelechy is Aristotle's term for the full actualization of a form. Processes of development are not endless; they have final stages at which the potentialities in question are realized and appropriate entelechies are reached. Saplings develop from acorns, and oaks develop from saplings, but nothing develops from oaks—except more acorns, which indicate that with oaks a final stage of development has been reached, for Aristotle believes that organic things reach this when they are able to reproduce their kind. Houses are constructed from bricks and mortar, but nothing is constructed from houses (at least not in the same sense of "constructed"), for finished houses are end products of construction.

"Actuality," Aristotle says, "is prior to potency,"[7] inasmuch as "from the potentially existing the actually existing is always produced by an actually existing thing, e.g., man from man, musician from musician. . . . Everything that is produced is something produced from something and by something, and that the same in species as it." The potential comes to be actual only by the agency of some actually existing thing of the same species. Thus the potential for human babies is actualized only by human parents, the potential for acorns is actualized only by oaks, the potential for a house is actualized not of course by another house but only by an artisan in whose mind there is a conception of an actual house "the same in species" as the one his hands are constructing. We have here the basis of Aristotle's view that the various species of natural organisms are fixed and beginningless. The priority of actuality to potentiality, as he understands it, implies that every baby must have parents of the same species, that like is produced only by like,[8] so that each species is fixed and can neither evolve into nor have evolved from any other species. And there cannot have been first parents of any species, parents who themselves were never babies, since "everything that is produced is produced *from something*"—that is, everything comes from a matter that already exists, and the "matter" of a parent is a baby. Aristotle disagrees, then, with the evolutionist views of earlier philosophers such as Anaximander, who believed that living things arose from mud, just as his adherents in recent times have opposed the evolutionary biology of which Charles Darwin is the best-known founder. But Aristotle's position is no less incompatible with a common interpretation of the Biblical account of Creation, according to which every species had a beginning with first parents.

When it is a question of the agency by which potentialities are realized, as in the case of parents and offspring, actuality is "prior" to potentiality in the sense of coming *earlier* in time. A creature who becomes a parent obviously exists before its offspring. But Aristotle says that there is another sense of "prior" in which actuality is "prior" to potentiality although it comes *later* in time. Here the actuality in question is the finished form or *entelechy* into which the potentiality tends naturally to develop. For an animal this is the mature creature into which the offspring itself will in favorable circumstances grow up. The finished form

---

[7] "Potency," as used here, means the same as "potentiality."

[8] In his *History of Animals*, however, Aristotle takes note of some creatures, including "a number of insects," who appear to emerge by "spontaneous generation" from "putrefying earth or vegetable matter," without having any parents at all.

is "prior" in the sense that it is the *reason why* the matter having the potentiality to achieve it exists in the first place. Offspring exist for a *purpose*—the purpose of becoming fully developed members of their species. "Matter exists in a potential state," Aristotle says, "just because it may come to its form." And the process of coming to its form is explained by reference to the form as the final "end" (*telos*) toward which the process is directed. "Everything that comes to be moves towards a principle, i.e., an end," which is to say that all coming-into-being, wherever in the world it occurs, is *goal-directed* and calls for *teleological* explanation. In all natural things there is an "innate impulse to change," that is, to develop continuously until their potentialities are actualized; and this "impulse" is like an unconscious determination to achieve fulfillment, to arrive at what is *best* from the point of view of "the essential nature in each case." Something analogous to intelligent human action, in which certain means are deliberately chosen in order to achieve certain ends, is found at every level of nature—in lower animals, in plants, even indeed in the changing of seasons. We are compelled to acknowledge that natural happenings occur with a purpose, for the sake of achieving "that which is best" in each species, because the alternative is to view them as occurring spontaneously, coincidentally, by chance, and that would plainly be inconsistent with the great *regularity* to be found in nature. Someone might say that natural happenings occur neither with purpose nor by chance but by necessity. Yet is there any real difference between saying that something happens "by necessity" and saying that it happens "by chance"? Aristotle thinks not. Either way, no *reason* is given for the occurrence of the thing. "By necessity" does not explain *why,* any more than "by chance" does; both amount to saying merely that something "just happens." Aristotle's analysis of these issues is best expressed in his *Physics* (much of which is concerned with points of metaphysics), where we find the following celebrated passage:

A difficulty presents itself: why should not nature work, not for the sake of something, nor because it is better so, but just as the sky rains, not in order to make the corn grow, but of necessity? What is drawn up must cool, and what has been cooled must become water and descend, the result of this being that the corn grows. Similarly if a man's crop is spoiled on the threshing-floor, the rain did not fall for the sake of this— in order that the crop might be spoiled—but that result just followed. Why then should it not be the same with the parts in nature, e.g., that our teeth should come up *of necessity*—the front teeth sharp, fitted for tearing, the molars broad and useful for grinding down the food—since they did not arise for this end, but it was merely a coincident result; and so with all other parts in which we suppose that there is purpose? Wherever then all the parts came about just what they would have been if they had come to be for an end, such things survived, being organized spontaneously in a fitting way; whereas those which grew otherwise perished and continue to perish, as Empedocles says his "man-faced ox-progeny" did.

Such are the arguments (and others of the kind) which may cause difficulty on this point. Yet it is impossible that this should be the true view. For teeth and all other natural things either invariably or normally come about in a given way; but of not one of the results of chance or spontaneity is this true. We do not ascribe to chance or mere coincidence the frequency of rain in winter, but frequent rain in summer we do; nor heat in the dog-days, but only if we have it in winter. If then, it is agreed that things are either the result of coincidence or for an end, and these cannot be the result of coincidence or spontaneity, it follows that they must be for an end; and that such things are all due to nature even the champions of the theory which is before us would agree. Therefore action for an end is present in things which come to be and are by nature.

Further, where a series has a completion, all the preceding steps are for the sake of that. Now surely as in intelligent action, so in nature; and as in nature, so it is in each action, if nothing interferes. Now intelligent action is for the sake of an end; therefore the nature of things also is so. Thus if a house, e.g., had been a thing made by nature, it would have been made in the same way as it is now by art; and if things made by nature were made also by art, they would come to be in the same way as by nature. Each step then in the series is for the sake of the next; and generally art partly completes what nature cannot bring to a finish, and partly imitates her. If, therefore, artificial products are for the sake of an end, so clearly also are natural products. The relation of the later to the earlier terms of the series is the same in both.

This is most obvious in the animals other than man: they make things neither by art nor after inquiry or deliberation. Wherefore people discuss whether it is by intelligence or by some other faculty that these creatures work—spiders, ants, and the like. By gradual advance in this direction we come to see clearly that in plants too that is produced which is conducive to the end—leaves, e.g., grow to provide shade for the fruit. If then it is both by nature and for an end that the swallow makes its nest and the spider its web, and plants grow leaves for the sake of nourishment, it is plain that this kind of cause is operative in things which come to be and are by nature. And since "nature" means two things, the matter and the form, of which the latter is the end, and since all the rest is for the sake of the end, the form must be the cause in the sense of "that for the sake of which."

In order to explain why any natural thing is the way it is, one must identify the end "for the sake of which" it exists. This is called its *final cause*. The final cause of any natural thing is the finished form which it tends naturally to achieve. Of course the precise form, finished or unfinished, that a thing has at any moment is essential to its condition at that moment and as such is called its *formal cause*. This is the aspect of form, however short of final, that gives to the thing's matter such specific character as it has at the time. The formal cause of an egg, just as an egg, would include its peculiar eggy shape, whereas its final cause is the mature form of chicken into which it may develop. The agent responsible for producing a thing in the first place, for beginning the process by which a potential thing becomes an actual thing, is called its *efficient cause*. The efficient cause of a fertile egg is a hen, with the assistance of a rooster. The matter from which a thing is produced, containing as it does the potential for the thing, is called its *material cause*. The material cause of a fertile egg is certain matter in the body of the hen (some of it contributed by a rooster).

These are Aristotle's famous Four Causes—final, formal, efficient, and material—all of which, he thinks, have to be identified in order fully to account for a thing. Aristotle observes, however, that final, formal, and efficient causes "often coincide," for "the 'what' and 'that for the sake of which' are one, while the primary source of motion is the same in species as these (for man generates man). . . ." In other words, a thing's formal cause (the distinctive form or "what" of it) will be identical with its final cause (the end "for the sake of which" it exists) when the thing has achieved its finished form. The formal cause of a mature chicken is the same as its final cause. And the efficient cause of a thing ("the primary source of motion") is the same *in species* as its final cause, since the efficient cause of a thing is an already-actualized member of the same species—another thing that already has the finished form which the thing it produces will aim to acquire also. Thus "man generates man" (via babies), and chicken generates chicken (via eggs).

Aristotle uses the term "motion" (*kinesis*) in a very wide sense to designate all development from potentiality to actuality, for any kind of change—in quality and magnitude as well as in location—which an efficient cause may bring about in any given matter. He believes that "motion" in this sense is everlasting. There never was a beginning of it, and there never will be an end to it. The whole world of motion is uncreated and indestructible. To think otherwise is to think that there could be a *time* before or after motion existed, but no such time is possible. Time is inseparably connected with motion, particularly with the periodic revolutions of the stars, so that a time at which there was or will be no motion is strictly out of the question. Nor can we avoid this conclusion by maintaining (as Plato may have done) that time can be conceived as simple beforeness and afterness, independent of all moving things, and that accordingly it would still make sense to speak of a time before or after all moving things existed. No, "there could not be a before and after," Aristotle says, "if time did not exist . . . [and] time is either the same thing as movement or an attribute of movement."

Now everlasting motion can hardly be supposed to occur all by itself. Everlasting motion is a continuous actualization of potentiality. Potentiality can be actualized only by the agency of something actual. Everlasting motion can therefore be actualized only by the agency of something eternally actual. The stars continuously move (as Aristotle believes) in circular orbits at uniform velocities; everlastingly their potential for doing this is realized, and there must be some agent responsible for realizing it—an agent that eternally exercises a moving power. (It is "sufficient to assume" just *one* such agent, Aristotle says.) There will be nothing merely potential about its nature, since it is possible for what is potential never to become actual, and it is *not* possible that the power responsible for everlasting motion could ever be other than actual. It is thus "a principle whose very essence is actuality." Since matter is the basis of potentiality in things, the agent "must be without matter," a pure individual *form* "which moves without being moved" (for to be moved is to change, and change requires matter). This supreme "unmoved mover" is what Aristotle calls God.

Plato believed that the cosmos was fashioned by a Divine Craftsman who, as a great soul, could be described as "self-initiating motion." Aristotle, however, thinks it plain that nothing could initiate its own motion. This would mean that it actualized its own potential, but it could not do this unless it was already actual in the respect in question. Thus it would have to be both potential and actual in the same respect at the same time, which is impossible. One might as well speak of "self-hatching chickens" as of "self-initiating motion." This is another reason, then, why God, the source of all motion, must himself be viewed as unmoved. If he moved, his moving would be produced either by himself, which is absurd, or by something else, in which case he would not be the source of all motion.

This of course only brings up the question of how anything unmoving could possibly produce motion. How could A move B if A were motionless? Certainly there is no way that this could happen by physical contact. But suppose that B is a creature with consciousness and that A is some object that B desired on sight to possess. In that event the mere presence of A, however motionless A may be, might very well stimulate motion in B. It is simply a matter of *final causation;* and so it is, Aristotle says, with God and the cosmos, for God "produces motion as being loved." A powerful magnetic attraction radiates from the Deity throughout the universe, as all things desire to associate themselves with the continuous and unchanging spiritual life that is his. The stars of the outermost sphere of heaven (the sphere has an "intelligence") come as close to this as they can by perpetually rotating in orbits that are perfectly circular. Their movement is communicated to all the lesser heavenly spheres (via the "intelligence" of each) that revolve around the earth, which is located at the exact center of the universe. So are night and day produced, and seasons of planting and harvest, and all the living things that move upon the earth—eternal like God at least as species.

All things move from love of God, whether they know this or not, but he takes no cognizance of them. He is an immaterial being whose actuality consists solely of thought. Because he is a changeless form, the contents of his thought do not change, and this means that he thinks of none of the things that change, not of stars as they wheel in their orbits, not of animals as they live and die. The object of God's thought must in any case be the best object possible, the "most divine and precious," and this can be none other than God himself. "Therefore," Aristotle says, "it must be of itself that the divine thought thinks (since it is the most excellent of things), and its thinking is a thinking on thinking." With this self-absorbed divinity Aristotle's metaphysics reaches its disappointing climax. If God is not the creator of the world (for the whole show has always existed), he is also not a benevolent providence concerned for the well-being of his creatures. In every sense of "unmoved" he is an "unmoved mover." And now it is clear why Aristotle believed that God could not be "jealous" of human attempts to gain wisdom in respect of the first principles of being. God, according to Aristotle, does not even notice.

How could Aristotle, having sharply criticized Plato for believing that forms exist apart from sensible things, turn around and argue that at least one such form exists and is God? Aristotle would probably say that God is not a form of which sensible things "partake," but one with which they desire to identify; and because many different things can obviously have the same aspiration, there is for him no problem of the kind that arises for Plato as to the way in which many sensible things could "partake" of one and the same form. Plato could reply that if Aristotle objects to "partaking" on the grounds that it is an "empty word" and a "poetical metaphor," it can hardly be less objectionable for Aristotle to speak of God as causing motion or development by being what sensible things "desire" also to be and the object of their "love." "Love" and "desire" are themselves metaphorical as far as things lacking consciousness are concerned, and Aristotle plainly says that most things lack consciousness.

Human Nature and Its Good

Soul

Consciousness is an attribute of those living things that are capable of at least sense-perception. Life of any sort is the function of what Aristotle calls "soul" (*psyche*). This he views (in his treatise *On the Soul*) as the *form* according to which, and for the sake of which, the matter of an organism is so structured that it naturally tends to develop and display the attributes of vitality found in mature members of its species. A rudimentary type of soul (called *nutritive* soul) is found in plants, where it figures as their power to take in nourishment, assimilate it, and grow. This power is incorporated by the higher type of soul (*sensitive* soul) found in animals, which besides nutrition is responsible for their powers of sense-perception, desire, and locomotion. The powers of both nutritive and sensitive soul are incorporated by the still higher type of soul (*rational* soul) found in human beings and thanks to which we are able both to achieve theoretical knowledge and to deliberate about alternative courses of action.

Now although this classification seems quite clear-cut, Aristotle recognizes that no sharp distinctions can in practice be drawn between the lifeless and the living, between plants and animals, or between animals and human beings. He does not believe that higher organisms historically evolved from lower ones, but he does believe that the scale from lower to higher is continuous, as witness this passage from his *History of Animals:*

> In the great majority of animals there are traces of psychical qualities or attitudes, which qualities are more markedly differentiated in the case of human beings. For just as we pointed out resemblances in the physical organs, so in a number of animals we observe gentleness or fierceness, mildness or cross temper, courage or timidity, fear or confidence, high spirit or low cunning, and, with regard to intelligence, something equivalent to sagacity. Some of these qualities in man, as compared with the corresponding qualities in animals, differ only quantitatively: that is to say, a man has more or less of this quality, and an animal has more or less of some other; other qualities in man are represented by analogous and not identical qualities: for instance, just as in man we find knowledge, wisdom, and sagacity, so in certain animals there exists some other natural potentiality akin to these. The truth of this statement will be the more clearly apprehended if we have regard to the phenomena of childhood: for in children may be observed the traces and seeds of what will one day be settled psychological habits, though psychologically a child hardly differs for the time being from an animal; so that one is quite justified in saying that, as regards man and animals, certain psychical qualities are identical with one another, whilst others resemble, and others are analogous to, each other.
>
> Nature proceeds little by little from things lifeless to animal life in such a way that it is impossible to determine the exact line of demarcation, nor on which side thereof an intermediate form should lie. Thus, next after lifeless things in the upward scale comes the plant, and of plants one will differ from another as to its amount of apparent vitality; and, in a word, the whole genus of plants, whilst it is devoid of life as compared with an animal, is endowed with life as compared with other corporeal entities. Indeed, as we just remarked, there is observed in plants a continuous scale of ascent towards the animal. So, in the sea, there are certain objects concerning which one would be at a loss to determine whether they be animal or vegetable.

Aristotle's position is that soul and body are related as form and matter, constituting a single individual substance. A human soul is therefore not to be viewed, in the way that Socrates and Plato viewed it, as a thing unto itself, related to the body as a craftsman is related to his tools. "We can wholly dismiss as unnecessary," Aristotle says, "the question whether the soul and body are one: it is as meaningless as to ask whether the wax and the shape given to it by the stamp are one, or generally the matter of a thing and that of which it is the matter." It would seem, then, that it would be no less meaningless to ask whether the soul could survive the body's demise. How could the shape of the wax continue to exist after the wax is gone? So it is only to be expected that Aristotle should say, "From this it indubitably follows that the soul is inseparable from its body. . . ." The surprising thing is how he continues this sentence: ". . . or at any rate that certain parts of it are (if it has parts). . . ." After all, it appears, not everything in a human soul may be inseparably related as form to the body. There may be something left over that could exist independently.

This, it turns out, is a component of the soul to which Aristotle gives no name, but which has come to be known as the *active intellect*. He identifies this by another of his analyses based upon the distinction between potentiality and actuality. Knowledge consists of the apprehension of necessary connections among the forms of things. Of course, before we actually achieve any knowledge, there must be in our souls the potentiality for achieving it; there must be something—call it the *passive intellect*—having the capacity for apprehending all forms in much the same way as a blank writing tablet is capable of having all kinds of things inscribed upon it. Now this potentiality for knowledge cannot actualize itself any more than a tablet can inscribe something upon itself. It can be actualized only by the agency of something in our souls that actually has knowledge already—knowledge of all connections among forms—and this is the *active intellect*. The process of acquiring knowledge may thus be described in general terms as the development by active intellect of the potentiality in passive intellect. Aristotle is silent about the details of this. Presumably he conceives of active intellect as somehow cut off from our ordinary consciousness (that is, from passive intellect), so that we are not aware of the knowledge it possesses, and yet as somehow in communication with our ordinary consciousness, so as to lead it on to awareness of forms. In any case, it is the active intellect in our souls that is separable from our bodies and survives death, for the actual and active is always, Aristotle says, "superior" to the potential and passive.

A staggering amount of controversy has accumulated over the centuries in regard to Aristotle's precise view of active intellect. Does he identify active intellect with the mind of God, and is it this which is really at work in our minds and the cause of our getting knowledge? Or does he instead identify active intellect with one of the lesser cosmic "intelligences" such as he associated with the heavenly spheres? Or does he perhaps take active intellect to be a strictly human affair, although the highest component of the soul? The second alternative may be the likeliest, but Aristotle's remarks on the subject are so sketchy that neither of the other alternatives can be positively ruled out. At all events, he is sufficiently clear on one point: he does not believe that the survival of active intellect means that *we* outlast death as personalities conscious of our individual identities. We could not do this unless after death we remembered our experiences in this life. Memories, however, are entirely the business of *passive* intellect, and that, Aristotle says, dies with the body. Only some part of the soul that is capable of growth could be the possessor of memories, because they obviously grow with experience. But active intellect, which is a thing fully actual, contains no potential for growth. It is the principle by which growth in the soul is supposed to be explained. As such, it is evidently quite impersonal and the same in everyone (the same at least in content).

In his treatise *On the Generation of Animals,* Aristotle says that active intellect is "something divine" that "enters from outside" into the semen of human fathers, whereby it is transmitted to their unborn offspring. In the Christian theology of St. Thomas Aquinas (1225–1274 A.D.), this was interpreted in keeping with the doctrine that each rational soul is "created by God at the end of human generation." But Aristotle does not himself speak of "creation"; he says nothing about the manner in which active intellect "enters from outside"; and he does not explain what in this connection he means by "divine."

Ethics

"Those . . . who deny that that which all creatures seek to obtain is good," Aristotle says, "are surely talking nonsense. For what all think to be good, that, we assert, is good; and he that subverts our belief in the opinion of all mankind will hardly persuade us to believe his own either." So it is that Aristotle takes the view, which he believes everyone takes, that happiness or well-being (*eudaimonia*) is the only thing good simply on its own account, the only thing complete and self-sufficient in its goodness, and that other things are good just insofar as they minister to this. The real problem, he says, is to determine what happiness or well-being consists of, because on this point there is much less agreement; and in his *Nichomachean Ethics*[9] he proposes that the solution is to be found by ascertaining the "function" of human nature. Now the function of any sort of thing is to be understood in terms of the actualization of its distinctive potentialities. And the potentialities that are distinctive of human nature, in contrast to vegetable and animal nature, are potentialities for roughly two sorts of rational activity: the *practical* activity of governing our appetites and emotions by principles of action that are recognized to be right, and the *theoretical* activity of inquiring after necessary truths in respect of "what is noble and divine." Excellence in the

---

[9] Called "Nichomachean" perhaps because the treatise was edited by Aristotle's son, Nichomachus.

sphere of practical activity is *moral virtue,* and it requires *practical wisdom (phronesis),* which is one main form of *intellectual virtue.* Excellence in the sphere of theoretical activity involves *philosophic wisdom (sophia),* which is the other main form of intellectual virtue. Aristotle's position, then, is that human happiness, "the good of man," consists in the achievement of these specially human forms of excellence and in the possession of them throughout a lifetime. This is the "ultimate end" to which "every art and every investigation, and likewise every practical pursuit or undertaking," is to be subordinated.[10]

Moral virtue, to consider it first, is a "fixed and permanent disposition of character" from which one deliberately chooses to do what is right "for its own sake" as an excellence of practical activity. One's natural capacity for acquiring this disposition is developed less by instruction than by practice, which forms in one the habit of behaving in the way in which virtuous persons behave. "We learn an art or craft by doing the things that we shall have to do when we have learnt it: for instance, men become builders by building houses, harpers by playing the harp. Similarly we become just by doing just acts, temperate by doing temperate acts, brave by doing brave acts . . . and no one can have the remotest chance of becoming good without doing them." In time one will see for oneself the rightness of doing them and will then begin to do them for that reason. Externally right behavior will eventually flow from an inwardly upright character, provided that one grows accustomed in childhood to doing what is externally right. "It is therefore not of small moment whether we are trained from childhood in one set of habits or another; on the contrary it is of very great, or rather of supreme, importance."

Excellence of character, in Aristotle's view, consists largely in being well-disposed in respect of one's appetites and emotions, so that one indulges them neither too much nor too little. To indulge them neither too much nor too little is to observe a "mean" regarding them, which puts one in a state that is "mean" in the sense of being "just right." The correct principles to follow here are not easy to determine. In fact, "the whole theory of conduct is bound to be an outline only and not an exact science"—unlike what we expect of theoretical knowledge—because "matters of conduct have nothing fixed and invariable about them, any more than have matters of health." It is just as well to face up to this at the

---

[10] It is customary to say that Aristotle's ethical theory is *teleological* because he is usually interpreted as holding that actions are right or wrong, not in and of themselves but only insofar as they are or are not conducive as "means" to the "end" (*telos*) of happiness or well-being. Happiness or well-being, however, is not for Aristotle a *result* separate from right actions; it *consists* of right actions, of an all-around excellence of activity, sustained over the course of one's years. Happiness or well-being is an "end" to which right actions are the "means" only in the sense that happiness is a complex whole of which right actions are the temporally successive elements. Analogously, one might say that a year is the "end" to which the days making it up are the "means." And Aristotle does maintain that particular actions in specific circumstances are right or wrong, noble or ignoble, in and of themselves.

outset, "for it is the mark of an educated mind to expect that amount of exactness in each kind which the nature of the particular subject admits." Still, there is such a thing as "hitting the mean" between excess and deficiency when it comes to appetites and emotions, and indeed to actions themselves; and a good deal can be done on the basis of this to specify the notion of a virtuous disposition and to prescribe some rules of thumb for securing one. The mean for one person may not be the same as the mean for another. How much is too much or too little will depend upon individual makeup and circumstances, just as it does in the case of food or exercise, where the right amount for an athlete is not the same as it is for someone of more sedentary occupation. The mean in question is of course the mean "relative to us"—to each of us individually. This said, it remains true that "virtue has the quality of hitting the mean," and all virtuous persons do regularly manage to hit it.

> For example, one can be frightened or bold, feel desire or anger or pity, and experience pleasure or pain in general, either too much or too little, and in both cases wrongly; whereas to feel these feelings at the right time, on the right occasion, towards the right people, for the right purpose and in the right manner, is to feel the best amount of them, which is the mean amount—and the best amount is of course the mark of virtue. And similarly there can be excess, deficiency, and the due mean in actions. Now feelings and actions are the objects with which virtue is concerned; and in feelings and actions excess and deficiency are errors, while the mean amount is praised, and constitutes success; and to be praised and to be successful are both marks of virtue. Virtue, therefore, is a mean state in the sense that it is able to hit the mean. Again, error is multiform (for evil is a form of the unlimited, as in the old Pythagorean imagery, and good of the limited), whereas success is possible in one way only (which is why it is easy to fail and difficult to succeed—easy to miss the target and difficult to hit it): so this is another reason why excess and deficiency are a mark of vice, and observance of the mean a mark of virtue: goodness is simple, badness manifold.[11]
>
> Virtue then is a settled disposition of the mind determining the choice of actions and emotions, consisting essentially in the observance of the mean relative to us, this being determined by principle, that is, as the prudent man [the man of practical wisdom] would determine it.

Such is Aristotle's formal definition of "moral virtue": it belongs to the genus "settled disposition determining choice" and to the species "in accordance with the mean relative to us as identified by practical wisdom." He continues:

> And it is a mean state between two vices, one of excess and one of defect. Furthermore, it is a mean state in that whereas the vices either

---

[11] Compare the opening sentence of Tolstoy's *Anna Karenin:* "All happy families are alike, but an unhappy family is unhappy after its own fashion."

fall short of or exceed what is right in feelings and in actions, virtue ascertains and adopts the mean. Hence while in respect of its substance and the definition that states what it really is in essence, virtue is the observance of the mean, in point of excellence and rightness it is an extreme.

Aristotle discusses a number of particular moral virtues in order to show how each consists in observing a mean. "The observance of the mean in fear and confidence," he says, "is Courage. The man that exceeds in fearlessness is not designated by any special name (and this is the case with many of the virtues and vices); he that exceeds in confidence is Rash; he that exceeds in fear and is deficient in confidence is Cowardly." In other words, Courage is a mean with respect to two emotions, fear and confidence, each of which is prone to extremes of excess and deficiency that combine in pairs to produce the vices of Rashness and Cowardice. Here is a diagram showing how Aristotle conceives the situation:

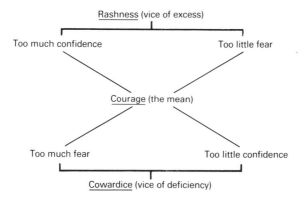

It is "easy to miss the target and difficult to hit it" because here there are *four* faulty extremes, "whereas success is possible in one way only." The same is true for many other moral virtues—for Temperance, which is a mean with respect to pleasures and pains (where Profligacy and Insensibility are the chief vices); for Liberality, which is a mean with respect to giving and getting money (where Prodigality and Meanness are the chief vices); for Greatness of Soul (or Self-respect), which is a mean with respect to honor and dishonor (where Vanity and Smallness of Soul are the chief vices); for Gentleness, which is a mean with respect to just one emotion, anger (where Irascibility and Spiritlessness are the chief vices); and so on. Aristotle recognizes, however, that the names of some emotions and actions "directly imply evil," so that there can be no question of observing a mean with respect to them. "Malice" and "adultery," for example, are names for wrongful excesses of emotion and of action respectively. "It is impossible, therefore, ever to go right in regard to them—one must always be wrong; nor does right or wrong in their case depend on the circumstances, for instance, whether one commits adultery with the right woman, at the right time, and in the right manner; the mere commission of any of them is wrong." This goes also for shameless-ness, envy, theft, and murder. Nevertheless, a number of emotions, ap-petites, and actions (viewed in the abstract) are neither good nor bad in themselves; there is a right object, time, manner, and amount—in short, a mean—with respect to each of them.

Hitting the mean is all the more difficult because it is usually more opposed to one vice than it is to another. We cannot simply make a point of keeping, so to speak, an equal distance from each vice. Courage, for instance, is more opposed to Cowardice (a vice of deficiency) than it is to Rashness (a vice of excess), and Rashness is generally the lesser of the two evils. Temperance is more opposed to Profligacy (a vice of excess) than it is to Insensibility (a vice of deficiency), and Insensibility is gen-erally the lesser of the two evils. Accordingly, we can take it as a kind of rule "to avoid that extreme which is most opposed to the mean"; and if err we must, we should endeavor "to take the least of the evils." Of course, one is likely by nature to be attracted more to some vices than to others—more to Profligacy, say, than to Insensibility—as we may learn by ob-serving which vices seem to us more pleasurable, or at any rate less unpleasurable, than their alternatives. Thus we can formulate a second rule, "to notice what are the errors to which we are ourselves most prone . . . and drag ourselves away in the opposite direction, for by steering wide of our besetting error we shall make a middle course." And this leads directly to a third rule: "We must in everything be most of all on guard against what is pleasant and against pleasure; for when pleasure is on her trial we are not impartial judges [and] if we roundly bid her be gone, we shall be less likely to err." Needless to say, it is not always easy to resist the temptations of pleasure; "but virtue, like art, is constantly dealing with what is harder, since the harder the task the better is suc-cess."[12]

Pleasure, Aristotle believes, naturally accompanies the unimpeded ex-ercise of any of our faculties of sensation and reason. Everyone desires pleasure who desires life itself, because life for humankind involves ac-tivities of sensation and reason which in normal health and circum-stances are pleasurable and which are augmented by being so. Pleasure comes with these activities as "a supervening perfection, like the bloom of health in the young and vigorous." This is not to say, however, that the accompanying pleasure is what makes these activities worth perform-ing. "There are many things which we should be eager to possess even if they brought us no pleasure, for instance, sight, memory, knowledge, vir-tue. It may be the case that these things are necessarily attended by

---

[12] Another translation of the same words: "But both art and virtue are always con-cerned with what is harder; for even the good is better when it is harder."

pleasure, but that makes no difference; for we should desire them even if no pleasure resulted from them." And in fact there are special circumstances in which pleasure certainly does not result from them, as Aristotle observes in regard to the virtue of Courage: "The death or wounds that it may bring will be painful to the courageous man, and he will suffer them unwillingly; but he will endure them because it is noble to do so, or because it is base not to do so." ("For to do noble and virtuous deeds is a thing desirable for its own sake.") If considerations of nobility and baseness can in extreme situations override considerations of pleasure altogether, they can also require us in everyday circumstances to forgo certain pleasures in favor of others; for pleasures differ in quality according to the moral value of the activities with which they are associated. "Since activities differ in moral value, and some are to be adopted, others to be avoided, and others again are neutral, the same is true also of their pleasures: for each activity has a pleasure of its own. Thus the pleasure of a good activity is morally good, that of a bad one morally bad. . . . The standard of everything is goodness, or the good man, *qua* good."

Of the pleasures that a good man finds "respectable," the best in quality are those that normally accompany the distinctively human activities of practical and theoretical reason. The excellent performance of *these activities* is what constitutes human happiness or well-being. For Aristotle, then, pleasure is a usual *accompaniment* of happiness or well-being, not the sum and substance of happiness or well-being. It is characteristic of a virtuous person to take pleasure in virtuous action. Of course, virtuous action is given scope and is all the pleasanter when one has the good fortune to be supplied with "certain external advantages" in the way of family background, personal appearance, financial success, and the like; but these are by no means essential.

> Great and repeated successes will render life more blissful, since both of their own nature they help to embellish it, and also they can be nobly and virtuously utilized; while great and repeated reverses can crush and mar our bliss both by the pain they cause and by the hindrance they offer to many activities. Yet nevertheless even in adversity nobility shines through, when a man endures great and repeated misfortune with patience, not owing to insensibility but from generosity and greatness of soul. And if, as we said, a man's life is determined by his activities, no supremely happy man can ever become miserable. For he will never do hateful or base actions, since we hold that the truly good and wise man will bear all kinds of misfortune in a seemly way, and will always act in the noblest manner that the circumstances allow, even as a good general makes the most effective use of the forces at his disposal. . . .

To act in the noblest manner that the circumstances allow, be the circumstances fortunate or unfortunate, calls for practical wisdom, which is the power of deliberating well about what is conducive to "the good life in general." Practical wisdom is an excellence or virtue of intellect which includes both knowledge of general principles and perceptiveness in re-gard to particular facts—general principles concerning the conditions of human happiness (especially principles relating to the mean in emotions and appetites) and particular facts pertaining to the application of these principles in given circumstances—from which one arrives at conclusions as to the right thing to do, on the right grounds, and at the right time. If moral virtue is a settled disposition determining choice in accordance with the mean relative to us, then the intellectual virtue of practical wisdom is our power of determining in any situation what the mean is. Without practical wisdom our natural capacity for a virtuous disposition is very likely to develop into something harmful. Practical wisdom supplies a virtuous disposition with the eyes, as it were, without which it would be blind and fumbling. "If a man of good natural disposition acquires Intelligence [practical wisdom], then he excels in conduct, and the disposition which previously only resembled Virtue will now be Virtue in the true sense." Aristotle accordingly says that Socrates was right up to a point: moral virtue *implies* practical wisdom, but it cannot be *identified* with practical wisdom as Socrates supposed—for the former is an excellence of character or disposition, whereas the latter is an excellence of intellect.

Aristotle wishes to take sharper exception to Socrates' view that one cannot knowingly do what one believes to be wrong. "This theory," Aristotle says, "is at variance with plain facts"—above all with the fact of what he calls "Unrestraint" ("Incontinence" in some translations), which is the giving in to seductions of gross appetite or emotion while knowing that it is wrong to do so. But the more Aristotle considers this phenomenon, the less reason he finds really to disagree with Socrates. Everything hinges upon the extent to which the Unrestrained person can be supposed to "know" that his or her Unrestraint is wrong; and when he gets down to it, Aristotle can think of only the following possibilities. At the time of yielding to temptation, the person may "know" in just a *potential* sense the wrongness of Unrestraint in general and in the case at hand: the knowledge, that is, may be at the back of the person's mind but not actually present in consciousness. This happens in an extreme way when the passion of the moment is so intoxicating that the person, like someone actually drunk, cannot be conscious of the knowledge, or recognize its importance, until sober again. "It is evident," Aristotle says, "that anger, sexual desire, and certain other passions actually alter the state of the body, and in some cases even cause madness." Alternatively, the person might be perfectly aware of the wrongness of Unrestraint in general but quite ignorant (not even potentially aware) of the fact that the sort of thing he or she is doing at the moment is really a case of Unrestraint. Or yet again, the person might be perfectly aware of the wrongness of Unrestraint in general but only *potentially* aware that the sort of thing in question is a case of it; and this potential knowledge may for the time being remain just potential because the person is overwhelmed by some emotion or desire.

Such are the possible ways in which Aristotle finds that one can "know" the wrongness of what one is doing while one is doing it, but in none of them is one fully aware of the wrongness. "We do seem," Aristotle admits, "to be led to the conclusion which Socrates sought to establish." This in turn would seem to imply that no one can *voluntarily* do what is wrong, which would mean that no one can be held *accountable* for doing what is wrong. Aristotle himself says that an action is not voluntary if one does it under compulsion or through ignorance of its nature, circumstances, or effects—ignorance, that is, that is not attributable to one's own negligence or carelessness. Now it might be said that carelessness could be a factor in each of the situations mentioned. One could be accountably careless for not being fully aware of the wrongness of Unrestraint in general and in the particular case at hand. One could be accountably careless for having allowed oneself to develop a character that is so susceptible to the intoxications of passion that one loses control of one's thoughts and actions. Aristotle, as a matter of fact, does say just these things; and he maintains that careless persons have no excuse for their carelessness. "Men are themselves responsible for having become careless through living carelessly, as they are for being unjust or profligate if they do wrong or pass their time in drinking and dissipation. They acquire a particular quality by constantly acting in a particular way. . . . The unjust and profligate might at the outset have avoided becoming so, and therefore they are so voluntarily, although when they have become unjust and profligate it is no longer open to them not to be so." But now the question arises again: did these people know "at the outset," when they began to act in the ways that formed their careless habits, that they were doing something wrong? Aristotle appears to want to hold that they did; but as we have seen from his analysis of Unrestraint, he is unable to discover an interpretation of the facts that really distinguishes his position from Socrates'.

A particularly notable feature of the *Nichomachean Ethics* is the extensive treatment given to *friendship,* in the wide sense of the Greek word *philia,* which includes any sort of kindly feeling (from liking to affection and love) between two persons, and which Aristotle considers "one of the most indispensable requirements of life":

Friends are an aid to the young, to guard them from error; to the elderly, to tend them and to supplement their failing powers of action; to those in the prime of life, to assist them in noble deeds . . . for two are better able both to plan and to execute. . . . Moreover, friendship appears to be the bond of the state; and lawgivers seem to set more store by it than they do by justice, for to promote concord, which seems akin to friendship, is their chief aim, while faction, which is enmity, is what they are most anxious to banish. And if men are friends, there is no need of justice between them; whereas merely to be just is not enough—a feeling of friendship also is necessary. Indeed the highest form of justice seems to have an element of friendly feeling in it.

In order to be friends, two persons "must feel goodwill for each other, that is, wish each other's good, and be aware of each other's goodwill." The basis of their mutual goodwill can be, roughly speaking, one or the other of three things: their *usefulness* to one another in broadly economic respects; the *pleasure* they derive from one another's company; and their regard for one another's *goodness*. Friendships based simply upon usefulness or pleasure last only so long as the persons involved are useful or sources of pleasure to one another. The "good" they wish each other is that they should *remain* useful or pleasure-giving, and should become even more so. Neither takes an interest in the other for the other's own sake. The fondness of each for the other derives entirely from the personal benefits each expects from the other. Such friendships, although hardly unimportant, are not of the finest type. Besides being precarious and self-interested, they can exist between persons of bad character. "The perfect form of friendship is that between the good, and those who resemble each other in virtue. For these friends wish each alike the other's good in respect of their goodness, and they are good in themselves; but it is those who wish the good of their friends for their friends' sake who are friends in the fullest sense, since they love each other for themselves and not accidentally [that is, not for temporary qualities such as usefulness or pleasurableness]. Hence the friendship of these lasts as long as they continue to be good; and virtue is a permanent quality. . . . Such friendships are of course rare, because such men are few." Naturally friends of this kind are useful to one another and enjoy being together; but they are useful because each wishes to facilitate the other's excellence, and their enjoyment comes with their doing so. "Amity consists in equality and similarity, especially the similarity of those who are alike in virtue; for being true to themselves, these also remain true to one another, and neither request nor render services that are morally degrading. Indeed they may be said to restrain each other from evil: since good men neither err themselves nor permit their friends to err. Bad men on the other hand have no constancy in friendship, for they do not even remain true to their own characters; but they can be friends for a short time, while they take pleasure in each other's wickedness."

The most interesting aspect of Aristotle's treatment of friendship is his view that friendly feelings for others derive from the feelings of regard that a person of good character has for himself or herself, "for a friend is another self." If one is virtuous, one so extends one's interests that the well-being of others becomes precisely as direct a matter of personal concern as one's own well-being. So it is that in a "friendship of virtue" each person promotes the other's true good, delights in the other's company, and shares in the other's joys and sorrows, just as each promotes his or her own true good, delights in his or her own company (for only persons of bad character dislike their own company), and feels his or her own joys and sorrows. Aristotle realizes that this position may be criticized on the grounds that it is egoistic: if "all the feelings that constitute friendship for others are an extension of regard for self," does not this mean that even the deepest love for others is only a form of love for oneself? Aristotle replies by pointing out that self-love is by no means a bad thing if the self one loves is the right kind of self—a self, that is, which is bent on securing the highest attainable degree of moral nobility, not on appropriating "the larger share of money, honors, or bodily pleasures." Just consider: "If all men vied with each other in moral nobility and strove to perform the noblest deeds, the common welfare would be fully realized, while individuals also could enjoy the greatest of goods, inasmuch as virtue is the greatest good. Therefore the good man ought to be a lover of self, since he will then both benefit himself by acting nobly and aid his fellows; but the bad man ought not to be a lover of self, since he will follow his base passions, and so injure himself and his neighbors."

"Virtue is the greatest good"—meaning *moral* virtue—does not, however, accurately express Aristotle's final view of human happiness or well-being. Toward the end of the *Nichomachean Ethics* he considers our power of apprehending first principles, such as those in metaphysics; and he finds that the proficient exercise of this, which constitutes the intellectual virtue of philosophic wisdom, is on several counts superior to moral virtue. It consists in contemplation of things that are eternal and unchanging, which are the best things of all. It is capable of being sustained longer than any of our other activities; it affords pleasure of unique purity and permanence; it is least dependent upon other persons and material goods; it aims at nothing beyond itself; and it is the only form of activity that can be ascribed to God. The contemplation of divine matters brings into play the element in us that is most akin to the divine, namely, our intellect, and thereby "so far as possible" we achieve immortality. The trouble, however, is that a life of contemplation only is "higher than the human level." We are composite creatures, with bodies and passions as well as intellects; and for the most part we are capable only of that "secondary degree" of happiness associated with moral virtue and practical wisdom, which concern the feelings and needs of our mortal nature. Nevertheless, we should pay no attention to "those who enjoin that a man should have man's thoughts and a mortal the thoughts of mortality"; instead, we should always do what we can to live in accordance with "the best part of us" and to have "cognizance of what is noble and divine."

In a practical field such as ethics, the aim is not to achieve theoretical knowledge of various matters but, rather, to carry out our findings in action. Thus it is not enough simply to know what virtue is; we must try to acquire it and to act accordingly, and thereby to become good. Treatises on ethics have some usefulness in this connection, as stimulating a desire for virtue in persons of generous natural disposition and good upbringing, but over others their influence is nil. "For it is the nature of the many to be amenable to fear but not to a sense of honor, and to abstain from evil not because of its baseness but because of the penalties it entails. . . ." Accordingly, it is essential that a community be governed by laws that promote good education for children and that provide sanctions against misconduct on the part of those adults who are "disobedient and ill-conditioned." Which laws are best for a given community is the subject of the science of legislation—a branch of *political science,* which deals with the whole question of the proper constitution of states. Political science is really the most authoritative of all the sciences, "for it is this that ordains which of the [other] sciences are to exist in states, and what branches of knowledge the different classes of citizens are to learn, and up to what point." Ethics, which investigates excellence of individual character, is itself subordinate to political science, which investigates the good of the whole state—"manifestly a greater and more perfect good, both to attain and to preserve." So Aristotle insists that the study of ethics leads straight to the study of politics.

Politics

An independent city-state (*polis*), such as Athens or Sparta, is in Aristotle's opinion the kind of political organization that has the greatest potential for fostering human happiness or well-being. Throughout his *Politics* he is concerned with "the state" in this sense. Human beings, he says, are "political animals" by nature, for only by sharing in the life of a community can their capacities be developed. Contrary to what the Sophists supposed, a state is not a mere creature of "convention" without any serious claim on the allegiance of its citizens. Human beings have of necessity always lived in communities of some sort—at least in families for assistance in meeting basic needs, perhaps in villages so as to achieve something more than a bare subsistence. And a state comes into being when villages pool their resources to form a community that is "large enough to be nearly or quite self-sufficing," so that not only life but a good life may be feasible. Because a good life is the natural "end" of a human being, the state is a natural form of human society. Anyone capable of a satisfactory existence apart from society must be "either a beast or a god." The capacity of human beings for speech, enabling them "to set forth the expedient and inexpedient, and therefore likewise the just and the unjust," is an unmistakable indication that nature has destined them for social life. Under conditions of law and justice, human beings are capable of becoming the best of animals; without law and justice, they are the worst of animals—the most savage, lustful, and voracious. But the rule of law and the administration of justice cannot be effective if a community's population is enormous: "A very great multitude cannot be orderly: to introduce order into the unlimited is the work of a divine power—of such a power as holds together the universe." Moreover, citizens must not be so numerous that they cannot all know one another, for then they would be unable to determine who among them is worthiest of public office. "Clearly, then, the best limit of the population of a state is the largest number which suffices for the purposes of life [that is, a good life], and can be taken in at a single view." In other words, a city-state on the Greek model is the best for size.[13]

Although this type of community is the object of Aristotle's attention, much of his *Politics* is still pertinent to the governing of modern nations. It is possible to be discouraged from appreciating this, however, by the shock of encountering within the first few pages an attempt to defend the institution of slavery. Aristotle presumes that human beings are distinguishable into two groups, one of them comprising persons who are born with the capacity for acting rationally on their own, the other comprising persons who are born with the capacity for acting rationally only when someone else tells them what to do. And he maintains that those in the second group should be subservient to those in the first for the same reason that an individual's body should be subservient to the soul. "That some should rule and others be ruled is a thing not only necessary, but expedient; from the hour of their birth, some are marked out for subjection, others for rule." This is in the best interests of all concerned. Those who are "slaves by nature" live the best lives of which they are capable when they serve as "living instruments" of those who by nature are "masters" and whose activity is thereby facilitated. "For that which can foresee by the exercise of mind is by nature intended to be lord and master, and that which can with its body give effect to such foresight is a subject, and by nature a slave; hence master and slave have the same interest." Slaves, having by themselves negligible capacity for rational action, "have no share in happiness"—unless perhaps they share vicariously in the happiness they make possible for their masters.

The inhumaneness of this position seems hardly the less for the qualifications Aristotle adds to it. He says that the distinction between natural slaves and natural masters is not always clear, that children of natural slaves are not always natural slaves, that persons are not to be treated as slaves merely on the basis that they have been conquered in war, that masters should not abuse their authority and should be "friends" with their slaves, that slaves should be reasoned with and not simply commanded, and that "liberty should always be held out to them as the reward of their services."

That Aristotle should attempt to justify slavery is not, however, really surprising. Slavery had existed from time immemorial all over the world. It was an entrenched institution of Greek society. Plato takes it for granted in his *Laws*. Aristotle may even have been viewed as something of a revolutionary for speaking against slavery "by right of military conquest," and the matter for wonder is that anyone in ancient Greece gave thought to slavery or questioned it at all. Until the Thirteenth Amend-

---

[13] Historians have disagreed widely about the probable population of Greek city-states. For example, the population of Athens in her prime has been put at anywhere from 200,000 to 400,000 or more. Perhaps only about a third of the total (whatever it was exactly) were citizens; the rest were slaves (somewhat more than a third) and resident-foreigners.

ment of 1865, slavery was not abolished in the Constitution of the United States. But the first person who is known to have condemned slavery was in fact a Greek, the playwright Euripides, who died about twenty years before Aristotle was born. "Slavery," he says in his *Hecuba:*

> That thing of evil, by its nature evil,
> Forcing submission from a man to what
> No man should yield to.

So radical a departure from the conventional view was not for Aristotle. His general satisfaction with existing Athenian institutions is also shown, much less objectionably, in his criticism of Plato's proposal in the *Republic* that government officials (the Guardians and Auxiliaries) be forbidden the ownership of private property. He seems to think that Plato believed it best for private property to be abolished entirely, whereas Plato in fact held that all except government officials should have it, in moderation, but what Aristotle says is interesting on its own account and in spite of this inaccuracy. He argues that the prevailing system of private property, if reformed and regulated in certain respects, is superior on several counts to a system in which people have everything in common.

There is always a difficulty in men living together and having all human relations in common, but especially in their having common property. The partnerships of fellow-travellers are an example to the point; for they generally fall out over everyday matters and quarrel about any trifle which turns up. So with servants: we are most liable to take offence at those with whom we most frequently come into contact in daily life.

These are only some of the disadvantages which attend the community of property; the present arrangement, if improved as it might be by customs and laws, would be far better, and would have the advantages of both systems. Property should be in a certain sense common, but as a general rule private; for when everyone has a distinct interest, men will not complain of one another, and they will make more progress, because everyone will be attending to his own business. And yet by reason of goodness, and in respect of use, "Friends," as the proverb says, "will have all things in common." Even now there are traces of such a principle, showing that it is not impracticable, but in well-ordered states exists already to a certain extent and may be carried further. For although every man has his own property, some things he will place at the disposal of his friends, while of others he shares the use with them. The Lacedaemonians, for example, use one another's slaves, and horses, and dogs, as if they were their own; and when they lack provisions on a journey, they appropriate what they find in the fields throughout the country. It is clearly better that property should be private, but the use of it common; and the special business of the legislator is to create in men this benevolent disposition. Again, how immeasurably greater is the pleasure, when a man feels a thing to be his own. . . . And . . . there is the greatest pleasure in doing a kindness or service to friends or guests or companions, which can only be rendered when a man has private property. These advantages are lost by excessive unification of the state. . . . No one, when men have all things in common, will any longer set an example of liberality or do any liberal action; for liberality consists in the use which is made of property.

Such legislation [abolishing private property] may have a specious appearance of benevolence; men readily listen to it, and are easily induced to believe that in some wonderful manner everybody will become everybody's friend, especially when someone is heard denouncing the evils now existing in states, suits about contracts, convictions for perjury, flatteries of rich men, and the like, which are said to arise out of the possession of private property. These evils, however, are due to a very different cause—the wickedness of human nature. Indeed, we see that there is much more quarrelling among those who have all things in common, though there are not so many of them when compared with the vast numbers who have private property.

Again, we ought to reckon not only the evils from which the citizens will be saved, but also the advantages which they will lose. The life which they [the citizens in Plato's *Republic*] are to lead appears to be quite impracticable. The error of Socrates [that is, of Plato in the *Republic*] must be attributed to the false notion of unity from which he starts. Unity there should be, both of the family and of the state, but in some respects only. For there is a point at which a state may attain such a degree of unity as to be no longer a state, or at which, without actually ceasing to exist, it will become an inferior state, like harmony passing into unison, or rhythm which has been reduced to a single foot. The state, as I was saying, is a plurality, which should be united and made into a community by education. . . .

If the institution of private property should be reformed instead of abolished, then should one of the reforms be the redistribution of property, so that everyone will have an equal amount of it? Some advocate this as a cure for crime: because no one would be in want (the argument runs), no one would be impelled to rob or steal in order to live. But Aristotle points out that the most serious crimes are not committed for necessities; they are committed from uncontrolled desires for nonessentials—for pleasure, money, and power far beyond anything needful. "Men do not become tyrants in order that they may not suffer cold." It is true that equalization of property would do something to keep people from quarreling, but it would not do much. The main cause of social unrest is the insatiable greed of humankind: "Men always want more and more without end; for it is of the nature of desire never to be satisfied, and most men live only for the gratification of it." Reformers must first of all come to terms with this. "The beginning of reform is not so much to equalize property as to train the nobler sort of natures not to desire more, and to prevent the lower from getting more; that is to say, they must be kept down, but not ill-treated."

Governments that adhere to strict principles of justice and endeavor to promote the best interests of all their citizens are the only "true" governments. There are three forms of these: *monarchy,* in which supreme authority is exercised by one man[14]; *aristocracy,* in which it is exercised by "more than one, but not many"; and *polity,* in which it is exercised by "the citizens at large," or more precisely, by males meeting a certain property requirement. Monarchy and aristocracy are governments by persons of exceptional all-around virtue. Polity is government by a larger group whose members have in common a narrower excellence—"military virtue"—for this is a perfection that the many who have little capacity for wisdom can share with the few who are blessed with more. To these "true" forms of government there correspond forms that are "defective and perverted" in which the rulers look to their own selfish interests and disregard the well-being of the state as a whole. *Tyranny* thus corresponds to monarchy, *oligarchy* to aristocracy, and *democracy* to polity. "For tyranny is a kind of monarchy which has in view the interest of the monarch only; oligarchy has in view the interest of the wealthy; democracy, of the needy: none of them the common good of all."

Oligarchs and democrats, unlike tyrants, do not simply cast aside all considerations of justice. They explicitly appeal to justice in support of their positions and programs, and they even agree that justice consists in equality of rights for equals and inequality of rights for unequals—a view which Aristotle himself accepts. What they disagree about is the test for determining who are equals and who are unequals. Oligarchs insist that the test is wealth and that only the wealthy should participate in the legislative, executive, and judicial functions of the state. Democrats insist that the test is free birth and that all who are not slaves should enjoy the same political rights. In Aristotle's opinion, however, both parties are mistaken, for the true test of equality is goodness and goodness alone, and only the best men available—"best" on the score of moral and intellectual virtue—are entitled to exercise the powers of government.

A state is not a mere society, having a common place, established for the prevention of mutual crime and for the sake of exchange. These are conditions without which a state cannot exist; but all of them together do not constitute a state, which is a community of families and aggregations of families [villages] in well-being, for the sake of a perfect and self-sufficing life. . . . Political society exists for the sake of noble actions, and not of mere companionship. Hence they who contribute most

[14] It is regrettable that Aristotle does not share Plato's estimate of the political capacity of women. "Although there may be exceptions to the order of nature," Aristotle says, "the male is by nature fitter for command than the female, just as the elder and full-grown is superior to the younger and more immature." He allows that women, unlike slaves, do possess a "deliberative faculty," but he swiftly dismisses it as "without authority" and quotes with approval a line from Sophocles: "Silence is a woman's glory."

to such a society have a greater share in it than those who have the same or greater freedom or nobility of birth but are inferior to them in political virtue; or than those who exceed them in wealth but are surpassed by them in virtue.

From this point of view, Aristotle says, the best form of government would be a monarchy in which a man of godlike excellence had supreme power. In the absence of such a man, the best government would be an aristocracy of several men of outstanding, if not divine, moral and intellectual virtue, who alone would enjoy full citizenship and who would take turns in ruling and in being ruled. Men such as these are hardly abundant either, and so the best that we are likely in practice to get is the form of government known as "polity," which does not require "a standard of virtue which is above ordinary persons," and which to all intents and purposes is government by the middle class.

In every state there are three classes—one rich, one poor, and one in the middle. Those in the middle are the best situated as far as morality is concerned, for moderate possessions are most conducive to that "disposition to choose according to the mean" in which moral virtue consists. They are "most ready to follow rational principle" in general; and as regards politics in particular, they are likeliest to desire public office neither too much nor too little, and they tend to be the most law-abiding. Rich people, by and large, "are neither willing nor able to submit to authority." Poor people do not know how to exercise authority, are given to all kinds of rascality, and "must be ruled like slaves." The rich despise the poor; the poor envy the rich. "Nothing can be more fatal to friendship and good fellowship in states than this." What is wanted is leadership by a strong middle class, neither envied by the poor nor envious of the rich, that both sides will trust to arbitrate between them.

> Thus it is manifest that the best political community is formed by citizens of the middle class, and that those states are likely to be well-administered in which the middle class is large, and stronger if possible than both the other classes, or at any rate than either singly; for the addition of the middle class turns the scale, and prevents either of the extremes from being dominant. . . . In that case there will be no fear that rich will unite with the poor against the rulers. For neither of them will ever be willing to serve the other, and if they look for some form of government more suitable to both, they will find nothing better than this, for the rich and poor will never consent to rule in turn, because they mistrust one another. The arbiter is always the one trusted, and he who is in the middle is an arbiter.

A polity is reached by steering a middle course between oligarchy and democracy; the idea is to take "a portion from each" and "put the two together." The best form of government, practically speaking, is therefore a "fusion" of two of the worst, or a "mean" between them in somewhat the same way as a moral virtue is a mean between two vices. Aristotle says disappointingly little about the constitution that should result from this, but he says enough to make it clear that he takes the Athenian constitution of 411 B.C. as a sort of model. This was drafted by the statesman Theramenes, around whom there had gathered a sizable party of men who were dissatisfied with the Athenian democracy on account of its mismanagement of affairs relating to the Peloponnesian War but who also wished to avoid the opposite extreme of oligarchy. They were able to get Theramenes' constitution adopted for about a year. This replaced the vast popular Assembly with a body of Five Thousand, elected from the middle class (to be eligible a man had to be able to furnish himself with certain military weapons) by representatives from each of the ten religious associations ("tribes") making up the citizenry of Athens. The system of paying citizens for rendering services to the state, a system essential to the democracy, was abolished. The Five Thousand were divided into four equal parts, and each part was to act as the governing Council for a year in turn and to elect magistrates and generals from its own number. Aristotle's high regard for this constitution was shared by Thucydides: "Indeed," Thucydides says, "during the first period of this new regime the Athenians appear to have had better government than ever before, at least in my time. There was a reasonable and moderate blending of the few and the many, and it was this, in the first place, that made it possible for the city to recover from the bad state into which her affairs had fallen."

One of the most interesting sections of the *Politics* is devoted to the causes and preventives of revolution. Aristotle traces the causes to one-sided notions of justice—to the belief of democrats that persons of free birth have equal rights in everything, to the belief of oligarchs that persons of unequal wealth have unequal rights in everything. The high-handedness to which the side in power is prone—persecution of the wealthy by democrats, oppression of the poor by oligarchs—tends to consolidate the opposition of the other side, which sooner or later will probably try to seize control at any cost. Reckless behavior on all sides is best prevented in a polity; but for a state in which the middle class is small, democracy or oligarchy "may yet be a good enough government" if only it will observe certain principles of which the wisdom has time and again been shown by the actual history of states. A spirit of obedience to law should be jealously maintained. No transgression is small enough to be tolerated. Special care should be taken that no one acquires too much power, whether in money or in friends, and anyone who does is to be exiled. An increase of prosperity in any part of the state is a danger which should be met by giving a certain amount of power to leading figures from opposite elements. Every state should above all be so constituted that its public officials cannot possibly make money out of their positions. An oligarchy must be particularly careful about this. "For the people do not take any great offense at being kept out of the government—indeed they are rather pleased than otherwise at having leisure for their private business—but what irritates them is to think that their rulers are stealing the public money." Everything possible should be done to insure that high offices are filled only by persons of outstanding administrative ability who will be loyal to the constitution and who are conspicuous for "virtue and justice of the kind proper to each form of government." To this end nothing is more important than an education that is adapted to the government in question. "The best laws, though sanctioned by every citizen of the state, will be of no avail unless the young are trained by habit and education in the spirit of the constitution, if the laws are democratical, then democratically, or oligarchically, if the laws are oligarchical."

Education is the subject with which Aristotle closes the *Politics*. "The citizen," he says, "should be molded to suit the form of government under which he lives." As this is a matter of the greatest common interest, education should be public, compulsory, and the same for all—for all male citizens, that is, not for women or for inhabitants of the state from whom citizenship is to be withheld. Slaves will not be citizens, nor will manual laborers, for it is Aristotle's position that they also are incapable of participating—as citizens should—in affairs of government. Manual laborers have no spare time for public service; and on top of this, Aristotle says, the work they do "absorbs" and "degrades" their minds to such an extent that they cannot be counted upon to exercise good judgment in relation to public interests. Children destined for citizenship must therefore be instructed in only those subjects by which their minds will be liberated instead of narrowed, and it is only with *liberal* education that Aristotle is concerned. Reading, writing, gymnastics, music, drawing, and so forth, are to be taught in such a way as to foster in children habits of good citizenship—"in the spirit of the constitution."

One detail of Aristotle's scheme of education is particularly worth mentioning. He would have children listen occasionally to music of the most "exciting and emotional" kind. Plato had in the *Republic* proposed to ban everywhere in society all except two forms of music—one expressive of courage, as he thought, the other expressive of temperance. Music of any other sort, Plato said, has an unstabilizing effect upon the soul, making it slack, moody, unrestrained, or what not. For the same reason he proposed to suppress all poetry except that praising gods and good men. Tragic drama is especially to be forbidden, on the grounds that the pity it calls up in us for the suffering hero in the play will encourage in us habits of self-pity. Aristotle disagrees with all this. He holds that exciting and emotional music, in moderation, is positively good for the soul. Like a medicine that purges us of an excess of some bodily "humor," sensational music purges the soul of excess emotions which otherwise would make for unhealthy psychological conditions. "For feelings such as pity and fear, or again, enthusiasm, exist very strongly in some souls and have more or less influence over all. Some persons fall into a religious frenzy, whom we see as a result of the sacred melodies—when they have used the melodies that excite the soul to mystic frenzy—restored as though they had found healing and purgation. Those who are influenced by pity or fear, and every emotional nature, must have a like experience, and others insofar as each is susceptible to such emotions, and all are in a manner purged and their souls lightened and delighted." The souls of children, then, are to be lightened and delighted, in the intervals of their classwork, by performances of suitably purgative compositions.

The same kind of purgation (*catharsis*), Aristotle says, is effected by attending the performance of a tragic drama. In the *Poetics,* where he analyzes the elements and structure of this form of literature, a tragedy is defined in these famous words: "A tragedy, then, is the imitation of an action that is serious and also, as having magnitude, complete in itself; in language with pleasurable accessories, each kind brought in separately in the parts of the work; in a dramatic, not in a narrative form; with incidents arousing pity and fear, wherewith to accomplish its catharsis of such emotions." A tragedy evokes our sympathy for an impersonated figure much like ourselves, not exceptional for either virtue or vice, who suffers unmerited misfortune because of some frailty or some error of judgment. The story of the play may be based more or less closely upon actual events, or upon what are commonly believed to have been actual events, as in the case of legends and myths. But these are poetically managed to heighten their dramatic effect. The relation between the frailty or error and the misfortune in the chief character's life is made to stand out by omitting from the play all details irrelevant to this and by modifying other details as necessary. The dramatist's aim is not simply to retell history in a "literary" way. It is to portray "a kind of thing that might happen"—a relation between events that is "universal" in the sense that it might occur in the life of any of us. The poetry of a tragic drama, then, is of wider significance and weightier concern than an historical account of what once happened to a particular individual. "Poetry," Aristotle says, "is something more philosophic and of graver import than history, since its statements are of the nature rather of universals, whereas those of history are singulars."

Although poetry was superior to history in his estimation, Aristotle was still keenly interested in historical research and writing. During his later days at the Lyceum, for example, he promoted among his associates a scheme for a vast collective work on the history of philosophy and the sciences. He was the first to see the need for historical writing of this kind—"intellectual history," as it is now called. Theophrastus took in hand that part of the project that concerned physical and metaphysical systems (from Thales to Plato); and the resulting eighteen books—now largely lost, but much quoted in works that survive—are our main source of information about the Pre-Socratic philosophers. Aristotle's importance as the pioneer promoter of intellectual history has seldom been appreciated.

What is owed to him in this regard has been eclipsed by what is owed to him in logic, metaphysics, ethics, politics, and the other fields in which "the mind of the school" has exercised an immeasurable influence. Much will be said of this influence below, particularly when we come to the Muslim, Jewish, and Christian thinkers of the Middle Ages. We have now to see the new directions taken by philosophy within a few years of Aristotle's death.

PART III

Hellenistic and Roman Philosophy

For nearly fifty years after the death of Alexander the Great (323 B.C.), his former generals and their descendants fought among themselves for control of his vast Macedonian Empire. By 276 B.C. the families of three of these generals—Ptolemy, Seleucus, and Antigonus—had each secured a portion of the empire: the Ptolemies were supreme in Egypt and Palestine, the Seleucids in Asia Minor and Syria, and the Antigonids in Greece and Macedon. The diffusion of Greek culture into Egypt and the Near East during the next two and a half centuries is signified by calling this the Hellenistic Age of ancient Western history, in contrast with the preceding Hellenic Age of cultural greatness in the original Greek territories.[1]

Before the Hellenistic period closed with the annexation of Egypt by Rome in 31 B.C., important developments in almost every field of the arts and sciences had occurred in the new regions of Greek influence—especially at Alexandria in Egypt, which the Ptolemies made their capital and which, thanks to their patronage, became the leading cultural center of the age. Athens, as we shall see, continued to attract philosophers, but she was not to have another of the caliber of Plato or Aristotle, and in intellectual vitality she was soon surpassed by Alexandria. There the Ptolemies sponsored two magnificent libraries that grew into a combined collection of about 700,000 volumes (or papyrus rolls). The librarians whom the Ptolemies employed were innovators of rigorous scholarship: the most famous of them, Aristarchus of Samothrace, is said to have written no fewer than 800 volumes of textual commentary. His critical editions of Homer's *Iliad* and *Odyssey* are responsible for the excellent texts of these

---

[1] "Hellenic" and "Hellenistic" both come from *hellen,* the Greek word for a Greek person.

works that survive today. Around the museum to which one of the libraries was attached there sprang up a university to which eminent scientists and mathematicians were drawn: Herophilus, the founder of scientific anatomy; Euclid, whose *Elements* was to be the textbook of geometry for 2,000 years; Apollonius of Perga, whose treatise on conic sections marked the culmination of Greek mathematics; Hipparchus, the first known systematic astronomer, who charted the positions of some 850 stars and who calculated the moon's distance from the earth (with remarkable accuracy, as regards the average distance); Eratosthenes, the astronomer who calculated the circumference of the earth (with an error of only about 170 miles); Aristarchus of Samos, the astronomer who first proposed the Heliocentric Theory—revived by Copernicus in the sixteenth century A.D.—according to which the earth orbits around the sun and the sun is at rest; and Archimedes—who studied in Alexandria but lived mostly in Syracuse—the mathematician, physicist, and inventor, whose many accomplishments included calculating the value of *pi* (the ratio of the circumference of a circle to its diameter).

Alexandria was equally notable as a center for the exchange and development of religious ideas. The medium for this was the common (or *koine*) idiom of Greek that became the international language of educated persons all around the Mediterranean, including the native Egyptians and the large Jewish colony in Alexandria. Since many Jews could no longer understand Hebrew, a translation of the Old Testament into Greek was made for them in Alexandria about 250 B.C. This is called the Septuagint, from the Latin word for "seventy;" because of the tradition that seventy (or seventy-two) scholars produced it in as many days. The Septuagint had the effect not only of reviving the faith of those who were Jews by heritage but also of converting thousands of pagans, Romans as well as Greeks, to Judaism. It is estimated that by the first century A.D. about 10 per cent of the population of the Roman Empire was Jewish—7 million out of 70 million, of which about 3 million were converts or descendants of converts. The Septuagint was subsequently adopted by the early Christians as their sacred Scripture and became so identified with Christianity that in the second century A.D. as many as three new Greek translations of the Old Testament were prepared by Jewish scholars for Jewish readers. Outstanding among the figures of Alexandrian Judaism was Philo, whose writings (to be discussed in Chapter 11) had a great influence upon Christian thought.

There also occurred in Alexandria a blending of Greek and Egyptian religious traditions by the process known technically as *syncretism*. Elements from Greek and Egyptian sources were deliberately combined to produce doctrine and ritual that would have the widest general appeal. The first Ptolemy had immense success in this respect with the cult of the god Serapis (or Sarapis), which he evidently introduced with a view to consolidating his political position. By associating himself with this god, who combined aspects of both Greek and Egyptian popular deities,

Ptolemy strengthened his hold upon Greeks and Egyptians alike. Serapis was a fusion of the Egyptian gods Osiris and Apis and of the Greek gods Hades and Zeus. He was worshipped along with his wife and sister Isis (identified with the Greek goddesses Athena and Demeter) and his son Horus. Serapis, Isis, and Horus tended, however, to be viewed as aspects of one and the same god. The story was that Serapis died and rose again in the form of Horus, whom Isis conceived after Serapis' death as she fluttered in the guise of a hawk over his corpse. All humankind may hope to rise again like Serapis, who is lord of eternity and judge of the departed, and also the healer of the sick. Isis, represented with the infant Horus in her arms, was worshipped as divine mother and queen of heaven, with candles before her shrine in the great Serapium that Ptolemy built. Many pledged themselves to her service. After lengthy preparations, they were initiated into her mysteries (which celebrated the death and resurrection of Serapis-Horus), took vows of celibacy, shaved their heads, and dressed in special linen garments. Horus, the only son of Serapis, was (like Apollo) god of the sun and interceded with his father on behalf of the souls of the deceased. The cult of Serapis-Isis-Horus gradually extended throughout the Mediterranean region and became one of the chief religions of the Roman Empire. Worship of Isis was particularly difficult for the Christian church to eradicate. It continued into the sixth century A.D. The philosopher Proclus (about 410–485 A.D.) mentions a statue of Isis which bore the inscription, "I am that which is, has been, and shall be. My veil no one has lifted. The fruit I bore was the Sun."

What became of Alexandria's great libraries? They were gradually destroyed by a series of disasters, beginning with a fire in one of them accidentally caused by Julius Caesar in 47 B.C. (he had intended only to burn a fleet in the nearby harbor). Alexandria itself began rapidly to decline in political and cultural importance toward the end of the third century A.D., when much of the city's commerce was lost in a general collapse of the Roman government and economy throughout the Mediterranean.

CHAPTER 8

Epicureanism

Meanwhile, in Athens around 306 B.C.—sixteen years after Aristotle's death—there appeared a philosopher with a message to which many persons listened with considerable relief. This was Epicurus; and the message was that anxiety about life beyond the grave, upon which cults such as Serapis' capitalized, may safely be dismissed as unnecessary—because there is no such life. The present life is the only one we have, and the gods leave us alone to enjoy it as best we can. Religious fears to the contrary have no rational basis.

Epicurus had been born in 341 B.C. of Athenian parents in a colony that Athens had established on the island of Samos. He took to philosophy at the age of fourteen, having found that his literature teachers "were not able to explain to him the passage about Chaos in Hesiod."[1] After study in various places with various philosophers, including followers of Plato and Democritus, Epicurus set up a school of his own in about 311 B.C. at Mitylene on the island of Lesbos. Soon, however, he moved the school to Lampsacus on the Hellespont. Disciples whom he attracted in these cities subsequently followed him to Athens, where he purchased for himself and his entourage a house complete with a garden—a garden destined to become (next to Eden itself) the most famous of gardens, for it was there that Epicurus discoursed upon the principles of his philosophy, and "the Garden" is the name by which his school was always to be known. There he remained for thirty-six years, until his death in 270 B.C., in spite of attempts on the part of certain of his followers to transplant him to one or another of the satellite gardens that they, as his missionaries, were beginning to establish around the Aegean Sea and even in Egypt. Epicurus' last will and testament, which has come down to us, stipulated that the house and garden in Athens were to be held in perpetual trusteeship for the use of his successors and their pupils. Epicurus also provided in his will for "the customary celebration of my birthday every year" and for "the assembly of my disciples which takes place on the

---

[1] Probably this passage from Hesiod's *Theogony:*

> Tell me these things, Olympian Muses, tell
> From the beginning, which first came to be?
> Chaos was first of all, but next appeared
> Broad-bosomed Earth, sure standing-place for all
> The gods who live on snowy Olympus' peak. . . .

twentieth of each month . . . in recollection of myself and Metodorus"—the latter an esteemed associate who had died a few years previously.

These remembrances of Epicurus were by no means grudgingly kept up by his followers. For generations they revered him almost as a god; and at least one of them, the Roman poet Lucretius (about 99–55 B.C.), was prepared on occasion to go even further: "He was a god—a god indeed . . . who first discovered that rule of life that is now called philosophy, who by his art rescued life from such a stormy sea, so black a night, and steered it into such a calm and sun-lit haven." Contrary to what this might suggest, however, there seems to have been nothing Olympian in Epicurus' manner. From all accounts he was generosity itself and considered his followers to be his friends. Persons from all quarters and of both sexes were made to feel welcome in his garden: we hear, for instance, of slaves and soldiers there, and of courtesans (the famous *hetaerae* of Athens), in addition to prominent citizens.

Epicurus is reported to have written over 300 volumes. Nothing but fragments of these have survived. The only complete writings of his that we have are three letters summarizing his views and a little work called *Principal Doctrines* consisting of forty short pithy maxims. These may be supplemented, however, by Lucretius' poem *On the Nature of Things* (*De Rerum Natura*), which faithfully reports Epicurus' views in 7,400 lines of choice Latin hexameter verse. By the time Lucretius composed his poem—about 200 years after Epicurus died—Epicureanism had become the most widespread of Greek philosophies. Cicero (106–43 B.C.), the Roman philosopher and statesman, observed that "not only Greece and Italy but all barbary seethes with that philosophy." A striking indication of Epicureanism's outreach was its adoption as the official court philosophy of the Seleucid emperor Antiochus IV, who is also noteworthy as the ruler against whom Judas Maccabeus led a revolt of the Jews in 168 B.C. Although the Jews strongly condemned the Epicureans, there is evidence that not even they escaped the influence of Epicurean ideas. Traces of them, according to some authorities, are to be found in the Old Testament Book of Ecclesiastes (probably composed shortly before 200 B.C.).

The Canonic

Epicurus divided his philosophy into three parts: the Canonic, the Physics, and the Ethics. In the Canonic he set forth the criteria (or "canons") of truth by which he thought inquiries in Physics and Ethics should be guided. He says that we may always be sure of obtaining truth in these fields if only we will attend to our immediate experiences of sensation and feeling, for these provide clear and authoritative tests both of our beliefs about nature and of our judgments about good and evil. Falsehood resides in our opinions when they are "contradicted or not confirmed" by our experiences, not in our experiences themselves. Epicurus was an *empiricist,* holding that all of our knowledge is based upon what we have experienced *(empeiria* is the Greek for "experience"), so that to deny the trustworthiness of our experiences is to deny the possibility of our having any knowledge at all. Someone may, of course, be prepared to assert that indeed we do not have any knowledge because our experience is deceitful, but of such a person there is this (from Lucretius) to be said:

> If anyone thinks that nothing can be known, he does not know whether even this can be known, since he admits that he knows nothing. Against such an adversary, therefore, who deliberately stands on his head, I will not try to argue my case. And yet, if I were to grant that he possessed this knowledge, I might ask several pertinent questions. Since he has had no experience of truth, how does he know the difference between knowledge and ignorance? What has originated the concept of truth and falsehood? Where is his proof that doubt is not the same as certainty?
>
> You will find, in fact, that the concept of truth was originated by the senses and that the senses cannot be rebutted. The testimony that we must accept as more trustworthy is that which can spontaneously overcome falsehood with truth. What then are we to pronounce more trustworthy than the senses? Can reason derived from the [supposedly] deceitful senses be invoked to contradict them, when it is itself wholly derived from the senses? If they are not true, then reason in its entirety is equally false.

Knowledge is built up from sense-experience by way of general concepts. These concepts are formed from our memories of the similarities and differences we have noticed among our experiences. The general concept of humans, for example, consists of a pattern of characteristic human features that we remember having frequently observed and to which we have attached the word *human* as a name. "Human" signifies nothing more than a recurring complex of observable qualities approximately the same for different persons; it does not signify a Platonic "form" distinguishable from these qualities and apprehensible by reason alone, nor does it signify an Aristotelian "essence" embodied in different persons as the "form" of their "matter" and abstractable by a process of induction. In order that we may be sure of meaning something when we use general terms such as "human," we should "keep all our investigations in accord with our sensations"—that is, we should constantly ask ourselves whether our terms refer to anything that has actually occurred in our sense-experience. Or in the case of ethical terms such as "good" and "evil," we should always bear in mind the feelings that accompany our sense-experience, for ethical terms have meaning only in reference to these feelings. General concepts are what Epicurus calls "anticipations" because when we hear the names attached to them we "anticipate" experiences of relevant sorts. Hearing "human," we think of the observable characteristics that distinguish humans from, s.ʉy, horses and cattle. Hearing "good," we think of the feelings by which (as Epicurus believes) our choices are invariably determined.

Epicurus borrows from Democritus his theory as to the way in which our senses come by information about the objects in our environment. What happens is that films of atoms are continually sent off from the surfaces of objects, and when these films make contact with the atoms composing our eyes, for example, the result is that we have visual images of the objects. These images are said to be *always true*, not in the sense that they are always exact replicas of objects but in the sense that our beliefs about objects will always be true if only we will interpret the images properly. It would perhaps be better if Epicurus and Lucretius were to say that images are not in themselves either true or false, that both truth and falsity pertain to our beliefs in respect of the exactness of images. But they are so concerned to absolve the images of responsibility for our false beliefs, and to place the blame upon our faulty reasoning, that they will have it said that all images are true. And when Lucretius says in the passage quoted on page 179 that "the senses cannot be rebutted," what he really means is that the information provided by the senses cannot *in general* be distrusted. He does not mean that each and every visual image is an exact replica of some object. He offers in fact a number of explanations, along the lines of the following, for images that are inexact:

> When we see the square towers of a city in the distance, they often appear round. This is because every angle seen at a distance is blunted or even is not seen as an angle at all. Its impact is nullified and does not penetrate as far as our eyes, because films that travel through a great deal of air lose their sharp outlines through frequent collisions with it. When every angle has thus eluded our sense, the result is as though the squared ashlars [the building-stones at the corners of the towers] were rounded off on the lathe—not that they resemble really round stones seen close up, but in a sketchy sort of way they counterfeit them.

If one took at face value Lucretius' statement elsewhere that "whatever the senses may perceive at any time is all alike true," it would seem that he is inconsistent with himself in implying here that the images we have of the city's towers are less accurate at a distance than when we are closer. What he ought to say, if he believes all images are true, is that the towers change from round to square as we draw near, not that our images gain in accuracy. Of course he does not say this. He believes, as we all do, that the towers remain the same and that only our view of them changes. But the crucial question is how we can justify our belief that they remain the same if all that we are ever immediately aware of is images. We would not have any way of inspecting the towers directly so as to check the images against them and to assure ourselves that *both* do not change. All the checking we could do would be of one image against another image. We would be in the position of someone who is asked to determine, just by looking at them, whether two photographs that are said to have been taken of the same person were not in fact taken of different persons, one of whom was cleverly disguised to look like the other.

Neither Lucretius nor Epicurus, in the writings we have, comes to grips with this sort of problem. Lucretius says merely that the comparative accuracy of images is "something to be discerned by the reasoning power of the mind." He does not discuss the tests to be employed or the way in which they could be authenticated in keeping with an empiricist theory of knowledge. And Epicurus is content to reiterate that the criteria of truth in matters of physics are sense-experience and the general concepts that arise from it, and that the criterion in matters of ethics is our feelings. We are told that when we proceed to form judgments by using general concepts, the rule to follow is that no judgment should be taken for true unless it is "confirmed or not contradicted" by the testimony of our senses or feelings.[2] Our beliefs should not be allowed to run ahead of our evidence. In any case in which there is not sufficient evidence for a decision either way, we must simply face up to the fact that there we have (in a famous Epicurean phrase) "a problem awaiting confirmation."

Physics

"Vain is the word of a philosopher," Epicurus says, "which does not heal any suffering of man." The philosophy of nature which constitutes Epicurus' physics is expressly offered in the interests of healing. He finds that the human species is plagued by anxieties and fears, especially concerning death and destructive forces of nature as these are superstitiously interpreted. The powers that menace humankind are attributed to gods of a particularly conceited and spiteful description who may yet, it is hoped, be persuaded to spare us if only we can somehow manage to please them. It is feared that when we die our troubles will hardly be over, because if we have failed to please them in this life, an eternity of punishment may await us in Hades. And it appears that we are indeed bound to fail, for we see even now that the gods visit terrible things upon the pious no less than the impious. The fear of death and of torment afterward is a sickness that works in us unconsciously, causing us to make life miserable for others as well as ourselves. Many try uncon-

---

[2]Going by this, we could guess that Epicurus might have said that our sense-experience at least does not *contradict* the supposition that objects remain the same while our visual images of them change. He might have commended this supposition on the grounds, say, that it is simpler than the supposition that both change, and also that it contributes to a more powerful explanation of the processes involved in the changing of our images.

sciously to rid themselves of this sickness by escaping from themselves into miscellaneous activities. Not knowing what they really want, they run from one thing to another, as though it were an answer just to keep moving. But hatred of themselves grows upon them because from themselves it is impossible to escape. In extreme instances, as Lucretius explains, the disease is totally corrupting:

> Consider . . . the greed and blind lust of power that drive unhappy men to overstep the bounds of right and may even turn them into accomplices or instruments of crime, struggling night and day with unstinted effort to scale the pinnacles of wealth. These running sores of life are fed in no small measure by the fear of death. For abject ignominy and irksome poverty seem far indeed from the joy and assurance of life, and in effect loitering already at the gateway of death. From such a fate men revolt in groundless terror and long to escape far, far away. So in their greed of gain they amass a fortune out of civil bloodshed: piling wealth on wealth, they heap carnage on carnage. With heartless glee they welcome a brother's tragic death. They hate and fear the hospitable board of their own kin. Often, in the same spirit and influenced by the same fear, they are consumed with envy at the sight of another's success: he walks in a blaze of glory, looked up to by all, while they curse the dingy squalor in which their own lives are bogged. Some sacrifice life itself for the sake of statues and a title. Often from fear of death mortals are gripped by such a hate of living and looking on the light that with anguished hearts they do themselves to death. They forget that this very fear is the fountainhead of their troubles; this it is that harasses conscience, snaps the bonds of friendship and hurls down virtue from the heights. Many a time before now men have betrayed their country and their beloved parents in an effort to escape the halls of Hell.

> As children in blank darkness tremble and start at everything, so we in broad daylight are oppressed at times by fears as baseless as those horrors which children imagine coming upon them in the dark. This dread and darkness of the mind cannot be dispelled by the sunbeams, the blinding shafts of day, but only by an understanding of the outward form and inner workings of nature.

Epicurus found in the atomism of Democritus the understanding of nature for which he was looking—a theory that at every point is "confirmed or not contradicted" by the testimony of sense-experience, and that clears away superstitious anxieties and fears. This he proceeded to adopt as his own, with a few significant modifications. A multitude of phenomena, from wind and evaporation to porosity and weight, speak in favor of material atoms and empty space ("void") as the fundamental constituents of reality. All the objects and processes of nature are to be explained by reference to aggregations and impacts of atoms, which individually are uncreated, unalterable, and indestructible. The atoms are infinite in number; space is infinite in extent. Countless worlds, some of them like ours, are formed and reformed as atoms collide in the void. Democritus had supposed that collisions occur because atoms naturally move at random in all directions. Epicurus, however, takes the position that atoms have weight (which Democritus denied) and so like raindrops fall downward in space along parallel lines.[3] They fall at a uniform speed in spite of differences in their weight, because space is a vacuum in which they encounter no resistance. It follows that atoms would never collide to form worlds unless they *swerve* a little from their vertical paths. If we drop some heavy object, we do not of course detect any swerve as it falls; but still it is possible that it diverges very slightly from the vertical, and no more than an infinitesimal divergence would be needed on the part of atoms for them to collide. Swerves, therefore, if not directly confirmed by our experience, are certainly not inconsistent with it. Atoms, therefore, spontaneously swerve, at quite indeterminable times and places, and thus they collide with others that in turn collide with others, bounding and rebounding until a great swirling cloud of them is accumulated and a world begins to take shape. Lucretius illustrates this stage of cosmic development by means of a beautiful analogy:

> Observe what happens when sunbeams are admitted into a building and shed light on its shadowy places. You will see a multitude of tiny particles mingling in a multitude of ways in the empty space within the light of the beam, as though contending in everlasting conflict, rushing into battle rank upon rank with never a moment's pause in a rapid sequence of unions and disunions. From this you may picture what it is for the atoms to be perpetually tossed about in the illimitable void. Besides, there is a further reason why you should give your mind to these particles that are seen dancing in a sunbeam: their dancing is an actual indication of underlying movements of matter that are hidden from our sight. There you will see many particles under the impact of invisible blows changing their course and driven back upon their tracks, this way and that, in all directions. You must understand that they all derive this restlessness from the atoms. It originates with the atoms, which move of themselves. . . . The movement mounts up from the atoms and gradually emerges to the level of our senses, so that these bodies are in motion that we see in sunbeams, moved by blows that remain invisible.

Everything that happens is an outcome of these "invisible blows" of atoms. Nothing is intelligently designed. Nothing happens for a purpose. "Our world has been made by nature through the spontaneous and casual collision and the multifarious, accidental, random, and purposeless congregation and coalescence of atoms whose suddenly formed combinations

---

[3] Epicurus recognizes that "up" and "down" are directions relative to us. He believes, however, that worlds are flat and are oriented parallel to one another, so that what "goes down" from our perspective in this world also "goes down" from the perspective of an observer in any other world.

could serve on each occasion as the starting-point of substantial fabrics—earth and sea and sky and the races of living creatures." Neither the constructive nor the destructive processes of nature are imputable to divine control or interference. "Nature is free and uncontrolled by proud masters and runs the universe by herself without the aid of gods." From gods we have nothing to fear; but this is not to say that gods do not exist, only that they—like everything else—are aggregates of atoms. The atoms of which the gods consist are of such an especially fine texture that films of them penetrate right through the bodies of mortals and impact directly upon the atoms of their minds. Thus are produced, particularly in sleep, those visions of the gods that account for the widespread belief in their existence. But the superstitious imagination of mortals has distorted their images of the gods with false attributions of unlimited power and vindictive temperament. In fact, as a less clouded vision will reveal, these holy beings have very limited power and no inclination to meddle in human affairs. "It is essential to the very nature of deity that it should enjoy immortal existence in utter tranquility, aloof and detached from our affairs. It is free from all pain and peril, strong in its own resources, exempt from any need of us, indifferent to our merits, and immune from anger." Though composed of atoms, the gods are immortal because they inhabit the spaces between worlds, where they are safe from collisions that could destroy them—"those quiet habitations, never shaken by storms nor drenched by rain-clouds nor defaced by white drifts of snow . . . [where] all their wants are supplied by nature, and nothing at any time cankers their peace of mind." The serene dignity of the gods is for us to revere and to emulate. It is no compliment to them for us to suppose that a world as imperfect as this one is any creation or concern of theirs. Nor can it be considered pious to prostrate ourselves before shrines of the gods or to offer them sacrifices. They have no use for such things. "True piety lies rather in the power to contemplate the universe with a quiet mind."

A quiet mind, coming as it does with an understanding of the true causes of natural phenomena, may be secure in the general assurance that these causes are one and all just impacts of atoms. Of course, we do not directly perceive impacts of atoms; we infer their existence from what we do perceive, as in the case of the motes in the sunbeam, encouraged by the knowledge that nothing but movements of matter can produce material changes. We cannot really think, Epicurus says, that any natural phenomenon comes about because of the activity of immaterial agents such as the gods are popularly supposed to be. It is impossible to conceive of one thing's producing any change with respect to another thing except by *physical contact,* which requires that both things be material. This is why we must believe that the "spirit" which animates a human body, and the mind which gives it intelligent direction, are alike composed of atoms—very small spherical atoms, which Lucretius associates with warmth, wind, air, and a fourth element "which is quite nameless."

We see them [spirit and mind] propelling the limbs, rousing the body from sleep, changing the expression of the face, and guiding and steering the whole man—activities that all clearly involve touch, as touch in turn involves matter. How then can we deny their material nature? You see the mind sharing in the body's experiences and sympathizing with it. When the nerve-racking impact of a spear gashes bones and sinews, even if it does not penetrate to the seat of life, there ensues faintness and a tempting inclination earthwards. . . . The substance of the mind must therefore be material, since it is affected by the impact of material weapons.

Although it is right for us to be confident that absolutely everything can in principle be accounted for along atomic lines, we cannot in practice expect to discover the precise causes for each and every phenomenon that occurs. Our knowledge of nature's "outward form and inner workings" will doubtless increase as investigation proceeds, and yet at any given time there will still be many things of which we do not know the true explanation. The best we can do in such cases is to develop alternative explanations that are consistent with the general theory of atoms, and to determine if we can which alternative is most probable. Epicurus finds that "phenomena of the sky," in particular, must be approached in this way: "They admit of more than one cause of coming into being and more than one account of their nature which harmonizes with our sensations." Concerning the sun, the moon, and the stars, of whose behavior we can observe little, we must construct probable explanations by analogy with earthly phenomena that we can observe at close hand. Thus, on the matter of the size of these heavenly bodies, we must remember that fires on earth, when seen at night from a distance, may appear to be either smaller *or larger* than they really are; and so the safe conclusion about heavenly bodies, which resemble fires, is that they are "either slightly greater than what we see or slightly less or the same size." Or to take something nearer to home, consider the rainbow, which in Homer is associated with Iris, goddess and messenger of the gods, but which in fact may be accounted for in several ways without "recourse to myth":

The rainbow is caused by light shining from the sun onto watery atmosphere: or else by a peculiar union of light and air, which can produce the special qualities of these colors whether all together or separately; from it, as it reflects back again, the neighboring regions of the air can take the tint which we see, by means of the shining of the light onto its various parts. The appearance of its round shape is caused because it is perceived by our sight at equal distance from all its points, or else because the atoms in the air or those in the clouds which are derived from the same air, are pressed together in this manner, and so the combination spreads out in a round shape.

If the rainbow is not a bridge between gods and mortals, neither is it true that mortals "were let down into the fields from heaven by a golden cord." Humankind arose from the earth, in the days when the earth was young, along with many curious species of creatures that have since died out because they were inadequately provided with means of protecting, nourishing, and reproducing themselves. In the old days, Lucretius says, many things were better than they are now: the weather was milder; fruits grew naturally in abundance; human beings were tougher and more adaptable and lived in the open. "They lived in thickets and hillside caves and forests and stowed their rugged limbs among bushes when driven to seek shelter from the lash of wind and rain." With the passage of time conditions worsened and humanity mellowed. Fire began to be used for warmth. Families began to live together and neighbors to form alliances for mutual protection. Languages developed as people indicated objects to one another with vocal utterances expressive of their feelings, using for convenience the same utterances for the same objects. Men of exceptional energy and ability became kings, founding cities and establishing citadels, and parceling out cattle and land among their favorites. Lesser men grew envious and resentful and schemed together to overthrow the kings.

> So the kings were killed. Down in the hot dust lay the ancient majesty of thrones, the haughty sceptres. . . . [And] the conduct of affairs sank back into the depths of mob-rule, with each man struggling to win dominance and supremacy for himself. Then some men showed how to form a constitution, based on fixed rights and recognized laws. Mankind, worn out by a life of violence and enfeebled by feuds, was the more ready to submit to the bondage of laws and institutions. . . . Ever since then the enjoyment of life has been tempered by the fear of punishment. . . . It is not easy for one who breaks by his acts the mutual compact of social peace to lead a peaceful and untroubled life.

The wearing out of mankind has accompanied a general wearing out of the earth, which already is far past her prime. No longer are the atoms that the earth throws off into space fully replenished by new ones coming in. "Everything is gradually decaying and nearing its end, worn out by old age." The whole substance and structure of the world, upheld through many ages, is nearing collapse, which may occur with "one ear-splitting crack." From the billions of atoms that will be dispersed in this cataclysm an identical world with identical creatures will one day be reassembled in the void. The entire process of growth and decay will be exactly duplicated. In fact all this has happened countless times in the past and will happen countless times in the future, for in infinite time the atoms in the universe must again and again fall into "the self-same combinations as now."[4] This goes as well for the atoms composing our bodies and minds,

[4] Actually, this could be true only if the atoms were limited in number, and Lucretius' position is that there are infinitely many of them.

which are dispersed in our individual deaths, to be reassembled when the earth emerges once more ages hence. Our lives down to the smallest detail have been lived, and will be lived, over and over. Of course, we do not remember having done before exactly what we are doing now, "for between then and now is interposed a breach of life, and all the atomic motions [associated then and now with our minds] have been wandering [in the interim] far astray from sentience," and "the chain of our identity has been snapped." Nevertheless, "all things are always the same," precisely the same, and "there is nothing new to look forward to." In the words of Ecclesiastes:

> Whatsoever has been is that which will be;
> And whatsoever has been done is that which will be done;
> And there is nothing new under the sun.
> Is there a thing of which it is said, "Lo, this is new"?
> It was already in existence in the ages
> Which were before us.

Death, feared by many as the beginning of a life worse than the one we have now, is in reality the end of our consciousness, a "return to sleep and peace," toward which we may and should look with quiet minds. The torments that are said to await us in Hades are present here and now if we are oppressed by superstitious fears of the gods, or if we have committed crimes for which we fear punishment from our fellow mortals, or if we defiantly refuse to acknowledge that the term of our existence is limited. An anxious lust for perpetual life saps the enjoyment that is possible for us. We should gracefully accept the inevitable.

Yet how can our attitude toward life and death be ours to change for the better if all of our thoughts are attributable to the falling and colliding of atoms? How can we have any choice in the matter? Lucretius is not without an answer. The movements of atoms, including those of which our minds are composed, are not wholly determined by their weight or by the impacts of other atoms. Each atom, remember, now and again spontaneously *swerves;* and when a mind-atom does this, we have a "voluntary action of the mind," an instance of "free will," by which the "bonds of fate" are broken and the "everlasting sequence of cause and effect" is interrupted. In such cases we "swerve from our course at no set time or place but at the bidding of our own hearts"—literally our hearts, for there mind-atoms are located, and from there voluntary motion is transmitted (via atoms of spirit) throughout the body and the limbs. So far Lucretius' view would seem to be a species of what today is called *indeterminism,* according to which human thoughts and actions are not entirely the effects of any causes (physical, physiological, or psychological), but his further remarks on the subject show him to be a kind of determinist—a psychological determinist—after all. He associates certain events in our minds with uncaused swerves of atoms; but these events, insofar as they relate to actions, are exclusively thoughts of *pleasure* to be derived from doing one thing or another. "We follow the path," he says, "along which we are severally led by pleasure." This is exactly in line with Epicurus' position that pleasure is to be considered the "end" of human life inasmuch as all persons instinctively pursue it and avoid pain, never deliberately choosing a lesser instead of a greater pleasure (when both are obtainable), or a greater instead of a lesser pain (when both are not avoidable). Such a theory of human motivation, which is called *psychological hedonism* (from *hedone,* the Greek for "pleasure"), is inconsistent with freedom of will—if one understands this to mean that we have genuine options with respect to the kinds of considerations that shall have decisive weight with us as we map out our actions. And if it is psychologically out of the question for our choices and avoidances to be functions of anything except "swerves" toward maximum pleasure (or at least toward minimum pain), what could be the point of saying that our choices and avoidances are "free"? The atoms in question are "free" in the sense that their swerves are spontaneous; but because, by curious coincidence, they happen always to agree on the sort of thing they prompt us to do, it is hard to see what difference it would make to us if their agreement were not spontaneous but was caused by their weight or by their collisions with other atoms.

Ethics

Our feelings should be our guide in matters of ethics, just as our sense-experience should be our guide in matters of physics. In point of fact, our feelings—specifically those of pleasure and pain—always *are* the guide we follow in matters of ethics; and so it would be futile to propose that we should be guided by anything else. "For we recognize pleasure as the first good in us," Epicurus says, "and from pleasure we begin every act of choice and avoidance, and to pleasure we return again, using the feeling as the standard by which we judge every good." Thus, in effect, Epicurus appeals to a hedonistic psychological theory of human motivation in support of a hedonistic ethical theory as to how it is best for human beings to live. Pleasure, he says, is "natural to us," insomuch that our happiness or well-being—"the good life"—can be conceived only in terms of it: "I do not know how I can conceive the good, if I withdraw the pleasures of taste, and withdraw the pleasures of love, and withdraw the pleasures of hearing, and withdraw the pleasurable emotions caused to sight by beautiful form." Sensuous pleasures such as these are fundamental. "The beginning and root of all good is the pleasure of the stomach. . . ."; that is to say, pleasure of the stomach may be taken as representative of the pleasures in question. Pleasures of the mind are of course recognized by Epicurus, but he maintains that they are all associated with memories of past sensuous pleasures and with anticipations of future ones. The satisfactions of physics, for example, are said to derive from the way in which an accurate understanding of nature enables us to face the future without fear of injury from the gods and so "attain our pleasures unalloyed." Friendship is said to be pleasurable, and is much recommended, on account of the sense of security, the "confidence of help," it affords.

From this it might seem that Epicurus embraces the principle attributed to the Assyrian King Sardanapalus—and also found in Ecclesiastes: "There is nothing good for man under the sun except to eat, drink, and be merry." Supporters as well as detractors have often taken Epicurus to be saying something like this, and today the word *Epicurean* is regularly used in a more or less Sardanapalian sense. Nothing could be more opposed, however, to what Epicurus has in mind. He takes the position that pleasure is needed, and normally sought, only when there is some pain or discomfort in respect of hunger, thirst, or other bodily deficiency. A process such as eating or drinking affords pleasure of an "active" type that reaches a natural limit of intensity and duration when the pain or discomfort is removed. Hunger or thirst may be satisfied with a variety of foods or drinks, and in this sense the pleasure of eating or drinking may be *varied,* but it cannot be increased or prolonged beyond the point at which hunger or thirst ceases to be felt—at least not without risking pains and disturbances that outweigh the pleasure. Active pleasures often seem indeed to promise more than this: "The flesh perceives the limits of pleasure as unlimited and unlimited time is required to supply it." Ever more money, power, recognition, and so on, are viewed as necessary in order to supply pleasure ever more abundantly. In fact, however, the "unlimitedness" of pleasure is quite illusory. The real needs of the body are met with simple provisions at modest expense. Anything more is unnecessary and in the long run pays diminishing returns. The point of view of "eat, drink, and be merry" fails to recognize that the greatest pleasures of which we are capable are "static" pleasures associated with states of bodily and mental equilibrium, free from agitations of inflamed appetite and capable of indefinite prolongation. Luxuries, if we have access to them, may on occasion be safely enjoyed, but only if we do not consider them essential.

Independence of desire [Epicurus says] we think a great good—not that we may at all times enjoy but a few things, but that, if we do not possess many, we may enjoy the few in the genuine persuasion that those have the sweetest pleasure in luxury who least need it, and that all that is natural is easy to be obtained, but that which is superfluous is hard. And so plain savors bring us a pleasure equal to a luxurious diet, when all the pain due to want is removed; and bread and water produce the highest pleasure, when one who needs them puts them to his lips. To grow accustomed, therefore, to simple and not luxurious diet gives us health to the full, and makes a man alert for the needful employments of life, and when after long intervals we approach luxuries, disposes us better towards them, and fits us to be fearless of fortune.

When, therefore, we maintain that pleasure is the end, we do not mean the pleasures of profligates and those that consist in sensuality, as is supposed by some who are either ignorant or disagree with us or do not understand, but freedom from pain in the body and from trouble in the mind. For it is not continuous drinkings and revellings, nor the satisfaction of lusts, nor the enjoyment of fish and other luxuries of the wealthy table, which produces a pleasant life, but sober reasoning, searching out the motives for all choice and avoidance, and banishing mere opinions, to which are due the greatest disturbance of the spirit.

Epicurus holds that, in and of themselves, or intrinsically, no pleasures are bad, and no pains are good. Yet some pleasures (say, of gluttony) are to be avoided, and some pains (say, of surgery) are to be chosen, because the former are not, and the latter are, valuable instrumentally as means to the pleasantest life possible overall. In general, active pleasures are to be subordinated to static ones because the pleasantest life consists in the static or stable conditions of "freedom from pain in the body and from trouble in the mind" (*ataraxia* is Epicurus' famous term for an untroubled state of mind). "By a scale of comparison," he says, "and by the consideration of advantages and disadvantages we must form our judgment on all these matters." This is really how our judgments *are* formed, to the extent that we are aware of the probable outcomes of our actions in respect of pleasure and pain. No one knowingly chooses a lesser pleasure in preference to a greater, or a greater pain in preference to a lesser. The trouble is that most persons have a poor understanding of such things, not that they fail to act on what understanding they have. They mistakenly perceive small pleasures available now as being equal to or greater than large pleasures available only later—and available only if they forgo the small ones now. They do not see that the pleasantest life is one from which desires that are impossible or risky to satisfy have been eradicated. They have no grasp of all-important distinctions among types of desires—for some desires (such as those for food and drink) are "natural and necessary" and have to be satisfied, whereas other desires (such as those for *special* foods or drinks) are "natural but not necessary" and do not have to be satisfied, and yet other desires (such as those for position and fame) are "neither natural nor necessary" and should definitely be suppressed. Moreover, few people sufficiently appreciate the role that traditional moral virtues (such as honor and justice) have to play in a life that would be pleasant.

Now *practical wisdom,* or prudence, consists precisely in sound judgment on all points of this sort. Without it, no one may expect to live the pleasantest life possible. With it, anyone may be assured of doing so.

Wherefore prudence is a more precious thing even than philosophy: for from prudence are sprung all the other virtues, and it teaches us that it is not possible to live pleasantly without living prudently and honorably and justly, nor, again, to live a life of prudence, honor, and justice without living pleasantly. For the virtues are by nature bound up with the pleasant life, and the pleasant life is inseparable from them. For indeed who, think you, is a better man than he who holds reverent opinions concerning the gods, and is at all times free from fear of death, and has reasoned out the end ordained by nature? He understands that the limit of good things is easy to fulfil and easy to attain, whereas the course of ills is either short in time or slight in pain: he laughs at destiny, whom some have introduced as the mistress of all things. He thinks that with us lies the chief power in determining events, some of which happen by necessity and some by chance, and some are within our control; for while necessity cannot be called to account, he sees that chance is inconstant, but that what is in our control is subject to no master, and to it are naturally attached praise and blame. . . . He does not believe that good and evil are given by chance to man for the framing of a blessed life, but that opportunities for great good and great evil are afforded by it. He therefore thinks it better to be unfortunate in reasonable action than to prosper in unreason. For it is better in a man's actions that what is well chosen should fail, rather than that what is ill chosen should be successful owing to chance.

Meditate therefore on these things and things akin to them night and day by yourself, and with a companion like to yourself, and never shall you be disturbed waking or asleep, but you shall live like a god among men.

Is it true, as prudence is said to teach us, that one can live most pleasantly if and only if one is virtuous—"virtuous," that is, in a standard sense of the term?[5] Naturally Epicurus is aware that many persons doubt this, having calculated that at least in their own cases a certain amount of vice is positively essential to the greatest pleasures of body and mind. Elsewhere he acknowledges that it is possible for their calculation to be correct, saying that "beauty and virtue and the like are to be honored, if they give pleasure; but if they do not give pleasure, we must bid them farewell." Prudence must therefore have been speaking loosely in teaching that the pleasant life is "inseparable" from virtue. But Epicurus is apparently convinced that the probability of vice's being conducive to the pleasantest life is never high enough to warrant anyone's betting on it, except perhaps in the most extraordinary of circumstances. He says that "to secure protection from men anything is a natural good by which you may be able to attain this end," which seems to authorize, in desperate situations, conduct that might be considered unjust or dishonorable by some conventional standards.

---

[5] Epicurus' thesis would be true just as a matter of definition if it derived from a refusal on his part to *call* anyone "virtuous" whose life is not as pleasant as it might be. His point, surely, is that those whom discerning persons besides Epicureans consider virtuous are the same as those who live most pleasantly.

The rule that Epicurus seems to have in mind is that we should do nothing for which, if others happen to find out about it, we would suffer more distress than we will suffer if we do not do it. It is with reference to some such rule that he sets forth his view that injustice in the sense of lawbreaking is generally inadvisable. Historically, laws have been established among people as pledges of mutual advantage to refrain from harming one another. Justice as a virtue of personal character is the disposition to honor such pledges as a matter of prudence, and laws are just or unjust to the extent that they actually are advantageous or disadvantageous for all concerned. Precisely which laws and form of government are best for a given community will depend upon its particular circumstances. Laws that were once advantageous and just may become the reverse as circumstances change, but to break even these, as long as they are still enforced, may (Epicurus implies) cause one more discomfort than obeying them. One can never be sure of escaping detection, and one's anxiety on this score may subtract heavily from one's peace of mind. "Even if he hides his guilt from gods and men," Lucretius says, "he must feel a secret misgiving that it will not rest hidden forever. He cannot forget those oft-told tales of men betraying themselves by words spoken in dreams or delirium that drag out long-buried crimes into the daylight."

Epicurus says that it is better for someone who acts reasonably to suffer bad fortune than for someone who acts unreasonably to prosper by good fortune. And one reason he gives for this seems to be that the reasonableness or unreasonableness of one's actions is in one's control and as such merits praise or blame, never mind whether one's actions happen to be favored by fortune. The quality of one's effort is morally what matters, not the success of the outcome insofar as that depends upon uncontrollable circumstances. But how is this consistent with the view that what matters is just how pleasantly one lives? An unreasonable person who really prospers lives more pleasantly, as "pleasantly" is normally understood, than a reasonable person who is truly unfortunate. Or is it Epicurus' position that unreasonable persons who prosper will always so mismanage their affairs that they will invariably have less pleasure than if they were reasonable but unfortunate? This is hard to believe. Or perhaps what he means is that the "untroubled mind" peculiar to reasonable persons gives them pleasure that can be neither augmented by good fortune nor diminished by bad fortune—pleasure that is always greater than any obtainable by unreasonable persons? This is not any easier to believe, and it does not fit well with what he says about chance sometimes affording "opportunities for great good"; but it is in the spirit of "the limit of good things is easy to fulfil and easy to attain, whereas the course of ills is either short in time [because death soon results] or slight in pain." It is also in keeping with a statement he is reported to have made about wise persons' being happy even if they are tortured on the rack. And among the fragments of his writings on ethics there is this: "Nature teaches us to pay little heed to what fortune brings, and when we are prosperous to understand that we are unfortunate, and when we are unfortunate not to regard prosperity highly, and to receive unmoved the good things which come from fortune and to range ourselves boldly against the seeming evils which it brings: for all that the many regard as good or evil is fleeting, and wisdom has nothing in common with fortune."

Why, then, should it be of any concern to the wise to make the most of "opportunities for great good" offered by good fortune, or to endeavor to lessen the suffering visited upon humankind by bad fortune? With an undisturbed mind one is to "live like a god among men." Epicurus believes, indeed, that it is consistent with maintaining an undisturbed mind for us to promote the interests of others. Our friendships, though they start from our own need of help and protection, lead in the end to our identifying the interests of our friends with our own interests—so much so that "for friendship's sake we must even run risks." No god, of course, would do this, as it would be incompatible with his or her serene indifference to human affairs.[6] But all apart from considerations of friendship, those who are wise have so accustomed themselves to frugal living that they "know better how to give than to receive"; and if they chance to have many possessions, they find it "easy to distribute them so as to win the gratitude of neighbors." The plain implication of this, however, is that possessions and the desire for them are worth little in the eyes of the wise, except as occasions for eliciting the grateful thanks of neighbors and thereby acquiring, no doubt, a measure of security in relation to them. Giving is for the wise preferable to receiving, because they do not want what they receive, not because they have a disinterested desire to bestow things of real value upon those less fortunate than themselves. Epicurus' notion of the correct godly attitude toward human affairs is always to be found in close conjunction with views that appear to show him struggling for a more generous and charitable perspective. On the whole, however, the godly attitude, as he understands it, seems to prevail. Lucretius expresses it only too clearly in a famous passage that has few equals for iciness:

> What joy it is, when out at sea the stormwinds are lashing the waters, to gaze from the shore at the heavy stress some other man is enduring! Not that anyone's afflictions are in themselves a source of delight; but to realize from what troubles you yourself are free is joy indeed. What joy, again, to watch opposing hosts marshalled on the field of battle when you have yourself no part in their peril! But this is the greatest joy of all: to stand aloof in a quiet citadel, stoutly fortified by the teaching of the wise, and to gaze down from that elevation on others wandering aimlessly in a vain search for the way of life, pitting their wits one against another, disputing for precedence, struggling night and day

---

[6] It is fortunate for us, Epicurus says, that the gods do not listen to our prayers. If they did, the human race would long ago have perished, inasmuch as people are always praying for evil against one another.

with unstinted effort to scale the pinnacles of wealth and power. O joyless hearts of men! O minds without vision! How dark and dangerous the life in which this tiny span is lived away! Do you not see that nature is clamoring for two things only, a body free from pain, a mind released from worry and fear for the enjoyment of pleasurable sensations?

The better to "stand aloof in a quiet citadel," Epicurus counsels us to "live unknown" in an economical manner with like-minded friends, avoiding if we can all involvement in politics and all competition with others, marrying or not marrying as our circumstances permit, but in any case remembering that "the pleasures of love never profited a man, and he is lucky if they do him no harm." We should be careful of our reputation and "do all things rightly according to the laws," not omitting to observe the religious customs of our community—even though we know them to be based upon erroneous beliefs about the gods. Above all, we should

become accustomed to the belief that death is nothing to us. For all good and evil consists in sensation, but death is deprivation of sensation. And therefore a right understanding that death is nothing to us makes the mortality of life enjoyable, not because it adds to it an infinite span of time, but because it takes away the craving for immortality. For there is nothing terrible in life for the man who has truly comprehended that there is nothing terrible in not living. So that the man speaks but idly who says that he fears death not because it will be painful when it comes, but because it is painful in anticipation. For that which gives no trouble when it comes is but an empty pain in anticipation. So death, the most terrifying of ills, is nothing to us, since so long as we exist death is not with us; but when death comes, then we do not exist. It does not then concern either the living or the dead, since for the former it is not, and the latter are no more.

Epicurus is said to have met his own death in a singularly serene frame of mind. He had endured many days of intense pain from a stone obstructing his urinary tract[7]; and when at length he was about to die, "he got into a bronze bath filled with hot water, and asked for a cup of unmixed wine, which he gulped down." Thus he expired; and his last words, we are told, were "Farewell, remember my teaching."

---

[7] A common cause of which is, one feels obliged to note, an improperly balanced diet. Epicurus seems to have lived mainly on bread and water. In a letter he asks that some preserved cheese be sent to him "that when I like I may have a feast."

CHAPTER **9**

Stoicism

Epicurus had been in Athens for five or six years when (about 300 B.C.) another philosopher there began to expound views that in some respects were diametrically opposed to his. This was Zeno of Citium.[1] Not pleasure, but virtue, Zeno said, is the highest good; and not random combinations of atoms, but God's holy ordinance is what forms and sustains the world. Thus began the Stoic school of philosophy, so called because Zeno delivered his lectures in a colonnade known as the *Stoa Poikile,* or Painted Porch (which the artist Polygnotus had decorated with a fresco of the fall of Troy).

Zeno was born in Citium on the island of Cyprus sometime around 336 B.C. He went to Athens in his early twenties, conceived a deep admiration for the Socrates of Xenophon's *Memorabilia,* and fell under the influence of first one and then another of the city's philosophers. Two of these made a particularly strong impression upon him. From Crates, a Cynic, he learned that even the penniless are kings if (like Socrates) they virtuously reign over their own passions, and that all persons, owing to their common humanity, are citizens of a city that encompasses the cosmos—a *cosmopolis*—where wisdom is the only law. Under Stilpo, a Megarian, he became acquainted with techniques of logic and with problems of knowledge, and he began to work out his own views on these subjects. Zeno's thoughts were shaped most of all, however, by the writings of a philosopher long dead, Heraclitus of Ephesus, who had said that the cosmos is sustained by an eternal fire in which there is a rational principle that governs the perpetual flux of events. This constituted for Zeno the metaphysical perspective from which he coordinated and developed the lessons of his teachers in Athens.

In his personal life Zeno seems to have followed the Cynics in emulating to a fault the simple habits of Socrates. We are told that he wore a thin cloak in all seasons, dined upon water and uncooked food, was oblivious to illness, and so forth. He is said to have been swarthy in appearance and to have had a slightly twisted neck. Despite a harshness of manner for which he was notorious, or perhaps because of it, he was honored highly by Athenian officialdom as a beneficial influence upon the young. The consistency of his personal practice with his philosophical theory excited general acclaim. This included his death by suicide (in

[1] Not to be confused with Zeno of Elea, the follower of Parmenides.

195

about 265 B.C.), a practice which, as we shall see, his theory by no means discouraged. The story is that Zeno, having tripped and broken a toe, interpreted the incident as a sign that God wished his life to end, and so hobbled home and killed himself. As we shall also see, the belief that such occurrences reveal God's will was a feature of the Stoic position, and the story may well be true.

Zeno's teachings were developed by Cleanthes of Assos (about 331–232 B.C.), who in his gentleness of manner was, but in his mode of dying was not, unlike Zeno; and by Chrysippus of Soli (about 280–206 B.C.), who was known as the "second founder" of the Stoic school owing to his systematic elaboration of its principles. But aside from a poem of Cleanthes' and a few fragments from Zeno and Chrysippus, none of the writings of these "Old Stoics" has survived. Information about them must be pieced together from scattered references in works of a later date, and it is usually impossible to tell from these who among Zeno, Cleanthes, and Chrysippus is to be credited with a given idea. Here the usual practice of referring to the early phase of Stoicism as if it were their joint production will mostly be followed. In Stoicism's last phase, during the first two centuries of the Roman Empire (from about 30 B.C. to 180 A.D.), it surpassed Epicureanism in popularity and attracted some gifted expositors whose works still exist. We shall sample these after we have recounted the views of the Old Stoics.

Logic

Philosophy for the Stoics, as for Epicurus, has three main subdivisions: Logic, Physics, and Ethics. The Stoics include in Logic much more investigation of principles of argument than Epicurus thought it worthwhile to include in his Canonic; but otherwise their Logic resembles his Canonic in containing much that today would be classified as theory of knowledge. The most important question for the Stoics is how we may arrive at truths of which we may be perfectly certain. Wisdom, as they see it, has nothing to do with mere opinions, which may be false and which tend to be weak and unstable. "The wise man never opines, never regrets, never is mistaken, never changes his mind." It is by one's command of Logic that one protects oneself from these errors. Logic is like the fence that one puts around a cultivated field to keep out the goats, whereas Physics is like the soil, and Ethics is like the crop.

Knowledge begins with impressions (*phantasiae*) of the senses, whereby the soul is imprinted with resemblances of objects—trees and horses, ships and people—in somewhat the same way as wax may be imprinted with a seal. Impressions to which the soul gives spontaneous "assent" as accurate resemblances of objects are called "apprehensive" (*cataleptic*) impressions—"apprehensive" in the sense that by grasping or apprehending them, the soul also grasps the objects from which they derive. These apprehensive impressions constitute the all-important criterion by which we may determine what truly exists and what does not. All our general concepts are built up, directly or indirectly, from apprehensive impressions; and all our knowledge consists of truths incorporating these concepts. One learns many concepts by being taught them, and others are formed by one's conscious effort; but there are concepts that every soul is naturally stimulated by sense impressions to form willy-nilly—concepts for which Chrysippus borrowed the name "anticipations" from Epicurus—for example, the concepts of goodness, justice, and God.[2] Wisdom, which alone is knowledge in the strict sense, entails a systematic ordering of propositions concerning apprehensive impressions, by which the propositions gain such force and clarity from being connected with one another that one's conviction of their truth becomes absolutely unshakable.

The foundation stones of the entire edifice of knowledge are the *cataleptic phantasiae,* which we immediately acknowledge to be faithful pictures of the world around us. An issue arises here that is similar to the one noted in connection with the "images" of Epicurus: how do we tell that a given impression is faithful and not distorted, illusory, or delusory? Zeno is said to have maintained that faithful impressions are recognized as such by virtue of bearing a "peculiar mark" that sets them apart, but precisely what this is he seems never to have succeeded in explaining. The school of Skeptics that flourished in Plato's Academy after about 280 B.C. tirelessly attacked the Stoics on this point. In Chapter 10 we shall see how the Stoics fared in the controversy.

The propositions that are systematized into knowledge are meanings (*letka*) expressed by *signs* such as vocal sounds and written words. That meanings and signs are distinguishable is plain when one reflects that two persons may see the same words, but only one of them may understand what the words mean, as when only one knows the language in question. Both meanings and signs are in turn to be distinguished from the objects to which reference is made when one asserts propositions. "This table is square" has a table as its object of reference—an actual physical or corporeal thing. The printed words are also corporeal, of course, for they are physical marks on paper; and in this both they and the table are unlike the meaning or proposition that the sentence is used to express. The meaning or proposition, the Stoics insist, is *not* corporeal: it is not a physical thing as tables and printed words are physical things; it cannot be pointed to in the way that they may be; it is *incorporeal.*

"This table is square" expresses, to be more precise, a *complete* meaning, a meaning that may be either true or false and must be one or the other. "This table" and "square," taken separately, express what the Stoics

---

[2]Because the Stoics, unlike Epicurus, believed that everyone has from birth a disposition to form the same anticipations, they were "empiricists" in a qualified sense of the term. All concepts are formed on the basis of sense-experience, but *which* concepts are formed is to an important extent determined in advance of sense-experience.

call *incomplete* meanings because by themselves they can be neither true nor false. The simplest complete meaning is a *simple proposition* such as "This table is square," which contains, as Aristotle said, just one subject term ("This table") and one predicate term ("square"). Complex meanings are formed when two different propositions, or two occurrences of the same proposition, are joined to make a *compound proposition,* for example, "This table is square, and this table is wooden."

Zeno's studies with Megarian philosophers in Athens made him familiar with their work on the logic of compound propositions. His own contributions to the subject appear to have been modest, but they stimulated Chrysippus to undertake investigations that were remarkably fruitful and that anticipated by over two thousand years some basic elements of modern propositional logic. For instance, Chrysippus maintains that any compound proposition is, to use the modern expression, "truth-functional" in that its truth or falsity as a whole is determined by the truth or falsity of the simple propositions of which it is composed. Thus a *conjunctive* proposition, formed when two simple propositions are connected by "and" (as in "Virtue is knowledge, and virtue may be taught"), is true if both of its simple propositions are true, and otherwise it is false. A *disjunctive* proposition, formed when two simple propositions are connected by "or" in the exclusive sense[3] (as in "Virtue is knowledge, or virtue is ignorance"), is true if just one of the simple propositions is true, and otherwise it is false. A *conditional* proposition, formed when two simple propositions are connected by "If . . . then . . ." (as in "If virtue is knowledge, then virtue may be taught"), is true according to the Stoics in every case except that in which the proposition following "If" (the *antecedent,* so called) is true and the one following "then" (the *consequent*) is false. (Nowadays this is known as the "material" interpretation of conditional propositions.)

A great many deductive arguments are valid because of the ways in which the simple propositions in them are connected by "and," "or," and "If . . . then. . . ." Chrysippus believes, however, that the logical forms of all these arguments may be reduced to just five basic forms—"indemonstrables," he calls them, because their validity, already as obvious as it could be, is not going to be made any more obvious by trying to prove or demonstrate them. Here are two of Chrysippus' indemonstrables,[4] which came to be known by the Latin names of "Modus Ponens" and "Modus

---

[3] "Or" in the *exclusive* sense means "either alternative, but not both, may be true." "Or" in the *inclusive* sense means "either alternative, and even both, may be true," as in the case of "Virtue is knowledge, or virtue is correct opinion." Inclusive disjunctions seem to have been introduced into Stoic logic sometime after Chrysippus.

[4] Those who are acquainted with modern logic may be interested to see the principles of all five forms (inference schema) in symbolic notation:

1. $((p \supset q) \& p) \supset q$
2. $((p \supset q) \& -q) \supset -p$
3. $(-(p \& q) \& p) \supset -q$
4. $(((p \vee q) \& -(p \& q)) \& p) \supset -q$
5. $(((p \vee q) \& -(p \& q)) \& -q) \supset p$

Tollens," respectively. The letters "*p*" and "*q*" stand for any two simple propositions; "not-*p*" and "not-*q*" stand for "*p* is false" and "*q* is false."

1. If *p*, then *q*.

  *p.*_____

  Therefore, *q*.

Example:
If virtue is knowledge, then virtue may be taught.
Virtue is knowledge._____
Therefore, virtue may be taught.

2. If *p*, then *q*.

  Not-*q.*_____

  Therefore, not-*p*.

Example:
If virtue is knowledge, then virtue may be taught.
It is false that virtue may be taught._____
Therefore, it is false that virtue is knowledge.

The conclusions of these arguments follow with necessity from their premises because of the ways in which the simple propositions in them are related to one another as units. In order to see that the conclusions follow, one does not have to take account of the internal structures of the simple propositions; one has only to notice the form of their overall arrangement. This is shown by the fact that the form may be represented by using *p* and *q* to stand for the propositions as wholes. Such is not the case, however, with a syllogism of the Aristotelian type, whose validity depends upon the way in which the *terms* within the simple propositions are related to one another. For example, the syllogism "All animals are mortal; all men are animals; therefore, all men are mortal" is valid because of the precise relations it asserts among "animals," "mortal," and "men," which cannot be brought to light if the propositions are considered simply as units. The argument-form "*p; q;* therefore, *r*" (there are *three* simple propositions involved) is not the form by virtue of which the syllogism is valid. Something is needed along the lines of "All B's are C's; all A's are B's; therefore, all A's are C's," which shows schematically how the terms are related.

It is to Chrysippus' credit that he saw the importance of systematically analyzing the forms of arguments such as (1) and (2), which Aristotle, on the evidence available, greatly underrated.[5] Chrysippus' achievement was

---

[5] Modern logicians have shown that the logic of propositions is more fundamental than Aristotle's logic of terms, inasmuch as the latter may be derived from the former, but not vice versa.

highly praised in antiquity; indeed it was even said that, if the gods used any logic, it would be his. But he would not have been pleased with the "if" in this because no Stoic supposed for a moment that the gods, or God, could be illogical. Principles of reasoning, which Logic investigates, reflect the operations in nature of Divine Reason, which operations Physics investigates. Since these operations are mainly to be understood as relations of causes to effects, which may be represented by conditional propositions ("If this happens, then that happens"), Chrysippus was especially interested in the logic of conditional propositions and of arguments incorporating them.

Physics

In the infinite void of the universe there is a solitary ball of matter. The outer layer of the ball is a fiery aether which contains stars. Inside the aether there is a sphere of planets, then a sphere of air and another of water, and then the earth, which is at the center of everything. Such is the world, the Stoics say, but only for the time being. There will come a day when the fiery aether will have drawn into itself all the water in the world, and everything will begin to burn, and eventually nothing will remain but fire. Water, air, and earth will have become fire. Then after a long period the fire will give birth to a new world, for the fire is "like a kind of seed, containing the reasons of all things and the causes of everything, past, present, and future"; and from the fire will come air, and from air will come water, and from water will come earth; and then from the mixture of these elements will come the multitudinous things of nature, including plants and animals and humans just like those in the present world. Even so did the present world emerge from the fire that consumed the previous world, and the previous one emerge from the fire that consumed the one previous to it. There is neither beginning nor end to the series of conflagrations and rebirths. Each new world is in every detail precisely like its predecessor, so that each person, for example, has existed and will exist over and over, living exactly the same life times beyond counting.

The everlasting cycle is totally attributable to the fiery aether, which fixes the periods of death and resurrection according to the law of its own nature, and which similarly governs the course of events during the life of each world. Distinguishable things exist in a world only because amounts of aether mixed with air serve as forces of cohesion and organization with respect to the inert elements of water and earth, binding determinate proportions of water and earth together into integrated wholes. And every alteration and movement that occurs is caused by the aether, which permeates the world and, depending on how much of it an organic thing possesses, appears as a power of growth (in plants), as a power of sensation and desire (the soul in animals), or as a power of rational thought and action (the soul in humans). A wise and virtuous human soul is the purest earthly manifestation of the aether, for the aether is perfect wisdom and virtue, as may be seen from the excellence of the world it produces. It is the soul of the world and makes the world a single living being of which humans, animals, plants, and all lesser things are just so many members. In fact the aether is God, Zeus, Providence, the Logos (or Word), Universal Reason, Nature, and King of Kings—to mention but a few of the names by which the Stoics refer to it.

So do the Stoics revive the old theory of Heraclitus, adding the notion of world-cycles in which he seems not to have believed, but to which his theory naturally lends itself. Only matter exists; its permanent form is fire; and fire is a divine intelligence that contains "rational seeds" or "seminal reasons" (*logoi spermatikoi*) from which, and for the sake of which, fire modifies itself into other forms of matter and into a world of manifold things. Since fire modifies itself, two aspects are distinguishable within it—an *active* aspect that causes the modifications, and a *passive* aspect that receives the modifications. The Stoics sometimes speak as if these were not just two aspects of the same thing but two independent "principles" that "combine"—the one being "God" and the other being "unqualified matter." The idea that anything could actualize its own potential is, Aristotle believed, a confused one. Perhaps the Stoics take account of this by occasionally saying not that the divine fire actualizes its own potential for modification into other forms of matter but that the divine fire is the actuality that realizes the potential for definite qualities in a separate "unqualified matter"—these qualities being the "roots" of Empedocles, namely, dryness, wetness, coldness, and hotness (associated with earth, water, air, and ordinary fire respectively).

If only matter exists, what becomes of *meanings,* which the Stoics consider to be immaterial or incorporeal? How can they be anything at all if nothing but matter exists? The answer lies in the Stoics' peculiar view that in the "order of nature" there are entities that do not "exist" but that nevertheless are "something." *Something,* in fact, is for them the highest genus of things; those things that "exist" (material things) form one species of this genus, and those things that do not "exist" (immaterial things) form the other species. Besides meanings, this other species includes the empty space outside the world (there is none inside) and the time that elapses between the end of one world and the beginning of the next. Empty space is "that which is capable of being occupied by an existent thing but is not so occupied . . ."; it is not itself an "existent thing." Time "exists" only when there is a world of objects in motion. Yet space without objects and time without motion are still *something;* otherwise the world could not be surrounded by an infinite void, and there could not be a series of worlds with intervals of time between them. Chrysippus says that the only time that "exists" is the present moment, inasmuch as time is an attribute of motion, and motion does not *now* occur in the past or in the future, though past time and future time are still *something* (they "subsist," he says, not "exist").

Human souls do "exist," for they are "bodies"—breaths "hot and fiery"—

which come from the ever-living aether, but they do not retain forever their individual identities. They live on for some time after their respective bodies have died, but sooner or later they are absorbed back into Universal Reason—sooner in the case of the wicked, later in the case of the virtuous, as some Stoics believe. All things are dissolved, of course, in the periodic conflagrations of the world. The career of each soul, whether here or hereafter, would seem to be determined by the comprehensive plan of the Logos, which under the name of Destiny or Fate is said to be an infinite series of causes which necessitate everything that occurs, "even our thoughts." Effects follow from causes with the same necessity as that with which conclusions follow from premises in valid arguments. Thus does the Law of Nature "command what is right," and God, who is Nature, knows the whole system of interrelated causes and "what every future event will be," including every event in the life of each person. Any freedom of the human will is therefore, on the face of it, out of the question.

Chrysippus, however, wishes to show that Fate and freedom of will are really compatible. He makes a distinction between "antecedent causes" and "principal causes," which distinction he illustrates by reference to a cylinder that has been set rolling. The "antecedent cause" of its rolling is the hand that pushed it, whereas the "principal cause" of its rolling is its round shape, for it could not be rolled if its shape were, say, cubical. The cylinder's rolling, then, is not entirely owing to outside factors over which, so to speak, it has no control; much also depends upon its own configuration. Analogously, the "antecedent causes" of human thoughts and actions do not fully determine what they are; "principal causes," which are a matter of individual initiative, are necessary as well. For example, in the case of an apprehensive impression, the "antecedent cause" is an object that imparts an image of itself to one's soul; but the "principal cause" is one's *spontaneous assent* to the image as a faithful replica of an object. If "antecedent causes" are attributable to Fate and "principal causes" (as far as we are concerned) to spontaneity of soul, then the power of Fate would appear to extend only to the circumstances or occasions of our thoughts and actions. But this is not quite what Chrysippus has in mind. The scope of our spontaneity is said to be limited much more narrowly: we are free only to wish, or not to wish, to do what Fate has determined that we *will* do in any case. Chrysippus and Zeno have a favorite illustration: "Suppose a dog to be tied to a wagon. If he wishes to follow, the wagon pulls him and he follows, so that his own power and necessity [Fate] unite. But if he does not wish to follow, he will be compelled to anyhow. The same is the case with mankind also. Even if they do not wish to follow, they will be absolutely forced to enter into the fated event."

To a certain extent we can foretell what Fate has in store for us. All things are in "sympathy" with one another, the Stoics say, in the sense that every occurrence is directly or indirectly connected as cause or effect with every other; and we are able to grasp many of these connections so as to make reliable predictions. By way of methods for grasping them, the Stoics enthusiastically subscribe to astrology, divination by augury, ecstatic prophecies, dream interpretation, and the like. Anything, rightly interpreted, is a "sign" of God's will (even Zeno's broken toe), but astrological forecasts are of greatest interest to the Stoics, as indeed they are to almost everyone at this time except Skeptics and Epicureans (Epicurus, of course, dismissed astrology as superstitious nonsense). A Chaldaean named Berossos is credited with introducing astrology to the Greeks on the island of Cos early in the third century B.C., and from there it spread swiftly around the Mediterranean like a plague. The connection between heavenly bodies and earthly events upon which astrology insists was quite in line with the Stoics' general theory and fitted perfectly with their belief that planets and stars are concentrations of fiery aether and as such call for particular veneration as expressions of Universal Reason. They believed, incidentally, that the end of the world will be signaled by the return of the planets to the same relative positions they had at the beginning of the world; but it is not clear whether or how they thought they knew what the beginning positions were.

Although their official view is that, strictly speaking, only one God exists, the Stoics on the whole are defenders of the prevailing polytheism. The belief in many gods cannot be entirely erroneous, they say, or else so many persons would not have been convinced of its truth. Besides, polytheism is the basis of popular morality, and we can ill afford to weaken that. Philosophers should strive to discover some interpretation of traditional mythologies that will show them to have been essentially on the right track. This will protect popular religion from the assaults of reckless modern critics, while also refining it of its coarser elements. The means whereby the Stoics aim to accomplish these ends is the method of allegorical interpretation, which they were the first to employ systematically. The guiding supposition of the method is that accounts of the gods express truths figuratively, not literally. The gods and their activities are *symbols* for actual things, processes, or personages. Apollo, Aphrodite, Hermes, and so on, are symbols for the sun and the planets, which truly are divinities of a sort. Other gods are symbols for atmospheric phenomena and for seasons of planting and harvest, and these also are manifestations of the Word. Still other gods are symbols for great human beings— heroes and benefactors in the old days whom God selected as his special instruments. The fundamental truth of the unity of God, who is Nature and Nature's Soul, is represented in its many aspects by the ancient stories. Working over these materials from their own point of view, the Stoics themselves produced some stirring devotional poetry. Here is Cleanthes' "Hymn to Zeus":

> O God most glorious, called by many a name,
> Nature's great King, through endless years the same;
> Omnipotence, who by thy just decree

Controllest all, hail, Zeus, for unto thee
Behoves thy creatures in all lands to call.
We are thy children, we alone, of all
On earth's broad ways that wander to and fro,
Bearing thine image wheresoe'er we go.
Wherefore with songs of praise thy power I will forth show.
Lo! yonder Heaven, that round the earth is wheeled,
Follows thy guidance, still to thee doth yield
Glad homage; thine unconquerable hand
Such flaming minister, the levin brand,
Wieldeth, a sword two-edged, whose deathless might
Pulsates through all that Nature brings to light;
Vehicle of the universal Word, that flows
Through all, and in the light celestial glows
Of stars both great and small. A King of Kings
Through ceaseless ages, God, whose purpose brings
To birth, whate'er on land or in the sea
Is wrought, or in high heaven's immensity;
Save what the sinner works infatuate.
Nay, but thou knowest to make crooked straight:
Chaos to thee is order: in thine eyes
The unloved is lovely, who didst harmonize
Things evil with things good, that there should be
One Word through all things everlastingly.
One Word—whose voice alas! the wicked spurn;
Insatiate for the good their spirits yearn:
Yet seeing see not, neither hearing hear
God's universal law, which those revere,
By reason guided, happiness who win.
The rest, unreasoning, diverse shapes of sin
Self-prompted follow: for an idle name
Vainly they wrestle in the lists of fame:
Others inordinately riches woo,
Or dissolute, the joys of flesh pursue.
Now here, now there they wander, fruitless still,
For ever seeking good and finding ill.
Zeus the all-bountiful, whom darkness shrouds,
Whose lightning lightens in the thunder-clouds;
Thy children save from error's deadly sway:
Turn thou the darkness from their souls away:
Vouchsafe that unto knowledge they attain;
For thou by knowledge art made strong to reign
O'er all, and all things rulest righteously.
So by thee honored, we will honor thee,
Praising thy works continually with songs,
As mortals should; nor higher meed belongs
E'en to the gods, than justly to adore
The universal law for evermore.

If everything is controlled by Zeus the all-bountiful, how is it that evils exist? Cleanthes offers an explanation here of the evil of human wickedness: it is "self-prompted" by those of us who wander after fame, riches, joys of the flesh, and so on, instead of guiding ourselves by God's universal law. The choice is up to us; God does not control this, and so it is not entirely accurate to say that he controls everything. God does, however, see to it that the evil we do is in some way made to "harmonize" with "things good," and the suggestion is that the world does not in the long run contain fewer goods than it would have contained if no one had chosen the path of darkness. Chrysippus has a different view of the matter— one more in keeping with Stoic fatalism. He argues that evil, both in the form of human wickedness and in the form of natural calamities, is *indispensable* to the existence of good. In the first place, he says, good and evil are contraries, and in general it is impossible for one of a pair of contraries to exist without the other. There can be no justice without injustice, no courage without cowardice, no pleasure without pain, no health without sickness—in short, no good of any kind without the correlative evil. "If you take away one, you take away the other." In the second place, many good things necessarily possess some features that are not always advantageous. For example, it is good that the human head should be of delicate construction, though as a result it is easily injured. In the third place, the greatest possible goodness of the world as a whole requires the presence in it of evils that throw particular goods into apt relief, just as "comedies have in them ludicrous verses which, though bad in themselves, nevertheless lend a certain grace to the whole play."

These explanations of evil were often to figure in the defenses of God's goodness (called "theodicies") of subsequent religious thinkers other than Stoics. But it is surprising that Chrysippus should be concerned to account for anything besides human wickedness, for (as we shall see) the Stoics in general believe that nothing else is intrinsically evil; and if that is correct, there are no other evils that could be shown to be indispensable to the existence of good. Consistency on this point, as on others, is not to be found in the Stoics.

Ethics

Our well-being or happiness, Cleanthes says, is won by living in accordance with God's universal law. Since this law, or the complex of laws known collectively as the Logos, constitutes the order of nature, the Stoics also say that our well-being depends upon living "in accordance with nature." We do this by furthering Destiny's purposes in matters that depend upon us, and by assenting or submitting to all that does not depend upon us in the knowledge that it is a necessary part of Destiny's plan for the best possible world, or at least will be harmonized by Destiny with Destiny's plan. To know Destiny's purposes is to be wise. Wisdom is the sum and substance of human excellence or virtue, because it is the perfection of the distinctive feature of human nature, namely, our capacity for rational understanding. To the extent that we achieve rational understanding, we will act accordingly, since (as Socrates maintained) we always do what we think is right. Vice or wickedness is a function of ignorance, and that alone is to be considered intrinsically evil. None of the other things commonly considered evil is really evil at all. Illness, poverty, ugliness, and so on, are not evil, for they can have no effect whatever upon the wisdom in which our well-being consists. We may of course experience pain in connection with bodily suffering and be fearful or sorrowful at the prospect of it in ourselves or in others. This, however, is a mistake. We would not experience pain, fear, or sorrow unless we judged that bodily suffering is an evil, which it is not. Our experience of bodily pleasure and of desire for it rests upon judgments no less mistaken as to what is good. Epicurus is in error: pleasure is far from being our highest good and the object of everything we do. It has no value at all, according to Chrysippus, and it is not the object of anything we do. As Aristotle said, pleasure is a by-product of certain activities whose objects are other than it; and in any case, the state of mind of a virtuous person is not correctly described as "pleasurable" but, rather, as "tranquil" (Zeno's term is "smooth"). Virtue alone is intrinsically good, and everything else is "indifferent" or "neutral," except for vice, which is evil. With this understanding we are prepared for whatever Destiny has in store for us: it will be all the same from the point of view of our inner tranquillity.

Tranquillity is a difficult achievement because virtue presupposes what the Stoics call *apathia,* that is, the complete eradication of irrational passions and emotions. And these have been encouraged in us from childhood by our parents and teachers and peers, who would have us think that indifferent things such as health, wealth, and pleasure are all-important. The instinctive impulse toward self-preservation that we have at birth is soon perverted by these social pressures: we get into the habit of thinking that indifferent things are essential to our well-being. This habit must be broken. We should realize that the delight we took as children in simply finding out about things, and our impatience with falsehood and deception, were expressions of a profoundly correct impulse. We should once again settle for nothing less than the truth and should enlighten ourselves accordingly by studies in logic and physics, whereby we will come to apprehend the awesome harmonious order of the world's constitution and to recognize that our well-being—our true "preservation"—lies in an unshakable attitude of cooperation and conformity with it. Such is the duty laid upon us by that "right reason" which is represented by the Logos and which is nature's law and the law of our nature.

Virtue and vice, the Stoics insist, differ in *kind,* not merely in *degree.* Good and evil are not to be described in quantitative terms. They are qualitative and absolute in the sense that where one is present, it is present fully and completely, and the other is totally absent. Aristotle was wrong in thinking that one vice (say, rashness) may be less evil than another (say, cowardice). All vices are equally evil, and (as Socrates said) they are all expressions of the one great vice of ignorance. Aristotle was also wrong in thinking that a virtue may be a mean between extremes of vice, and that it may be less opposed to one extreme than to the other (as when he said that courage is less opposed to rashness than to cowardice). All virtues are equally opposed to all vices, and they are all expressions of the one great virtue of wisdom. This we either have or do not have. There is no such thing as being more or less wise, virtuous, and tranquil. When it comes to ethics, a miss is as good as a mile, for all are equally foolish, depraved, and miserable who are any distance at all from wisdom. The transition from foolishness to wisdom is instantaneous: one achieves with suddenness a radical conversion of perspective in which harmony with the Logos becomes one's only concern. Such a virtuous disposition, once attained, can never be lost (except, Chrysippus says, in cases of mental disease). The happiness that results is equal to God's and is not increased by the time it lasts.

Wise persons, never numerous, are in the Stoics' opinion getting fewer and fewer. Be that as it may, certainly fewer persons would have been attracted to Stoicism if its spokesmen had kept to the strict position just described. Its popularity owed more than a little to concessions that were made to the frailties of the multitude. The abrupt distinction between the foolish and the wise was modified by recognizing and encouraging a third group in the middle—persons who are making progress toward wisdom and who thereby merit the title of "proficients." Moreover, the classification according to which virtue alone is intrinsically good, vice alone is intrinsically evil, and all other things are simply indifferent was amended by the introduction of a threefold classification of indifferent things. (1) Some indifferent things, though not essential to well-being, may be so employed as to enhance well-being. As such these things are in accordance with nature and are said to be "preferred," that is, usually preferable. Examples are life itself, health, pleasure, beauty, strength, wealth, fame, and noble birth. (2) Other indifferent things, though not necessarily destructive of well-being, are not normally conducive to it either. As such they are contrary to nature and are said to be "rejected," that is, usually not preferable. Examples are death, disease, pain, ugliness, weakness, poverty, obscurity, and ignoble birth. (3) Finally, still other indifferent things have no bearing at all upon our well-being and may be termed "indifferent" in a narrower sense. Whether one has an odd or an even number of hairs on one's head, or whether one holds out a finger straight or bent, is of no significance from the standpoint of one's happiness. Such things are neither in accordance with nature nor contrary to nature; they have neither value nor disvalue, but are absolutely neutral.

On the basis of this classification of indifferent things, the Stoics developed a secondary system of ethics suited to "proficients." Only the wise possess the virtuous attitude necessary for actions that are, in the strict sense, morally good. Those who are progressing toward wisdom, however, are capable of actions that have a subordinate type of value called "appropriateness." Appropriate actions are those that are calculated to achieve things "preferred" and avert things "rejected" when the Logos has determined that we do not have to renounce the one or acquiesce in the other. Exactly which actions are appropriate in various practical situations is best known to the wise, who have the fullest understanding of the ways of the Logos, and those of us who are merely on the road to wisdom will naturally seek their counsel. Thus we may acquire correct opinions from which we can perform as "simple" duties the actions that the wise, with their complete moral knowledge, perform as "perfect" duties. To this end, the Stoics evolved a vast literature of detailed moral advice.

Unlike Epicurus, the Stoics do not advise us to "live unknown." On the contrary, we should recognize that our rationality, as an expression of the Logos, relates us to all mortals and gods, and that consequently we are obligated to live for others. All rational beings stand under the same law of nature and have the same rights. It is evidence of this that we possess an instinctive impulse to associate with others and to benefit them—an impulse which shows up in the affection of parents for their offspring but which encompasses a wider and wider circle the more we realize that all of us are akin. Benevolence and justice without partiality, the two things most essential to a satisfactory social existence, are demanded by Nature. Our kinship with the whole of humanity is of far greater significance than our membership in a particular state. Differences among forms of government are entirely conventional. All persons are to be understood as having citizenship in the same great *polis* or City which is the cosmos—the Cosmopolis—whose one constitution and law is the Logos. Everyone without exception has a claim to our good will. Enemies are to be shown mercy and forgiveness. No one, in spite of Aristotle's arguments, is a "slave by nature." "We are born for society and intercourse, and for a natural partnership with our fellow men. . . . How inconsistent it would be for us to expect the immortal gods to love and cherish us, when we ourselves despise and neglect one another!"

Such, then, were the views of the Old Stoics of Greece. Now let us see how they were received in Rome.

Roman Stoicism

Greece came under the control of Rome in 168 B.C., and thereafter the Roman Senate was the final authority in settling disputes between the highly disputatious Greek cities. In 155 B.C. Athens considered that she had been grievously wronged by the city of Sicyon. It seems that Athens had raided the city of Oropus, that Oropus had sued for damages, and that Rome had referred the matter to Sicyon for arbitration. When Sicyon concluded that Athens should pay a heavy fine, Athens was furious and sent an embassy to Rome with the charge of inducing the Senate to reverse the decision. Three of Athens' most prominent philosophers were commissioned to present her case—Critolaus the Peripatetic, Carneades the Skeptic, and Diogenes the Stoic.[6] Their arguments before the Senate, and their public appearances on the side, created an immense sensation. Philosophy was suddenly all the rage, particularly among the Roman youth. "Most of the Romans," Plutarch says, "were gratified by this, and were well content to see their sons embrace Greek culture and frequent the society of such estimable men."

Certain conservative pillars of Roman society, however, were not prepared to see Greek culture embraced. Cato the Elder, who had been consul of Rome in 195 B.C. and afterward a censor, was representative of those who felt that an enthusiasm for philosophy was scarcely compatible with the grave and severe soldierly virtues that had given Rome her empire. Plutarch explains:

> Cato, from the moment that this passion for [philosophical] discussion first showed itself in Rome, was deeply disturbed. He was afraid that the younger generation might allow their ambitions to be diverted in this direction, and might come to value most highly a reputation that was based upon feats of oratory rather than upon feats of arms. So when the prestige of the philosophers continued to rise still higher . . . , Cato made up his mind to find some plausible excuse for clearing the whole tribe of philosophers out of the city. Accordingly he rose in the Senate and criticized the authorities for having kept in such long suspense a delegation composed of men whose powers of persuasion were so remarkable that they could obtain any verdict that they wished. "We ought to come to a decision as soon as possible," he declared, "and take a vote on their proposal, so that these distinguished men may return to their seats of learning and lecture to the sons of Greece, but leave the youth of Rome to give their attention to the laws and the magistrates, as they have done in the past. . . . "
>
> Cato . . . was opposed on principle to the study of philosophy. . . . His patriotic fervor made him regard the whole of Greek culture and its methods of education with contempt. He asserts, for example, that Socrates was a turbulent windbag, who did his best to tyrannize over his country by undermining its established customs and seducing his fellow-citizens into holding opinions which were contrary to the laws. . . . In [Cato's] effort to turn his son against Greek culture, he allowed himself an utterance which was absurdly rash for an old man: he pronounced with all the solemnity of a prophet that if ever the Romans became infected with the literature of Greece, they would lose their empire.

As Plutarch goes on to note, Cato's prophecy could not have been more mistaken: "For in the age when the city rose to the zenith of her great-

---

[6] Not the same as Diogenes the Cynic.

ness, her people had made themselves familiar with Greek learning and culture in all its forms." Stoicism in particular found favor in the highest ranks of Roman society not long after Diogenes—a successor of Chrysippus as head of the school—had paid his visit to Rome with the Athenian embassy. One of Diogenes' former pupils, Panetius of Rhodes (about 180–110 B.C.), spent seventeen years in close company with Scipio Aemilianus, a Roman military and political leader who gathered around him eminent Greek men of letters. Panetius instructed Scipio and his friends in Stoic philosophy, and thenceforth the most noted statesmen and scholars of Rome professed themselves to be Stoics—among others Rutilius Rufus, proconsul of Asia Minor, and Quintus Scaevola, the founder of Roman jurisprudence. Panetius' most important pupil was Posidonius of Apamaea (135–51 B.C.), who was a friend of many distinguished Romans and who opened a school on the island of Rhodes where he was visited by such personages as Pompey and Cicero.

Stoicism increasingly became the semi-official philosophy of the Roman establishment. The allegorical method by which the Stoics aimed to make polytheism intellectually respectable was seized upon by educated Romans who could not believe literally in the traditional religion of Jupiter, Juno, and Minerva but who nevertheless viewed it as the cement of Roman society. The Stoics' doctrine of the Cosmopolis seemed to many leading Romans an inspiring philosophical formulation of their designs for a world community under Roman law—an interpretation of the doctrine which Posidonius was especially responsible for encouraging. The Stoics' view of knowledge as a logical ordering of truths, and their methodical elaboration of rules of conduct for "proficients," was quite to the mind of the Romans, who felt that a systematic treatment of their morals, regulations, and laws was urgently required. The personal qualities enjoined by the Stoics—endurance, self-restraint, simplicity of habit, dedication to the community—were closely in line with the old Roman idea of *virtus* (a Latin word which, like the Greek *arete,* is very imperfectly translated by the English "virtue"). Here it is possible only to indicate some highlights of the important and complex developments of Stoic ideas during the final phase of the Roman Republic and the first two centuries of the Empire. Three principal figures are described in the following sections.

Cicero

Marcus Tullius Cicero was born in 106 B.C. of a well-to-do family in the central Italian hill-town of Arpinium (now Arpino) and was educated in law and philosophy at Rome, Athens, and Rhodes. His brilliance as a public speaker soon won him a formidable reputation as a trial lawyer in Rome and a prominent place in the Senate. During more than twenty years of political activity, Cicero conducted a losing campaign against the autocratic forces that sought to abolish the Republican system of Roman government and that succeeded in doing so, once and for all, when Julius

Caesar became dictator in 49 B.C. Caesar's assassination in 44 B.C., which Cicero applauded but was not a party to, resulted only in the ruthless committee-government or "Triumvirate" of Octavian, Lepidus, and Antony, in which Antony had the upper hand. Cicero excoriated Antony in speeches before the Senate, and in 43 B.C. Antony had Cicero murdered.

Cicero's deepest personal sorrow was occasioned by the death of his daughter Tullia, during pregnancy, in February of 45 B.C. He retired to his country house at Tusculum and immersed himself in literary activity—"the only way," he said, "I can get away from my misery." By November of 44 B.C. he had composed a dozen treatises, including such philosophical works as *Academics, On the Greatest Degrees of Good and Evil, Tusculan Disputations, On Fate, On the Nature of the Gods,* and *On Duties.* Also dating from this period are Cicero's famous essays *On Friendship* and *On Old Age.* In these works, and in others *On the State* and *On Laws* written a few years earlier, it was Cicero's plan to explain, in Latin for a wide Roman audience, the chief positions of the Greek philosophical schools. Having the practical bent that was characteristic of the Romans, he aimed further to show how philosophical principles may be applied to actual problems and to give examples from Roman experience. His success was complete. There has never been a more eloquent and effective popularizer. For centuries his writings were staples of education and made upon the Western mind an impression that may be estimated from a remark of John Adams, the second American president: "All the ages of the world," Adams said of Cicero, "have not produced a greater statesman and philosopher combined." As a contemporary scholar has observed: "The influence of Cicero upon the history of European literature and ideas greatly exceeds that of any other prose writer in any language. In most of the literary, political, religious, ethical, and educational controversies that have gravely agitated Western mankind, he has been passionately and incessantly quoted—usually by both sides."

The philosophy of Cicero is said to be "eclectic" because he arrived at it by developing and combining views that he selected as true or probable from various philosophical schools ("eclectic" derives from the Greek for "select"). He denied that any one philosophical school had a monopoly of the truth, and he tended to suspend judgment on matters about which different schools appeared to be in irreconcilable disagreement. Since an eclectic approach to philosophy was recommended in his day by those who had fallen heir to Plato's Academy—the "New Academy," it was called—Cicero considered himself a "New Academic." Nevertheless, when it came to moral and political philosophy, he was most in sympathy with a modified form of Stoicism—one that recognized the existence both of free will and of a " 'second-class' kind of goodness [for 'proficients'], which is not the exclusive possession of the hypothetical man of ideal wisdom, but is relevant to the whole of mankind." Of particular historical significance was Cicero's application to Roman jurisprudence of the Stoic notion of the law of nature. Over and above the written legal code pertaining to Roman citizens (the *jus civile,* in Latin) and that pertaining to foreigners (the *jus genitum*), there is, Cicero maintained, an unwritten code of natural law (the *jus naturale*) that is valid for all persons by virtue of their common humanity, and that is the ultimate standard of justice. No statute in the *jus civile* or *jus genitum* is to be recognized as a true law if it is unjust according to the *jus naturale.* This standpoint was incorporated by the jurists who, during the reign of the emperor Justinian (527–565 A.D.), codified Roman law in the *Corpus Juris Civilis,* which today is still the basis of most Continental European law.[7]

In *On Duties (De officiis),* the most influential of all his works, Cicero develops the Stoic position that law and ethics have a common foundation in the law of nature according to which all men are brothers. Here are some representative passages:

> To take something away from someone else—to profit by another's loss— is more unnatural than death, or destitution, or pain, or any other physical or external blow. To begin with, this strikes at the roots of human society and fellowship. For if we each of us propose to rob or injure one another for our personal gain, then we are clearly going to demolish what is more emphatically nature's creation than anything else in the whole world: namely, the link that unites every human being with every other. Just imagine if each of our limbs had its own consciousness and saw advantage for itself in appropriating the nearest limb's strength! Of course the whole body would inevitably collapse and die. In precisely the same way, a general seizure and appropriation of other people's property would cause the collapse of the human community, the brotherhood of man. Granted that there is nothing unnatural in a man preferring to earn a living for himself rather than for someone else, what nature forbids is that we should increase our own means, property, and resources by plundering others.
>
> Indeed this idea—that one must not injure anybody else for one's own profit—is not only natural law [*jus naturale*], an international valid principle: the same idea is also incorporated in the statutes [*jus civile*] which individual communities have framed for their national purposes. The whole point and intention of these statutes is that one citizen shall live safely with another. . . .
>
> The same conclusion follows even more forcibly from nature's *rational principle,* the law that governs gods and men alike. Whoever obeys this principle—and everyone who wants to live according to nature's laws must obey it—will never be guilty of coveting another man's goods or taking things from someone else and appropriating them for himself. For great-heartedness and heroism, and courtesy, and justice, and gen-

---

[7] A trace of the Roman *jus naturale* is contained in the opening paragraph of the Declaration of Independence, where it is said that the American people lay claim to "the separate and equal station to which the law of nature and of nature's God entitle them."

erosity, are far more in conformity with nature than self-indulgence, or wealth, or even life itself. . . .

So everyone ought to have the same purpose: to identify the interest of each with the interest of all. Once men grab for themselves, human society will completely collapse. But if nature prescribes (as she does) that every human being must help every other human being, whoever he is, just precisely because they are all human beings, then—by the same authority—all men have identical interests. Having identical interests means that we are all subject to one and the same law of nature: and, that being so, the very least that such a law enjoins is that we must not wrong one another. This conclusion follows inevitably from the truth of the initial assumption.

If people claim (as they sometimes do) that they have no intention of robbing their parents or brothers for their own gain, but that robbing their other compatriots is a different matter, they are not talking sense. For that is the same as denying their common interest with their fellow-countrymen, and all the legal or social obligations that follow therefrom: a denial which shatters the whole fabric of national life. Another objection urges that one ought to take account of compatriots but not of foreigners [thus denying the force of *jus genitum*]. But people who put forward these arguments subvert the whole foundation of the human community . . . which is a sin against the immortal gods, since they were the creators of the society which such men are seeking to undermine. . . .

Cases arise, however, in which it seems that it is greatly to one's personal advantage to do something that is wrong from the point of view of *jus naturale*. Cicero is anxious to explain that in every such case this can seem to be true only because of a mistaken conception of personal advantage. One's well-being consists in moral integrity, and nothing incompatible with this may be accounted truly advantageous.

When we encounter advantage in some plausible form, we cannot help being impressed. But close examination may reveal something morally wrong with this apparently advantageous action. In such a case the question of abandoning advantage does not arise, since it is axiomatic that where there is wrong there can be no true advantage. For nature demands that all things should be right and harmonious and consistent with itself and therefore with each other. But nothing is less harmonious with nature than wrongdoing: and equally, nothing is more in harmony with nature than what is truly advantageous. So advantage cannot possibly coexist with wrong. . . .

A man who has in mind an apparent advantage and promptly proceeds to dissociate this from the question of what is right shows himself to be mistaken and immoral. Such a standpoint is the parent of . . . desire for excessive wealth, for unendurable tyranny, and ultimately for the despotic seizure of free states. These desires are the most horrible and repulsive things imaginable. The perverted intelligences of men who are animated by such feelings are competent to understand the material rewards, but not the penalties. I do not mean the penalties established by law, for these they often escape. I mean the most terrible of all penalties: their own degradation.

Away, then, with the whole wicked, godless crowd of people who hesitate which course to follow—the course they know to be right, or deliberate immersion and self-pollution in sin and crime! For the mere fact of their indecision is an offence: some courses of action are wrong even to contemplate—merely to pause over them is evil. . . .

There is an ideal of human goodness: nature itself has stored and wrapped this up inside our minds. Unfold this ideal, and you will straightaway identify the good man as the person who helps everybody he can and, unless wrongfully provoked, harms none. . . .

Obviously we all aim at our own advantage: we find that irresistibly attractive. No one can possibly work *against* his own interests—indeed no one can refrain from pursuing them to the best of his ability. But seeing that our advantage can only be found in good repute, honor, and right, priority and primacy must be accorded to these. The advantage that goes with them should be interpreted as their indispensable accompaniment rather than as a glorious objective in itself.

Cicero illustrates these points with reference to a variety of actual cases in which there seems to be a conflict between right and advantage. The following humorous story appears in a section of *On Duties* where he is discussing fraudulent business practices:

A Roman gentleman called Gaius Canius, quite a witty and cultured man, once went to Syracuse, not on business but on holiday. . . . He often spoke of buying a little estate where he could invite his friends and enjoy himself without intrusion. When his intention became known, a Syracusan banker called Pythias disclosed his own possession of just such a property; this was not for sale, he said, but Canius could treat the place as his own if he wanted to. Pythias forthwith asked him to dinner there on the following day, and Canius accepted.

Now Pythias, being a banker, had people of all classes ready to oblige him. So he sent for some fishermen, and requested them to do their next day's fishing in front of his grounds; and he issued them full instructions. Canius arrived to dinner punctually, and Pythias gave him a sumptuous entertainment. Before their gaze there was a fleet of fishing-boats; each fisherman brought in his catch, which he then deposited at Pythias' feet. "Tell me, Pythias," said Canius, "what does this mean?—all these fish and all these boats?" "It is quite natural," Pythias replied. "All the fish and all the water in Syracuse are at this very spot; without this place of mine, the men could do nothing."

Canius became excited and pressed Pythias to sell him the property. Pythias showed reluctance at first; but finally—to cut the story short—he gave in. Canius was rich and wanted the estate, and he paid what

Pythias asked—and bought all its furnishings as well. Pythias clinched the agreement and entered the terms in his books.

On the following day Canius invited his friends to the house, and arrived early. As far as boats were concerned, he saw not so much as a single thole-pin. He inquired from his next-door neighbor if there was some fisherman's holiday which accounted for their invisibility. "I don't know of any," was the answer. "But nobody does fish here; so yesterday I couldn't think what had happened."

Canius was furious. But what was he to do? For at that time my friend and colleague Gaius Aquilius Gallus had not yet laid down the established forms of pleading in cases of criminal fraud. When Aquilius was asked what he meant by criminal fraud in this connection, he used to answer: *pretending one thing and doing another*—a masterly reply, characteristic of a lawyer so expert at framing definitions.

So Pythias and everyone else whose actions belie their words are ill-intentioned, faithless, and dishonest. Nothing that such vicious people do can possibly be advantageous. . . .

As I have said before—and it needs constant repetition!—there is a bond of community that links every man in the world with every other. . . . The existence of this . . . explains why [we] make a distinction between the civil law of the land and the universal law. The law of the land, it is true, ought to be capable of inclusion within the universal law, but they are not synonymous since the latter is more comprehensive.

Not that we possess any clear-cut, tangible images to show us what true, authentic Law and Justice really look like! We have only outline sketches. And the extent to which we allow ourselves to be guided even by these leaves a great deal to be desired. For at least they have the merit of derivation from the finest models—those which have been vouchsafed to us by nature and by truth. Think of the nobility of that formula: *that I be not deceived and defrauded because of you and because of trust in you*. And that other golden phrase: *between honest men there must be honest dealing and no deception*. . . .

This is not a question of the anger of the gods, which does not exist, but of right dealing and good faith.

Epictetus

The enthusiasm for Stoic ideas that generally characterized Roman officialdom was not shared by the despotic emperor Domitian, who in 89 A.D. banished all philosophers from Rome. He believed that philosophers in general were given to seditious activities and that some of them had supported an ill-starred revolt against his reign during the previous year. Stoics in particular came under suspicion because they taught that anyone who acquires political power receives it from God and is expected by Him to exercise it, as a servant of the people, for the benefit of all—a view scarcely consistent with the blind submission that Domitian required of his subjects in recognition of his own absolute authority. Certainly Domitian cannot have been pleased with Epictetus, who was the most notable of the Stoics whom he banished. Epictetus was known to say that his regard for the emperor was of exactly the same intensity as his regard for his water-pot. Nor can Domitian have been gratified with the numbers of Roman youths who continued to enroll in Epictetus' school at its new location of Nicopolis in northwestern Greece, but he seems to have given up trying to put Epictetus out of commission.

Born around 50 A.D. in Heiropolis, a city in the region of Asia Minor called Phrygia, Epictetus was the son of a slave-woman and was himself a slave in Rome of someone in Nero's retinue. He was allowed to study philosophy—not as strange as it might seem, for Roman families of high station customarily had slaves as tutors for their children. Eventually— when is uncertain—he was emancipated, as were many slaves who either purchased their freedom (as by saving from the stipends they often received) or were given it as a reward for faithful service.[8] It appears that Epictetus was lame, but nothing is known about how or when he became so. He is said to have lived with the simplicity befitting a Stoic and to have married in old age so as to adopt a child who was going to be "exposed" (in keeping with an appalling old practice) by parents who did not want it. Like Socrates, for whom he had the highest admiration, Epictetus wrote nothing; but his pupil Flavius Arrianus transcribed his lectures in eight books (the *Discourses,* of which four books have survived) and composed a short handbook (*Enchiridion*) of his main teachings. Epictetus was about eighty years old when he died around 130 A.D.

Epictetus' opinion of slavery? As a Stoic he of course maintained that all human beings have equal citizenship in the Cosmopolis by virtue of their common rationality, and thus he disagreed with Aristotle's view that some persons are "slaves by nature" owing to their congenitally inferior rationality. But neither Epictetus nor any other Stoic, from what we can tell, went so far as to advocate that slavery be abolished. To have pressed for any such fundamental change in Roman society would have run counter to two key elements of the Stoics' position (elements not easily squared with one another), namely, their grateful acceptance of everything in the world as a product of Divine Providence,[9] and their belief that anyone's particular circumstances, although perhaps not "preferred," are ultimately "indifferent." Epictetus insists indeed that slaves be decently treated—as when he says that one should not deal harshly with a slave who performs some service imperfectly, because the slave is one's brother in God. Yet he goes on to say that in mistreating a slave one is abusing the "place of authority" to which one has been "appointed" by God. Passing over the problem of how mistreatment of anyone is hu-

---

[8] So many were emancipated during Augustus' reign (27 B.C.–14 A.D.) that he, fearing the value of Roman citizenship would be cheapened, set thirty as the minimum age for emancipation.

[9] Or at least as employed by Providence in bringing about a world that is perfect as a whole.

manly avoidable if everything is determined by Providence, and the problem of why mistreatment *should* be avoided if everything is determined by Providence for the best, we may simply note that equal citizenship in the Cosmopolis does not for Epictetus entail a right to equal citizenship in Rome. Some persons are appointed to places of superiority, others to places of inferiority, and that (unless, God willing, one is emancipated) is that. But Epictetus admonishes masters and consoles slaves by enlarging upon the Stoic doctrine that one's position in life has nothing to do with the extent to which one is genuinely free. Freedom depends entirely upon willing what God wills, and that is something that any slave can do and any master may not (and then it is the master who is really the slave).

Following are some passages from Epictetus' *Discourses* in which basic themes of Stoicism find expression in lofty and forthright terms.

[*An Argument for God's Existence*] Each single thing that comes into being in the universe affords a ready ground for praising Providence, if one possesses these two qualities—a power to see clearly the circumstances of each, and the spirit of gratitude therewith. . . . If God had created colors and, in general, all visible things, but had not created a faculty to behold them, of what use would they be? . . . Who is it then that has adapted this to that, and that to this? Who is it that has fitted the sword to the scabbard and the scabbard to the sword? Is there no one? Surely the very structure of such finished products leads us commonly to infer that they must be the work of some craftsman, and are not constructed at random. Are we to say then that each of these products points to the craftsman, but that things visible and vision and light do not? Do not male and female and the desire of union and the power to use the organs adapted for it—do not these point to the craftsman [that is, to a Divine Craftsman]? But if these things are so, then the fact that the intellect is so framed that we are not merely the passive subjects of sensations, but select and subtract from them and add to them, and by this means construct objects, nay more, that we pass from them to others which are not in mere juxtaposition—I say are not these facts sufficient to rouse men's attention and to deter them from leaving out the craftsman? . . . How is it possible that objects so marvellously designed should have come into being by chance and at random?

[*Our Relation to God*] You are a fragment of God Himself, you have in yourself a part of Him. Why then are you ignorant of your high birth? . . . Will you not remember, when you eat, who you are that eat, and whom you are feeding, and the same in your relations with women? When you take part in society, or training, or conversation, do you not know that it is God you are nourishing and training? . . . You bear Him about within you and are unaware that you are defiling Him with unclean thoughts and foul actions. . . .

[*Our Vocation*] God makes one animal for eating, and another for service in farming, another to produce cheese, and others for different uses of a like nature, for which there is no need of understanding impressions and being able to distinguish them, but He brought man into the world to take cognizance of Himself and His works, and not only to take cognizance but also to interpret them. Therefore it is beneath man's dignity to begin and end where the irrational creatures do; he must rather begin where they do and end where nature has ended in forming us; and nature ends in contemplation and understanding and a way of life in harmony with nature. See to it that ye do not die without taking cognizance of these things.

[*The Benefit of Understanding*] When a man . . . has learnt to understand the government of the universe and has realized that there is nothing so great or sovereign or all-inclusive as this frame of things wherein men and gods are united, and that from it come the seeds from which are sprung . . . all things that are begotten and that grow upon the earth, and rational creatures in particular—for these alone are by nature fitted to share in the society of God, being connected with Him by the bond of reason—why should he not call himself a citizen of the universe and a son of God? Why should he fear anything that can happen to him among men? When kinship with Caesar or any other of those who are powerful in Rome is sufficient to make men live in security, above all scorn and free from every fear, shall not the fact that we have God as maker and father and kinsman relieve us from pains and fears?

[*The Penalty of Ignorance*] What punishment is there, you ask, for those who do not accept things in this spirit? Their punishment is to be as they are. . . .

[*Against Epicurus*] If Epicurus should come and say that the good must be in the flesh, that . . . means a long discussion; it means we must be taught what is the commanding faculty in us, what constitutes our substantial and true nature. If it is not probable that the good of the snail is in the shell, is it probable that man's good is in his body? Take yourself, Epicurus. What is the more masterly faculty you possess? What is it in you which deliberates, which examines everything, which examines the flesh itself and decides that it is the principal thing? Why do you light a lamp and toil for us, and write such big volumes? Is it that we may not be ignorant of the truth? Who are we? What concern have we with you? So the argument becomes a long one. . . .

[*The Uniqueness of Reason*] The reasoning faculty . . . alone of the faculties we have received is created to comprehend even its own nature; that is to say, what it is and what it can do, and with what peculiar qualities it has come to us, and to comprehend all other faculties as well. . . . [It is] the one blessing that is best of all and master of all, that and nothing else, the power to deal rightly with our impressions. . . .

What says Zeus? "Epictetus, if it were possible I would have made your body and your possessions (those trifles that you prize) free and untrammelled. But as things are—never forget this—this body is not yours, it is but a clever mixture of clay. But since I could not make it free, I gave you a portion in our divinity, this faculty of impulse to act and not to act, of will to get and will to avoid, in a word the faculty which can turn impressions to right use. If you pay heed to this, and put your affairs in its keeping, you will never suffer let or hindrance, you will not groan, you will blame no man, you will flatter none. . . .

[*A Clarification*] I do not mean that you may not groan, but do not groan in spirit.

[*The Aim of Education*] Education is just this—learning to frame one's will in accord with events. How do events happen? They happen as the Disposer of events has ordained them. He ordained summer and winter, fruitful and barren seasons, virtue and vice and all such opposites for the sake of the harmony of the universe. . . .

Remembering then that things are thus ordained we ought to approach education, not that we may change the conditions of life—that is not given to us, nor is it good for us—but that, our circumstances being as they are and as nature makes them, we may conform our mind to events.

[*One's Station and Its Duties*] Is it in your power to take the task you choose? No, a body is given you of such a kind, parents of such a kind, brothers of such a kind, a country of such a kind, a position in it of such a kind. . . . Have you not the resources to deal with what is given you?

[*Service to Others*] It is natural to man, as to other creatures, to do everything for his own sake; for even the sun does everything for his own sake, and in a word so does Zeus himself. But when he would be called "The Rain-giver" and "Fruit-giver" and "Father of men and gods," you see that he cannot win these names or do these works unless he does some good to the world at large: and in general he has so created the nature of the rational animal that he can attain nothing good for himself unless he contributes some service to the community. So it turns out that to do everything for his own sake is not unsocial. . . .

[*Indifferent Things*] The essence of good and evil lies in an attitude of the will.

What are external things then?

They are materials for the will, in dealing with which it will find its own good or evil.

How will it find its good?

If it does not value overmuch the things that it deals with. For its judgments on matters presented to it, if they be right, make the will good, and if crooked and perverse make it bad. This law God has ordained and says, "If you want anything good, get it from yourself."

Material things are indifferent, but how we handle them is not indifferent. . . .

How then are we to maintain the constant and tranquil mind, and therewith the careful spirit which is not random or hasty? . . .

We act very much as if we were on a voyage. What can I do? I can choose out the helmsman, the sailors, the day, the moment. Then a storm arises. What do I care? I have fulfilled my task: another has now to act, the helmsman. Suppose even the ship goes down. What have I to do then? I do only what lies in my power, drowning, if drown I must, without fear, not crying out or accusing heaven, for I know that what is born must needs also perish. For I am not immortal, but a man, a part of the universe as an hour is part of the day. . . .

A man must certainly cultivate skill in regard to some outward things: he need not accept a thing for its own sake, but he should show his skill in regard to it, whatever it be. . . . Sustenance and property are given to you by Another, who can take them away from you, yes and your bit of body as well.

It is for you, then, to take what is given you and make the most of it.

[*On Suicide*] Suppose someone made the room smoke. If the smoke is moderate I will stay: if excessive, I go out: for one must remember and hold fast to this, that the door is open. . . .

But let me not cast [my life] off without reason or from a faint heart, or for a casual pretext. . . . God wills it not: for He has need of a world like this, and of such creatures as ourselves to move upon the earth. But if He give the signal of retreat, . . . one must obey His signal as that of the general in command.

[*On Tenacity*] I will show you the sinews of a philosopher.
"What do you mean by sinews?"
Will to achieve that fails not, will to avoid that falls not into evil, impulse to act appropriately, strenuous purpose, assent that is not precipitate. This is what you shall see.

Marcus Aurelius

Domitian was assassinated in 96 A.D. Such was the resentment against him that his name was removed from all public inscriptions and all his decrees were annulled. Rome was now to have a succession of capable rulers—the "five good emperors" Nerva, Trajan, Hadrian, Antoninus Pius, and Marcus Aurelius—who fully accepted the Stoic position that an emperor is only the "first citizen" (*princeps*) of the state, divinely appointed as guardian of the public interest. Outstanding among these emperors was Marcus Aurelius, who introduced a number of wise and humane reforms while coping with an eruption of disasters—including a plague that is estimated to have carried off a quarter of the entire population, a famine resulting from huge agricultural losses caused by floods, and a series of barbarian invasions across the northern frontier of the Empire. Marcus was born in 121 A.D., was the adopted son as well as the son-in-law of

Antoninus Pius, and was emperor from 161 to 180 A.D. In his youth he was encouraged to study philosophy by Junius Rusticus, who was prefect of Rome and an admirer of Epictetus, and the result was that Marcus grew up to become Stoicism's last great representative and one of the most engaging philosophers of antiquity. Gibbon, in *The Decline and Fall of the Roman Empire,* says of him that

> his life was the noblest commentary on the precepts of Zeno. He was severe to himself, indulgent to the imperfections of others, just and beneficent to all mankind. He regretted that Avidius Cassius, who excited a rebellion in Syria, had disappointed him, by a voluntary death, of the pleasure of converting an enemy into a friend; and he justified the sincerity of that sentiment by moderating the zeal of the Senate against the adherents of the traitor. War he detested as the disgrace and calamity of human nature; but when the necessity of a just defense called upon him to take up arms, he readily exposed his person to eight winter campaigns on the frozen banks of the Danube, the severity of which was at last [in 180 A.D.] fatal to the weakness of his constitution. His memory was revered by a grateful posterity, and above a century after his death, many persons preserved the image of Marcus among those of their household gods.

Unfortunately no transcripts have survived of the popular lectures on Stoicism that Marcus periodically delivered—"in a more public manner," Gibbon feels, "than was perhaps consistent with the modesty of a sage or the dignity of an emperor." But what we have is undoubtedly more interesting—the contents of the little volume (called *Meditations*) in which Marcus was accustomed, both at home and on military campaigns, to make notes for his own reference of the thoughts that occurred to him. These notes reveal a personality of rare gentleness and refinement, on the one hand prone to feel that nothing in human life is of any value, but on the other hand finding strength to persevere with heavy responsibilities by taking Stoic principles to heart. Here are some typical passages, arranged so as to contrast these two tendencies in Marcus' reflections. First, the darker tendency:

> Think continually [Marcus says to himself] how many physicians are dead after often contracting their eyebrows over the sick; and how many astrologers after predicting with great pretensions the deaths of others; and how many philosophers after endless discourses on death or immortality; how many heroes after killing thousands; and how many tyrants who have used their power over men's lives with terrible insolence as if they were immortal; and how many cities are entirely dead, so to speak, Helice and Pompeii and Herculaneum, and others innumerable. . . . Always observe how ephemeral and worthless human things are, and what was yesterday a little mucus tomorrow will be a mummy or ashes.

Altogether the interval is small between birth and death; and consider how much trouble, and in company with what sort of people and in what a feeble body this interval is laboriously passed. Do not then consider life a thing of any value.

Soon, very soon, thou wilt be ashes, or a skeleton, and either a name or not even a name; but name is sound and echo. And the things which are much valued in life are empty and rotten and trifling, and like little dogs biting one another, and little children quarreling, laughing, and then straightway weeping. . . . To have good repute amidst such a world as this is an empty thing.

Such as bathing appears to thee—oil, sweat, dirt, filthy water, all things disgusting—so is every part of life and everything.

Look down from above on the countless herds of men and their countless solemnities, and the infinitely varied voyagings in storms and calms, and the differences among those who are born, who live together, and die. And consider, too, the life lived by others in olden time, and the life of those who will live after thee, and the life now lived among barbarous nations, and how many know not even thy name, and how many will soon forget it, and how they who perhaps now are praising thee will very soon blame thee, and that neither a posthumous name is of any value, nor anything else.

Consider that men will do the same things nevertheless, even though thou shouldst burst.

Thus the weary emperor, not a little exasperated by the intractability of human nature; but alongside notes such as these, we find others in which Marcus exhorts himself as a Stoic to carry on:

On every occasion ask thyself, What is there in this which is intolerable and past bearing? For thou wilt be ashamed to confess. In the next place remember that neither the future nor the past pains thee, but only the present. But this is reduced to a very little, if thou only circumscribest it, and chidest thy mind, if it is unable to hold out even against this.

Be like the promontory against which the waves continually break, but it stands firm and tames the fury of the water around it.

Men seek retreats for themselves, houses in the country, sea shores, and mountains; and thou too art wont to desire such things very much. But . . . it is in thy power whenever thou shalt choose to retire into thyself. For nowhere either with more quiet or more freedom from trouble does a man retire than into his own soul, particularly when he has within him such thoughts that by looking into them he is immediately in perfect tranquillity; and I affirm that tranquillity is nothing else than the good ordering of the mind. Constantly then give to thyself this retreat, and renew thyself; and let thy principles be brief and fundamental, which, as soon as thou shalt recur to them, will be sufficient to cleanse the soul completely, and to send thee back free from all discontent with the things to which thou returnest.

We ought then to check in the series of our thoughts everything that is without a purpose and useless, but most of all the overcurious feeling and the malignant; and a man should use himself to think of those things only about which if one should suddenly ask, What hast thou now in thy thoughts? with perfect openness thou mightest immediately answer, This or That; so that from thy words it should be plain that everything in thee is simple and benevolent, and such as befits a social animal, and one that cares not for thoughts about pleasure or sensual enjoyments at all, nor has any rivalry or envy or suspicion, or anything else for which thou wouldst blush if thou shouldst say that thou hadst it in thy mind.

It is peculiar to man to love even those who do wrong. And this happens, if when they do wrong it occurs to thee that they are kinsmen, and that they do wrong through ignorance and unintentionally, and that soon both of you will die; and above all that the wrongdoer has done thee no harm, for he has not made thy ruling faculty worse than it was before.

Reverence that which is best in the universe; and this [the Divine Reason] is that which makes use of all things and directs all things. And in like manner also reverence that which is best in thyself; and this is of the same kind as that. For in thyself also that which makes use of everything else is this, and thy life is directed by this.

Nature which governs the whole will soon change all things which thou seest, and out of their substance will make other things, and again other things from the substance of them, in order that the world may be ever new.

When bread is baked some parts are split at the surface, and these parts which thus open, and have a certain fashion contrary to the purpose of the baker's art, are beautiful in a manner, and in a peculiar way excite a desire for eating. And again, figs, when they are quite ripe, gape open; and in the ripe olives the very circumstance of their being near to rottenness adds a peculiar beauty to the fruit. And the ears of corn bending down, and the lion's eyebrows, and the foam which flows from the mouth of wild boars, and many other things—though they are far from being beautiful if a man should examine them severally—still, because they are consequent upon the things which are formed by nature, help to adorn them, and they please the mind; so that if a man should have a feeling and deeper insight with respect to the things which are produced in the universe, there is hardly one . . . which will not seem to him to be in a manner disposed so as to give pleasure.

Accept everything which happens, even if it seem disagreeable, because it leads to this, to the health of the universe and to the prosperity and felicity of Zeus. For he would not have brought on any man what he has brought if it were not useful for the whole.

Nor is it possible that [Providence] has made so great a mistake, either through want of power or want of skill, that good and evil should happen indiscriminately to the good and the bad. But death certainly, and life, honor and dishonor, pain and pleasure, all these things equally happen to good men and bad. . . . Therefore they are neither good nor evil.

Everything harmonizes with me which is harmonious to thee, O Universe. Nothing for me is too early or too late which is in due time for thee. Everything is fruit to me which thy seasons bring, O Nature: from thee are all things, in thee are all things, to thee all things return. The poet says, Dear city of Cecrops;[10] and wilt thou not say, Dear city of Zeus?

After Marcus Aurelius, the Stoic school declined into obscurity as Christianity came into prominence. Points of Stoic logic and physics continued to be discussed, and occasionally adopted, by philosophers from other schools. Stoic moral teaching became the common property of all, Christians and pagans alike, and was modified to suit a variety of religious and philosophical contexts. Stoicism paved the way for Christianity by the currency it gave to principles that were also to be advocated by Christians—that the world is governed by a Divine Providence, that the present frame of things will one day perish in a great conflagration, that human beings are brothers by virtue of their common relation to God, that God's law is the basis of rigorous moral standards that in particular require purity of intention, and that the worldly objects of most people's affection are hollow and worthless. But Christianity triumphed over Stoicism by proclaiming several principles that were foreign to the Stoics—especially the principle that "God so loved the world, that he gave his only begotten Son, that whosoever believeth in him should not perish, but have everlasting life."

---

[10] Cecrops, according to Greek mythology, was the founder and first king of Athens.

CHAPTER 10

Skepticism

Carneades

In 155 B.C., when the embassy from Athens appeared in Rome,[1] it was Carneades the Skeptic—not Critolaus the Peripatetic or Diogenes the Stoic—who attracted the greatest attention. The Romans already knew that Carneades was supposed to be the ablest philosopher and speaker of the day, and they were by no means disappointed with his performance. They were spellbound, Plutarch says, by the grace and charm with which he expressed himself. His public appearances drew large, enthusiastic audiences. His arguments before the Senate, in defense of Athens' plundering of Oropus, were breathtaking in their dexterity. "It was quite in keeping with the circumstances of the case," says the historian Theodor Mommsen, "when Carneades provided by thesis and counterthesis that exactly as many and as cogent reasons might be adduced in praise of injustice as in praise of justice, and when he showed in due logical form that with equal propriety the Athenians might be required to surrender Oropus and the Romans to confine themselves once more to their old straw huts on the Palatine." Such oratorical virtuosity was of course lost on Cato the Elder, whose limited patience with Greek philosophers was quickly exhausted by Carneades—and very properly, too, in Mommsen's opinion: "On this occasion at least Cato could not be found fault with, when he not only bluntly enough compared the dialectic arguments of the philosophers to the tedious dirges of the wailing-women, but also insisted on the Senate dismissing a man who understood the art of making right wrong and wrong right, and whose defense was in fact nothing but a shameless and almost insulting confession of injustice."

Carneades (about 214–129 B.C.), who was originally from Cyrene, became head of Plato's Academy probably sometime before his visit to Rome. The Academy had turned toward Skepticism a century earlier, under the direction of Arcesilaus of Pitane (roughly 316–242 B.C.), who was about twenty years senior to Zeno the Stoic, and whose overriding aim was to cast the greatest possible doubt upon Zeno's teachings (*dogmata*), which he found too "dogmatic" by far. Arcesilaus had himself been drawn to Skepticism by a certain Pyrrho of Elis (about 360–270 B.C.), who taught

---

[1] See p. 209.

that the key to happiness is to suspend judgment on every issue, in recognition of our inability to get beyond how things appear to us and to find out what the truth concerning them really is. It seemed to Arcesilaus that Socrates and Plato had actually been Skeptics: Socrates used to say that although it was certainly his mission to *look for* (*skeptesthai*, in Greek) the truth, he had as yet discovered only that he knew nothing;[2] and Plato evidently felt the same, for in his dialogues (as far as Arcesilaus could see) many issues are discussed pro and con, but no conclusions are definitely asserted. The Academy was persuaded by Arcesilaus that Skepticism was its true heritage, and there was indeed something to be said for this. The generally tentative and exploratory character of Plato's dialogues, especially his earlier ones, does seem skeptical—at least in comparison with the confident assertiveness of Stoic *dogmata,* according to which a wise man is one who "never opines, never regrets, never is mistaken, never changes his mind."

Although Carneades left no writings behind, the testimony of his disciples was that he found Epicureanism no less objectionable than Stoicism. There is a story that he was always so busy thinking out criticisms of these schools that he never once found it possible to accept an invitation to dinner. One thing that particularly exercised him was the way in which both Epicureans and Stoics kept insisting that knowledge derives from sense-experience, in spite of the obviously insurmountable difficulties that would be created for knowledge if their theories of sense-experience were correct. The Epicureans said that films of atoms are sent off from the surfaces of things and impinge upon the atoms composing our sensory organs, thus producing "images" of the things. The Stoics spoke in more general terms of our receiving "impressions" when representations of things impinge upon our souls, in a manner analogous to that in which wax receives the impress of a seal. But when they were asked how one is supposed to tell that a given image or impression accurately represents some object, neither the Epicureans nor the Stoics had a satisfactory reply. Though the Epicureans were fond of saying that all images are true, what they meant was that one's beliefs about the comparative accuracy of images would always be true if one examined the images properly; but instead of explaining what specific tests of accuracy one should employ, they referred vaguely to bringing "the reasoning power of the mind" to bear upon the matter. The Stoics had a notion that some impressions—"apprehensive" ones—bear a "peculiar mark" that immediately identifies them as accurate, so that one's soul spontaneously "assents" to them, without further ado, as foundation stones of knowledge. But Carneades, following Arcesilaus, points out that an equally spontaneous assent is often given to impressions that Stoics conceded to be inaccurate—impressions, for example, in dreams and hallucinations, by

---

[2] If Socrates had said that he was unsure whether he knew even that he knew nothing, his Skepticism, Arcesilaus pointed out, would have been complete.

which even a sage could sometimes be misled. This would never happen if accurate impressions bore some unmistakable internal hallmark of their accuracy. Evidently there is no such hallmark. Nor can there be any question of externally comparing images or impressions against the objects they purport to represent in order to determine how faithfully they do so. One has no access to objects independently of one's images or impressions—this is what the Epicureans and Stoics themselves maintained—and consequently it would be impossible for anyone to have reason to believe that sense-experience ever gives trustworthy information about objects. There is no criterion, either internal or external, by which accurate images or impressions can be distinguished from inaccurate ones. The logical outcome of these theories is complete Skepticism about sense-experience, and about knowledge generally insofar as sense-experience is supposed to be its basis.

Distrust of the senses can be traced back to Democritus, who denied that things possess any of the colors, sounds, smells, tastes, and temperatures that are conventionally attributed to them. By a strictly intellectual process, Democritus said, we discover that things are complexes of atoms having only shape, size, and position. This is the real truth about the physical world. Carneades, however, argues that the intellect is no more to be trusted than the senses. The wide differences between human opinions (upon which Xenophanes remarked), the equally good arguments that may be produced on both sides of every question (which Protagoras illustrated in his *Antilogiae*), show that our power of reasoning cannot be trusted to give us the truth about anything. Protagoras interpreted the situation incorrectly when he said that truth is *relative*—relative to the beliefs of each person. The theory that truth is relative, as witness Plato's plausible criticisms of it, is no less controversial than any other theory. If to every opinion a contrary can be opposed with equally good reasons, if in this sense there is an "equilibrium of reasons" on every issue, then a skeptical suspension (*epoche*) of judgment on every issue would seem the appropriate posture to adopt. In spite of what Aristotle and Chrysippus said, there are no self-evident "first principles" or "indemonstrables" that offer secure starting points or rules of procedure for our reasoning; and therefore nothing whatever can be proved. The attempt to prove any proposition inevitably leads to an infinite regress, for the premises of any argument *A* are disputable and require justification, but the same applies to any argument *B* given to prove the premises of *A,* and to any argument *C* given to prove the premises of *B,* and so on without end. More fundamentally, the very principles of logic that any argument takes for granted are themselves highly doubtful. Consider, for instance, the principle that every proposition is either true or false (and not both), which seems to be refuted by the proposition "I am lying," for (as was observed by Eubulides the Megarian) this is true only if it is false, and false if it is true.

Neither reason nor the senses, then, can ever be relied upon as instruments of knowledge. At least this is how it *seems*. As a Skeptic, Carneades naturally does not wish to assert positively that this is how it *is*, or to deny that further investigation might require him to revise his opinion. A dogmatic Skeptic, as he fully realizes, is a contradiction in terms—or at any rate would appear to be. Thus he anticipates Lucretius' point about Skepticism—"If anyone thinks that nothing can be known, he does not know whether even this can be known"—by admitting that of course this is so and by challenging critics to find anything wrong with it. A Skeptic suspends judgment on every issue, including the issue of the legitimacy of Skepticism.

There is an obvious objection to such wholesale Skepticism, which the Stoics were quick to seize upon: a complete suspending of judgment would entail a complete suspending of *activity,* and without activity (the activity of taking nourishment, for instance) no one could long exist. Before we act we must experience some impression to which we assent as accurate (the impression that here is nourishment and not poison, for instance), and therefore it is the height of absurdity for Skeptics to argue that accurate impressions can never with any confidence be identified. A complete Skeptic would exist—briefly—in a state of total paralysis.

Carneades is especially notable among Skeptics for his novel response to this objection. Certainty, he said, is not necessary for action; probability is enough, and a Skeptic can acknowledge that many impressions are probably accurate, even though one cannot be perfectly sure of them. An impression having sufficient vividness or clarity (*enargeia*) will by itself strike one as having some claim to accuracy. The probability that it is accurate will be increased, however, if it is found to square with a number of other impressions, and increased all the more if these other impressions are themselves vivid and clear. Suppose, for example, you have a clear visual impression that a cup of wine is on a table before you. Other impressions of smell, taste, and touch, the clearer the better, may confirm your visual impression: they go with it to form a coherent complex of impressions typical of cups of wine. The probability will then be high that your impression is accurate. This is enough for everyday purposes, although it is possible that you are mistaken and that what is before you is in fact a cleverly disguised cup of hemlock.

Cicero reports in his *Academics* that Carneades proceeded to interpret "wisdom" in terms of probability, holding that "the wise man will make use of whatever apparently probable impression he encounters, if nothing presents itself that is contrary to that probability, and his whole plan of life will be charted out in this manner." As far as theory is concerned, of course, the wise are equally doubtful of all impressions and give their assent to none; but in practice they permit themselves to be "aroused to action," and to answer questions affirmatively or negatively, on the basis of what seems to them most probable. Stoics, who hanker after certainty in all matters, should in candor admit that they themselves are "guided by probability" at every step—"in going on a voyage, in sowing a crop, in marrying a wife, in begetting a family, in ever so many things. . . ." in which a successful outcome is never more than probable.

The Stoics have a reply to this, which we may state on their behalf. How in practice, they ask, do the Skeptics really differ from them? If Skeptics accept as probable impressions that Stoics think are certain, their disagreement is minor in comparison with what initially it appeared to be. Having been bombarded with arguments to the effect that absolutely everything is doubtful, the Stoics are now told by Carneades that life may continue as before—except that everyone is to speak of degrees of probability instead of certainty. This seems an unexpectedly mild result, hardly worth all the preceding skeptical commotion about the total unreliability of both sense-experience and reason. But, also, this result, such as it is, seems hardly compatible with wholesale doubt about the attainability of truth. If Carneades is saying that there *is* such a thing as probability and that it *is* in practice an adequate substitute for certainty, then it appears that there are two things of which he is certain. Or is it his position that it is only probable that there is such a thing as probability? What sense could this make? Unless there *is* such a thing as probability, how could it be probable that there is?

Although our information (appropriately enough) is too scanty for confidence about Carneades' reaction to such criticisms, it appears that he did take account of them. He seems to have been anxious, first, to emphasize the differences between Skeptics and Stoics. He probably insisted most upon there being a wide difference between their characteristic attitudes. Stoicism, he thought, fosters an uncritical attitude of submission to authority—the authority of Zeno and the other Stoic "masters"—whereas Skepticism is a uniquely liberating position: "We are more free and untrammelled," Cicero says on Carneades' behalf, "in that we possess our power of judgment uncurtailed, and are bound by no compulsion to support all the dogmas laid down for us almost as edicts by certain masters." But other differences arose with respect to particular Stoic "dogmas" that Carneades seems to have declared less probable than their contraries. Thus he advanced an argument for freedom of will in opposition to the Stoics' belief in Destiny, having found nothing satisfactory in Chrysippus' attempt to show that the two are compatible. Carneades said that although every event in the world may have a cause, it does not follow that every event is "destined" in the sense of being produced by a cause that is linked into an infinite, divinely forged chain of causes. There may be *independent* causes that produce effects in the world quite on their own account, and the human will may be a cause of this kind—a self-determining cause (the notion of which gave the Stoics no qualms as far as the gods' wills were concerned).

In ethics also Carneades took issue with the Stoics. He represented himself as thinking that virtue is less likely to be our chief good than is enjoyment of those things that all of us have desired from infancy—health, unimpaired senses, freedom from pain, the good opinion of others, and so on. Everyone instinctively wants these "primary natural objects," and there is no use in the Stoics' pretending that they are able to view them as "indifferent." So convincing was Carneades on this subject, Cicero says, that he brought certain Stoics to confess that "a man of good breeding and liberal education would desire to have the good opinion of his parents and relatives, and of good men in general, and that for its own sake and not for any practical advantage. . . ."

But there is still the question how Carneades can have believed both that everything is doubtful and that some things are probable. And the testimony we have indicates that, after all, he did not believe both—he believed only that everything is doubtful, and his talk about probability in ethics and elsewhere was apparently just a tactic in his campaign to "combat the Stoics," as Cicero says. On the score of ethics, we are told that Clitomachus, who was Carneades' most eminent pupil, "used to declare that he had never been able to understand what Carneades did accept." As regards Carneades' statement that probability is in general a substitute for certainty, Clitomachus is reported to have said that "Carneades did not so much accept this view as advance it in argument." In other words, Carneades found probability useful in answering the Stoics' objection that Skepticism paralyzes action and in attacking various Stoic positions. He was not himself confident that there was anything in it.

One would prefer not to think that Carneades' low regard for Stoics, or his delight in winning arguments, betrayed him into unscrupulous practices of debate. Perhaps he admitted to the Stoics that he was doubtful about his theory of probability, and perhaps they then asked him why on earth he brought it up when they objected that Skepticism paralyzes action, and perhaps he had a plausible and candid reply. We cannot tell from the information we have. That he was not entirely above applying his Skepticism in what Henry Sidgwick calls "a morally dangerous manner" is clear enough from his chicanery in the Oropus case. On the other hand, however, there is evidence that Carneades was very much aware of the misuses to which the power of argument and reasoning can be put; and in light of this he appears to have been considerably more discriminating in matters of right and wrong than his role in the Oropus affair would by itself suggest. The dangerous potential of reason, as developed fully by humankind, was adduced by Carneades in criticism of the Stoic doctrine of Providence. Stoics argued endlessly that the gods care for human well-being and give help to individuals; but if human reason is a gift from the gods, Carneades said, then the benevolence of the gods is questionable indeed. His views on this were preserved in Cicero's dialogue on *The Nature of the Gods,* where they are presented (with appropriate Roman illustrations) by the character named Cotta. Cotta is addressing Balbus, a Stoic:

> Men use their reason both for good and evil. But it is only a few, and those rarely, who use it for good, while many use it constantly for evil. So that it would have been better if the immortal gods had not endowed

us with reason at all, rather than given us so calamitous a gift. . . . If the divine mind willed the good of men, when it endowed them with reason, then it willed only the good of those whom it also endowed with the power to use their reason well, whom we see to be few indeed, if any. But the gods would not will the good of a few men only. So it follows that they have not willed the good of any. . . .

If the gods gave man reason then they made him a villain. Villainy is merely reason allied to craft and deception for an evil purpose. So in your [Balbus'] view the gods become responsible for fraud, felony, and all misdemeanors of this sort; as none of them could be conceived or carried through without the use of reason. . . . So this divine gift of reason and foresight seems to have been imparted to corrupt mankind rather than to make them good.

You argue that man is to blame for all this and not the gods. . . . But [the gods] could have endowed men with reason in a form which would exclude all vice and crime. How then did the gods come to make such a mistake? We men bequeath an inheritance in the hope of passing on something of benefit to our sons. In this we can be mistaken. But how can a god make mistakes? . . .

This "Providence" of yours is blameworthy, who gave reason to those who she well knew would pervert it to an evil use. Perhaps you will say she did not know this? I wish you would say this, but you do not dare. For we all know how high you rate the name of "Providence"! . . .

If the gods had the good of the human race at heart, then they ought to have made all men good. If that were too much to ask, then they should at least do their best for those who are good. How did it come about that in Spain the Carthaginians defeated the two Scipios, the bravest and best of men? Why did Maximus have to bury the consul who was his own son? Why did Hannibal destroy Marcellus? . . . Time would fail me if I tried to list all the good men for whom things have turned out badly. So it would if I tried to mention all the wicked men who have prospered. Why should a Marius be seven times consul, and then die at a ripe old age in his own bed? Why should a cruel monster like Cinna have so long a lease of terror?

You may argue that in the end he paid the penalty for his crimes. But it would surely have been better if in the first place he had been prevented from killing so many of our best men rather than that he should himself be punished for it at some later time. Quintus Varius, a most desperate character, himself died an agonizing death. If this was the penalty he paid for stabbing Drusus and poisoning Metellus, it was well deserved. But it would have been better if both his victims had been saved. . . . So you see that if the gods do look down upon our human world, they make no difference in their judgment between good and bad. . . .

No house or estate can be regarded as an example of reason and discipline if good deeds go unrewarded and crimes unpunished. By the same token, there can be no divine guidance of human affairs if the gods make no distinction between good and evil. . . .

Balbus tells us that the gods, like human monarchs, cannot keep an eye on everything. This is not a true comparison. If a king knowingly connives at crime, then he is much to blame. And a god can never plead ignorance. . . .

You are always saying that there is nothing which a god cannot do, and do easily. As easily as a man can move his limbs in obedience to his thought and will, so you say the divine power of a god can create, set in motion, or transform anything at will. You do not offer this belief as a superstition and an old wives' tale, but as a reasoned proposition of physical science. . . . It follows from this theory of yours that this divine Providence is either unaware of its own powers or is indifferent to human life. Or else it is unable to judge what is best. Providence is not concerned with individuals. . . . It does not even care about nations. Nations? It does not even care about whole peoples and races, and so we need not be surprised if it shows contempt for mankind altogether.

Neither the substance nor the tone of these criticisms would incline one to suppose that Carneades personally believed in the existence of gods who have the welfare of individuals at heart. Nevertheless, it seems that he did, or said that he did. Cicero tells us that Carneades did not at all wish "to deny that the gods exist, which would ill become a philosopher, but to show that the Stoics have no real explanation of them." It was for him reason enough to affirm the gods' existence "that this was the traditional belief of our ancestors." The Stoics, who "despise authority and appeal to reason," fail to see that religion would be a poor affair if it needed bolstering by arguments, which always raise more questions than they answer and which in religion raise particularly baffling questions about Providence in relation to evil. "By these very arguments you cast doubt on something which to my mind is not doubtful at all."[3]

Not doubtful at all? Carneades was at once a Skeptic about all human beliefs and a confirmed traditionalist in religion? Having faulted the Stoics for submitting uncritically to the teachings of their own authorities, Carneades himself, when it came to religion, appealed to the authority of his ancestors? How can he possibly have reconciled these positions? It is tempting to speculate about the answers; but the fact of the matter is that, like Clitomachus, we are completely in the dark about what Carneades really thought.

Less than fifty years after Carneades' death, the Academy forsook Skepticism and reverted to "dogmatism" under the direction of Antiochus of Ascalon (about 130–69 B.C.). Cicero, who in 79 B.C. attended Antiochus' lectures in Athens, says that Antiochus was not in the least impressed by Carneades' attempts to show that Skepticism is a logically coherent

---

[3] A viewed shared by the Danish thinker, Søren Kierkegaard (1813–1855): "He who first invented the notion of defending Christianity in Christendom is *de facto* Judas No. 2; he also betrays with a kiss, only his treachery is that of stupidity. To defend anything is always to discredit it."

position. He thought it perfectly clear that probability presupposes certainty; that one cannot speak of inaccurate impressions and at the same time deny that they are distinguishable from accurate ones; and that it is contradictory to assert that everything is doubtful, since in doing so (whatever one may say) one cannot very well doubt one's own assertion. We may safely accept as true, Antiochus maintained, those positions upon which eminent philosophers have agreed; and in order to establish that they have agreed on all the most important points, he expounded Plato, Aristotle, and the Stoics in such a way as to show—with a good deal of inaccuracy—that their disagreements were relatively minor and mostly verbal. (Skeptics, of course, make the most of disagreements between philosophers.) Accordingly, Antiochus' own philosophy was an "eclectic" (or selective[4]) synthesis of the views of others. A Stoic element predominated in his ethics as in the ethics of Cicero after him.

Aenesidemus and Sextus Empiricus ⎯⎯⎯⎯⎯⎯⎯⎯⎯

There were those who believed that the Skeptics in the Academy had strayed from the original lines of Skepticism marked out by Pyrrho of Elis. A genuinely "Pyrrhonian" Skepticism should rise up, they thought, as the vestiges of "Academic" Skepticism faded away. Foremost among Pyrrho's latter-day followers was Aenesidemus of Cnossos (in Crete), who is believed to have taught in Alexandria during the second half of the first century B.C. Aenesidemus appears to have taken Carneades to task for having "dogmatized" to the extent of definitely asserting that everything is doubtful and that some things are probable whereas others are not. We have seen that Carneades, as represented by Cicero, did not mean definitely to assert either of these things, but Aenesidemus understood that he had done so and had thus fallen short of true Skepticism. In testimony concerning his writings (all of which have vanished), it is said that Aenesidemus went to great lengths in explaining that true Skeptics do not assert or "determine" or "lay down" anything whatever, "not even the laying down of nothing." He insisted that nothing is really asserted by such mottoes of Skepticism as "We determine nothing," "One statement is no more certain than another," "Every statement has its corresponding opposite," and the like. These mottoes, he said, are meant to convey only that Skeptics assent to nothing, not even to the statement that they assent to nothing. Skeptics advance arguments to show that "We assent to nothing" is as dubious a statement as any other, "so that after destroying others it turns round and destroys itself, like a purge which drives the substance out and then in its turn is itself eliminated and destroyed."

That the process of purging might be facilitated, Aenesidemus pre-

⎯⎯⎯⎯⎯⎯⎯⎯⎯

[4] See p. 211.

pared convenient lists of the various modes (*tropoi*) of skeptical argumentation. Especially famous are his Ten Tropes designed to induce suspension of judgment chiefly with respect to sense-experience. The Greek biographer Diogenes Laertius recorded them as follows:

The *first* mode relates to the differences between living creatures in respect of those things which give them pleasure or pain, or are useful or harmful to them. By this it is inferred that they do not receive the same impressions from the same things, with the result that such a conflict necessarily leads to suspension of judgment [there being no good reason to prefer the impressions of one sort of creature above the impressions of another]. For some creatures multiply without intercourse, for example, creatures that live in fire, the Arabian phoenix and worms; others by union, such as man and the rest. Some are distinguished in one way, some in another, and for this reason they differ in their senses also, hawks for instance being most keen-sighted, and dogs having a most acute sense of smell. It is natural that if the senses, e.g., eyes, of animals differ, so also will the impressions produced upon them; so to the goat vine-shoots are good to eat, to man they are bitter; the quail thrives on hemlock, which is fatal to man; the pig will eat ordure, the horse will not.

The *second* mode has reference to the natures and idiosyncracies of men; for instance, Demophon, Alexander's butler, used to get warm in the shade and shiver in the sun. Andron of Argos is reported by Aristotle to have travelled across the waterless deserts of Libya without drinking. Moreover, one man fancies the profession of medicine, another farming, and another commerce; and the same ways of life are injurious to one man but beneficial to another; from which it follows that judgment must be suspended.

The *third* mode depends on the differences between the sense-channels in different cases, for an apple gives the impression of being pale yellow in color to the sight, sweet in taste, and fragrant in smell. An object of the same shape is made to appear different by differences in the mirrors reflecting it. Thus it follows that what appears is no more such and such a thing than something different.

The *fourth* mode is that due to differences of condition and to changes in general; for instance, health, illness, sleep, waking, joy, sorrow, youth, old age, courage, fear, want, fullness, hate, love, heat, cold, to say nothing of breathing freely and having the passages obstructed. The impressions received thus appear to vary according to the nature of the conditions. Nay, even the state of madmen is not contrary to nature; for why should their state be so more than ours? Even to our view the sun has the appearance of standing still. And Theon of Tithorea used to go to bed and walk in his sleep, while Pericles' slave did the same on the housetop.

The *fifth* mode is derived from customs, laws, belief in myths, compacts between nations and dogmatic assumptions. This class includes considerations with regard to things beautiful and ugly, true and false, good and bad, with regard to the gods, and with regard to the coming into being and the passing away of the world of phenomena. Obviously the same thing is regarded by some as just and by others as unjust, or as good by some and bad by others. Persians think it not unnatural for a man to marry his daughter; to Greeks it is unlawful. The Massagetae, according to Eudoxus in the first book of his *Voyage round the World*, have their wives in common; the Greeks have not. The Cicilians used to delight in piracy; not so the Greeks. Different people believe in different gods; some in providence, others not. In burying their dead, the Egyptians embalm them; the Romans burn them; the Paeonians throw them into lakes. As to what is true, then, let suspension of judgment be our practice.

The *sixth* mode relates to mixtures and participations, by virtue of which nothing appears pure in and by itself, but only in combination with air, light, moisture, solidity, heat, cold, movement, exhalations, and other forces. For purple shows different tints in sunlight, moonlight, and lamplight; and our own complexion does not appear the same at noon and when the sun is low. Again, a rock which in air takes two men to lift is easily moved about in water or because, being light, it is made heavy by the air. Of its own inherent property we know nothing, any more than of the constituent oils in an ointment.

The *seventh* mode has reference to distances, positions, places, and the occupants of the places. In this mode things which are thought to be large appear small, square things round; flat things appear to have projections, straight things to be bent, and colorless colored. So the sun, on account of its distance, appears small, mountains when far away appear misty and smooth, but when near at hand rugged. Furthermore, the sun at its rising has a certain appearance, but has a dissimilar appearance when in mid-heaven, and the same body one appearance in a wood and another in open country. The image again varies according to the position of the object, and a dove's neck according to the way it is turned. Since, then, it is not possible to observe these things apart from places and positions, their real nature is unknowable.

The *eighth* mode is concerned with quantities and qualities of things, say, heat or cold, swiftness or slowness, colorlessness or variety of colors. Thus wine taken in moderation strengthens the body, but too much of it is weakening; and so with food and other things.

The *ninth* mode has to do with perpetuity, strangeness, or rarity. Thus earthquakes are no surprise to those among whom they constantly take place; nor is the sun, for it is seen every day. . . .

The *tenth* mode rests on interrelation, e.g., between light and heavy, strong and weak, greater and less, up and down. Thus that which is on the right is not so by nature, but is so understood in virtue of its position with respect to something else; for if that changes its position, the thing is no longer on the right. Similarly father and brother are relative terms, day is relative to the sun, and all things relative to our mind. Thus relative terms are in and by themselves unknowable. These, then, are the ten modes of perplexity.

A rearrangement of Aenesidemus' Tropes is helpful in summarizing them. Impressions *differ* very greatly, not only with different species of living creatures (1), not only with different human beings (2)—according to their different expectations (9) and ways of life (5)—but even in the case of the same person at the same time (as when sight conveys one impression and smell another) (3), and at different times owing to changes in the condition of one's body (4) and in one's location in relation to the object or objects in question (7). Impressions differ also because an object may vary in quantity or quality (8); because sizes, locations, degrees of intensity, and directions of movement are inherently relative (10); and because variations occur in the circumstances (air, light, and so on) in which objects are found (6). From among such a multitude of conflicting impressions we have no means of identifying those, if any, that are accurate. One impression is no more to be trusted than another. A suspension of judgment about all of them is the attitude indicated.

Also, however, suspension of judgment may *not* be the attitude indicated. All statements are doubtful. No argument may be viewed as cogent, and this goes for the Ten Tropes themselves. An assumption of the Tropes—notably of the seventh—is that in spite of appearances, nothing can possess contrary properties (such as squareness and roundness) at the same time; but this is questionable, as witness the *disagreement* (even among logicians) on the matter. If one tries to prove the assumption, one's proof (as Carneades pointed out) will make other questionable assumptions, and thus one will be launched into an *infinite regress*—ever constructing arguments to prove the premises of other arguments—unless indeed one falls at some point into *circular reasoning* and simply takes for granted something that one professes to be proving. If one realizes the futility of trying to prove the assumption, one might be inclined just flatly to assert it in the belief that it is self-evident and does not require a demonstration. But opponents will then be free to respond to such an unproved *hypothesis* by asserting that they find some contrary assumption self-evident. So it was that Aenesidemus suspended judgment on the issue of whether his Ten Tropes do in fact call for suspension of judgment. He held only that, as far as he was concerned, they appeared to do so.

The considerations just mentioned, far from telling against Skepticism, add a new dimension to the perplexity created by the Ten Tropes. Disagreement, Infinite Regress, Circular Reasoning, and Hypothesis are but four additional modes of attacking "dogmatism" of every kind.[5] And if we take the gist of the Ten to be the inescapable *relativity* of our sensory impressions, we may add this to the four new tropes for a set of five "supertropes" containing the whole arsenal of Skepticism in a compact form. Such a list of Five Tropes is said to have been drawn up by a successor of Aenesidemus' named Agrippa. Here is Diogenes Laertius' account of the Five:

---

[5] Actually, several of the Ten Tropes, especially the fifth, touch upon Disagreement.

Agrippa and his school add to them [Aenesidemus' Ten Tropes] five other modes [actually four], resulting respectively from [1] disagreement, [2] regress *ad infinitum,* [3] relativity [the gist of the Ten Tropes], [4] hypothesis, and [5] circular reasoning. The mode arising from [1] disagreement proves, with regard to any inquiry *whether in philosophy or in everyday life,* that it is full of the utmost contentiousness and confusion. The mode which involves [2] regress *ad infinitum* refuses to admit that what is sought to be proved is firmly established, because one thing furnishes the ground for belief in another, and so on *ad infinitum.* The mode deriving from [3] relativity declares that a thing can never be apprehended in and by itself, but only in connection with something else. Hence all things are unknowable. The mode resulting from [4] hypothesis arises when people suppose that you must take the most elementary of things as of themselves entitled to credence, instead of postulating them [that is, instead of conceding that they need proof]: which is useless, because someone else will adopt the contrary hypothesis. The mode arising from [5] circular reasoning is found whenever that which should be confirmatory of the thing requiring to be proved itself has to borrow credit from the latter, as, for example, if anyone seeking to establish the existence of pores on the ground that exhalations take place should take this (the existence of pores) as proof that there are emanations.

In practice the Five Modes work this way. If you make any definite statement, "whether in philosophy or in everyday life," a Skeptic will remind you that at least some persons will [1] disagree with it. Are there not some persons who will disagree with anything? The question now is whether you believe that the controversy between you and these persons can be decided one way or the other. If you say "no," you concede that judgment must be suspended on the issue, and the Skeptic has already won his point. If you say "yes," the Skeptic will ask *how* the controversy is to be decided. Suppose you say that you can offer good and sufficient reasons in favor of your statement. The Skeptic will then remind you that there is bound to be controversy about whatever you take as "good and sufficient reasons," so that you would have to produce reasons for your reasons [2] *ad infinitum.* But suppose you say that your reasons are based upon direct personal observation of certain relevant facts—facts as plain as the nose on one's face. Then the Skeptic will bring you to admit that the impressions of sense-experience differ greatly from one person to another and that one can never overcome the [3] relativity of one's own impressions so as to determine for sure what the facts objectively are. It may then occur to you that, after all, your original statement was perfectly obvious in itself—as plain as $2+2=4$—and that an attempt to justify it would really be superfluous. "My statement speaks for itself," you say. But the Skeptic will ask you what is to keep others from saying that, in their eyes, some contrary statement is perfectly obvious in itself. Is it not clear that your statement, like theirs, is a groundless [4] hypothesis?

"No, it is not," you say; "anyone with any sense would see that my statement is true, and therefore it is *not* a 'groundless hypothesis.' " The Skeptic will now ask you what you mean by "anyone with any sense." "Look," you say, "people who go around denying statements like that just have not got any sense." But this, the Skeptic will point out, is [5] circular reasoning. You have said that your statement is not a groundless hypothesis because anyone with any sense would agree with it; but unless someone believes that it is not a groundless hypothesis, you will not concede that he or she has any sense. This, of course, flagrantly begs the question. You may as well admit that you have no leg to stand on and join the Skeptic in suspending judgment about the whole matter.

A particular case of circular reasoning was especially interesting to Aenesidemus and his followers. They observed that in order to ascertain that any argument constitutes a demonstration of the truth of its conclusion, one would need a *criterion* by which such an argument could be identified. But in order to be confident that some proposed criterion is satisfactory, one would need an argument that constitutes a demonstration of its satisfactoriness. But obviously one could not ascertain that an argument demonstrates this unless one already had a criterion that one knew to be satisfactory. It would be circular to argue that because an argument meets some proposed criterion of what constitutes a demonstration, the argument therefore constitutes a demonstration that the criterion is satisfactory. Consequently, one cannot be confident that any proposed criterion is satisfactory, or that any argument constitutes a demonstration of the truth of its conclusion—and this goes for the argument just given.

The "problem of the criterion," as it is called, arises not only with respect to the soundness of arguments but also with respect to the more general issue of distinguishing true statements from false ones. Either you have a criterion for making this distinction or else you are completely at a loss when it comes to determining whether any given statement is true or false. Suppose, then, you declare that you are in possession of a criterion C by which this may be determined. You assert, in other words, the following statement $S:$ "C is a criterion by which true statements may be distinguished from false ones." Very well; but now there comes the question of how you can tell that S is true. Obviously it would be circular if you were to say that the truth of S is assured by virtue of its satisfying criterion C. Nor would it do for you to say that the truth of S is assured by virtue of its satisfying another and a higher criterion C^1, for this would involve you in an infinite regress. You would in effect assert statement $S^1:$ "C^1 is a criterion by which C is shown to be a criterion by which true statements may be distinguished from false ones." How, then, can you tell that S^1 is true? By means of yet another and a still higher criterion C^2? There would be no end to this. Result: it is impossible for you, for anyone, to determine whether any statement is true or false—and this goes for the present statement.

So radical a Skepticism would seem to have quite a numbing effect.

How could it possibly be consistent with recognizing—to say nothing of meeting—the demands of everyday life? Carneades, for all his talk about "probability" as an adequate practical guide, left his own students guessing what he really thought about this. The Pyrrhonian Skeptics, however, were much less mysterious, and a full account of what they said on the issue survives in the writings of one of their late representatives— Sextus Empiricus. Little is known about Sextus' life. He probably lived in the last half of the second century and the first quarter of the third century A.D.; he probably was a Greek; and he may have been a physician (a possible meaning of "Empiricus"). We do not know where he was born, where he lived, or where he taught. But his extant works—three books of *Outlines of Pyrrhonism* and eleven books *Against the Dogmatists (Adversus Mathematicos)*—contain more information about Greek Skepticism than any other source. Here are some selections from the first book of the *Outlines* in which he explains what for Pyrrhonians is the goal of Skepticism. (A disclaimer with which Sextus prefaces his book should be remembered throughout: "Of none of our future statements do we positively affirm that the fact is exactly as we state it, but we simply record each fact, like a chronicler, as it appears to us at the moment.")

Skepticism is an ability, or mental attitude, which opposes appearances to judgments in any way whatsoever, with the result that, owing to the equipollence of the objects and reasons thus opposed, we are first brought to a state of mental suspense and next to a state of "unperturbedness" or quietude. . . . "Suspense" is a state of mental rest owing to which we neither deny nor affirm anything. "Quietude" is an untroubled and tranquil condition of soul. . . .

The originating cause of Skepticism is, we say, the hope of attaining quietude. Men of talent, who were perturbed by the contradictions in things and in doubt as to which of the alternatives they ought to accept, were led on to inquire what is true in things and what false, hoping by the settlement of this question to attain quietude. . . . [But] we end by ceasing to dogmatize. . . .

When we say that the Skeptic refrains from dogmatizing we do not use the term "dogma," as some do, in the broader sense of "approval of a thing" (for the Skeptic gives assent to the feelings which are the necessary results of sense impressions, and he would not, for example, say when feeling hot or cold "I believe that I am not hot or cold"); but we say that "he does not dogmatize" using "dogma" in the sense, which some give it, of "assent to one of the non-evident objects of scientific inquiry"; for the Pyrrhonian philosopher assents to nothing that is non-evident. . . .

We follow a line of reasoning which, in accordance with appearances, points us to a life conformable to the customs of our country and its laws and institutions, and to our own instinctive feelings. . . .

We do not overthrow the affective sense impressions which induce our assent involuntarily; and these impressions are "the appearances." And when we question whether the underlying object is such as it appears, we grant the fact that it appears, and our doubt does not concern the appearance itself but the account given of that appearance. . . .

Adhering, then, to appearances, we live in accordance with the normal rules of life, undogmatically, seeing that we cannot remain wholly inactive. . . .

The Skeptic's end is quietude in respect of matters of opinion and moderate feeling in respect of things unavoidable. For the Skeptic, having set out to philosophize with the object of passing judgment on the sense impressions and ascertaining which of them are true and which false, so as to attain quietude thereby, found himself involved in contradictions of equal weight, and being unable to decide between them suspended judgment; and as he was thus in suspense there followed, as it happened, the state of quietude in respect of matters of opinion. For the man who opines that anything is by nature good or bad is for ever being disquieted [by a too eager pursuit of the one and a too fearful avoidance of the other]. . . . On the other hand, the man who determines nothing as to what is naturally good or bad neither shuns nor pursues anything eagerly; and in consequence he is unperturbed.

The Skeptic, in fact, had the same experience which is said to have befallen the painter Apelles. Once, they say, when he was painting a horse and wished to represent in the painting the horse's foam, he was so unsuccessful that he gave up the attempt and flung at the picture the sponge on which he used to wipe the paints off his brush, and the mark of the sponge produced the effect of a horse's foam. So, too, the Skeptics were in hopes of gaining quietude by means of a decision regarding the disparity of objects of sense and of thought, and being unable to effect this they suspended judgment; and they found that quietude, as if by chance, followed upon their suspense, even as a shadow follows its substance.

Tranquillity of soul, which for the Stoics was an accompaniment of virtue, is for Sextus an accompaniment of "mental suspense." The Stoics argued that tranquillity comes with viewing everything except virtue as undesirable or indifferent; Sextus argues that tranquillity comes with doubting whether anything at all is really desirable (even tranquillity) and by "assenting" only to those appearances which "induce our assent involuntarily." This answers the question how Skeptics are able to manage their practical affairs: they do (as they must) what compels their assent, however dubious it is from a philosophical point of view, and so live in accordance with their "instinctive feelings." It appears to Sextus that life on this basis will harmonize perfectly with "the customs of our country and its laws and institutions," though one might have supposed that he would find this rather less apparent. "Instinctive feelings" may stir one to all kinds of unorthodox activity (to leave it just at that). But perhaps what appears to him is that training in Skepticism has a tendency to extinguish any sympathy or zeal one might have for radical or revolutionary causes; and no doubt there is something, for better or worse, in this. Yet a Skeptic will not be a great partisan of orthodoxy either: "The man who determines nothing as to what is naturally good or bad neither shuns nor pursues anything eagerly." Stoics, for whom virtue is to be pursued eagerly, would find this attitude deplorably lukewarm; but for Sextus it is simply a question of "moderate feeling," to all appearances commendable in every way.

Pyrrhonian Skepticism is said to have had, even in its heyday, a comparatively small following. It died out entirely in the third century A.D., and for 1,200 years little was even known of it. In the fifteenth century, however, Sextus' *Outlines* and *Against the Dogmatists* were rediscovered. Pyrrhonian arguments then began to figure in religious and philosophical controversies that were to have a large hand in shaping the development of modern thought.

CHAPTER **11**

Philo of Alexandria

Germanicus, the Roman general, married his cousin Agrippina, and they had a son whom they called Gaius. The soldiers in Germanicus' legions adopted Gaius as their mascot, and to please them Agrippina let the boy wear little military boots. So it was that Gaius acquired "Little Boots" as his nickname. Time passed, and at twenty-five Little Boots became emperor of Rome—a good emperor, he seemed at first, but soon he contracted a severe illness that appeared to affect his sanity. During three and a half years, until one of his own guards killed him (in 41 A.D.), Little Boots committed atrocities so monstrous that his nickname is still a synonym for demented wickedness of the worst order. The Latin for "Little Boots" is *Caligula.*

Caligula's courtiers, alarmed by his increasing lust for power, tried to restrain him by pointing out that he was already more powerful than any other potentate on earth. This, however, only gave Caligula the idea that he was a god and should be worshipped accordingly. Statues of himself, he announced, were at once to be placed in sanctuaries throughout the Empire, including the Temple at Jerusalem. If the Jewish officials refused to comply, they were to be executed and their people made slaves. Naturally the officials refused, as compliance would have violated the First and Second Commandments,[1] but their courage moved the Roman provincial governor, Petronius, to see whether he could not persuade Caligula to change his mind. Fortunately, the ship bringing Petronius' own death-warrant was passed at sea by the ship bringing the news of Caligula's assassination. But Petronius' insubordination was not for the likes of Flaccus, provincial governor of Egypt, who seems to have tried to win Caligula's favor by persecuting the Jews with conspicuous zeal. At least a million Jews were living at this time in the vicinity of Alexandria. In 38 A.D. Flaccus issued a decree that deprived them of their legal status as resident aliens; and among his other enormities, he ordered the arrest and flogging of the members of the Jewish senate that had long before been authorized by the emperor Augustus for the direction of Jewish affairs. Thinking, wrongly, that Caligula must be better than Flaccus, the Alexandrian Jews in 40 A.D. sent an embassy to Rome in hopes of getting him to restrain their oppressors and to restore their civil rights. Caligula

[1] [I.] "Thou shalt have none other gods before [or besides] me.
[II.] Thou shalt not make thee any graven image. . . ."

242

refused. (The Jews were not to receive any redress of their grievances until Claudius became emperor in the following year.)

The head of the embassy was a distinguished religious philosopher, Philo Judaeus (about 20 B.C.–50 A.D.), of whose life little besides this incident is known. From it we can safely infer that Philo was a leading figure in the Jewish community of Alexandria. The quantity of Philo's writings enables us to infer almost as safely that he was free from pressing business for at least a considerable period, but no details are available as to his position or means of living. In one of the very few references to himself in his writings, he mentions that he had made a pilgrimage to the Temple at Jerusalem "to offer up prayers and sacrifices." Although Philo was contemporary with the origins of Christianity, and indeed is the only Jew of the period whose views are well known to us from his own writings, there is no evidence that he was aware of Jesus (about 4 B.C.–29 A.D.) or of the activities of Jesus' apostles. Philo is, however, one of our main sources of information about the Jewish communal order of Essenes, in which there has been increased interest since the discovery in 1947 and later of the Dead Sea Scrolls. Some scholars maintain that a group of Essenes produced the Scrolls and that certain passages in the Scrolls make it probable that Jesus and John the Baptist were Essenes (these are subjects of much debate).

No fewer than thirty-three of Philo's treatises have survived, most of them in their original Greek, but some in Latin and Armenian translations. These are mainly expositions of the Septuagint version of the Pentateuch—that is, of the Alexandrian Greek translation of the first five Old Testament books ("Pentateuch" means "five scrolls"), which in Jewish tradition are known as the Law or Torah and are attributed to Moses. Philo reverenced the Pentateuch as divinely inspired, but he also highly esteemed the Greek philosophers, especially Plato and the Stoics. It seemed to him that these philosophers had advanced positions that were in substantial agreement with the Pentateuch, and he took this as evidence that the Pentateuch was known to them; but he was also prepared, within limits, to interpret the Pentateuch allegorically in such a way as to bring it into harmony with the positions of these philosophers. The Stoics had given allegorical interpretations of the myths of Greek and Roman religion; Jewish scholars before Philo had given allegorical interpretations of the Scriptures; but Philo stands alone in his thoroughgoing use of the allegorical method to effect a far-reaching synthesis of Greek and Jewish thought. Efforts to achieve such a synthesis are characteristic of Hellenistic Judaism, and Philo is indisputably its greatest representative.

If Scripture is always to be understood literally, we will have to admit, Philo says, that sometimes it is "greatly at variance with truth." As a simple case in point, consider Genesis 4:16, where it is said (in the Septuagint version) that Cain, after killing his brother Abel, "went out from the face of God, and dwelt in the land of Naid [or Nod], over against Eden." God could not literally have a "face" unless He had a body, and if he had a body he would have bodily needs as we do, but this cannot be correct. God does not have needs; He is sufficient unto Himself; He is, in short, the *Self-Existent Being*—for such is Philo's understanding (and the Septuagint's rendering) of God's declaration to Moses in Exodus 3:14, "I am that I am." Nor can it literally be true that Cain "went out" from God's presence, as if there were places from which God is absent. Accordingly, "the only thing left for us to do," Philo says, "is to make up our minds that none of [these expressions] is literally intended and to take the path of figurative [allegorical] interpretation. . . ." And a reasonable interpretation of "went out from the face" is that it is a figurative way of saying that Cain committed the great sin of deliberately obscuring his own awareness of God, thus bringing down on himself the severest penalty, which is ever to be alone in spiritual wandering (*Naid* or *Nod* means "wandering").

The path of figurative interpretation, Philo says, is especially to be followed in connection with Moses' account in Genesis of the world's creation. This account is by no means simply a "mythical fiction," but on the other hand Moses cannot have intended for every word of it to be understood in a perfectly ordinary sense. We read, for instance, that God spent six days in creating the world, whereas on reflection, Philo thinks, we cannot but suppose that He actually created everything at once. The Almighty, unlike ourselves, does not have to do things seriatim. Moses certainly knew this, for he had both "attained the very summit of philosophy" and "been divinely instructed in the greater and most essential part of Nature's lore"; but he also knew how to couch his knowledge in symbolic terms appropriate to the intelligence of the general public. In the opening chapters of Genesis, Moses' chief concern, according to Philo, was to establish the basic point that the world, as God's creation, is providentially governed in keeping with Divine Law. An assurance of this is one's strongest incentive to observe the Law and thereby to become, in phraseology Philo borrows from the Stoics, "a loyal citizen of the world, regulating [one's] doings by the purpose and will of Nature. . . ." One may be confident that one's loyalty will not be in vain. "For it stands to reason that what has been brought into existence should be cared for by its Father and Maker." This much anyone can understand, and the account in Genesis is admirably suited to convey it, in preparation for the statements of Law that follow. The letter of the account, however, must not be pressed too closely.

Nevertheless, if we examine the account of creation from the point of view of its spirit—its symbolic meaning—we will discover an abundance of philosophical truths. For example, at the outset of Genesis we read that, when God began His creation, "the earth was a desolate waste, with darkness covering the abyss and a tempestuous wind raging over the surface of the waters." The "desolate waste" was transformed by God into an ordered universe. This is in keeping with the Stoic position that the cosmos is constituted by two "principles"—one a passive recipient of order, the other an active imposer of order. Of course Philo does not agree with the Stoics in identifying the active principle with fiery aether. God is not a special material element mixed in with other material elements; He stands over and above—or "transcends"—the entire realm of matter and in this respect is akin to the Divine Craftsman of Plato's *Timaeus,* who is a strictly spiritual agent and who imposed order upon the indefinite raw "matrix" of stuff in space because he was good and free from jealousy and desired that all things should be as much like himself as possible— which, Philo says, we "would not be wrong" to assign as God's motive in creating the world. The God of Genesis, however, is fully a creator in respects in which the Craftsman of the *Timaeus* is not. The Craftsman does not make the "matrix" upon which he works, nor does he make the forms which serve as his models in shaping it. Both of these eternally exist independently of the Craftsman whereas nothing exists independently of God. All things owe their existence to Him; He alone exists in His own right; He is *the* Self-Existent Being and as such so far transcends everything else that we cannot even begin to comprehend His nature. We can know that He exists and has the property of being wholly active and never passive; but we cannot define His essence, for that (on the Aristotelian view of definition which Philo accepts) would require us to identify Him as belonging to a species of some genus, and because He is fundamentally different from everything else, He does not belong to any species. God is in a class by Himself, above and beyond any positive conception we can form, and so we can properly speak of Him only in negative terms—in terms that set forth what He is *not.* "The active Cause," Philo says, "is the perfectly pure and unsullied Mind of the universe, transcending virtue, transcending knowledge, transcending the good itself and the beautiful itself." God is thus even more exalted than the highest of Plato's forms, which is the form of "the good itself and the beautiful itself."

At Genesis 1:26 we find: "Then God said, 'Let us make man in our image after our likeness. . . .' " Philo understands this to mean that the minds of human beings are patterned after an archetype or form that is a likeness of God's mind, and from this he infers that everything else was also created to resemble as closely as possible other appropriate archetypes or forms. What is true of the human mind as a part of the world, Philo says, must also be true of the whole of the world's contents: "This entire world perceived by our senses (seeing that it is greater than any human image) is a copy of the Divine image. . . ." Such is the way in which Philo finds a basis in Scripture for a modified version of Plato's theory of forms. The forms eternally exist as thoughts in God's mind, as His ideas for the "one great city" of the cosmos. As the first stage of His creative activity, God brought about an intelligible world in which the forms are located as an integrated system in a Mind (*Nous*) that is subordinate to God and that serves as God's instrument for further creation. Philo refers to this subordinate Mind as the Word or Logos of God. The second stage of creation involves the bringing into existence all at once of a sensible world of animate and inanimate things of every species, in accordance with all the forms comprehended in the Logos—a "beautiful copy," Philo says, of a "beautiful pattern." The material elements (in the "desolate waste") of which sensible things are made up were created "out of nothing," for although Plato and the Greek philosophers in general could not accept the notion of creation from nothing, Philo finds it required by God's omnipotence as the (only) Self-Existent Being.

Why did Philo think that God created the sensible world through an intermediary, the Word or Logos? Could not God have created everything directly? Part of the answer is that Philo seems to have taken very literally certain passages of Scripture in which "the word of the Lord" is referred to as if it were God's deputy. In Genesis creation takes place when God *says,* "Let there be light. . . ."; and in Psalm 33:6 this becomes "By the word of the Lord the heavens were made," which could be read as if "the word" were an agent whom the Lord had created to do His will. Such a reading is more strongly invited by Isaiah 55:11, where God says that as rain and snow come down from heaven and make the earth fruitful, "so shall my word be that which goes out of my mouth—it shall not return to me fruitless, without having done the thing that I pleased and accomplishing the purpose for which I sent it." If the Word of the Lord tends to be personified, the same is true of the Wisdom or Reason of the Lord, which in Proverbs is said to be that "by" which the Lord established the heavens and the earth (3:19–20), and which says of itself that "the Lord formed me [Wisdom] as the first of his works. . . . [And] when he traced the foundations of the earth, I was beside him . . ." (8:22, 29–30). Philo appears to have identified Wisdom with the Word and to have identified the Word with the "angel of the Lord" who appears at several places in the Old Testament (though in fact the "angel" is usually described not as a being subordinate to God but as an earthly manifestation of God Himself). The extent to which Philo was prepared to view the Word as a separate heavenly personage with a special divine commission is clear from the following passage:

> To his Word, his chief messenger [literally, *archangel*], highest in age and honor, the Father of all has given the special prerogative, to stand on the border and separate the creature from the Creator. This same Word both pleads with the immortal as suppliant for afflicted mortality and acts as ambassador of the ruler to the subject. He glories in this prerogative and proudly describes it in these words *"and I stood between the Lord and you,"*[2] that is neither uncreated as God, nor created as you, but midway between the two extremes, a surety to both sides; to the parent, pledging the creature that it should never altogether rebel against the rein and choose disorder rather than order; to the child,

---

[2] Actually these words (from Deuteronomy 5:5) were spoken by Moses, not by "the Word."

warranting his hopes that the merciful God will never forget his own work. For "I am the harbinger of peace to creation from that God whose will is to bring wars to an end, who is ever the guardian of peace."

Here we see another reason why Philo believed that God works through an intermediary. Creator and creature are "extremes," and the Word serves to bridge the gulf between them. God is eternal and unchanging. Human beings, along with all the other things in the world, are decidedly *not* eternal and unchanging. On the face of it, there could be no positive relation between two such radically dissimilar levels of existence. How could God deliver us from our afflictions, how could He have created us and all the other things in the first place, if He is eternal (nontemporal) and unchanging? Delivering and creating are activities, and activities are processes of change, and processes of change are temporal. Apparently, then, God is either not really eternal and unchanging or not really our Father and Creator. But Philo believes that Scripture has provided a way around this conclusion: God is eternal and unchanging, and He is our Father and Creator—*indirectly,* however, through the agency of the Word, the "first-born son" of God, which (or who) is neither uncreated nor created, neither eternal nor temporal, neither unchanging nor changing, but is "midway between."

This is at best a difficult notion. How could something be "midway between" the uncreated and the created? Must not anything be definitely one or the other? Philo tried to clarify the matter by making a distinction, which he adapted from the Stoics, between two aspects of the Logos or Word. The Stoics had conceived of the Logos as a single executive Reason that orders all things, but they had also viewed it as a complex of forces (associated with fiery aether) that bind together the elements of which physical objects are composed. Considered as a single executive Reason, the Logos is unchanging ("Nature's great King, through endless years the same," says Cleanthes in his "Hymn to Zeus"). Considered as a complex of cohesive forces ("pulsating through" things, Cleanthes says), the Logos changes because these forces are continually being redistributed as things arise and perish. Similarly, Philo distinguished within the Word its unchanging aspect as a single transcendent Mind comprehending the forms in unity with God, and its changing aspect as a complex of directive "powers" that "pervade" all things.[3] The Word both transcends the world and is immanent within the world ("immanent" meaning "pervasive"). As transcendent the Word shares in the nontemporal and unchanging character of God. As immanent the Word participates in time and change, for the material objects that it pervades are temporal and

---

[3] Occasionally Philo goes so far as to represent the Word's "powers" as separate agencies in their own right and to associate them with the stars, which he calls "manifest and visible gods" in the manner of Plato and the Stoics. A plurality of subordinate deities seems to Philo required by "let *us* make man in *our* image," as if God were addressing a number of assistants.

changing. Having these two aspects, the Word both resembles and differs from God (uncreated) on the one hand and the world (created) on the other. It is "midway between" them and relates them to one another through itself.

The Word's two aspects and intermediate position found their way into the Wisdom of Solomon. This book, which forms part of the Apocrypha of the Bible, may have influenced Philo, or he may have influenced whoever composed it (another subject of much debate). Most authorities believe that the Wisdom of Solomon was in any case composed long after the lifetime of Solomon (who lived in the tenth century B.C.) because for one thing it appears to make use of the Septuagint version of Isaiah; and some authorities believe that it dates from the first half of the first century A.D. The Word, addressed as Wisdom and personified as female, is praised in the following terms:

> Wisdom, the fashioner of all things . . .
> Penetrates and permeates everything. . . .
> She is the breath of the power of God,
> And a pure emanation of his almighty glory. . . .
> She is a reflection of the everlasting light,
> And a spotless mirror of the activity of God,
> And a likeness of his goodness.
> Though she is one, she can do all things,
> And while remaining in herself, she makes everything new. . . .
> She reaches in strength from one end of the earth to the other,
> And conducts everything well. . . .
> She glorifies her high birth in living with God,
> For the Lord of all loves her.
> For she is initiated into the knowledge of God,
> And is a searcher of his works. . . .
>
> God of my forefathers and merciful Lord,
> Who created all things by your word,
> And by your wisdom formed men . . .
> Give me [Solomon] the wisdom that sits by your throne. . . .
> You have chosen me out to be a king of your people. . . .
> You told me to build a sanctuary on your holy mountain,
> And an altar in the city where you dwell,
> A copy of the holy tent which you prepared in the beginning;
> And with you is wisdom, which knows your works,
> And was present when you made the world. . . .

On the one hand Wisdom is a unitary power who remains in herself and in company with God, of Whom she is the issue ("emanation") and image. On the other hand, like the divine fire of the Stoics, Wisdom permeates all things as their artificer and guide, investing humans with the power of making things (as, by implication, she does) that are copies of archetypes which she perceives in God's mind—the "holy tent," for example. Wisdom thus has one foot in the supernatural realm of timeless perfection and another foot in the natural realm of becoming and change.

There is a problem with this which should be mentioned. If God and the world require an intermediary to relate them, then so do the two aspects of Wisdom or the Word. Insofar as Wisdom has a side that is like God in being above time and change, there is the same difficulty in conceiving how this could be related to her temporal and changing side as there is in conceiving how God could be related to the world. But an intermediary between Wisdom's two sides would itself have the same two sides, and the difficulty would only recur, unless Philo is able to produce an altogether different notion of what makes an intermediary an intermediary. If an intermediary between Wisdom's nontemporal and temporal aspects must itself have these aspects, then there will have to be a subintermediary to relate them—a subintermediary with the same two aspects. An infinite series of would-be intermediaries thus opens out before us, with never a definitive intermediary to be found.

It is not surprising, then, that Philo does not always speak as if God and the world require an intermediary to relate them. He sometimes speaks instead of God's creating and ruling the world directly by "powers" that are aspects of Himself, not separate agents subordinate to Him. From this point of view, the Word is simply the system of forms that constitutes the intelligible world in God's mind and serves as His model in creating and ruling the sensible world. Creating and ruling, Philo says, are expressions of two of the Almighty's many powers. The power of creating the world is what "God" properly signifies; the power of ruling the world once it has been created is what "Lord" properly signifies. Neither "God" nor "Lord" adequately expresses the Almighty's essence, which transcends the world completely and far surpasses any of the powers we can conceive Him to possess. His powers are to Him as shadows are to a physical object; and as an object may cast two shadows at once, so does He manifest to our minds His powers as Creator and Ruler. Philo presents this analogy in the course of an allegorical interpretation of Genesis 18, where three mysterious visitors call upon Abraham as he sits "at the door of his tent in the heat of the day." One way of reading the passage is to identify one of the visitors as the Almighty and the other two as His attendants. Philo goes beyond this to view the two "attendants" as shadows cast by the Almighty under the noonday sun, and then he allegorizes as follows:

> Spoken words contain symbols of things apprehended by the understanding only. When, then, as at noontide God shines around the soul, and the light of the mind fills it through and through and the shadows are driven from it by the rays which pour all around it, the single object presents to it a triple vision, one representing the reality, the other two the shadows reflected from it. Our life in the light which our senses

perceive gives us a somewhat similar experience, for objects standing or moving often cast two shadows at once. No one, however, should think that the shadows can be properly spoken of as God. To call them so is loose speaking, serving merely to give a clearer view of the fact which we are explaining, since the real truth is otherwise. Rather, as anyone who has approached nearest to the truth would say, the central place is held by the Father of the Universe, who in the sacred scriptures is called he that IS ["I am that I am"] as his proper name, while on either side of him are the senior potencies [powers], the nearest to him, the creative and the kingly. The title of the former is God, since it made and ordered the All; the title of the latter is Lord, since it is the fundamental right of the maker to rule and control what he has brought into being. So the central Being with each of his potencies as his squire presents to the mind which has vision the appearance sometimes of one, sometimes of three: of one, when that mind is highly purified and . . . presses on to the ideal form which is free from mixture and complexity, and being self-contained needs nothing more; of three, when, as yet uninitiated into the highest mysteries, it is still a votary of the minor rites and unable to apprehend the Existent alone by itself and apart from all else, but only through its actions, as either creative or ruling.

Although Philo describes God and the Lord as the "senior potencies" and "squires" of the Father (the Existent, He that IS), he makes it clear that these are not really three separate divine persons. "God" and "the Lord" refer to the Father's own activities as creative and ruling—activities that express only limited aspects of His nature. This will be fully understood, Philo says, only by those few persons who have attained the highest knowledge. Many can understand that the world is ruled by a wise power and must have been created by one. This much indeed "the world teaches," for if we contemplate the regularity and purposeful arrangement of events in the world, we will come (Philo is sure) to no other conclusion. But what is too seldom realized is that it is not possible for us to capture the Existent with our concepts of Creator/God and Ruler/Lord. Insofar as we can be aware of His true nature at all, we should be aware that it quite overpowers our capacities of comprehension. Philo explains this in terms reminiscent of Plato's account in the *Symposium* of the soul's ascent to the ecstatic vision of absolute beauty:

> The human mind evidently occupies a position in men precisely answering to that which the great Ruler occupies in all the world. It is invisible while itself seeing all things, and while comprehending the substances of others, it is as to its own substance unperceived; and while it opens by arts and sciences roads branching in many directions, all of them great highways, it comes through land and sea investigating what either element contains. Again, when on soaring wing it has contemplated the atmosphere and all its phases, it is borne yet higher to the ether and the circuit of heaven, and is whirled around with the dances

of planets and fixed stars, in accordance with the laws of perfect music, following that love of wisdom which guides its steps. And so, carrying its gaze beyond the confines of all substance discernible by sense, it comes to a point at which it reaches out after the intelligible world, and on descrying in that world sights of surpassing loveliness, even the patterns and the originals of the things of sense which it saw here, it is seized by a sober intoxication, like those filled with Corybantic frenzy,[4] and is inspired, possessed by a longing far other than theirs and a nobler desire. Wafted by this to the topmost arch of the things perceptible to mind, it seems to be on its way to the Great King Himself; but, amid its longing to see Him, pure and untempered rays of concentrated light stream forth like a torrent, so that by its gleams the eye of the understanding is dazzled.

Philo continued throughout his writings to waver between conceiving of God as related to the world through one or more intermediaries and conceiving of Him as related to the world directly. The more Philo insisted upon God's transcendence of the world and upon our inability to comprehend His nature, the more an intermediary seemed to be required—an agent and ambassador and messenger "midway between." But an intermediary would have to combine in itself an aspect that transcends the world with an aspect that does not, and how it could do this is not easy to see. The notion of an intermediary proves to be no less difficult than the notion that God is directly related to the world. One cannot tell from Philo's writings whether he was fully conscious of this problem, but the lack of decisive clarity in his statements concerning the Logos probably did not escape him, and one feels in reading him that he was continually struggling for an adequate conception of God's relation to the world.

One of the greatest of all scholarly controversies has concerned the extent to which Philo's ideas figure in the New Testament. There is no explicit reference to Philo in the New Testament, and there is no external evidence that any of the authors represented in the New Testament was acquainted with Philo's writings. But certain passages in the New Testament are so reminiscent of Philo that some authorities have concluded that his works must have been known to the writers in question. The chief of these passages is the Prologue to the Gospel of John:

> In the beginning was the Word [Logos];
> the Word was in God's presence,
> and the Word was God.
> He was present with God in the beginning.

---

[4] Corybantes, in Phrygian mythology, were attendants of the nature goddess Cybele and accompanied her with wild dances and music. The priests of her cult were notorious for behaving likewise.

Through him all things came into being,
and apart from him not a thing came to be.
That which had come to be in him was life,
and this life was the light of men. . . .

He was in the world,
and the world was made by him. . . .

And the Word became flesh
and made his dwelling among us.
And we have seen his glory,
the glory of an only Son coming from the Father,
filled with enduring love.

Here, as in Philo, the Word—God's Son—is the power "through" whom the world was created, and as such the Word is both transcendent ("in God's presence") and immanent ("in the world").[5] The same function and attributes are assigned to Wisdom in the Wisdom of Solomon, and some authorities believe that the Prologue owes more to Wisdom than to Philo. But other authorities have concluded that Philo influenced the author of Wisdom, so that if the Prologue borrows from Wisdom, it indirectly borrows from Philo. The complicated debate on these points cannot be gone into here, and in any case the differences between Philo and the Prologue are as significant as the similarities. The Prologue says that the Word, although "with" God, also *was* God, whereas for Philo the Word, when personified, is a being *subordinate* to God. The Prologue says, in reference to Jesus, that "the Word became *flesh*," whereas it is unlikely that Philo conceived the Word as capable of being literally incarnated in a particular historical person. Philo says that it is the Word's function "to stand on the border and separate the creature from the Creator"; but according to the Prologue, the Word crossed the border completely "and made his dwelling among us." St. Augustine (354–430 A.D.) says in his *Confessions* that he found in Greek sources the equivalents of most Christian doctrines, "but I did not read in them that *the Word was made flesh . . ,*" and the consensus regarding Philo is that St. Augustine was correct.

Be Philo's relation to the New Testament as it may, there is no question that an important phase of the evolution of Christian doctrine was heavily indebted to him. The Greek Christians of Alexandria, beginning with Clement in the second century A.D., took their cue from Philo's confidence that Scripture and Greek philosophy are largely compatible.

---

[5] Compare St. Paul's Letter to the Colossians, 1:15–20: "He is the image of the invisible God, the first-born of all creation, for in him all things were created, in heaven and on earth, visible and invisible, whether thrones or dominions or principalities or authorities—all things were created through him and for him. He is before all things, and in him all things hold together. . . . In him all the fulness of God was pleased to dwell, and through him to reconcile to himself all things, whether on earth or in heaven, making peace by the blood of his cross."

Adopting Philo's allegorical method and guided by the Biblical interpretations he achieved with it, they undertook to interpret Christian beliefs within a framework of Platonic and Stoic ideas. No comparable development was inspired by Philo among Jewish thinkers, however, for in general Alexandria declined as a Jewish cultural center during the second century A.D., and intellectual ascendancy began to pass to the rabbis of the Jewish communities in Parthia (formerly Babylonia, now Iraq). Parthia was the main refuge for the Jews of Judea after the Romans ruthlessly suppressed their revolt under Simon bar Kochba in 135 A.D., and in Parthia the influence of Hellenistic ideas, even Jewish ones, seems to have been very slight.

CHAPTER 12

Plotinus

Some of the main themes of Greek philosophy culminated in the work of Plotinus (205–270 A.D.), who was born and raised in a provincial town of Egypt and went in his late twenties to study in Alexandria. He soon became devoted to a philosopher called Ammonius Saccus, whose pupil he remained for eleven years, and from whom he acquired a firm attachment to certain metaphysical and religious principles in Plato's dialogues. Ammonius encouraged Plotinus to interpret these principles in a special way and to supplement them with ideas borrowed from the Pre-Socratics, Aristotle, and the Stoics. The result was a "New Platonism" or "Neoplatonism," as Plotinus' philosophy is now called, though at the time he and his followers were known simply as "Platonists," for it was not supposed that they had significantly departed from Plato. Plotinus did not acknowledge finding anything to his purpose or liking in the views of Jewish or Christian thinkers, or in the Scriptures, and yet in some respects his position was similar to Philo's. St. Augustine came to adopt much of Plotinus' philosophy as a medium for presenting Christian doctrines, but Plotinus himself took Christians to task in his lectures (he was silent about them in his writings) for suggesting that Plato's grasp of ultimate reality was incomplete.[1]

Plotinus left Alexandria in his thirty-ninth year on a journey to the East with the aim of investigating the thought of Persia and India. Unfortunately, however, the trip was not a success. Plotinus had fallen in with a military expedition of the Roman emperor Gordian III, who was bent upon driving the Persians out of Mesopotamia. But in Mesopotamia Gordian was murdered by a conspiracy within his own camp; and Plotinus found it necessary to retire quickly from the region. This brought him to Rome (in 245), where he opened a school and began to attract a following in high places. Many members of the Senate are said to have attended his lectures. He found particular favor with the emperor Gallienus, whose several pursuits included philosophy but, sad to say, excluded diligent statesmanship. Gibbon says of Gallienus that "he was a master of several curious but useless sciences, a ready orator and elegant poet, a skillful gardener, an excellent cook, and most contemptible prince. When the great emergencies of the state required his presence and atten-

---

[1] Ammonius Saccus, incidentally, is said to have been reared as a Christian but to have become a pagan in later life.

tion, he was engaged in conversation with the philosopher Plotinus, wasting his time in trifling or licentious pleasures, preparing his initiation to the Grecian mysteries, or soliciting a place in the Areopagus of Athens." Plotinus' private opinion of Gallienus is unknown, but he is said to have tried to make full use of Gallienus' friendship. For example, there was a ruined town in the vicinity of Rome that Plotinus asked Gallienus to rebuild with a view to establishing a community there along the lines laid down in Plato's *Laws*. Although Gallienus was initially in favor of the project, some of his courtiers were not, and they contrived to change his mind. It would seem that they were jealous of Plotinus' influence. At any rate "Platonopolis," as the town was to have been called, never materialized.

A confirmed bachelor of weak health and abstemious habits, Plotinus nevertheless enjoyed a wide circle of friends and admirers, including a number of women in fashionable society. He was especially noted for his kindliness and charity, as illustrated by his taking orphaned children into his home and acting as their guardian. Plotinus would never tell anyone his precise birthday, for (unlike Epicurus) he did not want it to be celebrated; instead it was his custom to entertain his friends on the traditional birthdays of Socrates and Plato. His lectures took the form of conversations in which he encouraged his students to ask questions—a practice to which at least one of his students objected on the grounds that Plotinus' courses were "lacking in order" and encumbered with "a great deal of pointless chatter." These conversations were so much Plotinus' preferred mode of expression that he did not begin to compose his thoughts in writing until he was nearly fifty, by which time his eyesight was failing. The manuscripts he produced were difficult in style and unsystematic in arrangement. His pupil Porphyry undertook to improve at least their arrangement by organizing them into six groups of nine treatises each. These "groups of nine"—*Enneads*, in Greek—are what have come down to us. Porphyry also prepared a biography of Plotinus, which is the source of practically all that is known of his life.

The One

Plotinus' *Enneads* do not contain much in the way of explicit argument. One finds instead a wealth of conclusions and usually no more than brief indications of the reasoning by which Plotinus arrived at them. An important exception, however, is a well-developed argument concerning the function of *unity* in the constitution of *beings,* which leads Plotinus to the central thesis of his position. Any particular being, he points out, consists of a number of distinguishable elements, parts, or aspects. This is obviously true of bodily beings of every kind, for even the smallest of them has some size, and whatever has size necessarily has distinguishable parts. But this is also true of souls, for although souls have no size, they do have distinguishable elements in the form of various powers such as reasoning, perceiving, and desiring. The essential thing, of course, is that the constituents of a particular being are brought into a characteristic kind of *unity,* for without this it would not be *one* being of the sort it is. Detached fragments of matter do not constitute a body; dissociated powers do not constitute a soul; these must be *unified* in appropriate ways if such beings are to exist. It may further be noted that the more tightly the elements of anything are unified, the more fully it may be said to *have* being. A flock of geese, for example, has considerable unity, but not as much unity as the components of an individual goose; and so we may say of the goose that she is *more* of a being than the flock. The flock may be dispersed easily, but not the components of the goose: her being is much more substantial. In general, the degree of a thing's being is exactly equivalent to the degree of its unity; and we may rank the many beings of our experience on a scale of increasing unity-and-being, with clouds, say, near the bottom and stars nearer the top.

Perfect or absolute unity, however, is never attained by the objects of our experience. Even the most unified of bodies and souls have distinguishable elements within them, whereas perfect unity—absolute, unqualified *oneness*—excludes all multiplicity or diversity. Unity pure and simple cannot coexist with any plurality of aspects or parts. If by "Unity" (with a capital "U") we mean "absolute, unqualified oneness," and if by "Being" (with a capital "B") we mean "the being possessed in various degrees by the objects of our experience," we may describe the situation— as Plotinus does—by saying that Unity must be distinguished from Being.

Is "Unity" a name for anything more than an empty abstraction? Plotinus is sure that it is. If the beings of our experience *are* beings only to the extent that their elements are unified, does not this mean that they are beings only to the extent that they approximate absolute Unity? And what is an approximation to Unity if it is not (as Plato would say) a more or less limited *participation* in Unity? And how could anything participate in an empty abstraction? Unity, it is plain, is not only something real: it is the Supreme Reality, since beings *are* beings only by sharing in it. Individual beings have in common the unity that makes them individuals; this common possession of theirs implies that the same thing is present (more or less) to each of them; and this same thing is Unity, which accordingly is the Principle upon which the existence of individuals depends. Or look at it this way: as we move up the scale of increasing unity, knowing that this is also the scale of increasing being, how can we suppose that Unity itself is nothing, or is at best an empty abstraction? As the last word in oneness, Unity must be the last word in reality, responsible for Being but standing beyond Being—beyond the diversity within particular beings, beyond the diversity of the whole cosmos of particular beings. All diversity must somehow find its ultimate explanation in Unity; the many must somehow derive from the absolute One. Unity, the One, can only be God, the Father, the Good "beyond being" of which Plato spoke in the *Republic*.

Such is roughly how Plotinus, starting from the function of unity in the constitution of beings, arrives at the conclusion that Unity is incomparably real and is God. For Plotinus as for Philo, God transcends the world completely and far surpasses human comprehension. God is beyond description, for to describe anything is to specify the predicates that belong to some subject; but in Unity—in absolute, unqualified Oneness— there is no diversity whatever and therefore no distinction between subject and predicates. In saying that God is Unity, Plotinus does not mean that Unity is a predicate or characteristic of God; he means that "God" and "Unity" (or "the One") are interchangeable names for precisely the same thing. God does not have characteristics; He is the *author* of all characteristics and is Himself above and beyond them all. No name is really appropriate to God, since any name inevitably suggests a being that has certain characteristics. "God," "Unity," "the One," and so on, have only a rough fitness as names that direct our attention away from the world of multiplicity and toward its transcendent Source, of which we may achieve some imperfect vision but to which no words can do justice.

Plotinus, again like Philo, believes that we are in a position to say of God only what he is *not*—a procedure associated with what in later times was to be called "negative theology." We may confidently assert, for example, that God is *not* a being for whom anything can be good in the sense of meeting His needs. The Father of all being and every excellence can have no needs. We may also be sure that God Himself is *not* good in the sense of having goodness as a characteristic; He is superior to goodness-as-a-characteristic, which Plotinus says we may signify by saying that He is *the* Good, though we must understand this not as a characterization of God but as a way of stating that the well-being of all other things consists in communion with Him. It is equally certain that God cannot properly be described as thinking, willing, or engaging in any kind of activity. In absolute Unity there are no distinctions, whereas in thinking or willing the mind that thinks or wills is distinguishable from the objects that it thinks about or aims at. Any kind of activity implies a distinction between an agent that acts and an object that it acts upon, but for Unity this is out of the question. Even self-consciousness must be denied of God, for in self-consciousness one distinguishes between oneself-as-knowing and oneself-as-known, and Unity cannot do that. But this does not mean that God is ignorant of Himself; one can be ignorant only of some possible object of consciousness, but nothing can stand as an object of consciousness to the transcendent Author of all objects and all consciousness. He is beyond knowing and unknowing. God is the Alone and the Solitary in His complete unlikeness to everything else, for everything else is characterized by some form of multiplicity or diversity, but He who is the Father of multiplicity and diversity is One, indivisible, unchanging, eternal, and inconceivably greater than everything else.

Here are some passages from the Sixth of Plotinus' *Enneads* which bear upon points mentioned thus far:

It is in virtue of unity that beings are beings. . . .

What could exist at all except as one thing? Deprived of unity, a thing ceases to be what it is called: no army unless a unity: a chorus, a flock, must be one thing. . . . Take plant and animal: the material form stands a unity; fallen from that into a litter of fragments, the things have lost their being; what was is no longer there; it is replaced by quite other things—as many others, precisely, as possess unity. . . .

Anything that can be described as a unity is so in the precise degree in which it holds a characteristic being; the less or more the degree of the being, the less or more the unity [and vice versa]. . . .

Now the being of the particular is a manifold; unity cannot be a manifold; there must therefore be a distinction between Being and Unity. Thus a man is at once a reasoning living being and a total of parts; his variety is held together by his unity; man therefore and Unity are different—man a thing of parts against unity partless. Much more [the totality of all particular beings] must be a manifold and therefore distinct from the unity in which it is but *participant*. . . .

What then must The Unity be, what nature is left for it? . . . It cannot be a being. . . . Generative of all, The Unity is none of all; neither thing nor quantity nor quality nor intellect nor soul; not in motion, not at rest, not in place, not in time: it is the self-defined, unique in form or, better, formless, existing before Form was, or Movement, or Rest, all of which are attachments of Being and make Being the manifold it is. . . .

Awareness of this Principle [that is, of Unity] comes . . . by a presence overpassing all knowledge. . . . Our way . . . takes us beyond knowing. . . . In our writing and telling we are but urging towards it: out of discussion we call to vision: to those desiring to see, we point the path; our teaching is of the road and the traveling. . . .

Strictly no name is apt to it, but since name it we must there is a certain rough fitness in designating it as unity with the understanding that it is not the unity of some other thing [that is, the Unity that is God is not, like the unity of other things, a unity of distinguishable aspects or parts]. . . . It is great beyond anything . . . infinite not in measureless extension or numerable quantity [extension and quantity in general imply distinguishable parts] but in fathomless depths of power. . . . This is utterly a self-existent . . . supremely adequate, autonomous, all-transcending, most utterly without need.

Any manifold, anything beneath The Unity, is dependent: combined from various constituents, its essential nature goes in need of unity; but unity cannot need itself; it stands unity accomplished. . . .

The sovereignly self-sufficing principle will be Unity-Absolute, for only in this Unity is there a nature above all need whether within itself or in regard to the rest of things. . . . Cause to all, how can it acquire its character outside of itself or know any good outside? The good of its being can be no borrowing: This is The Good. . . .

Neither can it have will to anything; it is a Beyond-Good, not even to itself a good but to such things as may be of quality to have part with it. Nor has it Intellection; that would comport diversity: nor Movement; it is prior to Movement as to Intellection.

To what could its Intellection be directed? To itself?[2] But that would imply a previous ignorance; it would be dependent upon that Intellection in order to have knowledge of itself; but it is the self-sufficing. Yet this absence of self-knowing does not comport ignorance; ignorance is of something outside—a knower ignorant of a knowable—but in the Solitary there is neither knowing nor anything unknown. Unity, self-present, it has no need of self-intellection. . . . It is . . . the cause of [intellectual activity] in something else, and cause is not to be identified with caused: most assuredly, the cause of all is not a thing within that all.

This Principle is not, therefore, to be identified with the good of which it is the source: it is good in the unique mode of being The Good above all that is good.

Plotinus wishes it to be understood that his views are "no novelties, no inventions of today, but long since stated, if not stressed." "Our doctrine here," he says, "is the explanation of an earlier and can show the antiquity of these opinions in the testimony of Plato himself." Certainly Plato described the Good (in the *Republic*) as the transcendent source of both the reality and the intelligibility of everything other than itself; but the Good, for Plato, is not God—it is a *form* (the paramount form).[3] The supreme *deity* (in Plato's *Timaeus*) is the Craftsman, who exists *independently* of the forms and who takes the forms as his models in fashioning the sensible world. How the Craftsman could exist independently of the forms, if the Good (a form) is the source of everything other than itself, is a problem that Plato never cleared up. He said nothing further about the Good after mentioning it in the *Republic,* and in the *Republic* he said nothing about the Craftsman. Plotinus, in the belief that he is only giving an "explanation" of what Plato really meant, proceeds in effect to make Plato consistent: he adheres to the *Republic* in maintaining that the Good produces all reality, and thus he views the Craftsman—whom he calls "Intellect"—as *subordinate* to the Good. But Plotinus also goes beyond Plato in viewing the Good not as the paramount form but as God, the One who is author of *every* form. So, after all, there are some important innovations in Plotinus' position. Let us now see how he presents his views concerning Intellect and the forms.

---

[2] Here Plotinus is taking issue with Aristotle, who said that "it must be of itself that the divine thought thinks (since it is the most excellent of things), and its thinking is a thinking on thinking." (see p. 149.) Elsewhere Plotinus remarks that Aristotle, after correctly stating that God is the transcendent First, goes on to cancel God's primacy by attributing to Him self-consciousness, which implies diversity in God and calls for a higher principle of unity to account for it.

[3] See p. 91.

Intellect

Plotinus takes it as a general principle that anything perfect of its kind necessarily generates something a degree lower in perfection. God, who is perfection itself, necessarily generates Intellect (*Nous*, in Greek). He does not do this at any particular *time*, or through any sort of *activity*, or from any *constraint* or sense of *need*, for none of these terms is applicable to Unity. Nor in doing this does God subtract anything from His own perfection, which is strictly unlimited and so cannot be diminished however much is generated from it.[4] Intellect eternally "proceeds" or "emanates" from God in somewhat the same way as light comes from the sun, without (as Plotinus believes) the sun's changing or losing anything in the process. Self-sufficient and devoid of "jealousy," God in the superabundance of his power spontaneously "overflows," as it were, and Intellect is the immediate result.

What, then, is Intellect? Like God or the One, it is an incorporeal reality (or *hypostasis*, to use Plotinus' Greek term); but unlike the One, it is not unqualifiedly *one*. Intellect is a unity that comprises a *duality*, for Intellect is a timeless *knowing* in which a subject of knowledge is distinguishable from the objects it knows. The objects of Intellect's knowing are (a) the One and (b) itself. Intellect is what it is by virtue of its participating in Unity, and this it does by directly apprehending the One. So constituted, Intellect is aware of itself as containing patterns or forms of all possible beings less perfect than itself. As Philo located Plato's forms in a Logos subordinate to God, so Plotinus locates them in an Intellect, which is Plato's Craftsman viewed as subordinate to the Good. Intellect knows these forms by a comprehensive intuition, not by a sequential process of reasoning; and it knows them as a unified system—as an "intelligible cosmos," the best *image* of Unity—in which specific forms (forms of fish, for example) are encompassed by more general ones (such as the form of animal), and the more general ones are encompassed by the *most* general—the form of Being itself. The system of forms, as in Plato, is the realm of authentic Being; but among the forms Plotinus recognizes, as Plato apparently did not, forms of individuals (the man Socrates, for instance), which means that an eternal status and value are provided by Plotinus, more securely than by Plato, for particular souls. Plotinus views the forms as so organically related to one another, by virtue of their being diverse specifications of a supreme Unity, that to know any one is to know them all.

---

[4] Anything strictly unlimited remains unlimited no matter how much is "taken away" from it. For example, you can take away any number of integers from the series 0, 1, 2, 3 . . . , and you will still have infinitely many integers left over. There is no question of reducing the supply. But Plotinus warns that the unlimitedness of the One is not really comprehensible to us and in particular cannot be comprehended in terms of the *quantity* of anything (such as integers), since quantity implies a multiplicity of distinguishable components or elements, which the One does not possess.

Intellect, in its knowing of the forms, is conscious of itself as different from them; but it is also conscious of itself as *identical* with them. Aristotle had maintained that a human soul acquires knowledge of some object when its "thinking part" (its passive intellect) registers the object's essence or form—much as a tablet receives an inscription—so that the soul becomes "identical in character" with the object. Because the soul has the potential for knowing all forms, Aristotle said, there is reason to call it "the place of forms"; and the soul knows itself as a "place" where forms are realized. Plotinus adapts these notions to the case of Intellect, which he describes as not just identical *in character* with the objects it knows but identical in the numerical sense that it and they are *one and the same thing*. Intellect is the "place," the only "place," where the forms fully exist, but Intellect is also a knowing of the forms; and thus its knowing of them is a knowing of itself,[5] and it and they are one reality. "The unity they form," Plotinus says, "is two-sided; there is Intellect as against Being [that is, the forms, which constitute the realm of Being], the intellectual agent as against the object of intellection; we consider the intellective act and we have Intellect; we think of the object of that act and we have Being. Such difference there must be if there is to be any intellection; but similarly there must be identity (since, in perfect knowing, subject and object are identical). . . ."

The origin and character of Intellect are set forth in these passages from the Fifth and Sixth of Plotinus' *Enneads:*

> From such a unity as we have declared the One to be, how does anything at all come into substantial existence, any multiplicity? . . . Why has the Primal not remained self-gathered so that there be none of this profusion of the manifold which we observe in existence and yet are compelled to trace to that absolute unity? . . .
>
> All existences, as long as they retain their character, produce—about themselves, from their essence, in virtue of the power which must be in them—some necessary, outward-facing hypostasis continuously attached to them . . . thus fire gives out its heat; snow is cold not merely to itself; [in the case of] fragrant substances . . . as long as they last something is diffused from them and perceived wherever they are present.
>
> Again, all that is fully achieved engenders: therefore the eternally achieved engenders eternally an eternal being. At the same time, the offspring is always minor: what, then, are we to think of the All-Perfect [One] but that it can produce nothing less than the very greatest that is later than [subordinate to] itself? This must be the Divine Mind [Intellect, *Nous*], . . . that which sees the One on which alone it leans . . . [It] looks to the First without mediation—thus becoming what it is—and has that vision . . . as an immediate next with nothing intervening. . . .

[5] Hence, according to Plotinus, it is Intellect—not God, as Aristotle supposed—of whom we may say that "it must be of itself that the divine thought thinks. . . ."

[Intellect in its relation to the One] may be compared to the brilliant light encircling the sun and ceaselessly generated from that unchanging substance. . . .

The Intellect stands as the image of The One, firstly because there is a certain necessity that the first should have its offspring, carrying onward much of its quality, in other words that there be something in its likeness as the sun's rays tell of the sun. . . .

Unity . . . is the potentiality of all existence. . . . The items of this potentiality [that is, the forms] the divine intellection [Intellect] brings out, so to speak, from the unity [of God] and knows them in detail. . . .

It [Intellect] knows that its nature is in some sense a definite part of the content of the First [God]. . . . It sees that, as a member in some sense of the realm of division and part, it receives life and intellection and all else it has and is from the undivided and partless [that is, from God]. . . . As it comes into existence, all other beings must be simultaneously engendered—all the beauty of the Ideas [forms], all the gods of the intellectual realm. . . .

[Plato in the *Republic*] teaches . . . that there is an author of the Cause [an author of the Craftsman in the *Timaeus*], that is, of Intellect, which to him is the Creator who made the Soul [of the world]. . . . This author is to him [in the *Republic*] the Good, that which transcends Being. . . .

There exists a Principle which transcends Being; this is the One, whose nature we have sought to establish insofar as such matters lend themselves to proof. Upon the One follows immediately the Principle which is at once Being and Intellect. Third comes the Principle, Soul. . . .

If Being is identical with Intellect, even at that it is a manifold; all the more so when count is taken of the ideal forms in it; for the idea [or form], particular or collective, is after all a numerable agglomeration whose unity is that of a cosmos. . . .

Considered as at once thinker and object of its thought, it [Intellect] is dual, not simplex, not the Unity. . . . [Intellect is] that which, holding itself in the presence of the Good and First and looking towards that, is self-present also, self-knowing and knowing itself as all Being: thus manifold, it is far from being the Unity[6]. . . .

[Intellect] is a multiple but at once indivisible and comporting difference. . . . Intellect is not merely one; it is one and many. . . .

[Intellect's] knowing is not by search [reasoning] but by possession [intuition], its blessedness inherent, not acquired; for all belongs to it eternally and it holds the authentic eternity imitated by time. . . . Its entire content is simultaneously present in that identity: this is pure being in eternal actuality; nowhere is there any future, for every then

---

[6] Parmenides, as Plotinus understands him, correctly identified Intellect and Being but incorrectly supposed that this identity could be "the Primal One"—as if it were not also a multiplicity. A more adequate view, in Plotinus' opinion, is expressed by the Parmenides of Plato's dialogue, who recognizes the difference between oneness that is absolute and oneness that is also manyness.

is a now; nor is there any past, for nothing there has ever ceased to be: everything has taken its stand for ever, an identity well pleased, we might say, to be as it is; and everything, in that entire content, is Intellect and Authentic Existence; and the total of all is Intellect entire and Being entire. Intellect by its intellective act establishes Being, which in turn, as the object of intellection, becomes the cause of intellection and of existence to Intellect—though of course there is another cause of intellection [namely, God] which is also a cause to Being, both rising in a source distinct from either. . . .

The Intellect is, so to speak, shaped by the Ideas [forms] rising within it—or rather, it is shaped in a certain sense by the One and in another sense by itself, since its potential vision becomes actual and intellection is, precisely, an act of vision in which subject and object are identical.

Soul, Matter, and Evil

As the One eternally generates Intellect, so Intellect eternally generates an hypostasis that Plotinus calls "Soul" and identifies with "the soul of the cosmos" in Plato's *Timaeus*. Soul is an incorporeal reality that contemplates Intellect just as Intellect contemplates the One. Soul apprehends the system of forms contained in Intellect; but it apprehends the system not in the intuitive manner of Intellect itself but through a continual process of step-by-step reasoning. The movement of Soul's reasoning is what constitutes time, without beginning or end, and gives rise to motion in space. A higher part of Soul remains always in the presence of Intellect, contemplating the perfect forms of Being; but a lower part of Soul "descends" from this intelligible world and endeavors to shape a sensible world in accordance with images of the forms. On the principle that everything perfect of its kind necessarily generates something a degree lower in perfection, it is necessary that Intellect should generate Soul and that Soul should generate a sensible world of corporeal beings corresponding to all the possible forms of Being contained in Intellect. Each form specifies the unity characteristic of some kind of being. The lower part of Soul is the agency by which an image of each form of unity is realized in the material sphere. Thus the lower part of Soul pervades the material sphere as a principle of order and growth, and as such it may be called "Nature." (In assigning this separate role to Soul's lower part, Plotinus is actually treating it as a separate reality or hypostasis derivative from Soul proper.)

Plotinus says that Intellect may be viewed as a unity of many separate powers of intellect, or intelligences, one corresponding to each of the forms that Intellect knows. Similarly, he says, Soul proceeds from Intellect as a unity of many different souls, one corresponding to each form as the power that carries its image into sensible effect.[7] Thus arise the souls of human beings, along with souls of every degree of intelligence that operate in producing beings of every degree of unity throughout the natural world. Each soul, like Soul in general, has a higher and a lower part: its higher part remains in communion with Intellect, but its lower part communes with a body and is more or less weakened by its efforts to give form and direction to the matter of its body. Matter, like the raw "matrix" of Plato's *Timaeus,* is by itself absolute disunity and privation of form; it has no being in the sense in which "being" connotes something having at least a minimum of order and arrangement. The "nonbeing" of matter is evil in that it resists complete determination by souls, but it is the destiny of souls to try to impose lasting form upon the formless and to learn from their inevitable failure the wisdom of escaping from their "fallen" condition to full participation in the blessed life of Intellect. The cosmos as a whole, contrary to what Plato may have believed, is without beginning, nor will it have any end; and the great Soul that animates it does so without difficulty. Yet the particular contents of the cosmos, except for the celestial bodies that are gods, arise and change and perish in spite of the best efforts of particular souls to give them the permanence and stability of the forms. Earthly things are inherently unstable; human bodies are especially so. The more preoccupied human souls become with the needs of their bodies, the more infected they become with the formlessness that they can never eradicate from the matter of which their bodies are composed. This infection is sin, the root of all vices, which are just so many sorts of disunity in the soul.

Matter, Plotinus says, necessarily exists as the terminus of God's eternal outpouring of all degrees of unity-and-being; it is the nonbeing that is the limit of Being—the darkness, so to speak, into which the light radiating from the One fades away. If there must be a First, who is absolutely Good, then there must also be a Last, which is absolutely evil; and this Last is matter, indeterminate and never fully determinable. If God in the superabundance of His perfection is *beyond* Being, matter in its total privation of form is *beneath* Being—a purely negative principle, even less than a zero, of which nothing entirely perfect can be made. Evil in all its types is a function of this ineradicable negativity of matter and is never anything positive for which God could be blamed. But this way of viewing matter involves Plotinus in serious difficulties. If matter has any sort of status independently of God, as a kind of barrier or resistant medium which He encounters, then it cannot be true (as Plotinus believes) that God is the source of all that exists. But as evil and the source of evil, matter is the complete antithesis of God and could hardly be even

---

[7] Plotinus interprets the Stoic theory of "rational seeds" or "seminal reasons" (see p. 201) as pertaining to powers in souls for organizing sensible things according to the forms.

the last stage of His outpouring. Plotinus apparently would like to resolve this dilemma by saying that matter, as sheer formlessness, is nonbeing or privation of being, in which case it does not exist and the question of its origin does not arise. The trouble then, however, is to understand how something that does not exist could as such be evil and a source of evil—a barrier to the Good, a resistant medium in which it "fades away"—and Plotinus cannot be said to have explained this at all clearly.

Plotinus has, however, an alternative explanation of evil. According to this, evil comes about not because of matter but because the One, via Intellect and Soul, realizes in the cosmos all possible forms of being. Forms of being differ from one another in respect of strengths and weaknesses; they do not all possess the same or equivalent excellences; they may, in fact, be ranked on a continuous scale of overall excellence, where their places are determined by the balance of their respective assets and liabilities. Thus human beings rank higher than animals, inasmuch as the human capacity for reason is to be prized above physical strength, though the greater strength of certain animals is occasionally lethal to human beings. The point is that the cosmos contains all possible forms of being, and accordingly it contains all possible types and degrees of imperfection as well as perfection—of instability as well as stability, of danger as well as safety, of suffering as well as happiness, of injustice as well as justice, and so on. No creature may fairly complain of its situation in life, for the degree of its well-being is a function of its appropriate and necessary place in the great cosmic hierarchy of perfection. Our cosmos as a whole is the best and most beautiful cosmos possible—exactly because the One has not failed to furnish it with the richest possible variety of contents. As a painting may contain bits of color that individually are displeasing but that nevertheless contribute essentially to the beauty of the whole, so the cosmos contains many features which look individually as if they were flatly evil but which nevertheless contribute essentially to the goodness of the whole.

With this in mind, we can see an important respect in which Plotinus differs from Philo. Intellect and Soul, standing as they do between the One and the sensible world, are reminiscent of Philo's concept of the Logos as God's agent for creation and His emissary to humankind. But Intellect and Soul are not really intermediaries in the way in which Philo understood the Logos to be; they are not divine personages who intercede with the One on our behalf as the Logos "pleads with [the Father] as suppliant for afflicted mortality."[8] Intellect's attention is entirely absorbed in contemplation of itself and the One; Soul at its best contemplates Intellect; neither of them is concerned with human well-being. The evils with which mortals are afflicted are necessary features of a world

[8]See p. 246.

that must contain everything possible—in the interests of the greatest perfection of the whole—and therefore such evils can occasion no concern on the part of Intellect or Soul.

Following are passages, from the first five *Enneads,* dealing with Soul, matter, and evil:

> Treating in the *Timaeus* of our universe, [Plato] exalts the cosmos and entitles it "a blessed god," and holds that the Soul was given by the goodness of the Creator to the end that the total of things might be possessed of intellect. . . . There is a reason, then, why the Soul of this All should be sent into it from God: in the same way the soul of each single one of us is sent, that the universe may be complete; it was necessary that all beings of the Intellectual [that is, all the forms in Intellect] should be tallied by just so many forms of living creatures here in the realm of sense. . . .
>
> All that is Intellect has its being . . . in the place of Intellection, what we call the Intellectual Cosmos: but there exist, too, the intellective powers included in its being, and the separate intelligences—for Intellect is not merely one; it is one and many. In the same way there must be both many souls and one, the one being the source of the differing many just as from one genus there arise various species, better and worse, some of the more intellectual order, others less effectively so. . . .
>
> The total of things could not have remained stationary in the Intellectual Cosmos, once there was the possibility of continuous variety, of beings inferior but as necessarily existent as their superiors. . . .
>
> [It is] better for the Soul to dwell in the Intellectual, but given its proper nature, it is under compulsion to participate in the sense-realm also. There is no grievance in its not being, through and through, the highest; it holds mid-rank among the authentic existences, being of divine station but at the lowest extreme of the Intellectual and skirting the sense-known nature. . . . [The lower part of Soul, however, does not just "skirt" the sensible world—no,] it plunges in an excessive zeal to the very midst of its chosen sphere, [abandoning] its status as whole soul with whole soul, though even thus it is always able to recover itself by turning to account the experience of what it has seen and suffered here, learning, so, the greatness of rest in the Supreme, and more clearly discerning the finer things by comparison with what is almost their direct antithesis. . . . The experience of evil brings the clearer perception of Good.
>
> The outgoing that takes place in Intellect is a descent to its own downward ultimate: . . . operating necessarily outwards from itself . . . the need and law of Nature bring it to its extreme term, to Soul—to which it entrusts all the later stages of being while itself turns back on its course.
>
> The Soul's operation is similar: its next lower act is this universe: its immediate higher is the contemplation of the Authentic Existences [the forms in Intellect]. To individual souls such divine operation takes place

only . . . by a temporal process when, from the lower in which they reside, they turn towards the noblest; but that soul which we know as the All-Soul has never entered the lower activity, but immune from evil has the property of knowing its lower by inspection, while it still cleaves continuously to the beings above itself; thus its double task becomes possible; it takes hence and, since as Soul it cannot escape touching this sphere, it gives hither. . . .

Even our human soul has not sunk entire; something of it is continuously in the Intellectual Realm, though if that part, which is in this sphere of sense, hold the mastery, or rather be mastered here and troubled, it keeps us blind to what the upper phase holds in contemplation. . . .

Every soul has something of the lower on the body side and something of the higher on the side of Intellect.

The Soul of the All, as an entirety, governs the universe through that part of it which leans to the body side, but since it does not exercise a will based on calculation as we do—but proceeds by purely intellectual act as in the execution of an artistic conception—its ministrance is that of a laborless overpoising, only at its lowest phase being active upon the universe it embellishes. . . .

Soul . . . brings all to unity, making, molding, shaping, ranging to order. . . . By the power of the Soul the manifold and diverse heavenly system is a unit: through Soul this universe is a god: and the sun is a god because it is ensouled; so too the stars: and whatsoever we ourselves may be, it is all in virtue of soul. . . .

Soul is the author of all living things. . . . As the rays of the sun throwing their brilliance upon a louring cloud make it gleam all gold, so the soul entering the material expanse of the heavens has given life, has given immortality: what was abject it has lifted up; and the heavenly system, moved now in endless motion by the Soul that leads it in wisdom, has become a living and blessed thing; the soul domiciled within, it takes worth where, before the Soul, it was stark body—clay and water—or, rather, the blankness of Matter, the absence of Being. . . .

Sprung . . . from Intellect, Soul is intellective, but with an intellection operating by the method of reasoning. . . . Soul deals with thing after thing—now Socrates; now a horse: always some one entity from among beings—but Intellect is all and therefore its entire content is simultaneously present in that identity. . . .

The appetite for the divine Intellect urges [individual souls] to return to their source, but they have, too, a power apt to administration in this lower sphere . . . [and] there comes a stage at which they descend from the universal to become partial and self-centered. . . . Thus [the soul] has drifted away from the universal and, by an actual presence, it administers the particular. . . . It has fallen: it is at the chain: debarred from expressing itself now through its intellectual phase, it operates through sense, it is a captive; this is the burial . . . of the soul. . . . The soul has entered the body. . . . [This is] determined by an eternal law of nature . . . [but] still there is a twofold flaw: the first lies in the motive of the soul's descent (its audacity, its Tolma), and the second in the evil it does when actually here: the first is punished by what the soul has suffered by its descent: for the faults committed here, the lesser penalty is to enter into body after body . . . but any outrageous form of ill-doing incurs a proportionately greater punishment administered under the surveillance of chastising daimons. . . .

What comes into [the universe] from God is good; the evil comes from . . . the underlying matter, . . . that which underlies figures and forms and shapes and measures and limits, . . . which is unbounded in itself and absolutely formless. . . . Since not only the Good exists, there must be the last end to the process of going out past it, or if one prefers to put it like this, going down or going away: and this last, after which nothing else can come into being, is evil. Now it is necessary that what comes after the First should exist, and therefore that the Last should exist; and this is matter, which possesses nothing at all of the Good . . . [but is only] a sort of form of non-existence . . . something other than being. . . . For matter has not even being—if it had it would by this means have a share in Good; when we say it "is" we are just using the same word for two different things, and the true way of speaking is to say it "is not." . . .

The forms in matter are not the same as they would be if they were by themselves; they are formative forces immanent in matter, corrupted in matter and infected with its [formless] nature. . . . Matter masters what is imaged in it and corrupts and destroys it. . . . Matter spreads itself out under Soul and is illuminated [by Soul] . . . [but] matter darkens the illumination, the light from that source, by mixture with itself, and weakens it by itself offering it the opportunity of generation and the reason for coming to matter. . . . This is the fall of the soul, to come in this way to matter and to become weak, because all its powers do not come into action: matter hinders them from coming by occupying the place which soul holds and producing a kind of cramped condition, and making evil what it has got hold of by a sort of theft— until the soul manages to escape back to its higher state. So matter is the cause of the soul's weakness and vice: it is then itself evil before soul and is primary evil. . . .

[But there is also this to be said about evil:] Those . . . that censure the constitution of the Cosmos do not understand what they are doing or where their audacity leads them. They do not understand that there is a successive order [of levels or grades of being]; . . . that nothing is to be blamed for being inferior to the First; that we can but accept, meekly, the constitution of the total. . . . Since the higher exists, there must be the lower as well. The Universe is a thing of variety, and how could there be an inferior without a superior or a superior without an inferior? . . . Those that would like evil driven out from the All would drive out Providence itself. . . . The Intellect is the sovereign, making all. . . . It produces even what we know as evil: it cannot desire all to be good: an artist would not make an animal all eyes; and in the same way, the Intellect would not make all divine; it makes gods, [then] spirits . . . then men, then the animals; all is graded succession, and this in no spirit of grudging but in the expression of a Reason teeming with intellectual variety. We are like people ignorant of painting who complain that the colors are not beautiful everywhere in the picture; but the Artist has laid on the appropriate tint to every spot. Or we are censuring a drama because the persons are not all heroes but include a servant and a rustic and some scurrilous clown; yet take away the low characters and the power of the drama is gone; these are part and parcel of it.[9]

Ascent of the Soul

Soul necessarily descends from Intellect so as to shape a material universe, and human souls necessarily descend from Soul so as to administer particular bodies. The descent of human souls is a "fall," because their commerce with matter inevitably constricts their powers and narrows their vision—so much so that they lose sight of the higher part of themselves that remains in the realm of Intellect. They are mastered and troubled by bodily concerns; they become partial and self-centered; they live no longer in cognizance of the Good. Inevitable as it is that human souls should fall, Plotinus insists that they are still blameworthy for the audacity and zeal with which they throw themselves into bodily life and for the faults they commit therein—faults that can require punishment, as Pythagoras believed, by a whole series of incarnations. Although imperfection of every kind must exist in order that the universe may contain everything possible, fallen human souls are, in Plotinus' eyes, still accountable for their own imperfection and responsible for ridding themselves of it. Their paramount aim should be to restore themselves to the blessed condition they used to enjoy—when they joined with the universal Soul that, as Plotinus says, "dances round Intellect and looks to it, and in contemplating its interior sees God through it."

Fallen souls yearn, however unconsciously, for a vision of God. Plotinus, drawing upon Plato's *Symposium* and *Phaedrus,* says that this is shown by the way a fallen soul is naturally repelled by ugliness and attracted by beauty. All beauty in the world comes from the participation of things in the forms of Intellect, and Intellect flows from God, so that the soul's attraction to beauty is indirectly an attraction to God. Shapes, colors, and sounds have beauty to the extent that forms confer unity upon them. A fallen soul responds to beautiful things as to old friends recalling it to better days: it is reminded at least dimly of the perfect beauty of the forms and of the fuller manifestation of this beauty in achievements of the spirit—in virtuous conduct, in just institutions, in knowledge. In this

[9]Chrysippus, the Stoic, held a similar view. See p. 205.

way the soul is prompted to reflect that bodily preoccupations are to be disdained as unworthy of it. The soul should follow such promptings by "purifying" itself of (or "converting" itself from) corruptions of the flesh and rising to the practice of moral virtue, whereby with perseverance it can itself become beautiful and godlike—at one with its own higher part and with other souls in the divine unity of Soul. Thus firmly planted on the upward path to "the beloved Fatherland," the soul is prepared for the second stage of its ascent: this calls for philosophical dialectic in order that the realm of forms in Intellect may be grasped and contemplated in its perfect beauty as the source of all beauty. The soul proceeds from reasoning to intuition and participates as an intelligence in the unity of intelligences that is Intellect: here "all is transparent, nothing dark, nothing resistant; every being is lucid to every other . . . light runs through light. And each of them contains all within itself, and at the same time sees all in every other, so that everywhere there is all, and all is all and each all, and infinite the glory." At this point the soul, self-gathered in its purity, "carried out by the very surge of the wave of Intellect," is able at last to achieve a vision of the One—a vision in which the soul recognizes its "identity with the Divine."

> Thus we have all the vision that may be of Him and of ourselves; but it is of a self wrought to splendor, brimmed with the Intellectual light, become that very light, pure, buoyant, unburdened, raised to Godhood or, better, knowing its Godhood, all aflame then—but crushed out once more if it should take up the discarded burden. . . .
> The vision baffles telling; we cannot detach the Supreme to state it; if we have seen something thus detached we have failed of the Supreme which is to be known only as one with ourselves. . . .
> Fallen back again, we waken the virtue within us until we know ourselves all order once more; once more we are lightened of the burden and move by virtue towards Intellect and through the Wisdom in That to the Supreme. This is the life of gods and of the godlike and blessed among men, liberation from the alien that besets us here, a life taking no pleasure in the things of earth, the passing of solitary to solitary.

Those who live in purity and wisdom may expect to enjoy this vision perpetually, once death has freed their souls from the burden of their bodies. Meanwhile, if Plotinus' own experience is any indication, the vision can be attained comparatively seldom. Porphyry says that Plotinus, during the six years of their acquaintance, was "united to God" on just four occasions. But the sense of fulfillment afforded by the vision, however rare its occurrence, is ample recompense for the strenuous moral and intellectual discipline required for its achievement. Plotinus' last words, uttered to his physician as he lay dying (of a form of leprosy) at sixty-six, were: "Try to bring back the god in you to the divine in the All."

Schools of Neoplatonism _____

Followers of Plotinus proclaimed his doctrines, with various modifications, for more than three and a half centuries after his death. Porphyry (about 232–305), who appears to have taken over the direction of Plotinus' school in Rome, wrote many treatises with a view to explaining Plotinus' ideas in the clearest possible terms and to developing their full significance for ethics and religion. Porphyry also composed a number of commentaries on works of Plato and Aristotle, including an introduction (*Isagoge*) to Aristotle's *Categories* that exercised a powerful influence upon subsequent thinkers. Christianity seemed to Porphyry completely unacceptable, and he attacked it in no fewer than fifteen books—all copies of which were burnt in 448 by order of the Christian emperors Valentinian III and Theodosius II. Porphyry's pupil Iamblichus introduced Neoplatonism into Syria; and Iamblichus' pupil Aedesius carried it to Pergamum in Asia Minor. The emperor Julian (who reigned from 361 to 363) was tutored in his youth by associates of Aedesius, was converted from Christianity to paganism, and attempted while emperor to revive polytheism in Neoplatonic dress—for which he became known among Christians as "Julian the Apostate." He was encouraged and assisted in his apostasy by Sallustius, who maintained that the traditional Greek and Roman accounts of the gods should be allegorically interpreted as referring not really to a number of independent deities but to "essences" or "powers" of the One.

Neoplatonism appeared in Plato's Academy under the administration of Plutarch of Athens[10] (about 350–433), and it was a successor of Plutarch named Proclus (about 410–485) who produced the fullest and most systematic elaboration of Neoplatonic principles. Although Proclus was an opponent of Christianity, his presentation of Neoplatonism was given a kind of Christian interpretation around 500 by an individual (whose real identity is unknown) who managed to pass off his or her own writings as those of Dionysius the Areopagite—an Athenian who, according to Acts 17:34, was converted to Christianity by St. Paul sometime around 50 A.D. The treatises of "Pseudo-Dionysius," as this writer is now called, were much esteemed by Christian theologians during the Middle Ages. Another philosopher of great influence during the Middle Ages was Boethius (480–524)—a Roman, a Christian, and a Neoplatonist who studied at Athens and whose Latin edition of Porphyry's *Isagoge* became the standard medieval textbook on logic. But the Neoplatonists of the Academy were in general hostile to Christianity—so hostile that the emperor Justinian, himself a Christian, ordered the institution closed in 529.

A school of Neoplatonism was founded at Alexandria by Hierocles, a

---

[10] Not the same as Plutarch (of Chaeronea) the biographer and moralist, who lived from about 46 to 120 A.D.

pupil of Plutarch of Athens. The Alexandrian Neoplatonists came to be far more accommodating to Christianity than their Athenian counterparts; we even hear of a graduate of the school—Synesius of Cyrene—who (in 411) became a Christian bishop. Church authorities in Alexandria, however, were not always tolerant of Neoplatonists. Synesius' own teacher, a woman named Hypatia, was murdered in 415 by a fanatical mob of Christians who had taken their cue from the repressive policies of Cyril, the local bishop. Nevertheless, there continued to be Neoplatonists in Alexandria down to 642—the year in which the city was seized by Muslim Arabs.

PART IV

The Middle Ages

What are called the "Middle Ages"[1] of Western European history began with the disintegration of the Western Roman Empire in the fourth and fifth centuries after Christ and ended with the Renaissance and Reformation in the fifteenth and sixteenth centuries. During this period of roughly a thousand years, the Church of Rome came to be the dominant cultural force in Western Europe, insomuch that philosophy hardly existed where the Church did not support it as an adjunct of theology. Philosophy's dependence upon the Church and its service to theology were generally understood to have been mandated in unambiguous terms by the Bible itself. Reference was often made to Proverbs 9:3, where Wisdom, in the person of a noble hostess, is described as sending forth the maids of her household to summon all who are unwise to a great feast. Can Wisdom in this passage be other than theology—the science of sacred doctrine as revealed by God? And can Wisdom's maids be other than the several fields of philosophy—the sciences that proceed from natural human reason and that lead by rights to God? This was the interpretation favored by many, including St. Thomas Aquinas, who adduced it in the course of explaining that theology "can draw upon the philosophical sciences, not as though it stood in need of them, but only in order to make its teaching clearer. For it [theology] accepts its principles, not from the other sciences, but immediately from God, by revelation. Therefore it does not draw upon the other sciences as upon its superiors, but uses them as its inferiors and handmaidens. . . ."

As might be expected, however, not all Christian authorities were of the opinion that the Church had very much to gain from philosophy—even as theology's handmaiden. Dispute on the matter began very early, well before the Middle Ages; and because the issues involved are both interesting and fundamental, we shall begin with them from the beginning.

[1] *Medium aevum* in Latin, whence the adjective "medieval."

CHAPTER 13

St. Paul and the Early Christian Fathers

In the New Testament there is only one explicit reference to Western philosophers. This is found in Acts 17:18, where we are told that some Stoics and Epicureans heard St. Paul preaching in the marketplace at Athens and were puzzled by what he said concerning Jesus and the Resurrection. Desiring a fuller explanation, the philosophers took Paul to the Areopagus, where he obliged them by delivering a brief sermon to the effect that there is one God, in Whom we live and move and have our being, Who does not dwell in shrines and has no need of sacrifices, and Who has appointed a day in which He will judge the world in righteousness by a Man whom he has ordained and raised from the dead. Ignorance of these matters, Paul said, is no longer permissible. The Athenians must forsake their idolatrous worship of gods and goddesses. An altar in Athens dedicated "to an unknown god"—or as we might say, "to whom it may concern"—was in particular quite obsolete. The Athenians now knew—for Paul had told them—to Whom everything is of concern, and they should forthwith act accordingly, since God "now commandeth all men everywhere to repent." Such was Paul's sermon. It did not, however, entirely satisfy the Stoics and the Epicureans. They are said to have had especial difficulty with Paul's notion that anyone could literally be resurrected, body and soul, from the dead. Some of them simply mocked at this, while others wished to hear Paul speak further on the subject. Presumably it was the Epicureans who mocked and the Stoics who wished to hear more, because the latter, unlike the former, would have believed that at least one's soul is not extinguished by death; but at all events it does not appear that Paul said any more. He "departed from among them" and soon left Athens for Corinth.

The point of this episode, some have said, is that human wisdom at its best is incapable of apprehending truths of the greatest importance. As is illustrated by the incomprehension of the philosophers of Athens itself, Jesus' death and resurrection—as redeeming humankind from its sinful condition and giving hope of everlasting life—cannot be understood or appreciated from a strictly philosophical point of view. In general the truths pertaining to our deepest well-being and our ultimate salvation must be supernaturally revealed to us by God, for the natural exercise of our powers of reason can never bring us to them. Acceptance by faith of Divine revelation, not further philosophical inquiry, is the path for us to follow. It may not seem that this is necessarily the moral to be drawn from Paul's experience in Athens, since not *all* the philosophers he met there responded to his message with derision. But several remarks in Paul's letters, as some have believed, make it very clear that he himself had formed the lowest possible estimate of the "wisdom" of philosophers. In his First Letter to the Corinthians, for example, there is this famous passage: "Where is the wise? . . . Hath not God made foolish the wisdom of this world? For after that in the wisdom of God the world by wisdom knew not God, it pleased God by the foolishness of preaching [for instance, Paul's preaching] to save them that believe. For the Jews require a sign, and the Greeks seek after wisdom: but we preach Christ crucified, unto the Jews a stumbling block, and unto the Greeks foolishness; but unto them which are called, both Jews and Greeks, Christ the power of God, and the wisdom of God." And if this is not a plain enough indication of Paul's attitude toward philosophy, we have what certainly looks like an express warning against it in his Letter to the Colossians: "Beware lest any man spoil you through philosophy and vain deceit, after the tradition of men, after the rudiments of the world, and not after Christ."

Actually, however, these passages may not fully represent Paul's view of philosophy. There is evidence that he did not really intend to censure philosophy in general as nothing but dangerous folly. In his Letter to the Romans he seems to say that at least some truths of vital significance may be discovered by the ordinary exercise of our rational faculties. Pagans, he says, are "without excuse" in their idolatrous worship of statues of men and animals because the existence of God, and His invisible attributes of eternal power and deity, have all along been plainly discernible through His creation—through "things that are made" and that are commonly seen and known. Here Paul appears to maintain that God's existence and certain aspects of His nature may, and indeed should, be inferred from observable features of the world—as the Stoics, for example, characteristically sought to do.[1] Paul also states in his Letter to the Romans that the requirements of moral law may be known without special Divine assistance of the kind given to Moses on Mount Sinai. "For when the Gentiles, which have not the law [that is, the Law of Moses], do by nature the things contained in the law, these, having not the law, are a law unto themselves: which show the work of the law written in their hearts, their conscience also bearing witness, and their thoughts the meanwhile accusing or else excusing one another. . . ." If there are morally sensitive and responsible Gentiles, as this clearly says, then presumably in philosophical reflection upon their moral ideas and experience—following the example of Socrates—they can arrive at a reasoned understanding of the principles of morality. The Prologue to the Gospel accord-

---

[1] See Epictetus' argument for God's existence on p. 217.

ing to John says that God's Word, by Whom all things were made, is "the true Light, which lighteth every man that cometh into the world"; and this on the face of it means that everybody, or virtually everybody, is furnished as a matter of course with the ability to attain at least some knowledge of God's existence and God's commandments. Extraordinary revelations directly from God are not necessary for us to know everything that most concerns us. Philosophy from a Christian point of view thus has a leg to stand on, as Paul seems to say it does in his Letter to the Romans.

Whatever may have been Paul's settled appraisal of the worth of philosophy, the fact is that subsequent Christian spokesmen on each side of the question believed they found passages in his letters that supported their own appraisal. Those who believed that Divine revelation had *superseded* all other means of knowledge could cite: "God made foolish the wisdom of this world." Those who believed that Divine revelation might still be at least *supplemented* by philosophical reasoning could cite: "The invisible things of Him from the creation of the world are clearly seen, being understood by the things that are made." Both points of view are found in the writings of those early Christian thinkers who are called "Fathers of the Church."[2] The positions of some representative Fathers will now be briefly explained.

Justin Martyr

Christians were persecuted at intervals by Roman officials for about two and a half centuries—from the year 64 in the reign of Nero until 313, when Constantine the Great, the first Christian emperor, ordered toleration of all religions in his Edict of Milan. Even so conscientious and high-minded an emperor as Marcus Aurelius lent his authority to severe repressions. The Roman government tended to view any association among its subjects, however harmless that association might appear, as a likely source of seditious activity. How distrustful the government was in this respect may be gauged from the unwillingness of the emperor Trajan to authorize even the incorporation of a company of firemen for a town in Bithynia. Imagine, then, the dismay with which the government saw Christian churches springing up in cities and towns throughout the Empire and refusing on principle to apply for legal status by participating in the customary religious observances associated with the cult of the emperor. The imperial authorities understood that Christians actually pledged allegiance to a rival of the emperor: after all, they revered Christ as *Kurios* or "lord of the whole earth," whereas everyone knew that the

---

[2]The writings of the Fathers are called the Patristic Writings. "Patristic" comes from *pater,* the Latin for "father."

emperor alone was to be so regarded. Nor were official apprehensions at all dispelled by the intelligence that many Christians regarded the emperor as none other than Anti-Christ—the embodiment of depravity. So it was that membership in the Church was declared treasonous and dealt with as a capital offense.

Defenders of the Church endeavored both to persuade the Roman government that Christianity had a right to exist and to persuade the educated Roman public that Christianity was reasonable. The most famous of these defenders, or "Apologists" as they are called, is Flavius Justinus (about 100–164), who came to be known as Justin Martyr. Justin was born of pagan Greek parents in Neapolis (now Nablus, on the West Bank of the Jordan), studied philosophy in Ephesus, was converted to Christianity sometime in his late thirties, and went to Rome in order to open a school of Christian philosophy. He and some of his associates were martyred during the reign of Marcus Aurelius. His surviving works are the *Apology* for Christianity, which he addressed to the emperor Antoninus Pius (who seems to have been lenient in his treatment of Christians[3]), and the *Dialogue with Typho,* in which he represents himself in discussion with a Jewish thinker in Ephesus.

In his *Dialogue,* Justin advances the thesis that philosophy, when honestly pursued as a search for truth, is "the greatest possession, and most honorable before God, to whom it leads us and alone commends us." But many of those who have considered themselves philosophers have not, Justin says, really cared about truth: they have only identified themselves with one or another philosophical school in admiration of its founder or in fascination with the novelty of its doctrines. Justin himself sampled in his youth the wares of various philosophical schools, until at length he found what seemed to him the genuine article. Initially, he says, he attached himself to a proponent of Stoicism, but this man disappointed him by having too little to say on so important a subject as the nature of God. In hopes of learning more, he turned to an Aristotelian who certainly fancied himself as having more to offer but who was in fact chiefly interested in the fee that Justin was to pay him. Reflecting that anyone so preoccupied with money could hardly be a philosopher, Justin dropped the Aristotelian in favor of a noted Pythagorean. As was characteristic of his school, this Pythagorean had the virtue of deploring unspiritual concerns, but he also insisted that a thorough grounding in music, astronomy, and geometry was absolutely essential to a philosophical education. Justin was not strong in these subjects and hesitated to devote valuable time to getting them up. He felt that his search for truth had already been sufficiently protracted. But just when his sense of frustration was becoming oppressively acute, a happy idea suggested itself. "In my helpless condition," he says, "it occurred to me to have a meeting with the

---

[3] There is a remarkable description of the reign of Antoninus Pius in Walter Pater's *Marius the Epicurean,* Chapter XXII, "The Minor Peace of the Church."

Platonists, for their fame was great. I thereupon spent as much of my time as possible with one who had lately settled in our city—a sagacious man, holding a high position among the Platonists—and I progressed and made the greatest improvements daily. And the perception of immaterial things quite overpowered me, and the contemplation of ideas [or forms] furnished my mind with wings, so that in a little while I supposed that I had become wise; and such was my stupidity, I expected forthwith to look upon God, for this is the end of Plato's philosophy."

Plato's philosophy, Justin subsequently found, was neither wholly true nor the whole truth. Plato, in arguing that human souls are inherently and naturally immortal, had implied that immortality is not in God's gift. Plato seemed also to believe that one and the same soul may successively inhabit a number of different bodies. Justin came to think, after discussion with a Christian, that Plato had been in error on both of these points; and he further concluded that Plato's philosophy was incomplete in respects in which Christianity was not—respects having especially to do with God's Word as incarnated in Christ. The more he learned of Christianity, the more it struck him as "the true philosophy." Nevertheless, Justin continued to believe that there was much truth in Plato. Is not the Good in Plato's *Republic* (Justin asks) the same as God in the Scriptures? Did not Plato teach, as the Scriptures teach, that our souls have a special kinship to God, that we are responsible for our actions, and that we may expect a day of reckoning in a world to come? No doubt Plato, in spite of his errors, came closer to the truth that we know, for probably (Justin supposes) he was unwilling to present all his discoveries to people as hopelessly polytheistic as were most of the Greeks of his time. Socrates had met his death attempting "by the critical application of sound reasoning" to show his fellow Athenians (as Justin thinks) that the gods they worshipped were actually "wicked and unholy demons." As atheism and impiety were the charges leveled against Socrates, so they were the charges that the Roman government leveled against Christians; and yet Christians, like Socrates, have only tried to proclaim "the most true God, the Father of righteousness and moderation and the other virtues, the God who is without a trace of evil."

How was it possible that Socrates and Plato knew as much of the truth as they did? How did it happen that even Heraclitus and the Stoics occasionally caught glimpses of the truth? Justin believes, as Philo did before him, that part of the explanation is that Socrates, Plato, and the others were acquainted with the Pentateuch and so had the benefit of the wisdom of Moses. Beyond this, however, Justin follows St. Paul (at least one side of St. Paul) in believing that everyone is created with the capacity to discover by reasoning something of God's nature and God's commandments. Socrates and Plato, no less than Moses, had this capacity—and of course an uncommon resolve to exercise it. As we are told in the Gospel according to John, the light vouchsafed to all humankind flows from the Logos, who is both the Word by whom all things were created and (as the Stoics also maintained) the Divine Reason. Before the coming of Christ, Justin says, both Greeks and non-Greeks were able to discover bits and pieces of the truth because they possessed "seeds" of the Divine Reason (the "Spermatic Logos"); and some of these persons, certainly Socrates and Plato, may even be said to have been Christians—"Christians before Christ," one might call them. At Christ's coming, the whole Logos took shape and was made man, and it is in Christ's teaching that both Greek philosophy and Old Testament prophecy reach their completion. The seeds of truth that were scattered among the Hebrew prophets and the Greek schools are unified and fully developed in the Gospel of Jesus. As Justin says:

> I prayed and strove with all my might that I might prove a Christian: not because Plato's teachings are contrary to Christ's, but because they are not in all respects identical with them: as is the case with the doctrines of the others, the Stoics, the poets, and the prose authors. For each, through his share in the divine generative Logos, spoke well, seeing what was akin to it; while those who contradict them on the more important matters clearly have not obtained the hidden wisdom and the irrefutable knowledge. Thus, whatever has been spoken aright by any men belongs to us Christians; for we worship and love, next to God, the Logos which is from the unbegotten and ineffable God; since it was on our behalf that he has been made man, that, becoming partaker of our sufferings, he may also bring us a healing. For all those writers were able, through the seed of the Logos implanted in them, to see reality darkly.

Educated Romans may therefore understand that in Christianity the really valuable elements of their philosophical heritage are not only preserved but perfected. Contrary to what some critics have alleged, Christianity does not require blind faith in paradoxical teachings of which no one has ever heard; it is the fulfillment of a long and familiar tradition of reasoned inquiry into the nature of reality. There is no sharp distinction between theology and philosophy, between truths of faith revealed by God and truths of reason discovered by philosophers. All truths are truths of reason, the Divine Reason, and all truths of reason are revealed—revealed by the Divine Reason operating on a limited scale through philosophers but fully present in Jesus. As for the Roman government, Justin wishes to assure it that the refusal of Christians to worship the "genius" of the emperor implies no disrespect of the emperor's legitimate authority. Christians assiduously follow the injunction of Jesus to "render unto Caesar the things which are Caesar's, and unto God the things that are God's"—that is to say, Christians render worship unto God alone, but in all other things they obey the emperor, while also praying that his power will be guided by wisdom.

The feast of St. Justin—for his martyrdom under Aurelius led to his canonization—is celebrated by the Church every June 1st.

Tertullian

In the second century after Christ, a bizarre religious movement called "Gnosticism" came into vogue. This consisted of a dozen or more rival sects that represented themselves as having been entrusted with special knowledge (*gnosis,* in Greek) of the means whereby a privileged few could attain salvation. The basic idea was that in the bodies of *some* persons a soul is imprisoned that may yet escape to bliss in its heavenly home if only it acquires *gnosis* of the route. Especially useful, so it was claimed, are certain magical formulas by which a soul can neutralize the demonic powers who guard the gates of the planetary spheres that revolve between the earth and Paradise. The details of all this, which varied from one Gnostic sect to another, were pieced together from such miscellaneous sources as Babylonian astrology, Persian religion, Greek mystery cults, the Book of Genesis, Plato's dialogues, and Stoicism. Christ figured in Gnostic systems as the Redeemer who came down from heaven in order to divulge the saving *gnosis* and to strengthen the elect for their arduous ascent to the Father. The Redeemer was not believed to have formed one person with the man Jesus. Indeed, some Gnostics said that the human nature of Jesus was merely an illusive appearance which the Redeemer put on; others said that the Redeemer and Jesus were two different persons, divine and mortal respectively, and that the Redeemer entered into Jesus at the latter's baptism and withdrew at His crucifixion. Gnostics expressly rejected the notion that a Divine Being could be so closely identified with mortal flesh as to experience suffering. In their opinion, the Passion of Jesus was either another illusion created by the Redeemer or else the Redeemer, having taken leave of Jesus, did not experience it. Not only flesh but the material world in general seemed to Gnostics a thing of darkness and evil, hardly a suitable residence for the Redeemer, who of course belongs to the spiritual realm of light and goodness. According to one Gnostic teacher, the material world was created by "the God of the Jews"—a supposedly inferior, self-aggrandizing deity from whose clutches good human souls can escape thanks to the *gnosis* imparted by the "First-begotten Mind" of the "Unborn and Unnamed Father" who is truly the supreme deity.[4]

To the Fathers of the Church, the *gnosis* of Gnosticism was a hotchpotch of heresies calling for immediate refutation. If Christ is the fulfiller and fulfillment of God's will disclosed in the Old Testament, as the Gospel according to Matthew in particular maintains, then it cannot be right to belittle the God of the Jews. If the material world was created by God

---

[4] A collection of early religious texts, some of them distinctly Gnostic, was unearthed in 1945 near the Egyptian town of Nag Hammadi. Those wishing to see for themselves how Gnosticism's main themes were phrased by its disciples will find them expressed with especial vividness in the text entitled *The Second Treatise of the Great Seth.* This is included in *The Nag Hammadi Library,* translated into English (from the original Coptic) under the direction of James M. Robinson (New York: Harper & Row, 1977).

through the mediation of the Word, and if "the Word was made flesh and dwelt among us," as we are told in the Gospel according to John, then it cannot be right to disparage the material world or to deny that the Word formed one person with the man Jesus. If after the Crucifixion Jesus was resurrected and was seen in the flesh by His disciples, then the everlasting life which He promised to those who believe in Him must involve not just a disembodied immortality of the soul but a complete resurrection like His. Such in part were the considerations adduced by the Fathers, including Justin Martyr in a treatise that has not survived.

Some Fathers believed that the prime instigator of heresies, Gnostic and otherwise, was pagan philosophy. Unlike Justin, these Fathers saw little in Greek or Roman philosophy that looked as if it were an anticipation of the Gospel of Jesus. Plato, for instance, would certainly *not* have us think that the material world is wholly the creation of a Deity of infinite wisdom: in his *Laws,* at any rate, he finds the material world so beset with evils that he is prepared to ascribe them to at least one cosmic Soul who "companies with folly." And Plato would scarcely encourage us to see any merit in the notions of divine incarnation and bodily resurrection: in his *Phaedo* he states very plainly that bodies are constant sources of impurity and infection for souls and that "heaven will hardly permit" souls to attain wisdom until in death they are "released from the body's fetters." In brief, these Fathers said, there is much in Plato, and much in the rest of pagan philosophy, that is calculated either to encourage complete rejection of the Gospel or else to instill wrongheaded preconceptions of what the Gospel must mean. It is no wonder, then, that St. Paul told us to "beware lest any man spoil you through philosophy."

Outstanding among the Fathers who deprecated pagan philosophy as a source of heresies was Quintus Septimius Florens Tertullianus—Tertullian, for short. Born around 160 of pagan parents in the North African city of Carthage, Tertullian was educated for the law and became a successful trial attorney in Rome. He was converted to Christianity in 193 after witnessing the courage of Christians facing martyrdom. Tertullian was the first Christian theologian to write in Latin instead of Greek, and he composed numerous treatises explaining points of doctrine and attacking Gnostics and other heretics. The personality of Tertullian, as indicated by the singular style of his writings, is described by the noted Church historian Henry Chadwick: "Brilliant, exasperating, sarcastic, and intolerant, yet intensely vigorous and incisive in argument, delighting in logical tricks and with an advocate's love of clever sophistry if it will make the adversary look foolish, but a powerful writer of splendid, torrential prose." The torrent of Tertullian's prose discharged part of itself in a treatise addressed, and entitled, *To His Wife.* Here, curiously, he enlarges upon the theme of "how greatly second marriages detract from faith, and what a hindrance they are to sanctity." As nothing is known of either Tertullian or his wife after about 220, when his literary work seems to have ended, we do not know whether, if his wife outlived him, she remarried or not.

Tertullian's animadversions upon pagan philosophy are expressed in these celebrated words from his *Prescription Against Heretics:*

> Philosophy it is which is the material of the world's wisdom, the rash interpreter of the nature and the dispensation of God. Indeed heresies are themselves instigated by philosophy. From this source come the "aeons" [inferior heavenly powers], and I know not what infinite "forms," and the "trinity of man" in the [Gnostic] system of Valentinus, who was of Plato's school. From the same source came [the semi-Gnostic] Marcion's "better" god, with all his "tranquillity"; he came of the Stoics. Then, again, the opinion that the soul dies is held by the Epicureans; while the denial of the restoration of the body is taken from the aggregate school of all the philosophers; also, when matter is made equal to God, then you have the teaching of Zeno [the Stoic]; and when any doctrine is alleged touching a god of fire, then Heraclitus comes in. The same subject matter is discussed over and over again by the heretics and the philosophers; the same arguments are involved. Whence comes evil? Why is it permitted? What is the origin of man? and in what way does he come? Besides the question which Valentinus has very lately proposed—Whence comes God?—which he settles with the answer: From *enthymesis* [conception] and *ectroma* [abortion]. Unhappy Aristotle! who invented for these men dialectics, the art of building up and pulling down; an art so evasive in its propositions, so farfetched in its conjectures, so harsh in its arguments, so productive of contentions—embarrassing even to itself, retracting everything, and really treating of nothing! . . . The apostle [Paul] . . . expressly names *philosophy* as that which he would have us be on our guard against. . . . He had been at Athens, and had in his interviews (with the philosophers) become acquainted with human wisdom which pretends to know the truth, whilst it only corrupts it, and is itself divided into its own manifold heresies by the variety of its mutually repugnant sects. What indeed has Athens to do with Jerusalem? What concord is there between the Academy and the Church? what between heretics and Christians? Our instruction comes from "the porch of Solomon," who had himself taught that "the Lord should be sought in simplicity of heart." Away with all attempts to produce a mottled Christianity of Stoic, Platonic, and dialectic composition! We want no curious disputation after possessing Christ Jesus, no investigation after enjoying the gospel! With our faith, we desire no further belief. For this is our palmary faith, that there is nothing which we ought to believe besides.

Tertullian's position, then, is that the Gospel revealed by God in Christ wholly supersedes the "wisdom" of philosophers, which in any case has been discredited by the rancorous factions into which philosophers have split. In a way that reminds one of Carneades, Tertullian finds that the welter of arguments produced in philosophy on all sides of every question can lead only to the conclusion that philosophy leads nowhere. Faith alone can provide solid, soul-saving convictions—faith in the Gospel as interpreted by the Church according to the tradition bequeathed to it by the Apostles. Tertullian is aware that some persons have taken Christ's words "Seek and ye shall find" to mean that the Lord Himself supports philosophical research. But Tertullian is sure that this is not what Christ had in mind. That for which one ought to "seek," if one is not already aware of it, cannot be other than the Gospel of Christ; and when one has found this, one ought simply to believe it—and not go on "seeking" as philosophers go on arguing. "There is some one, and therefore definite, thing taught by Christ," Tertullian says, and "there can be no indefinite seeking for that which he has taught as one only definite thing." Having found and believed Christ's teachings, one has but to persevere in one's belief by believing also that "nothing else is to be believed, and therefore nothing else is to be sought." Further seeking, on the chance that one might find something of value in the teachings of others, is an unmistakable indication that one either has never really believed Christ's teachings or else has ceased to believe them. Is one to seek instruction from everybody who emerges professing to have novel truths to offer? At that rate one would perpetually be seeking and never finding, never believing. Such restless curiosity signifies that one is in conflict with oneself: in seeking one presumably wants to find, but in refusing really to believe anything at which one arrives, one evidently also does *not* want to find. "Away with the man who is ever seeking because he never finds," Tertullian says; "for he seeks there [in the mists of his own irresolution] where nothing can be found."[5]

Socrates, who was always seeking and never finding, who said at his trial that he was wiser than others only in knowing that he knew nothing, certainly did not qualify as a "Christian before Christ" in Tertullian's eyes. The "divine voice" that guided Socrates throughout his life[6] was obviously, Tertullian says, a pernicious demon. The Oracle at Delphi, in pronouncing Socrates the wisest of men, can only have been the voice of a fellow demon "which, you may be sure, neatly managed the business for his friend." Tertullian particularly deplores Socrates' conduct in prison on the day of his execution, when (according to Plato's *Phaedo*) he examined with his associates the case for immortality of the soul. A more inopportune time for philosophical discourse, Tertullian says, would be difficult to imagine: "For what could the soul of Socrates then contemplate with serenity?" Socrates should have paused to consider that anyone in his position would probably be driven by indignation or resentment to the purely vindictive conclusion that the tables will ultimately be turned on his oppressors. Yet Socrates would not pause; he allowed himself to proceed with the discussion and naturally finished by saying that he "ventured to believe" both in everlasting punishment for the souls

---

[5] St. Paul, in his Second Letter to Timothy (3:7), speaks of the folly of persons who are "ever learning, and never able to come to the knowledge of the truth."

[6] See p. 62.

of those who have committed "murders foul and violent" and in everlasting bliss for the souls of those who have "duly purified themselves with philosophy." But this simply is not, Tertullian says, how "the firm conviction of ascertained truth" is to be obtained on any subject. Of course, Socrates did not have the advantage of God's revelation in Christ—the one fully reliable source of truth—but (Tertullian implies) he should at all events have been wise enough to refrain in his last hours from skirmishing with his friends over immortality. So at least he would have avoided embracing falsehood, for the truth (Tertullian says) is that God is prepared to pardon even the vilest of crimes[7] and is far from having especial esteem for philosophers.

Tertullian does not wish to maintain that philosophers have never uttered any true statements at all. Occasionally, he admits, they have done so, but more or less as a matter of luck, and always with a large admixture of error. Seldom, he finds, have philosophers arrived at the right conclusions except on the basis of some very wrong reasons, and seldom have they started with entirely the right reasons without arriving at some very wrong conclusions. "The truth has at this rate," he says, "been wellnigh excluded by philosophers through the poisons with which they have infected it." Pagan philosophy must be reviewed with an eye to abstracting from it the modicum of arguments congenial to Christian conclusions, and the modicum of conclusions congenial to Christian arguments. Everything else—pagan arguments and pagan conclusions—must be discarded. The ultimate test of acceptability is "God's inspired standard" as disclosed in the Gospel, although in simple cases "mere human testimony" will suffice, "because plain evidence of this sort we must sometimes borrow from opponents when our opponents have nothing to gain from it." In other words, there are some relatively straightforward things in pagan philosophy that are not peculiarly pagan—certain patterns of argument, for example, that can be seen to be valid without special Divine assistance and that can actually be turned to good account in defending the Faith against pagan assaults. Elements of pagan philosophy itself may thus, Tertullian says, be employed to dispel the "noxious vapors" given out by all the rest of pagan philosophy.

Chances are that Tertullian borrows from an "opponent" in the statements for which he is most famous. These occur in his treatise *On Christ's Human Nature,* where during an attack upon the Gnostic denial of the humanity of Christ, he suddenly says: "The Son of God died; it must needs be believed because it is absurd. He was buried and rose again; it is certain because it is impossible."[8] It has often been supposed that Tertullian really is asserting that we are to believe in Christ's death and resurrec-

---

[7] In his treatise *On Repentance,* Tertullian says: "For all sins, whether committed by the flesh or by the spirit, whether by deed or will, He who has appointed a penalty by means of judgment has also promised pardon by means of penitence. . . ."

[8] Tertullian does not say (what he is commonly said to say): "I believe because it is absurd."

tion precisely because (as the *eternal* Son of God) His death and resurrection are absurd and impossible. But although Tertullian does of course maintain that doctrines essential to our salvation, such as these, cannot be made out by human reason, he probably does not mean that just this could be a reason for accepting them. In fact his famous statements seem to have been inspired by one of the sample "commonplaces of oratory" catalogued in Aristotle's *Rhetoric*. Speaking of a line of argument that "refers to things which are supposed to happen and yet seem incredible," Aristotle says: "We may argue that people could not have believed them, if they had not been true or nearly true: even that they are the more likely to be true because they are incredible. For the things which men believe are either facts or probabilities: if, therefore, a thing that *is* believed is improbable and even incredible, it must be true, since it is certainly not believed because it is at all probable or credible." Tertullian, in keeping with this, may well intend to suggest an argument to the effect that the Gospel narratives of Christ's resurrection must be true, because if Christ had not indeed risen from the dead, *so incredible a thing would hardly have been believed* by the many disciples who reported that they saw Him and who by all accounts expected nothing of the kind. As Aristotle points out, however, an argument of this type is "rhetorical" in the sense that it shows its conclusion to be at most only probable and is easily rebutted by an analogous argument for an opposite conclusion. Thus a Gnostic could argue (as in fact some Gnostics did) that Jesus was not really crucified, since—incredible as it is—witnesses known to Gnostics observed Him to switch places and exchange appearances with that Simon of Cyrene who is said in the Gospels to have carried the Cross. But Tertullian, recognizing the slippery character of this type of argument, may have been content to indicate that Christians can derive *as much* benefit from it as their opponents can, so that "our opponents have nothing to *gain* from it."

While Tertullian may find that some points of philosophy are not without their uses, his normal impulse is to think of philosophers in general as, at best, "huckstering wiseacres and talkers," and at worst, "patriarchs of heretics." The thought of heresy emanating from philosophy seems almost to haunt him. In the eyes of the Church, however, Tertullian himself drifted into heresy—heresy emanating not from philosophy but from a Phrygian revivalist by the name of Montanus. This man and his two assistants, Priscilla and Maximilla, announced that they were possessed of the Holy Spirit, and they proceeded to prophesy accordingly. The Lord, they declared, would shortly appear in Phrygia to reign for a thousand years; meanwhile Christians everywhere must reform themselves of the loose morals into which they had lapsed, and if Church authorities chose to disregard this information (as indeed they did), then it would be so much the worse for them. Priscilla and Maximilla, we are told, professed to speak for the Holy Spirit especially in prescribing "novelties in the form of fasts and feasts, abstinences and diets of radishes." This "New

Prophecy," as it was called, perfectly suited Tertullian's fiery and austere nature, and he left the Church in 213 (when he was about fifty-three) in order to join the movement. Nevertheless, many of Tertullian's reflections upon Christian beliefs were influential in the shaping of doctrines which the Church eventually declared orthodox. Of particular importance in this regard was his conception of Jesus as one *person* in whom there were two distinct *natures,* a human nature and a divine nature; and his conception of God as one *substance* in whom there are three distinct *persons:* the Father, the Son, and the Holy Spirit.

Clement of Alexandria, Origen

Tertullian's antagonism to philosophy was shared by some other Fathers of note. Tatian, who may have begun as a pupil of Justin Martyr, had arrived at a view very different from Justin's by the time (around 170) he composed his *Address to the Greeks:* "Obeying the commands of God," Tatian says, "and following the law of the Father of immortality, we reject everything which rests upon human opinion." And Arnobius denied the relevance of philosophy to Christianity by arguing in a treatise *Against the Pagans* (around 300) that human knowledge is strictly limited to the objects of sense-experience, so that only faith in Divine Revelation can give assurance of God's existence or of any human vocation or destiny that transcends this life.

A majority of the Fathers, however, were in agreement with the general outlook of Justin Martyr: Greek and Roman philosophy—above all the philosophy of Plato—was in many respects an anticipation of the Gospel and is still of value in leading educated persons to faith in the definitive wisdom of God's Word, which it may also serve to explain and clarify. Such, most notably, was the position of Titus Flavius Clemens, or Clement of Alexandria (about 150–213), and of Origenes Adamantius, or Origen (about 185–255). In Alexandria a Catechetical School was established to teach (*katechein,* in Greek) Christian principles to new converts. Clement served for a time as head of this school and taught that Scripture, allegorically interpreted in the manner of Philo, will be found to contain the true philosophy of which Platonic metaphysics, Aristotelian logic, and Stoic ethics were partial foreshadowings. In his *Stromata* (or *Miscellanies*), Clement draws upon Philo in interpreting the story of Abraham as an allegory upon the true relations between philosophy and religious faith. In Genesis it is said that, after Abraham and Sarah had for many years been childless, Sarah suggested to Abraham that he have intercourse with her Egyptian maid Hagar. Abraham did so, and when Hagar's pride in the result (a son, Ishmael) took the form of disdain for her mistress, Sarah sought and got Abraham's permission to send Hagar away—temporarily, as it turned out. (Later on, of course, Abraham begot

Isaac of Sarah.) What we have here, Clement says, is wisdom (Sarah) directing a man of faith (Abraham) to have intercourse with "secular philosophy" (Hagar) as instruction preliminary to "the faith and righteousness which are according to God" (fruitful intercourse with his true wife). A man of faith corrects secular philosophy (Hagar is admonished) from the point of view of wisdom (Sarah), which in all things selects only what is profitable.

Clement, surprisingly for a Father, finds something profitable to select from the philosophy of Epicurus. He believes that Epicurus' notion of "anticipations" may be viewed as a precursor of the Christian conception of faith. Knowledge, Epicurus maintained, is built up from sense-experience by way of general concepts which are "anticipations" in that they prompt us to anticipate fresh experiences of specific sorts. Clement argues more generally that without "anticipations," or "preconceptions" as he calls them, our attempts to discover truth in any field would lack direction. Before undertaking any investigation, we must form an idea of what we might find and of how we might find it. Such a "preconception," according to Clement, involves faith in the existence of that which we seek. Unless we *believe* that there is something to discover, we will never begin to look and so will never come to *understand* whatever is understandable. "Except ye believe, neither shall ye understand," Isaiah says; and just as this holds even for the objects of our sense-experience, so it holds all the more for our inquiries concerning the transcendent Creator of the entire universe. An "intuition" of God may be vouchsafed to those who strive for the demonstrative knowledge that is obtainable (as Clement believes) of His Son, who is Wisdom and Knowledge and Truth; but none would strive for this who did not first have faith that Wisdom exists. Hence: "No one shall learn aught without faith, since no one learns aught without preconception. . . . [Whereas] by starting from this faith, and being developed by it, through the grace of God, the knowledge respecting Him is to be acquired as far as possible."

Philosophy, which is to faith what Hagar was to Abraham, is so far from being useless, Clement says, that even if it *were* useless, the (surely useful) demonstration of its uselessness would show that it is *not* useless.

Origen, who succeeded Clement as head of the Catechetical School in Alexandria, went to unprecedented lengths in employing the allegorical method, aiming to detect in Scripture the principles of a comprehensive philosophical theology having many affinities with Neoplatonism. He is said to have attended, a year before Plotinus, the lectures of Ammonius Saccus; and it would seem that he was decisively influenced by the experience. Thus in his treatise *On First Principles,* Origen subscribes on the one hand to the scriptural view that God freely created the world at a certain time, and on the other hand to the Neoplatonic view that God, or the Good, necessarily exercises full creative power from eternity. Origen reconciles these views by arguing that "the world" in Scripture refers to the present world of visible things, whereas from eternity God has sustained by His creative energy all the invisible souls who "descend" to bodily habitations in the world. Other worlds existed before the present world,[9] and still others will exist afterward, until at length all souls have freely chosen (even if some must be "threatened") to become, with Christ's aid, as like to God as possible. All souls will ultimately be redeemed; none will suffer eternal punishment in Hell. As these and related views proved repugnant to the Church, Origen was eventually (in 553) condemned as a heretic. But for more than a century after his death, the evolution of Christian thinking, especially in the eastern portions of the Roman Empire, followed the lines—the sometimes conflicting lines—he had mapped out.

Concerning the relation of God the Son to God the Father, Origen seems to say different things in different places; and two opposite schools of thought, both citing Origen as an authority, soon fell into bitter conflict over the issue. One school, whose chief representative was Athanasius (about 295–373), maintained that the Son was eternally begotten of the Father and was, to use the Greek expression, *homoousion,* that is, of the same essential being or substance with the Father. The other school, whose chief representative was Arius (about 256–336), maintained that the Son was not eternally begotten of the Father ("the Son had a beginning") and was *homoiousion,* that is, only of similar substance with the Father. (Tertullian had said that the Son is of one substance with the Father, but he had also said that the Son had a beginning.) The controversy between the two sides became so disruptive that the emperor Constantine felt obliged to intercede; he summoned bishops to a general synod—the Council of Nicea in 325—in order to settle the matter once and for all. Arius and his followers were formally anathematized (denounced as accursed), and Athanasius' position was declared orthodox; but in fact it was not until the Council of Constantinople in 381 that the Arian Heresy was effectively stemmed. Had the Arians prevailed, the Church would really have abandoned the doctrine that God Himself (as opposed to a "similar" being) was incarnate in Christ and redeemed the world through His Passion.

---

[9] A view for which Origen finds a scriptural basis in Ecclesiastes 1:9–10, but this may in turn derive from Epicureanism. See pp. 178, 187.

CHAPTER 14

St. Augustine

Aurelius Augustinus—St. Augustine of Hippo—is preeminent among the Fathers of the Church. For centuries his thought dominated theological discussion in Roman Catholicism, and it also figured largely in the Protestant Reformation of the sixteenth century. Like Clement of Alexandria, but to much greater effect, St. Augustine sought a reasoned understanding of the contents of Revelation; and in the process he adopted positions that were to have no little influence upon the subsequent history of philosophy.

St. Augustine was born to parents named Patricius and Monica in 354 in Tagaste,[1] a small town in the Roman province of Numidia in North Africa. He received a thorough education in Latin literature and rhetoric—the customary preparation in those days for the law and for the Roman civil service—but he was still in his teens when Patricius died, and it was soon necessary for him to take a teaching position in order to support his family. He taught rhetoric, first at Tagaste, then at Carthage, Rome, and Milan. Although Patricius was a pagan until shortly before his death, Monica (later St. Monica) was a devout Christian and saw to it that her son was fully instructed in the Faith. But in his adolescence St. Augustine was sent to school in Carthage—"a hissing cauldron of lust" as he subsequently described it—where his boyhood faith gave way to worldly impulses and non-Christian ideas. How eventually he regained his faith, thanks to God's grace and Monica's devotions, is recounted in his famous *Confessions*. Wishing often that he could sometime—"but not yet"—live chastely, he lived with two mistresses and fathered an illegitimate son. Having been inspired by reading Cicero to search for wisdom, he delved hopefully into Manichaeism[2] and astrology—only to wind up on the brink of Skepticism. But then he heard the illuminating sermons of St. Ambrose, Bishop of Milan; and he began to study with great interest the teachings of Plotinus; and he reread with new eyes the letters of St. Paul, in which he discovered that "whatever truth I had found in the

---

[1] Now Souk-Ahras in Algeria, about forty miles inland from the port of 'Annaba (ancient Hippo).

[2] An ascetic religious movement founded by a Persian called Mani (about 216–276), who combined elements of Zoroastrianism, Buddhism, and Christianity in teaching that the world is a scene of perpetual conflict between two ultimate forces—one of light and goodness, the other of darkness and evil.

Platonists was set down here as well." The turning point of St. Augustine's life came in his thirty-second year. Intellectually reconciled to the Church, yet lacking strength of will to break his old incontinent habits, one summer day in 386 in Milan he was overwhelmed by his sense of helplessness. In the garden of the house where he was staying, he flung himself beneath a tree and wept. Then from a neighboring house came the voice of a child chanting the words, "Take and read; take and read." Understanding this as a divine command, St. Augustine opened the New Testament at random and read the first passage on which his eyes fell (Romans 13:13–14): "Let us conduct ourselves becomingly as in the day, not in reveling and drunkenness, not in debauchery and licentiousness, not in quarreling and jealousy. But put on the Lord Jesus Christ, and make no provision for the flesh, to gratify its desires." Suddenly St. Augustine's conversion was complete: "In an instant, as I came to the end of the sentence, it was as though the light of confidence flooded into my heart. . . ." It was from God, he believed, that the strength had come to subdue his wayward inclinations: "O Lord . . . it was your power that drained dry the well of corruption in the depths of my heart."

In 388 St. Augustine returned to Tagaste, where he established a small monastic community with the plan of devoting himself to writing. But in 391 his bishop, Valerius, prevailed upon him to accept ordination as a priest and to move to Hippo. When Valerius died in 396, St. Augustine succeeded him as Bishop of Hippo and remained in that post for the rest of his life. In spite of heavy episcopal duties, he managed to compose scores of treatises on a wide range of subjects, to conduct a vast correspondence with various notables—including popes and emperors—who sought his advice, and to write innumerable sermons of which hundreds have survived.

Hippo was besieged in 430 by an army of the Germanic tribe of Vandals. The Vandals had invaded the Roman Empire in 407 and had gotten into North Africa by way of Spain and the Straits of Gibraltar. St. Augustine and some other clergy stayed in Hippo for the attack, as there would be baptisms and last rites to administer during the frightful ordeal ahead. Death came to St. Augustine, at the age of seventy-six, before the Vandals broke through the defenses and burned down the city. It is reported that he died while reciting the Penitential Psalms.[3]

Faith and Reason _____

St. Augustine, like Clement of Alexandria, finds that the relation between faith and reason, or between belief and understanding, is exactly

[3] Psalms 6, 32, 38, 51, 102, 130, and 143 in the King James Version.

as Isaiah said: "Except ye believe, neither shall ye understand."[4] The famous words in which St. Augustine expresses the matter for himself are: "Understanding is the reward of faith. Therefore, seek not to understand that thou mayest believe, but believe that thou mayest understand." By "faith" or "belief" St. Augustine means our voluntary assent to, or agreement with, statements whose truth (if they are true) we do not directly and clearly apprehend. When we do directly and clearly apprehend the truth of some statement, then we "understand" it, and the power by which we do so is "reason"—"inferior reason" (conducive only to "knowledge") if the statement concerns something in the changing world of space and time, "superior reason" (conducive to "wisdom") if the statement concerns God or eternal principles. Superior reason involves the fixing of intellectual attention—the "gaze of the mind," as St. Augustine pictures it—upon objects that transcend space and time. To this end it is necessary that we "purify" our minds by following a course of conduct that will counteract our preoccupation with sensible things and accustom us to thoughts of intelligible things. The right course of conduct, in St. Augustine's view, is naturally set forth in the doctrines of the Church, which enjoin specific practices of worship and rules of behavior in keeping with Scripture. Until right living has purified the mind and prepared it for understanding, the doctrines of the Church must simply be believed on the Church's authority.

There are compelling reasons, St. Augustine says, for trusting in the Church's authority. After all, we have to think how unlikely it is that vast numbers of persons would have accepted the Church's teachings if her teachings were fundamentally erroneous. Of course, we might be deterred by numbers, thinking that little or no truth is likely to reside in doctrines professed by unphilosophical multitudes; but surely, St. Augustine argues, we are not prepared consistently to doubt what multitudes believe. In that case we would have to go to the absurd lengths of doubting that good health and honor and happiness are valuable, since virtually everyone believes they are valuable. Nor can we very well have any general objection to believing things on the authority of others. We all rely on authority in countless matters, including matters about which we could never personally know anything for certain. A favorite example of St. Augustine's is the belief that one's biological parents are in fact the man and woman who represent themselves as such. One cannot personally have made observations that would verify this belief beyond a shadow of doubt, for the relevant events occurred before one was aware of anything; and so one must hold the belief on authority—generally on the authority of the very man and woman who represent themselves (hon-

---

[4] This wording derives from the Septuagint Version—actually a mistranslation—of Isaiah 7:9. A more accurate translation of the original Hebrew is given in the King James Version: "If ye will not believe, surely ye shall not be established." The words were spoken to King Ahaz of Judah, who was in danger of being overthrown by a coalition of aggressors (Damascus and Israel).

estly or not) as one's biological parents. We are in a far better position than this, St. Augustine says, with respect to many, if not quite all, of the doctrines of the Church. Real knowledge of these, in due course, is possible. Having accepted them on faith and endeavored sincerely to live up to them, we may with instruction and God's help come to understand or comprehend them to our complete intellectual satisfaction. Christ's words "Seek and ye shall find," notwithstanding Tertullian's opinion to the contrary, promise knowledge—genuine philosophical insight—to those who begin by believing. There are people who, professing a sincere concern that we are too ready to believe, would try to dissuade us from accepting the Church's doctrines on the Church's authority. But the sincerity of these people's concern is something we can believe, if at all, only on these people's authority; and although they would hardly like us to question *that,* they cannot, St. Augustine is sure, give us any good reason for trusting in their authority and *not* in the Church's.

St. Augustine does not maintain that everyone is able in this life to achieve understanding of Christian principles. For the "uninstructed multitude," he says, belief has to suffice for the time being, although in the next life enlightenment will surely be vouchsafed to all the faithful. No one who lacks wisdom may be said to enjoy complete happiness or well-being. Educated persons should try to comprehend by reason the deliverances of Revelation, recognizing however that some of these, at least for the present, can be understood only as "possible and fitting," not as perfectly certain. St. Augustine's view of the respective offices of faith and reason is stated particularly well in his treatise *Of True Religion,* composed not long after he returned to Africa and took up monastic life in Tagaste:

A way of life agreeable to the divine commandments will purge the mind and make it fit to perceive spiritual things which are neither past nor future but abide ever the same, liable to no change. . . . All those things which to begin with we simply believed, following authority only, we come to understand. Partly we see them as certain, partly as possible and fitting. . . . [As examples of the latter] the Holy Incarnation, the birth from a virgin, the death of the Son of God for us, his resurrection from the dead, . . . the forgiveness of sins, the day of judgment, the resurrection of the body are not merely believed. . . . They are also judged to be part and parcel of [that is, as fitting in with] the mercy of the most high God, which he has shown towards the human race. . . .

Authority demands belief and prepares man for reason. Reason leads to understanding and knowledge. But reason is not entirely absent from authority, for we have got to consider whom we have to believe . . . what men or what books we are to believe in order that we may rightly worship God, wherein lies our sole salvation. Here the first decision must be this: Are we to believe those who summon us to the worship of many gods or those who summon us to worship one God? Who can doubt that we ought rather to follow those who summon us to worship one God? . . . In the realm of nature there is a presumption of greater authority when all things are brought into unity. In the human race a multitude has no power unless by consent, i.e., agreement in unity. So in religion the authority of those who summon us to unity ought to be greater and more worthy of being believed. . . .

We have heard that our predecessors, at a stage in faith on the way from temporal things up to eternal things, followed visible miracles. They could do nothing else. And they did so in such a way that it should not be necessary for those who came after them. When the Catholic Church had been founded and diffused throughout the whole world, on the one hand miracles were not allowed to continue till our time, lest the mind should always seek visible things, and the human race should grow cold by becoming accustomed to things which when they were novelties kindled its faith. On the other hand we must not doubt that those are to be believed who proclaimed miracles, which only a few had actually seen, and yet were able to persuade whole peoples to follow them.

Knowledge and God

Skeptics such as Carneades doubted that reasoning was profitable in any field and were inclined in religion (or so they said) simply to acquiesce in the beliefs of their ancestors. St. Augustine, in *reasoning* that the Church should be trusted in preparation for *"reasoning* about the divine and the invisible," was far from being a Skeptic. At one time, it is true, Skepticism had not been entirely unattractive to him. He had been drawn to Manichaeism partly because it promised ready knowledge of ultimate truths; and when he found that it by no means fulfilled this promise, he began to think that knowledge of any kind might be unattainable. But he saw that he could not keep up an attitude of complete Skepticism. If he were really to doubt everything, he would have to doubt even that he existed, and nothing to him could be more absurd. Supposing that Skeptics were correct in arguing that we may always be deceived in trusting our senses, in thinking that we are awake and not dreaming, sane and not mad, and so on, it would still be impossible to be deceived about our own existence. "If I am deceived, I am," St. Augustine says, "for he who does not exist cannot be deceived. . . . And since I am if I am deceived, how am I deceived in believing that I am? For it is certain that I am, if I am deceived. Since therefore I, the person deceived, should be, even if I were deceived, certainly I am not deceived in this knowledge that I am."[5]

---

[5] Descartes (1596–1650), whose "I think, therefore I am" would seem to have been inspired by St. Augustine, did not acknowledge such an indebtedness. In fact he may have drawn upon any of a number of writers who had borrowed St. Augustine's argument.

While St. Augustine is ready to argue that he could not be deceived about his own existence even though he were deceived about everything else, he is not actually prepared to suppose that he *is* deceived about everything else. As he argues in his treatise *On Free Choice of the Will,* we could hardly exist without being alive, which fact we may understand, so that besides our mere existence there are two further things of which we may be certain, namely, that we are alive and that we understand. And included in the understanding that we are alive is the awareness that we possess bodily senses of sight, hearing, smell, taste, and touch, each of them conveying its own characteristic data—colors, sounds, odors, flavors, and textures—that we discriminate and coordinate in the course of our experience.[6] Moreover, if we will only reflect upon the factors at work in our experience, we may be confident of much else. Indeed, we may see, St. Augustine believes, how very much our powers of reason can do by way of complementing faith with understanding.

Let us follow for a distance the argument in *On Free Choice,* supplementing it with related arguments in other works of St. Augustine's. This will illustrate his typical manner of dealing with a variety of philosophical points, often with great subtlety, in the course of a line of reasoning that is theological in orientation. St. Augustine is at his most original when arguing, as here, that the inner experience of the individual is the soundest basis for advancing to knowledge—or rather to wisdom—concerning God.

Consider what is involved in some ordinary experience such as seeing and touching an apple.[7] We are aware that with our eyes we perceive redness and roundness and that with our fingers we perceive roundness again, along with smoothness and coolness. We are also aware that these qualities belong to the same thing and that the roundness we see is the same as the roundness we touch. We may further be aware of *not* smelling or tasting this thing that we see and touch. But how, by what means, are we aware of all this? Is it simply by means of our eyes and fingers? St. Augustine thinks not. We can scarcely perceive by eyes and fingers, he says, that we are not smelling or tasting. We do not even perceive by eyes and fingers that we are seeing and touching; we do not literally see our seeing or touch our touching; we see colors and shapes, not our seeing, and we touch textures and shapes, not our touching. And not by eyes and fingers are we aware that colors we see belong to textures we touch, or that shapes we see are the same as shapes we touch. No, St. Augustine

---

[6] In response to Skeptics who contend that sensory data may all be "deceptive," St. Augustine follows the Epicureans in holding that none is deceptive in itself and that errors of perception arise instead from hasty judgments concerning sensory data. "We must confess," he says, "that not only our own senses, but those of other persons also, have added very much indeed to our knowledge." And who besides someone of perversely bad judgment, St. Augustine asks, is really "deceived" by the appearances Skeptics are so fond of citing—oars that look bent under water, towers that seem to move, and so forth?

[7] Our example, not St. Augustine's.

concludes, there must be within us something over and above our five bodily senses, some general capacity for apprehending whether and when these particular senses are functioning, and for integrating the data they convey into unified apprehensions of objects. Aristotle had identified such a capacity as our "common sense"—"common" because it accounts among other things for the awareness of qualities (such as shape) common to different bodily senses—but St. Augustine prefers to call it our "inner sense." It is this inner sense, he says, "to which all things are referred by the five familiar senses"; it "controls and as it were judges the bodily senses," functioning as a central monitor and clearinghouse in the mind for sensory data of all kinds.

On the principle that "what judges is better than what is judged," St. Augustine pronounces the inner sense a better thing than the bodily senses of which it is the judge. He does not, however, believe that it is the best of our powers. Many species of animals, he says, must also be supposed to have an inner sense. How could an animal move either to seek or to avoid something unless it were aware that it perceived, and how could it be aware that it perceived unless it had an inner sense as we do? Of course, this is not to say that any animal *understands* that it has an inner sense. In order to understand this, an animal would need to distinguish explicitly the qualities it perceives from its perceiving them, and its perceiving them from its awareness that it perceives them; and there is no evidence, St. Augustine believes, for thinking that any animal can make these distinctions. That *we* can make them, by "rational thought and reflection within the soul," is part of what it means for us to possess *reason* or *understanding*. And because it is by reason that we "judge" of the inner sense, in making the distinctions by which its existence is revealed in consciousness, reason is a better thing in us than the inner sense. Do we have in us any faculty better than reason? This would be so only if we had some faculty which judges of reason; but this we neither have nor need, for reason is self-reflective and discerns its own operations and appraises its own performance. The analysis of sense-experience by which the inner sense is disclosed is a perfect example—an exercise of reason that is self-aware and self-guiding. So St. Augustine concludes that reason is the best of our powers.

If reason is the best of our powers, it is also a power by which we know that it itself is still far from perfect. We know, for one thing, that reason is mutable or inconstant—"now struggling to arrive at truth, now ceasing to struggle, sometimes reaching it, and sometimes not." This inconstancy of reason is strikingly in contrast to the principles that reason struggles to apprehend. The principles of mathematics, to take the most obvious example, are apprehended (after struggle for many) as perfectly constant and unchangeable, as necessarily true and the same eternally and for everyone. A simple arithmetical truth such as $7 + 3 = 10$ will serve as an illustration. Unlike any of the things we perceive through our senses and to which we might apply it, and unlike any of our own processes of thought,

$7 + 3 = 10$ is absolutely immutable: "There has never been a time when seven and three were not ten," St. Augustine says, "nor will there ever be a time when they are not ten." Likewise for principles of logic such as "*A* must either be *B* or not *B*" (the Law of Excluded Middle), and for principles of value such as "the incorrupt is better than the corrupt," which in St. Augustine's view are no less immutable. Everyone acknowledges principles of these kinds as standards of judgment in both thought and action; no one in practice seriously supposes that they are doubtful or that they are matters for the individual for decide. We judge *according to* them, St. Augustine says, not *about* them. On reflection we realize that their immutable truth has nothing to do with us, for the best thing in us—our reason—is only too mutable. In short, we realize that their immutable truth is "something higher than our mind and reason."

Although immutable principles are higher than our minds, we grasp them nevertheless, and St. Augustine infers from this that our minds must be incorporeal in nature. He argues as follows. Immutable principles such as $7 + 3 = 10$ cannot be statements about the corporeal objects of our sense-experience, for all of these objects are mutable. To be divisible is to be mutable, and any corporeal object is divisible. Whatever is divisible is *many,* not strictly *one* or a numerical unity. Any number, however, contains numerical unity: 7, for example, contains it seven times ($7 = 7 \times 1$). Numbers, therefore, cannot be corporeal objects, and statements about numbers cannot be statements about corporeal objects (which exemplify numerical truths only approximately at best). The only alternative is that numbers are *incorporeal* entities and that arithmetical statements concern them. Incorporeal entities do not exist in space and cannot be apprehended by our bodily senses. We can apprehend them only by our mind and reason. But if our mind were not itself incorporeal, how could it apprehend anything incorporeal? To St. Augustine the conclusion is clear and inescapable: the human mind is not a "body," not an object in space, changeable though it is with respect to time. "If, by reason of some marvelous affinity of natures, bodily things are seen with bodily eyes," he says, "must not the mind by which we see such incorporeal things be neither a body nor anything like a body?"

We are in the position, then, of apprehending immutable truths with incorporeal minds, acknowledging that the eternal constancy of these truths puts them on a higher plane than our minds. Principles of mathematics, logic, and value are timeless and unchangeable, whereas our thoughts of these principles are temporal and transitory—"transitory thoughts of things not transitory," St. Augustine says. But how is it that timeless or eternal truths are what they are? Whence the immutable truth that each of them possesses? St. Augustine's understanding of the matter is indebted to a familiar tenet of Plato's: if two or more items are *F*, Plato thought, that is because there exists such a thing as "*F* itself"—the perfect *form* of *F*— to which these items have a certain common relation. For example, if the pages of this book are rectangular (more or less), that is because there exists such a thing as rectangularity itself to which these pages have a certain common relation—they "participate in" rectangularity, as Plato might say. St. Augustine, for his part, believes that if principles of mathematics, logic, and value are immutably true, that is because there exists such a thing as Immutable Truth itself to which these principles have a certain common relation. St. Augustine speaks of this relation as one of *containment:* "There is an Immutable Truth," he says, "in which all things that are immutably true are contained."

Immutable Truth, as "containing" things that are neither in space nor in time, must itself be something that transcends space and time. Yet something that transcends space and time cannot literally "contain" things of any kind, much less things not themselves either in space or in time. We know what it means for a gallon to "contain" quarts or for an hour to "contain" minutes, but what can it mean to say that Immutable Truth "contains" immutable truths? St. Augustine implicitly answers this question by the way in which he develops the rest of his argument. It turns out that Immutable Truth is to be understood as an eternal *Mind* and that particular immutable truths are to be understood as eternal *thoughts* of this Mind. It is a familiar figure of speech to say that our minds "contain" thoughts; and however difficult it may be to conceive of an eternal Mind and of eternal thoughts, to say that one would "contain" the other is natural enough. What St. Augustine says is that Immutable Truth can be none other than God (or His eternal Mind), unless indeed there exists something more excellent than Immutable Truth, in which case that will be God. God, of course, is understood to be "that to whom nothing is superior." St. Augustine plainly believes that nothing is superior to Immutable Truth, but he does not detail his reasons. Perhaps he has in mind an argument along the following lines: if you believe that there *is* something superior to Immutable Truth, surely you will believe that this is unchangeably the case; but whatever is unchangeably the case is immutably true, and is therefore "contained in" Immutable Truth, and is therefore *not* superior to Immutable Truth. The belief in question implies its own contradictory and so must be false. This may be what St. Augustine thinks. At all events, he is satisfied that he has proved the existence of Immutable Truth, and he leaves little doubt that in doing this he believes he has proved the existence of God, whose eternal Mind "contains" immutable truths. "God exists, truly and in the highest degree," St. Augustine says; "this indubitable fact we maintain, I think, not only by faith, but also by a sure though somewhat tenuous form of reasoning. . . ."

St. Augustine's view, then, comes to this: immutable truths exist as thoughts eternally present in God's mind, and the relevance of these truths to our knowledge of the world is owing to God's creating the world in accordance with His thoughts. God's thoughts, and the ideas therein, are "the primary forms, or the permanent and immutable reasons of real things, and they are not themselves formed; so that they are, as a consequence, eternal and ever the same in themselves, and they are contained in the divine intelligence. And since they never come into being or go out of it, everything that can come into being and go out of it, and everything that does come into being and goes out of it, may be said to be formed in accord with them." Plato had supposed that such "primary forms" or "reasons of things" exist in their own right, independently of the Divine Craftsman who looks to them as models in fashioning the world. But to St. Augustine it is inconsistent with God's unqualified supremacy to suppose that He looks to anything outside Himself for guidance in His creative activity. More acceptable to St. Augustine are the views of those "Platonic philosophers"—Plotinus and his followers—"who have recognized the true God as the Author of all things, the Source of the light and truth . . . [and who] have seen also that, in every changeable thing, the form which makes it that which it is, whatever be its mode or nature, can only *be* through Him who truly *is,* because He is unchangeable." Actually, Plotinus conceived of the forms as contained not in the Mind of God Himself but in the subordinate Intellect that eternally emanates from God. For Plotinus, God or the One, like the form of the good in Plato's *Republic,* transcends all knowing and all things knowable. On this Plotinus was in agreement with Philo, who (often at least) was inclined to think of the forms as ideas of a subordinate power, the Word or Logos or Son, who serves as God's intermediary in transactions with the world. St. Augustine himself, in fact, occasionally speaks of the Son of God as "Truth," and he certainly views the Son as "the mediator between God and men"; but it has to be remembered that, on the orthodox view which St. Augustine accepts, Son and Father are one God, even though the Son is begotten (eternally) of the Father. Both Son and Father may then be the Truth that contains all truths.

St. Augustine praises Plotinus and his school for recognizing that God is "the Source of the light of truth." Plato had attributed "the light of truth" not to God or a god but to the form of the good: as the sun by its light makes other visible objects visible, Plato said, so the form of the good, by something analogous to light, makes other intelligible forms intelligible. St. Augustine, mindful of what the Gospel says about "the true Light, which lighteth every man that cometh into the world," follows Plotinus in attributing to God the power of illuminating intelligible forms; and it is by reference to this that St. Augustine proposes to explain how we, with our changeable minds, manage to discern things that are unchangeable. He says that we are able to apprehend $7 + 3 = 10$, for example, because God—or Truth, or Christ our Teacher—makes its eternal necessity manifest to us "by a sort of incorporeal light of an unique kind." This Divine Light "illumines the inner man," "presides over our minds within us," and "makes us able to judge correctly." Much controversy was to arise over what St. Augustine means by this. Does he mean that the Divine Light discloses to us forms in God's Mind? If not, how could it enable us to apprehend $7 + 3 = 10$, if "7," "3," and "10" properly refer to forms in God's Mind? But if so, we would enjoy a remarkably close acquaintance with God—apprehending indeed the very content of His Mind—simply by thinking of a truth in arithmetic. St. Augustine himself, however, would be the first to insist that a knowledge of arithmetic, compatible as it is with impiety and vice, cannot by itself entail closeness to God. Perhaps, then, St. Augustine does not really mean that the Divine Light discloses to us forms in God's Mind. Maybe he means instead that we somehow arrive on our own at notions of 7, 3, and 10—notions that have a certain adequacy without deriving from an apprehension of forms in God's Mind—and then the Divine Light discloses to us the necessary *relation* expressed by $7 + 3 = 10$. Some have believed that this is his position. Problems also arise concerning it, including the problem of how notions that are not derived from an apprehension of forms in God's Mind could possibly, in St. Augustine's view, be adequate for us to apprehend a necessary relation. The fact is that St. Augustine's statements about the Divine Light are subject to various interpretations and have been variously interpreted.

Such is the way in which, according to St. Augustine, wisdom about God may be achieved when we begin by reflecting upon the factors at work in our experience. But what more specifically does St. Augustine say about God's nature and about God's relation to the world He creates?

Creator and Creation _____

St. Augustine does not wish to minimize the difficulty of thinking about God. We find it hard enough, he says, to make out the properties of objects we see and touch; we imperfectly understand the inner workings of our own minds or souls; so it is only to be expected that we should not readily or fully comprehend the Creator of all objects and souls. Because God, the Immutable Truth, transcends space and time, we cannot ascribe to Him any characteristics associated with space and time. This makes it far easier to say what God is *not* than what He is; and for St. Augustine, as for Philo and Plotinus, there is much to recommend an essentially negative approach to describing the Almighty.

> We may understand God, if we are able, and as much as we are able, as good without quality, great without quantity, a creator though He lack nothing, ruling but from no position, sustaining all things without "having" them, in His wholeness everywhere yet without place, eternal without time, making things that are changeable, without change of Himself and without passion. Whoso thus thinks of God, although he cannot yet find out in all ways what He is, yet piously takes heed, as much as he is able, to think of nothing of Him that He is not.

Consider the point that God "makes" changeable things but *not* in such a way as to involve any change on His own part. This is really to say that "makes," although correctly indicating that God is the originator of changeable things, cannot be understood literally to specify how God originates them. "Making" refers to a form of activity (say, carpentering); any form of activity is a process in time involving a sequence of changes (as in hammering and sawing) on the part of whoever performs the activity; but because God is not in time He cannot perform any activity or experience any change. If we are to be careful "to think nothing of Him that He is not," we have to acknowledge that, in His case, "making" designates a type of origination of things that is *not* making.

In view of the great difficulty of thinking about God, St. Augustine occasionally goes so far as to say that all we can know of Him is how we do *not* know Him. But we could not ascertain how we do not know Him, or how He is not to be conceived, unless it were possible for us to think of God in some positive terms that literally apply to Him. How could we know what anything is not unless we know at least something about what it is? And in fact St. Augustine does believe that we are in a position to say something affirmative and literally true about God. We may certainly say of God that He is "something than which there is nothing better or more sublime." Moreover, God's declaration to Moses, "I am that I am," can only mean (as Philo believed also) that God, and God alone, "falls most truly, without difficulty or hesitation, under the category of *Being*." All other things are changeable—they are "able not to be that which they had been"—and this means that their *being* is of a limited and relative type. It is God, in His unique unchangeability, "to whom certainly Being . . . most especially and most truly belongs." In line with this, we may also say that God is the *Selfsame*—"that which always exists in the same way; that which is not now one thing and again a different thing."

If all we could accurately say about God is that He is Being, the Selfsame, and "something than which there is nothing better or more sublime," our notion of Him would be exceedingly abstract. We should not be able to ascribe to Him the attributes of *personality* that are so essential a part of the Biblical conception of Him—attributes that are implied in calling Him "Him" and that include loving-kindness as Father, righteousness as Judge, and mercifulness as Redeemer. St. Augustine constantly refers to God in these terms; but sometimes he then goes right on to say that God is "incomprehensible to us," leaving us to wonder how he finds it possible to refer to God in these terms, or in any terms. In practice, however, he proceeds on the basis that if God made human beings in His image and likeness, as Genesis says, then the attributes of personality He gave to human beings must have some resemblance, however remote, to attributes of His own. We cannot be wholly misguided, then, if we ascribe to God certain attributes of personality that we conceive as vastly superior to, but not absolutely unlike, those we possess.[8] Thus a hu-

---

[8] "In your soul," St. Augustine says, "is the image of God . . . by the Word this image was stamped on it. . . . It now remains for you, then, to seek out what is of better worth than your soul. Higher indeed than this there is nothing save the Creator. Stretch upwards towards Him, do not despair, do not say: 'It is beyond me.' "

man father's love for his children may be taken as giving us some idea of God's relation to His creatures, although God is so far superior to the best of human fathers that our idea of Him as Father is just barely suitable.

St. Augustine's writings contain many attempts to achieve some comprehension of God's nature by means of analogies drawn from human experience. A famous example is St. Augustine's argument, in the *Confessions,* that something remotely akin to the *eternity* of God is to be found by examining the human consciousness of *time.* What prompts him to develop this argument is that some people, "steeped in error," have been asking what God was doing before He created the world. If God was doing nothing before He created the world, these people say, it is hard to see why He did not continue doing nothing; but granting that at some point He finally decided to create the world, was not this decision a *new thing* in His consciousness, so that all are in error who say that God is changeless and eternally the same? St. Augustine forbids himself the rejoinder, which he nevertheless mentions, that before God created the world, He was busy preparing Hell for people who ask questions of this sort. No, St. Augustine says, the question is a serious one, and it deserves a serious answer. The answer should be that although the world has existed for a limited time, there never was a time when it did not yet exist, and there was never a time when God had not yet willed to create it, because *time itself was created* with the creation of the world. "Periods of time come into being by means of the changes of things," St. Augustine says, and things that change are what God made in creating the world. It is not as if God had ages and ages of empty time on His hands before it occurred to Him to create the world. There was no "time before" He willed to create, and did create, time and the world together. In other words, time and the world came into existence a definite number of years ago (how many St. Augustine does not profess to know), but "God's will that there should be a creation was there from all eternity." The will to create represents no novelty in God's consciousness, no departure from His eternity. As for those who think otherwise:

> [They] have not learnt to understand you, Wisdom of God, Light of our minds. They do not yet understand how the things are made which come into being in you and through you. Try as they may to savor the taste of eternity, their thoughts still twist and turn upon the ebb and flow of things in past and future time. But if only their minds could be seized and held steady, they would be still for a while and, for that short moment, they would glimpse the splendor of eternity which is for ever still. They would contrast it with time, which is never still, and see that it is not comparable. They would see that time derives its length only from a great number of movements constantly following one another into the past, because they cannot all continue at once. But in eternity nothing moves into the past: all is present. Time, on the other hand, is never present all at once. The past is always driven on by the

future, the future always follows on the heels of the past, and both the past and the future have their beginning and their end in the eternal present. If only men's minds could be seized and held still! They would see how eternity, in which there is neither past nor future, determines both past and future time.

Time, which is "never still," is also a continuum in that any period of time we take as *present* is divisible into parts that are *not* present but past or future. Not even a minute can be present, for a minute is divisible into earlier and later seconds—the earlier being past, the later being future. Not even a second, or a tenth of a second, or a hundredth of a second, can be present, for these also are divisible into earlier and later parts. How, then, do we measure periods of time? We can hardly measure something that does not exist; but how can any period of time be said to exist if it is divisible into parts that either have already gone by (and so no longer exist) or else have still to arrive (and so do not yet exist)? St. Augustine ultimately concludes that we measure periods of time in our minds as we combine *memories* of what has happened with *expectations* of what is yet to come. Memories and expectations exist as objects of our attention; and our attention can persist in spite of time's continuous passage.

I say that I measure time in my mind. For everything which happens leaves an impression on it, and this impression remains after the thing itself has ceased to be. It is the impression that I measure, since it is still present. . . . The future, which [the mind] expects, passes through the present, to which it attends, into the past, which it remembers. No one would deny that the future does not yet exist or that the past no longer exists. Yet in the mind there is both expectation of the future and remembrance of the past. Again, no one would deny that the present has no duration, since it exists only for the instant of its passage. Yet the mind's attention persists, and through it that which is to be passes towards the state in which it is to be no more. So it is not future time that is long, but a long future is a long expectation of the future; and past time is not long, because it does not exist, but a long past is a long remembrance of the past.

Our attention is of course very limited in scope. For us a long memory might reach back to early childhood, but not to the beginning of the world; and a long expectation might stretch forward a number of years, but not so as to include an infinite future. Yet we can dimly imagine a mind of unlimited scope in which the past and the future are seized in their entirety—"seized and held steady" in an abiding attention that is "for ever still" and in which "all is present." The eternity of God, St. Augustine says, must afford Him a perspective upon the whole of time that is something like this. We are thus able to "glimpse the splendor of eternity" by imagining our own scope of attention indefinitely widened.

A definite time ago, St. Augustine believes, the world came into existence out of nothing by a free act of creation that God willed from eternity. The world has not "emanated" from God's own abundance, as Plotinus believed, by a necessary—and so beginningless—process of diffusion or overflowing. Nor has the world arisen, as Plato believed, from some raw material that God took in hand but did not Himself create. The matter of the world, formed in accordance with the forms in God's mind, did not come into being "out of" anything whatever. Matter that was formed just began to be, as God freely willed it to be, and so the world came about. As St. Augustine says, in words addressed to God:

> You created [all the things of the world] from nothing, not from your own substance or from some matter not created by yourself or already in existence, but from matter which you created at one and the same time as the things that you made from it, since there was no interval of time before you gave form to this formless matter. For the matter of heaven and earth is one thing, their form another. You created the matter from absolutely nothing and the form of the world from this formless matter. But you created both in one act. . . .

In Scripture there are seemingly incompatible statements about the Creation which St. Augustine wishes to reconcile. Ecclesiasticus, in the Apocrypha, speaks of God as having "created all things together."[9] But in Genesis it appears that God did not create all things together, inasmuch as there we are told that God made things—living things, for example—on successive "days."[10] St. Augustine proposes to harmonize these statements, at least as far as living things are concerned, by making a distinction. If we distinguish, he says, between *developed* things and *undeveloped* things, we may take it that Genesis refers only to the former, whereas Ecclesiasticus refers to both. We may suppose that in the beginning God created certain undeveloped "invisible seeds" which He "concealed in the corporeal elements of this world"—seeds that He wills to "burst forth" on subsequent "days" into developed plants and animals of various species. All things would thus have been created together, but some of them in germ, not in full flower, which then could blossom in succession, fish appearing on one "day," cattle appearing on the next, just as Genesis says. St. Augustine also refers to these invisible seeds as "original rules" or "seminal reasons" (*rationes seminales,* in Latin); they are counterparts in matter of God's ideas, making for the emergence and continuity of living species, and determining "what can come from what

---

[9]Such was the version St. Augustine knew. The American Translation has it that God "created all things alike" (Ecclesiasticus 18:1), so that the problem St. Augustine saw does not there arise.

[10]"As for these 'days,' " St. Augustine says, "it is difficult, perhaps impossible to think—let alone to explain in words—what they mean . . . since, according to Scripture, the sun was made [only] on the fourth day."

[forms of matter]." So the old Stoic notion of "seminal reasons," which Plotinus had already adapted for his own purposes, is refitted by St. Augustine for duty in a Biblical context.

God created the world and "saw that it was good," Genesis says; but because much in the world may look very evil to us, we may come to doubt or deny that a Being of infinite wisdom, power, and goodness can have created the world. St. Augustine himself, in his youth, had been attracted to the Manichees' view of the world as a field of endless combat between good and evil cosmic forces. Upon examining the writings of Plotinus, however, he began to think that an understanding of evil along Neoplatonic lines was compelling in itself and compatible with Christian doctrines. The extent to which St. Augustine's mature position on evil is indebted to Plotinus is clear in the following passages from *The City of God*—a work that St. Augustine did not start to compose until his fifty-ninth year.

Absolutely no natural reality is evil and the only meaning of the word "evil" is the privation of good. What, however, is true is that there is a hierarchy of created realities, from earthly to heavenly, from visible to invisible, some being better than others, and that the very reason of their inequality is to make possible an existence for them all. . . .

Since God is supreme being, that is, since He supremely *is* and, therefore, is immutable, it follows that He gave "being" to all that He created out of nothing; not, however, absolute being. To some things He gave more of being and to others less and, in this way, arranged an order of natures in a hierarchy of being. . . .

It is, in fact, the very law of transitory things that . . . some should be born while others die, the weak should give way to the strong and the victims should nourish the life of the victors. If the beauty of this order fails to delight us, it is because we ourselves, by reason of our mortality, are so enmeshed in this corner of the cosmos that we fail to perceive the beauty of a total pattern in which the particular parts, which seem ugly to us, blend in so harmonious and beautiful a way. That is why, in those situations where it is beyond our power to understand the providence of God, we are rightly commanded to make an act of faith rather than allow the rashness of human vanity to criticize even a minute detail in the masterpiece of our Creator. . . .

All natures, then, are good simply because they exist and, therefore, have each its own measure of being, its own beauty. . . . Beings not made for eternal life, changing for better or worse according as they promote the good and improvement of things to which, by the law of the Creator, they serve as means, follow the direction of Divine Providence and tend toward the particular end which forms a part of the general plan for governing the universe. This means that the dissolution which brings mutable and mortal things to their death is not so much a process of annihiliation as a progress toward something they were designed to become.

The conclusion . . . is that God is never to be blamed for any defects that offend us, but should ever be praised for all the perfection we see in the natures that He has made. For God is Absolute Being and, therefore, all other being that is relative was made by Him. No being that was made from nothing could be on a par with God, nor could it ever be at all, were it not made by Him.

In common with Plotinus, St. Augustine believes that reality or being admits of degrees, that goodness or perfection also admits of degrees, and that the degrees of the one correspond exactly to the degrees of the other. God, in His supreme reality, is supremely good. God's creatures, having reality of lesser degrees than God's, have correspondingly lesser degrees of goodness. The less the goodness, the more the *privation* of goodness. A privation of goodness, and only a privation of goodness, can be *evil*. It is inevitable, and no fault of God's, that His creatures should have less reality than He does, and should therefore have privations of goodness that are evils. If God's creatures had as much reality as He does, they would be "on a par with" Him—which is to say that they would not be creatures. On the one hand, no creature can be totally devoid of goodness because insofar as it has any reality at all it will have some degree of goodness. But on the other hand, no creature can be entirely free of evils, for all creatures have arisen from nothing—from utter privation of being— and traces of this, so to speak, inevitably cling to them. In the Greek philosophical tradition, it was generally taken as axiomatic that nothing can come from nothing. Plotinus conformed to this principle in maintaining that the world comes not from nothing but from the superabundant inner resources of the One. St. Augustine understands Scripture to proclaim that God freely created the world out of nothing; but he might be said to pay his respects to the traditional Greek view in holding that at least nothing *fully real* can come from nothing. Whatever is made from nothing, he thinks, is bound to suffer more or less from privation of goodness and reality.

Taking another cue from Plotinus, St. Augustine further maintains that evils—or privations of goodness—are unavoidable if the world as a whole is to be of the best. What is wanted is a hierarchy of creatures ranging from lesser to greater degrees of reality, or from greater to lesser degrees of privation. Such an ordered richness of contents is essential to a "total pattern" of the choicest beauty. Suffering and death seem deplorable to us only because we do not perceive how, in all their many forms, they have appropriate places in "the masterpiece of our Creator." It must be understood, or at any rate believed, that Divine Providence has a "general plan for governing the universe" in which evils, not unlike dissonances in music, only enhance the effect of a great cosmic harmony.

"Divine Providence," one might suppose, ought for a Christian to connote God's beneficent care for His creatures as individuals, not His employing them as means to achieve a beautiful but impersonal "total pattern." St. Augustine has often been criticized on this score. It is said that the Biblical view of Providence is actually nullified in St. Augustine's thought by his attempt to translate it into Neoplatonic terms. Plotinus did not conceive of the One, or of Intellect or Soul, as having a fatherly concern for the welfare of mortal beings. Evils, or "what we call" evils, are produced by Intellect, Plotinus says, because it is "the expression of a Reason teeming with intellectual variety," and variety without evil would be inartistic. If we are to think of Intellect as having anything analogous to human characteristics, we should think not of a father's devotion to his children but of an artist's preoccupation with strictly aesthetic values. St. Augustine would seem to imply agreement with this when he speaks of God as desiring a "hierarchy of created realities," costly as this is in "particular parts which seem ugly *to us*," including all the horrors of pestilence and famine. And it may seem only fair to ask how St. Augustine can possibly have found this understanding of God the same as the one in the Penitential Psalms he was reciting when he died. "Hear my prayer, O Lord, give ear to my supplications," says the last of these Psalms, "and of thy mercy cut off mine enemies, and destroy all them that afflict my soul: for I am thy servant." Do not one's enemies have their place in the "masterpiece of our Creator"?

St. Augustine, however, would doubtless reply that if the affliction of one's soul be part of God's plan, so may one's praying for deliverance from this evil. "Prayers," St. Augustine says, "are useful in obtaining those favors which [God] foresaw He would bestow on those who should pray for them." Not to pray for deliverance from some evil, when God foresaw that He would comply with the request, would obviously be a serious mistake. But it can hardly be supposed that there is no place in God's plan for requests He foresaw that He would *not* grant. God often does not bestow the favors for which He is asked. We may be sure, St. Augustine says, that this is always for the best, even if in given instances we cannot imagine how. "The providence of the Creator and Ruler of the world transcends human reckoning," although we can appreciate the point that if God complied with *every* request, "we might have the impression that God is to be served only for the gifts He bestows," in which case "the service of God would not make us religious, but rather covetous and greedy."

In speaking of God's foresight or foreknowledge, St. Augustine realizes that he brings up an issue troublesome to many. It would certainly appear that God must know everything that will happen, for His knowledge is infinite and infallible. But in that case God foresees every choice we will make, and this in turn would seem to imply that none of our choices is really up to us. How could we be responsible for (or free in) choosing to do A unless we *could* have chosen *not* to do A? And how could we have chosen not to do A if God, who cannot possibly be in error, knew that we *would* choose to do A? In other words, if it is impossible for God not to know that we will choose to do A, then is it not impossible for us to choose to do anything else? The answer that we should have expected from St. Augustine, in light of his analysis of God's eternity, is not in fact the one he gives. He ought to point out, but surprisingly does not, that we (and indeed he) speak very loosely in saying that God "foresees" our choices or knows what we "will" choose to do. Actually (St. Augustine should have said), God does nothing of the kind, since from the perspective of His eternity there is no future to be foreseen, no occurrence that has yet to happen. All the events in the history of the universe—past and future—are "seized and held steady" in the changeless *present* of the Divine Intelligence. So there can be no question of our choices' being necessitated by virtue of God's knowing, in advance and before we make them, what they will be. He does not know anything "in advance." His knowledge consists of what is eternally present to Him, and our choices are present to Him, all at once, *as* we make them. A difficult notion, no doubt, but is it not consistent with our being responsible for (or free in making) our choices?[11]

Appropriate as it would be for St. Augustine to take the line just indicated, what he does is something quite different. Speaking as if it were literally true that God "foresees" or "foreknows" all our choices, St. Augustine proceeds as if what he has to show is that this is not inconsistent with our choices' being causes of our actions. Our choices, as causes of our actions, belong to the "order of causes" which God "foresees" in the world. That our choices *are* causes of our actions is really guaranteed, St. Augustine says, by God's "foreseeing" them as such. Here, from *The City of God,* are the pertinent passages:

> From the fact that to God the order of all causes is certain, there is no logical deduction that there is no power in the choice of our will. The fact is that our choices fall within the order of the causes which is known for certain to God and is contained in His foreknowledge—for human choices are the causes of human acts. It follows that He who foreknew the causes of all things could not be unaware that our choices were among those causes which were foreknown as the causes of our acts. . . .
>
> Our wills have the power to do all that God wanted them to do and foresaw that they could do. Their power, such as it is, is a real power. What they are to do they themselves will most certainly do, because God foresaw both that they could do it and that they would do it, and His knowledge cannot be mistaken. . . .
>
> Our choices, therefore, are our own, and they effect, whenever we choose to act, something that would not happen if we had not chosen. . . .

[11] Such an argument was worked out, possibly under inspiration from St. Augustine, by Boethius, the Christian Neoplatonist mentioned on p. 271 and examined on pp. 318–322.

We are by no means under compulsion to abandon free choice in favor of divine foreknowledge, nor need we deny—God forbid!—that God knows the future, as a condition for holding free choice. We accept both. As Christians and philosophers, we profess both—foreknowledge, as part of our faith; free choice, as a condition of responsible living. . . .

No one sins because God foreknew that he would sin. In fact, the very reason why a man is undoubtedly responsible for his own sin, when he sins, is because He whose foreknowledge cannot be deceived foresaw that the man himself would be responsible for his own sin. No man sins unless it is his choice to sin; and his choice not to sin, that, too, God foresaw.

Assuming for a moment that it makes sense to say that God in His eternity "foresees" our choices, do St. Augustine's remarks make it clear that our choices would still be free? He holds that we are responsible for an action (or free in doing it) provided that it "would not happen if we had not chosen." He shows that there is no contradiction between (a) our not doing something unless we had chosen and (b) God's "foreseeing" that we would so choose. But does God's "foreseeing" that we would so choose imply that we *could not have chosen otherwise?* Our actions may be caused by our choices, so that our actions "would not happen if we had not chosen"; but if our choices are *unavoidable,* how can they or our actions be free? And are not our choices unavoidable if God unerringly knows, in advance and before we make them, what they will be? St. Augustine rather evades than addresses this—the most troublesome—aspect of the matter.

From St. Augustine's standpoint, however, questions of human freedom and responsibility cannot profitably be discussed in isolation from the facts, as he sees them, of sin and redemption. His actual position, it will shortly appear, is that the freedom of will possessed by us, who are descendants of Adam, is severely limited at best.

Sin and Redemption

In general St. Augustine's treatises are long-winded in the extreme, but scattered throughout them are compact statements in which his views are neatly and arrestingly crystallized. A selection of these, taken mainly from his *Confessions, Enchiridion,* and *City of God,* will represent in the liveliest way his interpretations of the familiar Christian doctrines of sin and redemption. St. Augustine's views on these subjects have had an incalculable effect upon Western religious thought; and they have been accepted or rejected, with much argumentation, by a number of important philosophers. Why they have received this amount of attention will be clear from the following:

All men are united by one purpose, temporal happiness on earth, and all that they do is aimed at this goal, although in the endless variety of their struggles to attain it they pitch and toss like the waves of the sea.

Those who try to find joy in things outside themselves easily vanish away into emptiness. They waste themselves on the temporal pleasures of the visible world. Their minds are starved and they nibble at empty shadows.

I wished no more for the manifold riches of this earth, things on which I should lose time, only to be lost in time myself.

There is no other good which can make any rational or intellectual creature happy except God.

The good things which you love are all from God, but they are good and sweet only as long as they are used to do His will. They will rightly turn bitter if God is spurned and the things that come from Him are wrongly loved.

O God of hosts . . . wherever the soul of man may turn, unless it turns to you, it clasps sorrow to itself. Even though it clings to things of beauty, if their beauty is outside God and outside the soul, it only clings to sorrow. . . . For they [things of beauty] continue on the course that is set for them and leads to their end, and if the soul loves them and wishes to be with them and find its rest in them, it is torn by desires that can destroy it. In those things there is no place to rest, because they do not last.

Man's will . . . is all-important. If it is badly directed, the emotions will be perverse; if it is rightly directed, the emotions will not be merely blameless but even praiseworthy. The will is in all of these affections: indeed, they are nothing else but inclinations of the will.

When I asked myself what wickedness was, I saw that it was not a substance [a cosmic force as the Manichees supposed] but perversion of the will when it turns aside from you, O God . . . and veers toward things of the lowest order.

Vices in the soul are nothing but privations of natural good.

The only cause of any good that we enjoy is the goodness of God, and . . . the only cause of evil is the falling away from the unchangeable good of a being made good but changeable, first in the case of an angel [Satan], and afterwards in the case of man [Adam].

By his [Adam's] sin the whole race of which he was the root was corrupted in him, and thereby subjected to the penalty of death. And so it happens that all descended from him, and from the woman [Eve] who had led him into sin, . . . were tainted with the original sin. . . .

In his [Adam's] person, human nature was so changed and vitiated that it suffers from the recalcitrance of a rebellious concupiscence and is bound by the law of death.

God, the Author of all natures, but not of their defects, created man good; but man, corrupt by choice and condemned by justice, has produced a progeny that is both corrupt and condemned.

No man is free from sin, not even a child who has lived only one day on earth. . . . If babies are innocent, it is not from lack of will to do harm, but from lack of strength.

The rule of sin is the force of habit, by which the mind is swept along and held fast even against its will, yet deservedly, because it fell into the habit of its own accord.

It may be that all men desire to be happy, but because "the impulses of nature and the impulses of the spirit are at war with one another," so that they "cannot do all that their will approves,"[12] they fall back upon what they are able to do. . . . Their will to do what they cannot do is not strong enough to enable them to do it.

It was by the evil use of his free will that man destroyed both it and himself. . . . And hence he will not be free to do right, until being freed from sin, he shall begin to be the servant of righteousness.

There is nothing else that now makes a man more miserable than his own disobedience to himself. Because he would not do what he could, he can no longer do what he would.[13] . . . Neither his spirit nor even his body obeys his will.

It is . . . no strange phenomenon partly to will to do something and partly to will not to do it. It is a disease of the mind, which does not wholly rise to the heights where it is lifted by the truth, because it is weighted down by habit. So there are two wills in us. . . .

[12] St. Augustine is quoting from St. Paul's Letter to the Galatians 5:17. It is to St. Paul that St. Augustine is most indebted for his conceptions of sin and redemption. See especially the Letter to the Romans, Chapters 5 through 9.

[13] Compare St. Paul (Romans 7:19): "For the good that I would I do not: but the evil which I would not, that I do."

A man's free choice avails only to lead him to sin, if the way of truth be hidden from him. And when it is plain to him what he should do and to what he should aspire, even then, unless he feel delight and love therein, he does not perform his duty, nor undertake it, nor attain to the good life.

There are two causes that lead to sin: either we do not yet know our duty, or we do not perform the duty that we know. The former is the sin of ignorance, the latter of weakness.

Our first parents only fell openly into the sin of disobedience because, secretly, they had begun to be guilty. Actually, their bad deed could not have been done had not bad will preceded it; what is more, the root of their bad will was nothing else than pride.

If one seeks for the efficient cause of their evil will, none is to be found. . . . An evil will is the efficient cause of a bad action, but there is no efficient cause of an evil will . . . it was made bad by itself.

The evil [of a man's evil will] arises not from the fact that the man is a nature [that is, a reality, which as such is good], but from the fact that the nature was made out of nothing.

No one . . . need seek for an efficient cause of an evil will. Since the "effect" is, in fact, a deficiency, the cause should be called "deficient." The fault of an evil will begins when one falls from Supreme Being to some being which is less than absolute. Trying to discover causes of such deficiencies . . . is like trying to see darkness or hear silence. . . .

The very defection [from God] is deficient—in the sense of having no cause.

[Nevertheless] even what is done in opposition to [God's] will does not defeat His will. For it would not be done did He not permit it (and of course His permission is not unwilling, but willing). . . .

He judged it better to bring good out of evil than not to permit any evil to exist.

As He foresaw that man would make a bad use of his free will, that is, would sin, God arranged His own designs rather with a view to do good to man even in his sinfulness. . . .

That one sin [of Adam's], admitted into a place [the Garden of Eden] where such perfect happiness reigned, was of so heinous a character that in one man the whole human race was originally and . . . radically condemned; and it cannot be pardoned and blotted out except through the one Mediator between God and men. . . .

There was need for a Mediator, that is, for a reconciler, who, by the offering of one sacrifice . . . should take away this wrath.

A mediator between God and man must have something in common with God and something in common with man. . . . Jesus Christ . . . appeared on earth between men, who are sinful and mortal, and God, who is immortal and just. Like man he was mortal: like God, he was just.

As man, he is our Mediator; but as the Word of God, he is not an intermediary between God and man because he is equal with God, and God with God, and together with Him one God.

In His one person the Word was joined with a body and a rational soul. Wherefore, so far as He is God, He and the Father are one; so far as He is man, the Father is greater than He. . . . God without beginning; man with a beginning, our Lord Jesus Christ.

Just as each individual man unites in one person a body and a rational soul, so Christ in one person unites the Word and man.

Although He Himself [Christ] had never lived the old life of sin, yet by His resurrection He typified our new life springing up out of the old death in sin.

[The preceding point, incidentally, has no small bearing upon our understanding of world history.] Some philosophers have [held that there are] cycles of time, in which there should be a constant renewal and repetition of the order of nature [so that] the world shall at fixed intervals die out, and be renewed so as to exhibit a recurrence of the same phenomena. . . . Far be it, I say, from us to believe this. For once Christ died for our sins and, rising from the dead, He dieth no more. . . . [These philosophers] know not how the human race and this mortal condition of ours took its origin, nor how it will be brought to an end [at the Last Judgment]. . . .

Baptism in Christ is nothing else than a similitude of the death of Christ, and . . . the death of Christ on the cross is nothing but a similitude of the pardon of sin. . . .

In order . . . that we might receive that love whereby we might love, we were loved while as yet we had no love ourselves.

[However,] not all, nor even a majority, are saved. . . .

It is [God's] grace alone that separates the redeemed from the lost, all having been involved in one common perdition through their common origin.

As for those who, out of the mass of perdition caused by the first man's sin, are not redeemed through the one Mediator . . . they too shall rise again, each with his own body, but only to be punished with the devil and his angels.

When reprobate angels and men are left to endure everlasting punishment, the saints shall know more fully the benefit they have received by grace. . . . For it is only of unmerited mercy that any is redeemed, and only in well-merited judgment that any is condemned.

He has predestined His chosen ones in such a manner that He Himself has even made ready the volitions of those whom He has already endowed with free choice.[14]

If this divine assistance, whereby the will is freed, were granted for its merits, it would not be a "grace"—a gratuitous gift—for it would not have preceded the willing.

O Lord . . . the good that I do is done by you in me and by your grace: the evil is my fault; it is the punishment you send me.

The grace of God [is] that by which alone men are delivered from evil, and without which they do absolutely no good thing, whether in thought, or will and affection, or in deed; not only in order that they may know by the manifestation of the same what should be done, but moreover in order that by its enabling they may do with love what they know.

Assistance was bestowed on the weakness of man's will, that it might be unalterably and irresistibly influenced by divine grace. . . .

The mercy of God is necessary not only when a man repents, but even to lead him to repent.

I have no hope at all but in thy great mercy. . . . Thou commandest continence. Grant what thou commandest and command what thou wilt!

This last passage, from St. Augustine's *Confessions,* is noteworthy for the distress it gave to one reader in particular. In the year 400 a British monk by the name of Pelagius went to Rome and was appalled at the loose conduct he saw there. An immediate reform in Roman behavior was not only imperative, he declared, but also quite feasible. The Romans needed only to try harder, much harder, to keep God's commandments. God has not commanded the impossible. With real effort, anyone can lead a more virtuous life. The popularity in Rome of St. Augustine's *Confes-*

[14]Compare St. Paul (Romans 8:29, 9:18): "For whom he did foreknow, he also did predestinate to be conformed to the image of his Son. . . . Therefore hath he mercy on whom he will have mercy, and whom he will he hardeneth."

sions, however, did not strike Pelagius as a sign that real effort was on the increase. Especially unfortunate, he felt, was this passage about continence (or sexual self-restraint) being strictly a gift of God's mercy. Can thinking that so much depends upon God be anything besides an excuse for sloth? It is, Pelagius said, "blind folly and presumptuous blasphemy" to suppose that our God-given powers are too weak by themselves for virtuous initiatives such as would merit God's support.

Following the sack of Rome in 410 by Alaric and the Goths, Pelagius shifted operations to St. Augustine's vicinity in North Africa. Between 412 and 415 St. Augustine composed no fewer than five treatises attacking the views of Pelagius. At the Council of Carthage in 417 the views of Pelagius were condemned as heretical. Some eighteen bishops who refused to denounce the Pelagian Heresy were removed from office. Pelagius himself went off to Palestine, and nothing is known of him after 418.

Meanwhile, the sack of Rome had come as a tremendous shock to citizens everywhere in the Empire. How could the city, once invincible, have become so vulnerable to attack? Those Romans who still were pagan tended to blame the many who had joined the Church. Rome succumbed to the barbarians, they said, because she had turned away from the gods who had made her great. The age-old worship of Jupiter, Juno, and Minerva had been prohibited after 391 by order of the Christian emperor Theodosius I. As early as 382 the Senate House in Rome had been divested of its altar to the Goddess of Victory. Given this kind of sacrilege, pagans said, the destruction of Rome had been simply a matter of time.

Such were the pagan allegations that prompted St. Augustine to write *The City of God.* Nearly half of this monumental volume is occupied with showing the bankruptcy of Roman polytheism and with arguing that the hardships and cruelties meted out by the Goths came from that Divine Providence Who employs war both to reform the corrupt and to test the virtuous. In the remainder of the book St. Augustine develops his interpretation (or "philosophy") of world history as a struggle between those upon whom God's grace has been bestowed and those from whom it has been withheld. These two populations constitute, spiritually speaking, two different "societies" or "cities"—the City of God (represented on earth by the true members of the Church) and the City of Satan (exemplified by Babylon and Rome). The interplay between the citizens of the two cities is the mechanism by which the great drama of history unfolds, from the Fall through the Resurrection to the Last Judgment. Thus St. Augustine advances an interpretation of world history, with a sweep of unprecedented breadth, that prefigures many attempts in more recent times to identify an underlying pattern in the vast complex of events. A few selections:

> For all the difference of the many and very great nations throughout the world in religion and morals, language, weapons and dress, there

exist no more than . . . two kinds of society, which according to the Scriptures,[15] we have rightly called the two cities. One city is that of men who live according to the flesh. The other is of men who live according to the spirit.

Two societies have issued from two kinds of love. Worldly society has flowered from a selfish love which dared to despise even God, whereas the communion of saints is rooted in a love of God that is ready to trample on self. . . . In the city of the world [or the city of Satan] both the rulers themselves and the people they dominate are dominated by the lust for domination; whereas in the City of God all citizens serve one another in charity. . . .

So long . . . as the heavenly city is wayfaring on earth, she invites citizens from all nations and all tongues, and unites them into a single pilgrim band. She takes no issue with that diversity of customs, laws, and traditions whereby human peace is sought and maintained . . . provided only that they do not stand in the way of the faith and worship of the one supreme and true God.

There is no such thing as a human heart that does not crave for joy and peace. . . . Even while waging a war every man wants peace, whereas no one wants war while he is making peace. And even when men are plotting to disturb the peace, it is merely to fashion a new peace nearer to the heart's desire; it is not because they dislike peace as such.

The peace of the political community is an ordered harmony of authority and obedience between citizens. The peace of the heavenly City lies in a perfectly ordered and harmonious communion of those who find their joy in God and in one another in God. Peace, in its final sense, is the calm that comes of order.

Sinful man hates the equality of all men under God and, as though he were God, loves to impose his sovereignty on his fellow man. He hates the peace of God which is just and prefers his own which is unjust.

[God] meant no man . . . to have dominion over man. . . . When subjection came, it was merely a condition deservedly imposed on sinful man. . . . Sin is the primary cause of servitude, in the sense of a social status in which one man is compelled to be subjected to another man. . . . Such, then, as men now are, is the order of peace. Some are in subjection to others, and while humility helps those who serve, pride harms those in power.

The heavenly City, so long as it is wayfaring on earth, not only makes use of earthly peace but fosters and actively pursues along with other

---

[15] For example, Psalm 46:4: "There is a river, the streams whereof shall make glad the city of God, the holy place of the tabernacles of the most High."

human beings a common platform in regard to all that concerns our purely human life and does not interfere with faith and worship. Of course, though, the City of God subordinates this earthly peace to that of heaven. For this is not merely true peace, but strictly speaking, for any rational creature, the only real peace. . . . When this peace is reached, man will no longer be haunted by death, but plainly and perpetually endowed with life, nor will his body, which now wastes away and weighs down the soul, be any longer animal, but spiritual, in need of nothing, and completely under the control of our will.

Although they [the two cities] are now, during the course of time, intermingled, they shall be divided at the last judgment; the first, being joined by the good angels under its King, shall attain eternal life; the second, in union with the bad angels under its king, shall be sent into eternal fire.

To tell the truth, I have no real notion of what eternal life will be like, for the simple reason that I know of no sensible experience to which it can be related. Nor can I say that I have any mental conception of such an activity, for, at that height, what is intelligence or what can it do? In heaven, as St. Paul assures us, "the peace of God . . . surpasses all understanding." Certainly, it surpasses ours.

In spite of this last passage, St. Augustine was not always reluctant to suggest, on the basis of experiences of his own, what eternal life may be like. He describes in his *Confessions* an incident that occurred in conversation with Monica, his mother. She had been with him in Milan from the time of his break (in 384) with the Manichees. In 387, following St. Augustine's conversion and baptism, they were on their way back home to North Africa. They stopped at the port of Ostia near Rome for a few days of rest before their sea voyage. At a window of their rooms, as they looked upon the garden in the courtyard below, they began to speak of "what the eternal life of the saints will be like." Their thoughts ranged from the earth to the heavens, and then to their own souls, and then "passed beyond" to the place of that Wisdom by which all things are made but which is not itself made. "And while we spoke of that eternal Wisdom, longing for it and straining for it with all the strength of our hearts, for one fleeting instant we reached out and touched it." And when they resumed their conversation, they said that eternal life must afford such a vision, not just for an instant, but changelessly and forever.

Not long afterwards, Monica took to her bed with a fever. Ostia had an evil reputation for malaria, and possibly she was infected with the disease. St. Augustine tells us only that "on the ninth day of her illness, when she was fifty-six and I was thirty-three, her pious and devoted soul was set free from the body."

CHAPTER 15

Medieval Philosophers in Profile

Between St. Augustine of Hippo and St. Thomas Aquinas, the greatest figures of European philosophy in the Middle Ages, there elapsed a period of about eight hundred years. During this long interval many thinkers appeared—Muslim and Jewish as well as Christian—who contributed to the development of philosophy in the West. Here we can survey only some of the more prominent of these thinkers, and we can consider only their most characteristic ideas.

Christian Philosophers

Boethius

In the century following St. Augustine's death, the Western territories of the Roman Empire came under the control of Germanic tribes. The leaders of these tribes generally wished not to destroy but to take over the apparatus of Roman government. Ultimately they proved incapable of maintaining the old political structures, and Western Europe was plunged into an age of social turmoil and cultural darkness. But for a time, in some regions, life went on much as usual. Italy had the good fortune to be ruled for thirty-seven years (489–526) by Theodoric the Great, king of the Ostrogoths, who respected Roman institutions, preserved Roman laws, and appointed Romans to civil offices. Theodoric chose as one of his chief ministers a cultivated Roman aristocrat by the name of Anicius Manlius Torquatus Severinus Boethius (about 480–525)—the same Boethius whom we have already noted as a prominent Christian Neoplatonist.[1] Boethius tells us that he desired a role in government because he subscribed to Plato's view that justice in a state requires philosophers at the helm. Theodoric, however, came to feel that Plato's view, insofar as it applied to Boethius, had little to recommend it. Boethius got embroiled (as he himself relates) in "bitter and irreconcilable quarrels with . . .

---

[1] See p. 271.

those in power"; and the king of the Ostrogoths was not the man to be patient with this. We cannot now determine precisely what quarrels led to Boethius' downfall, but certain it is that, around his forty-third year, he was incarcerated on a capital charge of disloyalty. Deplorable as it may have been of Theodoric, and disastrous as it was for Boethius, this event nevertheless had, as it turned out, a thoroughly beneficial result for philosophy in the Middle Ages. While in prison awaiting execution, Boethius composed *The Consolation of Philosophy;* and aside from the Bible, no volume was more highly regarded by medieval European philosophers or was more of a stimulus to their reflections. Boethius largely borrowed his arguments in the *Consolation* from Greek philosophers— especially from Plato, the Stoics, and Plotinus—and when, in Europe, not long after Boethius' death, most of the works of these philosophers dropped out of sight, the *Consolation* became one of the few sources of information about them. It remained so until the rediscovery of the Classics in the twelfth century and after.

At the start of the *Consolation,* Boethius says that he was bewailing his misfortune and wishing for death when suddenly there appeared to him a woman of majestic countenance holding a sceptre in one hand and some books in the other. This, he soon realized, was none other than Philosophy herself, come to console him in his grief and despair. In a manner that was kindly yet firm, she proceeded to question him in order to determine how his sorrow, which she viewed as a sickness, could best be treated. It came out that although Boethius did still believe the general proposition that God governs the world, he had been so distracted by his predicament that he had "forgotten" virtually everything else that he used to maintain. Philosophy then knew what she had to do. By "reminding" Boethius of certain specific truths concerning God's governance and human destiny, she would restore him to a sound and serene frame of mind.

Boethius should reconcile himself to his misfortune, Philosophy says, by reflecting that misfortune is actually better for anyone than prosperity. Misfortune, unlike prosperity, encourages one to see that true happiness depends not upon external advantages, which at any time may be taken away, but upon one's inner state of mind, for the mind is immortal and in its rationality is akin to God, who intends for it to rise above all earthly things. From this broadly Stoic line of argument, to which she devotes a good deal of attention, Philosophy passes to considerations of a more Platonic or Neoplatonic kind. We know that the objects at which most persons aim—wealth, status, bodily pleasure, and so on—will not give them the secure and complete happiness that everyone desires. Such "goods" are very imperfect. But the existence of imperfect things implies the existence of something perfect as their source: "For Nature does not take its start from what is defective and imperfect, but proceeding from the consummate and absolute, it gradually degenerates [as Plotinus maintained] into what is lower and weaker." That which is "consummate and absolute" is the highest good, or the Good, which is the highest happiness, and which must be identical with God ("than Whom nothing is better"). True happiness for us consists in our becoming as God-like as possible. With these points in mind, Philosophy says, Boethius can understand that God does not, in spite of appearances, allow the wicked (say, Theodoric) to have any real power over the virtuous (say, Boethius). The more wicked a person is, the "lower and weaker" are the goods the person goes after, and the "lower and weaker" is the person who goes after them. To have real power is to do what one wills, but to be wicked is to pursue imperfect goods that make for imperfect happiness, and no one wills to be imperfectly happy. So the wicked, in not doing what they will, have no real power (as Plato argued in his *Gorgias*). Or may it be supposed that the wicked knowingly and willingly desert the Good and stoop to evil?

> But they lose in this way [Philosophy says] not only power, but existence altogether. For those who abandon the end [God or the Good] common to all things which exist must in the same measure cease to exist. It may seem strange to some that I maintain that evil men, though constituting the majority of mankind, do not exist; yet it is true. For while I do not deny that evil men are evil, I do deny that they "are," in the pure and full sense of the term "existence." You may say, for instance, that a corpse is a dead man, but you cannot call it simply a man; in like manner I grant that wicked men are bad, but I cannot allow that they exist in the full sense. For a thing exists which keeps its proper rank in the order of being and preserves its nature; when it falls away from this nature it relinquishes also its existence, which is grounded in its nature. . . . As goodness alone can raise a man above the level of humanity (to God-likeness), so evil of necessity lowers beneath that level those whom it has ejected from their human status. The result is that you cannot hold him to be a man whom you see transformed by vices.

Boethius, surprisingly, is not quite satisfied with the conclusion that wicked people are either relatively powerless or not fully existent. It still disturbs him that God "sends hardships to the good and grants the wishes of the bad." Philosophy has to remind him that, as a creature of limited understanding, he naturally cannot expect to comprehend God's reasons for everything. He should sometimes be content with the general assurance that a good Governor orders the universe for the best. This, however, raises a further difficulty in Boethius' mind. If God orders everything, then does He not know in advance what choices we will make, and does this not make our choices necessary and unavoidable, so that we have no freedom of will? Philosophy responds with the ingenious argument that we have already mentioned in connection with St. Augustine's discussion of this problem. The *eternity* of God, she says, is "the complete possession of an endless life enjoyed as one simultaneous whole," which means that all events—past, present, and future—are in God's awareness all at once. Thus He does not know anything "in advance." He sees as present what for us is yet to come. This does not impose necessity upon our choices any more than does our awareness of someone's present activity impose necessity upon it.

A curious feature of the points that Boethius (or Philosophy) makes in the *Consolation* is the absence from them of anything distinctively Christian. Not once does Boethius even mention Christ's name; and he says nothing about the doctrines of sin and redemption, death and resurrection, in which one might have expected him, as a Christian *in extremis,* to find particular consolation. His arguments are so completely in the spirit of Greek philosophy that one would hardly guess from them that he not only was steeped in Church doctrine but had actually written treatises on the Trinity and on Christ's divine and human natures. This raises questions about the depth (or duration) of Boethius' faith, or at least about his view of the relation between pagan philosophy and Christian beliefs; but neither from Boethius nor from any source concerning him can we discover sure answers. His readers in the Middle Ages seem not to have felt that there was any problem: they evidently believed that the lessons of Philosophy in the *Consolation* were perfectly consistent with Scripture, and they let it go at that. Possibly the truth of the matter, as one authority has suggested, is that Boethius' pagan philosophy and his Christian faith "existed unmixed side by side in his thought."

As a young scholar, Boethius conceived the plan of translating into Latin the entire works of Plato and Aristotle. He further intended to show that on fundamental issues Plato and Aristotle were in agreement. Exactly how far he got with all this is uncertain; but we know that at least he managed to translate, and to write commentaries on, Aristotle's six logical treatises (in the *Organon*) and Porphyry's[2] introduction (or *Isagoge*) to one of these treatises (the *Categories*). Such was the scarcity of books in the earlier Middle Ages that virtually nothing was known of Aristotle beyond Boethius' translations of, and commentaries on, just two of the logical treatises (the *Categories* and *On Interpretation*) and the *Isagoge* of Porphyry. (Of Plato nothing was known in the early Middle Ages except an incomplete Latin translation of the *Timaeus*.) Boethius' commentary on the *Isagoge*—actually the second of his two commentaries thereon—came to have especial importance for medieval philosophers. In this work Boethius discusses some issues mentioned by Porphyry concerning the notions of genus and species. These issues, as Boethius articulates them, were to be the basis of a great controversy in the philosophical schools of the twelfth century. The controversy will be related in the section on Peter Abelard. Here it behooves us simply to observe that Boethius, the final representative of Roman philosophy in the old Greek tradition, but also the instigator of philosophizing by the "Scholastics" in

[2] Porphyry was Plotinus' pupil and successor. See p. 271.

the medieval schools, is customarily described as "the last of the Romans, and the first of the Scholastics."

John Scotus Eriugena

Not until three centuries after Boethius was there another philosopher of importance in Western Europe. John Scotus Eriugena (about 810–877) was born in Ireland and studied at an Irish monastery. (The Irish were at that time called "Scoti," and "Eriugena" meant "of the people of Erin.") Ireland, on account of its remoteness, was spared most of the warfare of the sixth, seventh, and eighth centuries; and Irish monasteries were centers of learning, notable especially for keeping up the study of Greek. Sometime in the 840s Eriugena was summoned to Paris by Charles the Bald, king of the Franks. Charles followed the example of his grandfather Charlemagne in assembling scholars in his Palace (or Palatine) School, the better to encourage a revival of learning in the great Frankish empire. Eriugena was commissioned to translate into Latin the writings of certain Greek Fathers of the Church, including the writings then attributed to St. Paul's convert, Dionysius the Areopagite, but now attributed to someone—"Pseudo-Dionysius"—of a much later date.[3] The strongly Neoplatonic interpretation of Christian doctrines given by Pseudo-Dionysius was the chief influence upon Eriugena when he began, early in the 860s, to set down his own views in an extended dialogue *On the Division of Nature*. St. Augustine, Boethius, and such Greek Fathers as Maximus the Confessor and Gregory of Nyssa also figured prominently in Eriugena's thoughts. Nevertheless, there was considerable originality in the synthesis Eriugena made of the ideas he borrowed; and against the philosophical barrenness of the era, he stands out as a thinker of exceptional energy. If we were to believe a famous story about him, however, we should have to infer that he did not always enjoy popularity as a teacher. The end of Eriugena came about, so it is said, when students in one of his courses—displeased because he "forced them to think"—stabbed him to death with their pens. But modern authorities consider this story unlikely.

Eriugena uses the term "Nature," in *On the Division of Nature*, to denote the whole of reality, including both "things that are" and "things that are not." By "things that are not" he means in part (and oddly enough) things that have a standing in reality, but a standing either above or below the level of principles we can grasp "by intellect alone" (which is the level of "things that are"). God is above this level, material objects are below, in keeping with the usual Platonic and Neoplatonic teachings. Nature, so conceived as the sum total of everything, may be "divided," Eriugena says, into four "species": (1) "Nature which creates and is not created" (a species which includes only God, the uncreated Creator), (2)

---

[3]See p. 271.

"Nature which creates and is created" (includes only the Divine Ideas, which as prototypes of creatures are lodged in the eternally begotten Word or Son, "through" Whom, the Gospel tells us, "all things were made"), (3) "Nature which is created and does not create" (includes all things "made"— angels, men, animals, plants, and so forth), and (4) "Nature which neither creates nor is created" (God again, now considered not as the originator of things but as their final destination, inasmuch as all things will ultimately be reunited, more or less, with Him).

A problem with this scheme, from the standpoint of orthodox Christianity, is that in classifying both (1) God and (3) creatures as species of the same totality ("Nature"), it seems at odds with the doctrine that God is of a wholly different order from His creatures, that He transcends them absolutely. How consistently Eriugena adhered to this doctrine is one of the main questions about him. When he argues that God is beyond our comprehension, he certainly appears to commit himself to the sharpest possible distinction between Creator and creatures. We can know *that* God is, Eriugena says, but not *what* God is. To describe the basic "what" of anything is to describe its essential characteristics, its essence or form; but as God is the *author* of all characteristics, He surpasses them all. "Goodness," "wisdom," and so on, may be affirmed of God only in metaphorical senses. Because goodness and wisdom are manifested in the world, we may conclude that the Creator of the world is *not less* than good and wise; but because goodness and wisdom are characteristics of which God is the author, we also have to conclude that He is *more* than good and wise. Eriugena follows Pseudo-Dionysius in saying that we may think of God as "*super*good," "*super*wise," and so on, provided that we understand these terms to have no positive significance beyond the idea that God surpasses description in these or any terms. Accordingly, since no terms applicable to creatures are literally applicable to God, between creatures and God there is an immeasurable distance.

This distance appears to be bridged, however, when Eriugena explains how he construes the Scriptural doctrine of Creation. He finds it illuminating in this connection to take account once again of "St. Dionysius," who advanced the thesis that, in creating all things, God *creates Himself*. Here is what Eriugena says:

> What is said "to be made" in anything is the divine nature, which is not something other than the divine will. For in [the unity or simplicity of God's nature] being is not something other than willing, but in establishing all things He sees are to be made, His being and willing are one and the same. For example, one could say that the movement of the divine will comes down to this: that those things which exist, exist. To that extent it creates all things, bringing them forth from nothing, so that they may be in being from nonbeing. On the other hand, it [God's nature] is created because except for it nothing exists essentially, for it is the essence of all things. Just as there is no natural good be-

sides it, but everything which is called good is good by participating in the highest good, so everything which is said to exist does not exist in itself, but by participating in that nature which truly exists. . . . The divine nature, being invisible in itself, reveals itself in all things which exist and consequently it is not improperly said to be made. . . . That nature which creates all things and can be created by nothing is for all that "created" in a marvelous fashion in all those things which stem from it. Just as the [human] mind's intelligence, intention, or purpose, or whatever you wish to call this innermost movement of ours, when it finds expression first in thought, then through sense images, and finally in sensible signs like words or gestures, not unreasonably can be said to be made, so too the divine essence, which as subsisting in itself transcends every intellect, can justly be said to "be created" in those things which are made by it, in it, through it, and for its sake, so that it is able to be known in these things by the intellect, if they be intellectual, or by the senses, if they be sensible, by those who investigate this essence by proper study.

In other words, since God alone is uncreated, He alone exists on His own account, which is to say that He alone exists "truly" or "essentially." Everything else exists in creaturely dependence upon His will. But His will is identical with His being[4], for in Him are no distinctions, so that dependence upon His will is dependence upon His being. Now dependence upon His being can be understood (Eriugena thinks) only as *participation in* His being. Creatures must exist by virtue of participating in God's being, in His nature or essence. And if we view the situation from God's end, we have to say that His essence is to some extent "expressed" in the creatures He causes to "stem from" it. The world of creatures is therefore a *theophany*—that is, a visible manifestation, however partial, of God's very nature. Eriugena, following Pseudo-Dionysius, is prepared to go even further: as a human intellect is actualized in thinking and speaking, so God's essence is "created" in the creatures made "in" it.

How could God possibly transcend His creatures if they exist by participating in His essence? Eriugena undoubtedly had no intention of denying God's transcendence. More than once he expresses strong agreement with the orthodox interpretation of Genesis, according to which God created all things from nothing, and which implies that God is radically other than His creatures. But Eriugena's references to the doctrine of creation from nothing occur in the course of argumentation that, as in the preceding passage, is really governed by the Neoplatonic conception of the world as an emanation from God's own superabundant inner resources. Eriugena plainly was unable to see how the world could be dependent upon God otherwise than by "participating in" God's essence, or "flowing from" it, as he says elsewhere, using another Neoplatonic met-

---

[4]Or rather with His *"super*being," for strictly speaking, of course, God is "beyond being."

aphor. In one place he suggests, having previously shied away from suggesting, that "nothing" in "creation from nothing" might actually be understood as referring to God's essence, which surpasses our powers of intellect and so may be listed first among "things that are not." Of course, this would completely reverse the sense in which the doctrine of creation from nothing was, and is, normally understood. Eriugena's indecision as to the aptness of identifying "nothing" with God is a symptom of the underlying difficulty he certainly had, and possibly felt, in reconciling the Creator in the Bible with the Good in Neoplatonic metaphysics. In fact the two, on any standard interpretation of either, are simply irreconcilable.

It is small wonder that *On the Division of Nature* was in the end condemned (in 1226 by Pope Honorius III, who described it as "pullulating with worms of heretical perversity") on the grounds that it embodied and encouraged the heresy of pantheism. If "pantheism" is understood in a wide sense to mean the doctrine that the world is a mode of God's being or essence, then there is in Eriugena, whether he intended it or not, a great deal that is distinctly pantheistic. This is not surprising in view of his esteem for Pseudo-Dionysius as one who had personally been instructed in the Faith by no less an authority than St. Paul. The error of this identification, and hence the appropriateness of "Pseudo," was not generally conceded until long after the Middle Ages; and the grand scale on which Eriugena attempted to work out a Christian philosophical theology, drawing upon what he took to be the soundest of philosophical sources, is undeniably impressive.

St. Anselm of Canterbury

Eriugena's death (in about 877) occurred when dynastic rivalries and civil wars were beginning to break up the empire of the Franks. The result was a disorganized mass of feudal principalities ill prepared to repel foreign invaders, who soon appeared in the particularly brutal form of the Scandinavian Vikings. As pagans the Vikings felt no compunction in plundering churches and monasteries, which they found easy and attractive prey. In consequence the intellectual life based upon churches and monasteries was nearly extinguished on the Continent (and was completely extinguished in Eriugena's native Ireland). It may therefore seem strange that the scene now shifts to the coastal region of France ruled after 911 by Vikings called "Normans" (or "Norsemen"); but these people rapidly assimilated the language, customs, and religion of France, and around 1040 learning in "Normandy" experienced a revival. It was in about this year that an Italian theologian by the name of Lanfranc established a school at the Benedictine monastery in the Norman town of Bec.

The school at Bec became one of the most famous of medieval schools, thanks largely to one man whom Lanfranc attracted there. This was St.

Anselm (1033–1109), an Italian of noble family who had spent a carefree youth of travel and schooling in Burgundy before ending up in Bec as a monk and a disciple of Lanfranc. During his years at Bec (1060–1093), St. Anselm composed several dialogues and treatises that won wide acclaim for him and for the school, including the *Monologion* (or *Soliloquy*) and the *Proslogion* (or *Discourse*), for which he is especially celebrated in philosophy. In 1078 St. Anselm was made abbot of the monastery. Lanfranc had been made Archbishop of Canterbury after William, Duke of Normandy, won the throne of England in 1066. When Lanfranc died, William's son and successor, the unscrupulous William Rufus, left the see of Canterbury vacant, as this gave him the use of some sizable revenues. But a severe illness caused William Rufus to repent of his sins and to conceive a strong desire to fill the vacancy with none other than St. Anselm. Expecting the worst of a monarch whose piety fluctuated with his health, St. Anselm removed to Canterbury (in 1093) only because he was coerced into doing so. Soon he was on bad terms with William Rufus and was enlisting papal support in an effort to free the Church from the king's control, particularly from the king's control over the appointment and investment of bishops. The sixteen years of St. Anselm's tenure as archbishop were crowded with controversy and with comings and goings between England and Rome. Ultimately he employed the threat of excommunication to force the king—by then Henry, brother of William Rufus—into a compromise favorable to the Church. Or so it seemed to St. Anselm. There are those who maintain that the king was really the gainer. As it worked out, the king appointed bishops and invested them with temporal powers, whereupon the archbishop invested them with spiritual powers. St. Anselm died in 1109 at the age of seventy-six. He was canonized in 1494.

St. Anselm's object in his dialogues and treatises is to arrive at conclusive arguments by which he can "understand" the Christian teachings he accepted on faith. In the spirit of St. Augustine, and of St. Augustine's (and Clement's) interpretation of Isaiah, St. Anselm insists that faith—or belief in religious truths as divinely revealed—is a precondition of understanding and of having things to understand. "I do not seek to understand that I may believe," he says, "but I believe in order to understand." So devoted to St. Augustine did St. Anselm profess himself to be that "the second Augustine" became, very aptly, a common description of him. Peculiar to St. Anselm, however, was a conviction that deductive methods of proof, as set forth in Boethius' rendering of Aristotle's logic, could provide understanding by way of "necessary reasons" for doctrines of the greatest difficulty. Thus he tries to demonstrate the truth even of such doctrines as the Trinity and the Incarnation, which most later theologians were to view as prime examples of indemonstrable matters of faith. But St. Anselm's basic plan of using logical techniques to illuminate the content of faith was followed, if not quite so far, by the Medieval Scholastics in general.

The most famous and original of St. Anselm's arguments is to be found in his *Proslogion*. There he says that he had long been in search of some one argument that would be sufficient by itself to demonstrate God's existence. In his earlier *Monologion,* St. Anselm had offered several arguments for God's existence; but he came to feel that perhaps these were excessively complicated. Could he not devise something fresh and compellingly simple? Many were his attempts to do this, and no fewer were his failures; then one day, just as he was about to abandon hope, the argument for which he had been looking suddenly "offered itself" to him. It would seem that St. Anselm had been thinking of St. Augustine's (and Boethius') notion of God as "something than which there is nothing better," when it occurred to him that this notion allows of the possibility that a being better than God, though there *is* none, might still be conceivable. Of course this possibility is hardly countenanced in Scripture.[5] So it would be more accurate to think of God not as something than which nothing *is* better but as something than which nothing *could conceivably be* better. And St. Anselm may have noticed or remembered that St. Augustine himself once spoke this way in a treatise *On the Moral Behavior of the Catholic Church and of the Manichees,* where he characterized God as a being "than which nothing better can be or be conceived" (in Latin: *quo esse aut cogitari melius nihil possit*). Such may well have been St. Anselm's reflections when his argument "offered itself." At any rate, the improved notion of God as something than which nothing better is conceivable, however and whenever St. Anselm seized upon it, is the key notion in his argument. But often he prefers to use "greater" instead of "better" and to say that God is "that than which nothing greater can be conceived" (*aliquid quo nihil maius cogitari possit*).

St. Anselm presents his argument more or less in the form of an indirect address to the "fool" of Psalm 14 who "hath said in his heart, there is no God." Surely, St. Anselm says, such a fool can hear and understand the words "that than which nothing greater can be conceived," and he will have to admit that what he understands has at least an existence as an idea in his mind or understanding. All that the fool can in this case deny is the existence *outside* of his mind or understanding of what exists in it. But can the fool really do this? Not according to St. Anselm. Here is his argument:

> [1] Hence, even the fool is convinced that something exists in the understanding, at least, than which nothing greater can be conceived. For when he hears of this he understands it, and whatever is understood exists in the understanding. [But] assuredly that than which nothing greater can be conceived cannot exist in the understanding alone.

---

[5] Where we are told, concerning "the depths of God," that "what no eye has seen, nor ear heard, nor the heart of man conceived" had perforce to be revealed to us by the Holy Spirit if we were to conceive of it at all.

For suppose that it exists in the understanding alone: then it can be conceived to exist in reality, which is greater.

[2] Therefore, if that than which nothing greater can be conceived exists in the understanding alone, [then] the very being than which nothing greater can be conceived is [after all] one than which a greater can be conceived. But obviously this is impossible. Hence, there is no doubt that there exists a being than which nothing greater can be conceived, and it exists both in the understanding and in reality.

[3] And it [that than which nothing greater can be conceived] assuredly exists so truly that it cannot be conceived not to exist. For it is possible to conceive of a being which cannot be conceived not to exist; and this is greater than one which can be conceived not to exist. Hence if that than which nothing greater can be conceived, can be conceived not to exist, it is not that than which nothing greater can be conceived. But this is an irreconcilable contradiction. There is, then, so truly a being than which nothing greater can be conceived to exist, that it cannot even be conceived not to exist; and this being thou art, O Lord, our God. . . .

[4] Whatever else there is, except thee alone, can be conceived not to exist. To thee alone, therefore, it belongs to exist more truly than all other beings, and hence in a higher degree than all the others. . . . Why, then, has the fool said in his heart, there is no God, since it is so evident to a rational mind that thou dost exist in the highest degree of all? Why except that he is dull and a fool?

It would have been more accurate to introduce these passages by saying, "Here are his arguments"; for St. Anselm actually states two arguments here, not just one as he seems to have supposed. Paragraphs [1] and [2] contain one argument, and paragraphs [3] and [4] contain another.[6] Both arguments have the same (valid) logical form, Modus Tollens:

> If p, then q.   (where "p" and "q" stand for any
> Not-q.   two propositions)
> Therefore, not-p.

Here is the argument in [1] and [2], with "NG" used to abbreviate "that than which nothing greater can be conceived":

If God as NG *does not exist* in reality but only as an idea in one's mind or understanding, then something can be conceived which is greater than NG (namely, something which *does* exist in reality and not only as an idea in one's mind or understanding).

But it is false (because contradictory) that something can be conceived which is greater than NG (which would imply that NG is *not* NG).

---

[6] [1] and [2] appear at the end of Chapter II of the *Proslogion;* [3] and [4] constitute Chapter III.

Therefore, it is false that God as NG does not exist in reality but only as an idea in one's mind or understanding.

And here is the argument in [3] and [4]:

If God as NG *can be conceived not to exist*—and so does not exist *necessarily*—in reality, then something can be conceived which is greater than NG (namely, something which *cannot* be conceived not to exist—and so *does* exist necessarily—in reality).
But it is false (because contradictory) that something can be conceived which is greater than NG

Therefore, it is false that God as NG can be conceived not to exist—and so does not exist necessarily—in reality.

Notice that the argument in [1] and [2] turns upon the notion that a thing is greater if it exists in reality than if it does not, whereas the argument in [3] and [4] turns upon the notion that a thing is greater if it *necessarily* exists in reality than if it does not. And this is a very important difference between the two arguments.

The argument in [3] and [4] has often been disregarded: and the one in [1] and [2]—reformulated in various ways—has often been called simply "Anselm's argument" (or *the* "Ontological Argument," to use the coinage of the German philosopher Immanuel Kant[7]). It seems likely, however, that despite the difference we have noted between them, St. Anselm himself regarded the argument in [1] and [2] as just a preliminary statement of the argument of [3] and [4], so that we should take the latter to be the argument he really wished to advance. The propriety of this seems especially clear from St. Anselm's answer to an objection that was raised "on behalf of the fool" by a certain Gaunilon, monk of Marmoutier. Are we seriously to suppose, Gaunilon asked, that the existence in reality of God, or that than which nothing greater can be conceived, follows from the simple thesis that a thing is greater if it exists, not only as an idea in our minds, but also in reality? Very well, Gaunilon said, then we may argue with equal justice that a lost island of surpassing bliss exists somewhere in the ocean—an island than which none greater is conceivable—inasmuch as it too is greater if it exists, not only as an idea in our minds, but also in reality. Yet who would be the greater "fool"—the man who accepts such an argument, or the man who offers it?

In answer to Gaunilon, St. Anselm says that only God is such that His nonexistence is *inconceivable*. However excellent the lost island is conceived to be, its nonexistence is still conceivable. The implication of St. Anselm's answer is that he wishes to be interpreted as holding not (as

---

[7] "Ontological" because the argument purports to prove God's existence from the concept of His nature or *being* (as that than which nothing greater can be conceived), and "ont-" derives from the Greek for "being."

[1] and [2] would have it) that a thing is conceived to be greater than otherwise if it is conceived to *exist* but (in line with [3] and [4]) that a thing is conceived to be greater than otherwise if it is conceived to *exist necessarily,* so that its nonexistence is inconceivable. It has often been said of St. Anselm that he proceeded on the basis that "existence is a perfection"—a perfection in the sense that a thing is conceived to be greater or more excellent than otherwise if it is conceived to exist[8]—but it appears that what he really wished to say was that *necessary existence* is a perfection, and of course one belonging to God alone. Why God alone? Why should not the lost island also be something whose nonexistence is inconceivable? Because, as St. Anselm explains, even the best of islands—an island than which none greater is conceivable—would have to be conceived as existing in *time.* Time is composed of distinguishable parts (hours, for example); and whatever is composed of distinguishable parts can be, St. Anselm says, "dissolved in concept"—that is, we can conceive of its having any number of its parts subtracted from it. Hence, even if we suppose that the island exists, we can still conceive of the nonexistence of any of the parts of time in which it exists, thereby conceiving of it as nonexistent in those times. Moreover, it is conceivable that, notwithstanding our memories to the contrary, there was no time before (say) twelve noon yesterday, so that even if the island has existed since then, it did not exist before. And it is conceivable that there will be no time after (say) twelve noon tomorrow, so that even if the island exists now, it will not exist after then. In general, time and everything in it (however excellent) can be conceived to have a beginning and an end, and therefore time and everything in it can be conceived not to exist before it begins or after it ends. But God, or that than which nothing greater can be conceived, cannot (St. Anselm argues) be conceived to have a beginning or an end, for whatever can be conceived to have a beginning or an end is certainly not that than which nothing greater can be conceived.

St. Anselm makes his subtlest observations in connection with the point that God could have neither beginning nor end. As it would be greater to have neither a possible beginning nor a possible end, but to exist for all eternity with absolute necessity, there could be (St. Anselm says) no possible beginning or end to that than which nothing greater can be conceived. And this is to say that if God does *not* exist, then since he could not possibly *begin* to exist, His existence would be impossible. On the other hand, if God *does* exist, then since He could not possibly *cease* to exist, His nonexistence would be impossible. But really there can be no "if" about God's existence provided that we conceive of Him as that than

----

[8] A view of which the now standard criticism was first given by the French philosopher Gassendi (1592–1665) in reference to Descartes: "Existence is a perfection neither in God nor in anything else; it is rather that in the absence of which there is no perfection. . . . Hence neither is existence held to exist in a thing in the way that perfections do, nor if the thing lacks existence is it said to be imperfect (or deprived of a perfection), so much as to be nothing."

which nothing greater can be conceived. We cannot without contradiction conceive of Him in these terms and yet not conceive of Him as existing necessarily. Such is the argument as St. Anselm develops it in his reply to Gaunilon:

> If that being [than which none greater is conceivable] can even be conceived to be, it must exist in reality. For that than which a greater is inconceivable cannot be conceived except as without beginning. But whatever can be conceived to exist, and does not exist, can be conceived to exist through a beginning. Hence what can be conceived to exist, but does not exist, is not the being than which a greater cannot be conceived. Therefore, if such a being can be conceived to exist, necessarily it does exist. . . .
>
> If it can be conceived at all, it must exist. For no one who denies or doubts the existence of a being than which a greater is inconceivable, denies or doubts that if it did exist, its nonexistence, either in reality or in the understanding, would be impossible. For otherwise it would not be a being than which a greater cannot be conceived. But as to whatever can be conceived, but does not exist—if there were such a being, its nonexistence, either in reality or in the understanding, would be possible. Therefore, if a being than which a greater is inconceivable can even be conceived, it cannot be nonexistent. . . .
>
> Hence he who conceives of a being than which a greater is inconceivable, does not conceive of that whose nonexistence is possible, but of that whose nonexistence is impossible. Therefore, what he conceives of must exist; for anything whose nonexistence is possible is not that of which he conceives.

Is it quite certain, however, that we are able to conceive of that than which nothing greater can be conceived? Gaunilon thought not. He said that the words "that than which nothing greater can be conceived" point to something so unique and incomparable that he, for one, could on hearing them detect nothing in his understanding beyond a kind of groping for their significance. He could readily conceive the nonexistence, he said, of that of which he had no more understanding than this. St. Anselm, however, felt that Gaunilon was exaggerating. Surely, St. Anselm said, we can form *some* conception of that than which nothing greater can be conceived, for otherwise we could not understand things about it as we do (the impossibility of its *beginning* to exist, for example). Cannot we compare greater and lesser goods and thereby arrive at the conception of a good than which nothing better is conceivable? And "is this not to form a notion, from objects than which a greater is conceivable, of the being than which a greater cannot be conceived?" But suppose that Gaunilon is right in saying that this being cannot be conceived. We would hardly be in a position to say this unless we could indicate what it is that cannot be conceived; and we would indicate this, as Gaunilon himself does, by using the words "that than which nothing greater can be conceived." These words, then, cannot be devoid of significance, even if we cannot comprehend what they refer to. "So when one says, 'that than which nothing greater is conceivable,' undoubtedly what is heard [the verbal description] is conceivable and intelligible, although that being itself, than which a greater is inconceivable, cannot be conceived or understood." And St. Anselm believes that the intelligibility of the verbal description is all that his argument requires.

To pursue this issue further would take us beyond St. Anselm into an investigation of problems of meaning and definition that it is best to discuss in connection with the philosophers who dealt with them. The main criticisms and defenses of the arguments of the *Proslogion* are to be encountered in St. Thomas, Duns Scotus, Descartes, Spinoza, Leibniz, Hume, Kant, and Hegel, to name only some of the notable philosophers who found it necessary to take a stand with or against St. Anselm. Like the paradoxes of Zeno, the arguments of St. Anselm have stimulated a vast amount of controversy, and they continue to do so today.

Peter Abelard

Not long after Pope Urban II launched the First Crusade to free the Holy Land from the Muslims, the young Peter Abelard came up to Paris from his ancestral château, Le Pallet, in Brittany. The year was about 1100 (nine years before the death of St. Anselm), and Abelard (1079–1142) was about twenty-one. He had decided against a military career, having acquired a consuming interest in philosophy and a powerful command of what he described as "the weapons of dialectic."[9] His sights were set on a position in Paris at the cathedral school of Notre Dame, for this was the outstanding school of the day, and Abelard was nothing if not self-confident. But in Paris the trouble with Abelard soon became clear: although an immense success with students, he as often as not made enemies of others by embarrassing them mercilessly in debate. He seldom lost an argument or an opportunity for getting into one, and so annoying was he to Church authorities that they tended to see in him only an arrogant nuisance of doubtful religious orthodoxy. To make a long story short, this "Socrates of France" (as one of his admirers characterized him) was repeatedly caused to retire from Paris and to set up schools of his own in safer places. Twice he was condemned to silence by Church councils—at Soissons in 1121, when he was forty-two, and at Sens in 1140, when he was sixty-one and already suffering from the affliction (possibly Hodgkin's Disease) of which he was to die within two years. Abelard's main antagonist at Sens was the Cistercian abbot Bernard (later St. Ber-

---

[9] Dialectic or logic was classed with grammar and rhetoric in the basic *trivium* of the standard medieval curriculum for higher education. The more advanced *quadrivium* comprised geometry, arithmetic, astronomy, and music. Beyond these lay the still more advanced studies of theology, canon law, and medicine.

nard) of Clairvaux, who viewed Abelard as a danger to the faith of young people. The suspicion that Abelard was really a skeptic in religion had been created in the minds of many Churchmen by a book called *Yes and No* (*Sic et non*) that he had written years before. There, in a manner that could not but seem impudent, he had proposed a series of 158 questions and then simply listed the conflicting answers given to them by various Church Fathers. He had said that the purpose of the book was to sharpen the wits of his young readers and to encourage them to seek for the truth. But naturally his critics condemned the book as skeptical in intent and as subversive of respect for religious authority. (A certain Peter Lombard [1100–1160] subsequently produced a volume called *Sentences* in which he followed Abelard's scheme but tried to reconcile the Fathers. This became a standard textbook of theology, whereas Abelard's *Yes and No* was burned after the Council at Sens.)

Abelard's misfortunes, of which he wrote the story in his *Historia calamitatum,* included a cruel assault upon his person. During his heyday in Paris, when he was about thirty-five, he fell in love with Heloise, the young niece of a canon of Notre Dame. She reciprocated and soon was pregnant. A son was born. A secret marriage was arranged with, as they believed, the consent of the uncle. In fact the uncle was furious and heaped abuse upon Heloise for continuing to see Abelard. Abelard removed Heloise from the uncle's house and placed her in a convent for safekeeping. The uncle took revenge by ordering his henchmen to break into Abelard's room one night and to castrate him.

Heloise became a nun and Abelard a monk. The letters they exchanged in later years constitute some of the most famous correspondence in history. Here is a sample, from one of her letters to him:

> The pleasures of lovers which we shared have been too sweet—they can never displease me, and can scarcely be banished from my thoughts. Wherever I turn they are always there before my eyes, bringing with them awakened longings and fantasies which will not even let me sleep. Even during the celebration of the Mass, when our prayers should be purer, lewd visions of those pleasures take such a hold upon my unhappy soul that my thoughts are on their wantonness instead of on prayers. I should be groaning over the sins I have committed, but I can only sigh for what I have lost. Everything we did and also the times and places are stamped on my heart along with your image, so that I live through it all again with you.

Abelard's importance in philosophy, however, derives mainly from his role in the medieval controversy over universals. A universal is that which may be common to many particular things. The medieval controversy, stimulated in large part by certain passages in Boethius, concerned that which is common (and peculiar) to the members of a species and to the species within a genus. A species such as *human* has individuals such as

Socrates and Plato as its members. What sort of thing do these individuals have in common, so that they belong to the same species? A genus such as *animal* includes species such as *human, horse,* and *dog*. What sort of thing do these species have in common, so that they belong to the same genus? And how is "in common" to be understood in this connection? These were the basic issues in the controversy.

Boethius, in the second of his commentaries on Porphyry's *Isagoge* (Introduction to Aristotle's *Categories*), called attention to a passage in which Porphyry asks, without venturing to decide, whether genera and species are more than figments of the mind, and if they are, whether they are corporeal or incorporeal, and whether they exist in or apart from sensible particulars. In effect Porphyry is asking about the nature and status of universals—the common elements—by virtue of which individuals are classified into species and species are included within genera. Abelard's contribution was to revive and give currency to something like Aristotle's answers to these questions. Boethius had outlined Aristotle's answers (without committing himself to them), but for long their merits were unrecognized by medieval thinkers (as they seem to have been unrecognized by Boethius, whose *Consolation* follows Plato in such matters).

The earlier medieval thinkers were prone to reason as follows. In saying "Socrates is a human" and "Plato is a human," we say the same thing about both Socrates and Plato. "Human," in other words, has the same meaning in both statements. But "human" could not have the same meaning in both statements unless in both it stood for one and the same thing. And this one thing for which "human" stands must be something that actually exists, not something that is just a figment of the mind, or else the statements in question could not be (as they plainly are) objectively true. Of course, "human" stands for a *species*—the species rational animal (to state humankind's form or essence or nature). This species, then, must have actual existence as *one thing*. It must be a single independent reality, that is, it must be one *substance,* of which individual humans are manifestations or modifications—"accidental" modifications in the sense that men differ from one another not in their fixed underlying essence or nature (rational animal) but only in their variable surface accidents (height, weight, color, location, and so on). That which is common (and peculiar) to all the individuals denoted by "human"—the universal in question—is this unitary substance of which they all partake, or in which they all share. And so it is with any other term, say, "horse" or "dog," that denotes a species of creatures. That which is common to the members of any species is the unitary substance of the species itself, which constitutes the nature or essence of the members. A similar process of reasoning establishes that *genera* are unitary substances of which species are modifications. In "a human is an animal" and "a horse is an animal," the predicate "animal" stands for the same reality—the genus animal of which human and horse partake. That which is common (and peculiar) to the species of any genus—the universal in question—is the unitary substance of the genus itself, which constitutes the nature or essence of the species.

Extreme Realism is the name given to the view that universals have objective reality as unitary things (substances). Plato advocated a type of Extreme Realism in arguing that what individuals of a kind have in common is a relation to a single *form* that exists apart from them and of which they are, so to speak, copies. The early medieval type of Extreme Realism differed from Plato's in taking universals to be forms (or essences or natures) not separate from individuals of a kind but manifested therein in something like the way in which the same underlying bone structure can be manifested in different faces. A defect of this analogy is that no two faces have literally one and the same bone structure; that is, there is no question of a *numerical* identity of structure, only of a close similarity; whereas this type of Extreme Realism holds that different individuals are manifestations of literally one and the same form, essence, or nature. This may seem a very strange view. It may help to remember that it was motivated by the belief that a general term such as "human" must stand for *one* objective reality if it is to mean the same thing when predicated of different individuals.

A problem with Extreme Realism, from the orthodox Christian point of view, is that it leads naturally to pantheism. If individuals are manifestations of species, and if species are manifestations of genera, then if there is *one all-embracing genus,* everything else is a manifestation of it. Suppose we maintain that *Being* is the all-embracing genus, inasmuch as what is common to all the things of the world—individuals, species, and narrower genera included—is that they exist or have Being. Extreme Realism would then have us view Being as the unitary substance of which all other things are manifestations. Another short step would bring us to identify Being with God on the grounds that Being is the source of all other things, which is what God is. We would then view the world as a theophany, as a manifestation of God, adopting pantheism and rejecting the Scriptural teaching that God radically transcends His creatures. Eriugena was led into pantheistic modes of thought, or at least of expression, because some such line of reasoning was invited by the Extreme Realism of the Neoplatonic sources he regarded so highly.

Despite its pantheistic tendencies, Extreme Realism was long believed to be compatible with, or even required by, certain doctrines of the Church. Consider the doctrine of Original Sin as formulated by St. Augustine: "By [Adam's] sin the whole race of which he was the root was corrupted in him, and thereby subjected to the penalty of death." How could Adam's sin be inherited by his descendants? Extreme Realism readily furnishes an answer: all human beings are manifestations of the same human nature or essence, accidental modifications of the unitary substance of humankind; the sin of Adam corrupted this substance, so that each new member of the species, as he or she is conceived, inherits the corruption. Such a view is especially associated with a man called Odo, who was

Bishop of Cambrai (and died in 1113). Another doctrine believed to be illuminated by Extreme Realism was the doctrine of the Trinity, according to which Father, Son, and Holy Spirit are three Divine Persons but are also one God. This gains in intelligibility, it was argued, if we understand that what Father, Son, and Holy Spirit have in common—their Divine Personhood—is a unitary substance, much as what the multitude of humans have in common—their nature or essence, rational animal— is a unitary substance. (The Nicene Creed of the Church, as formulated in 374, declares that the Son is "of one substance with the Father.") St. Anselm appears to have maintained such a position, although the correct interpretation of him on this point is controversial.

There came a reaction to Extreme Realism toward the end of the eleventh century. The instigator of this is usually considered to have been Roscelin (about 1050–1120), a teacher of logic in several French schools and probably one of the teachers of Abelard. Because his treatises have been lost, and because testimony about them is scanty, Roscelin's precise views are difficult to determine. But it is clear that he rejected the notion that genera and species are unitary substances. Perhaps he did so for the reason—found in Aristotle's *Categories*—that unitary substances cannot be predicates, but only subjects of predication; so that animal and human, which are predicates, cannot be unitary substances. In saying "Socrates is a man," Aristotle held, we do not attribute to Socrates a *thing* (a unitary substance) called "man"; we attribute to him a complex *characteristic* (a predicate)—humanity. At all events, Roscelin had a strong conviction that independent existence belongs only to concrete individuals (such as Socrates and Plato), not to that which may be common to concrete individuals (such as humanity). He may even have denied, as against Aristotle, that concrete individuals have characteristics in common. So extreme a position is implied, on the face of it, by a statement reported of him to the effect that "universals are merely *word sounds.*" This seems to mean that nothing is really common to any group of individuals named by a general name (such as "humans") except the uttering of that name in reference to all of them. The individuals would in that case certainly not have it in common that they were all manifestations of one and the same substance; but they would also not even have any characteristics in common. All that they would have in common is their being called by the same name. If this is what Roscelin believed, then he was a proponent of an extreme form of what is called *Nominalism* with respect to universals (from *nomina,* the Latin for "names"), according to which actual existence belongs not to universals but only to individuals, which have nothing whatever in common aside from the general names that may be given to groups of them. One problem with this position, as it stands, is that it does not allow of any *reason* for giving a name to a group of individuals. Why, for instance, should a group have been given the general name "human" if nothing were common to the members of the group before they were so named (and nothing were common to them afterward except their being so named)? And why view them as members of a distinctive group (or species) in the first place? Another problem, which some of Roscelin's critics believed he ran into, concerned the Trinity. How could three Persons be one God if individuals in general (that is, Divine Individuals included) have nothing in common except names? Would not the three Persons in fact be three separate Gods? Roscelin is said to have denied (successfully as far as Church authorities were concerned) that anything of the kind was implied by his position. For all we know about his position, however, there may well have been justice in the accusation of "Tritheism."

Meanwhile, in spite of Roscelin's criticisms, the advocates of Extreme Realism continued to promulgate the "Old Doctrine" (*antiqua doctrina*), as Abelard called it. William of Champeaux, who died as bishop of Châlons in 1120, was an outstanding case in point. Abelard encountered him in Paris at the time when William was teaching at the cathedral school. Mindful probably of the lessons of Roscelin and of the pertinent passages in Boethius, Abelard objected to William's version of the Old Doctrine on the grounds that it violated an old principle—the principle that nothing can have contrary characteristics at the same time. William, like his predecessors, wished to maintain that one and the same substance of animal, for example, is manifested in the several species of the genus—in horse as well as in human. But if that were so, Abelard pointed out, animal would have contrary characteristics at the same time: it would be *irrational* because it would constitute the nature of horse, and it would be *rational* because it would also constitute the nature of human. William, like his predecessors, wished also to maintain that one and the same substance of human, for example, is manifested in the several members of the species—in Socrates as well as in Plato. But this would entail, as Abelard also observed, that one and the same thing, human, would be in different places at once: it would be where Socrates is because it would constitute his nature; and at the same time it would be where Plato is because it would also constitute his nature. Or inasmuch as Socrates would manifest numerically the same substance as Plato, he would be identical with Plato; and then Plato would be in two places at once. Absurd consequences such as these, which can be multiplied at will, demonstrate the falsity of Extreme Realism. "It is manifest," Abelard says in his *Glosses on Porphyry,* "that the opinion in which it is held that absolutely the same essence [or nature] subsists at the same time in diverse things, lacks reason utterly."

William responded to Abelard's criticisms by modifying his theory. He now said that individuals belong to a species not by virtue of manifesting an identical nature but by virtue of *not* manifesting *different* natures. The species consists of a unitary substance that is present in its members in a state of "undifferentiation" (*indifferenter*), so that the members may be regarded as the same, not "essentially," but "indifferently." What precisely William meant by this is hard to tell. He may have meant that

Socrates and Plato represent not numerically the same thing but two exactly *similar* things, as far as their basic human nature is concerned. If so, he did indeed modify his theory. Otherwise Abelard was probably correct in his charge that William's new position differed only verbally from his old one.

In the early part of the twelfth century, we find departures from Extreme Realism, less equivocal than William's, by thinkers who saw the force of criticisms such as Abelard's. Joscelin of Soissons maintained that a species is simply a *collection* of individuals. Walter of Mortagne and Adelard (not Abelard) of Bath maintained that to speak of genera and species is to refer to *states* or *aspects* of individuals. These and other views (too numerous to mention) were attempts to reconcile the Nominalist thesis that actual existence belongs only to individuals with the Extreme Realist thesis that genus and species are notions having an objective basis. But the most satisfactory compromise between the claims of Nominalism and of Extreme Realism was the one—reminiscent of Aristotle—arrived at by Abelard himself.

In his *Glosses on Porphyry,* Abelard accepts Aristotle's definition of a universal as "that which is of such a nature as to be predicated of many." The absurd consequences of Extreme Realism, as Abelard has spelled them out, show that what can be predicated of many is certainly not a *thing* (a unitary substance). The only alternative, Abelard believes, is to understand "what can be predicated of many" as referring to certain *words*—"universal words" such as "animal" and "human." But Abelard does not mean to subscribe to the view (possibly advanced by Roscelin) that what can be predicated of individual humans, for example, is merely the spoken word "human." Such an extreme of Nominalism fails to take into account that a spoken word is itself a kind of *thing*—a sound in the air—and no thing can be predicated of another thing. ("Socrates is a sound in the air, namely, the sound of 'human' " is plainly a confusion.) Abelard's position, at its clearest in the second edition of his *Glosses,* is that "what can be predicated of many" refers to the *significance* or *meaning* of a universal word. And this meaning, according to Abelard, consists in a *universal idea* or *conception* associated with a universal word.

A universal conception is obtained, Abelard says, by abstracting from particular things a "general and indiscriminate image" of some characteristic they are alike in possessing. Such an image is "indiscriminate" in the sense that it contains nothing that discriminates, or distinguishes, between particular things having the characteristic. A general and indiscriminate image of rational animality, for instance, can be abstracted in reflection upon basic likenesses between individuals; and so we come by a meaning for "human" that can be "predicated of many" without discriminating between individuals. This meaning is unitary and distinct from individuals; but it is a conception of ours, not an independent thing of which individuals are "copies" or "accidental modifications." From the standpoint of individuals, rational animality is an essential characteristic or form that is "fused together" with their bodily substance. This characteristic is numerically different in each instance. That is, each person has his or her own essence (or form or nature) of rational animality; there is not a numerically identical essence in which everyone somehow "shares" or "participates." The rational animality of Socrates is one affair, and the rational animality of Plato is another affair. Socrates and Plato are, however, exactly *alike* in respect of rational animality; and it is this *likeness* that is abstracted to constitute the universal conception associated with the word "human."

Abelard is aware that he may appear to be open to one criticism especially. It is likely to be said that his account of universal conceptions really makes them false or empty. Any conception in which something is viewed otherwise than it exists is false or empty; and according to Abelard, a universal conception is one in which a characteristic that exists only as particularized in a multiplicity of individuals is abstracted therefrom and viewed (otherwise than it exists) as a unity separate and apart. On Abelard's theory, then, universal conceptions are false or empty. It would have been better for him to have reflected more carefully upon the merits of Extreme Realism, according to which there exist unitary essences of "human," "animal," and so on, exactly corresponding to our universal conceptions. In answer to this, Abelard says that there is an all-important difference between considering something *separately* and considering it as *separated*. By a process of abstraction we consider rational animality, for example, *separately* from the individuals of whom it is the essential characteristic; but this does not mean that we have to consider rational animality as something actually *separated* from individuals. We need do nothing of the sort; and if we do not, then we do not view things "otherwise than they exist" in such a way as to fall into error. Extreme Realists are right to maintain that if our universal conceptions are not to be false or empty, they must correspond to objective realities. But these objective realities cannot be supposed to be unitary things distinct from individuals, for this notion leads to absurdity. It is quite enough that these objective realities are the likenesses of essential characteristics that actually exist between the objects of our experience. This kind of *Moderate Realism* (for such is the name usually given to theories of the Abelardian type) provides for the accuracy of universal conceptions, and of the notions of genus and species formed from universal conceptions, by holding that they are simply abstractions of the real similarities to be found among the creatures of the world. *Why* creatures exhibit similarities enabling us to classify them into species and genera is a question to which Abelard is content to give the orthodox answer. God created and sustains the world according to patterns of species and genera which are *ideas* in His mind (not independent substances of the sort in which Extreme Realists believe).

Extreme Realism lingered on after Abelard passed from the scene, but he had dealt it a mortal blow. Moderate Realism became the reigning doctrine; and it was generally believed, with Abelard, that a universal—or that which may be common to many particular things—has a threefold status: "before" things (*ante rem*) as a pattern in God's mind; "in" things (*in re*) as a characteristic in which things are alike; and "after" things (*post rem*) as a universal conception formed in our minds by abstracting the likeness. But this particular way of putting the matter was not Abelard's; it was borrowed from the Muslim philosopher Avicenna, who will be before us shortly.

Muslim Philosophers

In 570, some 140 years after St. Augustine's death, the prophet Muhammad was born in the Arabian city of Mecca. Orphaned at an early age, brought up by relatives, Muhammad went to work in the caravan trade and in time became the agent of a wealthy widow named Khadija. On business for her, he traveled often to Syria and Palestine, where probably he came into contact with Jews and Christians. So favorable was Khadija's impression of Muhammad in all respects that she married him in 596, whereupon he, now a man of substance, retired from mercantile activity. An incident some years earlier, in which Muhammad settled a dispute between three sheiks in the temple at Mecca, had prompted him to think that he might have the gifts to become a religious leader. The prevailing polytheism of Arabia had long seemed to him superstitious and uncivilized—an encouragement to vice and to the vendettas that were a conspicuous feature of the tribalism of the region. Khadija's wealth enabled Muhammad to direct all his energies to the pursuit of spiritual truth, and he began to frequent a lonely spot in the vicinity of Mecca for solitary prayer and meditation. There messages came to him from a voice he identified as that of the Archangel Gabriel. The burden of these messages was that there is no God but Allah [10] and that Muhammad is His prophet—last and greatest, or "the Seal," of a series of prophets including Abraham, Moses, and Jesus. Muhammad was given to understand that it is sacrilegious of Christians to think that in the absolute unity of God there could somehow be a Trinity of Persons. Except for himself, Muhammad believed, no one had been favored with a fuller revelation of God's will than Jesus. But Muhammad also believed that to attribute divine status to any human being is inconsistent with recognizing that all are equally bound to surrender or submit themselves unconditionally to Allah. This surrender or submission, and the perfect peace that comes with it, is what "Islam" means. It was the religion of Islam that Muhammad believed himself called to establish, and he began to preach accordingly.

[10]"Allah" derives from the Arabic *al* ("the") and *Illah* ("God"). Thus, "There is no God but Allah" means "There is no God but *the* God."

As far as the powerful aristocrats of Mecca were concerned, Muhammad's preaching was simply a menace to the status quo, and they plotted to do away with him. In the nick of time, Muhammad and a companion fled from Mecca and went north to Medina. The year (622) of this Flight (the *Hegira*) was adopted as the beginning of the Muslim[11] calendar, for then commenced Muhammad's astounding success, initially at Medina and subsequently back at Mecca, in unifying the Arabian tribes into a strong Muslim commonwealth. The momentum of religious fervor he imparted to his followers was such that, within a century of his death (in 632), they had seized for Islam virtually all the inhabited lands from India through North Africa to Spain. The entire Western world might today be ruled by Muslims had not their conquest been halted in 732 at Tours, about 120 miles southwest of Paris, by the Franks under Charles Martel. But there was never any truth to the old allegation that Jews and Christians who came under Muslim rule were forcibly converted to Islam. In fact one reason for the Muslims' rapid territorial gains was the tolerance they displayed toward Jews and Christians, whom Muhammad classed with Muslims as "peoples of the Book" on account of the large measure of authentic Revelation he detected in the Old and New Testaments. Muhammad's successors—the sovereign *caliphs*—allowed Jews and Christians to practice their faiths on payment of a tribute.

No very intricate system of doctrines was communicated by Muhammad. The revelations vouchsafed to him over twenty-three years, as reported in Islam's bible, the Koran, stress the unqualified oneness, power, knowledge, and benevolence of Allah; the perfection of the world Allah has created; the accountability of persons for their deeds; and the judgment to be rendered by Allah on a day of reckoning, when one's eternal happiness will hang in the balance. Whether one will be sent to Heaven or to Hell will depend upon whether one has followed in this life the "straight path" indicated by what came to be called the Five Pillars of Islam, namely, (1) recital with conviction of the Confession of Faith ("There is no God but Allah, and Muhammad is His prophet"), (2) constancy in praying (normally five times a day), (3) almsgiving (2½ per cent of one's capital annually), (4) fasting from sunrise to sunset during the month of Ramadan (commemorating Muhammad's call to prophecy as well as the Hegira), and (5) pilgrimage to Mecca at least once in one's lifetime (health and finances permitting).

These clear and simple teachings, however, were soon given a complicated new setting by Muslim thinkers imbued with Greek philosophical ideas. Before the rise of Islam, there were already Christian schools in Mesopotamia, Persia, and Syria at which the study of Greek philosophy and science was kept up. In the eighth and ninth centuries, the Muslim caliphs who ruled these regions ordered translations to be made of the

---

[11] "Muslim" is the adjective corresponding to "Islam" as well as the name for an adherent of Islam.

Greek texts into Arabic; and so it happened that Muslim thinkers had access to works of Plato and Aristotle at a time when Christian thinkers in Europe did not. (When these works did finally reappear in Western Christendom, beginning in the twelfth century, it was thanks mainly to Muslim sources in Sicily and Spain.) Aristotle was of particular interest to Muslim philosophers, but they tended to read Aristotle as if he were a Neoplatonist. They did this partly because they possessed Greek commentaries on Aristotle that interpreted him Neoplatonically, and partly because they mistakenly believed that Aristotle was the author of two works actually of Neoplatonic origin—the so-called *Theology of Aristotle* (really an abstract of three of Plotinus' *Enneads*) and the *Book of Causes* (really an abstract of a work by Proclus, the Athenian systematizer of Neoplatonism from whom Pseudo-Dionysius borrowed). Geographically the Muslim philosophers fell into two groups, an earlier group in Baghdad and a later group in Spain. The group in Baghdad included Al-Kindi (about 800–870), Al-Razi (died in 923 or 932), Al-Farabi (875–930), Avicenna (or Ibn Sīnā, 980–1037), and Algazali (or Al-Ghazālī, 1058–1111). The group in Spain included Ibn Masarrah (883–931), Ibn Bājjah (about 1070–1138), Ibn Tufayl (1100–1184), and Averroes (or Ibn Rushd, 1126–1198). Here the outstanding figure in each group, Avicenna and Averroes, will be considered. Algazali will also be taken into account, because he was the most notable critic of attempts to interpret Muslim doctrines from the standpoint of a Neoplatonized Aristotelianism.

Avicenna

Avicenna (Abū 'Ali al-Husayn ibn Sīnā, to give him his Arabic name) was born in 980 of Persian parents in a village near Boukhara, now Buchara in southern Russia. One of the most precocious children on record, he had assimilated virtually all existing knowledge and had begun to practice medicine by the time he was sixteen. Philosophy presented him with just one obstacle—the *Metaphysics* of Aristotle, which he read forty times, we are told, without making sense of it. Luckily he found a commentary of Al-Farabi's that enabled him to understand Aristotle's arguments; and as it turned out, a large number of Avicenna's metaphysical views were adaptations of Aristotle's. Avicenna had a checkered career as physician and minister (or *vizier*) to various provincial potentates in the Caliphate of Baghdad. Through all his political ups and downs (which included a term of imprisonment) he steadfastly pursued his philosophical and scientific investigations, writing more than a hundred treatises in Persian and Arabic on logic, mathematics, physics, medicine, and metaphysics, among other subjects. A Latin translation of his chief medical treatise, *The Canon of Medicine,* was in Europe the standard reference in the field down to the seventeenth century. His most important philosophical work, *The Book of Healing* (healing for the soul, that is), was partly translated into Latin and had a powerful effect upon Christian philosophers in the thirteenth century. In the Muslim world his influence during the Middle Ages was great. Avicenna died in 1037 at the age of fifty-seven while accompanying the Emir of Ispahan on a military expedition.

Avicenna subscribed to Aristotle's view of metaphysics as the study of "Being as Being." From a suggestion of Plotinus', he developed an ingenious illustration of the thesis that Being is a primary and inescapable idea. This occurs as part of Avicenna's celebrated Argument of the Flying Man. Avicenna asks us to imagine a man suddenly created with full powers of understanding but floating in empty space in such a way (blindfolded, and so on) that he can perceive nothing through his senses, not even his own body. The man would still know, Avicenna insists, that he exists or has Being; and this shows that Being is an idea of the most basic type, acquired willy-nilly through self-consciousness, if not through sense-experience (which incidentally we see not to be necessary to self-consciousness).

"Being" in the fullest sense, however, applies for Avicenna only to God or Allah, since to Him alone it belongs, in virtue of His very nature or essence, to exist *necessarily*. The creatures of the world, in all their many species, have being of a lower order, since their existence is not necessary but only *possible* as far as their own natures or essences are concerned. For them, but not for God, essence and existence are two different things: *what* any species essentially is (its essence) does not of itself determine *that* it is (its existence). For example, we cannot tell whether some species of bird exists just by considering a definition giving the characteristics supposedly constituting its nature or essence. It is one question what the essential characteristics are of any species of creature, and it is another question whether there ever were, or still are, any actual members of the species. But if no species of creature exists by virtue of its own nature, how is it that species exist nevertheless? Avicenna sees nothing to recommend the answer that one species is produced by another, which in turn is produced by another, and so on perhaps indefinitely. All species are merely possible in themselves, and no relations between them can explain why they do not all remain mere possibilities instead of becoming actualities. The only explanation, Avicenna says, is that something must *necessarily* exist that actualizes the possible existence of creatures. Of course, Avicenna holds that this Necessary Being is God. The existence of any species of creature (only possible in itself) must ultimately be explained, Avicenna argues, by reference to a Divine Cause whose nonexistence is strictly impossible.

This line of argument was to be borrowed by several Jewish and Christian thinkers, notably by Maimonides and St. Thomas. A result of it, in Avicenna's case, was that it led him to diverge from orthodox religious doctrines. Having concluded that God exists necessarily, and so without beginning, Avicenna was not prepared to suppose that any of God's attributes could be other than necessary and without beginning. Thus he maintained that the attribute of being the world's Creator belongs necessarily to God, so that there could be no beginning to, and no free choice in, God's creating the world. The world, then, must have existed from eternity, contrary to what the Koran teaches, and nothing about the world could have been created differently. And in line with this, Avicenna says that every created species, though not necessary by virtue of its own nature or essence, *is* necessary by virtue of its being part of a world-system that God could not have created otherwise. Moreover, within the world system, each particular thing or event is linked into a chain of causes and effects, which chain is necessarily what it is because the Necessary Being necessarily produces it.

Actually God does not, according to Avicenna, produce the world *directly*. In Neoplatonic fashion, Avicenna conceives of the world's multiplicity as emanating from the unity of God through a series of intermediary Intelligences. The last and lowest of these Intelligences, associated with the sphere of the moon, is responsible for the world of terrestrial matter with its forms, and it also has the function of actualizing the human potential for knowledge. From some ambiguous remarks of Aristotle's,[12] Avicenna generates an imposing theory to the effect that it is this lunar Intelligence, also known as the Agent Intelligence, that enables us (after suitable sense-experience) to grasp the forms of things in abstraction from their matter. The Agent Intelligence is said to "illumine" our minds by "radiating" forms into them, thus providing us with the universal conceptions upon which our knowledge depends. But Avicenna, unlike Aristotle, does not view the impersonal Agent Intelligence as so much responsible for our thoughts that we have nothing of our own, so to speak, that could survive the death of our bodies. He does believe in the immortality of individual souls, although he tends to interpret the graphic Muslim doctrines of Heaven and Hell as referring to extremes on the scale of theoretical knowledge.

That we have souls capable of existing apart from our bodies is shown, Avicenna believes, by the Argument of the Flying Man. The Flying Man knows that he exists, though he has no awareness of his body or indeed of anything else having the properties of space. In other words, he conceives of himself (of his *self*) without conceiving of anything material; so that in affirming the existence of himself, he does not affirm the existence of anything he conceives to be material. On the general principle that "what is affirmed is *other than* what is not affirmed," Avicenna concludes that the self whose existence the man affirms is other than something material—that the self is a thing *immaterial* in nature or essence. This immaterial thing, the man's soul, obviously *may* exist apart from whatever is *other than* it—the man's body and material things in general.[13]

---

[12] See the discussion of Aristotle's distinction between passive and active intellect on pp. 151–152.

[13] Descartes, particularly in the Second and Sixth of his *Meditations,* argues for a radical distinction between mind and body in a way that may indirectly be indebted to this argument of Avicenna's.

The possibility of the soul's immortality is thus established, but for all of us, not just for the Flying Man. He is simply a graphic illustration of what is true of us; for although we have sense-experience of our bodies, which he does not, we can still conceive of ourselves without conceiving of our bodies, or of anything else having the properties of space. We must so conceive of ourselves, according to Avicenna, if we would understand our ability to have such basic concepts as those of Being, necessity, and possibility. These concepts are perfectly simple in that they cannot be divided or analyzed into component concepts (as the concept of horse can be analyzed into "large solid-hoofed herbivorous mammal with long mane and tail"). An indivisible concept, Avicenna argues, could not be received in one's soul if that were something material, for whatever is in something material is divisible.[14] Everyone's soul, then, must be immaterial and hence capable of existing apart from the body.

An even stronger conclusion may be obtained, Avicenna says, by reflecting upon the soul's immateriality. We can show not only that the soul is capable of surviving the body's demise but that it must do so. As something immaterial, the soul is not divisible into parts; it is unitary and simple in its incompositeness. And since it is unitary and simple, the soul cannot have in its essence two different things such as (a) the actuality of persistence before the body dies and (b) the potentiality of corruption when the body dies. Here, in characteristically abstract and technical style, is how Avicenna argues:

> Everything which might be corrupted through some cause has in itself the potentiality of corruption and, before corruption, has the actuality of persistence. But it is absurd that a single thing in the same sense should possess both, the potentiality of corruption and the actuality of persistence; its potentiality of corruption cannot be due to its actual persistence, for the concept of potentiality is contrary to that of actuality. . . . These two concepts, then, are attributable to two different factors in the concrete thing. Hence we say that the actuality of persistence and the potentiality of corruption may be combined in composite things [such as a body]. . . . But these two concepts cannot come together in simple things [such as a human soul]. . . . I say in another absolute sense that these two concepts cannot come together in a simple thing whose essence is unitary. This is because everything [such as a body] which persists and has the potentiality of corruption also has the potentiality of persistence, since its persistence is not necessary. When it is not necessary, it is possible; and possibility is of the nature of potentiality. Thus the potentiality of persistence is in its very substance. But, of course, it is clear that the actuality of persistence of a thing is not the same as its potentiality of persistence. Thus its actuality of per-

---

[14] It may be said that an indivisible concept could be received in some indivisible *point* of a material soul; but Avicenna replies that a point is nothing but the extremity of a line, and any line is divisible.

sistence is a fact which happens to the body when it has the potentiality of persistence. Therefore that potentiality does not belong to something actual but to something of which actual existence is only an accident and does not constitute its real essence. From this it necessarily follows that its [the body's] being is composed of a factor the possession of which gives actual existence to it (this factor is the form in every concrete existent), and another factor which attains this actual existence but which in itself has only the potentiality of existence (and this factor is the matter in the concrete existent).

So if the soul is absolutely simple and is not divisible into matter and form [and of course its simplicity and immateriality have already been demonstrated], it will not admit of corruption.

Very well, but Muhammad did not teach merely that the soul is incorruptible. He was given to understand that everyone would be resurrected from the dead in body as well as in soul. The Koran could hardly be more explicit about this: "The trumpet shall be blown; and behold, from their graves unto the Lord shall they slip out. . . . Verily, the pious shall be in gardens and pleasure, enjoying what their Lord has given them; for their Lord will save them from the torments of hell. 'Eat and drink with good digestion, for that which ye have done,' reclining on couches in rows. And We will wed them to large-eyed maids. . . . And We will extend to them fruit and flesh such as they like." Avicenna thought that here as elsewhere the Koran should be read as couching the truth in figurative terms intelligible to the multitude. Bodily resurrection is only a symbol, with appeal for untrained minds, of the truth that souls (alone) are incorruptible. But not every Muslim thinker was ready to believe that, on points as fundamental as this, the truth was widely different from the literal meaning of the Koran.

Algazali

Chief among the opponents of Avicenna was a fellow Persian, Algazali (Abū Hāmid ibn Muhammad al-Ghazālī, 1058–1111). A native of Tūs, near Mashhad in what now is northeastern Iran, Algazali (like Muhammad) was only a child when his parents died; but he received a good education, the upshot of which was that he became a teacher of jurisprudence and theology. In his early thirties, under the patronage of a vizier, he was appointed to a notable university in Baghdad, where he soon found himself gaining influence in politics along with celebrity as a lecturer. Then a strange thing happened. He suddenly developed an impediment of speech that prevented him from lecturing. At the same time, he began to be afflicted with indigestion so acute that he could scarcely bring himself to eat. As Algazali explains in his autobiographical *Deliverance from Error,* such were the physical symptoms of a conflict that had been growing within him for months. The more he delighted in his influence and popularity, the more he had feared God's disfavor of his worldliness. "I saw for certain," he says, "that I was on the brink of a crumbling bank of sand and in imminent danger of hellfire unless I set about to mend my ways." But like St. Augustine in a similar situation, Algazali could not do what he knew he ought—the first step being to remove himself from Baghdad. When he could bear the strain no longer, he "sought refuge with God most high as one who is driven to Him, because he is without further resources of his own." And God "made it easy," he says, "for my heart to turn away from position and wealth, from children and friends."

After settling some money on his family, Algazali (now thirty-six) went into Syria and joined the Sufis—an ascetic Muslim order of mystics (named for their distinctive garments of *suf,* wool). Meditation and spiritual exercises were his main concerns during the sixteen years of life that were left to him; but also he produced a multitude of writings on theology, law, philosophy, and Sufism. His greatest theological work, *The Revival of the Religious Sciences,* came to be regarded as authoritative by conservative Muslims, and is still so regarded today. Algazali died at home in Tüs, not long after returning there to establish a Sufi community.

In philosophy Algazali is especially important as a critic of the Neoplatonic interpretation of Aristotle's views that Avicenna and others tried to read into Muslim doctrines. The better to master these people's arguments, Algazali wrote an impartial summary of them that he called *The Tendencies of the Philosophers.* A Latin translation of this work, minus the preface in which Algazali stated his purpose in writing it, came into Christian circles in the thirteenth century and was there mistaken for an account of views with which Algazali agreed. How very mistaken this was may be gauged from the title of the book he wrote next—*The Incoherence of the Philosophers*—a book of which Christian thinkers did not learn until the fourteenth century. The especial object of Algazali's attack in *The Incoherence* was Avicenna, whom he understood to have advanced three theses in particular that were both unsound in themselves and inconsistent with the Koran. First, Avicenna had argued that only the soul survives death, whereas the doctrine of bodily resurrection is asserted by the Koran in unmistakable terms. Second, Avicenna had believed that a hierarchy of Intelligences is interposed between God and the world, so that God, for His part, would apparently know only the ultimate principles of things (universals such as rational animality), not their particular instances (such as Muhammad and Khadija); whereas the Koran plainly says that God is immediately aware of individuals and guides them according to His Providence. Third, Avicenna had held that the world emanates eternally and of necessity from God (via the heavenly Intelligences), whereas nothing could be clearer than the Koran's insistence that God freely created everything out of nothing at a definite point in the past.

Algazali saw little coherence in Avicenna's tendency, under Neoplatonic inspiration, to deny God's free and personal control over the events of the world. As we saw, Avicenna maintained on the one hand that noth-ing in the world is necessary in itself, but on the other hand that every-thing is linked into a chain of causes and effects that could not possibly have been otherwise (since the chain necessarily emanates—via Intelli-gences—from the Necessary Being). One consequence of this is that mir-acles are impossible, for a miracle consists in God's causing something to happen other than what would have happened in the usual course of events, and God could not do this if the "usual" course of events is in fact an unbreakable chain of causes and effects. That miracles do occur, however, is clear above all (to any orthodox Muslim) from the very existence of the Koran, for Muhammad—as he himself insisted—was an unschooled man who could not have produced, without Divine instruction, a book of un-rivaled wisdom and beauty. Algazali, accordingly, proceeded to criticize in detail the notion of cause and effect that led Avicenna to deny the possibility of miracles. The power of Algazali as a critic is exemplified best by his arguments on this subject.

On grounds of both logic and observation Algazali held that causes and effects, or types of events identified as such, have no necessary connection between them. God may therefore alter the usual course of events by performing any miracles He thinks fit. If there were a necessary connec-tion between a cause X and an effect Y, then it would be impossible for an event of the X type to occur without an event of the Y type's occurring (and vice versa). Algazali uses the example of (X) bringing a flame into contact with a piece of cotton and (Y) the combustion of the cotton. Is it impossible for X to occur without Y's occurring, so that a miracle along these lines would be out of the question? If it *were* impossible, Algazali says, then as a matter of logic, the affirmation of "X occurs" together with the denial of "Y occurs" would be a *contradiction*. But there can be no contradiction in saying of two different statements that one is true and the other false, and what we have here are two different statements, "X occurs" and "Y occurs." A contradiction consists in simultaneously affirm-ing and denying the same thing, as in "Socrates is a Greek; and also Socrates is not a Greek," and we find nothing like this in the present case. Just as an event of the X type is *other than* an event of the Y type, so a statement about the occurrence of the one is *other than* a statement about the occurrence of the other. Thus "X occurs" and "Y occurs" do not logically follow from one another in the sense that to affirm one while denying the other would be contradictory. So we see that, in point of logic, there is no necessity in relations of cause and effect. "According to us," Algazali says, "the connection between what is usually believed to be a cause and what is believed to be an effect is not a necessary connec-tion: each of the two things has its own individuality and is not the other, and neither the affirmation nor the negation, neither the existence nor the nonexistence of the one is implied in the affirmation, negation, exis-tence, or nonexistence of the other. . . ."

So much, then, for purely logical considerations. Does observation of so-called "causes" and "effects" disclose any necessary relation between them? Algazali thinks not. Observe any "cause" and its "effect" as closely as you please, and you will still not observe that the "effect" *must* occur if the "cause" occurs. You see a piece of cotton touched by a flame. You see the cotton begin to burn. But you do not see that it is impossible for the cotton not to burn. All you see is that, as a matter of fact, the cotton does begin to burn at the time when the flame begins to touch it. In other words, what you really observe is just that the two events—flame touching, cotton burning—are *simultaneous,* not that the one necessitates the other. As Algazali puts it, "observation proves only a simultaneity, not a causation," if by "a causation" we mean "a necessary connection."

These arguments of Algazali's are similar to, and antedate by roughly six centuries, arguments for which Malebranche (1638–1715) and Hume (1711–1776) are undeservedly more famous. It was not Algazali's intention (any more than it was Malebranche's) to deny that every event in the world has a necessitating cause, only to deny that the cause is some other event in the world. "In reality," Algazali says, "there is no other cause but God," if by "cause" we mean "that upon which an event follows necessarily." If the Almighty in His freedom wills that some event should occur in the world, then that event cannot possibly fail to occur; and every event that does occur in the world is willed by Him. A miracle is something He wills to happen that is other than what we have come to expect from the order in which He usually wills things to happen.

Algazali's case for the possibility of miracles is built of philosophical arguments directed against the Neoplatonic Aristotelians, Avicenna among them, whom Algazali thought of as "the philosophers." His esteem for "the philosophers," very low during a period of skepticism in his days at Baghdad, did not greatly increase over the years. In *The Deliverance from Error,* his view of "the many philosophical sects and systems" is that "the defect of unbelief affects them all." He does not think that irreligious ideas are native to all parts of philosophy, only to metaphysics, but he finds that acquaintance with any part tends to foster in people an intellectual arrogance hardly compatible with the "godly fear" necessary in complete surrender to Allah. Logic, for example, is not in itself at odds with the doctrines of Islam; its methods are in fact useful in refuting views at odds with these doctrines, as witness Algazali's critique of Avicenna. But those who pride themselves upon their mastery of logic are prone, Algazali says, to disparage the religious (and other) beliefs of ordinary mortals who are unacquainted with the technical niceties of the subject. Moreover, students of logic, impressed with the clarity and force of logical principles, are apt to assume that these principles lend support to "infidel doctrines" in metaphysics advocated by teachers of logic. Actually, however, logical conditions of proof cannot be satisfied in metaphysics, where the many disagreements among philosophers show, Algazali believes, that on ultimate issues nothing more than conjecture is to be expected of the human intellect. And even if some intellects were capable of more than this, philosophy would still be a "baneful and mischievous influence" upon the general public, to whom any philosophical thesis is credible if it is advocated by a sufficiently impressive personality. "It is customary with weaker intellects thus to take the men as criterion of truth and not the truth as criterion of the men." Hence Algazali proposes that philosophical writings be kept out of general circulation in the interests of public spiritual safety. "Just as the poor swimmer must be kept from the slippery banks, so must mankind be kept from reading these books. . . ."

From his own period of philosophical study, Algazali emerged with a frame of mind which could, he felt, have been worse, but not any better in view of the limitations of philosophy. He was sure of the existence of God, and of the authority of the Koran, "not through any carefully argued proofs, but by reason of various causes, coincidences, and experiences which are not capable of being stated in detail." This, he realized, was as far as he or anyone could get "by way of intellectual apprehension." The Sufis held out to him the promise of much further progress if he would follow "the mystic way" that leads on beyond reason and intellect. And Algazali found this promise fulfilled upon his completion of the requisite purifications of body and spirit. He says:

> There were revealed to me things innumerable and unfathomable. This much I shall say about that in order that others may be helped: I learnt with certainty that it is above all the mystics who walk on the road of God; their life is the best life, their method the soundest method, their character the purest character; indeed, were the intellect of the intellectuals and the learning of the learned and the scholarship of the scholars, who are versed in the profundities of revealed truth, brought together in the attempt to improve the life and character of the mystics, they would find no way of doing so; for to the mystics all movement and all rest, whether external or internal, brings illumination from the light of the lamp of prophetic revelation; and behind the light of prophetic revelation there is no other light on the face of the earth from which illumination may be received.

An indescribable "immediate experience" of God is the end of the mystic way. At lower stages of the way, mystics "behold angels and the spirits of the prophets; they hear these speaking and are instructed by them," which instruction includes "what is to be in the future." Just as we have in intellect a power of apprehending things (mathematical truths, for example) that are beyond the ken of the senses, so we also have a "special faculty of prophecy" that enables us, when duly purified, to apprehend things beyond the ken of intellect. To those who refuse to believe that we possess any such faculty, Algazali replies by observing that something analogous to it, after all, is presupposed by the generally accepted view of dreams. In dreams (so it was widely supposed in those days) we may apprehend the future either explicitly or in symbols. Since this obviously involves something in us beyond ordinary powers of intellect, where is the difficulty in believing that a similar but far richer faculty of prophecy is at work in mystical experience?

According to an old Muslim tradition, in every century there will appear a great reviver of Islam. Algazali came to believe that, for the sixth Muslim century (the twelfth century A.D.), Allah had chosen him for this office. At first it might not have seemed that many would share Algazali's view of his mission. The Muslim scholars of the time tended to resent his suggestion that they were insufficiently God-fearing, and the initial effect of his writings was more to ruffle tempers than to rekindle faith and devotions. Before long, however, he began to be paid the kind of homage that ultimately led to his being revered as a saint and ranked as the greatest of Muslim theologians.

Averroes

Algazali's great authority as a theologian was achieved despite criticisms leveled against him by Averroes (1126–1198), the foremost Muslim philosopher in Spain. Averroes (Abū al-Walīd Muhammad Ibn Ahmed Ibn Rushd) came from a family of prominent judges in Córdoba and was for many years himself a judge, first in Seville and then in Córdoba. He moved in high society and enjoyed the favor of the sultan of Marrakesh, whose Almohad Dominions included much of southern Spain (where Seville and Córdoba are) in addition to much of northern Africa (where Marrakesh is). The sultan took an interest in matters philosophical and scientific, and it was he who commissioned the three (short, intermediate, and long) sets of commentaries on Aristotle for which Averroes was best known, and for which he was called "The Commentator" in Christendom. The story goes that, early in their acquaintance, Averroes was asked by the sultan to explain what Aristotle thought about the eternity of the world; and Averroes played it safe by pretending not to know, until it was clear that the sultan did not disapprove of philosophy. Like Avicenna, Averroes had absorbed an education of encyclopedic scope; and his duties as a judge did not prevent him from writing, along with the Aristotle commentaries (thirty-eight in all), a number of works on politics, religion, metaphysics, logic, astronomy, and medicine. Such was his knowledge of medicine that he was summoned to Marrakesh in 1182 to serve as the sultan's personal physician. In 1195 his fortunes suffered a temporary reverse. Having somehow incurred the displeasure of Muslim religious officials (the details of the episode are unclear), Averroes, at sixty-nine, was advised or directed by the sultan to retire to a remote village in Spain. After a year or so, when the trouble had blown over, he returned to Marrakesh in honor, and in time for his death at seventy-two.

Perhaps the religious authorities felt that Averroes was inclined to overrate dangerously the significance of Aristotle. More than once Averroes had gone on record with statements such as "the doctrine of Aristotle is the supreme truth, because his intellect was the limit of human intellect." And this sort of thing could easily have struck the authorities as inconsistent with a proper regard for Muhammad and the Koran. Certainly Averroes did not think that the human intellect, as represented by Aristotle at any rate, had the limitations attributed to it by those who shared Algazali's conservative theological standpoint. He replied to Algazali's *Incoherence of the Philosophers* by producing a treatise called *The Incoherence of the Incoherence,* in which he answered point for point the arguments by which Algazali tried to show that philosophical methods cannot furnish knowledge of the highest truths (which are apprehensible, Algazali says, only by a "special faculty of prophecy"). But Averroes also denied that the findings of philosophy could really be in conflict with the revelations of the Koran or with the theological doctrines derived therefrom. The basic agreement of religion and philosophy, notwithstanding appearances of disagreement, was the thesis he tried to prove in his famous *Decisive Treatise Determining the Nature of the Connection Between Religion and Philosophy.*

Averroes argues in the *Decisive Treatise* that philosophy has the full support of the Koran. He points out that many verses in the Koran urge us to reflect upon the world from the standpoint of its being God's handiwork. The clear implication of these verses, Averroes says, is that persons of philosophical ability should seek to demonstrate God's existence and attributes on the basis of knowledge concerning the beings in the world. To this end it is essential to know the conditions of demonstration and to be acquainted with any relevant existing arguments that satisfy these conditions. A study of Aristotle's logic, physics, and metaphysics is accordingly imperative, for his logic sets forth the conditions of demonstration, and his physics and metaphysics contain relevant arguments that satisfy these conditions. (Averroes personally believed that the one conclusive proof of God's existence was Aristotle's argument for an Unmoved Mover.[15]) The "books of the ancients," Averroes says with Aristotle chiefly in mind, consist of precisely that to which the Koran directs us, namely, "theoretical study which leads to the truest knowledge of God."

Those capable of theoretical study constitute "the best class of people," Averroes believes, but their number is small. Most people, he thinks, are incapable of forming abstract conceptions or of understanding philosophical demonstrations: they think in pictures, and they are persuaded by rhetorical arguments that appeal to their emotions and imagination. Nothing more clearly indicates the miraculous origin of the Koran, Averroes says, than the unparalleled effectiveness with which it "takes care of the majority" by means of arresting "images and likenesses" of the

[15] See pp. 147–148.

truth. Consider, for instance, the galvanizing effect upon unsophisticated people of the Koran's vivid descriptions of a Heaven of bodily pleasure for the virtuous and of a Hell of bodily suffering for the wicked. Of course, in these and similar instances it is only to be expected that philosophical reasoning will lead "the elite" (as Averroes calls them) to conclusions at odds with the "apparent meaning" of the Koran—only with the "apparent meaning," however, because in every such case allegorical interpretation will uncover in the Koran an "inner meaning" consistent with the philosophical conclusion. If the Koran contains nothing but the truth, and if it summons "the elite" to demonstrate the truth philosophically, then what "the elite" demonstrate cannot conflict with the Koran, "for truth does not oppose truth but accords with it and bears witness to it." Allegorical interpretation of the Koran will reveal, as necessary, its harmony with philosophical conclusions. Not that the general public is to be informed of the "inner meanings" of the Koran: this would produce among "the masses" only confusion and unbelief.

Theology, as Averroes sees it, has the office of furnishing probable (or "dialectical") arguments for doctrines deriving from the "apparent meaning" of the Koran. There are persons, he says, for whom rhetorical argument is too unsophisticated to be convincing, but for whom demonstrative argument is too sophisticated to be intelligible, and theology is the thing for them. It wins or solidifies their assent to Islam with arguments of medium difficulty showing that the Koran's teachings, even in their "apparent meaning," are rationally probable, and more probable than their contraries.

Thus Averroes classifies people according to which of the three kinds of argument (identified by Aristotle [16]) their abilities and temperaments enable them to understand. There is a small class of people who can handle the demonstrative arguments of philosophy; there is a somewhat larger class for whom the dialectical arguments of theology are suitable; and there is a huge class unable to appreciate anything except the rhetorical arguments of preachers and prophets. Averroes does appear to have seriously supposed that the theologians of his day would acquiesce in this scheme and in the relegation of their field to the second class; and no doubt he was mistaken.

Averroes' view of the relation between religion and philosophy has often been misunderstood. He has been credited with, or accused of, saying that religion and philosophy cannot be in conflict because each has its own kind of truth, so that religion may teach one thing and philosophy may teach something to the contrary, and both things may be true. For example, religion may tell us that God created the world from nothing a definite number of years ago, and philosophy may tell us (does tell us, as Averroes agrees with Aristotle in thinking) that God has produced the world from eternity; but there would be no real conflict between these

[16] See p. 132.

two positions, since the first would be "true for" religion and the second would be "true for" philosophy. This so-called Double-Truth Theory was attributed to Averroes by certain Christians in the thirteenth century, but the error of doing so is very clear from the *Decisive Treatise,* where Averroes explicitly maintains that the truth as philosophy demonstrates it may be accommodated in religion by allegorical interpretation of any Scriptural passage whose "apparent meaning" does not already accommodate it. In other words, Averroes holds that nothing may be considered literally true in religion that differs from the demonstrated conclusions of philosophy. Such is the sense in which he means that religion and philosophy are in basic agreement.

Philosophy, for Averroes, is personified by Aristotle. Although Averroes tends to interpret Aristotle in a Neoplatonic fashion, he does not go as far in that direction as Avicenna did. This is well illustrated by Averroes' disagreement with Avicenna over the issue of how God is related to His creatures. Avicenna followed Plotinus in maintaining that God, in His absolute unity, could not directly bring about a plurality of beings. The vast gulf between God's unity and the world's plurality, Avicenna said, must be bridged by a series of Intelligences, the highest of which emanates directly from God and in turn produces a lower Intelligence, which in turn produces a lower, and so on, until there emerges the so-called Agent Intelligence, which is the party responsible for actualizing forms in material things and in human consciousness. Averroes, for his part, does not dispute the existence of a hierarchy of Intelligences, which he associates with the spheres of the heavenly bodies. But Averroes does dispute the notion that God could directly produce only one of these Intelligences. In arguments of great complexity, he tries to show the inapplicability to God of the principle that "from the one only the one can proceed"; and he concludes that "out of the one [God] all things proceed by one first emanation." That is, all the Intelligences come directly from God in one eternal surge of "emanation," which means that there is no "emanation" in the usual Neoplatonic sense whereby every Intelligence except the highest stems from a higher Intelligence, not directly from God. Averroes believes that this view of the matter is in line with what Aristotle meant when he said that God is to the world-order what a general is to his army. The disposition of an army depends upon the orders of its general, which he issues to all his adjutants directly. Similarly, the order in the world depends upon the intelligence of its Maker, which He causes to be expressed in the form of Intelligences all stemming from Him directly.

There has long been controversy regarding Averroes' precise stand on the issue of life after death. Many have understood him to deny (with Aristotle) that there is anything immortal about humankind except the *impersonal* Agent Intelligence in which we all share insofar as we apprehend forms or universals latent in our sense-experience. According to this view of him, Averroes thinks that we are distinguished as individuals only by our bodies and by the experiences they afford us, so that our individual consciousness is extinguished upon the death of our bodies. Our souls are the seat of a passive intelligence which the Agent Intelligence activates, but Averroes (disagreeing with Avicenna) denies that our souls are purely spiritual entities: they are, as Aristotle said, the forms of our bodies in something like the way in which the imprint of a seal is the form of a piece of wax. Therefore, our souls have not an independent status of the kind that would enable them to survive the body's death. Such is the position that has often been attributed to Averroes. He was condemned for it, along with Aristotle, in thirteenth-century Christendom,[17] and today he is still sometimes said to have espoused it. Actually, however, in *The Incoherence of the Incoherence* (not translated from the Arabic until the fourteenth century) Averroes plainly states that he does believe in personal immortality. Under Stoic inspiration, he advances the thesis that when our earthly bodies die, they are replaced by new bodies composed of a "subtle matter" that he identifies with the "animal warmth which emanates from the heavenly bodies." In this way Averroes accommodates both the Muslim doctrine of the resurrection of the body and the Aristotelian doctrine that a human soul cannot survive without a body. We shall be resurrected with bodies of an incorruptibly celestial type.

Of the criticisms of Algazali in Averroes' *Incoherence of the Incoherence,* perhaps the most important are those concerning Algazali's denial of necessary relations of cause and effect (in the interests, as Algazali said, of allowing room for miracles). Averroes does not believe that it is possible to *prove* that such relations exist. The principle that all events have necessary causes (by way of other events) seems to him so primary a principle that there is none more primary from which it could be shown to follow. It must, he says, be taken as self-evident. But he does believe that something may be done to defend the principle dialectically, that is, by showing that absurd consequences follow from denying it. In one particularly subtle argument, he maintains (in so many words) that if we cannot apprehend necessary relations of cause and effect, then we cannot identify anything as being of one kind rather than another. To identify anything as being of one kind rather than another (as being cotton rather than asbestos, for example) is to conceive of it as having a specific nature all its own. To conceive of anything as having a specific nature all its own is to judge that under such-and-such conditions it will always act, or react, in such-and-such a way (as cotton, unlike asbestos, will always burn under certain conditions). To judge that under such-and-such conditions something will always act, or react, in such-and-such a way is to understand that its actions, or reactions, are necessarily related as causes, or effects, to other occurrences (as the cotton's burning is necessarily the

---

[17] Averroes and Aristotle were also condemned for denying that the world was created from nothing at a definite time in the past.

effect of its being touched with a flame). Or to put it the other way around, necessary relations of cause and effect are presupposed by our judgments that things will always act, or react, in the same ways under the same conditions; and these judgments are essential to our identifications of things as being of particular kinds. (If what we took to be cotton acted, or re-acted, in different ways under the same conditions, the term "cotton" would in fact have no particular significance.) Accordingly, either we must af-firm that there are necessary relations of cause and effect, or we must deny that anything may be identified as being of one kind rather than another. That the latter alternative is unacceptable should be clear, Av-erroes thinks, from a little reflection upon what it means. If nothing may be identified as being of a particular kind, then nothing whatever exists, for "a thing of no particular kind" is a contradictory expression and can apply to nothing whatever. A thing's identity, the nature of its oneness as a thing, its very being as a thing, consists in its being of one kind rather than another. And as Averroes puts it, "If the nature of oneness is denied, the nature of being is denied, and the consequence of the denial of being is nothingness."

What, then, did Averroes make of the problem that so concerned Alga-zali? If there are necessary relations of cause and effect between all the events in the world, then is it not impossible for Allah to perform mira-cles, that is, to bring about events for which there are no causes in the world? Will not the miraculous origin of the Koran itself have to be de-nied, contrary to Averroes' own argument that nothing short of a miracle could have produced Scripture that so well "takes care of the majority"? Averroes' remarks about this have an ambiguity such as may often be found in what he says about traditional Muslim beliefs. "The clearest of miracles is the Venerable Book of Allah," Averroes says, "the existence of which is not an interruption of the course of nature assumed by tradi-tion, like the changing of a rod into a serpent, but its miraculous nature is established by way of perception and consideration for every man who has been or who will be till the day of resurrection. And so this miracle is far superior to all the others. Let this suffice for the man who is not satisfied with passing this problem over in silence. . . ." But if the in-sights Muhammad believed he was given by Allah were not interruptions of the course of nature, in the sense that they had no natural causes, how were they miraculous? Evidently this was a question that Averroes wished only to appear not to have passed over in silence.

Muslim philosophy in Spain, like the Muslim dominion in Spain, did not long survive Averroes' death in 1198. On July 16, 1212, at Las Navas de Tolosa, a great army of the Almohad Muslims was destroyed by the combined forces of the Christian kings of Castile, Portugal, Aragon, and Navarre. The Muslims' power was broken, and a complete Christian re-conquest of Spain was only a matter of time. Córdoba, the center of Mus-lim culture in the West, was seized in 1236 by Ferdinand III of Castile. The works of Averroes, from then on of little moment in Muslim intellectual history, were conveyed to the European universities, where, at Paris especially, Latin translations of his commentaries on Aristotle were much studied and much debated by 1250.

Jewish Philosophers

Philo of Alexandria (about 20 B.C.–50 A.D.), the outstanding Jewish philosopher of the Hellenistic period, had considerable direct influence upon Christian Fathers but little or none upon Jewish thinkers. Within a century of Philo's death, the focus of Jewish intellectual life began to shift from Alexandria to Babylonia,[18] where Palestinian Jews found refuge from Roman persecution. In Babylonia three Jewish academies, or yeshivas, were established in the interests of perpetuating the tradition of expounding the Torah in unwritten interpretations known collectively as the Oral Law. These academies, located at Sura, Pumbedita, and Nehardea, existed for over 800 years (from the third to the eleventh centuries). By the time Babylonia came under Muslim control, shortly after Muhammad's death in 632, the academies had completed the monumental task of transcribing the Oral Law in the compilation known as the Babylonian Talmud. The rabbis at the academies, preoccupied though they were with Talmudic scholarship, did not fail to observe the interest in Greek philosophy that Muslim theologians began to display at the end of the eighth century. And in the tenth century, the head (or gaon) of the academy at Sura, a man named Saadia ben Joseph, was prompted by the Muslims' example to develop his own philosophical defenses for certain Scriptural positions. The *Book of Doctrines and Beliefs* that Saadia produced (in 933) is generally regarded as the first major work of medieval Jewish philosophy. After Saadia there came a series of Jewish philosophers, living in Muslim lands, writing mostly in Arabic, philosophizing under the inspiration of Muslim uses of Greek ideas. Like their Muslim counterparts, the Jewish philosophers of the Middle Ages fell into two groups, Eastern and Western, although in the Jews' case the Western group, in Spain, was much the more numerous. Besides Saadia the Eastern group included Isaac ben Solomon Israeli (about 855–955), Joseph ben Abraham (dates uncertain; probably born early in the eleventh century), and Jeshua ben Judah (dates also uncertain, but he was a pupil of Joseph ben Abraham). The Western group included Solomon ibn Gabirol (about 1022–1070), Bahya ibn Pakuda (late eleventh century), Abraham

---

[18] Although "Parthia" would, strictly speaking, be more accurate, "Babylonia" is the name customarily used when referring to the region around the lower Tigris and Euphrates rivers (in modern Iraq) in which the Jews settled in the second century A.D. Babylonia vanished from the political map when her last king surrendered to the Persians in 538 B.C. The Parthians held sway in the region from the second century B.C. until early in the third century A.D., when the Sassanids took it over.

bar Hiyya (early twelfth century), Joseph ibn Zaddik (died in 1149), Judah Halevi (about 1085–1141), Moses ibn Ezra (1078–1138) and his brother Abraham (1092–1167), Abraham ibn Daud (about 1110–1190), and Moses Maimonides (or ben Maimon, 1135–1204). Here Saadia and Maimonides will be considered, for with Saadia medieval Jewish philosophy made a formidable beginning, and with Maimonides it reached its great culmination. But it should at least be mentioned that in Judah Halevi the medieval Jewish philosophers had a critic of the same incisive type as the Muslim philosophers had in Algazali (from whom indeed Halevi borrowed much of his inspiration).

Saadia

Saadia ben Joseph, the father of medieval Jewish philosophy, was born in 882 at Dilaz in Egypt. After schooling in Egypt and Palestine, and while still a young man, Saadia won renown as a spokesman for orthodox (and Babylonian) Jewish causes. He supported the party of the rabbis—the Rabbanites—in their opposition to the sect of Karaites, who rejected the Talmud in the belief that it was insufficiently faithful to the letter of Scripture. He also supported the rabbis of Babylonia against the rabbis of Palestine in a debate the ostensible issue of which concerned the Jewish calendar, but the real issue of which was whether the rabbis of Babylonia were to supersede the rabbis of Palestine as the dominant religious authorities in Jewish life. The Babylonian side prevailed. In recognition of his services, Saadia was appointed to teach at the academy in Sura, about sixty miles from Baghdad. A few years later, in 928, when he was forty-six, he was made gaon of the institution. Saadia brought the academy to new heights of scholarly distinction, in spite of having much to endure from a controversy that swirled around him in which the leading parts were played by a jealous gaon of the academy at Pembedita, a weak exilarch (secular head) of the Jewish community in Babylonia, and a corrupt caliph of Baghdad. Suffice it to say that Saadia was compelled to spend some time in Baghdad (934–938) until matters sorted themselves out, and then he was reinstated as gaon at Sura, where he died in 942 at the age of sixty.

Saadia's writings were numerous and diversified. He was an innovator in translating much of the Old Testament into the Arabic language, which then was the vernacular of Jews in the East. He prepared commentaries on the Talmud and on several books of the Old Testament; he produced a Hebrew dictionary, an arrangement of the Jewish liturgy, and a number of polemical works directed against the Karaites and others. He wrote ten or more books on topics in Jewish jurisprudence. One of the most celebrated of his works dealt with a certain *Book of Creation* that had been ascribed to Abraham, the patriarch in the Bible, and which came to form part of the basis of the Jewish mystical tradition known as Kabbala (or Cabala). From the standpoint of philosophy, however, Saadia's *Book of Doctrines and Beliefs* was his greatest achievement, and it is of this that an account must now be given.

In its general plan and style of argument, Saadia's *Book of Doctrines and Beliefs* resembles works produced in the ninth century by what is called the Mu'tazilite school of Muslim thinkers. These Mu'tazilite writings contributed to the development of the major Muslim philosophical systems, such as Avicenna's, but the Mu'tazilites' use of Greek materials was not controlled by the overriding Neoplatonic perspective so characteristic of most subsequent Muslim philosophy. Saadia followed the Mu-'tazilites in drawing freely upon Greek philosophers of all schools for such insights and arguments as would serve his purpose of explicating and defending the truths communicated by Divine revelation. The result was not a metaphysical system really alien, like Neoplatonism, to the general outlook of the Old Testament, but an assortment of arguments giving a rationale for views that may plausibly be said to be expressed or implied in the Law and the Prophets.

Divine revelation is necessary, Saadia says, because many persons cannot discover religious truths by reasoning, and also because those who can need guidance in the meantime. It is part of our condition as creatures that everything we do is subject to time. It takes time for us to discover the truth, at least when the truth (as in the case of God) is not apparent to our senses or judgment and must be inferred, step by careful step, from what is apparent. Reasoning is a gradual process, often hindered by doubts and perplexities. If what we strive by reasoning to establish are truths of a religious nature, then until such time as we have managed to establish some of them we would have none to guide or encourage our thoughts and our daily activities, not unless we believed we had them by revelation. Thus it behooves us to believe in revelation; but it also behooves us, insofar as we are able, to discover conclusive arguments for what we accept as revealed. We owe it to ourselves and to God, Saadia says, to fix our true beliefs firmly in our minds by discovering the reasons why they are true. Otherwise we may let them slip away.

Scripture tells us that, a finite time ago, God created all things from nothing. This is the clear meaning, Saadia says, of such passages as "In the beginning God created the heaven and the earth" (Genesis 1:1) and "I am the Lord that maketh all things; that stretcheth forth the heavens alone; that spreadeth abroad the earth by myself" (Isaiah 44:24). The question is whether it is possible to demonstrate philosophically that God exists as the Creator of all things from nothing. Saadia is confident that it is possible. In fact he gives several arguments, the most important of which is an argument concerning time. The world cannot always have existed, Saadia maintains, because past time, and past processes of generation in time, must have had a beginning. Here is what he says:

> I know that time is threefold: past, present, and future. Although the present is smaller than any instant, I take the instant as one takes a

point and say: if a man should try in his thought to ascend from that point in time [the present moment], to the uppermost point [the remotest past moment], it would be impossible for him to do so [if past time were *infinite*, because] it is impossible for thought to penetrate to the furthest point of that which is infinite [there being no such point]. The same reason will also make it impossible that the process of generation should traverse an infinite period down to the lowest point [the present moment] so as ultimately to reach us. Yet if the process of generation did not reach us, we would not be generated, from which it necessarily follows that we, the multitude of created beings, would not be generated and the beings now existent would not be existent. And since I find myself existent, I know that the process of generation has traversed time until it has reached us, and that if time were not finite, the process of generation would not have traversed it. . . .

If we fail to admit the existence of something which has nothing prior to it [a first moment of time, a first process of generation in time], it is impossible for us to accept the fact that there exists anything at all. For if we consider in our mind that one thing comes from another thing, we have to predicate the same thing of the second as of the first, and say that it could only have come into being from a third thing; the same predicate must again be made of the third thing, namely, that it could only have come into being from a fourth thing, and so on *ad infinitum*. Since, however, an infinite series cannot be completed, it follows that we are not in existence. But, behold, we are in existence, and unless the things which preceded us were finite (in number), they could not have been completed so as to reach us.

If the things that preceded us must be finite in number, then the moments of past time, and the world as the complex of things and processes in time, must have had a beginning. The beginning of the world and time could not just have happened. There must, Saadia says, be some explanation. And it is no explanation to say that the world and time brought themselves into existence. Things that are nonexistent cannot do anything, much less create themselves. Nor is it an explanation to say that a primitive matter might have given rise, by itself and out of itself, to the world and time. Anything material, however primitive, exists in time and so could not be that from which time began. The world and time must therefore have an immaterial Creator who is independent of (or transcends) the world and who is independent of time (or eternal). Exactly *one* Creator is indicated, because the world (that is, the universe) is itself one in the sense that its parts cannot be separated; and a unitary effect implies a single, unitary cause. Perhaps, however, the Creator did not make the world from nothing as Scripture implies? Perhaps the Creator made the world out of Himself, so that it "emanated" from Him as the Neoplatonists suppose? Saadia expresses strong disagreement with this type of view. He finds it most unlikely, to say the least, that an

Eternal Being would, or could, transform some part of His own essence into material things subject to time and to the vicissitudes of time. Saadia is prepared to admit that it is not easy to conceive of the world as having been created out of nothing. But he believes that it is far more difficult to conceive of the (temporal) world as an emanation out of an Eternal (nontemporal) Being. As for the alternative that God might have made the world and time out of a pre-existing primitive matter, we have already seen that nothing material could be that from which time began or was made to begin. The conclusion has to be that God made the world and time from nothing.

Such, briefly put, is one of Saadia's arguments for the existence of God as the Creator of the world. In regard to God's nature, Saadia says that He must be omnipotent if He creates all things from nothing; and He must be omniscient if He is able (as He is, being omnipotent) to create that which is perfect; and He must possess life if He possesses omnipotence and omniscience. But it is essential to understand, Saadia says, that omnipotence, omniscience, and life are not three different things in God's nature.[19] God's nature as Creator is absolutely unitary. The terms *omnipotence, omniscience,* and *life* are not names of distinguishable elements of the Creator's nature, but elucidations of what "Creator" means. (These terms also, Saadia says, indicate how creatures are related to the Creator.) It is a limitation of language that we have to speak of the Creator as though His omnipotence were one thing and His life another, and as though His possession of the one implied His possession of the other. But they are not two different things, and we do not really infer the one from the other. With our reason we discover, in one act of thought, that the concept of Creator involves that which—though it is perfectly simple—cannot be stated except, imperfectly, by using several terms.

Reason tells us, Saadia says, that God cannot in any literal sense be compared to human beings. The many anthropomorphic expressions in the Bible have to be understood figuratively. When we read, for example, the prayer of Hezekiah, "Lord, bow down thine ear, and hear: open, Lord, thine eyes" (II Kings 19:16), we are not to think that God literally has an ear, or ears, and eyes, or that Hezekiah—a vigorous opponent of idolatry (see II Kings 18:14)—really meant that He does. The Bible fully supports what reason tells us about such language. Deuteronomy (4:15–19) expressly warns us against supposing that God has any "manner of similitude" to animals, humans, or heavenly bodies. The philosophical explanation of this is not hard to find. Aristotle has taught us that the world consists of substances and the attributes of substances—attributes that may be classified into quantities, qualities, relations, places, times, positions, states, actions, and affections. God, in creating the world from nothing, created the entire substance-attribute scheme of things; and so

---

[19]Some such mistaken notion, Saadia believes, was the basis for the Christian doctrine of the Trinity.

it could scarcely be correct to characterize Him in terms of this scheme. He transcends the world. Substance, quantity, quality, and so on, are the categories of things in the world. Therefore, He transcends these categories, which is to say that He has no "manner of similitude" to us or to any of the other beings of His creation. And in speaking of God's unity, we should understand that "unity" in His case means the absence in Him of the distinctions, present throughout His creation, between substance and attributes, and between one attribute and another.[20]

It was characteristic of the members of the Mu'tazilite school to concern themselves with upholding two things in particular: God's unity and God's justice. The Mu'tazilites were thus known as the "Men of Unity and Justice." Saadia, having followed them in upholding God's unity, proceeds now to the matter of God's justice. What Saadia aims to provide on this score is a reasoned defense of the Scriptural assurances (Psalm 145:9 is an example) that God, whose goodness prompted Him to create the world, does good to humankind in spite of appearances to the contrary, and rewards or punishes individuals according to their deserts.

In vindicating God's justice, Saadia wishes first to make it clear that we have nothing to complain of in the human nature He has given us. Each of us, he says, has a soul distinguishable from the body but created with and in the body. The body is the necessary instrument of the soul's activity and as such is good for the soul. The Neoplatonists, and indeed Plato, seriously erred in thinking that association with the body harms the soul and represents a "fall." Of course, the soul is harmed by sin, Saadia says, but sin results from the soul's misuse of its freedom, not from its being equipped with a body. The soul and the body form a natural whole. The soul's health requires not ascetic denial of bodily needs and appetites but system and proportion in satisfying them. The rational element of the soul (and about this Plato was right) should have mastery over the appetitive and spirited elements that arise in the soul owing to its connection with the body. Mastery of appetite and spirit, however, does not consist in the attempt to eradicate them as if they were inherently evil. God has given them to us, Saadia says, that we may regulate them with good sense and reason according to the commandments and prohibitions He has sent down, and thereby become worthy of the everlasting happiness He has promised.

It might be said that God, in His omnipotence, could have bestowed everlasting happiness upon all of us from birth, which surely would have been kinder of Him than making us earn it by obeying all sorts of difficult commandments and prohibitions. But Saadia cannot agree with this. "My answer to this objection," he says, "is that, on the contrary, the order instituted by God, whereby everlasting happiness is achieved by man's labors in fulfillment of the Law, is preferable. For Reason judges that one

---

[20] Saadia does not, as we shall see that Maimonides does, develop the implication of these points, namely, that we may say of God only what He is *not*.

who obtains some good in return for work which he has accomplished enjoys a double portion of happiness in comparison with one who has not done any work and receives what he receives as a gift of grace." Moreover, the Divine laws communicated to us through Moses and the other prophets are by no means whimsical or despotic. This is clearly true of that class of laws that we may call Laws of Reason, as the rightness of these is confirmed by the immediate approval they elicit from our faculty of reason. Saadia finds that the Laws of Reason may conveniently be classified into four kinds according to the general principles of which they are the expressions:

(1) I maintain that Reason bids us to respond to every benefactor either by returning his kindness if he is in need of it, or by offering thanks if he is not in need of recompense. Now since this is a dictate of Reason itself, it would not have been fitting for the Creator (be He exalted and glorified) to waive this right in respect of Himself, but it was necessary that he should command His creatures to worship Him and to render thanks unto Him for having created them. (2) Reason further lays down that the wise man should not permit himself to be vilified and treated with contempt. It is similarly necessary that the Creator should forbid His servants to treat Him in this way. (3) Reason further prescribes that human beings should be forbidden to trespass upon one another's rights by any sort of aggression. It is likewise necessary that the Wise should not permit them to act in such a way. (4) Reason, furthermore, permits a wise man to employ a workman for any kind of work and pay him his wages for the sole purpose of allowing him to earn something; since this is a matter which results in benefit to the workman and causes no harm to the employer.

If we put together these four points, their total is tantamount to a summary of the laws [that is, the Laws of Reason] which our Lord has commanded us.

It is true, Saadia says, that there is another class of Divine laws— Laws of Tradition (or Revelation), as they may be called—whose binding character is not immediately apparent to our faculty of reason. In fact we should not be aware of these laws at all had they not been revealed to us, for what they command or prohibit are matters that seem, to our reason (at any rate initially), completely indifferent. What Saadia has in mind are such commandments as those concerning ceremonial purity and observance of the Sabbath, and such prohibitions as those against eating certain foodstuffs and having sexual intercourse with "certain categories of women" (incestuous relations are what is meant). Two things, Saadia believes, may be said about Laws of Tradition in the interests of showing that they are not, after all, without a rationale. First, because Isaiah (42:21) has told us that "the Lord was pleased, for his righteousness' sake, to magnify his law and make it glorious," we may take it that Laws of Tradition, in all their abundance, have been given us so that our reward might be all the greater for obeying them as well as the Laws of

Reason. The more services we perform to deserve God's reward, the greater His righteousness in rewarding us and the greater the reward itself. "That which belongs to the things commanded by God [in Laws of Tradition] assumes the character of 'good,' and that which belongs to the things forbidden by Him [in other Laws of Tradition] assumes the character of 'evil,' on account of the Service thereby performed." Second, it also has to be said that most Laws of Tradition turn out, "upon closer examination," to have "some slender moral benefits and rational basis," "some minor and partial motives of a useful character." Laws of Tradition, when we really come to think about them, are generally found to commend themselves to reason on account of certain genuine, if limited, practical advantages. (We are leaving out of account, for the moment, their advantages from the point of view of our standing with the Almighty.) For example, Saadia says that one good reason for observing the Sabbath, and the holy days, too, is that "it enables us to desist from our work at certain times and obtain a rest from our many travails." The prohibition against eating certain animals has, among other things, this to be said for it: "It prevents people from worshipping any of the animals, since it is unthinkable that one should worship either what serves for food or [as in the case of the prohibited animals] what one declares as impure." And concerning the prohibition against sexual intercourse with "certain categories of women," Saadia says that one of its purposes is "to prevent men from being attracted only by those women who are of beautiful appearance and rejecting those who are not, when they see that their own relatives do not desire them." (A gallant reason for prohibiting incest.)

Unless we have freedom of will, and thereby are responsible for our actions, how could God be just in punishing those who disobey His laws? But if God is omniscient and knows in advance how we will act in a given case, how can we have freedom of will? Saadia tries to solve this problem by arguing that God's knowledge of how we will act does not *determine* how we will act. God's knowledge, Saadia says, does not cause anything to exist. All things would have existed from eternity, if God's knowledge causes things to exist, because He knows all things from eternity. Needless to say, all things have not existed from eternity; and so it must be false that God's knowledge causes things to exist. Accordingly, the freedom of which we are all conscious in our actions is not to be considered illusory on account of God's knowing what we will do. We should think of it this way: in our case what God knows from eternity is that we will choose of our own free will to do certain things. That our choices are up to us is unmistakably implied in Scripture, if there should be any doubt of confirmation from that quarter. Saadia cites Deuteronomy 30:19: "I call heaven and earth to record this day against you, that I have set before you life and death, blessing and cursing: therefore choose life, that both thou and thy seed may live."

Appearances would frequently suggest that God's blessing and cursing are unjustly distributed. We seem often to see the righteous miserable and the wicked prospering. Saadia has no intention of evading this problem. The righteous, he says, are persons whose deeds are predominantly good and whose souls, in consequence, are relatively pure. The wicked, on the other hand, are those whose deeds are predominantly bad and whose souls, in consequence, are relatively impure. We may have every confidence that in the *next* world God will fully reward the righteous and fully punish the wicked. It is reasonable to suppose, however, that in *this* world God punishes the righteous for their few bad deeds and pays the wicked for their few good ones. This accounts for the appearance of injustice on God's part. It is only an appearance, because any happiness enjoyed by the wicked in this life is as nothing in comparison to the misery they will suffer, everlastingly, in the next life. Saadia does not deny that some righteous persons have to endure in this life an amount of suffering that is greatly out of proportion to any bad deeds they might have done. In these instances, he says, we can believe only that the disproportionate suffering endured here earns all the more happiness in the hereafter. (This is also the basis on which Saadia tries to account for the sufferings of little children.)

Saadia believes that there is much to assure us of another life after this one. Scripture lends its authority to the idea, as witness the story of Abraham and Isaac. Isaac, Saadia says, would not have consented to be sacrificed by Abraham (Genesis 22:9), and God would not have commanded Abraham to sacrifice him (Genesis 22:2), if Isaac had not believed in, and if God did not have in store, another life after this one. What Scripture implies reason confirms: the good things of this life are too mixed with evils, the righteous are too often persecuted in their pursuit of justice, the unrighteous are too seldom punished enough if at all, for us to believe that this life can be the only life we shall have. No one, however prosperous and honored, is really contented and at peace in this world. What could be the reason for this, if it is not that the soul intuitively apprehends and longs for the other world which is destined for it? Such is the only explanation compatible with what we know of God's wisdom and goodness. As for the condition of the soul in the next world, Saadia argues that it will inhabit a resurrected body, inasmuch as in this world soul and body have been complementary parts of one's personality as a whole. And the day of resurrection will come, he believes, when Messiah, son of David, has appeared and has reassembled the faithful in Palestine.

For a century or more after Saadia's death in 942, Babylonia—strictly speaking, in this period, the Caliphate of Baghdad—continued to be of the greatest cultural importance to both Jews and Muslims. During the twelfth century, however, intellectual leadership among the Jews was assumed by the newer yeshivas in Spain. The city of Baghdad itself, with its glorious record of contributions to civilization, was destroyed in 1258 by a horde of the Mongols. They razed the city to the ground and slaughtered over three quarters of a million of the inhabitants.

Maimonides

At one o'clock in the afternoon of March 30, 1135, Moses ben Maimon, or Maimonides,[21] was born in Córdoba, Spain. That the very hour of his birth was handed down, whereas not even the year is known for many another medieval thinker, is indicative of the veneration in which Maimonides has always been held. He was educated at Córdoba, principally by his father, in Biblical and Talmudic studies, and in philosophy and the sciences. When he was thirteen, he and his family left Córdoba and traveled about, settling for a time at Fez in North Africa and then finally, when he was thirty, in Cairo. It appears that the Almohad Muslims then dominant in Córdoba and Fez were intolerant of everyone, other Muslims included, who did not subscribe to their own fundamentalist form of Islam. Life in Cairo was distinctly better for Maimonides and his family, as Cairo was the capital of the far more enlightened and liberal Fatimid Muslims. A livelihood for the family was provided by Maimonides' older brother, David, a merchant; but when David perished in a shipwreck in the Indian Ocean, the role of breadwinner fell to Maimonides. Like Avicenna and Averroes, he turned to the practice of medicine. In time he acquired such standing as a physician that he was appointed to attend upon the court of the sultan Saladin (deposer of the Fatimids, but a cultivated man and a patron of learning). As a medical celebrity Maimonides was known to King Richard I ("The Lionhearted"), who tried to persuade him to leave Saladin and to come to the English court. (Richard had as little success in this as he did in his efforts to take Jerusalem from Saladin in the Third Crusade.) Maimonides married the sister of one of Saladin's aides, and in 1186 their son Abraham was born.

Busy as he was with his medical practice, Maimonides found time for a great quantity of writing. His codification of the Talmud, in fourteen volumes with the general title of *Misneh Torah* ("Second Torah"), would have been, one might have supposed, the work of a lifetime. For Maimonides it was the work of ten years. He also wrote Talmudic commentaries, a treatise on logic, several medical books (including an important one on hygiene), and his great philosophical work, *The Guide for the Perplexed*. His fame as a rabbi surpassed his fame as a physician. He was made spiritual head (nagid) of the Jewish community of Egypt. Among Jews everywhere he was regarded as an authority to be consulted on difficult points of Jewish law. "From Moses to Moses," it was said, "there has arisen no one like Moses."[22] His death at seventy, on November 13, 1204, was mourned by Jews throughout Europe, Africa, and the Middle East. From Cairo his remains were taken for burial to Tiberias on the Sea of Galilee, where his tomb may still be viewed.

Maimonides' *Guide for the Perplexed,* published in Arabic in 1190, is

---

[21] Among Jews he is usually called "Rambam," which is an acronym formed from the initial letters of "Rabbi Moses ben Maimon."

[22] That is, from the Moses of the Bible to Moses Maimonides there has arisen no one like Moses Maimonides.

not (in spite of its title) addressed to all who happen to be perplexed, but only to well-educated persons made uneasy in their faith by apparent conflicts between truths of religion and truths of philosophy. He takes it for granted that his readers have a good knowledge of the Scriptures, of Talmudic literature, and of philosophy. In general he tries to dispel the perplexity in question by showing that genuine truths of philosophy are entirely consistent with a deeper meaning, if not with the literal meaning, of the Scriptures and the Talmud. The deeper meaning he frequently uncovers by employing the allegorical method of interpretation, a method in use since the time of the Old Stoics. Maimonides' originality in this respect lies in the great thoroughness with which he employs the method in the interests of harmonizing the Old Testament and the Talmud with a somewhat Neoplatonic version of Aristotle. Like Averroes, his older contemporary,[23] Maimonides had arrived at the twofold conclusion that persons with the requisite gifts of intelligence and temperament are actually commanded by Scripture to study metaphysics, and that Aristotle represent the best that metaphysics has to offer. Moses in the Bible prayed, "Show me thy way, that I may know thee, that I may find grace in thy sight" (Exodus 33:13); and this, to Moses Maimonides, means that God's especial favor is reserved for those who know Him, insofar as He is knowable, with the certainty and accuracy afforded by the methods of metaphysics. To the end that even persons of modest intellect may have a tolerably accurate conception of God, Maimonides formulated a creed embodying what he took to be the essential minimum of correct philosophical principles. Unlike Averroes, then, he did not believe it always a mistake to impart philosophical conclusions to the multitude. But he does make it clear that he expects for his *Guide* a very limited readership. On an early page he mentions a reference in the Psalms (82:5) to people who "walk on in darkness." Who are these people? "They are the multitude of ordinary men," Maimonides says; "there is no need to notice them in this treatise." The better to ensure its inaccessibility to "ordinary men," Maimonides gave the *Guide* an arrangement and a style that only the sophisticated would be likely to fathom.

In the Talmud, as Maimonides knows, there are statements that might appear to condemn the pursuit of metaphysics. A case in point: "Whoever pries into four things had better not come into the world, namely, what is above and what is below, what was before and what will be after." But Maimonides says that such statements do not really prohibit any and all reasoning about ultimate issues; they prohibit only the abuse of it by persons of inadequate training and unruly impulse who do not appreciate the limits to what reasoning can demonstrate. And unlike Averroes, Maimonides does believe that, even in the instance of an Aristotle, the human intellect has some signal limitations. For example, Maimonides denies that it is possible to demonstrate either that the world has always

---

[23] Maimonides became acquainted with Averroes' writings only in his later years, by which time his own views were more or less fixed.

existed (as Aristotle and Avicenna tried to do), or that the world was created a finite time ago (as Saadia and the Mu'tazilites argued). Saadia said that time itself necessarily had a beginning, since it is contradictory to think that an infinite amount of it could have elapsed before the present moment. Aristotle said that a beginning of time was impossible, since that would imply a time before there was any time. Plato believed, some authorities have said, that a beginning of time does not imply a time before time, but just a "before" in which time as periodic motion was not. Deep into the past we may trace the innumerable arguments of philosophers about time and the world's beginning. "Philosophers have for the last three thousand years been divided on that subject," Maimonides says; and we may therefore safely conclude that "this question, namely, whether the universe has been created or is eternal, cannot be answered with mathematical certainty; here the human intellect must pause." For his own part, Maimonides will maintain his adherence to the Biblical doctrine of creation: "I accept the latter," he says, "on the authority of Prophecy, which can teach things beyond the reach of human speculation."

When metaphysics cannot strictly demonstrate what Prophecy (or Revelation) teaches, it may still do something, Maimonides believes, by way of showing that Prophecy has more to be said for it than against it. In favor of the doctrine of creation we may cite the evidence of intelligent design in the world, for this is best explained, in Maimonides' view, on the supposition of a Creator who, following a plan He had previously devised, made the world from scratch. But suppose we assume, just for the sake of argument, that the world was *not* created, that it has always existed. Even on that assumption, Maimonides says, we can still demonstrate that God exists and is unique and incorporeal; and thus we shall dispel the perplexity of those at a loss to see why God's existence is not an open question if a beginning of the world, as taught in the Bible, cannot be conclusively proved in philosophy. If a beginning of the world could be demonstrated, everyone would agree that God's existence is certain, for a beginning would imply a Creator who began it. So in proving God's existence on the assumption that the world did *not* have a beginning, we show that His existence is certain either way. Such is the ingenious strategy of argument that Maimonides maps out.

Maimonides presents four arguments for God's existence. For none of them does he claim originality. All of them, he says, have been employed by "the philosophers," which means, as he uses the expression, Aristotle and the Muslim thinkers who found in Aristotle their main inspiration. Nevertheless, there is novelty in the detail and rigor of Maimonides' formulations of the arguments; and it was his formulations that caught the attention of some other notable philosophers, including St. Thomas Aquinas. Three of these four arguments—the first three given below[24]—are

---

[24] In Maimonides' exposition the arguments as we have numbered them occur in the sequence (1), (3), (4), (2).

variations on Aristotle's argument for an unmoved mover. The fourth is substantially Avicenna's argument for a necessary being. The first three are here rather drastically reduced to their elements and restated in simpler terms than Maimonides uses.

(1) *Argument from Motion:* We observe throughout the world a great many changes in the qualities and relations of things, including, of course, changes of place. Let us say (with Aristotle) that all of these changes are instances of *motion*. Let us assume (in temporary agreement with Aristotle) that motion is eternal in the sense that it has always occurred and will always occur. This eternal motion of the world could not occur all by itself. In the case of anything in motion (a bowling ball, say), there is something else—a *mover* (a bowler perhaps)—that moves it. Now, clearly, the eternal motion of the world implies nothing less than an eternal mover of the world. But consider: if this eternal mover were itself in motion, its motion would have to be accounted for by reference to another eternal mover, and so on *ad infinitum,* unless at some point in the hierarchy of eternal movers we come to one that does not move, an unmoved mover. Actually it is impossible for there to be a literally infinite hierarchy of eternal movers (Maimonides takes this as axiomatic). Consequently, there must be an unmoved eternal mover responsible for the eternal motion of the world. This unmoved eternal mover must be incorporeal because any corporeal thing that produces motion (for example, the arm of the bowler) is itself in motion at the time. The incorporeal unmoved eternal mover cannot reside within the world, as if it were a soul in a body, because a soul that moves its body is itself in motion at the time (as the soul of the bowler goes where it moves the bowler's body to go).[25] Accordingly, the incorporeal unmoved eternal mover completely transcends the world. This being is eternal in the strict sense that it is not subject to time, for there is no time without motion. There can be just *one* such being, since incorporeal beings (as Maimonides believes) can be different from one another only by residing in different bodies or by being related to one another, in a hierarchy, as cause and effect (one "emanating" another). And what has here been proved is the existence of a being that transcends all bodies and is not a subordinate member of some hierarchy of movers. To prove the existence of an unique transcendent incorporeal unmoved eternal mover is to prove the existence of God.

(2) *Argument from Potentiality and Actuality:* We observe throughout the world things existing potentially and then becoming actualities. Always, let us assume, this has been and will be going on. The eternal actualization of potential in the world has to be accounted for in terms of something—an *agent*—that eternally keeps it up. If this eternal agent had itself any potential that became actualized, this would have to be accounted for by reference to another eternal agent, but . . . And from

---

[25] Maimonides believes that the world has an outermost heavenly "sphere" that continuously rotates and communicates motion to the spheres inside. Thus the unmoved mover would not be unmoved if any of it resided within the spheres of the world.

here the argument proceeds along the lines of (1) above, arriving at the conclusion that there exists a supreme agent, namely God, who is unique, incorporeal, and completely, eternally actual. (Aristotle would not have considered this a different argument from (1), since he understood "motion" to designate all development from potentiality to actuality, including that represented by changes in the qualities and relations of things.)

(3) *Argument from Two Elements:* Aristotle subscribed to the principle that when we find two elements present together in something, but also find one of them existing elsewhere by itself, then we may conclude that the other also exists elsewhere by itself. Maimonides gives the example of a mixture of honey and vinegar. Having observed honey and vinegar in combination, and then having observed honey existing by itself, we can infer with confidence that vinegar also exists by itself, even if we have not actually observed it by itself. An argument of this type, Maimonides says, may be given for the existence of an unmoved mover. The two elements of *causing motion* and *being moved* are often found together in the same object. A water wheel, for example, combines both elements: it causes motion in the apparatus to which it is connected while it is being moved by the water falling over it. But we also find the element of *being moved* existing by itself. A weather vane, for example, has the element of being moved (by changes in the direction of the wind); but it lacks the element of causing motion in something else. It stands to reason, then, that the element of *causing motion* also exists by itself. There must be something that causes motion without being moved—an unmoved mover. Analysis will show that this unmoved mover must be incorporeal, transcendent, and unique (see argument (1) above); and these are the attributes of God.

(4) *Argument from Temporary Things:* Here the demonstration turns not upon the notions of moving and being moved but upon the notions of necessary and temporary (or contingent) existence. Maimonides argues, as Avicenna did (in somewhat different terms), that the existence of temporary things—things with possible beginnings and ends—implies that there is something whose existence is necessary, so that it could not possibly have a beginning or an end. Analysis will show, he believes, that this necessary being is God. The argument is given below in Maimonides' words, with clarifications inserted in brackets.

There is no doubt that many things actually exist, for example, things perceived with the senses. Now there are only three cases conceivable, namely, either all these things are without beginning and without end, or all of them have beginning and end, or some are with and some without beginning and end. The first of these three cases is altogether inadmissible, since we clearly perceive objects which come into existence and are subsequently destroyed. The second case is likewise inadmissible, for if everything had but a temporary existence all things might be destroyed, and that which is enunciated of a whole class of things as possible is necessarily actual. [That is, if each thing that exists could possibly cease to exist, then there could come a time (if time is infinite) when everything has ceased to exist. Actually that time would already have come, at some point in the infinite reaches of past time, for a possibility that *everything* is supposed to have (such as the possibility of ceasing to exist) is not really a possibility if in infinite time it is never realized.] All things must therefore come [must already have come] to an end, and then nothing would ever be [nothing would now be] in existence, for there would not exist [after everything ceased to exist] any being to produce anything. Consequently nothing whatever would exist [if all things have a temporary existence]; but as we see things existing, and find ourselves in existence, we conclude as follows: Since there are undoubtedly beings of a temporary existence, there must also be an eternal being that is not subject to destruction, and whose existence is real, not merely possible. . . .

The existence of this being is necessary, either on account of itself alone or on account of some external force. In the latter case its existence and non-existence would be equally possible [as far as its own nature was concerned], but its existence would be necessary on account of the external force. That force would then be the being that possesses absolute existence [that is, the being that exists by virtue of its own necessity]. It is therefore certain that there must be a being which has absolutely independent existence [which exists by virtue of its own necessity], and is the source of the existence of all [other] things. . . . This is a proof the correctness of which is not doubted, disputed, or rejected, except by those who have no knowledge of the method of proof. We further say that the existence of anything that has independent existence is not due to any cause, and that such a being does not include any plurality whatever [for if it had distinguishable elements, it would exist by virtue of whatever produces their combination, not on its own account, not by virtue of its own necessity]. Consequently it cannot be a body, nor a force residing in a body [because bodies and their forces have causes and components]. It is now clear that there must be a being with absolutely independent existence, a being whose existence cannot be attributed to any external cause, and which does not include different elements; it cannot therefore be corporeal, or a force residing in a corporeal object; this being is God.

Maimonides goes on to argue that there could not be more than one God, that is, more than one being that exists by virtue of its own necessity. If there were two Gods, they would have something in common (their Godliness), because otherwise they would not be alike in being Gods. And one of the two Gods, at least, would have an element not possessed by the other, because that would be required to differentiate them. Unless the two Gods were different in some respect, they would not be two. So one of the two Gods, at least, would "include a plurality" in having two distinguishable elements, Godliness and an element not possessed by the other God. But we have already seen that there cannot be a plurality in a necessary being. To put it simply, there would have to be something over and above the God-with-two-elements that accounted for the combination of the two elements that make Him up; and thus He would not exist by virtue of His own necessity. Since the supposition that there are two Gods (beings that exist by virtue of their own necessity) implies that at least one of them does *not* exist by virtue of His own necessity, this supposition is false. There cannot be more than one God. In His absolute simplicity and independence, Maimonides says, God is the only member of His species and "has therefore nothing in common with any other being."

God's radical unlikeness to any other being is a matter upon which Maimonides tirelessly insists. In this respect he follows Plotinus, not Aristotle. Aristotle ascribed to God an activity of self-reflective thinking not wholly unlike certain of our own processes of thought. But Maimonides, like Plotinus, will not allow that there is the faintest analogy between God and anything else. We cannot, he says, ascribe any positive attributes to God. We can state only what God is *not*, as when we say that He is "incorporeal" (meaning "not corporeal"). This follows from Maimonides' conception of God's unity or simplicity. Saadia had the same conception but did not fully develop its implications. God's unity, on this understanding of it, is such that no attributes are distinguishable in His nature. And in that case God's nature cannot be described, since to describe the nature of anything is to specify one or more of its attributes. Maimonides concedes that it is possible to refer to God, after a fashion, in terms of His relation to the world. This is done by means of so-called "attributes of action," such as "Maker of the world," but these are descriptions not of God's nature but of what He does—His "action." For the rest, our statements about God have to be negative in form ("God is not corporeal"), or else couched in terms of "negative attributes" ("God is incorporeal"). Maimonides hastens to assure us, however, that the more we really understand of what God is not, the closer we come to a knowledge of what He is. That we cannot assign positive attributes to God does not mean that we must forever be in the dark about His nature. By denying positive attributes of Him, or by asserting negative ones, and the more the better, we exclude from consideration things other than God and thus narrow the field, so to speak, until we have located His metaphysical vicinity. The value of philosophical training in enabling us to do this is one of the chief things in its favor from Maimonides' standpoint. He explains:

> It is generally accepted among theologians, and also among philosophers, that there can be a great difference between two persons as regards the knowledge of God obtained by them. Know that this is really the case, that those who have obtained a knowledge of God differ greatly from each other; for in the same way as by each additional [positive] attribute an object is more specified, and is brought nearer to the true

apprehension of the observer, so by each additional negative attribute you advance toward the knowledge of God, and you are nearer to it than he who does not negative, in reference to God, those qualities which you are convinced by proof must be negatived. . . .

I will give you . . . some illustrations. . . . A person may know for certain that a "ship" is in existence, but he may not know to what object that name is applied, whether to a substance or to an accident; a second person then learns that the ship is not an accident; a third, that it is not a mineral; a fourth, that it is not a plant growing in the earth; a fifth, that it is not a body whose parts are joined together by nature; a sixth, that it is not a flat object like boards or doors; a seventh, that it is not a sphere; an eighth, that it is not pointed; a ninth, that it is not round-shaped nor equilateral; a tenth, that it is not solid. It is clear that this tenth person has almost arrived at the correct notion of a "ship" by the foregoing negative attributes, as if he had exactly the same notion as those have who imagine it to be a wooden substance which is hollow, long, and composed of many pieces of wood, that is to say, who know it by positive attributes. But you must be careful, in what you negative, to negative by proof, not by mere words, for each time you ascertain by proof that a certain thing, [popularly] believed to exist in the Creator, must be negatived, you have undoubtedly come one step nearer to the knowledge of God. . . .

There is a great danger in applying positive attributes to God. . . . Every perfection we could imagine, even if existing in God in accordance with the opinion of those who [incorrectly] assert the existence of attributes [in Him], would in reality not be of the same kind as that imagined by us, but would only be called by the same name . . . it would in fact amount to a negation. Suppose, for example, that you say He has knowledge, and that [His] knowledge, which admits of no change and of no plurality, embraces many changeable things; His knowledge remains unaltered, while new things are constantly formed, and His knowledge of a thing before it exists, while it exists, and when it has ceased to exist, is the same without the least change: you would thereby declare that His knowledge is not like ours; and similarly that His existence is not like ours. You thus necessarily arrive at some negation, without obtaining a true conception of an essential attribute; on the contrary, you are led to assume that there is a plurality in God, and to believe that He, though one essence, has several unknown attributes. For if you intend to affirm them, you cannot compare them with those attributes known by us, and they are consequently not of the same kind. You are, as it were, brought by the belief in the reality of the attributes to say that God is one subject of which several things are predicated, though the subject is not like ordinary subjects, and the predicates are not like ordinary predicates. This belief would ultimately lead us to associate other things with God, and not to believe that He is One.

Not to believe in the absolute unity of God, Maimonides says, is not to believe in God at all. And this would put one at a serious disadvantage when it comes to the next life because what survives the death of one's body, as Maimonides understands the matter, is only as much of one's consciousness as has been invested, in this life, in true beliefs about the world in relation to the Creator. The more one rises above true belief and approximates to a knowledge of God, the more of oneself there will be—in the form of "acquired intellect"—capable of entering into eternal life. Moral virtue, of which Maimonides gives an account much like Aristotle's, is also necessary; but its value resides in its being a condition of intellectual perfection. Maimonides derives from his Neoplatonic sources a theory to the effect that what "joins us to God" is the Active Intelligence, tenth in a series of Intelligences subordinate to God,[26] which actualizes our potential for knowledge. Our "link" with God via the Active Intelligence is strengthened insofar as we do, and weakened or even broken insofar as we do not, strive to perfect in ourselves "the love of God"; and "man's love of God," Maimonides says, "is identical with his knowledge of Him." The supreme importance that Maimonides attaches to intellectual perfection is expressed very clearly in the conclusion of a parable he tells concerning a king (God) and his subjects (humankind): "Those who have succeeded in finding a proof for everything that can be proved, who have a true knowledge of God, so far as a true knowledge can be attained, and are near the truth, wherever an approach to the truth is possible, they have reached the goal, and are in the palace where the king lives. . . . When you have mastered Metaphysics, you have entered the innermost court, and are with the king in the same palace."

All the laws of the Bible, Maimonides thinks, have the purpose of fostering, directly or indirectly, the love that consists in knowledge of God. It is not the case that some laws—Laws of Tradition, as Saadia called them—have little or nothing in the way of beneficial purposes discoverable by reason. All of God's commandments, in Maimonides' view, are what Saadia called Laws of Reason, for we can discover by careful reflection what the reason for each of them is. Maimonides has little patience with the notion that the Divine character and origin of a law are only the plainer if the good to be realized by obeying it is a mystery to us. The "weak-minded persons" to whom this seems plausible hardly pay a compliment to the Creator in supposing that He would do what no sensible man or woman would do, namely, give orders that defy understanding. No, God's laws in their entirety are for our benefit, and Maimonides undertakes to show in every case how this is so. Some laws, he finds, have the immediate purpose of inculcating a correct understanding of God and

---

[26] Unlike his Neoplatonic sources, Maimonides does not believe that God has eternally emanated the Intelligences that bridge the gulf between Him and the world. He thinks that God created the Intelligences, and with them the world, from nothing a finite time ago: "The creative act of the Almighty in giving existence to pure Intelligences, endows the first of them with the power of giving existence to another, and so on down to the Active Intellect [or Intelligence], the lowest of the purely spiritual beings."

His relation to the world. This understanding is the highest end of humankind. Other laws are intended to promote social justice and moral virtue, which are prerequisites to achieving the highest end. In short, the laws in the Bible may be classified into "those which spread truth," "those which regulate our social conduct," and "those which teach morals." "These three principles," Maimonides says, "suffice for assigning a reason for every one of the Divine commandments."

Maimonides' confidence that reason enables us to understand God's purposes so thoroughly, and his assignment of supreme value to intellectual perfection, did not meet with the approval of all the Jewish philosophers who came after him. He had vigorous opponents as well as supporters. Hasdai Crescas (1340–1410) is especially notable among those who argued that Maimonides had gone too far in interpreting Jewish principles from an Aristotelian perspective. Nevertheless, Maimonides' *Guide* was by far the greatest single influence upon the development of later medieval Jewish philosophy. As one authority has put it: "In the post-Maimonidean age all [Jewish] philosophical thinking is in the nature of a commentary on Maimonides, whether avowedly or not." Soon after Maimonides published the *Guide* (in 1190), it was translated into Latin and began to be studied by Christian philosophers. Ideas and arguments in the *Guide* were eagerly adopted by such figures as William of Auvergne, Bishop of Paris (about 1180–1249), Alexander of Hales (about 1185–1245), and Albertus Magnus (1206–1280), the teacher of St. Thomas Aquinas. The use that St. Thomas made of the *Guide* brought some of Maimonides' chief positions permanently into the mainstream of Christian philosophical discussion.

CHAPTER 16

St. Thomas Aquinas

Some Background: St. Bonaventure

During the twelfth and thirteenth centuries, Western European civilization advanced on many fronts. These High Middle Ages featured a revolution in agriculture, a revival of commerce, the reemergence of towns as centers of finance and manufacture, the development of strong central governments in England and France, and reforms in the Roman Catholic Church which brought the Papacy—especially during the pontificate of Innocent III (1198–1216)—to new heights of power and prestige. On the score of cultural achievements, this period was one of the most fertile in history. In architecture the Romanesque and Gothic styles were brought to perfection in great French cathedrals such as those at Caen and Chartres. A flowering of poetic literature, in vernacular languages as well as in Latin, culminated in the *Divine Comedy* of Dante Alighieri (1265–1321). Historical writing flourished on an unprecedented scale and achieved a high standard in such works as the *Deeds of Frederick* by Otto of Freising (uncle of the subject, Frederick I Barbarossa). The Greek classics, through Muslim sources in Sicily and in Spain, were recovered for study in Christendom and were made accessible in Latin translations. Universities evolved from cathedral schools in Italy and in France, and at Paris especially the Greek classics were an incitement to philosophical investigation, while at Bologna scholarship focused upon the neglected Justinian *Corpus* of Roman Law. Scientific learning, partly under the inspiration of Muslim treatises in mathematics, astronomy, and medicine, was revived by Roger Bacon at Oxford and Paris, by Leonard of Pisa (a notable mathematician), by Constantine the African (founder of an important medical school at Salerno), and by a number of others. St. Dominic (1170–1221) and St. Francis of Assisi (1182–1226) founded the religious orders that bear their names; and Dominicans and Franciscans became rivals in learning, invaded the universities, and figured prominently as members of the faculties.

All of the most important Christian thinkers of the later Middle Ages were either Dominicans or Franciscans; all of them were associated at one time or another with the University of Paris (chartered in 1200); and all of them endeavored to come to terms with the newly discovered works of Aristotle. Available at Paris by 1250 were Aristotle's main works on logic, physics, metaphysics, and ethics, together with Muslim commentaries on them, and various Muslim and Jewish treatises in which Aristotelian themes were developed. Avicenna, Algazali, Averroes, and Maimonides, among others, were represented. This abundance of fresh material, covering a wide range of philosophical topics, but from non-Christian standpoints, presented no small challenge to Christian thinkers. St. Augustine had for centuries been viewed in the West as the authoritative philosopher-theologian. How were men steeped in St. Augustine going to deal with Aristotle and with Aristotle's Muslim and Jewish followers? What happened, roughly speaking, was that the Franciscan thinkers—notably St. Bonaventure (1221–1274)—adhered fairly closely to the tradition of St. Augustine and adopted a more or less critical attitude toward Aristotle, particularly in metaphysics; whereas the Dominican thinkers—notably St. Thomas Aquinas (1225–1274)—revolutionized Christian philosophy by reconciling Aristotle with the doctrines of the Church.

St. Bonaventure[1] said of Aristotle that "we follow him where he spoke well, not where he was in the dark." But Aristotle was entirely in the dark, as it seemed to St. Bonaventure, when it came to the chief point of metaphysics, which is that God possesses ideas of all possible creatures and produces the world employing these ideas as archetypes or models or exemplars. Plato, St. Bonaventure believed, had an inkling of the truth in his theory that sensible things are copies or imitations of separate intelligible forms. Plotinus, he felt, came closer to the truth when he located these forms in the Intellect that proceeds from the One. St. Augustine, however, achieved the fullest insight into the matter when he identified these forms as ideas contained in the Word of God, which is the expression of God that proceeds from God's knowledge of Himself, and which is the medium of creation. Aristotle, on the other hand, went wide of the mark in criticizing Plato for viewing forms as existing apart from particular sensible things, for unless they so existed (St. Bonaventure points out), they could hardly stand as exemplars in the Word of God. Having made this fundamental mistake, Aristotle proceeded to adopt the erroneous positions that follow from it. He believed that the world was eternal, not created, which would stand to reason, St. Bonaventure says, if there were no exemplars in God's mind (or in the Word) for Him to

---

[1] St. Bonaventure, Giovanni di Fidanza, was born in Tuscany in 1221, entered the Franciscan Order while a young man, studied and then taught (theology) at the University of Paris, became head (Minister General) of the Franciscans in 1257, and was made bishop as well as cardinal in 1273, a year before his death at fifty-three. Much of St. Bonaventure's energy was devoted to keeping peace among Franciscans, who had fallen into sharp disagreement over the mission of the Order. At one point he even found it necessary to imprison the man who had preceded him as Minister General and who indeed had recommended him for the position. His writings include *Commentary on the Sentences of Peter Lombard, Retracing the Arts to Theology, Journey of the Mind to God,* and *Conferences on the Hexaemeron* (that is, lectures on the six days of creation, in which occur the criticisms of Aristotle to be mentioned here).

follow in creation. Aristotle also believed that God thinks only of Himself, as of course He would do if He had no ideas of things other than Himself, in which case He could exercise no providence over the world, and whatever happened in the world would be—"as the Arabs maintain"—the outcome of strictly natural causes. Finally, St. Bonaventure says, Aristotle's belief in the eternity of the world appears to have led him, or at any rate Averroes,[2] to conclude that human individuality is an illusion, that there is but one imperishable intellect in all humankind (if the world had no beginning, so the argument goes, there would already have existed an infinity of persons, so that if each had his or her *own* imperishable intellect, an infinity of these would now exist, whereas an infinity of things cannot exist at the same time).

Aristotle and his Muslim followers, in St. Bonaventure's view, illustrate how far from the truth philosophers can stray when they are not guided by the light of faith. As St. Augustine said, understanding is the reward of faith—the reward of believing in certain fundamental doctrines on the Church's authority as revealed by God. It is only to be expected, St. Bonaventure says, that pagan or infidel philosophers will err in their reasoning, that they will mistake partial truths for the whole truth, that they will subscribe to downright falsehoods. Consider the issue of whether the world is eternal or was created. Aristotle, and Averroes after him, concluded that the world is eternal; but Averroes at least ought to have known better, since as a Muslim he was certainly acquainted with the doctrine of creation as given in the Koran. And with St. Augustine, St. Bonaventure maintains that the doctrine of creation will be seen to have reason on its side if only one will trust it enough really to explore and investigate what can be said in its behalf. Among the arguments that St. Bonaventure offers in this connection is one reminiscent of Saadia. If the world had no beginning, he says, an infinite multitude of days would have come and gone before the present day; but since it is impossible for an infinite multitude to be exhausted, the present day could never have arrived; and since it plainly *has* arrived, the world must after all have had a beginning. (And so the previous argument, to the effect that human individuality is an illusion because the world is eternal, falls to the ground.) Solid arguments such as this, in support of articles of faith, will not be found or appreciated, St. Bonaventure says, by philosophers having no real faith in the articles. These people will be apt, when faced with an Aristotle, either to throw over Christian doctrines or to suppose that these doctrines can expect little or no support from philosophy. It is equally essential, St. Bonaventure says, to grasp the fact that some very important religious truths cannot be arrived at by reasoning but can only be revealed to us supernaturally. The Trinity of Persons in the Unity of God's Nature is a prime example. A philosopher such as Aristotle or Av-

---

[2] Actually Averroes himself did not subscribe to this view (see pp. 354–355), but he attributed it to Aristotle, whose opinions on the matter are unclear (see pp. 151–152).

icenna, who arrives by reasoning at God's Unity but who does not go on to supplement this conclusion with the revealed doctrine of the Trinity, stops short of the whole truth. And he falls into error insofar as his conception of the Unity is such as to prompt him to reject—were he to consider it—the doctrine of the Trinity. St. Bonaventure does not deny that philosophical reasoning can in theory give us truths independently of faith, but he does deny that philosophers will in practice generally investigate the right issues, or avoid untrue or half-true conclusions, unless they philosophize in the light of faith.

St. Thomas Aquinas, who did not share St. Bonaventure's poor opinion of Aristotle's metaphysics, also did not share St. Bonaventure's poor opinion of the prospects of philosophizing without reliance upon faith. Aristotle, in St. Thomas's eyes, produced a largely satisfactory metaphysical system; and inasmuch as Aristotle was a pagan, evidently it was not impossible for a pagan to achieve many sound philosophical views. St. Bonaventure's opposition to Aristotle owed much, St. Thomas believed, to mistaken philosophical notions of St. Bonaventure's own. This was particularly true when it came to the question, answered in the negative by Aristotle, of whether the world had a beginning. St. Bonaventure held that the world cannot have been created if it did not have a beginning, so that in denying a beginning Aristotle perforce denied creation. St. Bonaventure further believed that the necessity of a beginning could be demonstrated and that Aristotle could thus be refuted. St. Thomas, however, did not think that St. Bonaventure or anyone else had succeeded in demonstrating that the world must have had a beginning; nor could St. Thomas see why creation of the world would be impossible unless the world had a beginning. Could not the world have been created from eternity? "Creation from eternity" seemed to St. Bonaventure a contradiction in terms: "creation," he thought, implies a time before which there was nothing, whereas "from eternity" denies that there was such a time. St. Thomas replied that a time before which there was nothing is not required by the idea that God creates everything from nothing, because God could have been doing this always. The Book of Genesis, as of course St. Thomas knew, tells us that God has not done this always, that God created the world a definite time ago; and this is a truth that we must accept on faith, correcting Aristotle accordingly. Analysis will show that Aristotle came no closer to proving the eternity of the world than St. Bonaventure came to proving the opposite. Philosophy, St. Thomas believed, cannot settle the issue one way or the other. But hostility to Aristotle, on account of his belief in the eternity of the world, is not an appropriate response to the profoundest philosopher yet to appear—"*the Philosopher*," St. Thomas called him. Aristotle *could* have been right about the eternity of the world, for all that philosophical reasoning can tell us on the matter; and his arguments for God's existence, as well as his arguments on hosts of other topics, will be found to be both sound in themselves and consistent with Christian doctrines. In fact, St. Thomas believed, Christian doctrines find in Aristotle's system a perfect instrument for their articulation and defense, and St. Thomas set himself to show that this was the case. The result was a monumental system of St. Thomas's own, in which the ideas of Aristotle (together with ideas of Aristotle's Muslim and Jewish followers), and the ideas of the tradition of St. Augustine, were rethought in relation to one another, modified considerably in process of analysis by an intellect of unsurpassed penetration, and fused into a synthesis of great originality.

Life and Method

St. Thomas Aquinas was born in 1225 at Roccasecca, near Aquino, about halfway between Rome and Naples (and in the vicinity of Arpino, Cicero's birthplace). He was the seventh son of Teodora and Landolfo, Count of Aquino, who sent him to school at the Benedictine monastery of Monte Cassino, a short distance from Roccasecca, where his uncle was abbot. When he was about fourteen, he went on to the University of Naples, which had recently been founded by Frederick II, Holy Roman Emperor, to whom St. Thomas's family, on his father's side, was distantly related. While at Naples he was attracted to the Dominican Order, which at nineteen he entered in spite of the objections of his family; whereupon St. Thomas's brothers, in hopes of bringing him to quit the Dominicans, kidnapped him and held him at Roccasecca for more than a year. Apparently his brothers would stop at nothing in their efforts to induce him to abandon his monastic vows. We are told that they sent into his room one night a woman of beautiful appearance and easy virtue, whom St. Thomas promptly frightened away with a firebrand snatched from his hearth. At length, in 1245, St. Thomas managed to escape from his brothers and to make his way to Paris. At the university there he came under the influence of a German Dominican scholar by the name of Albert, later known as St. Albert the Great (Albertus Magnus), who possessed vast learning and a strong interest in Aristotle. After three years in Paris, St. Thomas accompanied Albert to Cologne, where Albert was to set up a Dominican school; but after three years in Cologne, St. Thomas (now twenty-seven) returned to Paris, took a master's degree, and began to lecture on theology. His reputation rose to such heights that, in 1259, he was summoned to serve as professor and advisor in the court of the Pope. The remaining fifteen years of St. Thomas's life were mostly spent in Rome or its vicinity; but he did for a time return to lecture in Paris, and at the end he was a professor at the University of Naples. He died at forty-nine (March 7, 1274) on his way from Naples to a Church council at Lyons in France. He had gotten as far as Fossanova, a Cistercian abbey south of Rome, where the guesthouse in which he died can still be seen.

St. Thomas's appearance and personality have been well described by G. K. Chesterton:

> St. Thomas was a huge heavy bull of a man, fat and slow and quiet; very mild and magnanimous but not very sociable; shy, even apart from the humility of holiness; and abstracted, even apart from his occasional and carefully concealed experiences of trance or ecstasy. . . . [He was] so stolid that the scholars, in the schools which he attended, regularly thought he was a dunce ["the Dumb Ox" was his schoolmates' name for him]. . . . [He] came out of a world where he might have enjoyed leisure, and he remained one of those men whose labor has something of the placidity of leisure. He was a hard worker, but nobody could possibly mistake him for a hustler. He had something indefinable about him, which marks those who work when they need not work. For he was by birth a gentleman of a great house, and such repose can remain a habit, when it is no longer a motive. But in him it was expressed only in its most amiable elements . . . in his effortless courtesy and patience.

St. Thomas's great magnanimity, as well as his immense scholarship, were conspicuous in the controversies in which he took part, so that even his opponents were inclined to revere him. At Paris during his final visit there (1269–1272), he was confronted with some faculty at the university who interpreted Aristotle, after the manner of Averroes, in ways inconsistent with Christian doctrines. Headed by Siger of Brabant (about 1240–1284), these "Latin Averroists," as they have been called, were associated with propositions (on account of which St. Bonaventure had dismissed Aristotle's metaphysics) such as the eternity of the world and the unity of the intellect in all human beings. Exactly what Siger and the others made of these things is hard to determine. Did they themselves believe that Aristotle had really proved the eternity of the world, and if they did, was it their view that the Christian doctrine of creation was somehow *also* true? (The Latin Averroists have often been said to have held a Double–Truth Theory of this sort, according to which two opposed statements could both be true, one true "in philosophy," the other true "in theology.") Or did they think that the eternity of the world, although a conclusion to which the best human reasoning—as in Aristotle—is inevitably driven, should nevertheless be accounted false in favor of Divine revelation to the contrary? Whatever their precise attitude, the Latin Averroists certainly expounded Aristotle in ways that made him seem irreconcilable with the teachings of the Church. This only revived and heightened the anxieties of Church officials, who from time to time had issued prohibitions, more or less disregarded at Paris, against the teaching of Aristotle's metaphysics. St. Thomas, of course, vigorously opposed the Latin Averroists and endeavored to establish, as one recent authority has put it, "an interpretation of Aristotle that was moderate and acceptable in Christian schools."

All the same, it was some of the Latin Averroists who were the first to go on record, in a joint letter written on the occasion of his death, as believing him to have been a saint.

Forty-eight years later the Church agreed. St. Thomas was canonized in 1323. In 1270 and again in 1277, the Bishop of Paris had formally "condemned" a number of propositions attributable to the Latin Averroists and a few attributable to St. Thomas. Needless to say, however, the censure of St. Thomas was rescinded by the time of his canonization; and from then until now his theological and philosophical views have been held in especial esteem within the Catholic Church. A long series of papal endorsements culminated in 1879 in the encyclical *Aeterni Patris*, wherein Pope Leo XIII accorded a kind of official status to the teachings of the Angelic Doctor (for such was the title given him in 1567 by Pope Pius V). Here is part of what Leo XIII had to say:

> Far above all other Scholastic Doctors towers Thomas Aquinas, their master and prince. . . . Rightly and deservedly he is reckoned a singular safeguard and glory of the Catholic Church. . . . There is no part of philosophy which he did not handle with acuteness and solidity. He wrote about the laws of reasoning; about God and incorporeal substances; about man and other things of sense; and about human acts and their principles. What is more, he wrote on these subjects in such a way that not one of the following perfections is wanting: a full selection of subjects; a beautiful arrangement of their divisions; the best method of treating them; certainty of principles; strength of argument; perspicuity and propriety in language; and the power of explaining deep mysteries.
>
> Moreover, carefully distinguishing reason from Faith, as is right, and yet joining them together in a harmony of friendship, he so guarded the rights of each, and so watched over the dignity of each, that, as far as man is concerned, reason can now hardly rise higher than she rose, borne up in the flight of St. Thomas; and Faith can hardly gain more helps and greater helps from reason than those which St. Thomas gave her.

St. Thomas's writings, in the original Latin, fill twenty-five volumes. Included are letters, devotional works, sermons, and lectures; commentaries on Aristotle, Boethius, and Pseudo-Dionysius; a number of short works on special topics in philosophy and theology (*On the Eternity of the World* and *On Being and Essence* are examples); and the great comprehensive treatises for which he is especially famous, the *Summa contra Gentiles* and the *Summa Theologiae*. The term *summa* connotes an ordered synthesis of knowledge covering a wide field. In the *Summa contra Gentiles*, written from 1259 to 1264 during his sojourn at the papal court, St. Thomas produced a synthesis of theology and philosophy designed, as tradition has it, to guide Dominican missionaries in arguing against (*contra*) the infidels (*Gentiles*) in Spain—these "infidels" being the Muslims. In the *Summa Theologiae* (or *Theologica,* to give the time-honored misspelling, which we too shall follow hereafter), St. Thomas aimed to systematize theology for beginners in the subject. He began this work around 1264, and although it runs to five volumes in one standard edition, it was never completed. A few months before he died St. Thomas stopped writing. Something had happened to him while he was celebrating Mass. "I can write no more," he said to a friend. "I have seen things which make all my writings like straw." He did not explain further.

Pope Leo XIII commended St. Thomas for his "method of treating" a "full selection of subjects." What St. Thomas did was to perfect the method used by other thinkers in the medieval schools—the "Scholastic Method"—and to apply it to a multiplicity of topics arranged in a tightly-ordered fashion. The *Summa Theologica,* for example, takes up scores of specific issues classified under appropriate headings and divided carefully into subordinate issues. At the outset of the *Summa Theologica* we find, under the general heading of "God and the Order of Creation," some eight subdivisions, the first of which is "God: the Divine Unity." Under "God: the Divine Unity" are grouped twenty-six "Questions," the first of which is "The Nature and Domain of Sacred Doctrine." Under "The Nature and Domain of Sacred Doctrine" are grouped ten "Articles," the first of which is "Whether, Besides the Philosophical Sciences, Any Further Doctrine Is Required?" As a sample of St. Thomas's method, here in its entirety is this—the

FIRST ARTICLE
Whether, Besides the Philosophical Sciences, Any Further Doctrine Is Required?

We proceed thus to the First Article:—

Objection 1. It seems that, besides the philosophical sciences, we have no need of any further knowledge. For man should not seek to know what is above reason: *Seek not the things that are too high for thee (Ecclus.* iii.22). But whatever is not above reason is sufficiently considered in the philosophical sciences. Therefore any other knowledge besides the philosophical sciences is superfluous.

Objection 2. Further, knowledge can be concerned only with being, for nothing can be known, save the true, which is convertible with being. But everything that is, is considered in the philosophical sciences—even God himself; so that there is a part of philosophy called theology, or the divine science, as is clear from Aristotle. Therefore, besides the philosophical sciences, there is no need of any further knowledge.

On the contrary, It is written (*2 Tim.* iii.16): *All Scripture inspired of God is profitable to teach, to reprove, to correct, to instruct in justice.* Now Scripture, inspired of God, is not a part of the philosophical sciences discovered by human reason. Therefore it is useful that besides the philosophical sciences there should be another science—i.e., inspired of God.

I answer that, It was necessary for man's salvation that there should be a knowledge revealed by God, besides the philosophical sciences investigated by human reason. First, because man is directed to God as to an end that surpasses the grasp of his reason: *The eye hath not seen, O God, what things Thou hast prepared for them that wait for Thee (Isa.* lxiv.4). But the end must first be known by men who are to direct their thoughts and actions to the end. Hence it was necessary for the salvation of man that certain truths which exceed human reason should be made known to him by divine revelation. Even as regards those truths about God which human reason can investigate, it was necessary that man be taught by a divine revelation. For the truth about God, such as reason can know it, would only be known by a few, and that after a long time, and with the admixture of many errors; whereas man's whole salvation, which is in God, depends upon the knowledge of this truth. Therefore, in order that the salvation of men might be brought about more fitly and more surely, it was necessary that, besides the philosophical sciences investigated by reason, there should be a sacred science by way of revelation.

Reply Obj. 1. Although those things which are beyond man's knowledge may not be sought for by man through his reason, nevertheless, what is revealed by God must be accepted through faith. Hence the sacred text continues, *For many things are shown to thee above the understanding of man (Ecclus.* iii.25). And in such things sacred science consists.

Reply Obj. 2. Sciences are diversified according to the diverse nature of their knowable objects. For the astronomer and the physicist both prove the same conclusion—that the earth, for instance, is round: the astronomer by means of mathematics (i.e., abstracting from matter), but the physicist by means of matter itself. Hence there is no reason why those things which are treated by the philosophical sciences, so far as they can be known by the light of natural reason, may not also be treated by another science so far as they are known by the light of the divine revelation. Hence the theology included in sacred doctrine differs in genus from that theology which is part of philosophy.

Exactly this type of treatment is to be found in each of the hundreds of "Articles" in the *Summa Theologica.* First St. Thomas states the question at issue and outlines "Objections" in the form of answers to the question that he believes to be either wholly or partly incorrect. Next, often appealing to Scripture, he indicates ("On the contrary . . .") an answer to the question that is at odds with the answers of the "Objections"—usually an answer with which he agrees (as when he cites Scripture), but sometimes an answer he finds only partly correct. Then he proceeds ("I answer that . . .") to develop his own view of the matter, taking into account the opposing standpoints just presented; and in conclusion he replies one by one to the "Objections." With amazing perseverance St. Thomas does this on issue after issue, in volume after volume of the *Summa Theologica.* Hardly anyone escapes his notice, from the Pre-Socratics down to Averroes and Maimonides, from the earliest Fathers of the Church down to St. Bonaventure—virtually everyone comes in for consideration, favorable or otherwise, in some apt connection. Few indeed are the philosophers who have paid this kind of attention to what their predecessors have said.

Faith and Reason

Pope Leo XIII commended St. Thomas not only for his rigorous method but also for "carefully distinguishing reason from Faith . . . and yet joining them together in a harmony of friendship. . . ." And the First Article of the *Summa Theologica* indicates the direction taken by St. Thomas in distinguishing, yet joining, faith and reason. By faith we appropriate revealed truths pertaining to divine matters upon which our eternal salvation depends. Some of these revealed truths are also, for some persons, ascertainable by reasoning; and such reasoning is the concern of metaphysics under the heading of *philosophical* (or *natural*) theology. Other revealed truths are not, for any human being, ascertainable by reasoning; but they may be elucidated, and criticisms of them may be rebutted; and such are the concerns of *sacred* (or *dogmatic*) theology. "Articles of Faith," as St. Thomas uses the expression, are revealed truths *not* ascertainable by reasoning; whereas revealed truths that *are* so ascertainable are "Preambles" to the Articles. God's existence and unity are among the Preambles.[3] The doctrines of the Trinity and of Creation are among the Articles. Principles of logic, and philosophical methods of analysis generally, are of use in sacred theology for spelling out and systematizing the implications of Articles of Faith, and for neutralizing attacks upon the Articles. Although Articles of Faith cannot be proved, "authority based on divine revelation" affords every assurance that in themselves (though not to us) they are certain in the highest degree. We may therefore be confident that criticisms of the Articles are never conclusive but are always "arguments that can be answered." The utility of philosophical methods for this and other theological purposes does not mean, however, that the "philosophical sciences" are helps of which sacred theology "stands in need." Sacred theology is the noblest of the sciences, owing to the supreme importance of its subject matter and the unrivaled certitude of its principles (the Articles), and "philosophical sciences" are to be viewed simply as its "inferiors and handmaidens." "Other sciences," St. Thomas says, "derive their certitude from the natural light of human reason, which

[3] If we can grasp a demonstration of God's existence, we no longer have *faith* that He exists—we *know* that He exists. But if God's existence were classified as an Article of Faith, then in knowing that He exists we would not be assenting to an Article of Faith. It is to avoid this unhappy consequence that St. Thomas prefers to view God's existence as a Preamble to the Articles.

can err, whereas this science [sacred theology] derives its certitude from the light of divine revelation, which cannot err. . . ." Therefore, "whatsoever is found in the other sciences [such as philosophy] contrary to the truth of this science must be condemned as false." It follows from this that philosophy can never come into any real conflict with sacred theology, because the superior certitude of revelation gives sacred theology the right to adjudicate in any controversies with her that philosophers may start. But St. Thomas did not take the attitude that sacred theology has to watch with a jealous eye the exercise of "natural reason" in the philosophical sciences. Divine revelation, as a matter of God's grace, is perfectly harmonious with the conclusions of natural reason at its best. "Grace does not destroy nature, but perfects it." Sacred theology raises philosophy up into the highest of services, where truths of reason join with the truths of revelation to form an organic unity as befits their common origin, for both are gifts of God.

Natural reason at its best, in St. Thomas's view, is to be found in the works of Aristotle; and now we shall see something of how St. Thomas uses and develops Aristotle's ideas.

Metaphysical Principles

Following Aristotle, St. Thomas views the natural world as consisting of a multiplicity of concrete individual substances (animals, vegetables, and minerals), each of which has characteristics in the ten categories of substance, quantity, quality, relation, place, time, position, state, action, and affection. For any given individual substance certain characteristics are essential, inasmuch as losing them would amount to a complete loss of identity on the part of the substance. These essential characteristics, which fall under the category of substance, constitute the substance's essence or definition (as "rational animality" is the essence of a human being). Other characteristics, called "accidents," are not essential to a substance, since it can gain or lose them without losing its identity (as someone may move from one place to another without ceasing to be a human being, and the same human being). When something loses the characteristics that constitute its essence, what happens is called a "substantial change"—a new substance coming into existence where the old one was before. The firebrand that St. Thomas took from his hearth when the beautiful woman appeared in his room was undergoing a substantial change—from wood into the substances of smoke and ashes. Now the smoke and ashes, to focus for a moment upon them, did not come into existence from nowhere; they were transformations of the wood, very different in form from the wood, but actualizations of potential within the wood nevertheless. There must then have been, underlying (so to speak) the distinctive woody characteristics of the wood, something representing the potential of becoming smoke and ashes. This underlying something is called "matter," in contrast to the "forms" of wood, ashes, smoke, and whatever else this matter may have the potential to become. The same distinction may be observed in the case of any substance one cares to consider. Each of them consists of (a) an underlying matter representing the potential for change and (b) a form currently actualized in the matter—this form consisting in the characteristics that make up the essence or definition of the substance in question.

In view of the many radical transformations undergone by substances in the natural world, it seemed plausible to St. Thomas (as well as to Aristotle) that any of these substances is capable of changing into any other by a more or less lengthy series of intermediate changes. But this could not be true unless the matter underlying substances is "prime matter" in the sense of lacking any definite characteristics of its own. If the matter had any definite characteristics of its own, there would be something that it could *not* become, namely, any substance lacking those definite characteristics. And what we have to account for is the capacity of any substance to be transformed, indirectly if not directly, into any other. The matter of a substance, as representing the potential for an indefinite amount of substantial change, must be perfectly indefinite and characterless in itself; it must be "pure potentiality." This leads St. Thomas to depart from St. Augustine, who took the view (adapted from the Stoics) that matter contains "seminal reasons," that is, inchoate forms (like seeds) according to which different quantities of matter are induced to develop along different specific lines, especially into living things.[4] Matter would not be *pure* potentiality if it had any such built-in predispositions to assume some forms to the exclusion of others.

Prime matter never exists by itself. Anything that exists by itself has some characteristics or other, some form; whereas prime matter has no characteristics—is merely the potential within a substance for any number of different characteristics. Prime matter is always combined with some form or other to constitute a substance (some animal, vegetable, or mineral). But it is equally true that the forms or essences of substances—natural substances, that is—never exist by themselves. With Aristotle and against Plato, St. Thomas maintains that forms or essences exist only in combination with matter as aspects of individual substances. Another way of putting this is to say that forms require "individuation" in order to exist. They exist as "individuated" in the matter of particular concrete substances.

How is it that there can exist a number of individuals of the same species? The human species, for example, comprises a multitude of different individuals, but how is this possible? The form or essence of the human species, rational animality, is not different in each individual. Rational animality is a universal, the same for every individual, and that

[4] See pp. 304–305.

which is the same for every individual can hardly account for the possibility of there being a number of individuals. No, the explanation cannot reside in the form; it must instead reside in the matter. There can be a number of individuals of the same form because in each case the form is imposed upon, or is in union with, a separate quantity of prime matter. Or since it is inaccurate to think of prime matter as having characteristics, including the characteristics of space implied in speaking of separate quantities of it, let us say rather that prime matter, as pure potential generally, is in particular the potential for there being separate quantities of stuff, such as the bodily material having, in humans, the form of rational animality. It is for roughly these reasons that St. Thomas, following Aristotle, views matter as the "principle of individuation"—the principle owing to which there can exist a number of individuals having the same form. "Wherever there are many individuals under one common species," St. Thomas says, "the distinction of many individuals is due to individual matter which stands apart from the nature of the species."

So far we have been considering the nature of things in the corporeal world, where substances exist as compositions, or "composites," of matter and form. But St. Thomas believes that there is also a realm of incorporeal creatures—the angels—that exist not as composites of matter and form, but only as forms, spiritual forms. The existence of angels is not for St. Thomas an Article of Faith; it is capable of proof, based on the hierarchy discernible among the forms of things. At the bottom of the scale are the forms of inorganic substances; next come the forms of vegetative life, then the forms of animal life, then the form of rationality—the rational soul—in humankind. At the top of the scale is God, the Creator of all. But is there not a hiatus in the hierarchy between humankind and God? A human being is a created composite of matter and a rational soul. God is uncreated, incorporeal, and incomposite. It stands to reason, St. Thomas thinks, that between humankind and God are beings, created and composite like humankind, but incorporeal like God. Such are the angels. But if angels are incorporeal how can they be composite?[5] Human beings are composite in that the form (the rational soul) of each is united with a body. Angels, however, have no material component, in St. Thomas's view of them; and so he must find, with reference to the purely spiritual character of angels, some new distinction of elements or aspects. What St. Thomas does is to bring in a distinction more fundamental than the distinction between matter and form—a distinction applicable to creatures in general, be they incorporeal or corporeal. This is the distinction between *essence* and *existence,* and it is of great importance to St. Thomas's system in general, not only in regard to angels.

Al-Farabi and Avicenna, the Muslim philosophers, had long before made

---

[5] Another question: how can the species of angels contain a number of members if matter, which angels lack, is the principle of individuation? To make a long story short, St. Thomas's answer is that although there are many angels, each belongs to a *different* species.

a distinction between essence and existence. Much of what they said on the subject is adopted by St. Thomas. Except for God, so the argument goes, nothing exists *necessarily*. No finite substance, whether corporeal or incorporeal, is such that *what* it is (its essence) entails *that* it is (its existence). The essence of something consists in the characteristics that define or determine its nature, what sort of thing it is, or what sort of thing it would be if it existed. To reflect upon the essence of something is not by itself to know whether that thing exists. "Any essence is understandable," St. Thomas says, "without anything being known about its existing." Consider the phoenix, which is St. Thomas's example. The phoenix is defined as a bird that lives for 500 years and then consumes itself in fire, only to rise renewed from the ashes. A creature of this nature is perfectly conceivable. But the nature or essence we conceive is one thing; the actual existence of such a creature is another thing. The phoenix happens not to exist. Human beings, on the other hand, happen to exist; and yet the story with them is the same. The nature or essence of humanity, and the actual existence of human beings, are two different matters. The essence of humanity represents the possibility, or rather the "potency," of the actual existence of human beings. Existence is the actualization of the essence, nature, or form of humanity—or as St. Thomas puts it, "existence is the act by which the form is." Using "act of being" instead of "act of existence," St. Thomas says: "This act of being that I am talking about is the most perfect of all things; and this is obvious from the fact that act is always more perfect than potency. . . . For humanity, or the form of fire, can be considered as existing in the potency of matter, or even as in the power of an agent, or even as present in understanding—but the fact that it has actual being makes it actually existent."

Every actual finite substance, then, is constituted by two principles, an essence or form determining what it is, and an act of existence determining that it is. Even an immaterial "intelligence" such as an angel is composed of these two principles. An angel is not composed of form and *matter,* for there is no matter in an angel, "but composition of form and *existence* is there." This solves the problem of how angels can be composite (and so lower than God) while also being incorporeal (and so higher than humans), but more important, it also suggests a kind of argument for God's existence. If existence is different from essence in every finite substance, so that none exists necessarily, it follows that the nonexistence of all finite substances is possible. This prompts one to wonder how it is that finite substances do in fact exist. Can their existence be accounted for otherwise than as owing to some being whose nonexistence is impossible, in that its existence is not different from its essence? And can this being be other than God? St. Thomas develops such an argument (in his "third way" of proving God's existence, to which we shall come in a moment), but first he examines the much more direct argument, given by St. Anselm, that God's necessary existence immediately follows, without any consideration of finite substances, from the very notion of God's unrivaled greatness.

St. Thomas agrees with St. Anselm that God, the Being than which nothing greater can be thought, must be thought of as existing necessarily. (If we thought of God as not existing necessarily, then we could think of something greater than God, namely, something that does exist necessarily.) Yet St. Thomas does not agree with St. Anselm that we may therefore conclude, without further ado, that God actually exists. God's *non*existence outside our thoughts is compatible, St. Thomas says, with any conception of Him that we may form in our thoughts, even with the conception of Him as existing necessarily. "Granted that . . . by this name *God* is signified something than which nothing greater can be thought, nevertheless, it does not therefore follow that . . . what the name signifies exists actually, but only that it exists mentally [in the thoughts of whoever thinks of it]." St. Anselm could reply that we are not thinking of God, the Being than which nothing greater can be thought, if we understand the term *God* to signify what may or may not exist outside our thoughts. (What both exists in our thoughts and necessarily exists in reality is greater than what exists in our thoughts and may or may not exist in reality.) St. Thomas, however, believes that our conception of God is not by itself adequate for us to know even that God *may* exist in reality—that His existence is possible. God, if He existed, would exist necessarily, which means that His existence would not be different from, would be identical with, His essence. But can we really understand how God's existence could be the *same* as His essence? St. Thomas thinks not. We could understand this, and so be assured of its possibility, only if God's essence were a thing into which we had some real insight; and such insight is out of the question, at least in our present life. "God cannot be seen in His essence by one who is merely man, except he be separated from this mortal life. The reason is [that] the mode of knowledge follows the mode of the nature of the knower. But our soul, as long as we live in this life, has its being in corporeal matter; hence it knows naturally only what has a form in matter, or what can be known by such a form. Now it is evident that the divine essence cannot be known through the nature of material things." *That* God is, and is necessarily, is indeed capable of proof, according to St. Thomas, but not sheerly on the basis of some conception we have formed of *what* He is, of His essence, since none of our ideas is at all adequate to His "what."

Human knowledge, in the present life, is built up from sense-experience. We abstract from our experience of corporeal objects the forms or essences that determine their natures, that constitute them members of determinate species and genera. These forms or essences, in abstraction from the particularizing matter in which they are embodied, are universals such as "humanity," "animality," and "rationality." We employ these universals in judgments—"Socrates is a human," "Humans are rational animals"—whereby we achieve knowledge of the corporeal objects of our experience.[6] All the same, St. Thomas does not believe that our knowledge is limited to the corporeal objects of our experience. He argues that we may also know something of incorporeal objects insofar as the existence of these is implied by certain features of corporeal objects. God's existence, for example, is implied by the contingency and finitude everywhere characteristic of corporeal objects. The world of corporeal objects bears unmistakable signs of being the effect of a supernatural Cause, a Creator, Himself necessary and unlimited. Our notion of God in this life will always be imperfect by virtue of our having to think of Him in terms drawn from our experience of the world. God's essence or nature is quite beyond our intellectual grasp. But to the extent that the natural world manifests His existence, we can know Him indirectly and by analogy. It is a question of *reasoning from effect to cause,* and of understanding the cause (God) as well as we can on the basis of indications in the effect (the corporeal world).

Arguments for God's Existence

Some five arguments for God's existence are briefly presented by St. Thomas in his *Summa Theologica.* They all have a "traditional" flavor, deriving as they do from Aristotle and from such Aristotelian thinkers as Avicenna and Maimonides. They all conform to the same general pattern, appealing to certain broad features of the world of our experience, and inferring from these features a Cause to account for them. First the arguments themselves, and then some further comments. "The existence of God," St. Thomas says, "can be proved in five ways," as follows:

[1] The first and more manifest way is the argument from motion. It is certain, and evident to our senses, that in the world some things are in motion. Now whatever is moved is moved by another, for nothing can be moved except it is in potentiality to that towards which it is moved; whereas a thing moves inasmuch as it is in act. For motion is nothing else than the reduction of something from potentiality to actuality. But nothing can be reduced from potentiality to actuality, except by something in a state of actuality. Thus that which is actually hot, as fire, makes wood, which is potentially hot, to be actually hot, and thereby moves and changes it. Now it is not possible that the same thing should be at once in actuality and potentiality in the same re-

[6]Unlike St. Augustine, St. Thomas does not believe that the human mind requires some special illumination from God in order to apprehend necessary truths (such as $7 + 3 = 10$), for these also, he says, involve universals abstracted from sense-experience; and the "natural light" of our ordinary power of understanding perfectly equips us to grasp them. St. Thomas does believe, however, that a special "light of grace" is necessary for us to apprehend truths (the Articles of Faith) that cannot be arrived at by abstracting universals from sense-experience.

spect, but only in different respects. For what is actually hot cannot simultaneously be potentially hot; but it is simultaneously potentially cold. It is therefore impossible that in the same respect and in the same way a thing should be both mover and moved, i.e., that it should move itself. Therefore, whatever is moved must be moved by another. If that by which it is moved be itself moved, then this also must needs be moved by another, and that by another again. But this cannot go on to infinity, because then there would be no first mover, and, consequently, no other mover, seeing that subsequent movers move only inasmuch as they are moved by the first mover; as the staff moves only because it is moved by the hand. Therefore, it is necessary to arrive at a first mover, moved by no other; and this everyone understands to be God.

[2] The second way is from the nature of efficient cause. In the world of sensible things we find there is an order of efficient causes. There is no case known (neither is it, indeed, possible) in which a thing is found to be the efficient cause of itself; for so it would be prior to itself, which is impossible. Now in efficient causes it is not possible to go on to infinity, because in all efficient causes following in order, the first is the cause of the intermediate cause, and the intermediate is the cause of the ultimate cause, whether the intermediate cause be several, or one only. Now to take away the cause is to take away the effect. Therefore, if there be no first cause among efficient causes, there will be no ultimate, nor any intermediate, cause. But if in efficient causes it is possible to go on to infinity, there will be no first efficient cause, neither will there be an ultimate effect, nor any intermediate efficient causes; all of which is plainly false. Therefore it is necessary to admit a first efficient cause, to which everyone gives the name of God.

[3] The third way is taken from possibility and necessity, and runs thus. We find in nature things that are possible to be and not to be, since they are found to be generated, and to be corrupted, and consequently, it is possible for them to be and not to be. But it is impossible for these always to exist, for that which can not-be at some time is not. Therefore, if everything can not-be, then at one time there was nothing in existence. Now if this were true, even now there would be nothing in existence, because that which does not exist begins to exist only through something already existing. Therefore, if at one time nothing was in existence, it would have been impossible for anything to have begun to exist; and thus even now nothing would be in existence—which is absurd. Therefore, not all beings are merely possible, but there must exist something the existence of which is necessary. But every necessary thing either has its necessity caused by another, or not. Now it is impossible to go on to infinity in necessary things which have their necessity caused by another, as has already been proved in regard to efficient causes. Therefore we cannot but admit the existence of some being having of itself its own necessity, and not receiving it from another, but rather causing in others their necessity. This all men speak of as God.

[4] The fourth way is taken from the gradation to be found in things. Among beings there are some more or less good, true, noble, and the like. But *more* or *less* are predicated of different things according as they resemble in their different ways something which is the maximum, as a thing is said to be hotter according as it more nearly resembles that which is hottest; so that there is something which is truest, something best, something noblest, and, consequently, something which is most being, for those things that are greatest in truth are greatest in being, as it is written in [Aristotle's] *Metaphysics, ii.* Now the maximum in any genus is the cause of all in that genus, as fire, which is the maximum of heat, is the cause of all hot things, as is said in the same book. Therefore there must also be something which is to all beings the cause of their being, goodness, and every other perfection; and this we call God.

[5] The fifth way is taken from the governance of the world. We see that things which lack knowledge, such as natural bodies, act for an end, and this is evident from their acting always, or nearly always, in the same way, so as to obtain the best result. Hence it is plain that they achieve their end, not fortuitously, but designedly. Now whatever lacks knowledge cannot move towards an end, unless it be directed by some being endowed with knowledge and intelligence; as the arrow is directed by the archer. Therefore some intelligent being exists by whom all natural things are directed to their end; and this being we call God.

In each of the five arguments, St. Thomas mentions some observable fact about the world and maintains that we can account for it only in reference to God as conceived in accordance with some description that "everyone understands" to fit Him alone. In [1] the fact in question is that *motion* occurs in the world—"motion" in the wide Aristotelian sense of potentialities becoming actualities, as when things with the potential for hotness become actually hot. In [2] attention shifts to *efficient causality,* observed whenever a change in one thing (such as the turning of a crank) produces a change on the part of another thing (the raising of a bucket, say). In [3] consideration goes to the existence of *contingent* things— "things that are possible to be and not to be"—which really includes everything in the world (inasmuch as existence is different from essence in every finite substance). In [4] the matter for discussion is the *different degrees of perfection* in things, their greater or lesser value on one count or another (nobility, truth, and so on). In [5] the focus is upon *goal-directed processes* involving nonrational things, as when an acorn "moves towards an end" in developing into an oak. For each of these facts, St. Thomas assumes, there must be a reason why it is the way it is, why it *is* at all. None of them, he argues, is self-explanatory. In the last analysis, he says, they all have to be accounted for in relation to God—God as Unmoved Mover in [1], God as Uncaused Cause in [2], God as Necessary Being in [3], God as Absolute Perfection in [4], and God as Intelligent

Governor in [5]. Now if the only adequate explanation of these facts is God, and if these facts *are* facts (as everybody would admit), God's existence has been proved, indirectly, by reasoning "from effect to cause."

Space does not permit a detailed examination of these arguments, but a few additional points about them should be noted. In [1], [2], and [3] it looks as if St. Thomas is arguing that the world cannot always have existed. He says that it is impossible to "go on to infinity" in finding [1] movers for what moves, [2] causes for effects, and [3] necessary things to account for things not necessary. This seems to mean that there cannot have been in past time an infinite series of things (movers, say), so that the world must have had a beginning and a First Mover, for example, to begin it. As we have already seen, however, St. Thomas (unlike St. Bonaventure) does not think that a beginning of the world can be proved. He *believes* that the world had a beginning, but he views this as an indemonstrable Article of Faith, and he cautions against trying to prove it lest unbelievers be given "occasion to ridicule" by arguments that are bound to be fallacious. St. Bonaventure, for instance, subscribed to the argument that an infinite series of past days would mean that the present day could never have arrived, inasmuch as an infinite series cannot be traversed. St. Thomas replies that even if it were true that the world had no first day, the present day would still be only a finite number of days later than any particular past day, so that really there would be nothing impossible about getting to the present from any point, however remote, in the past. To speak of an infinite number of days having to be "traversed" makes it seem as if, starting a long time ago, an endless number of days would have had to be gotten through before today could have arrived; but this is simply a confusion, since between any two days, however far apart, the number of days would be finite. Nor does St. Thomas find any theoretical difficulty in the notion of a cause-effect series of infinite length in time, a series in which every member has an infinite number of predecessors. Consider, for instance, the relation of parents to children: for anything that reason alone can tell us, St. Thomas says, every parent may have been a child; we are not compelled by the sheer logic of the situation to infer that there was a first parent, an Adam who had no parents and was created directly by God. The procreative relation constitutes what St. Thomas calls an *accidental* series of causes and effects—"accidental" in the sense that the procreative activity of any given pair of parents does not, when and as it occurs, depend upon the procreative activity of *their* parents. Woman *A* and man *B* would not exist except for the procreative activity of their parents, but the procreative activity here and now of *A* and *B* does not depend upon any procreative activity here and now on the part of *A*'s or *B*'s parents. The fact that *A* and *B* now are causes (of children) is independent of the fact that *A* and *B* were themselves effects of previous causes (their parents). Any cause-effect series of this sort, St. Thomas says, may theoretically be without a beginning. What St. Thomas believes to require a beginning are cause-effect series of a very different sort, which he calls cause-effect series *per se.* A series *per se* consists of several distinguishable members related as causes and effects that *exist at one and the same time,* not (as with the procreative relation) one after the other. In a series of this type, each member *depends upon* another contemporary with it. Woman *A,* for example, would not be alive did not the sun keep the earth's temperature within tolerable limits—her existence now depends upon this happening now. But the sun would not be keeping the earth's temperature within tolerable limits unless it were burning certain substances at a fairly constant rate, and this would not be happening unless a number of other factors were also operating now. *This* is the kind of series in which, as St. Thomas believes, it is "impossible to go on to infinity." Whether we are dealing with causes in the sense of efficient causes, or in the sense of agents of motion, or in the sense of necessary things (accounting for things not necessary), so long as they form a series of contemporaneous members in which each depends upon another, there cannot be an infinite number of them. There must be a First (or Uncaused) Cause, an Unmoved Mover, and a Necessary Being ("having of itself its own necessity").

Why is it "impossible to go on to infinity" in any cause-effect series in which the members exist at the same time? What St. Thomas says in [1], [2], and [3] might seem to boil down to this: unless there were a First Cause (Mover, and so on) not dependent upon anything else, then really there could be no series of contemporaneous causes in which one cause depends upon another, and so no effect resulting from such a series. ("If in efficient causes it is possible to go on to infinity, there will be no first efficient cause, neither will there be an ultimate effect [since "to take away the cause is to take away the effect"], nor any intermediate efficient causes. . . .") But this way of putting it seems just to assume that an infinite series of the sort in question is impossible; it does not appear to explain why it is impossible. What St. Thomas means to convey, however, is probably something more like this: unless there were a First Cause (Mover, and so on) not dependent upon anything else, then a series of contemporaneous causes in which each cause depends upon another could not really serve to *account for* any effect said to follow from the series. But a cause-effect series that does not account for any effects is hardly a genuine cause-effect series. It is actually a contradiction in terms. Whatever the elements of the series may be, they cannot be considered *causes,* inasmuch as a cause is precisely that which accounts for something as an effect. Why, then, cannot a series of contemporaneous causes account for anything unless, instead of being infinite, it leads up to a First Cause? Because only then is the existence of the series itself intelligible. Were it true that every cause depended upon another, there would be no final explanation for the series. No matter how high in the series we went, we would always be referred to yet another cause for the cause we had reached, but *always* to find causes for causes is never to arrive at a sufficient reason for the existence of any of them. The chain of causes must ultimately depend upon a Cause which does not depend upon anything else if the existence of the chain is to be adequately explained. The existence of a First Cause has thus been proved, for it is only in reference to a First Cause that a sufficient reason can be found for the many series of contemporaneous causes observed in the world. Such, reading between the lines, is probably St. Thomas's meaning in [1], [2], and [3]—only substitute "Unmoved Mover" and "Necessary Being" for [1] and [3].

In [4] we have an argument similar in spirit to [1], [2], and [3], inferring an ultimate Cause for certain observable data; but here the data are in the realm of value. We observe different degrees of perfection in things, St. Thomas says, and these imply the existence of a supremely perfect Being as their source. The argument relies upon Plato's view that when a number of things possess the same quality to various limited degrees, they do so by virtue of a common relation of dependence upon a single perfect form of that quality. The pages of this book are more or less rectangular because they all "participate," as Plato would say, in the form of rectangularity. St. Augustine, remember, developed on this basis an argument concerning truth: the various immutable truths that we apprehend derive their truth from one Immutable Truth (identified with the Mind of God) in which they all participate, or in which, as St. Augustine put it, they are all "contained." In the same vein, St. Thomas holds that the relative truth, goodness, nobility, and so on of things in the world is owing to their dependence upon an Absolute Truth, Goodness, Nobility, and so on. The passages in Aristotle to which St. Thomas refers in [4] are more reminiscent of Plato's theory of forms than one might expect, given Aristotle's criticisms of that theory. For instance, Aristotle says that the "most true" is "that which causes derivative truths to be true." St. Thomas follows Aristotle in arguing that there is "something truest" that is also "most being," in other words, that there is an Absolute Truth which is also Supreme Being. This conclusion depends upon an Aristotelian principle often stated as "truth is convertible with being"—"convertible" in that what is true is identical with what exists or has being. Many today would believe that this represents a confused way of thinking because it is common now to consider truth a property of statements, which of course may refer to what really exists, but which are not identical with what they refer to. But look at the matter this way: if one believes that to apprehend truth is to apprehend forms; and if one believes that forms are the ultimate realities because it is by participating in them that other things exist; then one will find it natural to say that (a) apprehending the truth is the same as (b) apprehending what really exists. A short further step will then bring one to say that truth itself is the same as what really exists, or that truth is the same as being. And if one believes that there is one ultimate form of Truth upon which all other truths depend, one will believe that this is identical with an ultimate Being, a Supreme Being, upon which all other beings depend. "This," St. Thomas says, "we call God."

In [5] St. Thomas argues that there must exist an Intelligent Governor of the world to account for the existence of goal-directed processes or activities on the part of unintelligent things. Consider the acorn. When an acorn develops into an oak, the matter of the acorn undergoes certain changes which are the *means* whereby an oak comes about. The oak, however, is not a means whereby something else comes about, not naturally at any rate; it is the *end* of a process of natural development. Now surely the end here has some controlling relation to the means, for how can the means (the changes within the acorn) be understood if not as determined or directed by the end (the oak to be achieved)? But how could an end, as yet unachieved, direct the means to its own achievement? Could it do so otherwise than as an *idea* according to which some intelligence directs the means? But as acorns are unintelligent, the intelligence in question will have to be outside the acorn. The hosts of cases like this in the natural world require us to infer that "some intelligent being exists," an Intelligent Governor outside the world, "by whom all things are directed to their end." The acorn/oak illustration is an instance of what is called "internal finality"—where activity directed toward an end (*finis,* in Latin) is internal to, occurs within, an individual substance and represents an unfolding of its own distinctive potential. There is another kind of finality, however, and in the *Summa contra Gentiles* St. Thomas appeals to it as furnishing another argument for an Intelligent Governor. This is "external finality," which consists in the ordering of a number of diverse things so as to achieve an end external to their own individual natures. St. Thomas finds external finality in the vast system of things in the world at large. Here is his very brief statement of this additional argument: "Contrary and discordant things cannot, always or for the most part, be parts of one order except under someone's government, which enables all and each to tend to a definite end. But in the world we find that things of diverse natures come together under one order, and this not rarely or by chance, but always or for the most part. There must therefore be some being by whose providence the world is governed. This we call God."

St. Thomas believes, then, that the existence of an Unmoved Mover, an Uncaused Cause, a Necessary Being, an Absolute Perfection, and an Intelligent Governor may be proved. These names will be understood, by all who believe in God, to belong to Him and to Him alone; and so the five arguments will be viewed by them as proofs of His existence. St. Thomas is aware, however, that someone who does not already believe in God may not, and need not, view any of these arguments as proving *God's* existence. God is supposed to be, for one thing, an *immaterial* being; and none of the five arguments, as it stands, demonstrates that something immaterial exists. Thus St. Thomas proceeds, in the article of the *Summa Theologica* immediately following the one containing the five proofs, to argue that an Uncaused Cause, an Unmoved Mover, and so on, cannot be material or bodily in nature. And in subsequent articles St. Thomas rules out any kind of *composition,* whether of essence and existence, form and matter, genus and difference, or substance and accidents, so that perfectly simplicity or unity is attributable to the Uncaused Cause or Unmoved Mover, who thereby is shown the more clearly to be the God of Christian doctrine. In still further articles St. Thomas presents arguments respecting God's goodness, limitlessness, wisdom, and so on. We cannot recapitulate what he says on all of these matters, but the depth of his analysis and his sensitivity to important issues may be illustrated by noting a few of his points. Of particular interest is what St. Thomas says about the difficulties in the way of human efforts to comprehend God's nature.

God's Nature

We saw that St. Thomas finds us incapable of knowing God's nature or essence, at least in this life, because our knowledge is limited by its origin in sense-experience. Even if our knowledge were not limited in this way, however, there would still be a formidable problem. There cannot in any case be a *definition* of God, St. Thomas says; and insofar as we feel that we have not comprehended what we have not defined, we shall never feel that we have comprehended God. The reason why God cannot be defined is that there cannot in His regard be a distinction between genus and difference, and yet (as Aristotle said) it is only by specifying genus and difference that anything is defined. Human beings belong to the genus "animal" and are distinguished from other animals by the difference of rationality. "Rational animal," in giving the genus and difference of the human species, is a concise definition of the nature or essence of humanity. Now when it comes to God's nature, what we have to say is that it is His nature to exist, that His essence is the same as His existence. If it were not His nature to exist, so that He did not exist necessarily, God would owe His existence to some cause external to Himself; and this cannot be correct if He is the First (or Uncaused) Cause. But if it is God's nature or essence to exist, the only genus to which He could belong, if He belonged to any, would be the genus "existent" or "being." To put this differently: if in stating the genus of something we refer to its nature or essence, then in God's case we would refer to His existence because that *is* His essence. So God, on this showing, would be a member of the genus "being." St. Thomas believes, however, that "the Philosopher" (that is, Aristotle) was right when he said that "being" cannot be a genus. Why not? Well, reflect that any genus is differentiated into species by factors not already contained in the genus considered by itself. The genus animal, for example, is differentiated into the species vertebrates, arthropoda, mollusks, and so on, by factors not already contained in the genus as such—otherwise the species would not really be different. The species are distinguished from one another by differences, and in stating the differences we obviously describe factors that the species do not have in common, factors in addition to the common features indicated when we refer only to the genus. But for the supposed genus "being" no differentiating factor could be found that was not already contained in the genus, because any such factor would have to exist (how could a nonexistent factor distinguish anything?), and to exist is to be in the genus "being." In other words, we could not state any differences by which species of the supposed genus "being" could be distinguished, since whatever we proposed as a difference would, in existing, already be contained in the genus and would therefore not really be a difference. Of course, a genus under which there could be no species is a thoroughly confused idea, like the idea of a parent who could have no offspring. Being cannot be a genus. "So we are left," St. Thomas says, "with no genus to which God could belong," from which it follows that God cannot be defined.

To say that God cannot be defined amounts to saying that He cannot be distinguished from other beings in terms of differences between His nature and their natures. It is impossible, that is, to identify essential characteristics that God possesses and that other beings do not possess. St. Thomas does think, however, that it is possible to identify essential characteristics that other beings possess and that God does *not* possess. By denying these characteristics of God, we are able to obtain some notion of His nature, although not a definition of it. For guidance in determining which characteristics to deny of God, we should consider which are incompatible with His being an Uncaused Cause, an Unmoved Mover, a Necessary Being, and so on. "Unmoved Mover" indicates not God's nature but a way in which the world (or the motion in the world) depends upon Him (as the ultimate cause of motion). And we can identify characteristics that could not belong to the ultimate cause of motion—materiality, for one (any material cause of motion is itself moved—changed in some respect—in the process of moving something else). On this basis we are able to determine that God could not be composite, limited, contingent, temporal, and so on. A progressively less inadequate understanding of God's nature may thus be achieved by the process of "negative predication," determining what is *not* His nature. Moses Maimonides, as St. Thomas points out, took the position that this "negative way" of conceiving God's nature is the only way open to us.

St. Thomas is not prepared to agree with Maimonides completely. While many terms applied to God have really a negative significance, others are plainly intended to be positive. St. Thomas accordingly tries to explain how there can be an "affirmative way" of conceiving God's nature—a way that does not purport to give a definition of His nature, but which nevertheless yields some slender positive information about it. Little of the usual conception of God would remain if "good" and "wise" were inapplicable to Him, but "good" and "wise" are not equivalent to negative terms as are "immaterial" and "infinite," which amount to "not material" and "not finite." "Good" and "wise," whether used of God or of human beings, mean a great deal more than "not evil" and "not unintelligent." But how can we be right in predicating "good" and "wise" of God if these terms derive their meaning for us, as they do, from our own moral experience and intellectual endeavor, and if in any case God's unity or simplicity is such as to exclude, as it does, the distinction in Him between subject and predicate, which distinction is made in saying "God (subject) is good (predicate)"? St. Thomas's answer is that the imperfect goodness and wisdom of God's creatures may be taken to represent or mirror the perfection of these qualities in Him as their Creator, so that "good" and "wise" cannot be wholly out of place in statements about Him, although in statements about Him these terms cannot be understood to mean precisely the same as what they mean in statements about His creatures. In short, "good" and "wise" are not *equivocal* terms (with entirely different meanings) when applied to both creatures and Creator, nor are they *univocal* terms (with precisely the same meanings) when applied to both. "Good" and "wise" belong to a third category: they are *analogical* terms. A term is analogical when it is used in reference to generically different things between which there is still some analogy or resemblance. For instance, the term "faithful" may be applied to a dog as well as to a man, because a dog can exhibit attitudes and behavior which resemble to some extent those we associate with human faithfulness. The two meanings of "faithful" are different but not dissimilar. Of course, human faithfulness is here the standard of comparison, and the dog's faithfulness consists in an approximation to this. When human beings are viewed in relation to God, the situation is reversed. Human goodness and wisdom are the approximations—very distant approximations—to qualities in God that we mean to signify in calling Him "good" and "wise," but of which we can form only the dimmest of notions, even dimmer than a dog's notion of human qualities. How may we be confident that "good" and "wise" signify something in God at least remotely analogous to what they signify in human life? Because human beings are effects of God's creative activity, and "any perfection found in an effect," St. Thomas says, "must be found also in the cause of that effect . . . and in a more perfect manner when cause and effect are not of the same sort. . . ." St. Thomas goes on to say: "Since God then is the primary operative cause of all things, the perfections of everything must pre-exist in Him in a higher manner." This includes the perfections we signify in saying that someone is "good" or "wise." These must "pre-exist transcendentally" in God.

Creator and Creation

This brings us to the subject of God's office as Creator, about which we can only sketch a few of St. Thomas's views. He says that there must pre-exist in God not only the perfections of everything but also *ideas* of everything, if He creates and directs everything with perfect intelligence. These ideas, which are the forms of things, are "models" according to which God works in making particular things and in governing their development; and so they are also His means of knowing everything that takes place in the world. St. Thomas speaks as if, in formulating this position, he is following Aristotle as well as St. Augustine. In fact Aristotle, no believer in Divine creation, did not believe that God thinks of anything other than Himself and His own thinking; nor would Aristotle have subscribed to St. Thomas's notion that God, in knowing His own Divine essence, thereby has knowledge of creatures as representing only so many types and instances of "participation in" or "imitation of" His essence. These expressions of Plato's are used by St. Thomas when he attempts to explain how the simplicity of God's essence is compatible with His having a multitude of ideas of creatures. St. Thomas says that God's ideas of creatures are really just one act of knowledge, which consists in God's knowing His own essence as capable of being "participated in" or "imitated" by a multitude of creatures. What God knows may thus be manifold, although His means of knowing same is unitary. "Many models are understood through the self-same essence."

God's purpose in creation, St. Thomas says, is to "communicate His perfection, which is His goodness" by bringing into existence outside of Himself a universe of things which is "best as a whole." What is best as a whole is a hierarchy of beings with different degrees of goodness, showing the manifold ways in which God's perfection is communicable. "The universe would not be perfect," St. Thomas says, "if only one grade of goodness were found in things." It follows that corruptible as well as incorruptible things will exist, and that suffering and death will occur, not because God wills these evils as such but because of the "privations" inherent and unavoidable in creatures of different grades of goodness. "Thus God, by causing in things the good of the order of the universe, consequently, and as it were by accident [that is, incidentally, as an incidental accompaniment], causes the corruptions of things." In speaking of what is "best as a whole," St. Thomas does not mean that God could not have created a better universe than the one He did create. His point is that it is best for different grades of goodness to be found in things, not that the present universe is the best God could have made containing different grades of goodness. Owing to His infinite power, "God can make something better than each thing made by Him," and this goes for the universe as a whole. There could not be a "best possible universe," because God can create a universe better than any given universe. Why God created precisely the universe He did create, instead of a better one, is not something He has given to us to know. We may be sure that the present universe exists because of God's goodness, but any of an indefinite number of other universes would be equally consistent with His goodness. "The divine goodness is an end exceeding created things beyond all proportion," St. Thomas says; "therefore, the divine wisdom is not so restricted to any particular order that no other scheme of things could proceed from it."

It might be said that if God has infinite power or omnipotence, then He could have created a scheme of things having a rich variety of grades of goodness, but *not* having the privations that lead to suffering and death. An obvious reply to this, a reply with which St. Thomas would probably agree, is that such a scheme of things is impossible. Different grades of goodness in things, in any possible universe, would necessarily involve corruptibility of some kind and therefore counterparts of suffering and death as we know them.[7] It is contradictory to think that there could be the one without the other. "A universe in which things have different grades of goodness but in which no thing is corruptible" is, like "a surface which is square but does not have four sides," a contradiction in terms. Nothing can have contradictory properties at the same time; this is an application of the law of contradiction recognized since Aristotle. But does not this entail that God's power is limited? How can God be omnipotent if He is subject to the law of contradiction? St. Thomas gives a celebrated answer to this in the course of explaining what "omnipotence" should be understood to mean. Here are the relevant paragraphs, which show St. Thomas at his analytical best:

All confess that God is omnipotent; but it seems difficult to explain in what His omnipotence precisely consists. For there may be a doubt as to the precise meaning of the word "all" when we say that God can do all things. If, however, we consider the matter aright, since power is said in reference to possible things, this phrase, *God can do all things*, is rightly understood to mean that God can do all things that are possible; and for this reason He is said to be omnipotent. Now according to The Philosopher a thing is said to be possible in two ways. First, in relation to some power; thus whatever is subject to human power is said to be possible to a man. Now God cannot be said to be omnipotent through being able to do all things that are possible to created nature; for the divine power extends farther than that. If, however, we were to say that God is omnipotent because He can do all things that are possible to His power, there would be a vicious circle in explaining the nature of His power. For this would be saying nothing else but that God is omnipotent because He can do all that He is able to do.

It remains, therefore, that God is called omnipotent because He can do all things that are possible absolutely; which is the second way of saying a thing is possible. For a thing is said to be possible or impossible absolutely, according to the relation in which the very terms stand

---

[7] This seems to be implied when St. Thomas says: "One grade of goodness is that of the good which cannot fail. Another grade of goodness is that of the good which can fail in goodness. These grades of goodness are to be found in being itself." By "being itself" St. Thomas appears from the context to mean "created being in which different grades of goodness are realized."

to one another: possible, if the predicate is not incompatible with the subject, as that Socrates sits; and absolutely impossible when the predicate is altogether incompatible with the subject, as, for instance, that a man is an ass.

It must, however, be remembered that since every agent produces an effect like itself, to each active power there corresponds a thing possible as its proper object according to the nature of that act on which its active power is founded; for instance, the power of giving warmth is related, as to its proper object, to the being capable of being warmed. The divine being, however, upon which the nature of power in God is founded, is infinite; it is not limited to any class of being, but possesses within itself the perfection of all being. Whence, whatsoever has or can have the nature of being is numbered among the absolute possibles, in respect of which God is called omnipotent.

Now nothing is opposed to the notion of being except non-being. Therefore, that which at the same time implies being and non-being is repugnant to the notion of an absolute possible, which is subject to the divine omnipotence. For such cannot come under the divine omnipotence; not indeed because of any defect in the power of God, but because it has not the nature of a feasible or possible thing. Therefore, everything that does not imply a contradiction in terms is numbered among those possibles in respect of which God is called omnipotent; whereas whatever implies a contradiction does not come within the scope of divine omnipotence, because it cannot have the aspect of possibility. Hence it is more appropriate to say that such things cannot be done, than that God cannot do them. Nor is this contrary to the word of the angel, saying: *No word shall be impossible with God (Luke* i.37). For whatever implies a contradiction cannot be a word, because no intellect can possibly conceive such a thing.

As a matter of faith, St. Thomas accepts the Biblical doctrine that God created the world a finite time ago. From eternity God willed to create the world; but He willed to create it not from eternity but with a beginning in time. The world was created from nothing, *ex nihilo,* not from God's own substance, which is unchangeable, and not out of some independently existing raw material, for God alone has independent—that is, necessary—existence. The world came into being instantaneously, not over some period of time, for time is a function of motion and was itself created with the creation of the world of moving things. So far St. Thomas's view of creation and the Creator is a reformulation of doctrines familiar from St. Augustine. More original with St. Thomas is the rigor with which he expresses a conclusion, seemingly strange but inevitable on his premises, to the effect that the Creator has no "real relation" to His creatures.

In order to see how St. Thomas arrives at this conclusion, it is necessary to focus on the terminology he employs. As St. Thomas uses the expression, *A* has a "real relation" to *B* when *A* would not be exactly the same, or indeed would not exist at all, without that relation to *B*. A son has such a real relation to his mother, since he would not exist were it not for the relation of "being son of" that he has to her. His mother also has a real relation to him, since although her existence does not depend upon his, her life and experience would not be exactly the same without the relation of "being mother of" that she has to him. There is another sort of relation, which St. Thomas calls a "relation of reason," which *A* has to *B* when *A* would be exactly the same without that relation to *B*. Imagine that you are looking at an oak. The oak has to you the relation of "being looked at," but would not the oak be exactly the same if you never looked at it? St. Thomas, at any rate, would say so. He would call the oak's relation to you a "relation of reason" because it consists simply in your, or some rational creature's, *thinking* of the oak in relation to you. The relation of "being looked at" is not, St. Thomas would say, "due to something real in" the oak. It is a matter of the oak's "being thought of in a particular way." You of course would not be exactly the same if you never looked at that oak. No two oaks are the same, and the texture of your experience would be at least slightly different without the relation of "looking at" that you have to the particular oak in question. So while the oak does not have a real relation to you, you nevertheless have a real relation to the oak.

How, then, do matters stand between the Creator and His creatures? Needless to say, His creatures have a real relation to Him. Were it not for the relation of "being creatures of" that they have to Him, they simply would not exist. The serious question is whether the Creator has a real relation to His creatures. Would He be exactly the same without the relation of "being Creator (or First Cause, or Intelligent Governor) of" that He has to His creatures? St. Thomas says that He would. "Being related to creatures is not a reality in God," because creatures exist in time, they arise and change and perish, whereas God is timeless and changeless, Absolute Perfection, the Necessary Being, exactly the same for all eternity. "God is altogether outside the order of creatures." His relations to creatures, any of the relations we signify by such terms as "causing," "knowing," and "governing," which imply that He is active in time, are mere relations of reason, which consist in "our way of thinking of Him." It is a natural and permissible way of thinking, St. Thomas says, because "we cannot express the reality in creatures [their dependence upon God] without talking as though there were matching relations [in time to creatures] also in God." We creatures in time have a real relation to God, and we express this by speaking of God in terms ("loving" is another example) that are drawn from our experience and that attribute to Him an activity and a responsiveness in time relative to us and to other creatures. This is unobjectionable, St. Thomas says, as a way of articulating our dependence upon God. Yet we should remember that, in literal truth, everything would be the same with God if He had created some other universe, or no universe at all. "In God, relation to the creature is not a real relation."

A paradoxical conclusion, this might appear. How could there be no real relation to creatures on the part of the Being who "so loved the world, that he gave his only begotten Son"? But it is not as if Scripture never speaks of the unchangeableness of God, "with whom is no variableness, neither shadow of turning." The situation is complicated. On the one hand, it is hard to think that God's relation to His creatures is not "real," that nothing in Him is different from what it would have been had He not caused any creatures to exist, that He is not affected for better or worse by what His creatures do or suffer, that He is unresponsive to the good and evil in the world when and as they arise. On the other hand, it is difficult to conceive of the Most Perfect Being as not existing necessarily, if His existence is possible at all, and difficult to conceive of anything's being different, of anything analogous to change by way of activity or responsiveness, in what necessarily exists and is Absolute Perfection. The issues involved may be traced back to Plato's *Republic,*where Socrates takes Homer to task for depicting the gods as appearing on earth in various disguises. Surely, Socrates says, a divine being must be perfect in every way. Because that is so, any change on the part of a god could only be a change for the worse. No one, god or man, would deliberately make himself worse; nor could a god be affected by anything that happens outside himself. "Things in the most perfect condition," Socrates says, "are least affected by changes from outside." A god's nature, in view of its unqualified perfection, "would be the last thing to suffer transformations." But St. Thomas, in carrying this out to its logical conclusion, may prompt one to think that Socrates' treatment of Homer was perhaps overly abrupt.

St. Bonaventure criticized Aristotle for holding that God thinks only of Himself. St. Thomas reads Aristotle as really anticipating St. Augustine's view, which St. Thomas himself accepts, that the Mind of God contains ideas of creatures which He employs as models in creating the world, and which constitute the means whereby He knows and governs what happens in the world. It would seem, however, that this way of speaking cannot be taken literally if in fact God has no real relations to His creatures. What could God's knowing and governing amount to, as far as He is concerned, if nothing in Him, or in His Mind, is different from what it would have been if He had not created the world at all? How is St. Thomas's conception of God an improvement over Aristotle's in the major respect in which St. Bonaventure found Aristotle's deficient?

Ethics, Immortality, Freedom ⸻

One of the relations of reason that St. Thomas believes we are bound to attribute to God is a relation of "being governor or director of" that

He has to His creatures. As an architect directs the building of a house in accordance with a model he has in mind, so the Creator "governs all the acts and movements that are to be found in each single creature" in accordance with the "exemplar of the divine wisdom" that is like a model in His mind. This exemplar may be viewed as God's *eternal law* for the best possible ordering of everything in the world He has chosen to create. The Supreme Good, which is God, is communicated as much as possible to the world by the shaping of events in keeping with this eternal law. So it is that the "whole community of the universe is governed by the divine reason," and governed "to the common good." As far as we human beings are concerned, the eternal law ordains our cooperation in pursuing that perfection that is the fulfillment of the distinctive potential of rational creatures. This perfection consists in the contemplation of truth, and the highest truth, which is the essence of God Himself. Our ultimate happiness, our deepest well-being, reside in the blessed condition, or beatitude, of an eternal vision of the essence of God. Consciously or unconsciously, we all desire to achieve this end, for we all desire the fullest happiness, and the fullest happiness for us in fact consists in nothing other than such a communion with the Almighty. Beyond philosophical methods of knowing, which cannot bring us to God's essence, beyond even faith, which gives knowledge that "resembles hearing rather than seeing," the vision of God's essence is possible only if our minds are "wholly freed from the senses, either by death or by rapture," and only if God assists us by increasing our intellectual power. In the present life we are able to know how to conduct ourselves in a manner conducive to natural happiness here and consistent with the supernatural beatitude for which we hope hereafter. The "rule and measure" for human action consists in "dictates of practical reason" that "partake of" the eternal law and make up what St. Thomas calls the *natural moral law*. We may learn of the natural moral law and its requirements by reflecting upon our natural inclinations toward happiness and upon the shortcomings of happiness deriving from anything (bodily gratification, wealth, power, and so on) other than the greatest realization of our rational nature. Yet because human intelligence is not always reliable, and is in any case limited in scope, God has made known to us a *divine law* for our surer and fuller guidance. The divine law comprises the Old Law given to Moses, which concerns our "sensible and earthly good," and the New Law promulgated by Christ, which concerns our "intelligible and heavenly good."

If the final end or good of humankind consists in eternal contemplation of God, does St. Thomas have an argument for immortality? He has several arguments, in fact, but his chief argument is this. A human being is composed of matter and form, like any other natural creature. The form in this case is a human soul, which is the principle of life in the body, not only of life in the nutritive and sensitive respects in which plants and animals have life, but also life in the way of intellectual activity. Considering this intellectual activity, we can see that the soul is both incorporeal and subsistent (a substance, something existing on its own account). Human beings have the intellectual capacity of knowing any and every kind of corporeal thing (animal, vegetable, or mineral). They would not have this capacity, however, if the soul itself were some kind of corporeal thing. For the soul would then have a specific corporeal constitution that would limit what it could apprehend, in the way that eyes are limited by their specific corporeal constitution to the perception of color (not also sounds, smells, and so on). The soul must therefore be something incorporeal; it must be a principle unto itself, distinguishable from the body, of intellectual activity or operation. For the soul to be this, it must have existence on its own account; it must be a substance in its own right, since "only that which subsists in itself can have an operation in itself." But to say that the soul subsists in itself is to say that its existence is not a function of the body (or of anything else except God's creative activity), so that the soul cannot be corrupted—cannot be decomposed or otherwise perish—through the corruption of the body (or of anything else). Perhaps, however, the soul could be corrupted through itself, if not through anything else? "This is impossible," St. Thomas says, "not only as regards the human soul, but also as regards anything subsistent that is a form alone." A subsistent form, by definition, is a principle of activity or operation that exists on its own account. Its separation from something that has depended upon it will bring about the corruption of that other thing. But it could corrupt itself only if it could separate itself from itself, which is impossible. Accordingly, since the soul is not corruptible either through itself or through some other thing, it must be incorruptible, that is, immortal. Such is the main argument St. Thomas gives for immortality. One question among the many that could be raised at this juncture is how St. Thomas could believe that a soul retains its individual identity in separation from the body, if he also believes that matter is the principle of individuation within a species. He is not without an answer to this—a complicated answer whose existence should be mentioned, even though it cannot be recounted here. In any case, St. Thomas does not believe that, after the body has died, the soul remains forever in separation from it. He believes, in keeping with his interpretation of Scripture, that there will come a time when the body will be resurrected and reunited with the soul, but not in such a way as to impede the soul's beatific vision of God.

If the Creator "governs all the acts and movements that are to be found in each single creature," does St. Thomas try to explain how human beings can nevertheless be held morally accountable for their actions? Yes, he does. Human beings have freedom of choice, he says, inasmuch as they decide how to act by making comparative judgments of the alternative courses of action open to them. Thus "by his free choice man moves himself to act." God, the First Mover of everything, moves the individual's moving of himself or herself; but St. Thomas does not find this incompatible with freedom on the part of the individual. There would be an incompatibility, he says, only if the individual's decisions and actions were made necessary by God's causing them; but God is not limited to causing things to happen necessarily. He is also able to cause things to happen *contingently,* and that is what He does in regard to human decisions and actions. It is true, St. Thomas says, that the human will has been so orientated by the Creator that everyone necessarily desires the fullest happiness, which consists in the beatific vision of Himself. But the desire for happiness is voluntary in the sense that it is experienced as the natural inclination of one's will, not as something coercively imposed from without. We always aim to do what we believe will maximize our happiness; but the connection between our greatest happiness and "those things which are of God" is not so compellingly clear to us that we cannot fail to understand, or choose to disregard, what we should do to come closer to Him. The choice of *means* to happiness is what we are free in, at least when, as often happens, none of the alternatives open to us seems unambiguously better than the rest. In weighing the pros and cons of different courses of action, and then in choosing one to pursue, we exercise our power of free will. St. Thomas cannot, however, leave it at this. Human nature, he goes on to say, "is corrupted in us after the sin of our first parent"; and our power of free will is accordingly too weak for us, without the assistance of God's grace, to persevere in obeying God's laws to the exclusion of self-centered inclinations. Such is the corruption of human nature, St. Thomas says, that "free choice can be turned to God only when God turns it." The difficult problems this raises hardly need spelling out. Suffice it to say that St. Thomas is aware of these problems and tries to solve them in terms of a kind of cooperation of free will and grace. Because the issues in question pertain more to his theology than to his philosophy, we shall not further broach them here. For the sake of argument, let us take it that St. Thomas is able to defend, consistently with his other positions, the thesis that human beings are free in (and so responsible for) their choices of means to happiness.

A human action is "good absolutely," St. Thomas says, when and only when it achieves a suitable (or "due") object or result, in suitable circumstances, and with a suitable end in view. Suppose, to use St. Thomas's example, you give alms to someone; the object of your action is the transference of money to a needy person. So far so good; but suppose further that it were one of the circumstances that you had stolen the money in the first place, or that the end you had in view was the gaining of a reputation for generosity. Your action would not then be good absolutely, even though it were good in its object, because the circumstances or the end in view would be unsuitable. To say that an action is unsuitable in its object, its circumstances, or its end is to say that it is bad—bad absolutely if unsuitable in all three respects. Every human action, St. Thomas maintains, is either good or bad; none is simply indifferent or neutral in respect of moral value. This is because some end is aimed at in every human action—if the action is a deliberate undertaking as opposed to a mere reflex like a sneeze—and the end at which one aims will be either suitable and hence good, or unsuitable and hence bad. But St. Thomas does not say that we have an obligation to do an action simply because it would be suitable if we did it, for there may be no unsuitableness in not doing it.

How does St. Thomas define "suitable" and "unsuitable" as regards human actions? He says that the object, circumstances, and end of an action are suitable when they are, and unsuitable when they are not, "in accordance with reason," by which he means "in accordance with the natural moral law that God has established for us as His creatures." The natural moral law has a first principle—"good is to be done and promoted, and evil is to be avoided"—which, St. Thomas says, is as self-evident as an elementary principle of logic. From this principle, and from observing the inclinations that God has implanted in human nature, we may go on to discover the more specific principles of natural moral law, as St. Thomas here explains:

> This is the first precept of [natural moral] law, that *good is to be done and promoted, and evil is to be avoided.* All other precepts of natural law are based upon this; so that all the things which the practical reason naturally apprehends as man's good belong to the precepts of the natural law under the form of things to be done or avoided.
>
> Since, however, good has the nature of an end, and evil, the nature of the contrary, hence it is that all those things to which man has a natural inclination are naturally apprehended by reason as being good, and consequently as objects of pursuit, and their contraries as evil, and objects of avoidance. Therefore, the order of the precepts of the natural law is according to the order of natural inclinations. For there is in man, first of all, an inclination to good in accordance with the nature which he has in common with all substances, inasmuch, namely, as every substance seeks the preservation of its own being, according to its nature; and by reason of this inclination, whatever is a means of preserving human life, and of warding off its obstacles, belongs to the natural law. Secondly, there is in man an inclination to things that pertain to him more specially, according to that nature which he has in common with other animals; and in virtue of this inclination, those things are said to belong to the natural law which nature has taught to all animals, such as sexual intercourse, the education of offspring, and so forth. Thirdly, there is in man an inclination to good according to the nature of his reason, which nature is proper to him. Thus man has a natural inclination to know the truth about God, and to live in society; and in this respect, whatever pertains to this inclination belongs to the natural law: e.g., to shun ignorance, to avoid offending those among whom one has to live, and other such things regarding the above inclination.

By the ordinary exercise of reason, human beings may grasp various principles of the natural moral law and perceive the obligation to live by them for the sake of achieving the ends (making for happiness) that human nature prompts everyone to apprehend as good. Because human nature remains basically the same from century to century and from region to region, St. Thomas believes, these principles are not subject to change and have long been acknowledged by people everywhere. The Ten Commandments include some prime examples of the sort of principles St. Thomas has in mind. The better to ensure their general recognition, God has revealed (through Moses) the Ten Commandments to us; but "Thou shalt do no murder" and "Thou shalt not steal," for example, are discoverable without great difficulty through normal human processes of reflection. St. Thomas does not for a moment deny that the complexities of actual circumstances call for practical good sense in applying such principles. Is it stealing if we do not return property entrusted to us by its owner? Suppose the owner has in the meantime gone out of his mind and would harm himself or others with the property (a knife, say)? The rule "Return property entrusted to you" may follow from the principle "Thou shalt not steal," but obviously the rule has exceptions. The same thing goes for other rules—"secondary precepts," St. Thomas calls them—that follow from other principles: although applicable in the majority of cases, they are not applicable in all. *Conscience* is the name St. Thomas gives to the activity of determining the pertinence of moral rules to particular cases. We should use our best judgment in applying the rules to decide what to do in the circumstances in which we find ourselves, and we would be wrong not to act accordingly even when our best judgment happens (unavoidably) to be mistaken. In short, an erring conscience is still to be obeyed. "Since conscience is the dictate of reason, the application of theory [moral rules] to practice, the inquiry, *whether a will that disobeys an erroneous conscience is right,* is the same as, *whether a man is obliged to follow a mistaken conscience.* Now because the object of a volition is that which is proposed by the reason, if the will chooses to do what reason considers to be wrong, then the will goes out to it under the guise of evil. Therefore it must be said flatly that the will which disobeys the reason, whether true or mistaken, is always in the wrong."

We should always do what in good conscience we believe to be right. The settled disposition (or "habit") of doing this, mindful of the pertinent parts of the natural moral law and of the given circumstances, is what it means to be morally virtuous. "Every virtuous act," St. Thomas says, "has these four traits: controlled knowledge, right intention, unwavering purpose, and sense of situation." Following Aristotle, St. Thomas analyzes moral virtue into a number of distinguishable but mutually supportive dispositions to "hit the mean" between excess and deficiency in satisfying our appetites and in giving expression to our emotions. Following Plato, St. Thomas views wisdom, courage, temperance, and justice as the "cardinal" virtues, the main species of moral virtue; and he sees in wisdom—practical wisdom or prudence—the "chief effective control of human activity." Prudence is the one intellectual virtue (good habit of intellect) absolutely essential to moral goodness, and thus it is also a moral virtue. "For moral virtue is a habit of making a good choice. Here two conditions are called for, a good intention of the end, which moral virtue provides by giving us a bias to what is reasonable, and a right taking of means, which implies that the reason takes good counsel, makes the right selection, and commands the right course, all of which functions attach to prudence. . . . Moral virtue in consequence requires understanding of principles. As theory works from true premises, so prudence presupposes a true sense of background, for it is the right idea of dealing with a human situation." Prudence is the disposition to choose the best means by which our conduct *in general* may "keep the reasonable measure," whereas courage consists in a measured "firmness of spirit," temperance in a measured control of "one's own personal lusts and pleasures," and justice in measured dealings with others "under the aspect of what is owing to them."

Moral virtue perfects us for those actions by which we can attain the natural happiness possible without special divine assistance. The fullest happiness, however, is a supernatural happiness, experienced in communion with God, to which moral virtue alone cannot bring us. If we are to be directed to this, we must "receive from God some additional principles" in the form of *theological virtues,* three in number, namely, faith, hope, and charity. "Theological" is the appropriate name for these virtues, St. Thomas says, "first, because their object is God, inasmuch as they direct us rightly to God; secondly, because they are infused in us by God alone; thirdly, because these virtues are not made known to us, save by divine revelation, contained in Holy Scripture." *Faith* pertains to truths (the Articles of Faith) that surpass all human methods of discovery; and that which these truths specify as our highest end surpasses what we can possibly *hope* to attain by any human means; and that which would be strictly impossible of attainment could not be the object of *charity* or love. The special grace of God gives truths of faith and faith in these truths, gives hope of eternal beatitude, gives charity, which is "the friendship of man for God." In friendship with God, and in benevolence toward humanity for the sake of God, a person's moral virtues are supplemented, not supplanted, for "grace does not destroy nature, but perfects it."

To return to moral virtue, we may note that St. Thomas has no very high opinion of attempts by philosophers and others to give specific moral advice. The concrete situations of life, he says, are not nearly enough alike for that. "The factors are infinitely variable, and cannot be settled either by art or precedent. Judgment should be left to the people concerned. Each must set himself to act according to the immediate situation and the circumstances involved." Nevertheless, St. Thomas does believe that a certain amount of general guidance may be given for the prudent planning of conduct. He himself gives a good deal of it, and in some rather surprising areas. In connection with the virtue of modesty, for example, he has this to say: "Ornament should befit a person's condition and intention. If a woman decks herself out decently according to her rank and station, and comports herself unpretentiously according to the custom of her country, then she will be acting with modesty, the virtue that sets the style for making an entrance and sitting down and indeed for all deportment. This covers also her actions to please the husband she has or should have, and to keep him away from other women." The dry humor of "has or should have" is not uncharacteristic of St. Thomas.

Politics

St. Thomas agrees with Aristotle that a social existence is natural to humankind—"man is a social and political animal"—because a division of labor is needed to supply the necessities and conveniences of life, and because communication is needed to foster the activities of intelligence distinctive of the species. Government is no less natural than society, St. Thomas says, since a common ruling power is needed in the interests of directing, for the common good, the activities of individuals who tend, as is only human, to be preoccupied with personal concerns. St. Thomas does not take the view, to which St. Augustine was inclined, that government is needed at all only because human sinfulness on the score of "lust for domination" (as St. Augustine put it[8]) achieves through government a tolerable stability. Even if humankind had never "fallen" and become sinful, St. Thomas says, some persons would still be more gifted than others at directing affairs for the common good, and by rights they should exercise authority. It is true that, were it not for human sinfulness, certain institutions of government—an army to repel foreign enemies, a criminal justice system to insure domestic tranquillity—would be unnecessary. Yet a government, in St. Thomas's view, is responsible for more than merely keeping the peace; it should also promote the well-being of the people by seeing that adequate provision is made of the means of civilized life and by furnishing generally the unified direction required for effective cooperation.

In a treatise *On Princely Government,* St. Thomas maintains that the best form of government is monarchy. Peace and cooperation among a plurality of citizens depend upon a kind of unity among them; and this unity, St. Thomas says, is more likely to be achieved and maintained by government that is exercised not by a plurality but by one person. A plurality who exercise government are, as history shows, only too likely to disagree among themselves and to produce disunity among the people. "That which is itself a unity can more easily produce unity than that which is a plurality. . . . So government by one person is more likely to be successful than government by many." As the members of the human body are moved by one member (the heart, as St. Thomas believes), as

[8] See p. 316.

the powers of the human soul are subject to one power (reason), as the world at large is governed by one Creator and Lord, so there is a "natural pattern" unmistakably indicating the superiority of monarchy over other forms of human government. "Government by a king is the best." St. Thomas concedes that should a king degenerate into a tyrant, substituting his private interest for the common welfare of the citizens, then the *worst* form of government would come about. "Just as it is better for a power which is productive of good to be more united, it is more harmful for a power which is productive of evil to be united rather than divided." But the extremes of tyranny, St. Thomas says, are likelier to result from the breakdown of pluralistic forms of government than from the corruption of a king. It is harder, he believes, for a king to lose sight of the common interest than for the members of a pluralistic government to do so, because the latter tend to be absorbed by their own disagreements and rivalries, sometimes so absorbed as to be capable of fomenting civil war—historically the usual antecedent to tyranny. St. Thomas is far from denying, however, that safeguards should be adopted to minimize the danger of kings' becoming tyrants. His fullest statements about this occur in the *Summa Theologica,* where he makes it plain that what he favors is a *constitutional* monarchy, in which the power of the king is limited by that of magistrates elected by the people, and in which the king is himself subject to the laws that he, as the people's representative, is charged with promulgating and upholding. A king who becomes tyrannical may be deposed, but not assassinated, St. Thomas says, since assassination, in all likelihood, would only make matters worse. An attempt at assassination that failed would doubtless make the tyrant all the more tyrannical, whereas an attempt that succeeded would probably result in a seizing of power by someone no less unsavory than the tyrant. The point, however, is to take from the start every precaution against tyranny: "In the first place it is necessary that whoever of the possible candidates is proclaimed king shall be of such character that it is unlikely he will become a tyrant. . . . Next, a monarchy should be so constituted that there is no opportunity for the king, once he is reigning, to become a tyrant. And, at the same time, the kingly power should be so restricted that he could not easily turn to tyranny."

Kingly power, exercised for the benefit of the whole people, comes ultimately from God, St. Thomas says, and confers upon the king a "singular likeness to God." "A king does in his kingdom what God does in the universe," which is to govern and to administer justice so that the best condition of the whole may be realized and preserved. For human society the best condition is a "fullness of life." That means, as far as temporal affairs are concerned, a life according to virtue, with a sufficiency of material goods; and the promotion of this is the king's particular duty. The king "must, in governing, be concerned, by laws and by advice, by penalties and by rewards, to dissuade men from evildoing and to induce them to do good; following thus the example of God, who gave to men a law, and rewards those who observe it but punishes those who transgress." As God governs the world in keeping with his eternal law, so a king should govern his kingdom in keeping with sound human law.

Human law, when sound, consists for St. Thomas in regulations derived from the natural moral law for the purpose of establishing a "scheme of common happiness" in a community or state. The power to enact human laws belongs "either to the whole people or to the public authority [the king with his magistrates] who is the guardian of the community." Of course, a law must be promulgated, or officially made known, if people are to be obliged to obey it. Thus St. Thomas defines "law" as "an ordinance of reason made for the common good by the public personage who has charge of the community, and promulgated." Individuals may reasonably be enjoined by law to do what promotes the well-being of the community as a whole, because individuals are related as parts to this whole, and "each part is for its whole as imperfect for perfect." But to say that the individual "is for" the community or state is not, for St. Thomas, to say that the individual is to be viewed merely as an instrument for realizing some impersonal end (such as the "Good of the State"). "Men are principals, not merely instruments. It is true that parts are for the whole, not the whole for the parts. But rational creatures have an affinity to the whole, for, in a sense, each is all. They are not made for anyone's utility." In extreme situations law may require, for the common good, sacrifices of an extreme kind on the part of individuals (soldiers in war, for example); but in the life to come, when the community of the faithful see all things together in the vision of God, when "each is all" in mirroring in his or her soul the perfection of all, then it will be plain that none were "merely instruments," that all were "principals."

The proper task of human legislators, according to St. Thomas, is to work out applications of the natural moral law and to encourage compliance therewith by determining suitable rewards or penalties. Theft, for example, is forbidden by the natural moral law; but precisely what kinds of activity are to count as "theft," and the penalties to be paid for them, are matters for reasonable legislation to establish. It is essential, St. Thomas says, for legislators to bear in mind the capacities of the people for whom laws are to be enacted. There is no point in enacting laws against vices from which only persons of uncommon virtue can be expected to abstain. "Human law is enacted on behalf of the mass of men, the majority of whom are far from perfect in virtue. For this reason human law does not prohibit every vice from which virtuous men abstain; but only the graver vices from which the majority can abstain; and particularly those vices which are damaging of others, and which, if they were not prohibited, would make it impossible for human society to endure: as murder, theft, and suchlike, which are prohibited by human law." Moreover, there can be no question of enacting laws against bad intentions, even with respect to the graver vices, for God alone is competent to judge intentions. It is external actions, done of course knowingly, that should be of concern to human legislators and judges. "Human law does not punish the man who meditates murder but does not commit it, though divine law does punish him. . . ." But to this it must be added that "whatever a man does in ignorance he does accidentally, and in consequence both human and divine law must consider the question of ignorance in judging whether certain matters are punishable or pardonable."

Human laws are unjust, and so are not really laws at all, when they are inconsistent either with the natural moral law or with the divine law. St. Thomas explains in a famous passage of the *Summa Theologica:*

> Laws may be unjust for two reasons. Firstly, when they are detrimental to human welfare [as defined by the natural moral law]. . . . Either with respect to their object, as when a ruler enacts laws which are burdensome to his subjects and which do not make for common prosperity, but are designed better to serve his own cupidity and vainglory. Or with respect to their author; if a legislator should enact laws which exceed the powers vested in him. Or, finally with respect to their form; if the burdens, even though they are concerned with the common welfare, are distributed in an inequitable manner throughout the community. Laws of this sort have more in common with violence than with legality; for as St. Augustine says, in the *De Libro Arbitrio [On the Free Choice of the Will]* (I, 5): "A law which is not just cannot be called a law." Such laws do not, in consequence, oblige in conscience, except, on occasion, to avoid scandal or disorder. . . .
>
> Secondly, laws may be unjust through being contrary to divine goodness: such as tyrannical laws enforcing idolatry, or any other action against the divine law. Such laws may under no circumstances be obeyed: for, as it is said (*Acts* V, 29): "We must obey God rather than man."

Unlike the principles of divine law and of the natural moral law, St. Thomas says, human law is subject to change. Experience can bring a more accurate understanding of what, in the given circumstances, effectively promotes the common well-being; and then certain laws may well be found in need of refinement or replacement. But the circumstances of a community or state may also change in such a way as to require changes in its laws, occasionally very basic changes. St. Thomas mentions the case of a people who, having laws under which they elect their own public officials, allow the electoral process to become in time so corrupt that government "falls into the hands of dishonorable and vicious men." It would then be right, St. Thomas says, for the franchise to be restricted to "the few and honest" who can be trusted to manage things better. Yet St. Thomas cautions against changing any laws unless the advantages from doing so are clear and great. He points out that people's respect for law in general is largely a function of custom, so that respect for law is always to some extent weakened when custom is set aside by changes in the law. "Thus human law should never be changed unless the benefits which result to the public interest are such as to compensate for the harm done. This may be the case if the new statutes contain great and manifest advantages; or if there is urgent necessity due to the fact that the old law contains evident injustice, or its observance is excessively harmful." Custom, St. Thomas goes on to say, is as much a manifestation of human reason and will as the explicit words of a legislative enactment; and if words can change laws, so can custom, and without weakening the coercive power of law. "Law can be changed and explained by means of actions many times repeated, such as result in custom: and it can thus happen that new customs arise, which have the validity of law; in the sense that such exterior actions, frequently verified, clearly manifest the interior movements of the will and the concept of reason. For whatever is done frequently would seem to result from a deliberate judgment of reason. In this sense custom has the power of law, it may annul law, and it may act as the interpreter of law."

How does St. Thomas view the relation between Church and State? In line with the prevailing medieval outlook, he sees no sharp separation between the two. Church and State, the ecclesiastical and political establishments, are for him just complementary sides of one Christian society. Governmental authorities are responsible for upholding and defending the Catholic Church, as the only true church, and ecclesiastical authorities have the right to expect their civil counterparts to follow the Church's guidance in ordering temporal affairs with an eye to spiritual needs and requirements. St. Thomas reasons as follows. A king, with his magistrates, is responsible for promoting a fullness of life for the people as a whole; and because a full life is one lived according to virtue, a king is responsible for encouraging virtuous living (even though he cannot hope to eradicate every vice through legislation). Now since the final end or good of humankind is to attain, through virtuous living in this life, eternal beatitude in the next life, "the king's duty is to promote the welfare of the community in such a way that it leads fittingly to the happiness of heaven; insisting upon the performance of all that leads thereto, and forbidding, as far as is possible, whatever is inconsistent with this end." But what leads to the happiness of heaven is the concern of the officials of the Church, to whom God has entrusted the administration of His divine law pertaining to spiritual matters. Kings, therefore, in their management of temporal affairs, "must be subject to priests," and subject especially to "the High Priest, the successor of Peter and Vicar of Christ, the Roman Pontiff." As the body is subject to the soul, or as the philosophical sciences are subject (as "handmaidens") to sacred theology, so the temporal authority of kings is subject to the spiritual authority of the Church. "Therefore, there is no usurpation of power if a spiritual Prelate should interest himself in temporal affairs with respect to those things in which the temporal power is subject to him. . . ." St. Thomas indicates clearly enough what he means by this. It is within the Pope's authority, he says, to direct temporal rulers to take measures against infidels and heretics whom the Church has identified as likely to corrupt the faith of Catholics. Incorrigible heretics, upon excommunication from the Church, are to be turned over to secular authorities for "extermination." Jews may be allowed to practice their faith, but secular authorities should see to it that on all occasions they are "distinguished from other persons by some particular dress." Infidels other than Jews "are in no-wise to be tolerated, unless perhaps to avoid some evil. . . ." A king who lapses from the Faith and fails to perform the secular services the Church expects of him is liable to excommunication, in which case "his subjects are *ipso facto* absolved from his rule and from the oath of fealty which bound them to him." It is in temporal affairs such as these, according to St. Thomas, that a spiritual Prelate may rightly interest himself; and as a matter of fact, medieval popes certainly did take an interest in them. In 1076, a century and a half before St. Thomas was born, Pope Gregory VII excommunicated the Holy Roman Emperor Henry IV, with the result that feudal lords desirous of overthrowing Henry revolted against him, and for three years Germany was torn by civil war. In 1209, Pope Innocent III launched a crusade against the heretical sect of Albigenses in southern France, with the result that as many as a million suspected heretics were slaughtered, and the brilliant culture of Provence was destroyed. In 1215, at the Fourth Lateran Council called by Innocent III, it was ordered that Jews were not to hold public office, were to remain off the streets on Church festival days, and were always to wear a distinctive badge on their clothing.

Historians have observed that religious unity, as involving intolerance of religious differences, was a key but ominous factor in the recovery of Western Europe from the anarchy following the collapse of the Roman Empire. G. G. Coulton, for example, apropos of St. Thomas, has this to say:

> Just as the peasants of the Dark Ages were glad, on the whole, to rally round the nearest fighting man, and even commit their liberties to him, so they were quite content to rally round the priest. The Church . . . with its strong sense of social solidarity, gave them neighborly and religious warmth. . . . Her ordinary ceremonies, and many of her beliefs, since they had sprung to so great an extent from the multitude, were therefore acceptable and comfortable to the multitude. It is noteworthy that, in the Dark Ages, heresy seems to have been always unpopular; heretics were often lynched, and sometimes, apparently, not even by priestly initiative. Anything rather than anarchy; and the average man, quite apart from his uncultured dislike of anything strange and perplexing, realized dimly that these dissidents were not strong enough, either numerically or individually, to rebuild Church or State if either were destroyed. . . . The passion for outward unity was one of the main forces in Medieval reconstruction; it was the most obvious rallying point in Church and State. . . . This idea of unity outlasted the Dark Ages; it may even be said to have attained to its most definite expression only

when these were past, and when the world had settled down into the comparative stability of the thirteenth century. By that time, two generations of great thinkers had toiled to weave the accepted beliefs of their day into one harmonious philosophic whole; and then came the temptation to stiffen into self-satisfied repose. . . . Given the premises which were accepted by hierarchy and laity alike, Aquinas was impeccably logical in proving that it is the Christian's duty to remove obstinant nonconformists at any cost, even at that of the stake. But to lynch in the heat of passion is one thing, to kill by implacable logic is another; and the Inquisition [formally established by Pope Gregory IX in 1233] was never popular, even among men whose ancestors had with their own hands cast the heretic into an extemporised bonfire. Its unpopularity increased when it became evident how definitely it was nourished by the fines and confiscations imposed upon rich heretics; and, again, how fatally it lent itself (as in the cases of the Templars and Joan of Arc) to purely political purposes.

St. Thomas, then, in his own support of religious intolerance, was not so much a man of his time as a Churchman of his time, going against an incipient current of social change. Someone of his magnanimity, whose writings are otherwise remarkable for wise and humane observations, might well have been expected to evince some reluctance, at least, over having to speak for the barbarous practices in question.

CHAPTER 17

Three Late Medieval Minds

Among the contemporaries and immediate successors of St. Thomas, there were some who worked along lines very different from his; and there were others who pursued similar themes but with results more or less at odds with his. The outstanding figure in the first group was Roger Bacon. The leading figures in the second group were John Duns Scotus and William of Ockham. The death of Ockham, in the middle of the fourteenth century, came as the medieval period was giving way to the Renaissance. Ockham's thought can fairly be viewed as the last important expression, if a rather hectic expression, of a characteristic medieval mind.

Roger Bacon

When Christopher Columbus, in the second half of the fifteenth century, investigated the feasibility of sailing west to reach the Orient, he was encouraged to make the attempt partly by some geographical observations of a thirteenth-century Franciscan friar. This was Roger Bacon (1214–1292), the most famous medieval forerunner of the rise of modern natural science. In addition to geography, Bacon probed into a miscellany of subjects that are associated today with the physical and biological sciences, and that were impressively represented in his day by the newly discovered scientific works of Aristotle and of Aristotle's Muslim followers. Although Bacon made some important scientific contributions of his own, particularly in the field of optics, he himself was less a scientist than a publicist for science, concerned to promote the advancement of science for what he saw as its beneficial applications. With the kind of remarkable foresight sometimes thought to have been peculiar to Leonardo da Vinci (a contemporary of Columbus), Bacon anticipated such technological achievements as flying-machines and self-propelling vehicles and boats. Yet the greatest advantages that Bacon expected from science were advantages to the Church, in the way of confirming Scriptural doctrines and bringing more people to the Faith. In the course of presenting his theologically oriented program for science, Bacon expressed significant views on the nature and importance of scientific method—views not less significant than those of his more celebrated namesake, Francis Bacon (1561–1626).

419

Roger Bacon was born in 1214 in the English village of Ilchester, about 30 miles south of Bristol. He was educated at Oxford in the standard medieval "arts" curriculum, comprising the *trivium* of grammar, rhetoric, and logic, and the *quadrivium* of arithmetic, geometry, astronomy, and music. Then for several years Bacon lectured on philosophy, on Aristotle in particular, at the University of Paris. When he was about thirty-three (around 1247) he returned to Oxford and began a long period of investigation into sciences[1] and languages, during which period he also joined the Franciscan Order. Bacon's interest in sciences and languages had been awakened above all by a curious volume entitled the *Secret of Secrets* that he had discovered in Paris. Purportedly written by Aristotle for Alexander the Great, and accepted as such by Bacon, the *Secret of Secrets* was actually a work of anonymous Neoplatonic authorship that had long been in circulation among the Muslim philosophers. It speaks of a universal science revealed by God to the Hebrews, and transmitted to Aristotle via the Chaldeans and Egyptians, in which are disclosed all the secrets of nature—but in veiled language intelligible only (with linguistic training) to the virtuous and pious. Bacon seems to have been drawn to the Franciscans both because he hoped they would support his research and because he sought virtue and piety. In the event, Franciscan officials were not much interested in Bacon's scientific program and were flatly opposed to the evangelical brand of piety that, as they soon saw, Bacon found especially congenial. There had arisen within the Franciscan Order a left-wing movement that took its inspiration from one Joachim of Flora, a Calabrian monk (died around 1200) who preached the imminent arrival of Anti-Christ, defeat of whom would usher in an age of universal love. Bacon's outspoken support of the "Joachites" led (in about 1257) to his being transferred from Oxford to the Franciscan headquarters in Paris, where, he says, "My superiors and brothers, disciplining me with hunger, kept me under close guard and would not permit anyone to come to me. . . ." (At this time the chief Franciscan superior, or Minister General, was none other than St. Bonaventure.) Nevertheless, word of Bacon's work toward a universal science reached Pope Clement IV, who (in 1266) was sufficiently intrigued to ask Bacon in confidence to send him something he had written. With great speed Bacon produced an *Opus Maius* (Greater Work) and two supplementary treatises, *Opus Minus* and *Opus Tertium*. Unfortunately, Clement IV soon died, and Bacon was once again without a patron. But he was allowed to return to Oxford, where he resumed his studies, completed further scientific works as well as Greek and Hebrew grammars, and became increasingly an embittered critic of what he perceived as the Church's moral laxity and intellectual poverty. It appears that his harsh criticisms led in the 1280s to another period of confine-

---

[1] Especially influential with Bacon were the writings on mathematics and optics of Robert Grosseteste (1168–1253), Bishop of Lincoln after 1235, but formerly Chancellor of Oxford University.

ment. What exactly happened is not clear. At any rate he was back at work—this time on a *Compendium of Theology*—when he died in 1292 at seventy-eight.

Bacon had a low opinion of most of the philosophers and theologians of his day, including St. Thomas Aquinas. His critical remarks about St. Thomas and the others do not as a rule suggest that he attended very closely to what they said, only that he felt he knew enough about them to see that they neglected the scientific studies he considered essential. He begins his *Opus Maius* by undertaking to explain why virtually everyone, even among the supposedly learned, has remained in the "deepest shadows of error" and has been "blind to every gleam of wisdom." The prevailing ignorance, Bacon says, can be traced to four chief obstacles in the way of grasping truth, namely, "submission to faulty and unworthy authority, influence of custom, popular prejudice, and concealment of our own ignorance accompanied by an ostentatious display of our knowledge." The last obstacle is the worst, Bacon points out, for it really is the basis of the first three obstacles. Because everyone wants to appear wise and to avoid appearing ignorant, everyone, or almost everyone, resorts to convenient "authorities" to defend whatever he or she happens to believe. This in turn plays into the hands of everyone's tendency to go on believing, as a matter of custom or habit, whatever he or she has taken any trouble to defend ("since every man loves his own labors"). And "since no man errs for himself alone, but delights in spreading his madness among his neighbors," the habitual false beliefs of one person "take possession" of others and so contribute to popular prejudice. It has often been wryly observed that Bacon himself cites several "authorities"—Aristotle, Cicero, Seneca, Avicenna, Averroes, and so on—in the course of his discussion of the obstacles to knowledge in general and the obstacle of "authority" in particular. Bacon states clearly, however, that in his view there have been some genuine authorities, not many, but a few—the saints of the Church and "the perfect philosophers and other men of science." These are not the "authorities" invoked by the multitude, to whom perfection in anything, whether in virtue or in knowledge, is simply irksome. Variety and novelty, rather than the perfection of truth, is what most people want. Such indeed is the frailty of human nature that even the minority who seek perfection, in the "rich fulness of the virtues and sciences," are usually saddened when they discover it, "for it delights very few of us."

Knowledge, Bacon says, can be acquired in two ways—by reasoning and by experience. These are not alternatives, however, for experience is necessary if conclusions of reasoning are to be apprehended as true.

Reasoning draws a conclusion and makes us grant the conclusion, but does not make the conclusion certain, nor does it remove doubt so that the mind may rest on the intuition of truth, unless the mind discovers it by the path of experience; since many have the arguments relating to what can be known, but because they lack experience they neglect the arguments, and neither avoid what is harmful nor follow what is good. For if a man who has never seen fire should prove by adequate reasoning that fire burns and injures things and destroys them, his mind would not be satisfied thereby, nor would he avoid fire, until he placed his hand or some combustible substance in the fire, so that he might prove by experience that which reasoning taught. But when he has had actual experience of combustion his mind is made certain and rests in the full light of truth. Therefore reasoning does not suffice, but experience does.

Experience, Bacon goes on to say, is essential not only to confirm and impress upon us the conclusions of sound reasoning. It is essential also if we are to disconfirm and to disabuse ourselves of the conclusions of unsound reasoning. Bacon mentions in this connection some fallacies popular at the time—that diamonds cannot be broken except by goat's blood, that hot water freezes more quickly than cold—which can readily be disconfirmed by "anyone who makes the experiment." Of great concern to Bacon are the superstitious notions encouraged by magicians and others who deal in "incantations, invocations, conjurations, sacrifices, and cults." The effect of such hocus-pocus is to draw people away from the Church, by making them think, for example, that the miracles in the Bible were "conjurations" of magic, not acts of God. Genuine phenomena of nature, Bacon says, are far more wonderful than the fraudulent performances of sorcerers; and furthermore, an awareness of these phenomena is conducive to faith. Faith calls upon us to believe what in many instances we cannot understand, but so does our experience of natural phenomena, many of which we cannot understand although experience assures us that they are genuine. The more we discover of the amazing facts of nature, the more subdued will be the intellectual pride that inhibits faith. Understanding, as St. Augustine said, follows upon believing, as regards those revealed doctrines that we are capable of understanding. The same thing is true, according to Bacon, with reference to phenomena of nature, which we must accept—on good authority if not on the basis of our own experience—before we can proceed to perform experiments in the effort to discover what exactly the facts are and how they are to be explained. Using "experience" in a wide sense to mean any direct confrontation with data that lay claim to our acceptance, Bacon says that "experience is of two kinds." First, there is the experience, which everyone acknowledges, of confronting natural phenomena by means of the senses. Second, there is the experience, which Christians acknowledge even though they may never personally have had it, of confronting truths by divine revelation concerning both natural and spiritual matters. Revealed truths concerning natural matters, Bacon says, supply essential help in understanding the frequently baffling phenomena we experience through our senses. The "holy patriarchs and prophets," whom God especially favored with revelation, should be closely examined from this point of view. Scripture, in other words, should be found to contain, albeit in summary and esoteric terms, many useful indications of the whys and wherefores of natural phenomena. And if observation bears out the indications in Scripture, this will indirectly help to confirm the authenticity of Scriptural revelations in general, including the revelations pertaining to spiritual matters. An *Experimental Science* must therefore be cultivated in the interests of systematically confirming true beliefs, disconfirming false beliefs, eradicating superstition, and upholding the Faith.

Experimental Science, Bacon says, has three great "prerogatives" or "dignities" that distinguish it from other fields of study. The first of these prerogatives is that Experimental Science "investigates by experiment" the conclusions arrived at in other fields. By "experiment" Bacon means both planned experiments and careful observations of things and events as they naturally happen. He does not mean, however, that in fields other than Experimental Science no appeal is made to observation. Even in mathematics, he thinks, observations of a kind play an essential role, as witness the many references to illustrative diagrams in geometry and to written calculations in arithmetic. Bacon's point is that in other fields the observations cited are almost always very limited in scope. He notes, for example, that in the field of natural philosophy, as practiced by Aristotle and Avicenna, a phenomenon would usually be explained by reference to principles based upon little observation beyond that of the phenomenon in question. Consider Aristotle's explanation of the rainbow. Aristotle observed rainbows in the spray of oars as well as rainbows in the sky, and he reasoned that rainbows could in general be accounted for in terms of the reflection of sunlight from droplets of water. Now a "diligent experimenter," Bacon says, will submit this explanation to the test of further experience, taking into account the rainbow effects of crystals, say, and of glass vessels filled with water. When this is done, as it was (soon after Bacon's death) by Theodoric of Freiberg in famous experiments with hexagonal prisms and with water in glass globes, it can be shown that Aristotle's explanation was along the right lines but was seriously incomplete. Light is not just reflected by water; it also is refracted or bent in the process, and this refraction accounts for the colors in the rainbow and for double rainbows. Theodoric's improvement upon Aristotle's explanation was an impressive illustration of Bacon's first prerogative. In all the natural sciences of today, it is standard procedure to test a proposed explanation (an hypothesis) by a number of meticulous observations, if possible by observations made in the course of controlled experiments. Bacon, however, thinks of this testing as something to be done by one grand Experimental Science, which has the office of investigating explanations of natural phenomena advanced by any of the separate fields of study ("sciences") recognized in his day. He has astrology and alchemy in mind, and indeed he expects and promises much of them, as well as theology ("revealed science"), natural philosophy ("speculative science"), astronomy, medicine, and agronomy.

The second prerogative of Experimental Science, as Bacon conceives it, is the coordination and synthesis of results from the separate fields investigated in accordance with the first prerogative. The separate fields have much to contribute to one another, Bacon believes; and it is the business of Experimental Science, having tested the findings of these fields, to serve as their coordinator. Medicine seems to Bacon a field that particularly stands to gain by incorporating results from elsewhere. He notes that "in these times" few people live for more than forty-five or fifty years, whereas the Bible tells us that people once lived much longer. The trouble has been that "scarcely one physician in a thousand" has given the slightest attention to the "rules of health"—to nutrition, as we should say, and to hygiene in general, both mental and physical. The regimen for retarding and mitigating the effects of old age consists in "the proper use of food and drink, of motion and rest, of sleep and wakefulness, of elimination and retention, of the air, and in the control of the passions of the mind." What Aristotle, Avicenna, and others have said on these matters should be tested and, if found correct, incorporated into the practice of medicine, which for too long has dealt in dubious "remedies." Useful information of a nutritional kind could surely be obtained, Bacon says, from close observation of the diets of animals, for animals "in many ways avoid a premature death." Not that Bacon is opposed to manufactured medicines. In fact he sets great store by what "Aristotle in the book of *Secrets*" has to say about a "perfect medicine," the prescription for which was made known by divine revelation to Adam and his sons. Bacon believes that a chief ingredient of this elixir of life is some substance (the "philosopher's stone") discoverable by alchemy with the help of Experimental Science, which substance would also transmute base metals into gold. Lest Bacon be thought particularly credulous for his keen interest in alchemy, it is worth mentioning that the possibility of "transmutation" was accepted down to the seventeenth century by a number of distinguished men of science—including Boyle and van Helmont—and that Paracelsus (1493–1541), a great pioneer of chemical medicine, was himself an alchemist.[2] Bacon's vision of a general science that would coordinate the findings of particular sciences might seem all the more pertinent in our time, when specialization in science has been carried to great lengths. Also of even more value today would be a plan Bacon had for providing nonspecialists with a concise compendium of scientific knowl-

---

[2] Alchemy had a theoretical basis, respectable enough at the time, in Aristotle's doctrine that any substance of a given kind consists of (a) a form distinctive of it and (b) an "ultimate substratum" (or "prime matter") that is the same for every kind of substance. The alchemist tried, usually for mercury, to isolate (b) from (a) and to impose a new form—of gold, say—upon (b) by means of a "principle" (the "philosopher's stone") derived usually from sulfur. So it was hoped to transmute or convert one kind of substance into another. Today, from the very different theoretical perspective of modern nuclear physics, it has been found that certain chemical elements—radioactive ones— naturally convert into others (as radium spontaneously converts into an isotope of lead) and that artificial processes of nuclear fission and fusion can bring about transmutation (as uranium-235 can be transmuted by fission into krypton and barium). Conceivably, gold could be produced by nuclear fission or fusion from some other element(s), but the gold so produced might be radioactive.

edge, explaining in clear and systematic outline the current state of each science. Bacon realized that, even in his time, no one person could produce such a compendium. His idea was that "prelates and princes" should underwrite its preparation by a team of specialists.

The third and supreme prerogative of Experimental Science, Bacon says, consists in the practical application of scientific knowledge for beneficial purposes. Which purposes are beneficial is to be determined, in his view, in accordance with a properly religious moral philosophy, to which Experimental Science as a whole should be subordinate. Today the practical application of scientific knowledge is assigned to the various fields of engineering and technology, which are distinguished from the "pure" sciences engaged in "basic research." Bacon's position, we could say, is that the various fields of engineering and technology should be encompassed and coordinated by one Experimental Science respectful of Christian values, which will promote, direct, and evaluate the basic research of the pure sciences. By virtue of its third prerogative, Bacon says, Experimental Science "has the same relation to the other sciences as the science of navigation to the navigator's art"; or to use another analogy, Experimental Science "directs other sciences as its handmaids." Practitioners of Experimental Science, as Bacon describes them, will perceive the possibilities of beneficially applying developments within the separate sciences, will encourage and test these developments, and will work out the practical applications. Among the discoveries Bacon foresees are "perpetual baths" and "ever-burning lamps," which have been approximated in modern times by systems of plumbing and by incandescent bulbs. Sad to relate, Bacon also foresees, and champions, military uses of "the force of the salt called saltpeter" (potassium nitrate, a constituent of gunpowder), weapons that "act by means of an infection," a petroleum preparation that "burns up whatever it meets" and "can be extinguished only with difficulty, for water cannot put it out," and so on. One might wonder how the use of these things is consistent with a respect for Christian values, but Bacon believes that the Bible itself may indicate their advantages. When Gideon with a small force overcame the Midianites (Judges 7:16–32) by stunning them with a great noise outside their camp as they slept, did he not employ saltpeter or something akin to it? The noise it makes, Bacon says, "exceeds the roar of sharp thunder, and the flash exceeds the greatest brilliancy of the lightning accompanying the thunder." To Bacon's way of thinking, the Church has in this sphere a definite responsibility: "The Church should consider the employment of these inventions against unbelievers and rebels, in order that it may spare Christian blood, and especially should it do so because of future perils in the time of Antichrist, which with the grace of God it would be easy to meet, if prelates and princes promoted study and investigated the secrets of nature and of art."

Bacon happened not to be wrong in his sense of impending "perils." During the five or six decades after his death (in 1292), such misfortunes befell Western Europe that many believed the "time of Antichrist" had indeed arrived. A general economic crisis, with spiraling inflation and a collapse of agriculture leading to famine (1315–1317), was followed by an attack of bubonic plague—the Black Death (1346–1350)—which carried off about a third of the entire population of Europe. A kind of social hysteria was produced by these calamities. Civilized restraints broke down; superstition was rife; enormities of every sort were committed. Jews were massacred, in the belief that they had caused the plague (by poisoning the wells, it was said). Peasants and artisans were oppressed by the insolvent nobility; peasants and artisans revolted; the revolts were ruthlessly put down. England and France began the Hundred Years' War (1337–1453), with disastrous results for people caught in the path of the contending armies. On top of all this, the Church declined as a force for European political unity when the Papacy, under the domination of Philip IV of France, was removed from Rome to Avignon, where it remained from 1309 to 1377.

Historians have tended to see a reflection of these dislocating events in the philosophy of the period. St. Thomas's grand synthesis of theology and philosophy, of faith and reason, it is said, came apart along with the disintegration of European society and culture in general. Early signs of the breakup are said to appear in the writings of Duns Scotus, to be followed by the complete dissociation of faith and reason in the writings of William of Ockham. But this way of conceiving the philosophy of the fourteenth century is not, of course, wholly accurate or impartial. St. Thomas continued to have, and even now continues to have, a number of loyal supporters. In their minds, St. Thomas's synthesis certainly did not "come apart." Moreover, those inclined to agree more with William of Ockham than with St. Thomas will view the ideas of the former not as a manifestation of cultural decline but as an important contribution to human thought. What all parties can agree to is that Duns Scotus and William of Ockham raised some basic issues which greatly influenced the subsequent history of theology as well as philosophy and which need to be addressed by supporters of St. Thomas.

John Duns Scotus

In about 1266, John Duns Scotus was born somewhere in Scotland,[3] precisely where is much disputed by Scottish historians. Scotus entered the Franciscan Order in his youth, studied and then taught at both Oxford and Paris, and died at Cologne in 1308, when he was about forty-two. One of the few definite facts about Scotus's life is that he incurred

---

[3] "Scotus" meaning "the Scot." In Scotus's time, unlike Eriugena's, only Scotsmen—not Irishmen also—were in Latin called *Scoti*.

the displeasure of the king of France. The king, Philip IV, levied a tax upon the French clergy, the better to finance his armies. Pope Boniface VIII protested. Scotus supported the Pope. The king banished Scotus from France for a year or so (1303–1304).

Notwithstanding the shortness of his life, Scotus produced a vast quantity of writings. These mostly consist of commentaries and questions on such texts as the *Metaphysics* of Aristotle and the *Sentences* of Peter Lombard. One version of his commentary on the *Sentences,* entitled the *Oxford Commentary (Opus Oxoniense),* is the main source for his philosophical views. In style Scotus's writings are uniformly abstract, technical, colorless, and prolix. His followers imitated his style to such a fault that their nickname, "Dunsmen," became during the Renaissance a byword for ineptitude—and this is the origin of "dunce." But the closeness of Scotus's reasoning and the subtlety of his analysis won him the title of *Doctor Subtilis,* attracted the attention of many an important later philosopher, and drew high praise from Gerard Manley Hopkins in a famous poem on "Duns Scotus's Oxford." Here is the final stanza:

> Of reality the rarest-veinèd unraveller; a not
> Rivalled insight, be rival Italy or Greece;
> Who fired France for Mary without spot.

The last line refers to Scotus's spirited defense in Paris of the doctrine of the Immaculate Conception, according to which the Virgin Mary, though conceived naturally, was from the moment of her conception free from any taint of original sin.

Not in philosophy, but in theology, Scotus says, can we discover the ultimate end of humankind and the means of attaining it. The end is supernatural beatitude, "the face-to-face vision and enjoyment of God," and philosophy alone would not bring us to entertain even the possibility of this. Aristotle himself admits as much, Scotus believes, for did not Aristotle hold that in philosophy the objects of our knowledge are universals abstracted from our sense-experience of material things? And how could we have occasion or reason to think, without divine revelation, that any such universal could enable us to apprehend a nonmaterial Being? Avicenna, as Scotus knows, maintained that philosophical considerations by themselves suffice to make us realize that experience furnishes all of us with a concept of being in general, applicable to God as well as to creatures. But Scotus is sure that if Avicenna had not been a religious man, he would never have realized that he had this idea. "He has mixed his religion—that of Mohammed—with philosophical matters," Scotus says. Such is the fallen condition of human nature, in Scotus's view, that only divine revelation could inspire us to think that we are capable of the dimmest awareness of anything nonmaterial. The necessary assurance, however, is to be found in St. Paul's First Letter to the Corinthians (13:12): "For now we see through a glass, darkly; but then face to face: now I know in part; but then I shall know even as also I am known." Dark as it may be, any awareness now of God's existence implies the ability to form a concept of being that is not restricted to material things. Thus revelation in First Corinthians indicates to us—as the Koran really indicated to Avicenna—that our experience of material things must occasion in us a concept of being applicable also on the supernatural level. And this is to say that experience must provide us with a concept of being that is univocal (as opposed to equivocal[4]) in the sense that it conveys the same meaning in respect of both God and creatures. Here Scotus parts company with St. Thomas, according to whom there is only an *analogy* between the (necessary and infinite) "being" of God and the (contingent and finite) "being" of creatures. St. Thomas's view, as Scotus understands it, ought to have led St. Thomas to conclude that we can know nothing whatever of God. Our concepts derive from our sense-experience—Aristotle, St. Thomas, and Scotus are at one in this. But then it follows, Scotus says, that we cannot even conceive of God unless the concept of being we derive from sense-experience is as applicable to Him as to material things, notwithstanding the fact that His being is unique in its necessity and infinitude. "Every inquiry concerning God presupposes," Scotus says, "that the intellect has the same univocal concept which it takes from creatures."

Being, Scotus says, is so simple and basic a concept that it cannot be defined in terms of any simpler or more basic concepts. Scotus does proceed to make it clear, however, that by "being" he understands no more than *logical possibility.* That is, for Scotus the concept of being in general is the concept of whatever *can* exist in the sense that no logical contradiction is involved in the supposition of its existence. Thus the concept of being does not apply to squares without four sides, since "square without four sides" involves a contradiction, and nothing of the kind could possibly exist. On the other hand, the concept of being does apply to unicorns, for although unicorns happen not to exist, no contradiction is involved in the supposition of their existence. Scotus observes that being, even when conceived in this minimally positive fashion, can be said to have various characteristics. Of particular interest are the "disjunctive characteristics" that Scotus ascribes to being—characteristics expressed in phrases having an "either/or" (disjunctive) form. He says, for example, that being has the characteristic that it is *either necessary or contingent,* because whatever could have being would fall into the one category or the other, would exist either necessarily (as God is supposed to do) or else contingently (as creatures do). Similarly, we can say of being that it is either infinite or finite, either actual or potential, either capable of causing or capable of being caused, and so on. This last characteristic—either capable of causing or capable of being caused—is especially important to Scotus, since

---

[4]See p. 400, for the use of these terms in St. Thomas.

he employs it in constructing an argument for God's existence that he considers perfectly conclusive.

Briefly put, Scotus's argument for God's existence runs as follows. Being is either capable of causing or capable of being caused. Because "being" signifies logical possibility, the foregoing statement amounts to saying that the logically possible things are either things capable of acting as causes or things capable of being caused. Things capable of acting as causes are called "effective" things by Scotus, and things capable of being caused are called "effectible" things. In these terms, the principle in question is that the logically possible things are either effective or effectible. (An egg, for example, is effectible, whereas a hen is effective as its producer.) Scotus next proceeds to maintain that if something is effectible, then there must be something else that is effective in its regard, because a thing could not effect or produce itself, nor could a thing be effected or produced by nothing at all. The all-important question now arises: could every effective thing also be effectible? If so, there would be an infinite series of things in which each thing is effectible by another. Scotus takes it as axiomatic that such a series is out of the question. "An ascending infinity," he says, "is impossible." By "ascending" he means a hierarchical series of things existing at the same time, where each thing is effected (produced or maintained) by another "above" it. (For example, an egg is laid by a hen, while the hen is sustained by the oxygen in the air, while the air is prevented from escaping the earth by forces of gravity, while forces of gravity are kept in operation by . . .) Like St. Thomas, Scotus finds nothing impossible in the idea of an infinite (beginningless as well as endless) series of things occurring one after the other, in temporal succession, although he believes that divine revelation assures us that the world had a beginning. But if an "ascending infinity" is impossible, the conclusion has to be that something effective but not effectible, a "first effective being," has being at least in the sense of logical possibility. The *actual existence* of a first effective being can be demonstrated, Scotus believes, on the basis of some further considerations. A first effective being, in not owing its existence to anything else, would "exist from itself." That such a being *can* exist has already been shown, but how *can* it exist if it does *not* exist? To say that something can exist, although it happens not to exist, is to say that at some point it could conceivably come into existence. A being that exists from itself, however, could hardly come into existence, because whatever comes into existence does not exist from itself but from the productive activity of something else that brings it into existence. No, the nonexistence of a first effective being is flatly inconsistent with the demonstrated possibility of its existence. Accordingly, a first effective being, namely God, must actually exist. In Scotus's words: "The unconditionally first causally effective being can exist from itself, and therefore, it does exist from itself. Because what does not exist from itself, cannot exist from itself. . . ."

This very abstract argument is reminiscent of St. Thomas's argument for an Uncaused Cause. Scotus believes that his argument gives a stricter demonstration than St. Thomas's, however, because he appeals throughout only to necessary truths concerning logical possibility, whereas St. Thomas begins from a contingent truth of observation (concerning efficient causality in the natural world). In fact, Scotus's argument proceeds more along the lines followed by St. Anselm, who had already argued that if God *can* exist (as determined by His existence being conceivable), then He *does* (necessarily) exist. Scotus is prepared to endorse St. Anselm's own original version of the argument, provided that it is "touched up"—Scotus says "colored"—at a key point. What is needed is to supplement St. Anselm's argument with an additional premise to the effect that God's existence *is* conceivable because *no contradiction* is to be found in St. Anselm's apt characterization of God as "that than which nothing greater can be conceived."

God exists necessarily. From the mere possibility of God's existence we can deduce the impossibility of His nonexistence. Creatures, on the other hand, do not exist necessarily. As "effectible" things created by God in His freedom, creatures have an existence that is contingent. Such is Scotus's position. St. Thomas, of course, also believed that God's existence is necessary and that creatures' existence is contingent. Following Avicenna, St. Thomas attributed the contingent existence of creatures to a difference in their case between essence and existence. Any creature that could exist, St. Thomas said, would have some specific nature or other as constituted by a definition or essence ("rational animal," for instance). But whether any such thing (Socrates, for instance) has actual existence cannot be determined just by reflecting upon the definition or essence in question. Essence and existence, as far as creatures are concerned, are two different matters. Now Scotus, for his part, certainly acknowledges a distinction between essence and existence as regards creatures, but at the same time he insists that essence and existence are not strictly *different*. "It is simply false," Scotus says, "that existence is something different from essence." If the two were actually different for a creature, how could the creature have essential *unity* as an individual? Surely, Scotus says, it cannot be that essence and existence are different "factors" or "principles" of which an individual is somehow "composed." An individual that was "composed" in this way would be an accidental unity, not truly *one* as an individual. The contingent existence of creatures requires us to recognize in them only a *formal* distinction between essence and existence, not a *real* distinction amounting to an actual difference. This is enough to account for the fact that the essence of a creature does not include (and therefore necessitate) its existence.

Here we have an idea for which Scotus is famous—that we can detect in things formal distinctions that are not real distinctions. He makes use of this idea in formulating several of his philosophical and theological positions. Let us try to see more clearly what he means. A "real distinction," as Scotus uses the expression, is found whenever two things are seen to be capable of existing independently of one another, so that one could exist in separation from the other, and one could continue to exist even if the other ceased to exist. For example, there is a real distinction between two adjoining logs in a woodpile, since they can be separated from one another (and from the rest of the logs in the pile) without detriment to either, and one of them could be burned to ashes without the other's being affected in the least. In sharp contrast to this, a "formal distinction" is found when something is discovered to have *aspects* that are such that (a) we can think of one without thinking of the other, but (b) they could not possibly be separated, not even, as Scotus insists, by the infinite power of God. Essence and existence are aspects of this type. We can think of Socrates' essence as a rational animal without thinking of his existence, and vice versa. His existence is neither identical with nor included within his essence (as if he existed "by definition"). Nevertheless, his essence and his existence are but inseparable aspects of the concrete unitary individual that is Socrates. The distinction is formal, not real, but Scotus does not mean by this that the distinction is merely a figment of the mind. He believes that formal distinctions are real enough in the sense that inseparable yet distinguishable aspects are genuinely present in things, whether we happen to be aware of them or not.

Formal distinctions, Scotus maintains, are to be discovered throughout the entire field of existence. God's attributes—goodness, wisdom, and so on—are not really but just formally distinct from one another and from God's nature. Similarly, the powers of the human soul—nutrition, sensation, and intellection—are not really but just formally distinct from one another and from the soul itself. In any creature whatsoever there is a very basic formal distinction between the common nature it shares with other members of its species and the individuating difference on account of which the common nature belongs to the creature as a separate individual.

Scotus does not agree with St. Thomas's position that prime matter is the principle of individuation—the principle owing to which there can exist a number of different individuals having the same nature (or essence, or form). Prime matter, according to St. Thomas, is supposed to be perfectly indefinite and characterless; but nothing indefinite and characterless, Scotus argues, could be what makes the difference between individuals having the same nature. Socrates and Plato are alike as human beings by virtue of possessing the common nature of rational animality. St. Thomas would have it that what makes Socrates one individual and Plato another is that rational animality combines with prime matter to produce Socrates in one place and Plato in another place. But this, Scotus says, cannot be what happens. Rational animality, in and of itself, is not a number of different individuals. Prime matter is indefinite and characterless. How, then, could a "combination" of the two possibly give rise to different rational animals? The real story, Scotus says, must be that something is added to rational animality in Socrates' case that makes it *his* rational animality and not Plato's, whereas in Plato's case something is added to rational animality to make it *his* rational animality and not Socrates'. The "something" in each case must be *peculiar* to the individual (not another element of the form or common nature he shares with the other) and must be *definite* (unlike prime matter). The "something" in each case Scotus calls the "individuating difference"—in Latin, the *haecceitas,* the "thisness," by which a common nature is "contracted" to become *this* individual's nature. Now Scotus insists that there is a formal, but not a real, distinction between (a) the individuating difference peculiar to Socrates and (b) the common human nature that Socrates shares with Plato. There is a formal distinction, since we can think of (b) without thinking of (a), which we do in forming the universal concept of rational animality in abstraction from the individuating differences among actual human beings. But there is not a real distinction, since (b) cannot exist apart from (a) other than as a concept in our minds. Scotus, that is to say, does not subscribe to the view that common natures or essences have (or could have) reality on their own account, independently of the individuals whose natures or essences they are. Plato and the Extreme Realists whom Abelard criticized held different forms of this view, but Scotus agrees with Aristotle, Abelard, and St. Thomas in rejecting it. As we shall see in a moment, however, William of Ockham could find as little merit in Scotus's view as in that of the Extreme Realists.

In conclusion, we should take note of Scotus's disagreements with St. Thomas on the important topics of freedom of will, moral obligation, and immortality. On each of these topics Scotus advances a view according to which the human intellect has less competence or influence than St. Thomas believed. It was St. Thomas's position that all of us, as a matter of psychological necessity, strive to attain that which our *intellects* present to us (however inadequately) as the fullest happiness. We have freedom of will with respect to our choices of means to happiness, St. Thomas said, but not with respect to the pursuit of happiness itself. Here intellect dominates. Scotus maintains that although we indeed have an inclination toward happiness, it is *not* necessary that we always accede to it, as witness our ability to will that which *justice* requires irrespective of considerations of personal advantage. The human will, on Scotus's analysis, is unique among created agencies in that it has an "innate liberty" and is not determined by its nature to act always in a specific way—in the way, for example, that intellect points out as conducive to personal happiness. (Without this liberty, Scotus observes, we could hardly fulfill the Biblical injunction to love our neighbor—to will *another's* advantage—in a disinterested manner.) In line with this, Scotus further maintains that our sense of obligation to live in accordance with moral principles cannot be understood, as St. Thomas was prone to understand it, in terms of an intellectual appreciation that so to live is conducive to our personal happiness. Scotus says that the obligatory force of moral principles, and the sinfulness of violating them, consists in the fact that they confront us with what God *wills* or *commands* us to do, never mind what we happen to think about our personal road to happiness. As regards immortality, St. Thomas argued that our intellectual activity must be attributed to an incorporeal soul that, as a "substance" in its own right, cannot be corrupted through the corruption of the body. Scotus replies that although our intellectual activity may be *likely* to belong to a soul that is a substance in its own right, neither St. Thomas nor anyone else has strictly demonstrated that intellectual activity—be it ever so incorporeal—*cannot* depend upon the body for its existence. In short, St. Thomas's argument may be probable, but it is not conclusive. A definite assurance of immortality comes through faith, not through reason.

William of Ockham carries much further this tendency of Scotus's to narrow the office of reason or intellect in relation to will and to faith.

William of Ockham

William of Ockham was born in the village of Ockham, not far from London, in about 1290. A Franciscan from his youth, like Scotus, Ockham was educated at Oxford and Paris and looked forward to an academic career. All went according to plan until 1324, when he was accused of heresy and summoned to stand trial at Avignon (where the Papacy had been relocated by Philip IV of France). As the trial dragged on, Ockham was drawn into a controversy then raging in Avignon between the Franciscan Minister General, Michael of Cesena, and Pope John XXII. At issue was the rule of strict poverty upheld by the "Spiritual" party of Franciscans—and by Michael and Ockham. The furor created by this controversy overshadowed Ockham's heresy trial (which was never concluded) and reached such a pitch of intensity in 1328 that Ockham, with Michael, fled from Avignon to avoid arrest. At the price of excommunication from the Church, they availed themselves of the protection of Louis of Bavaria, whom the Pope had alienated by denouncing his election as Holy Roman Emperor. The story goes that Ockham said to Louis: "Defend me with your sword, and I will defend you with my pen." For almost twenty years Ockham resided at Louis's court in Munich, where he published tirelessly on the theme of the independence of the State in relation to the Church. After Louis's death in 1347, however, Ockham appears to have sought a reconciliation with the Pope, who then was Clement VI, but whether this was formally accomplished is not known. Ockham died at Munich, probably of the Black Death, around 1349.

In the years preceding his excommunication, Ockham produced a number of works on logic, natural philosophy, and theology. The most important of these, as far as philosophy is concerned, are the *Summa of Logic* and *On the Four Books of the Sentences* (Ockham's commentary on the *Sentences* of Peter Lombard). After his move to Munich, Ockham devoted most of his writing to political subjects. The chief work of this period is the *Dialogue on the Power of the Emperor and the Pope.*

Ockham is most frequently remembered today for something called "Ockham's Razor." This is a principle to the effect that when trying to explain anything, we should always choose the simplest explanation that will fit the facts. Usually the principle is given as "entities are not to be multiplied beyond necessity." This precise wording has yet to be found in Ockham's extant writings, but we do find him saying that "plurality is not to be assumed without necessity." The principle is not original with Ockham.[5] As a matter of fact, none of his predecessors would have looked with favor upon an explanation of something in terms of more factors than are strictly necessary to account for it. The real issue is *what* factors are necessary, and here Ockham is indeed often in disagreement with his predecessors. More than one of their theories seemed to him unwarrantably complex.

The razorlike effects of Ockham's analysis are best observed in his famous treatment of universals. Because Scotus's view of universals is the main object of Ockham's criticism, a little more must now be said about Scotus's view. Scotus had argued that two factors are present in each individual of a given species: (a) the *common nature* that the individual shares with the other member of its species and (b) the *individuating difference* added to the common nature to make it *this* individual's nature. In Socrates, for example, there is (a) the common nature of rational animality that he shares with the rest of the human species and (b) the individuating difference peculiar to Socrates that, as Scotus said, "contracts" rational animality into the unique form of Socrates. Between the common nature and the individuating difference, Scotus said, there is a formal distinction, not a real distinction, for although we can think of the one without thinking of the other, they are not literally separable from one another. Rational animality cannot exist independently of the individuals whose nature it is, although we can form by abstraction from individuals a universal concept of rational animality in which we do not think of any particular individual. Here, however, Scotus saw a problem—a version of the old problem of "the one and the many." The universal concept of rational animality is numerically one: it is one concept in the mind of anyone who thinks of it. But the common nature of rational animality is not numerically one, since it is always "contracted" by individuating differences into a multiplicity of particular individuals. How, then, can the universal concept be applicable to the individuals? How can that which is *one* be truly affirmed of *more* than one, as when

[5] It can be traced at least as far back as Aristotle, who appealed to it on several occasions, notably when he said that it is "sufficient to assume" just *one* Unmoved Mover to account for the motion in the world. Incidentally, Ockham's Razor is also known as the "Principle of Parsimony."

we say "Socrates and Plato are instances of rational animality"? Or to put it the other way around, how can *two* (Socrates and Plato) be instances of *one* (the universal concept of rational animality)? Scotus answered by making use of a notion of Avicenna's. A common nature, Avicenna said, can be considered absolutely by itself, and then it is seen to be neither one thing nor many things, but to be capable of being both. It is capable of being one thing as a universal concept in the mind. It is capable of being many things when multiplied in different individuals. In and of itself, however, the common nature is simply indifferent to oneness and manyness. Now Scotus believed that this indifference to oneness and manyness on the part of the common nature (considered by itself) provides a kind of *bridge* between, on the one hand, the unitary concept of the common nature and, on the other hand, the many individuals into which the common nature is multiplied. Thanks to this bridge, a common nature that is multiplied into many individuals can nevertheless be said to have a kind of unity, "less than numerical" but *not unlike* the numerical unity of a concept. This is what makes it possible for us to apply to the individuals our concept of the common nature; this is how *one* can be truly affirmed of *more* than one.

Ockham rejects the foregoing theory lock, stock, and barrel. There are, he says, no such things as common natures, and consequently there is no need to find for them a mysterious unity that is "less than numerical." Scotus himself would have denied the existence of common natures had anyone convinced him that they would be separable from individuals. The Extreme Realism of early medieval philosophers, which Abelard had attacked, was not for Scotus. He was hardly prepared to believe that an abstraction such as rational animality could have reality on its own account, outside of our minds and independently of individual human beings. Accordingly, Ockham proceeds to argue that rational animality could indeed have independent reality if Scotus were correct in thinking that it is something distinguishable from individuals. Ockham sees nothing whatever in Scotus's notion that two things can be formally distinct without being really distinct (and therefore separable). If rational animality were something capable of being "abstracted" from individuals and conceived separately from them, Ockham says, then it could *exist* separately from them, at least by virtue of the infinite power of God. Whatever is logically possible God can do, and it is logically possible for things we conceive separately to exist separately. Scotus wanted to say that there is no *numerical* distinction in Socrates between (a) the common nature of rational animality that Socrates shares with Plato and (b) the individuating difference peculiar to rational animality in Socrates' case. We think of (a) without thinking of (b), according to Scotus, but in reality (a) and (b) are one and the same. Ockham replies that they cannot possibly be one and the same: "That *a* and *b* are one thing, that *a* is not really distinguished from *b,* and yet that the intellect divides *a* from *b,* by thinking of *a* and not thinking of *b,* or conversely, is impossible." Scotus erred in failing to recognize the relevance here of a fundamental principle. If *a* and *b* are numerically identical, Ockham says, then whatever is true of *a* is also true of *b;* and if something is *not* true of *a* that is true of *b*, or vice versa, then *a* and *b* are numerically *different*. Scotus plainly believed that something is not true of a common nature that is true of an individuating difference: he believed that, for any common nature *C* and any individuating difference *D*, it is not true that *C* is formally distinct from *C*, whereas it is true that *D* is formally distinct from *C*. Therefore, on Scotus's own showing, a common nature and an individuating difference could not be one and the same, and hence they could, at least if God so desired, be actually separated. Because Scotus was not prepared to accept the possibility of such a separation, he would be compelled to abandon his theory of common natures and of universal concepts as mental abstractions of common natures.

Ockham believes that Scotus's basic mistake lay in thinking that the members of any species must *jointly possess* something—a "common nature" in which they share alike and that accounts for their likeness. To take this line is to confront one problem after another in understanding how the common nature can be related to the members of the species, how it can be "individuated" into them, how it can be one while they are many, and so on. All such problems are avoided, Ockham says, if from the beginning we adopt the standpoint that the members of a species are alike not *in* something but simply "by means of themselves." We should start from the position that the basic realities in the world are individual substances with individual characteristics. Next we should understand that things are classifiable into species because individual substances happen to have characteristics that resemble one another. We should view the resemblances between the characteristics of individual substances as a fundamental fact about them, not to be explained by reference to some universal thing (such as a "common nature" having an unheard-of "less than numerical" unity in a plurality of individuals). Our possession of universal concepts is perfectly intelligible without our supposing that something universal exists outside our minds. A universal concept is nothing more than a "kind of mental picture" of individual substances we perceive through our senses. What happens, we may suppose, is that "the intellect, seeing a thing outside the mind, forms in the mind a picture resembling it"—a picture of Socrates, for example. The intellect can remove from the picture of Socrates the features that distinguish Socrates from other individuals subsequently encountered, leaving only the features by which all human beings are alike. The mental picture will then resemble an indefinite number of individuals as they resemble one another, and so it can indifferently stand for or signify any and all of them. "And this can be called a universal, because it is a pattern and relates indifferently to all the singular things outside the mind. Because of the similarity between its being as a thought-object and the being of like things outside the mind, it can stand for such things. And in this way a universal . . . is only a kind of mental picture."

Such is the view of universals that Ockham advances as the simplest that will fit the facts. Or almost the simplest. He was later inclined to think that it is unnecessary to suppose that the intellect needs to form a mental picture in order to produce something in the mind similar to a class of resembling things outside the mind. The intellect's very act of conceiving, Ockham came to think, can be what indifferently resembles— "by some kind of assimilation"—any and all of an indefinite number of resembling things. On this theory, a universal concept is simply an act of the intellect, with reference to particular resembling things, by which we "do not refer more to one thing than to another."

"Nominalism" has long been the name usually given to Ockham's view (or views) of universals. "Conceptualism" would be a better name, however, for he believes that universals are not just names (*nomina*) given to classes of particular things, but concepts (mental pictures or acts of conceiving) that resemble classes of particular things that resemble one another. The similarities between Ockham's views and Abelard's "Moderate Realism" (wherein universals were also taken to be mental images or pictures) might seem to make it appropriate to give this name to Ockham's views as well. But Ockham disagrees with Abelard on a very important point. Abelard believed, like St. Augustine before him and like St. Thomas and Scotus after him, that the reason why the world contains species of things—classes of individuals who resemble one another in essential respects—is that God creates things in accordance with ideas of species that are like patterns or models in His mind. Ockham disagrees with this for several reasons, one of which is that it is simply unnecessary to suppose that God works from models in creating things. In His infinite power, God can create things directly, and there is no call for us to imagine Him doing otherwise. Naturally we have to think that God, in His infinite knowledge, knows from eternity everything He proposes to create, but there is no reason to believe that this knowledge of His depends upon models. Ockham's position, therefore, offers no metaphysical explanation for the existence of species beyond the observation that God simply decided to create them. It just happens to be the fact that God creates individuals who resemble one another in essential respects. No "because" is available in terms of ideas in God's mind. This is the main difference on the subject between Ockham and St. Thomas, for St. Thomas did not believe in common natures as Scotus did and was himself a kind of "Conceptualist" except for believing that species reflect God's ideas. (So that "Moderate Realism," understood as including the doctrine that species reflect God's ideas, is a better name for St. Thomas's position than "Conceptualism," understood as denying this doctrine.)

God's omnipotence or infinite power, to which we have twice noticed Ockham appealing, comes up about as often as the Razor in the course of his arguments. Some of his most distinctive positions result from his refusal to allow any compromise of the principle that God can do whatever is logically possible. For example, Ockham maintains that no natural occurrence can be shown for certain to have a natural cause, since God can produce any occurrence directly, and what we suppose to be the natural cause may have no real connection with the occurrence at all. Any natural occurrence and its supposed natural cause can be conceived separately; what can be conceived separately can exist separately, at least by virtue of God's omnipotence; therefore, God can bring about any natural occurrence separately from, or without employing, its supposed natural cause. The most we are ever in a position to say, with respect to supposed natural causes of kind *A* and natural occurrences of kind *B,* is that *A*'s *can* produce *B*'s. Whether a particular *A* is the actual cause of a particular *B* depends upon there being no miraculous interruption by God of the usual course of nature. This position, reminiscent of Algazali, was carried further by one of Ockham's younger contemporaries, Nicholas of Autrecourt (born around 1300). Nicholas argues that we cannot be certain that the course of events in nature will be in the future as it has been in the past, so that no amount of past experience of *A*'s in relation to *B*'s can definitely assure us that *A*'s will continue to have any relation (such as "can produce") to *B*'s in the future.[6]

A startling application of the principle of God's omnipotence is found in Ockham's discussion of sense-experience. All of our knowledge of the world, Ockham says, is based upon the immediate apprehension—the "intuitive cognition"—of particular objects as present to our senses. Thus do we know whether or not something exists. But the question arises whether God in His omnipotence could produce in one's mind the act of believing that one is immediately apprehending some object when in fact no such object exists. And Ockham answers this question in the affirmative. Since we can conceive separately (a) the act of believing that one is immediately apprehending some object and (b) the object itself, it follows that (a) can exist while (b) does not, at least by virtue of the omnipotence of God. Ockham's critics not unnaturally took him to be implying that God is capable of deceiving us. Such in substance was one of the charges of heresy brought against him. Heretical or not, Ockham's position suffers from the defect that he nowhere explains how we can tell whether God has miraculously produced (a) in the absence of (b). Pierre d'Ailly (1350–1420), a cardinal of the Church, addressed this issue in a general way by arguing that although each of our perceptions could be miraculously produced by God, it is likely that most of them are produced by the natural objects we take ourselves to be perceiving. After all, Pierre d'Ailly said, miracles would have little significance unless they were relatively infrequent. It is *probable,* therefore, if not quite certain, that our sense-experience is largely reliable.

Probability is the most that Ockham can see in arguments for God's existence. The argument that Ockham himself prefers is a variation upon the second of St. Thomas's five arguments—the argument that efficient

---

[6] Algazali, Ockham, and Nicholas anticipate, but have seldom been given proper credit for anticipating, the similar views on causality of Malebranche and Hume. See pp. 348–349.

causality in the world implies an Uncaused Cause. Ockham speaks in terms of the *conserving* of one thing by another in the world as implying a First Conserver. There cannot, he says, be an infinite number of contemporaneous things, each of which is conserved (or maintained in existence) by another. There must be at least one Conserver not conserved by anything other than itself. But the trouble, Ockham believes, is that we cannot strictly prove that there is just *one* First Conserver. There may be another world than ours with its own First Conserver; indeed there may be any number of other worlds and other First Conservers. The simplest hypothesis would be that there is just one First Conserver for all worlds, if there are worlds other than ours, but Ockham does not believe that an hypothesis can be *proved* merely on the basis of its comparative simplicity. Simplicity is a point in favor of an hypothesis with respect to its probability. If we are to have certainty that there is just one God, *the* First Conserver, this must come from faith, Ockham says; it cannot come from reason. God's omnipotence and limitlessness must also be matters of faith, if we are to be certain of them, for we can hardly prove that He is omnipotent and limitless if we cannot prove that He is unique. (Two or more gods could not each possess all power or be in other respects unlimited in respect of one another.) Consistently with his position that certainty about God's omnipotence is a function of faith, Ockham does not believe that appeals to God's omnipotence can figure in philosophical demonstrations of positive conclusions, only in negative arguments showing what cannot be demonstrated.

Immortality of the human soul, like the omnipotence and limitlessness of God, is not something Ockham believes we can demonstrate. He finds that all the more plausible arguments for immortality, including St. Thomas's, contain steps that after all are doubtful. St. Thomas held that the human soul, as a principle of intellectual operation, can only be a self-subsistent incorporeal entity. But this, Ockham says, is doubtful. If we consult our experience of intellectual activity—of understanding and willing—we do not find anything that obviously belongs to a self-subsistent incorporeal entity. On the contrary, our experience would seem to indicate clearly enough that understanding and willing are activities of a "corporeal and corruptible form." Can we prove otherwise, irrespective of our experience, and without making use of any doubtful assumptions? Ockham is sure that we cannot. He maintains that a definite assurance of immortality can be achieved only through faith.

Freedom of will, on the other hand, is in Ockham's opinion a plain fact of experience. Neither the deliverances of reason nor the promptings of appetite are irresistible, Ockham says. We are free to will or not to will whatever our intellects tell us is right or whatever our feelings incline us to find pleasurable. However strong the force of habit, it is never too strong for us to will something contrary to habit. Unless we had such freedom, we would not have the experience we do of moral obligation—the experience of having the duty to live by certain principles because they are right, not because we are necessarily inclined by appetite to live by them, and not because, having concluded that they are right, we find that living by them has an intellectual appeal that our wills cannot withstand. Freedom of will is a prerequisite of our being responsible for our actions, so that praise or blame for them can be in order. "No act is blameworthy," Ockham says, "unless it is in our power," and that our actions are in our power "can be known evidently through experience, that is, through the fact that every man experiences that however much his reason dictates something his will can will it or not will it [and] however intense may be the pleasure in the sensitive appetite, the will can . . . will the opposite."

The principles by which we ought to live, Ockham says, have been ordained by God, and their obligatory force derives from their status as His commandments. Ockham believes that moral principles have in fact no other status than as general specifications of what God wills us to do. "By the very fact that God wills something, it is right for it to be done." God *could* will very different principles from the ones that He does will, for God in His omnipotence can will whatever is logically possible, and very different principles are logically possible. Having rejected the view that God creates things in accordance with models in His mind, Ockham naturally rejects St. Thomas's account of moral principles as specifications of an immutable natural law that stems from God's model for humanity. Nor does Ockham think it makes sense to suppose that God could be obligated to command one principle as opposed to another. An omnipotent Being, in Ockham's view, could not have obligations, for nothing could confront infinite power as having independent authority. What God commands, then, is not right because it conforms to an intrinsically valid standard that God acknowledges and upholds; what God commands is right simply because it is what God freely chooses to command.[7] Such is Ockham's position on moral principles—a "voluntaristic" position, so called because the Divine will ("will," *voluntas* in Latin) is taken to be the ultimate standard of morality. A consequence for Ockham, or so it would seem, is that moral principles cannot be discovered by reason but can only be accepted by faith as divinely revealed. Whether Ockham drew this conclusion is difficult to determine; sometimes he appears to imply that reason can, at least to some extent, make out the principles that God has established.

In any event, the school of thinkers who followed Ockham—who followed Ockham's "new way" (*via moderna*), as they liked to call it—were quite prepared to draw the conclusion that moral principles are undiscoverable by reason. These people were prepared in general to carry to an extreme the distrust of reason implicit in Ockham's emphasis upon the

---

[7] In Plato's *Euthyphro,* Socrates asks Euthyphro whether piety, which the gods love, is pious because the gods love it, or whether the gods love it because it is pious. Ockham's view is in line with the first alternative. Euthyphro subscribed to the second.

omnipotence of God. It is a curious fact that this religious doctrine was employed by philosophical theologians in such a way as to alienate and impoverish the spheres of philosophy and theology. In philosophy it became a fashion to maintain that nothing is really certain except for the immediate data of sensation and introspection and for such propositions as cannot be denied without logical contradiction (so that divine omnipotence cannot falsify them). In theology, correspondingly, there was a strong tendency to maintain that few of the Church's traditional teachings can really be demonstrated, because the denials of few of them are logically contradictory. Gone by the boards, for these Ockhamists, was St. Thomas's conception that "grace perfects nature" by elevating human reason into the service of sacred theology. If no proposition is to be fully trusted unless divine omnipotence could not falsify it, philosophy has little of her own to offer to theology, and little remains of theology as distinguished from simple faith. The effects of Ockhamism during the declining phase of the Middle Ages have often been described, but perhaps the best description is that of David Knowles:

> The truths of "natural" theology, which had formed the chains binding the dictates of reason to the declarations of revelation, melted into thin air. Neither the existence of God, nor the immortality of the soul, nor the essential relation between human action and its moral worth, could be held to be demonstrable by the reason. The essentially supernatural life of the Christian, seen in action in divine faith and love, and derived from a totally new and God-given principle of grace which had inspired and dominated the work of an Anselm, a Bonaventure, or a Thomas, was now relegated, as unknowable and inexpressible, to the purely religious sphere of belief, and in practice ignored. The Ockhamists drew as sharp a line as did Thomism between the realm of reason and the realm of faith, but unlike Aquinas, who here stood fully in the line of traditional Christian theology, they did not regard the life of grace as a prolongation and elevation of the natural powers directed by a new principle. Grace for them, like the immortal soul itself and the new life of the Christian, was lifted out of the purview of the Christian thinker into that of the Christian believer, and the affirmations of faith were of no interest or value to the Christian philosopher. Consequently theology, the ordered, speculative theology of the schools, disappeared. The preacher and the pastor might use the Creeds and the Scriptures; the theologian was left with an unknowable and absolutely free God. Theologians had always distinguished between God's way of acting as revealed in Scripture and the commands of Christ and the general government of the world, and his "absolute" power, but their interests had always lain with God as known to us by reason or revelation, and the "absolute" power was no more than a formal saving clause. The Ockhamists, on the other hand, were not interested in what to them had no intellectual content, and concentrated all their attention on what may be called the "pure mathematics" of God's absolute power.

It remains only to note that a general weariness with the logic-chopping arguments of Scotists and Ockhamists was a main factor in the renewal of interest in classical literature during the Renaissance. An Italian scholar and poet by the name of Francesco Petrarca (1304–1374), who happened to be in Avignon while Ockham was on trial there, became the leading figure among those Renaissance "humanists" who felt that the best hope for religious philosophy lay in a return to Greek and Roman models of good sense and good writing. The prevailing preoccupation with dialectical methods and technical issues seemed to Petrarca laughably juvenile in comparison with the mature practical wisdom and the edifying eloquence of someone like Cicero. With Petrarca's program of recovering a classical perspective such as Cicero's, there began—around 1350—a new epoch in the history of Western philosophy.

Bibliography

Listed are the sources to which reference is made in the Notes following.

Abelard, Peter. *The Letters of Abelard and Heloise* [includes the *Historia calamitatum*]. Translated by Betty Radice. Penguin Classics, 1974.

Algazali. *The Faith and Practice of al-Ghazali* [includes the *Deliverance from Error*]. Translated by W. M. Watt. London: Allen and Unwin, 1951.

Allan, D. J. *The Philosophy of Aristotle*. Rev. ed. London: Oxford University Press, 1963.

Aristophanes. *The Comedies of Aristophanes*. Translated by James Hickie, 2 vols. London: Henry G. Bohn, 1853.

Aristotle. *Aristotle Selections*. Edited by W. D. Ross. New York: Charles Scribner's Sons, 1955.

———. *The Basic Works of Aristotle*. Edited by Richard McKeon. New York: Random House, 1941. Contains translations from *The Works of Aristotle Translated into English,* edited by J. A. Smith and W. D. Ross, 12 vols. Oxford: Clarendon Press, 1908–1952.

———. *Nichomachean Ethics*. Translated by H. Rackham. Rev. ed. Loeb Classical Library, 1934.

Augustine, Saint. *The Works of Aurelius Augustinus*. Edited by Marcus Dods, 15 vols. Edinburgh: T. & T. Clark, 1871–1876.

Anselm, Saint. *Basic Writings*. Translated by S. N. Deane. 2nd ed. La Salle, Ill.: Open Court, 1962.

———. *On Christian Doctrine*. Translated by D. W. Robertson. Library of Liberal Arts, 1958.

———. *The City of God*. Translated by Gerald G. Walsh, Demetrius B. Zema, Grace Monahan, and Daniel J. Honan, 3 vols. New York: Fathers of the Church, 1950–1954; abridged version, edited by Vernon J. Bourke, Garden City, N.Y.: Doubleday Image, 1958.

———. *Confessions*. Translated by R. S. Pine-Coffin. Penguin Classics, 1961.

443

————. *Augustine: Earlier Writings.* Translated by J. H. S. Burleigh. London: SCM Press, 1953.

————. *The Enchiridion on Faith, Hope, and Love.* Translated by J. F. Shaw. Chicago: Regnery, Gateway, 1961.

————. *The Essential Augustine.* Edited by Vernon J. Bourke. 2nd ed. Indianapolis: Hackett, 1974.

————. *On Free Choice of the Will.* Translated by Anna S. Benjamin and L. H. Hackstaff. Library of Liberal Arts, 1964.

————. *Homilies on the Gospel of John.* Translated by H. Browne and J. H. Parker. Oxford: Library of the Fathers of the Holy Catholic Church, 1848.

Averroes. *On the Harmony of Religion and Philosophy* [the *Decisive Treatise*]. Translated by G. F. Hourani. London: Luzac, 1961.

————. *Tahafut Al-Tahafut: The Incoherence of the Incoherence.* Translated by S. Van Den Burgh, 2 vols. London: Luzac, 1969.

Avicenna. *Avicenna's Psychology: Kitab al-Najat, Bk. II, Ch. VI.* Translated by F. Rahman. London: Oxford University Press, 1952.

Bacon, Roger. *Opus Maius.* Translated by R. B. Burke, 2 vols. Philadelphia: University of Pennsylvania Press, 1928.

Barrett, C. K., ed. *The New Testament Background: Selected Documents.* London: SPCK, 1956; New York: Harper Torchbooks, 1961.

Bettenson, Henry, ed. *Documents of the Christian Church.* 2nd ed. London: Oxford University Press, 1963.

Bettenson, Henry, ed. and trans. *The Early Christian Fathers.* London: Oxford University Press, 1956.

Bevan, Edwyn. *Hellenism and Christianity.* 1921. Reprint ed. New York: Arno, 1967.

Bible. *The Holy Bible.* King James Version. Cambridge: Cambridge University Press, n.d.

————. *The New Oxford Annotated Bible.* Revised Standard Version. New York: Oxford University Press, 1973.

————. *The Complete Bible: An American Translation.* Translated by J. M. Powis Smith et al. (O.T.) and Edgar J. Goodspeed (N. T.). Chicago: University of Chicago Press, 1939.

————. *The Gospel According to John I–XII.* Translated by Raymond J. Brown. The Anchor Bible. Garden City, N.Y.: Doubleday, 1966.

————. *The Wisdom of Solomon.* Translated by David Winston. The Anchor Bible. Garden City, N.Y.: Doubleday, 1979.

Boethius. *The Consolation of Philosophy.* Translated by James J. Buchanan. New York: Ungar, 1957.

Bréhier, Émile. *The History of Philosophy: The Hellenistic and Roman Age.* Paris, 1931. Translated by Wade Baskin. Chicago: University of Chicago Press, 1965.

Brewer's Dictionary of Phrase and Fable. Edited by I. H. Evans. New York: Harper & Row, 1970.

Burtt, Edwin Arthur. *The Metaphysical Foundations of Modern Science.* Rev. ed. New York: Humanities Press, 1931; Garden City, N.Y.: Doubleday Anchor, 1955.

Bury, J. B. *A History of Greece.* Rev. ed. Modern Library, n.d.

Butterfield, Herbert. *The Origins of Modern Science*. Rev. ed. New York: Collier, 1962.

Campbell, Robin. Introduction to *Seneca: Letters from a Stoic*. Penguin Classics, 1969.

Carcopino, Jerome. *Daily Life in Ancient Rome*. Translated by E. O. Lorimer. New Haven: Yale University Press, 1940.

Chadwick, Henry. *The Early Church*. Harmondsworth: Penguin, 1967.

Chesterton, G. K. *Saint Thomas Aquinas*. London: Sheed and Ward, 1933; Garden City, N.Y.: Doubleday Image, 1956.

Cicero. *De Finibus*. Translated by H. Rackham. 2nd ed. Loeb Classical Library, 1931.

――――. *De Natura Deorum, Academica*. Translated by H. Rackham. Loeb Classical Library, 1933.

――――. *The Nature of the Gods*. Translated by Horace C. P. McGregor. Penguin Classics, 1972.

――――. *Selected Works*. Translated by Michael Grant. Rev. ed. Penguin Classics, 1971.

Copleston, Frederick. *A History of Philosophy*. 9 vols. Westminster, Md.: Newman Press, 1946–1974; Garden City, N.Y.: Doubleday Image, 1962–1977.

Vol. 1, pts. 1 and 2, *Greece and Rome*.

Vol. 2, *Medieval Philosophy;* pt. 1, *Augustine to Bonaventure;* pt. 2, *Albert the Great to Duns Scotus*.

Vol. 3, *Late Medieval and Renaissance Philosophy;* pt. 1, *Ockham to the Speculative Mystics;* pt. 2, *The Revival of Platonism to Suarez*.

Coulton, G. G. *The Medieval Scene*. Cambridge: Cambridge University Press, 1930.

Cowell, F. R. *Life in Ancient Rome*. New York: Putnam's, Capricorn, 1975.

Creasy, Sir Edward S. *The Fifteen Decisive Battles of the World*. 5th ed, 1854. Everyman's Library, 1960.

De la Mare, Walter. *The Complete Poems of Walter de la Mare*. New York: Knopf, 1970.

Descartes, René. *The Philosophical Works of Descartes*. Translated by Elizabeth S. Haldane and G. R. T. Ross, 2 vols. Corrected ed. Cambridge: Cambridge University Press, 1931.

Dimont, Max I. *Jews, God, and History*. New York: New American Library, 1962.

Diogenes Laertius. *Lives and Opinions of Eminent Philosophers*. Translated by R. H. Hicks, 2 vols. Loeb Classical Library, 1925.

Dodds, E. R., ed. and trans. *Select Passages Illustrating Neoplatonism*. London: SPCK, 1923.

Easton, Stewart C. *Roger Bacon and His Search for a Universal Science*. New York: Columbia University Press, 1952; reprint ed., Westport, Conn.: Greenwood Press, 1970.

Eaton, Ralph M. *General Logic*. New York: Charles Scribner's Sons, 1931.

Encyclopedia Britannica. 11th ed. New York, 1911.

Encyclopedia of Philosophy. Edited by Paul Edwards. New York: Macmillan and Free Fress, 1967.

Enslin, Morton Scott. *Christian Beginnings,* Pts. 1 and 2. New York: Harper & Row, 1938; Harper Torchbooks, 1956.

Epictetus. *The Discourses and Manual.* Translated by P. E. Matheson. Oxford: Clarendon Press, 1917.

Epicurus. *Epicurus: The Extant Remains.* Translated by Cyril Bailey. Oxford: Clarendon Press, 1926.

Frankfort, H. and H. A., John A. Wilson, and Thorkild Jacobsen. *The Intellectual Adventure of Ancient Man.* Chicago: University of Chicago Press, 1946; reprint ed., *Before Philosophy,* Harmondsworth: Penguin, 1949.

Frazer, Sir James George. *The New Golden Bough.* Edited by Theodor Gaster. New York: S. G. Phillips, 1959.

Freeman, Kathleen. *An Ancilla to the Pre-Socratic Philosophers.* Cambridge, Mass.: Harvard University Press, 1947.

Gibbon, Edward. *The Decline and Fall of the Roman Empire.* Edited by Oliphant Smeaton, 3 vols. Modern Library, n.d.

Gilson, Etienne. *History of Christian Philosophy in the Middle Ages.* New York: Random House, 1955.

————. *Reason and Revelation in the Middle Ages.* New York: Charles Scribner's Sons, 1938.

Guthrie, W. K. C. *A History of Greek Philosophy.* 5 vols. Cambridge: Cambridge University Press, 1962–1978.

Vol. 1, *The Earlier Presocratics and the Pythagoreans.*

Vol. 2, *The Presocratic Tradition from Parmenides to Democritus.*

Vol. 3, *The Fifth-Century Enlightenment.*

Vol. 4, *Plato: The Man and His Dialogues: Earlier Period.*

Vol. 5, *The Later Plato and the Academy.*

Hadas, Moses. *Hellenistic Culture: Fusion and Diffusion.* New York: Columbia University Press, 1959; Norton, 1972.

Hamilton, Edith. *The Greek Way.* New York: Norton, 1942.

Hawkins, D. J. B. *A Sketch of Medieval Philosophy.* London: Sheed and Ward, 1947; reprint ed., Westport, Conn.: Greenwood Press, 1968.

Herodotus. *The Histories.* Translated by Aubrey de Sélincourt. Penguin Classics, 1954.

Hesiod. *Theogony, Works and Days.* Translated by Dorothea Wender. In *Hesiod and Theognis,* Penguin Classics, 1973.

Homer. *Iliad.* Translated by Robert Fitzgerald. Garden City, N.Y.: Doubleday Anchor, 1974.

————. *Iliad.* Translated by E. V. Rieu. Penguin Classics, 1950.

Hopkins, Gerard Manley. *Poems.* 3rd ed. Oxford: Oxford University Press, 1948.

Hügel, Baron Friedrich von. *Essays and Addresses on the Philosophy of Religion.* New York: Dutton, 1921; reprint ed., Westport, Conn.; Greenwood Press, 1974.

Hume, Robert E. *The World's Living Religions.* Rev. ed. New York: Charles Scribner's Sons, 1959.

Husik, Isaac. *A History of Medieval Jewish Philosophy.* Philadelphia: Jewish Publication Society of America, 1916; reprint ed., New York: Atheneum, Temple Books, 1969.

Hyman, Arthur, and James J. Walsh, eds. *Philosophy in the Middle Ages: The Christian, Islamic, and Jewish Traditions.* Indianapolis: Hackett, 1973.

Jones, W. T. *A History of Western Philosophy: The Medieval Mind.* 2nd ed. New York: Harcourt, Brace, 1969.

Josephus. *The Jewish War.* Translated by G. A. Williamson. Rev. ed. Penguin Classics, 1970.

Kierkegaard, Søren. *Fear and Trembling* and *The Sickness Unto Death.* Translated by Walter Lowrie. Princeton: Princeton University Press, 1941; Garden City, N.Y.: Doubleday Anchor, 1954.

Kirk, G. S. *The Nature of Greek Myths.* New York: Penguin, 1974.

———, and J. E. Raven. *The Presocratic Philosophers: A Critical History with a Selection of Texts.* Corrected ed. Cambridge: Cambridge University Press, 1963.

Knowles, David. *The Evolution of Medieval Thought.* Baltimore: Helicon Press, 1962; New York: Random House, Vintage, n.d.

LaMonte, John L. *The World of the Middle Ages.* New York: Appleton-Century-Crofts, 1949.

Latourette, Kenneth Scott. *A History of Christianity.* Rev. ed., 2 vols. New York: Harper & Row, 1975.

Leo XIII, Pope. *Aeterni Patris.* 1879. In *The "Summa Theologica" of St. Thomas Aquinas,* 1911. Reprint ed., New York: Benziger, 1947.

Lovejoy, Arthur O. *The Great Chain of Being: A Study of the History of an Idea.* Cambridge, Mass.: Harvard University Press, 1936; New York: Harper Torchbooks, 1960.

Lucretius. *The Nature of the Universe.* Translated by R. E. Latham. Penguin Classics, 1951.

McKeon, Richard, ed. *Selections from the Medieval Philosophers.* 2 vols. New York: Charles Scribner's Sons, 1929–1930.

Maimonides, Moses. *The Guide for the Perplexed.* Translated by M. Friedländer. 2nd ed. rev. London: Routledge, 1904; reprint ed., New York: Dover, 1956.

Malcolm, Norman. "Anselm's Ontological Arguments," *Philosophical Review* 69 (1960). In *The Ontological Argument: From St. Anselm to Contemporary Philosophers,* ed. Alvin Plantinga, Garden City, N.Y.: Doubleday Anchor, 1965.

Marcus Aurelius. *The Meditations.* Translated by George Long. London: G. Routledge & Sons, 1862.

Mommsen, Theodor. *The History of Rome.* Translated by W. P. Dickson, 4 vols. Everyman's Library, 1911.

Morison, Samuel Eliot. *Christopher Columbus, Mariner.* New York: Mentor, 1955.

Morrow, Glenn R. "Plato and the Rule of Law," *Philosophical Review* 59 (1941). In *Plato: A Collection of Critical Essays II,* ed. Gregory Vlastos, Garden City, N.Y.: Doubleday Anchor, 1971.

Murray, Gilbert. *Five Stages of Greek Religion.* 3rd ed. Boston: Beacon, 1951; Garden City, N.Y.: Doubleday Anchor, 1955.

Nettleship, Richard Lewis. *Lectures on the "Republic" of Plato.* 2nd ed., 1897. Reprint ed., New York: St. Martin's, 1964.

448 *Bibliography*

New Columbia Encyclopedia. New York: Columbia University Press, 1975.

Noss, John B. *Man's Religions.* 4th ed. New York: Macmillan, 1969.

Oates, Whitney J., ed. *The Stoic and Epicurean Philosophers.* Modern Library, 1940.

Philo. *Philo.* Translated by F. H. Colson and G. H. Whitaker, 10 vols. (2 supp. vols. translated by Ralph Marcus.) Loeb Classical Library, 1929–1962. (*On the Account of the World's Creation Given by Moses,* in Vol. 1; *On the Posterity of Cain,* in Vol. 2; *Who Is the Heir of Divine Things?,* in Vol. 4; *On Flaccus,* in Vol. 9.)

Plato. *The Collected Dialogues of Plato, Including the Letters.* Edited by Edith Hamilton and Huntington Cairns. Bollingen Series no. 71. Corrected ed. New York: Pantheon, 1963.

———. *The Dialogues of Plato.* Translated by Benjamin Jowett. 3rd ed. Oxford: Clarendon Press, 1892.

———. *The Last Days of Socrates* [*Euthyphro, Apology, Crito, Phaedo*]. Translated by Hugh Trendennick. Penguin Classics, 1954.

———. *Laws.* Translated by A. E. Taylor. Everyman's Library, 1934.

———. *Letter VII.* Translated by L. A. Post. In *Thirteen Epistles of Plato.* Oxford University Press, 1925.

———. *Phaedo.* Translated by R. Hackforth. Cambridge: Cambridge University Press, 1955.

———. *Phaedrus.* Translated by R. Hackforth. Cambridge: Cambridge University Press, 1952.

———. *Plato's Examination of Pleasure (the "Philebus").* Translated by R. Hackforth. Cambridge: Cambridge University Press, 1945.

———. *Protagoras and Meno.* Translated by W. K. C. Guthrie. Penguin Classics, 1956.

———. *Republic.* Translated by Francis MacDonald Cornford. Oxford: Clarendon Press, 1941.

———. *Statesman.* Translated by J. B. Skemp. New Haven: Yale University Press, 1952.

———. *Symposium.* Translated by W. Hamilton. Penguin Classics, 1973.

———. *Plato's Cosmology (the "Timaeus").* Translated by Francis MacDonald Cornford. New York: Humanities Press, 1937.

Plotinus. *The Enneads.* Translated by Stephen MacKenna. 2nd ed., rev. by B. S. Page. London: Faber and Faber, 1956.

———. *Plotinus.* Vol. 1. Translated by A. H. Armstrong. Loeb Classical Library, 1966.

Plutarch. *Lives of the Grecians and Romans.* In *The Rise and Fall of Athens* (1960) and *Makers of Rome* (1965), translated by Ian Scott-Kilvert; and *Fall of the Roman Republic* (rev. ed., 1972), translated by Rex Warner. Penguin Classics.

Quasten, J., et al., eds. *Ancient Christian Writers.* Westminster, Md.: Newman Press, 1946–1961.

Roberts, Alexander, and James Donaldson, eds. *Ante-Nicene Fathers.* Buffalo, 1885–1896; reprint ed., Grand Rapids, Mich.: Eerdmans, 1956.

Ross, W. D. *Aristotle: A Complete Exposition of His Works and Thought.* 5th ed. New York: Barnes & Noble, 1953; Meridian, 1959.

Rossiter, Stuart. *Rome and Environs.* Edited by Atla Macadam. 2nd ed. The Blue Guides. London: Ernest Benn, 1975.

Rostovtzeff, Michael I. *Rome.* Translated by J. D. Duff. Corrected ed. Oxford: Oxford University Press, 1928; reprint ed., ed. Elias J. Bickerman, New York: Oxford Galaxy, 1960.

Saadia. *Book of Doctrines and Beliefs.* Translated by Alexander Altmann. London: East and West Library, 1946.

Sandmel, Samuel. *Philo of Alexandria.* New York: Oxford University Press, 1979.

Saunders, Jason L., ed. *Greek and Roman Philosophy After Aristotle.* New York: Free Press, 1966.

Schaff, Philip, ed. *A Select Library of the Nicene and Post-Nicene Fathers.* New York: The Christian Literature Co., 1887–1892.

Schopenhauer, Arthur. *The World as Will and Idea.* Translated by R. B. Haldane and J. Kemp, 3 vols. London: Routledge, 1883.

Sextus Empiricus. *Outlines of Pyrrhonism.* Translated by R. G. Bury, 3 vols. Loeb Classical Library, 1933.

Shapiro, Herman, ed. *Medieval Philosophy: Selected Readings from Augustine to Buridan.* Modern Library, 1964.

Sidgwick, Henry. *Outlines of the History of Ethics.* 6th ed. London: Macmillan, 1931; Boston: Beacon, 1960.

Standard Dictionary of Folklore, Mythology, and Legend. 2 vols. New York: Funk & Wagnalls, 1949.

Suetonius. *The Twelve Caesars.* Translated by Robert Graves. Penguin Classics, 1957.

Taylor, A. E. *Plato: The Man and His Work.* 7th ed. London: Methuen, 1960.

Thomas Aquinas, Saint. *Basic Writings.* Translated by Laurence Shapcote. Edited by Anton C. Pegis, 2 vols. New York: Random House, 1945.

———. *Philosophical Texts.* Translated by Thomas Gilby. London: Oxford University Press, 1951; reprint ed., Durham, N.C.: Labyrinth Press, 1982.

———. *The Pocket Aquinas.* Edited by Vernon J. Bourke. New York: Washington Square Press, Pocket Books, 1960.

———. *Selected Political Writings.* Translated by J. G. Dawson. Edited by A. P. D'Entrèves. Totowa, N.J.: Barnes & Noble, 1981.

———. *On the Truth of the Catholic Faith [Summa contra Gentiles].* Bk. 1, *God.* Translated by Anton C. Pegis. New York: Doubleday Image, 1955.

———. *Summa Theologiae.* Vol. 1, *The Existence of God.* Pt. 1, Questions 1–13. Edited by Thomas Gilby. Cambridge: Blackfriars, 1964, 1969. New York: Doubleday Image, 1969.

Thucydides. *The Peloponnesian War.* Translated by Benjamin Jowett, 2 vols. 2nd ed. rev. Oxford: Clarendon Press, 1900.

———. *The Peloponnesian War.* Translated by Rex Warner. Penguin Classics, 1954.

Tolstoy, L. N. *Anna Karenin.* Translated by Rosemary Edmonds. Penguin Classics, 1954.

Weinberg, Julius R. *A Short History of Medieval Philosophy.* Princeton: Princeton University Press, 1964.

Wheelwright, Philip, ed. and trans. *The Presocratics.* New York: Odyssey, 1966.

William of Ockham. *Philosophical Writings.* Translated by Philotheus Boehner. Edinburgh: Nelson, 1957.

Wilson, Edmund. *Israel and the Dead Sea Scrolls.* New York: Farrar, Straus, and Giroux, 1978.

Windelband, Wilhelm. *A History of Philosophy.* Translated by James H. Tufts. 2nd ed. New York: Macmillan, 1901; reprint ed., 2 vols., New York: Harper Torchbooks, 1958.

Wippel, John F., and Allen B. Wolter, eds. *Medieval Philosophy: From St. Augustine to Nicholas of Cusa.* New York: Free Press, 1969.

Xenophon. *Recollections of Socrates [Memorabilia]* and Socrates' Defense Before the Jury. Translated by Anna S. Benjamin. Library of Liberal Arts, 1965.

Zeller, Eduard. *Outlines of the History of Greek Philosophy.* Translated by L. R. Palmer. 13th ed. Revised by William Nestle. New York: Humanities Press, 1931; Meridian, 1955.

Notes

Part I: The Pre-Socratic Philosophers _____

Chapter 1: The Ionians

Egyptian and Mesopotamian theogonies: see Frankfort et al., 51–70, 182–199. Hesiod, *Theogony,* trans. Wender, 26. World in Homer: see Kirk and Raven, 10–11. Okeanos in Homer: *Iliad,* bk. 14; cf. Kirk and Raven, 15–19. Some have conjectured: Kirk and Raven, 12–15.

The Milesians:
Thales. Probable indebtedness to theogonies: see Kirk, *Nature of Greek Myths,* 295. Full of gods: KR 93 ("KR" = Kirk and Raven; "93" = the boldface number given to this item in KR). Will of Zeus: *Iliad,* 1, trans. Rieu, 23. Decree of fate: *Iliad,* 15, trans. Rieu, 276–277. As under a great storm: *Iliad,* 16, trans. Fitzgerald, 389. The deathless gods: Hesiod, *Works and Days,* trans. Wender, 66.

Anaximander. The surviving sentence-fragment: KR 112. Separated off: KR 123. Like bark: KR 123. Kirk's appraisal: KR, p. 100.

Anaximenes. Rather poetical: KR 103. Felting: KR 144. Relaxed: KR 146. The surviving sentence: KR 163. Sneezes and yawns: Frazer, 151. Gaster, in Frazer, 214. Genesis 49:33–50:1 (King James Version).

Xenophanes. Gift of value, etc.: trans. Wheelwright, 35 (item no. 22). One god: KR 173. Isaiah 45:18 (King James Version).

Heraclitus. All things are beautiful: KR 209. War is the father: KR 215. Right is strife: KR 214. Everliving fire: KR 220. An exchange for fire: KR 222. Always was: KR 220. All things are steered: KR 230. Death to become water: KR 232. Dry is wisest: KR 233. Immortal mortals: KR 242. Gives a sign: KR 247. All laws nourished by one: KR 253. Searched out myself: KR 249.

Chapter 2: The Italians

Pythagoras. Eleusinian communion: Frazer, 358. Antiquity of Pythagorean theorem: Guthrie, 1:217. Aristotle, *Metaphysics*, 986a1 (Ross). Guard-House of Zeus: KR 329. Copernicus, Kepler: see Burtt, 49–63.

Parmenides. Quite grey-headed: Plato, *Parmenides*, 127b, trans. Guthrie, 2:1. Unshaken heart: KR 342. Noein: see Guthrie 2:15–20. It is the same thing: Frag. 2, trans. Guthrie, 2:14. Things that are not are: KR 346. Footnote on Way of Seeming: *Encyclopedia of Philosophy*, s.v. "Parmenides of Elea," by D. J. Furley. It is not lawful: KR 350. Bounded on every side: KR 351. That which can be spoken: KR 345.

Zeno. Then nearly forty: Plato, *Parmenides*, 127b (Jowett). Arrogance: Guthrie, 2:80.

Melissus. The story goes: Plutarch, *Pericles*, trans. Scott-Kilvert, in *Rise and Fall of Athens*, 191. Melissus, son of Ithagenes: ibid., 192. Body, thickness, bulk: KR 391. Of the same kind that the One is: KR 392.

Chapter 3: The Pluralists

Empedocles. Hail friends: Wheelwright, 102. A double tale: KR 423. Whole-natured forms: KR 442. Man-faced oxen: KR 446. Ceaseless flux, effluences: KR 456. With earth see earth: KR 454. Holy, unspeakable mind: KR 467. Fugitive and wanderer: KR 471. Already have I once: KR 476. Prophets, bards; sharing with the other immortals: KR 477. On problem of immortality, see Raven, KR, pp. 358–359.

Anaxagoras. Walter de la Mare, "Miss T.," *Complete Poems*, 146. How could hair: KR 511. All things have a portion: KR 508. Of the small no smallest: Frag. 3, trans. Guthrie, 2:289. Each thing both large and small: KR 499. Not even color: KR 496. Separating off: KR 503. Finest of all things: KR 503. All alike: KR 503. Here, where the earth now is: KR 516. Red-hot stones: KR 529. Controls all things: KR 503. A portion of everything except Mind: KR 509, emphasis added. Aristotle, *Metaphysics*, 984b15 (Ross). Plato, *Phaedo*, 97c, 98b–c. (Jowett). Aristotle, *Meta.*, 985a15 (Ross).

Leucippus and Democritus. Most traveled man: Wheelwright, 34. Naked philosophers: KR 551. No one knew me: Wheelwright, 33. Good morning: Diogenes Laertius, in Wheelwright, T 28. Nothing occurs at random: KR 568. The void exists: KR 554. Those that are fine go out: KR 562. Footnote on weight: see KR 574 and discussion on pp. 415–416. Some are angular: KR 581. The many does not come: KR 578. Certain images: KR 588. By convention: KR 589. Constant delay: *Gnomae*, 81 (Freeman). Good and true: Wheelwright, 27. Magnanimity: Wheelwright, 23. Long time dying: *Fragments on Ethics*, 160 (Freeman). Poverty under democracy: *Frags.*, 251 (Freeman). Wrongdoer more unfortunate, Cause of error: *Gnomae*, 45 (Freeman). Boyle, Bacon, Gassendi: see Butterfield, 142–150, and Burtt, 168–169.

Part II: The Great Days of Athens

Isaiah 44:24, 28 (King James Version). Herodotus, *Histories*, 5, trans. Sélincourt, 353. Creasy, *Fifteen Decisive Battles*, 20. Thucydides, *Peloponnesian War*, 2, 37–41 (Jowett).

Chapter 4: The Sophists

Protagoras. Political virtue: Plato, *Protagoras*, 324a. (All translations from Plato in this chapter are Jowett's.) Will learn that which he comes to learn, Their money's worth: *Protag.*, 318e–319a, 328b. Thinking of nothing: Plato, *Theaetetus*, 167a–b. Man is the measure: *Theaet.*, 152a. Whatever appears to a state: *Theaet.*, 167c. Stronger/weaker: Aristotle, *Rhetoric*, 1402a20. Better, not truer: *Theaet.*, 167b. Lawgivers in the olden time: *Protag.*, 326d. A teacher of this sort: *Protag.*, 328b.

Gorgias. Large sum of Athenian money: Plato, *Hippias Major*, 282b. I may add: Plato, *Gorgias*, 448a. Amused by promises to teach virtue: Plato, *Meno*, 95c. To speak and persuade: *Gorgias*, 452e. In contending with adversaries: Wheelwright, 2. When persuasion joins with speech, Mental agility is what determines, Not because of the truth: Wheelwright, 9. To conquer in speaking, Escape clean from, How pleasant it is: Aristophanes, *Clouds*, trans. Hickie, 1:121, 136–137, 174.

Callicles. Justice consists: *Gorgias*, 483d. Would trample underfoot: *Gorgias*, 484a–b. Luxury, intemperance, licence: *Gorgias*, 492c. Think it over: Thucydides, *Peloponnesian War*, 5, 3, trans. Warner, 365.

Chapter 5: Socrates

Life and Character. Cicero, *Tusculan Disputations*, 5, 4, 10, trans. Guthrie, 3:418–419. Pupil of Archelaus: Cicero, *Tusc.*, 5, 4, 10. Distrust, etc., of science: Xenophon, *Memorabilia*, 1, 1, 12. Oracle of Delphi: Plato, *Apology*, 21a. (All translations from Plato in this chapter are Jowett's.) Like a father: *Apol.*, 31b. Less for money, more for wisdom: *Apol.*, 29e. Interrogate and examine: *Apol.*, 29e–30a. Plutarch, *Aristides*, 1. Equivalent of slavery: Xenophon, *Mem.*, 1, 2, 6–7; 1, 2, 5 (Benjamin). Like a pelican: Plato, *Symposium*, 221b. Ready to bite him: Plato, *Theaetetus*, 151c. Dire are the pangs: *Theaet.*, 151a–b.

Socrates' Method. Virtues numberless: Plato, *Meno*, 71e–72a. Did I not ask you: *Meno*, 79b–c. Aristotle, *Metaphysics*, 987b1 (Socrates' seeking the universal); 1078b25 (Socrates' use of induction), trans. Ross. Alcibiades at wit's end: *Sym.*, 216a–c.

Socrates' Views. Everyone wants the good: Xenophon, *Mem.*, 3, 9, 4; Plato, *Gorgias*, 468b, 499e; *Alcibiades I*, 124d. I know my transgressions: Psalm 51:3 (Revised Standard Version). Excerpt from Plato's *Euthydemus*: 278e–282a (see also *Meno*, 87e–89a). Protagoras on courage: Plato, *Protagoras*, 329e. Unity of virtue: *Protag.*, 349b; Xenophon, *Mem.*, 3, 9, 4–5 (Benjamin). Footnote: avoid cobblers, etc.: *Mem.*, 1, 2, 37 (Benjamin). Unexamined life: *Apol.*, 38a. Excerpt from *Alcibiades I*: 128a–134e (considerably condensed). Far more miserable a companion: *Gorgias*, 479b. I do nothing but: *Apol.*, 30a. Divine Intelligence: Xenophon, *Mem.*, 4, 3, 13; 1, 4, 18; 1, 4, 17 (Benjamin). Either in life or: *Apol.*, 41d. A change and migration: *Apol.*, 40c. Knows nothing on subject: *Apol.*, 29b. Excerpt from *Apol.*: 40c–42a. Ruling an art: *Protag.*, 319b; Xenophon, *Mem.*, 1, 2, 9. Those who know how to rule: *Mem.*, 3, 8, 10 (phrasing slightly altered). The laws speak: Plato, *Crito*, 50a–b. No retaliation: *Crito*, 49c–d. Unrighteousness runs faster: *Apol.*, 39a.

The Minor Socratics. I possess Lais: Frag. 57a–g, trans. Guthrie, 3:495. The good is one, Things opposed to the good: Diogenes Laertius, 2, 106, trans. Guthrie, 3:500.

Chapter 6: Plato

Knowledge and Its Objects. Aristotle on Plato and Cratylus: *Metaphysics*, 987a30. Protagoras refutes himself: *Theaetetus*, 171a–c. (All translations from Plato in this chapter, unless otherwise attributed, are Jowett's.) No more knowledge than what is not: *Theaet.*, 182e. Excerpts from *Theaet.*: 184b–186a (putting "salty" for "saline"; emphasis added), 186a–187a. Must know something that is: *Republic*, 476e. Ambiguousness of sensible objects: *Rep.*, 497b. Cooking-pot: *Hippias Major*, 288d. In some point of view ugly: *Rep.*, 479b. Returning what we have borrowed: *Rep.*, 331c. Relativity of actions and laws: *Rep.*, 479e. Tossing about: *Rep.*, 479d. Darker than knowledge: *Rep.*, 478c. Example of equality: *Phaedo*, 94d–e. Excerpt on true philosophers: *Rep.*, 475–476d (putting "shape" for "form" at 476b and "form" for "idea" at 476d). Nettleship, 345. The animals which we see: *Rep.*, 510a. The eye of the mind: *Rep.*, 510e. Intelligence described: *Rep.*, 511b–c (putting "forms" for "ideas"). Task tremendous: *Rep.*, 511c. The good beyond being: *Rep.*, 509b (Cornford). Eye of soul lifted up: *Rep.*, 540a (Cornford). No way to put it in words: *Letter 7*, 341c–d (Post). Striving to be like: *Phaedo*, 75a–b (Hackforth). Myth of the Cave: *Rep.*, 514a–518c (putting "intelligible" for "intellectual" and "form" for "idea" at 517b). One thing ready to fight for: *Meno*, 86b–c (Guthrie).

Ethics. I tried to persuade: *Apology*, 36c (Trendennick). Inborn disposition: *Rep.*, 485a (Cornford). Inward measure and grace: *Rep.*, 486d (Cornford).

Pleasures of the body: *Rep.*, 485e (Cornford). Lost in the mazes: *Rep.*, 484b (Cornford). Neither hath the eye: Isaiah 64:4 (King James Version). Heredity in the *Laws:* 775d–e. Multitude never philosophical: *Rep.*, 494a (Cornford). The worthy remnant: *Rep.*, 496a–b (Cornford). Miraculous interposition: *Rep.*, 492e (Cornford). Excerpt from *Sophist:* 227e–229a. Self-initiating motion: *Laws*, 896a. Like a stream: *Rep.*, 485d. A many-headed beast: *Rep.*, 589b (Cornford). Myth of the Charioteer: *Phaedrus*, 246a–b, 253d–254e. The just man: *Rep.*, 443d–e. A ridiculous question: *Rep.*, 445a–b. Truest pleasures of which they are capable: *Rep.*, 596d (Cornford). Excerpt from *Philebus:* 21a–22b (putting "desirable" for "eligible" at 21d, 21e, 22b). By far the truest: *Phi.*, 58a. Good and innocent: *Phi.*, 63a. Measure and proportion: *Phi.*, 64e. Consort with health and temperance: *Phi.*, 63e–64a ((Hackforth). Instead of a mess: *Phi.*, 64e (Taylor, 433). King of heaven and earth: *Phi.*, 30c, 28c. The eternal nature found: *Phi.*, 66a. A touch of immortality: *Symposium*, 206c (Hamilton). A woman wise: *Sym.*, 201d. Diotima's speech: *Sym.*, 210a–212a (putting "goal" for "cause" at 211a). Home at last: Edith Hamilton, *Greek Way*, 224.

Politics. Nettleship on reciprocity: 71; see *Rep.*, 396b–370c. Household gear: *Rep.*, 373b (Cornford). Efficient soldiers: *Rep.*, 374c (Cornford). What naturally fitted for: *Rep.*, 536e (Cornford). From military defense to political leadership: *Rep.*, 414a–b. They will depart to the Islands: *Rep.*, 540a–b. Until philosophers are kings: *Rep.*, 473c–d. Heads of a hydra: *Rep.*, 426e. Better than their forebears: *Rep.*, 424a–b (Cornford). Excerpts from *Statesman:* 294a–c, 295b–296a, 297a–b, 301d–e (this trans. by Skemp), 297d–e, 300b–e, 301a (putting "philosophical" for "one scientific" at 301a), 302b, e, 303a–b. Both forms in a measure: *Laws*, 693d–e. On highway to ruin: *Laws*, 715d. Apt to imagine: *Laws*, 768b. Morrow, in Vlastos, 156. If a man were born: *Laws*, 875c–d.

Soul and Cosmos:

Human Immortality. Best and most irrefutable: *Phaedo*, 85c (Hackforth). Excerpts from *Phaedo:* 93a–94b, 94b–95a. *Phaedrus:* 245c–246a. *Laws:* 894c–895b. Would collapse into immobility: *Phaedrus*, 245d–e (Hackforth). When she has regained: *Rep.*, 611c (Cornford). In the meadow: *Gorgias*, 524a. Because they have the power: *Gor.*, 525d. A spectacle and a warning: *Gor.*, 525c. A hard thing: *Gor.*, 526a. Most likely a philosopher: *Gor.*, 526c.

The Divine Craftsman. Psalm 19:1 (King James Version). Marvelous intelligence: *Philebus*, 28d. Past finding out: *Timaeus*, 28c. Everything that becomes: *Tim.*, 28a. He was good: *Tim.*, 29e–30c. Diluted to the second and third degree: *Tim.*, 41d. Gods, children of gods: *Tim.*, 41a–d. Secondary causes: *Tim.*, 46d. Chance effects: *Tim.*, 46e. Prime cause: *Tim.*, 46d. God invented and gave: *Tim.*, 47b–c. Necessity, errant cause: *Tim.*, 47e, 48a. Creation is mixed: *Tim.*, 48a. Persuaded necessity: *Tim.*, 48a. Form and number: *Tim.*, 53b. Things not fair and good: *Tim.*, 53b–c. Contrary to nature: *Tim.*, 82a. Few are the goods: *Republic*, 379d. A moving image of eternity: *Tim.*, 37c–38b. Existed before the heaven: *Tim.*, 92c (Cornford). I John 2:15 (King James Version). Here at last: *Tim.*, 92c (Cornford).

Chapter 7: Aristotle

The mind of the school: Ross, 10. Sin twice: Ross, 14. Brilliant dryness: Schopenhauer, 2:21. Every realm is marvelous, etc.: *On the Parts of Animals,* 645a15–20. (All translations from Aristotle, unless otherwise attributed, are by the various hands who contributed to the Clarendon Press volumes edited by Smith and Ross.)

Logic and Method. In the doer: *Metaphysics,* 1025b20. Training in logic: *Meta.,* 1005b1. Inquires into demonstration: *Meta.,* 1059b15. Excerpt from *Categories:* 1b25–2a1 (emphasis added). Predicables: *Topics,* 101b10–102b25. Reasoning, kinds of argument: *Topics,* 100a25–101a1. Identity of middle term: *Prior Analytics,* 25b35 ff. The middle is the cause: *Posterior Analytics,* 90a5 ff. Quick wit: *Post. An.,* 89b10 ff. Opinion is unstable; scientific knowledge is not: *Post. An.,* 89a5, 88b30. Excerpt on induction: *Post. An.,* 99b35–100b5. Objects nearer to sense: *Post. An.,* 72a1. Symbolic logic carries forward: Eaton, 2.

Metaphysics. Wise man knows all: *Meta.,* 982a5. The good in each class: *Meta.,* 982b5 (Ross in *Selections*). For it is owing to their wonder: *Meta.,* 982b10–983a1. Investigates being as being: *Meta.,* 1003a20. On which the others depend: *Meta.,* 1003b15. Affections or processes or: *Meta.,* 1003b5–10. Of substances the philosopher must grasp: *Meta.,* 1003b15. Class with certain qualification: *Categories,* 3b15. From among things other than substances: *Cat.,* 4a10–20. Ultimate substratum: *Meta.,* 1029a20. Footnote on primary substratum: *Physics,* 192a25. Compound of form and matter: *Meta.,* 1029a25–30. Empty words, poetical metaphors: *Meta.,* 991a20. Plato on one/many problem: *Parmenides,* 130e–131e. Illustrations of potentiality/actuality: *Meta.,* 1048a30–1048b1. Actuality prior to potency: *Meta.,* 1049b5. Footnote on spontaneous generation: *History of Animals,* 539a20. Everything that is produced: *Meta.,* 1049b25. Just because it may come to its form: *Meta.,* 1050a15. Everything that comes to be: *Meta.,* 1050a5. Innate impulse to change: *Physics,* 192b15. The essential nature in each case: *Phy.,* 198b5. That which is best: *Phy.,* 194a30. Excerpt on purpose in nature: *Phy.,* 198b15–199a30. Causes often coincide: *Phy.,* 198a25. Could not be a before and after: *Meta.,* 1071b5–10. Sufficient to assume just one: *Phy.,* 295a10. Its essence is actuality, without matter: *Meta.,* 1071b20. Moves without being moved: *Meta.,* 1071a25. As being loved: *Meta.,* 1072b1. Of itself that it thinks: *Meta.,* 1074b30.

Human Nature and Its Good:
 Soul. Nutritive, sensitive, rational: *On the Soul,* 412a1–415a10. Excerpt on continuity between higher and lower: *History of Animals,* 588a1–588b10. We can dismiss as unnecessary: *Soul,* 412b5. It indubitably follows, or at any rate: *Soul,* 413a1. Active and passive intellect: *Soul,* 430a10–25. Something divine, from outside: *On the Generation of Animals,* 736b25. St. Thomas, *Summa Theologica,* I, 118, 2.
 Ethics. Those who deny: *Nichomachean Ethics,* 1172b35–1173a1. (All

translations from the *Nichomachean Ethics,* unless otherwise attributed, are Rackham's.) Function of human nature: 1097b30. What is noble and divine: 1177a15. The good of man: 1098a15. Ultimate end, every art and investigation: 1094a20. Fixed and permanent disposition: 1105a30. Learn an art or craft, no one can have the remotest chance: 1103a30–1103b1, 1105b10. Not of small moment whether: 1103b20–25. An outline only, nothing fixed: 1104a1. Mark of educated mind: 1094b20–25. Relative to us: 1106b35. Quality of hitting the mean: 1106b15. Footnote: Tolstoy, *Anna Karenin,* 13 (Edmonds). Excerpt on moral virtue: 1106b15–1107a5. Courage: 1107a30–1107b1. Diagram regarding courage adapted from Allan, 172. Directly imply evil: 1107a5–10. Adultery with right woman: 1107a10–15. The least of the evils: 1109a35. Steering wide of besetting error: 1109b1–5. Bid pleasure be gone: 1109b5–10. The harder the task: 1105a5–10 (another translation in footnote: Ross's). Pleasure a supervening perfection: 1174b30. Should desire them even if no pleasure resulted: 1174a1–5. Painful to courageous man: 1117b5. Desirable for its own sake: 1176b5. Pleasures differ, the standard: 1175b20–25, 1176a15. Pleasures respectable: 1176a20. External advantages: 1099b1. Great and repeated successes: 1100b25–1101a1. The good life in general: 1140a25. A man of good natural disposition: 1144b10. At variance with plain facts: 1145b25. It is evident that: 1147a15. We do seem: 1147b15. Men are themselves responsible: 1114a1–5, 15–20. Indispensable requirement, friends are an aid: 1155a1, 10–15, 20–25. Must feel good will: 1156a1. Perfect form of friendship: 1156b5–10, 25. Amity consists in equality: 1159b1–10. Another self: 1166a30. An extension of regard for self: 1168b5. Larger share of money, etc.: 1168b15. If men vied in nobility: 1169a5–10. Immortality so far as possible: 1178a1. Higher than human level: 1177b25. Those who enjoin: 1177b30. The nature of the many: 1179b10. Disobedient, ill-conditioned: 1180a10. Ordains which sciences exist: 1094a25–1094b1. A greater and more perfect good: 1094b10.

Politics. Political animals: *Politics,* 1253a1. Large enough: 1252b25. Beast or god: 1252a25. Set forth the expedient: 1253a15. Multitude cannot be orderly: 1326a30. Best limit of population: 1326b20. That some should rule: 1254a20. Slaves by nature: 1254b15. Living instruments: 1253b25. That which can foresee: 1252a30. Have no share in happiness: 1280a30. Liberty should be held out: 1330a30. Euripides, *Hecuba,* 1. 330 (Edith Hamilton). Excerpt regarding private property: 1263a15–1263b35. Not tyrants from cold: 1267a10. Desire never satisfied: 1267b1–5. The beginning of reform: 1267b5. More than one, but not many: 1279a35. The citizens at large: 1279a35. Footnote: male fitter for command: 1259b1; woman's deliberative faculty without authority: 1260a10; silence: 1260a30. Military virtue: 1279b1. Tyranny a kind of monarchy: 1279b5–10. State not mere society; for the sake of noble actions: 1280b30, 1281a1–5. Monarchy best: 1288a1. A standard of virtue: 1295a25. Most ready to follow: 1295b5. Fatal to friendship in states: 1295b20. Thus it is manifest; in that case there will be: 1295b35–40, 1296b40–1297a5. A portion from each: 1294a30. Constitution of 411 B.C.: Ross, 251. Details of constitution: Bury, 476. Thucydides, *Peloponnesian War,* 8, trans. Warner, 547. May yet be: 1309b30. The best laws, though sanctioned: 1310a15. The citizen should be moulded: 1337a10. Absorbs and degrades: 1337b10. Music exciting and emotional: 1342b1. For feelings such as pity and fear: 1342a5–15. A tragedy, then: *Poetics,* 1449b20–25. Kind of thing that might happen: *Poetics,* 1451a35. Poetry is something more: *Poetics,* 1451b5.

Part III: Hellenistic and Roman Philosophy ⎯⎯⎯⎯⎯

Jewish population of Roman Empire: see Dimont, 113. Greek translations for Jewish readers: see Enslin, 83–84. Cult of Serapis: see Hadas, 189 ff.; *Standard Dictionary of Folklore,* s.v. "Serapis," "Isis," "Horus"; *New Columbia Encyclopedia,* s.v. "Serapis," "Isis." Isis inscription: *Brewer's Dictionary,* s.v. "Isis."

Chapter 8: Epicureanism

Were not able to explain to him: Diogenes Laertius, *Life of Epicurus,* trans. Bailey, in Oates, 53. (All translations from Diogenes Laertius on Epicurus and from Epicurus himself are Bailey's, in Oates, and the page references here are to Oates.) Hesiod's *Theogony,* trans. Wender, 26–27. The customary celebration: Diogenes Laertius, 57. He was a god: Lucretius, *The Nature of the Universe,* trans. Latham, 171. (All translations from Lucretius are Latham's.) Cicero, *De finibus,* 2, 15, 49, trans. Hadas, 17. Epicureanism in Ecclesiastes: see Hadas, 140–141.

The Canonic. Contradicted or not confirmed: Epicurus, *Letter to Herodotus,* 6. If anyone thinks: Lucretius, 145. Keep all our investigations: *Herod.,* 4. Images always true: Lucr., 145. When we see the square towers: Lucr., 141. Something to be discerned: Lucr., 142. Confirmed or not contradicted: *Herod.,* 6. Problem awaiting confirmation: Diogenes, 61.

Physics. Vain is the word: Frag. 54, p. 49. Plagued by anxieties: *Herod.,* 13–15; Lucr., 218–219. Unconscious attempts: Lucr., 128–129. Excerpt on greed and lust for power: Lucr., 97–98. Epic. on "up" and "down": *Herod.,* 9. The swerve: Lucr., 66–67. Observe what happens (sunbeams): Lucr., 63–64. Our world has been made: Lucr., 91. Nature is free: Lucr., 92. Gods' limited power: Lucr., 219. It is essential to: Lucr., 79. Those quiet habitations: Lucr., 96. Imperfection of world: Lucr., 197. True piety: Lucr., 208. Physical contact: *Herod.,* 11. Which is quite nameless: Lucr., 103. We see them propelling: Lucr., 101. Phenomena of the sky: Epic., *Letter to Pythocles,* 19. Either slightly greater: *Pyth.,* 20. Recourse to myth: *Pyth.,* 20. Rainbow: *Pyth.,* 25. Golden cord: Lucr., 94. Lived in thickets: Lucr., 200. Kings were killed: Lucr., 206. Everything is decaying: Lucr., 95. Ear-splitting crack: Lucr., 174. Self-same combinations: Lucr., 122. Between then and now, chain of identity: Lucr., 122, 121. All things the same: Lucr., 124. Ecclesiastes: 1:9–10 (Smith and Goodspeed). A return to sleep: Lucr., 123. Voluntary action, free will, bonds of fate, everlasting sequence, swerve at no set time: Lucr., 67–68. We follow the path: Lucr., 67. Pleasure the end: Diogenes, 63. Never deliberately choose a lesser: Frag. 16, p. 40; *Letter to Menoeceus,* 31; Diogenes, 61.

Ethics. For we recognize pleasure: *Letter to Menoeceus,* 31–32. Natural to us, the good life: *Menoec.,* 32, 30. I do not know how: Frag. 10, p. 46. Beginning and root: Frag. 59, p. 50. Attain pleasures unalloyed: *Principal Doctrines,* 12, p. 36. Confidence of help: Frag. 34, p. 41. Ecclesiastes: 8:15 (Smith and Goodspeed). Active/static: Frag. 1, p. 44; Diogenes, 63. The flesh perceives: *Pr. Doc.,* 20, p. 36. Excerpt on independence from desire: *Menoec.,* 32. By a scale of comparison: *Menoec.,* 32. Types of desires: *Pr. Doc.,* 29, p. 37. Excerpt on prudence: *Menoec.,* 32–33. To be honored if they give pleasure: Frag. 12, p. 46. To secure protection: *Pr. Doc.,* 6, p. 35. Justice and injustice: *Pr. Doc.,* 33, 34, p. 38. Even if he hides: Lucr. 206. Happy on the rack: Diogenes, 62. Nature teaches us: Frag. 77, p. 51. For friendship's sake: Frag., 28, p. 41. Footnote on the gods and our prayers: Frag. 58, p. 50. Know better how to give: Frag. 64, p. 42. Easy to distribute: Frag., 86, p. 52. What joy it is: Lucr., 90. Pleasures of love never profited: Frag. 51, p. 43. Do all things rightly: Frag. 57, p. 50. Become accustomed: *Menoec.,* 31. Nature of his illness, etc.: Diogenes, 56–57. Footnote: that I may feast: Frag. 39, p. 48.

Chapter 9: Stoicism

Logic. The wise man never: Cicero, in J. von Arnim, *Stoicorum veterum fragmenta* (hereafter cited as "SVF"), I, 54a, trans. Saunders in *Greek and Roman Philosophy After Aristotle,* p. 61. (All translations from SVF are Saunders's, and the page references given here are to Saunders.) Logic like a fence: Diogenes Laertius, SVF II, 38b, p. 61. Peculiar mark: Cicero, SVF I, 60, p. 66. Stoic inference schema: *Encyclopedia of Philosophy,* s.v. "Logic, History of," by C. Lejewski.

Physics. Like a kind of seed: Eusebius, SVF I, 98, p. 92. Principles that combine: Diogenes Laertius, SVF II, 300, p. 80; Achilles Tatius, SVF I, 85c, p. 80. Something: Seneca, SVF II, 332, p. 81; Alexander Aphrodisias, SVF II, 329, p. 81. Empty space, time: Sextus Empiricus, SVF II, 505, p. 88; Philo, SVF II, 511, p. 89. Subsist: Plutarch, SVF II, 518, 519, p. 89. Souls are bodies: Nemesius, SVF II, 773a, p. 97. Even our thoughts: Plotinus, SVF II, 946, p. 102. Identity of causal and logical necessity: Plotinus, SVF II, 946, p. 102. Command what is right: Cicero, SVF I, 162a, p. 102. What every event will be: Cicero, SVF II, 944, p. 102. Antecedent vs. principal causes: Cicero, SVF II, 974, pp. 108–109. Suppose a dog: Hippolytus, SVF II, 975, pp. 109–110. Berossos and astrology: see Murray, *Five Stages,* pp. 137–138. Cleanthes' "Hymn," trans. Adam, in Oates, 591–592. If you take away one: Chrysippus, Frag. 1169, in Barrett, p. 64. Comedies have in them: Plutarch, *De Comm. Notit.* 1065d, trans. Copleston, 1, 2, 136.

Ethics. In accordance with nature: Clement of Alexandria, SVF I, 180, p. 111. Distinctive feature of human nature: Seneca, SVF III, 200, p. 123. Pain, etc., functions of judgment: Diogenes Laertius, SVF III, 407, 412, p. 127; Galen,

SVF III, 461, p. 128. No value to pleasure: Cicero, SVF III, 154, p. 120; Sextus Empiricus, SVF III, 155, p. 120. Tranquil, smooth: Strobaeus, SVF III, 16, p. 113. Apathia: Diogenes Laertius, SVF III, 448, p. 128. Instinctive impulse towards self-preservation: Seneca, SVF III, 169; Cicero, SVF III, 182, 188, 189; pp. 120–122. Virtue and vice differ in kind: Cicero, SVF III, 72, p. 115; Diogenes Laertius, SVF III, 536, p. 130. All equally foolish unless fully wise: Plutarch, SVF III, 539, p. 131. Proficients: see Zeller, 241. Simple vs. perfect duties: see Bréhier, 63. No slaves by nature: Seneca, SVF III, 351, p. 127. We are born for: Cicero, SVF III, 342, p. 126.

Roman Stoicism. Cato quotations: Plutarch, *Cato the Elder,* 22, 23, trans. Scott-Kilvert, in *Makers of Rome,* 144–146. Influence of Panetius through Scipio's circle: see Bréhier, 129; Mommsen, 3:406. Posidonius and Cosmopolis doctrine: see Campbell, Introduction to *Seneca: Letters,* 16.

Cicero. The only way: quoted by Grant in *Cicero: Selected Works,* 86. John Adams: quoted by Grant, 30. Influence of Cicero: Grant, 164. Excerpts from *On Duties,* III, trans. Grant: To take something away, Indeed this idea, The same conclusion, 166–167; So everyone ought, If people claim, 168; When we encounter, A man who has in mind, Away, then, 171–172; There is an ideal, 187–188; Obviously we all aim, 200; A Roman gentleman, 180–181; As I have said before, Not that we possess, 184–185; This is not a question, 201.

Epictetus. Domitian and Stoicism: see Rostovtzeff, 206–207. Emperor and water-pot: *Discourses of Epictetus,* 1, 19, trans. Matheson, in Oates. (All translations from *Discourses* are Matheson's.) Emancipation of slaves: see Cowell, 108. Augustus on emancipation: see Carcopino, 60. Appointed place of authority: *Dis.,* 1, 13. Genuine freedom: *Dis.,* 4, 1. Excerpts from *Dis.:* Argument for God's Existence, 1, 6; Our Relation to God, 2, 8; Our Vocation, 1, 6; The Benefit of Understanding, 1, 9; The Penalty of Ignorance, 1, 12; Against Epicurus, 1, 20; The Uniqueness of Reason, 1, 1: A Clarification, 1, 19; The Aim of Education, 1, 12; One's Station and Its Duties, 1, 29; Service to Others, 1, 19; Indifferent Things, 1, 29; 2, 5; On Suicide, 1, 25, 29; On Tenacity, 2, 8.

Marcus Aurelius. Five good emperors and Stoicism: see Rostovtzeff, 207–208. Gibbon, ch. 3, Modern Lib. 1:69–70. Excerpts from *Meditations,* trans. Long, in Oates. Think continually: 4, 48. Altogether the interval: 4, 50. Soon, very soon: 5, 33. Such as bathing: 8, 24. Look down: 9, 30. Consider that: 8, 4. On every occasion: 8, 36. Be like the promontory, 4, 49. Men seek retreats: 4, 3. We ought then: 3, 4. It is peculiar to man: 7, 22. Reverence that which is best: 5, 21. Nature which governs: 7, 25. When bread is baked: 3, 2. Accept everything: 5, 8. Nor is it possible, 2, 11. Everything harmonizes: 4, 23. God so loved: John 3:16 (King James Version).

Chapter 10: Skepticism

Carneades. Plutarch, *Cato the Elder,* trans. Scott-Kilvert, in *Makers of Rome,* 145. Mommsen, 3:403. Arcesilaus and Stoicism: Cicero, *Academica,* 1, 44. (All translations from *Academica* are Rackham's.) Socrates and Plato as Skeptics: *Acad.,* 1, 45–46; 2, 74. Epicureanism no less objectionable than

Stoicism: *Encyclopedia of Philosophy,* s.v. "Skepticism," by Richard Popkin. Dreams and hallucinations: *Acad.,* 2, 76–90. Untrustworthiness of reasoning: see Windelband, 1:200–201. No self-evident first principles: see Windelband, 1:201. I am lying: *Acad.,* 2, 95–96. Not a dogmatic Skeptic: *Acad.,* 2, 28, 110. Obvious Stoic objection: *Acad.,* 2, 39. Enargeia: see Windelband, 1:207. The wise man: *Acad.,* 2, 99 (putting "impression" for "presentation"). Theory vs. practice: *Acad.,* 2, 99, 109. Stoics have a reply: see *Acad.,* 2, 105. Two things of which he is certain: see *Acad.,* 2, 28–29, 109–111. Probability probable: see *Acad.,* 2, 110. We are more free: *Acad.,* 2, 8. On free will: Cicero, *De Fato,* 5, 9; 11, 23; 14, 31. Ethics, primary natural objects: Cicero, *De Finibus,* 2, 35; 3, 51, 57 (Rackham). A man of good breeding: *De Fin.,* 3, 57 (Rackham). To combat the Stoics: *Acad.,* 2, 131. Clitomachus had never been able: *Acad.,* 2, 139; cf. *De Fin.,* 2, 42. Carneades did not so much accept: *Acad.,* 2, 78; cf. 2, 108, 113. Sidgwick, *Outlines,* 93. Excerpts from Cicero, *The Nature of the Gods,* trans. McGregor: 3, 69–70, 75, 76, 78, 79–81, 81–82, 85, 90, 92–93. Did not wish to deny gods' existence: *Nature of Gods,* 3, 44; cf. Ross, intro. to McGregor's trans., 50. That this was the traditional belief, By these very arguments you cast doubt: *Nature of Gods,* 3, 9–10. Kierkegaard, *Sickness,* 218. Antiochus on Carneades: *Acad.,* 2, 28–29, 33–36, 41–44.

Aenesidemus and Sextus Empiricus. Carneades a dogmatist: Sextus, *Outlines,* 1, 1; cf. *Encyclopedia of Philosophy,* s.v. "Aenesidemus," by P. H. Hallie. Aenesidemus' Ten Tropes: Diogenes Laertius, *Pyrrho,* 79–88, trans. Hicks. Summary rearrangement: following Windelband, 1:201. Agrippa's Five Tropes: Diogenes Laertius, *Pyrrho,* 88–89, trans. Hicks (putting "regress" for "extension" and "circular reasoning" for "reciprocal inference"; emphasis added to "whether in . . ."). Criterion of demonstrative argument: Diogenes Laertius, *Pyrrho,* 90. Excerpts from Sextus' *Outlines,* trans. Bury: bk. 1, chs. 1, 4, 6, 7, 8, 10, 11, 12. Small following of Pyrrhonism: see Zeller, 300.

Chapter 11: Philo of Alexandria

Caligula, Petronius, Flaccus, etc.: see Suetonius, *Caligula,* 22; Josephus, *Jewish War,* 2, 184–187, 192–203; Philo, *On Flaccus,* 73 ff. First and Second Commandments: Deuteronomy 5:7–8 (King James Version). To offer up prayers: Sandmel, 34. Essenes, Dead Sea Scrolls, etc.: see Wilson, 132 ff. Allegorical interpretations by Jews before Philo: see Enslin, 89. Greatly at variance, Take the path: *On the Posterity of Cain,* 1–2. (All translations from Philo are those of Colson and Whitaker.) Self-Existent Being in Philo and Septuagint: see Barrett, 182, 209. Mythical fiction: *On the Account of the World's Creation Given by Moses* (hereafter cited as *"C"*), 56. Created everything at once: *C,* 3. Moses attained summit, Divinely instructed: *C,* 2. Loyal citizen of world: *C,* 1. It stands to reason: *C,* 2. Earth a desolate waste: Genesis 1:2 (Smith and Goodspeed). In keeping with Stoic position: *C,* 2. God fully a creator: *C,* 5. Unknowability of God's essence: see *Encyclopedia of Philosophy,* s.v. "Philo," by H. A. Wolfson. Pure and unsullied Mind: *C,* 2. Genesis 1:26 (Smith and Goodspeed); Philo's interpretation: *C,* 23. This entire world: *C,* 6. The one great city: *C,* 4. First stage of creation: *C,* 4–5. Beautiful copy: *C,* 4. Created desolate waste: *C*, 7; cf. Wolfson, op. cit. On Word and Wisdom as personified: see Brown, 521. Psalm 33:6, Isaiah 55:11, Proverbs 3:19–20, 8:22, 8:29–30 (Smith and Goodspeed). Angel of the Lord: see Genesis 15:7, Numbers 22:23, Psalm 34:7. To his Word, his chief messenger: *Who Is the Heir of Divine Things?*, XLII. First-born son: Sandmel, 95. Word's powers pervade all things: see Winston, 60 (for Philo references). Manifest and visible gods: *C*, 7, 24. Wisdom of Solomon, date and relation to Philo: see Winston, 23, 59. Excerpts from Wisdom: 7:22, 24, 25, 27; 8:1, 3–4; 9:1–2, 4, 7, 8–9 (Smith and Goodspeed). Creating and ruling, two of many powers: Sandmel, 59–60. At door of his tent: Genesis 18:1 (Revised Standard Version). Spoken words contain symbols: *On Abraham*, 119–122. The world teaches: see Wolfson, op. cit. The human mind evidently occupies: *C*, 23. Excerpts from Prologue to Gospel of John: 1:1–4, 10, 14 (Brown). Colossians 1:15–20 (Revised Standard Version). Philo and incarnation: see Sandmel, 155. St. Augustine, *Confessions*, 7, 9 (Pine-Coffin). Philo and the New Testament: see Brown, 519–524.

Chapter 12: Plotinus

Plotinus on Christians: Porphyry, *Life of Plotinus*, trans. Armstrong, 16, 1–10. Ammonius Saccus perhaps once a Christian: see Armstrong, *Plotinus 1*, pp. 8–9, n. 1. Gibbon on Gallienus: ch. 10, Modern Lib. 1:238. Platonopolis: Porphyry, *Life*, 12, 1–10. Plotinus' lectures: Porphyry, 3, 35.

The One. Excerpts concerning the One: It is in virtue: Ennead 6, Tractate 9, Ch. 1. (All translations from Plotinus, unless otherwise attributed, are MacKenna's.) Now the being: 6, 9, 2. What then must: 6, 9, 3. Awareness of this: 6, 9, 4. Strictly no name: 6, 9, 5. It is great beyond anything: 6, 9, 6 ("elsewhere," in footnote concerning Aristotle, is 5, 1, 9). Our doctrine here: 5, 1, 8.

Intellect. Footnote on incomprehensibility of One in quantitative terms: see 5, 5, 10. Aristotle on acquisition of knowledge: *On the Soul*, 429a15, 25, 429b5. The unity they form: 5, 1, 4 ("Intellect" has been put in place of MacKenna's "Intellectual-Principle" throughout our excerpts). Excerpts concerning Intellect: From such a unity: 5, 1, 6. There exists a principle: 5, 1, 10. If Being is identical with Intellect: 6, 9, 2. [Intellect] is multiple: 6, 9, 5. Not merely one: 6, 8, 3 (footnote on Parmenides: see 5, 1, 8). [Intellect's] knowing is not by search: 5, 1, 4. The Intellect is, so to speak: 5, 1, 5.

Soul, Matter, and Evil. Excerpts concerning Soul, matter, and evil: Treating in the *Timaeus:* 4, 8, 1. All that is Intellect: 4, 8, 3. The total of things: 4, 8, 3. [It is] better for the soul: 4, 8, 7. Even our human soul: 4, 8, 8. Soul brings all: 5, 1, 2. Sprung from Intellect: 5, 1, 3. Soul deals with: 5, 1, 4. The appetite for: 4, 8, 4. [This is] determined by: 4, 8, 5. What comes into [the universe] from God: 1, 8, 7 (Armstrong). That which underlies: 1, 8, 3 (Armstrong). Since not only: 1, 8, 7 (Armstrong). A sort of form of nonexistence: 1, 8, 3 (Armstrong). For matter has not: 1, 8, 5 (Armstrong). The forms in matter: 1, 8, 8 (Armstrong). Matter spreads itself out: 1, 8, 14 (Armstrong).

Those that censure: 2, 9, 3. Since the higher exists: 3, 3, 7. The Intellect is the sovereign: 3, 2, 11.

Ascent of the Soul. Dances round Intellect: 1, 8, 2 (Armstrong). Ugliness and beauty: 1, 6, 2. Purifying, converting: 1, 6, 6; 1, 3, 1. Beloved Fatherland: 1, 6, 8. All is transparent: 5, 8, 4. Carried out by the very surge: 4, 8, 1 (Armstrong in Preface to *Plotinus 1,* 27). Identity with the divine: 4, 8, 1. Thus we have all: 4, 9, 9. The vision baffles telling: 6, 9, 10. Fallen back again: 6, 9, 11. Four occasions in six years: Porphyry, *Life,* 23, 15. Try to bring back: Porphyry, 2, 25.

Schools of Neoplatonism. Sallustius on polytheism: see Murray, *Five Stages,* 174, 191, 196.

Part IV: The Middle Ages

St. Thomas and Proverbs 9:3: *Summa Theologica,* 1, 1, 5, trans. Shapcote, ed. Pegis.

Chapter 13: St. Paul and the Early Christian Fathers

Has appointed a day: Acts 17:31. To unknown god: Acts 17:23 (Revised Standard Version). Now commandeth: Acts 17:30 (King James Version). Where is the wise: I Corinthians 1:20–24 (KJV). Beware lest: Colossians 2:8 (KJV). Without excuse: Romans 1:20 (KJV). For when the Gentiles: Romans 2:14–16 (KJV). The true light: John 1:9 (KJV). The invisible things: Romans 1:20 (KJV).

Justin Martyr. Trajan and firemen: Gibbon, ch. 16, n. 14, Modern Lib. 1:451. Persecution of Christians: see Latourette, 1:84. The greatest possession, it occurred to me: *Dialogue with Typho,* 2, in Roberts and Donaldson. Disagrees with Plato on soul: see Chadwick, 76. The true philosophy: Chadwick, 75. Plato closer than we know: Chadwick, 76. Socrates' reasoning, Demons: *Apology,* 1, 5, trans. Bettenson, in *Early Fathers,* 80. Most true God: *Apology,* 1, 4, Bettenson, 81. Philosophers knew Pentateuch: see Chadwick, 76. Everyone has capacity to discover: Chadwick, 76. Christians before Christ: *Apology,* 1, 46, Bettenson, 83. I prayed and strove: *Apology,* 2, 13, Bettenson, 87–88. Render unto Caesar: Matthew 22:21 (King James Version); *Apology,* 1, 17, Bettenson, 82.

Tertullian. Gnosticism: see especially Bevan, "The Gnostic Redeemer," in *Hellenism and Christianity.* The God of the Jews: Basilides as reported by St. Irenaeus, in Bettenson, *Documents,* 36. Word made flesh: John 1:24 (King James Version). Soul who companies with folly: Plato, *Laws,* 897b (Taylor). *Phaedo:* 67b, 67d (Hackforth). On Tertullian's personality: Chadwick, 91. On second marriages: *Ad Uxorum,* 1, 7, Bettenson, *Early Fathers,* 217. Excerpt from *Prescription,* 7, in Roberts and Donaldson (putting "investigation" for "inquisition"). Seek and ye shall find: Matthew 7:7 (King James Version); *Prescription,* 8. Christ taught one thing, nothing else to believe or seek: *Prescription,* 9. Away with the man: *Prescription,* 11. Footnote: 2 Timothy 3:7 (King James Version). Socrates' voice and Delphi: *On the Soul,* 1, in Roberts and Donaldson. What could Socrates then contemplate: *Soul,* 1. Ventured to believe, etc.: *Phaedo,* 114d, 113e (Jowett). Footnote: *On Repentance,* 4, in Bettenson, *Early Fathers,* 210. The truth has at this rate: *Soul,* 2. God's inspired standard, Human testimony, Plain evidence: *Soul,* 2. Noxious vapors: *Soul,* 3. *On Christ's Human Nature:* 2, 5, Bettenson, *Early Fathers,* 19–20. Aristotle's *Rhetoric:* 1400a5 (Roberts); see *Encyclopedia of Philosophy,* s.v. "Tertullian," by R. M. Grant. Wiseacres, patriarchs: *Soul,* 3. Diets of radishes: Hippolytus, in Bettenson, *Documents,* 77. Person of Jesus, etc.: see Latourette, 1:145–146.

Clement of Alexandria, Origen. Tatian rejects human opinion: *Address,* 32, quoted in Gilson, *Reason and Revelation,* 12. Arnobius: see Windelband, 1:225. Clement on Abraham: *Stromata,* 1, 5, in Roberts and Donaldson. Clement on anticipations: *Stromata,* 2, 4. Except ye believe: Isaiah 7:9 (on Clement's trans.). Intuition of God: *Stromata,* 5, 1, Bettenson, *Early Fathers,* 236. Demonstrative knowledge of Son: *Stromata,* 4, 25, Bettenson, *Early Fathers,* 234. No one learns without faith: *Stromata,* 2, 4, in Roberts and Donaldson. Starting from faith, *Stromata,* 7, 10. Philosophy not useless: *Stromata,* 1, 2. Origen: *First Principles,* 3, 5–6, in Roberts and Donaldson. Both sides in Arian controversy cited Origen: see Latourette, 1:152. Tertullian denied coeternity: Bettenson, *Early Fathers,* 21. The Son had a beginning: Arias to Eusebius, Bettenson, *Documents,* 39.

Chapter 14: St. Augustine

Taught to support family: see Chadwick, 216. Hissing cauldron: *Confessions,* 3, 1. (All translations from the *Confessions,* unless otherwise attributed, are Pine-Coffin's.) Not yet: *Conf.,* 8, 7. Whatever truth: *Conf.,* 7, 21. Take, read: *Conf.,* 8, 12. Romans 13: Revised Standard Version. In an instant: *Conf.,* 8, 12. O Lord: *Conf.,* 9, 1.

Faith and Reason. Understanding, reward of faith: *On the Gospel of St. John,* 29, 6, trans. Browne and Parker, in *Homilies.* Faith, belief: *On the Spirit and the Letter,* 21.54; *On Free Choice,* 2, 6. Understanding, Reason, Gaze of mind: *On the Trinity,* 12, 14.21–23. Purification: *On Order,* 2, 9.27; *Of True Religion,* 7.13. Not doubt what multitudes believe: *On the Value of Believing,* 15–16. Belief concerning parents: *Conf.,* 6, 5. Seek and find: *Choice,* 2, 6. Sincerity of critics: *Choice,* 2, 5. Uninstructed multitude: *On Order,* 2, 9.26. Excerpts from *Of True Religion:* 7.13, 8.14, 24.45, 25.46, 25.47, trans. Burleigh, in *Earlier Writings.*

Knowledge and God. If I am deceived: *City of God,* 11, 26 (Dods). Descartes: see *Discourse on Method,* 4; *Reply to Objections,* 4 (2nd para.); Weinberg, *Short History*, 34, n. 5. Cannot exist unless alive: *Choice*, 2, 21. Bodily senses: *Choice*, 2, 43. Footnote on Academic Skeptics: We must confess: *Trinity*, 15, 22.21 (Dods); see also *Against the Academics*, 3, 10–11; *Of True Religion*, 33.62; and Copleston, 2, 1, 168. Inner sense: *Choice*, 2, 27, 48. (All translations from *On Free Choice*, unless otherwise attributed, are Benjamin and Hackstaff's.) What judges is better: *Choice*, 2, 48. Animals have it: *Choice*, 2, 30. Reason our best: *Choice*, 2, 53. Now struggling: *Choice*, 2, 55. Never been a time: *Choice*, 2, 8. Principles of logic: *Against the Academics*, 3, 10. Principles of value: *Choice*, 2, 10. According to, not about: *Choice.*, 2, 12. Higher than mind: *Choice*, 2, 13. Numerical unity: *Choice*, 2, 8. If, by reason: *How Great Is the Soul?*, 13, trans. Wolter, in Wippel and Wolter. Transitory thoughts: *Trinity*, 12, 14.23 (Dods). Immutable Truth: *Choice*, 2, 12. That to whom: *Choice*, 2, 6. God exists truly: *Choice*, 2, 15. The primary forms: *Eighty-three Disputed Questions*, q. 42.6, trans. Bourke, in *Essential Augustine*, 62. Looks to nothing outside Himself: *Eighty-three*, q. 46.2. Platonic philosophers have recognized: *City*, 8, 5–6 (Dods). Son as Truth: *The Teacher*, 11, 38. Mediator: *City*, 21, 16. A sort of incorporeal light: *Trinity*, 12, 15.24 (Dods). Illumines inner man, Presides over mind: *The Teacher*, 12, 40; 11, 38, trans. Burleigh, in *Earlier Writings*. Makes us able to judge: *City*, 11, 27, trans. Walsh et al., as abridged by Bourke. Issues concerning Divine Illumination: see Copleston, 2, 1, 75–78.

Creator and Creation. We may understand God: *Trinity*, 5, 1.2 (Dods). All we know is how we do not know: *On Order*, 2, 18.47. Something than which: *On Christian Doctrine*, 1, 7, 7 (Robertson). I am that I am, Being: *Trinity*, 5, 2.3 (Dods). The Selfsame: *On Psalm 121*, 3.5, trans. Bourke, in *Essential Augustine*, 143. Incomprehensible to us: *Conf.*, 1, 4. Footnote: In your soul is the image: *On Psalm 32*, Serm. 3, 16, in Quasten et al. Steeped in error: *Conf.*, 11, 10. Busy preparing Hell: *Conf.*, 11, 12. Time itself was created: *Conf.*, 11, 13. Periods of time come into being: *Conf.*, 12, 9, trans. Bourke, in *Essential Augustine*, 108. Does not profess to know how many: *City*, 12, 13–18. God's will there from eternity: *Conf.*, 11, 10. Have not learnt to understand you: *Conf.*, 11, 11. I say I measure: *Conf.*, 11, 27–28. You created from nothing: *Conf.*, 13, 33. Exegetical basis of seminal reasons theory: see Copleston, 2, 1, 91–92. Footnote: Ecclesiasticus 18:1 (Smith and Goodspeed). Genesis 1:20–26. Footnote on "days": *City*, 11, 6–7 (Walsh et al.). Invisible seeds concealed, Original rules: *Trinity*, 3, 8.13 (Dods). Seminal reasons, What can come from what: *Literal Commentary on Genesis*, 9, 17.32, trans. Bourke, in *Essential Augustine*, 103; cf. Weinberg, 39. Examines Plotinus on evil: *Conf.*, 7, 9. Excerpts on evil from *City:* 11, 22; 12, 2; 12, 4; 12, 5 (Walsh et al.). Augustine often criticized on Providence: e.g., Jones, *Medieval Mind*, 95–97; Lovejoy, *Great Chain*, 67. Hear my prayer, O Lord: Psalm 143: 1, 12 (King James Version). Prayers useful: *City*, 5, 10 (Walsh et al.). Providence transcends our reckoning: *City*, 1, 28 (Walsh et al.). We might have the impression: *City*, 1, 8 (Walsh et al.). Footnote on Boethius: see *On the Consolation of Philosophy*, 5. Excerpts concerning free will: *City*, 5, 9–10 (Walsh et al.).

Sin and Redemption. All men are: *Conf.*, 13, 17. Those who try, I wished no more: *Conf.*, 9, 4. There is no: *City*, 12, 1. (This and subsequent translations from the *City of God*, unless otherwise attributed, are those of Walsh et al.) The good things: *Conf.*, 4, 12. O God: *Conf.*, 4, 10. Man's will: *City*, 14, 6. When I asked: *Conf.*, 7, 16. Vices in the, The only cause: *Enchiridion*, 23. (All translations from the *Enchiridion* are Shaw's.) By his sin: *Ench.*, 26. In his person: *City*, 13, 3. God, the author: *City*, 13, 14. No man is: *Conf.*, 1, 7. The rule of sin: *Conf.*, 8, 5. It may be: *Conf.*, 10, 23. It was by: *Ench.*, 30. There is nothing: *City.*, 14, 15. Footnote: Romans 7:19 (King James Version). It is no: *Conf.*, 8, 9. A man's free: *Spirit and the Letter*, 5, trans. Bettenson, in *Documents*, 54. There are two: *Ench.*, 81. Our first parents: *City*, 14, 13. If one seeks, The evil arises: *City*, 12, 6. No one need: *City*, 12, 7. The very defection: *City*, 12, 9. [Nevertheless] even what: *Ench.*, 100. He judged it: *Ench.*, 11. As he foresaw: *Ench.*, 104. That one sin: *Ench.*, 48. There was need: *Ench.*, 33. A mediator between, As man, he: *Conf.*, 10, 42–43. In his own person: *Ench.*, 35. Just as each: *Ench.*, 36. Although He Himself: *Ench.*, 41. Some philosophers have: *City*, 12, 13 (Dods). Baptism in Christ: *Ench.*, 52. In order that: *On the Grace of Christ*, 26.27 (Dods). [However] not all: *Ench.*, 97. It is God's grace: *Ench.*, 99. As for those: *Ench.*, 92. When reprobate angels: *Ench.*, 94. He has predestined, If this divine assistance: *Retractations*, 9.2, 9.4, trans. Bourke, in *Essential Augustine*, 177. O Lord: *Conf.*, 10, 4. The grace of God: *On Admonition and Grace*, 2.3, in Schaff. Assistance was bestowed: *On Corruption and Grace*, 34, trans. Bettenson, in *Documents*, 55. The mercy of God: *Ench.*, 82. I have no hope: *Conf.*, 10, 29, trans. Bettenson, in *Documents*, 54. Pelagius: blind folly: *Letter to Demetriadem*, 16, trans. Bettenson, in *Documents*, 52. Goths' cruelties and Providence: *City*, 1, 1. For all the difference: *City*, 14, 1. Two societies have issued: *City*, 14, 28. So long as: *City*, 19, 17. There is no such: *City*, 19, 12. The peace of: *City*, 19, 13. Sinful man hates: *City*, 19, 12. [God] meant no man: *City*, 19, 15. The heavenly City: *City*, 19, 17. Although they [the two cities]: *Literal Commentary on Genesis*, 11, 15.20, trans. Bourke, in *Essential Augustine*, 201. To tell the truth: *City*, 22, 29 (citation from Philippians 4:7). What the eternal life, And while we spoke: *Conf.*, 9, 10. Malarial Ostia: see Rossiter, 314. On the ninth day: *Conf.*, 9, 11.

Chapter 15: Medieval Philosophers in Profile

Christian Philosophers:
Boethius. Bitter quarrels: *Consolation*, bk. 1, prose 4. (All translations from *Consolation* are Buchanan's.) For nature does not: *Con.*, 3, 10. Than Whom nothing better: *Con.*, 3, 10. But they lose: *Con.*, 4, 2, 3. Sends hardships: *Con.*, 4, 5. The complete possession: *Con.*, 5, 6. One authority: McKeon, *Selections*, 1:65.

John Scotus Eriugena. Use of "Nature": *On the Division of Nature*, 1, 1, trans. Wolter, in Wippel and Wolter, 118–119. By intellect alone: *Div.*, 1, 6, Wolter, 121. Divided: *Div.*, 1, 1, Wolter, 118. God incomprehensible, etc.: *Div.*, 1, 10–14. Excerpt on creation: *Div.*, 1, 12, Wolter, 124–125. Flowing from: *Div.*, 3, 4; see Copleston, 2, 1, 140. God's essence as nothing: *Div.*, 3, 19; see Copleston, 141. Previously shied away from this: *Div.*, 3, 5, Wolter, 133–134.

Pullulating with worms: see *Encyclopedia of Philosophy*, s.v. "Pantheism," by A. MacIntyre.

St. Anselm of Canterbury. Some think king was gainer: see LaMonte, 304. I do not seek: *Proslogion*, 1. (All translations from St. Anselm are Deane's.) Offered itself: *Pros.*, Preface. Hypothesis regarding Anselm and Augustine: see *Reply to Gaunilon*, 5. What no eye has seen: 1 Corinthians 2:9 (Revised Standard Version). *On the Moral Behavior*, 2, 11, 24, cited by Malcolm, in Plantinga, 142, n. 11; the translation here has been furnished by my colleague, Prof. Frederick Purnell, Jr. Excerpts from *Pros.* 2 and 3. Gaunilon's island: *In Behalf of the Fool*, 6 (Deane). Anselm's *Reply:* see especially 3. Gassendi: in Descartes, 2:186 (Haldane and Ross). Dissolved in concept: *Reply*, 1. Excerpts from *Reply:* 1 and 9. Gaunilon professes inability to conceive: *In Behalf*, 4. Anselm's rejoinder: *Reply*, 1 and 8. Is this not to form, So when one says: *Reply*, 8.

Peter Abelard. "Socrates of France": see Hyman and Walsh, 165. Possibility of Hodgkin's Disease: see Radice, Intro. to *Letters*, 41. The pleasure we shared: Letter 3 (Heloise to Abelard), trans. Radice, 133. Porphyry's questions as reported by Boethius: *Second Edition of Commentaries on the Isagoge*, 1, 10, in McKeon, 1:91. Boethius in *Consolation* follows Plato: see bk. 5, prose 4. How early medieval thinkers were prone to reason: see Hawkins, 40–49. Odo of Cambrai: see Copleston, 2, 1, 162. Nicene Creed of 374: in Bettenson, *Documents*, 26. Anselm on Trinity: see Copleston, 2, 1, 163. Roscelin perhaps indebted to Aristotle: see Windelband, 1:296. Merely word sounds: reported by John of Salisbury, *Metalogion*, 2, 17, trans. McGarry, in Hyman and Walsh, 167. Roscelin and Trinity: see Gilson, *History*, 154, n. 88, n. 89. Abelard on absurdities in William's theory: *Glosses on Porphyry*, trans. McKeon, in *Selections*, 1:222–227; see Copleston, 2, 1, 168. It is manifest: *Glosses*, trans. McKeon, 1:227. William's modified theory: *Glosses*, trans. McKeon, 1:227–228; see Gilson, *History*, 154, Copleston, 2, 1, 169. Abelard accepts Aristotle's definition (*On Interpretation*, 17a38): *Glosses*, trans. Wolter, in Wippel and Wolter, 191. Words predicable of many: *Glosses*, trans. Wolter, 191. Meaning associated with words: *Glosses*, trans. Wolter, 195; see Copleston, 2, 1, 171. General, indiscriminate image: *Glosses*, trans. Wolter, 195. Fused together: ibid., 198. No numerically identical human essence: ibid., 193. Anticipates criticism: ibid., 199. Separately/separated: ibid., 200. Ideas in God's mind: see Copleston, 2, 1, 172.

Muslim Philosophers. Muslims' treatment of Jews and Christians during conquest: see LaMonte, 104.

Avicenna. Plotinus' suggestion: *Enneads*, 4, 8, 1. Flying Man: Copleston, 2, 1, 216; Weinberg, 112–113. God's necessary existence: Copleston, 217. Essence vs. existence: Weinberg, 114–115. Argument for God's existence: Copleston, 217; Weinberg, 115. Creation necessary: Copleston, 217; Weinberg, 115, 117. God creates indirectly: Copleston, 218; Weinberg, 116. Agent Intellect and immortality: Copleston, 218–219; Weinberg, 117, 120. Flying Man and immortality: Gilson, *History*, 198, 202; Weinberg, 119. What is affirmed other than what is not: Gilson, 191, 198. Simple concepts and soul's immateriality: Gilson, 202; Avicenna, *The Deliverance: Psychology*, 6, 9, in Hyman and Walsh, 256. Footnote on indivisible point in material soul: Gilson, 202. Proof of immortality: *Deliverance*, 6, 13, trans. Rahman, in Hyman and Walsh, 260. Passages from Koran: 36:51, 15:17–22, 9:249, trans. Rodwell, in Robert E. Hume, 235.

Algazali. I saw for certain: *Deliverance from Error*, 3, 4 (Watt). Sought refuge with God, Made it easy: ibid. Muslim regard for *Revival:* see Noss, 544, 548. No necessity in causal relations: Weinberg, 123; Algazali as quoted in Averroes, *Tahafut Al-Tahafut*, trans. Van Den Bergh, 1:517. Only a simultaneity: Weinberg, 123–124; Algazali as quoted by Averroes, 1:518. God the only cause: Weinberg, 124. Algazali's period of skepticism: see Hyman and Walsh, 263. The many philosophical sects, The defect of unbelief, Godly fear, Infidel doctrines, No proofs in metaphysics, Customary with weaker intellects, Just as a poor swimmer: *Deliverance*, 3, 2 (Watt). Not through proofs, By way of intellectual apprehension, There were revealed to me, Immediate experience, Behold angels and spirits: *Deliv.*, 3, 4. What is to be, Special faculty: *Deliv.*, 4 (Watt). Dreams: *Deliv.*, 4. Revered as saint: see Noss, 548.

Averroes. Retirement to Spain and return: see Hyman and Walsh, 286; *Encyclopedia of Philosophy*, s.v. "Averrroes," by Stuart MacClintock. Aristotle the supreme truth: quoted in Gilson, *History*, 220. Only proof of God is Aristotle's: Weinberg, 135; *Tahafut Al-Tahafut*, trans. Van Den Bergh, 1:261. Books of ancients, Theoretical study which leads: *Decisive Treatise*, trans. Hourani, ch. 1. Best class of people: ibid., ch. 2. Takes care of majority: ibid., ch. 3. Images and likenesses: ibid., ch. 2. The elite: ibid., ch. 3. Apparent vs. inner meaning: ibid., ch. 2. Truth does not oppose truth: ibid. The masses not to be informed: ibid., ch. 3. From the one, Out of the one: *Tahafut*, 1:107. Aristotle on general: *Tahafut*, 1:106 (see Aristotle, *Metaphysics*, 1075a10–15). Sometimes still said to deny immortality: for example, Hyman and Walsh, 285. Actually affirms it: Weinberg, 138–139. Subtle matter, Animal warmth: *Tahafut*, 1:357. Principle of causality self-evident: Weinberg, 134–135. Necesary causal relations presupposed by identifications of kinds: *Tahafut*, 1:318 (see also Van Den Bergh's fourth note to this page). If the nature of oneness is denied: ibid. Clearest of miracles is Venerable Book: ibid., 1:315. A question Averroes wished to avoid: see Van Den Berg's fourth note to 1:315. Christian reconquest of Spain: LaMonte, 293, 514–515.

Jewish Philosophers. Halevi's indebtedness to Algazali: see Husik, 132–133.

Saadia. Gaon of Pumbedita, the exilarch, and the caliph: see *Encyclopedia Britannica*, 11th ed., s.v. "Seadiah." Should seek reasons for revealed truths: see Husik, 26–28. Genesis 1:1; Isaiah 44:24 (King James Version). I know that time is threefold, If we fail to admit: *Book of Doctrines and Beliefs*, ch. 1, secs. 2, 3 (Altmann). Disagrees with emanation: Husik, 31. Footnote on Saadia and Trinity: see Husik, 33–35. Insight into God's unity: Husik, 33. II Kings 19:16; Deut. 4:15–19 (King James Version). God transcends Aristotle's categories: Husik, 35–37. On soul and body: Husik, 37–38, 47. My answer to this objection: *Book*, 3, 1 (Altmann). I maintain that reason bids us: ibid., 3, 2. Examples of Laws of Tradition: ibid. Isaiah 42:21 (Revised Standard Version). That which belongs, Upon closer examination: *Book*, 3, 2 (Altmann).

Some minor and partial motives: ibid. Enables us to desist, Prevents people from worshipping animals, Prevents men being attracted only by: ibid. On freedom of will: Husik, 41–42. Deut. 30:19 (King James Version). On divine reward and punishment: Husik, 42–43. On the next life: Husik, 43–45.

Maimonides. Originality of allegorical interpretation: see Husik, 302. Footnote on knowledge of Averroes' writings: see Hyman and Walsh, 359. Exodus 33:13 (King James Version): see Maimonides, *Guide,* 1, 54, and Husik, 243. Why he formulated creed: see Weinberg, 155–156. Psalm 82:5 (King James Version). They are the multitude: *Guide,* Intro. (Friedländer). (All translations from the *Guide* are Friedländer's.) Arrangement and style of *Guide:* see Husik, 241–242. Whoever pries into: Mishna, Hagigah, ch. 2, quoted in Husik, 244. Limitations of human intellect: *Guide,* 2, 1. Philosophers for three thousand years, This question cannot be answered: *Guide,* 1, 71. I accept the latter: *Guide,* 2, 16. In favor of creation: see Weinberg, 153, and Husik, 271. Assumes eternity of world for argument's sake: *Guide,* 1, 71; see Weinberg, 152. Arguments for God's existence: *Guide,* 2, 1. On uniqueness of God: see Husik, 260. Has nothing in common: *Guide,* 2, 1. Attributes of action: *Guide,* 1, 52. It is generally accepted, I will give you some illustrations, There is a great danger: *Guide,* 1, 59, 60. On what survives death: see Weinberg, 155; *Guide,* 3, 51, 54. Joins us to God, Link: *Guide,* 3, 51. Love of God, Identical with knowledge: *Guide,* 3, 51. Those who have succeeded: *Guide,* 3, 51. Footnote on emanation: *Guide,* 2, 11; see Weinberg, 154. On intelligibility of all divine laws: see Husik, 294–299. Weak-minded persons: *Guide,* 3, 31. Classification of laws: ibid. These three principles: ibid. One authority: Husik, 312.

Chapter 16: St. Thomas Aquinas

Some Background: St. Bonaventure. Where he spoke well: St. Bonaventure, *Conferences on the Hexaemeron,* vis. 1, dis. 3, trans. Walsh, in Hyman and Walsh, 421. St. Bonaventure on faith and reason: see Copleston, 2, 1, 274–279. St. Bonaventure vs. St. Thomas on creation from eternity: see Copleston, 2, 1, 295; 2, 2, 85–86.

Life and Method. Related to Frederick II: see Latourette, 1:509. The woman in his room: see Chesterton, 64–65. St. Thomas described by Chesterton: 20–22. Moderate and acceptable: Bourke, *Pocket Aquinas,* xviii. Latin Averroists declared him saint: Bourke, xviii. *Aeterni Patris:* see Leo XIII in Bibliography. Could write no more: Chesterton, 141. First Article of *Summa Theologica* ("*ST*" hereafter): trans. Shapcote, ed. Pegis, in *Basic Writings* (the source of all translations from St. Thomas in this chapter not otherwise attributed).

Faith and Reason. Articles, Preambles: *ST,* pt. 1, quest. 2, art. 2; see Copleston, 2, 2, 33. Authority based on divine revelation, Arguments that can be answered: *ST,* 1, 1, 8. Handmaidens: *ST,* 1, 1, 5. Other sciences derive certitude: *ST,* 1, 1, 5. Whatsoever is found: *ST,* 1, 1, 6. Grace does not destroy: *ST,* 1, 1, 8. Organic unity of faith and reason: see Gilson, *Reason and Revelation,* 84.

Metaphysical Principles. See Copleston, 2, 2, ch. 33. Rejects St. Augustine's seminal reasons: Copleston, 47. Wherever there are many individuals: *Disputed Questions on Spiritual Creatures,* 1, reply to Obj. 9; trans. Bourke, *Pocket Aquinas,* 175. Any essence is understandable: *On the Composition of Essence and Existence in Created Substances,* trans. Wolter, in Wippel and Wolter, 332. Existence is the act: *Summa contra Gentiles,* 2, 30; trans. Copleston, 51. This act of being: *Disputed Questions on the Power of God,* 7, 2; trans. Bourke, *Pocket Aquinas,* 154. But composition of form and existence is there: *On the Composition,* trans. Wolter, 330. Granted that by this name: *ST,* 1, 2, 1. Cannot be seen in His essence, except: *ST,* 1, 12, 11. Footnote on natural light, light of grace, St. Augustine: *ST,* 1–2, 109, 1.

Arguments for God's Existence. The five ways: *ST,* 1, 2, 3. Reference in fourth way is to Aristotle's *Metaphysics,* 993b30. Occasion to ridicule: *ST,* 1, 46, 2. Possibility of infinite series in past time: *ST,* 1, 46, 2. Accidental vs. per se series: *ST,* 1, 46, 2. Aristotle on "most true": *Metaphysics,* 993b25. Argument from external finality: *Summa contra Gentiles,* 1, 35; trans. Pegis, *On the Truth;* in Shapiro, 366–367.

God's Nature. Aristotle on "being" not a genus: *Metaphysics,* 998b20–25. So we are left: *ST,* 1, 3, 5; trans. Gilby. On Maimonides and negative predication: *ST,* 1, 13, 2. Equivocal, univocal, analogical: *ST,* 1, 13, 5. Canine faithfulness: see von Hügel, *Essays and Addresses,* 102–103. Any perfection found in an effect, Since God then is the primary operative cause: *ST,* 1, 4, 2; trans. Gilby. Pre-exist transcendentally: *ST,* 1, 13, 5; trans. Gilby.

Creator and Creation. Models: *ST,* 1, 15, 2. His means of knowing: *ST,* 1, 15, 1. Many models are understood: *ST,* 1, 15, 2. Communicate His perfection: *ST,* 1, 44, 4. Best as a whole: *ST,* 1, 47, 2. Universe would not be perfect: *ST,* 1, 47, 2. Thus God by causing: *ST,* 1, 49, 2. Can make something better: *ST,* 1, 25, 6. The divine goodness is an end: *ST,* 1, 25, 5. Footnote: One grade of goodness is: *ST,* 1, 48, 2. Excerpt concerning omnipotence and law of contradiction: *ST,* 1, 25, 3. Time created with motion: *ST,* 1, 46, 1, 3. No real relation, His terminology: *ST,* 1, 45, 3; 1, 13, 7. Due to something real in, Being thought of in a particular way: *ST,* 1, 13, 7; trans. Gilby. Being related to creatures, God is altogether outside, Our way of thinking, We cannot express: *ST,* 1, 13, 7; trans. Gilby. In God, relation to the creature: *ST,* 1, 45, 3. So loved the world: John 3:16 (King James Version). With whom is no variableness: James 1:17 (King James Version). Socrates on Homer: Plato, *Republic,* 380e, 381b; trans. Cornford.

Ethics, Immortality, Freedom. Governs all acts and movements: *ST,* 1–2, 93, 1. Whole community of universe: *ST,* 1–2, 91, 1. To the common good: *ST,* 1–2, 90, 2. Perfection consists in contemplating God's essence: *Summa contra Gentiles,* 3, 37; in *Basic Writings.* Faith resembles hearing: *Summa contra Gentiles,* 3, 40. Wholly freed from the senses: *Summa contra Gentiles,* 3, 47. Must increase our intellectual power: *Summa contra Gentiles,* 3, 53. The rule and measure: *ST,* 1–2, 91, 1, 2. Sensible and earthly, Intelligible and heavenly: *ST*, 1–2, 91, 5. Argument for immortality: *ST*, 1, 75, 2. Only that which subsists: *ST*, 1, 75, 2. This is impossible: *ST*, 1, 75, 6. Not without an answer: *Summa contra Gentiles*, 2, 55. Resurrection of the body: *ST*, 3, 75, 1. By his free choice: *ST*, 1, 83, 1. God causes some things to happen contingently: *ST*, 1, 22, 4. Human will orientated towards happiness: *ST*, 1, 82, 1. Those things which are of God: *ST*, 1, 82, 2. Free in choice of means to happiness: *ST*, 1–2, 13, 6. Corrupted in us after the sin: *ST*, 1–2, 109, 2. Turned to God only when: *ST*, 1–2, 109, 7. Good absolutely: *ST*, 1–2, 18, 4. Every action good or bad: *ST*, 1–2, 18, 9. Excerpt on discovery of principles of natural moral law: *ST*, 1–2, 94, 2. Conscience: *ST*, 1, 79, 13. Erring conscience to be obeyed: *ST*, 1–2, 19, 5; trans. Gilby, in *Philosophical Texts*, #812. Every virtuous act, Chief effective control: Disputations, *de Virtuibus Cardinalibus*, 1; trans. Gilby, *Texts*, #849, #874. Moral virtue a habit of making good choice: *ST*, 1–2, 58, 4; trans. Gilby, *Texts*, #867. Keep the reasonable measure, Firmness of spirit, One's own personal lusts, Under the aspect of what: *ST*, 2–2, 47, 7; 123, 2; 141, 8; 23, 3; trans. Gilby, *Texts*, #973, #981, #988, #1007. "Theological" appropriate because: *ST*, 1–2, 62, 1. Friendship of man for God: *ST*, 2–2, 23, 1. The factors are infinitely variable: Commentary, *II Ethics, lect. 2;* trans. Gilby, *Texts*, #786. Ornament should befit: Commentary, *in Isaium,* 3; trans. Gilby, *Texts*, #1001.

Politics. Man social and political animal: *On Princely Government* (hereafter *"PG"*), 1, 1; trans. Dawson, in *Selected Political Writings*, ed. D'Entrèves. All subsequent translations from *PG* used here are Dawson's. That which is itself a unity: *PG*, 1, 2. Natural pattern: *PG*, 1, 2. King is best: *PG*, 1, 3. Just as it is better: *PG*, 1, 3. Constitutional monarchy: *ST*, 1–2, 105, 1. As people's representative: *ST*, 1–2, 96, 5. In the first place it is necessary: *PG*, 1, 6. Singular likeness to God: *PG*, 1, 9. Fullness of life: *PG*, 1, 14. Must in governing: *PG*, 1, 15. Scheme of common happiness: *ST*, 1–2, 90, 2; trans. Gilby, *Texts*, #1039. Either to the whole people or: *ST*, 1–2, 90, 3; trans. Gilby, *Texts*, #1040. Ordinance of reason for common good: *ST*, 1–2, 90, 4; trans. Gilby, *Texts*, #1037. Each part is for its whole: *ST*, 1–2, 90, 2; trans. Gilby, *Texts*, #1039. Men are principals: *Summa contra Gentiles*, 3, 111–16; trans. Gilby, *Texts*, #1043. How each will be all: Disputations, II *de Veritate,* 2; trans. Gilby, *Texts*, #1117. Human law enacted on behalf of the mass of men: *ST*, 1–2, 96, 2; trans. Dawson, 68. Does not punish man who meditates murder: *ST*, 1–2, 100, 9; trans. Dawson, 74–75. Whatever a man does in ignorance: *ST*, 1–2, 100, 9; trans. Dawson 74. Excerpt concerning unjust laws: *ST*, 1–2, 94, 6; trans. Dawson, 69. Dishonorable and vicious men: *ST*, 1–2, 97, 1; trans. Dawson, 72. Human law should never be changed unless: *ST*, 1–2, 97, 2; trans. Dawson, 73. The king's duty: *PG*, 1, 15. Subject to priests: *PG*, 1, 14. Therefore there is no usurpation: *ST*, 2–2, 60, 6; trans. Dawson, 84. Extermination: *ST*, 2–2, 11, 3; trans. Dawson, 79. Distinguished by some particular dress: *On the Government of Jews,* trans. Dawson, 48. In no-wise to be tolerated: *ST*, 2–2, 10, 11; trans. Dawson, 78. His subjects are ipso facto absolved: *ST*, 2–2, 12, 2; trans. Dawson, 80. Excerpts from Coulton, *Medieval Scene,* 154, 155, 152–153, 156.

Chapter 17: Three Late Medieval Minds

Roger Bacon. Columbus found Bacon's geographical observations in Pierre d'Ailly's *Imago Mundi;* see *Encyclopedia Britannica*, 11th ed., s.v. "Roger Bacon"; and Morison, 19. My superiors and brothers: S. E. Easton, *Roger Bacon,* 134. Four obstacles to truth: *Opus Maius*, 1, 1; trans Burke, 1:4. (*"OM"* hereafter refers to Burke's translation.) Since every man, Since no man: *OM*, 1, 9 (Burke 1:20). The perfect philosophers: *OM* 1, 1 (1:5). Rich fulness, Delights few: *OM*, 1, 3 (1:9–10). Reasoning draws a conclusion: *OM*, 6, 1 (2:583). Anyone who makes the experiment: *OM*, 6, 1 (2:584). Incantations, invocations: *OM*, 6, 12 (2:632). Experience of two kinds: *OM*, 6, 1 (2:585). Holy patriarchs and prophets: *OM*, 6, 1 (2:585). Indirect confirmation of Scriptures: see Easton, 173. Investigates by experiment: *OM*, 6, 2 (2:587). Even in mathematics: 6, 1 (2:583). Aristotle on rainbow: *Meteorologica*, 395b27–360a25. Diligent experimenter: *OM*, 6, 2 (2:589). Second prerogative as coordinator: see Easton, 181–183. In these times: *OM*, 6, 12 (2:619). Scarcely one physician: *OM*, 6, 12 (2:617). The proper use of food: *OM*, 6, 12 (2:618). Aristotle in *Secrets: OM*, 6, 12 (2:621). Perfect medicine: *OM*, 6, 12 (2:624). Boyle, van Helmont, Paracelsus: see *Encyclopedia Britannica*, 11th ed., s.v. "Alchemy." Prelates and princes: Easton, 183. Has same relation, Directs other sciences: *OM*, 6, 12 (2:633). Perpetual baths, etc.: *OM*, 6, 12 (2:629). Saltpeter, etc.: *OM*, 6, 2 (2:629–630). The Church should consider: *OM*, 6, 12 (2:634).

John Duns Scotus. Face-to-face vision: *Ordinatio*, Prologue; trans. Wolter, in Shapiro, 447. He has mixed: ibid., 453. For now we see: King James Version. Univocity of being: see Copleston, 2, 2, 224, 228. Every inquiry presupposes: *Opus Oxoniense*, trans. Walsh, in Hyman and Walsh, 563. Being indefinable: see Copleston, 222, and Weinberg, 217. Disjunctive characteristics of being: see Copleston, 223–224, and Weinberg, 219–220. Ascending infinity: Hyman and Walsh, 565; see Copleston, 256–257. First effective being, Exists from itself: Hyman and Walsh, 566. The unconditionally first: Hyman and Walsh, 566. Colored, That than which: Hyman and Walsh, 571 (putting "conceived" for "thought"). It is simply false: *Opus Oxon.*, trans. Copleston, 233. Not truly one as individual: see Weinberg, 227. Scotus on matter as principle of individuation: see Copleston, 239. Individuating difference: see Weinberg, 227–228, 246–247; and Copleston, 239–240. Scotus not Extreme Realist: see Copleston, 234. Justice: see *Encyclopedia of Philosophy*, s.v. "Duns Scotus," by A. B. Wolter. Moral obligation: see Copleston, 270. Immortality: see Copleston, 266.

William of Ockham. Defend me: Boehner, xv. Plurality not to be assumed: see Weinberg, 239. Footnote: Aristotle, *Physics*, 259a12; see Weinberg, 239, n. 1. Scotus's theory of universals: see Weinberg, 227–228, 246–247. That *a* and *b* are one thing: *Sentences*, 1, d. 2, q. 3, H, trans. Weinberg, 249. If *a* and *b* are numerically identical: see Weinberg, 247–248. For any common nature *C:* see Boehner, 38. By means of themselves: see Weinberg, 250. Kind of mental picture, The intellect, seeing, And this can be called: trans Boehner, 41. Some kind of assimilation: trans. Boehner, 45. Do not refer more to one thing: trans. Boehner, 44. Unnecessary to suppose God works from models: see Copleston, 3, 1, 100–103. Ockham on causality: see Weinberg, 260. Nicholas of Autrecourt: see Weinberg, 274. Ockham on sense experience: see Weinberg, 257–259. Heresy charge: see Copleston, 76, 78. Pierre d'Ailly: see Weinberg, 286. Argument to First Conserver: see Copleston, 95. Omnipotence principle used negatively: see Weinberg, 241. Corporeal and corruptible: trans. Boehner, 144. No act blameworthy unless, However intense, By the very fact: trans. Copleston, 113, 115, 116. God has no obligation: see Copleston, 117. Seems to imply that reason can discern moral principles: see Copleston, 120. Excerpt from Knowles, *Evolution of Medieval Thought*, 328–329.

Index